"This is the book that I have been looking for in my teaching that incorporates the most comprehensive and up-to-date management aspects and policy issues surrounding the nonprofit scholarly and practitioner community. By addressing current events/trends/movements affecting the field, such as the impacts of the global pandemic, social media, societal/political division; and enhanced societal awareness (social justice, diversity, equity, and inclusion), this book will play its pioneering role to lead the discourse and critical thinking much needed at this critical juncture in this field. I commend the book editors' remarkable job bringing distinguished articles and chapters that critically review, practically resolve, and insightfully comprehend complex issues/challenges facing nonprofits. Nonprofit practices and research evidently evolve and advance thanks to such efforts contributed by dedicated editors and chapter authors of this seminal book."

Bok Gyo Jeong, *Department of Public Administration,*
Kean University

"*Understanding Nonprofit Organizations* edited by Drs. J. Steven Ott and Lisa Dicke is a wonderful textbook for my nonprofit management class. This book covers all critical aspects of governance and operations of nonprofit organizations and supplements the conceptual discussions with case studies, which is perfect for students learning about nonprofit management. The introductions to each section of the book by the editors summarize and highlight the section's significance and implications for practice. This book is a great one-stop resource as it compiles literature surrounding the most salient nonprofit management topics that students need to know about. I have been using this book in my graduate class for a long time and will continue using it as it is updated with more relevant nonprofit management topics."

Karabi C. Bezboruah, *Associate Professor and Director of PhD programs at*
The University of Texas at Arlington

"*Understanding Nonprofit Organizations* provides an effective overview of critical, contemporary challenges facing today's nonprofit managers and complements that with interesting case studies to highlight these real-world issues. This book helps students and nonprofit managers create more successful, equitable nonprofit organizations. It is a must-read for anyone interested in nonprofit organizations."

Rebecca Nesbit, *University of Georgia*

"These chapters are written by leading scholars and professionals, people who know their topics very well, and they are organized and presented in a way that brings important clarity to the management of this new generation of nonprofit organizations. We are fortunate to have this valuable resource to inform our work in these exciting and promising times."

David O. Renz, *from the Preface to* Understanding
Nonprofit Organizations, 4th Edition

Understanding Nonprofit Organizations

There are no easy solutions to the complexities faced by nonprofit leaders and managers. This textbook addresses the governance, leadership, and management functions of the thousands of organizations in the nonprofit sector that provide an enormous range of services. This thoroughly revised fourth edition of *Understanding Nonprofit Organizations* does not simply recount and summarize seminal literature; it presents 19 of the most important and informative articles, chapters, and essays written about the workings of nonprofit organizations, alongside 18 case studies that illustrate the complex governing, leading, and managing issues raised in the chapters.

The introductions that open each of the nine parts of this book explore important issues and concepts, provide context, and explain what students should be looking for as they read each of the chapters. Each part introduction has been extensively rewritten or updated to address recent movements and changes in the nonprofit field, including the impacts of the COVID-19 pandemic on all aspects of nonprofit organizations' functions and ability to raise funds, increasing social and political divides within countries and communities, the gains and problems that have arisen with dramatic expansion of social media, and the need for justice, equity, diversity and inclusion in our organizations and our society.

Understanding Nonprofit Organizations provides a cohesive set of relevant readings for a course on nonprofit organizations and management, and instructors and students will appreciate the original case studies that parallel the major themes presented. The book is also designed for individuals who are hoping or planning to move into paid or voluntary leadership and management positions in nonprofit organizations—as well as for those already involved with nonprofits seeking to improve their skills and understanding of their chosen field.

Lisa A. Dicke is Professor of Public Administration at the University of North Texas, USA.

J. Steven Ott is Professor Emeritus of Political Science and Public Affairs at the University of Utah, USA.

Understanding Nonprofit Organizations

Governance, Leadership, and Management

Fourth Edition

Edited by
LISA A. DICKE AND J. STEVEN OTT

With case studies by
C. KENNETH MEYER

Routledge
Taylor & Francis Group

NEW YORK AND LONDON

Designed cover image: © Getty Images

Fourth edition published 2023
by Routledge
605 Third Avenue, New York, NY 10158

and by Routledge
4 Park Square, Milton Park, Abingdon, Oxon, OX14 4RN

Routledge is an imprint of the Taylor & Francis Group, an informa business

© 2023 Taylor & Francis

The right of Lisa A. Dicke, J. Steven Ott and C. Kenneth Meyer to be identified as the authors of the editorial material, and of the authors for their individual chapters, has been asserted in accordance with sections 77 and 78 of the Copyright, Designs and Patents Act 1988.

First edition published by Westview Press 2001
Third edition published by Routledge 2016

Library of Congress Cataloging-in-Publication Data
Names: Dicke, Lisa A., 1960– editor. | Ott, J. Steven, editor.
Title: Understanding nonprofit organizations : governance, leadership, and management / edited by J. Steven Ott and Lisa A. Dicke ; with case studies by C. Kenneth Meyer.
Description: Fourth edition. | New York : Routledge, 2023. | Includes bibliographical references.
Identifiers: LCCN 2022054921 (print) | LCCN 2022054922 (ebook) | ISBN 9781032481937 (hardback) | ISBN 9781032471259 (paperback) | ISBN 9781003387800 (ebook)
Subjects: LCSH: Nonprofit organizations—United States. | Voluntarism—United States.
Classification: LCC HD2769.2.U6 U53 2023 (print) | LCC HD2769.2.U6 (ebook) | DDC 658/.0480973—dc23/eng/20230104
LC record available at https://lccn.loc.gov/2022054921
LC ebook record available at https://lccn.loc.gov/2022054922

ISBN: 978-1-032-48193-7 (hbk)
ISBN: 978-1-032-47125-9 (pbk)
ISBN: 978-1-003-38780-0 (ebk)

DOI: 10.4324/9781003387800

Typeset in Garamond
by Apex CoVantage, LLC

Contents

I   Governance of Nonprofit Organizations   1

II   The Legal Framework (Jared C. Bennett)   43

IX   Accountability and Evaluation   349

Figures and Tables

Figures

Tables

Foreword

Leaders and communities across the globe are asking more and more of nonprofit and nongovernmental organizations—more with regard to creativity, more with regard to responsiveness, more with regard to impact and results. This was true prior to the global pandemic that began to grip the world in 2020, but it's even more true as we make our way beyond the pandemic and the resulting economic recession. These are exciting and challenging times for this sector, rife with opportunity but also laden with new kinds of challenges, needs, and threats, and the sector's capacity to deliver on its promises and to serve our communities and citizens well hinges directly on the effectiveness of its leaders and managers. Nonprofits serve in roles of pivotal significance in the shared-power global environment of today, and their leaders and managers must be adept at assessing and addressing the needs and challenges posed by an environment characterized by greater variation and complexity, coupled with cycles of change that are deeper and faster than we traditionally have known. The pace of change and the extent of that change demand of those in nonprofit leadership and management roles the flexibility, agility, and capacity to discern and leverage the conditions of today's fluid environments. And it all must be grounded in a solid base of knowledge, skill, and ability.

Thus, I am delighted that Steve Ott, Lisa A. Dicke, and their colleagues have prepared the fourth edition of this valuable book, *Understanding Nonprofit Organizations*, as a resource to help inform and educate those who lead and manage nonprofit organizations. An undertaking of this magnitude is very demanding, so we are fortunate that Steve, Lisa, and their colleagues have invested their time and energy in the creation of the next generation of this important volume.

This fourth edition arrives at a very interesting and important time. After having moved beyond the recession that gripped the economies of the world around 2010 and the changes it caused, the sector experienced nearly a decade of increased growth and sustainability. Even with the ongoing challenges of a dynamic global and local environment (physical, social, political, and technological), many nonprofits and their leaders achieved a degree of preparedness and alignment that resulted in some degree of stability. To be sure, the smallest of nonprofits continued to struggle with sustainability, and the fortunes of the sector (like the global economy at large) seemed to diverge with a small but very influential percentage of organizations acquiring significant wealth while the rest scrambled for the remainder. But overall, there was a sense of significance and relevance as more communities and constituencies looked to the third sector to address their needs.

And then came the next generation of challenge, with disruption of a magnitude and scope unlike anything experienced by the sector in the modern era. The global COVID pandemic and associated recession that began in 2020 caused exceptional disruption to the sector and ushered in a fundamentally new era of unique demands and expectations for the governance, management, and operation of nonprofit and nongovernmental organizations throughout the world. The impacts varied significantly within the sector, with certain subsectors (notably, health and human services) experiencing dramatic increases in demand for services and aid while other subsectors (notably, arts and culture organizations) found it necessary to essentially close key elements of their operations, many for months and some for years. A notable percentage found it necessary to close.

Health and human services organizations, as in the Great Recession (circa 2009–2011), continue to be challenged by the "triple whammy" of an abrupt increase in demand for essential emergency aid and services, plus an abrupt and dramatic shift in the resource environment (particularly in the nature and form of both philanthropic and governmental financial support), plus an equally abrupt and extreme demand for and shortage of the human and other resources essential to their effective response to the needs of their clients and communities (especially personnel, both paid and volunteer). Further, the sector experienced a dramatic redistribution of resources almost overnight. Even as many frontline emergency aid and safety net nonprofits received a rapid infusion of large amounts of money in the form of government aid and philanthropic investments, other mission categories (such as arts and culture organizations) experienced major and nearly immediate drops in revenues. Even as the urgent and most significant life-and-death consequences of the pandemic moderated, the residual effects of the disruptions and imbalances caused by pandemic relief measures have left large segments of the nonprofit economy (notably, those organizations not among the most wealthy) in substantial disarray.

Indeed, while certain economic indicators of the post-pandemic economy show improvement, the overall state of the nonprofit sector throughout much of the world appears to be nearly as precarious as it was at the height of the Great Recession. As of 2021, reports from US-based organizations (O'Leary, 2021; Martin et al., 2021) document that 75 percent of "lifeline" nonprofits and 50 percent of all nonprofits continue to experience high demand for services; almost half (45 percent) of the surveyed organizations report that they have been unable to meet demand. Indeed, 88 percent

altered their program offerings, 58 percent reduced programs and services, and more than 37 percent reduced staff hours (31 percent laid off or furloughed staff). Increasingly, nonprofits in such straits have stopped using waiting lists or queues for services and simply tell aid seekers they cannot be served. These organizations have been financially challenged as well: 57 percent report that revenues have decreased; those that rely on earned income have experienced a 69 percent decline in revenue, and arts organizations' declines have averaged a 77 percent drop. Perhaps not surprisingly, 39 percent of nonprofits also report that their operating costs have increased.

Of perhaps even greater long-term import are the talent leadership and human capital challenges that US employers (including nonprofits) have experienced in the waning days of the pandemic/recession, including a concurrent US phenomenon some have labelled the "Great Resignation." The Great Resignation refers to the fact that a notable share of the US workforce (about 47.4 million workers, or about 3 percent of the entire US workforce (Laker, 2022)) declined to return to their prior workplaces when economic activity increased, and employers called employees back to work. While attributed to many causes, the key issues in the US nonprofit sector are reported by nonprofit workers in care fields and professions, who report feeling great stress, lack of support (including child care), and "burnout" (especially in health and human services nonprofits). By the end of 2021, more than 42 percent of US nonprofits reported vacancy rates of greater than 20 percent (O'Leary, 2021), a critical problem given these agencies' high demands for services. These conditions exist for nonprofits and nongovernmental organizations in other parts of the world, often for dramatically different conditions. As economies and even nations fail their citizens, the people of nonprofits are pressed into service to aid larger-than-ever numbers of refugees and others who need humanitarian aid, often providing assistance under increasingly harsh and hostile conditions. Even as they often are mistrusted by both those at home and those seeking refuge as they seek to provide a middle ground, nonprofits and NGOs continue to be relied on for provision of the most basic of human services and care.

These are exceptionally challenging times for those who govern, lead, and manage non-profits. It is not hyperbole to assert that our communities' safety nets are fraying, the level of stress throughout the sector is significant and unsustainable, and the potential for relief appears to be very spotty for the large majority of nonprofits that are small to mid-size organizations. (In the US, only 8 percent of nonprofits have annual budgets greater than $1 million (Delaney & O'Leary, 2022).) Many of the organizations in this vital sector are in very fragile condition, and it is going to take a strong new generation of governance, leadership, and management to redevelop and sustain them.

Most concur that these trends affirm that the nonprofit world is changing (and being changed) in relatively fundamental ways, although they are simply the most recent versions of findings from earlier reports. Nonprofit sector scholar Lester Salamon (2010), who lauded the sector's resilience, has written that the context of nonprofit leadership and management has changed so much that it is not at all the same work as in the past. Some aspects have become easier, yet even in 2010 he described much as having become significantly more complex and difficult. Salamon identifies four key types of challenges confronting the sector:

- The challenges of *finance*, ranging from governmental retrenchment to the changing nature of public support to a decline in the share of private giving relative to nonprofit need;
- The challenges of more and different kinds of *competition*, ranging from intra-sector competition among nonprofits for time, talent, and

treasure to inter-sector competition among nonprofits and for-profits for attention, credibility, and business as they jockey for the opportunity to provide services in an increasingly ambivalent marketplace;
- The challenges of *effectiveness*, which arise from the increased demands that nonprofits demonstrate and prove their performance, results, and accountability; and
- The challenges of *technology* as new and increasingly sophisticated digital technologies and social media become available to both the sector and a good share of its constituents, leading to heightened expectations for new levels of communication, engagement, and responsiveness—and to new definitions of effectiveness (Salamon 2010, 97).

Many others have issued studies and reports that chronicle in similar ways the changes and challenges confronting sector leaders and managers. Melissa Campos, Heather Gowdy, and their associates described, in a 2009 assessment prepared for the James Irvine Foundation, that the nonprofit sector was at a unique point in time, "an inflection point" that was driving fundamental reshaping of the sector. The conditions of the post-pandemic world of nonprofit leadership and management match well the trends they discussed, although each is more present in today's world than they found in 2009! They asserted that successful nonprofit leaders and managers must build their capacity to be attuned to rapid and continual shifts such as these as they prepare to manage strategically in the fundamentally new operating environment that is emerging from the *convergence* of five central trends (and especially, they stress, from the interaction of these five converging trends):

- Demographic shifts that redefine participation, including the emergence of increasingly intergenerational and multicultural workplaces that must effectively address issues of engagement, inclusion, and equity;

- Technological advances, including the rise of social media and new ways of communicating, that demand greater openness and transparency and both enable and require nonprofits to strategically leverage and facilitate collaborative engagement;
- Growing networks (technological as well as social) that allow dialogue, work, and even decision making to be organized in multiple new and relatively more fluid ways;
- Rising interest in civic engagement and volunteerism, reflecting both growing expectations for new levels and multiple forms of engagement and heightened expectations that nonprofits will create opportunities better tailored to the contributions of volunteers with these interests and expectations; and
- A blurring of sectoral boundaries as nonprofits, for-profits, and even governmental agencies compete and collaborate in increasingly diverse ways that both enhance and sometimes confuse opportunities for the creation of private wealth and social capital.

These dynamics are challenging, yet they are not necessarily negative. Effective nonprofit leaders and managers are being both innovative and strategic as they explore ways to navigate these changes. For example:

- The realization that it is impossible to operate as they have in the past has led many nonprofit organizations and their leaders to fundamentally rethink what they do and how they do it. At best, nonprofits achieve greater focus as they clarify the core of their mission and then seek innovative ways to address it;
- Many nonprofit organizations, as they experience the problems posed by their traditional revenue strategies, are rethinking their business and revenue models. The exceptional growth in interest in nonprofit social entrepreneurship reflects a new level of creativity as many nonprofits employ different and more diverse ways to fund and finance their work;

- New forms of organizing are being explored and tested, particularly via the expanded use of creative forms of alliances and networks. There is expanded involvement in service-delivery networks as nonprofits recognize that they cannot achieve their results alone;
- There is growing use of hybrid forms of organization that extend across and blur traditional sector boundaries. Such organizations blend the practices of business, government, and nonprofits to achieve results that cannot be achieved in any single sector;
- New and richer ways of understanding and ensuring accountability are being developed at both the organizational and system levels to complement those that operate within programs. Systems are being developed in ways that more effectively gather and employ data to document and enhance performance and effectiveness at both the organizational and program levels of operation;
- Smaller nonprofits are investing in increasingly sophisticated yet lower-cost software that makes it feasible to become more effective in strategy and planning, decision making, constituent relations, and financial and performance management processes;
- Nonprofits are taking marketing more seriously and bringing more sophisticated practices to marketing and branding (which are no longer just euphemisms for fundraising and selling). These practices include adapting and employing social media and other emerging approaches and technologies to enhance constituent relations, communications, alliance and relationship building, and transparency and accountability at relatively low cost;
- Savvy nonprofits also are proactively addressing the human resources facets of nonprofit leadership and management, from developing new leadership talent to succession planning to changing how they engage new generations in their work—for example, by tapping the strong interest of many young people in community-building activities. These agencies

are creating new ways for young adults from all types of backgrounds to become more engaged in service in the sector;

- Increasing numbers are taking advantage of the phenomenal growth in the number and scope of programs in nonprofit leadership and management—both formal degree programs at the bachelor's and master's degree levels and various certificate and other nondegree programs—to build the capacity of both current and aspiring leaders; and
- New forms of leadership and governance are being explored and developed as nonprofit organizations and their leaders work to capitalize on all these trends and dynamics.

Needless to say, these conditions demand the best of even the most experienced nonprofit executives and boards. This is not an easy time to run a nonprofit, and this fourth edition offers important knowledge and insight to those who choose to lead and manage in this new era of nonprofit service.

Some question whether there is any substantive difference between "nonprofit management" and management in other types of organizations. After all, most of the nonprofit management functions explained in this volume are germane to the successful management of any organization. So is there a difference? At core, whether in nonprofit or for-profit organizations, the central purpose of management is the same. However, there are unique dimensions to nonprofit management that are important to recognize because they have a distinct impact on the success of those who do this work (Renz 2016, 741–744).

- *The unique legal context*: To state the obvious, the nonprofit sector in the United States and most other nations of the world is legally distinct from the other sectors. It is neither for-profit business nor government, even as it carries certain characteristics of each, and this difference in legal context is significant to the practice of management. Most notably, it limits the range of strategic options available to the leadership team;

- *The unique ownership structure*: One of the legal differences that becomes significant to management is that of organizational ownership. In the United States and many other nations, it is generally not possible to own (that is, to have an equity stake in, such as stock) a nonprofit charitable organization. In practical terms, the typical US charity is "owned" by the community or segment of the community that it exists to serve. Thus, its governing board and management must act as stewards of the assets of the organization on behalf of the community, even as there is no singular clear external source of accountability or control over the affairs of the organization. Such diffusion of control and accountability creates both unique opportunities and complications for nonprofit management;

- *The unique financial and capital structure*: Further complicating the unique work of nonprofit management is the financial context for a typical nonprofit organization, which often will be much more complex than it is for for-profit businesses of similar size. The typical nonprofit's complicated mix of clients and markets, which correlates directly to complicated business models grounded in diverse and inconsistent funding and financing models, makes the work of nonprofit management distinctive. The typical for-profit business gets its financial support from a relatively uncomplicated set of sources; nonprofits increasingly must fund and finance their operations with a mix of philanthropic resources and earned income derived from a relatively diverse set of sources. Each source imposes its own expectations for operations, management performance, and organizational accountability. Among the most demanding are the governmental sources, since acceptance of funds from government typically intensifies the demands for procedural as well as performance accountability; and

• *The unique accountability context*: Legal and ownership differences blend with the unique political and cultural context of the nonprofit sector to further complicate the work of nonprofit management. One characteristic of the nonprofit organization's diffuse and unclear accountability is that the typical organization has multiple significant stakeholders, most of whom think that they are, or should be, "in charge." These stakeholders bring diverse and conflicting performance expectations to bear on the organization and, therefore, on its management team. In today's environment of heightened concern for accountability and performance, the management team cannot afford to overtly ignore most such expectations, even when they are inconsistent. Thus, one of the most challenging tasks of nonprofit management is to craft a course of action that strikes a reasonable balance among the divergent and shifting expectations and demands of the organization's multiple stakeholders. To meet this challenge, management must have exceptional political sophistication and sensitivity to the external environment. Further, efficiency in the social sector cannot be assessed as it is in business. A sector that serves to address the expressive and artistic needs of a community cannot legitimately be judged by the same criteria brought to bear on those that serve instrumental functions. Indeed, this is where part of the accountability paradox of the sector arises—because many seek to turn the sector into a purely instrumental form. (In its own way, government has done more to create this dynamic than any other part of society.) For many communities, the important value of the sector extends far beyond that of a service provider.

These distinctions are relatively subtle, yet they are very real and very significant, and the failure to understand and address their implications is potentially disabling to the unprepared nonprofit leader or manager.

Some worry, as we continue to develop the professional capacity of the sector's management, that the distinctive character of nonprofits in civil society will be lost. Indeed, there can be some rather dark sides to the professionalization of the management of the nonprofit sector. But there is no reason to believe that this must be the case. Indeed, drawing on a key marketing concept, we can and must remember to regularly and clearly articulate the key differentiators that distinguish nonprofit organizations from all others. If professionalization and education are implemented appropriately, the sector will not lose its way because, at core, effective management must be grounded in and defined by mission accomplishment. So the challenge, in difficult times, is never to forget why we do what we do. I am optimistic that we are very unlikely to forget our mission—our volunteers and donors and community leaders will not let this happen. Although the sector's public trust ratings are lower than I'd like, it remains true that the average citizen values the nonprofit sector and considers it an essential part of a viable society. We know this in no small part because, year after year, we continue to see people across the globe coming together to invest their time and resources to advance the work and impact of the millions of nonprofits (a good share of them all-volunteer organizations) that exist to address their community's needs, interests, and aspirations.

It is through the effective practice of leadership and management that the organizations of the third sector will continue to grow and develop in their capacity to successfully address the needs of a diverse and complicated world. Fortunately, the new generation of nonprofit managers preparing to lead these important organizations understands the increasingly complex nature of the work of nonprofit management.

I congratulate and thank Steve Ott, Lisa A. Dicke, and their colleagues for once again taking on the work of preparing this new and substantially updated edition. It is a welcome contribution to the literature of the nonprofit sector because it explains and illustrates in useful terms what we need to know about nonprofit organizations, how they function, and how they can effectively be led and managed. This new edition has been revised to help leaders and managers understand and address the trends, needs, and dynamics described in this foreword, with new chapters and cases on innovation, networked organizations, social entrepreneurship, and the changing philanthropic and resource environments. These chapters are written by leading scholars and professionals, people who know their topics very well, and they are organized and presented in a way that brings important clarity to the management of this new generation of nonprofit organizations. We are fortunate to have this valuable resource to inform our work in these exciting and promising times.

David O. Renz

Midwest Center for Nonprofit Leadership
Henry W. Bloch School of Management
University of Missouri–Kansas City
February 2022

References

Campos, Melissa Mendes, Alex Hildebrand, David La Piana, and Heather Gowdy, *Convergence: How Five Trends Will Reshape the Social Sector*. San Francisco: James Irvine Foundation (2009).

Delaney, Tim, and Amy Silver O'Leary, "Rising Interest in Nonprofit Dissolutions and Mergers." Blogpost. National Council of Nonprofits. February 16, 2022.

Laker, Benjamin, "From the Great Resignation to the Great Return. Bringing Back the Workforce?" Blogpost. *Forbes*. February 2, 2022.

Martin, Hannah, Kate Gehling, and Ellie Buteau, *Persevering Through the Crisis: The State of Nonprofits*. San Francisco: Center for Effective Philanthropy (2021).

O'Leary, Amy Silver, "The Data Show What We Know: The Nonprofit Helpers Need Help." Blogpost. National Council of Nonprofits. November 23, 2021.

Renz, David O., "Conclusion." In *The Jossey-Bass Handbook of Nonprofit Leadership and Management, 4th ed.*, edited by D. O. Renz, 734–745. San Francisco: Jossey-Bass. (2016).

Salamon, Lester M., "The Changing Context of Nonprofit Leadership and Management." In *The Jossey-Bass Handbook of Nonprofit Leadership and Management*, 3rd ed., edited by David O. Renz, 77–100. San Francisco: Jossey-Bass. (2010).

Preface

Understanding Nonprofit Organizations is a collection of 22 of the most important and informative articles, chapters, and essays written about the workings of nonprofit organizations. This Fourth Edition also includes 18 cases that illustrate the complex governing, leading, and managing issues and challenges raised in the readings.* They are also intended to encourage critical thinking.

There are no easy solutions to the problems and complexities faced by nonprofit leaders and managers today. The world around nonprofits has changed dramatically since our Third Edition. The social activism, advocacy, and responses to societal divides require nonprofits to reorder their perspectives. Together, the introductions to each part, the chapter readings, and the case studies provide opportunities for readers to learn about, reflect on, and analyze circumstances; grapple with solutions; and provide solid rationales for the decisions they make and the positions they take.

This book addresses the governance, leadership, and management functions of the thousands of organizations in the nonprofit sector that engage in a surprisingly wide array of activities and provide an enormous range of services—mostly for the purpose of either improving aspects of the quality of life or preventing its deterioration. In our opinion, this volume includes some of the most insightful and interesting literature that can be found about nonprofit organizations. We hope that you will agree.

Understanding Nonprofit Organizations does not simply tell the readers what the authors of readings have written. It presents their work in their own words. It is designed for individuals who are hoping or planning to move into paid or voluntary leadership and management positions in nonprofit organizations, as well as for those who are already involved with nonprofits and want to learn more about their workings.

It provides a cohesive set of readings for a course on nonprofit organizations and management. Instructors and students will also appreciate the collection of case studies that parallel the major themes presented. The book may be used as the primary text in graduate courses and upper-division undergraduate levels, but it also may be used as a supplement to other texts.

All the introductory essays and reprinted readings attempt to answer two defining questions:

- What is distinctive about the governance, leadership, and management of nonprofit organizations? and
- What has caused nonprofit leadership and management to be distinctive?

Each part of this volume attempts to provide rich answers to these two defining questions by addressing a set of long-standing operating functions and issues from a variety of contemporary perspectives. The introductions that open each of the nine parts introduce important issues and concepts, place them in the context of the environment, and explain what students should be looking for as they read the reprinted chapters. To reflect major changes in the environment around nonprofits in the 2020s and shifts in managerial concerns, the parts in the Fourth Edition have been updated from the Third Edition to address current movements in the nonprofit field, including, for example:

- The impacts of the pandemic on all aspects of nonprofit organizations' functions and ability to raise funds;
- Increasing social and political divides within the country and communities;
- The gains and problems that have arisen with the dramatic expansion of social media; and
- Increased consciousness of the need for justice, equity, diversity, and inclusion in our organizations and our society.

Understanding Nonprofit Organizations focuses on internal organizational issues and the environmental forces that affect them. Theories and concepts of the nonprofit sector are the topics of our companion book, *The Nature of the Nonprofit Sector*, now also in its Fourth Edition and also edited by us with Routledge.

A listing of the parts, the titles, and the authors and dates of the readings in the Table of Contents reveals the scope and depth of the book's coverage—and thus, its usefulness for graduate and upper-division undergraduate courses in nonprofit organizations and management.

Although we fully expect to be criticized for excluding other excellent articles and writers, it will be more difficult to criticize the inclusions. We selected these readings that are among the best or that best inform the parts. The authors of these readings are thoughtful and perceptive. Some are relatively new to the field, and many have written about the management of nonprofit organizations for many years.

Our goals for this edition are to:

- Create a clear vision of what this collection of essays and readings will accomplish;
- Include only previously published readings that tell their stories accurately and understandably;
- Edit and condense the reprinted readings to make them more readable and to help students focus on the central ideas that make these readings worthwhile;

- Provide frameworks in our introductions that provide clarity about the most important topics addressed in each part; and
- Let the authors speak for themselves.

The nonprofit sector as we know it is a unique, mostly democratic phenomenon. The governance, management, and leadership functions of its organizations share similarities with businesses and government agencies but also differ in many important respects. Over the past several decades, however, a blurring of the lines between organizations in the nonprofit, government, and business sectors has eroded some of the distinctiveness of nonprofit organizations and some aspects of their governing, leading, and managing functions. Most nonprofit organizations have become more businesslike and/or more government-like in important ways.

Some changes in managing and leading nonprofit organizations are because of recent changes in our society and technology. There is no doubt that the array of challenges facing the nonprofit sector currently may be of a magnitude beyond any in the sector's history.[1] The pandemic has made it considerably more difficult to build and maintain networks and collaborations with members, donors, and allies. Zoom and Zoom-similar meetings cannot bring people together with the same feelings of connection as face-to-face meetings. Donations to nonprofits in many subsectors have plummeted since the start of the pandemic.[2] Concerns have grown about the long-term viability of nonprofits due to pandemic-related decreases in funding.[3] In order to remain robust, the leaders and managers of nonprofit organizations must rise to these challenges. They must be solidly grounded while remaining able to act quickly and effectively. They must be attuned to strategic thinking, building and participating in strong collaborations, and acting with professionalism and able to use information technology effectively and engage in innovative entrepreneurship. Social media should be a tool in every nonprofit's toolbox for helping managers respond to the challenges.[4]

Success in the nonprofit sector in the 2020s, however, requires even more of its leaders. As those familiar with the field have learned, governing boards and executives must also respect the distinctiveness of the nonprofit sector's history and traditions—including its deep commitment to justice, equality, diversity, and inclusion. Those at the helm of nonprofits are expected to contribute to the health of their communities and to guide their organizations with care and altruistic hearts.

Criteria for the Selection of Readings

Several criteria were used to make final selections about readings to include in this book. The first "test" that any reading had to pass was an unequivocal "yes" answer to two questions: Should the serious student of the nonprofit sector be expected to be able to identify the authors and their basic themes—the crux of their arguments? Does the reading provide a reason or reasons why the governance, leadership, or management of nonprofit organizations is distinctive?

The second criterion was related to the first: each reading had to make a statement. This criterion did not eliminate controversial readings; quite the contrary, it simply required that a reading cannot be ignored. Third, the chapter had to be readable—not written in technical jargon. Last, the reading had to advance the purposes for this volume substantively. It had to address issues, ideas, or innovations that are important to the governance, leadership, or management of nonprofit organizations.

In sum, this book is about the internal structures and workings of nonprofit organizations, not macro issues and macro theories, which are represented in the many interesting readings about the nonprofit sector in our companion book, *The Nature of the Nonprofit Sector*.[5] Most of the readings we have reviewed recently fit cleanly into and contributed substance to either *Understanding Nonprofit Organizations* or *The Nature of the Nonprofit Sector*. Most decisions about where they belonged were easy to make. Decisions about readings on intersectoral relations and international nonprofit organizations were the most difficult.

The Case Studies

The case studies that are included in this Fourth Edition complement the topics raised in each part. They will help students develop a deeper appreciation for the decisions and dilemmas that arise in the management and leadership of nonprofit organizations through the scenarios depicted in the cases. Instructors are encouraged to use the cases to stimulate class discussions, to help students recognize and engage with the challenges nonprofit managers and leaders face, and to hone and strengthen their critical thinking skills. The names and places used in the cases are fictitious, but the scenarios are not. Those who have been working in the nonprofit field will quickly realize that the situations and circumstances are "all too realistic." But familiarity does not lead to prescription! Such are the challenges—and excitement—of governing, leading, and managing nonprofit organizations.

We sincerely hope you will enjoy this book!

Lisa A. Dicke
University of North Texas

J. Steven Ott
University of Utah

Notes

* We use "chapters" and "readings" interchangeably throughout this preface. All "chapters" are previously published readings—book chapters, articles, and reports.

1. Lester M. Salamon, Stephanie L. Geller, and Kasey Spence, "Impact of the 2007–09 Economic Recession on Nonprofit Organizations," Listening Post Project Communique 14 (Baltimore, MD: Johns Hopkins Center for Civil Society Studies, 2009), 5.

2. Michael Theis. "Americans Giving More to Health Causes Since the Pandemic and Cutting Back on Environment and Education." *The Chronicle of Philanthropy* (April 29, 2020). www.philanthropy. com/article/americans-giving-more-to-health-causes-since-the-pandemic-and-cutting-back-on-environment-and-education/

3. Sarah O'Brien reported that the wealthy did not decrease giving in 2020. In "Here's How the Pandemic Changed Charitable Giving by Wealthy Households in 2020." *CNBC* (May 13, 2021.) www.cnbc.com/2021/05/13/heres-how-pandemic-changed-charitable-donations-from-the-wealthy.html

4. Katie Sehl, "Social Media for Nonprofits: 11 Essential Tips for Success." *Hootsute.* (September 21, 2020). https://blog.hootsuite.com/social-media-for-nonprofits/

5. J. Steven Ott and Lisa A. Dicke, eds., *The Nature of the Nonprofit Sector,* 4th ed. New York: Routledge (2021).

Acknowledgments

Space and propriety limit our statements of appreciation, but intellectual contributions that absolutely must be acknowledged include Stephen R. Block, University of Colorado–Denver; Kirsten Grønbjerg, Indiana University–Bloomington; David O. Renz, University of Missouri–Kansas City; Jesus Valero, University of Utah; Hee Soun Jang, Yu Shi, and Laura Keyes at the University of North Texas; Marina Saitgalina at Old Dominion University; and Ashley E. English at Texas Christian University. We also thank our wonderful colleagues in the ASPA Section on Nonprofits, the NASPAA Nonprofit Management Education Section, and ARNOVA, who have provided invaluable input and unflagging support and encouragement.

We acknowledge and thank C. Kenneth Meyer at Drake University for his collaboration on this Fourth Edition of *Understanding Nonprofit Organizations*. His generous contributions of the case study exercises and thoughtful suggestions have improved the volume and helped make the project a joy to undertake and complete. He and his colleagues have been wonderful to work with. Our appreciation also goes to Valencia Prentice, PhD, alumni of and Mohamed Bamanie, PhD, alumni of University of North Texas for authoring a case study on fund development. Coleen Franckowiak and Christopher Byrd at the University of North Texas supported this project throughout, and Floyd Rosenkranz also provided exceptional support and encouragement.

In addition, we extend special appreciation to Jared Bennett, who updated his introduction to Part II, "The Legal Framework," and Michele Cole, who wrote the original chapter "Capacity Building: Strategies for Successful Fundraising," included in Part V. Our Routledge representatives Laura Varley, Elizabeth Hart, and Marie Roberts have been exceptional. Finally, we owe a special debt of gratitude to David Gies and Jay Shafritz, co-collaborators in editing the 1990 book *The Nonprofit Organization: Essential Reading.*[1] Their ahead-of-the-times ideas and insights helped shape our thinking about the nonprofit sector and its organizations—and thus also the original concept for this book.

Note

1. David L. Gies, J. Steven Ott, and Jay M. Shafritz, eds., *The Nonprofit Organization: Essential Readings* (Fort Worth, TX: Harcourt Brace, 1990; originally published by Brooks/Cole, Pacific Grove, CA). This book is now out of print.

PART I

GOVERNANCE OF NONPROFIT ORGANIZATIONS

Governance is an umbrella term that includes the ultimate authority, accountability, and responsibility for an organization. Nonprofit organizations are governed through complex sets of functional roles and procedures that are defined in laws and tax codes, influenced by numerous external constituencies, and shaped to fit their own missions, structures, activities, personalities, policies, and procedures.[1] The governance of a nonprofit organization is a product of its purposes, people, resources, contracts, clients, boundaries, community coalitions and networks, and actions as prescribed (or prohibited) in its articles of incorporation and bylaws, state laws and codes, and the US Internal Revenue Service (IRS) codes and rules.[2]

A nonprofit organization that incorporates becomes a *corporation* and therefore is similar in many ways, "in the eyes of the law," to a for-profit business.[3] Corporations are *artificial persons*, groups of individuals who obtain legal identities and legal standing through the act of incorporation or, in some cases, through the act of legally associating—that is, forming and filing with a state as *associations*. The statutes of nonprofit incorporation differ somewhat from state to state, but all specify that the *board of trustees* (also referred to as the *board of directors*) is the ultimate point of responsibility and accountability for a nonprofit organization.[4] In some states, the laws are even more detailed and define specific responsibilities of boards. The courts have also been active in defining the basic responsibilities of boards. In the landmark 1974 *Sibley Hospital* case, for example, the Federal District Court for the District of Columbia held (among other things) that the board of trustees is responsible for active supervision of a nonprofit corporation's managers and for overseeing its financial management.[5] In 2002, the American Competitiveness and Corporate Accountability Act (commonly known as the Sarbanes-Oxley Act) was signed into law. The purpose of the act was to rebuild trust in America's corporate sector after a series of high-profile accounting scandals. Although very few provisions of Sarbanes-Oxley are directly applicable to nonprofit boards of trustees, it has served as a warning to all boards: "If nonprofit leaders do not ensure effective governance of their organizations, the government may step forward and also regulate nonprofit governance."[6] Ten general principles in the Sarbanes-Oxley Act are not directly aimed at nonprofit boards of directors, yet all are worth considering for students of nonprofit organizations. These include a clear identification of the role(s) of a board, the importance of independent directors, the activities and responsibilities of audit committees, governance and nominating committees, compensation committees, the disclosure and integrity of institutional information, ethics and business conduct codes, executive and (when applicable) director compensation, monitoring compliance and investigating complaints, and document destruction and retention. Each of these principles is

DOI: 10.4324/9781003387800-1

a matter of concern for a board of directors that collectively and, more recently, individually, are responsible for ensuring the health and fiscal integrity of the organization and compliance with legal directives. Two provisions of Sarbanes-Oxley do pertain directly to nonprofits:

> Board members are supposed to know what the organizations they oversee are actually doing; fiduciary responsibility has meaning and consequences for board members; there is a relationship between good governance and organizational effectiveness; and . . . institutional funders and individual donors should be legitimately concerned with and attentive to nonprofit governance.[7]

By statute, a nonprofit organization's articles of incorporation and bylaws must specify the composition of the board, its responsibilities, and the rules and procedures under which the board will govern. The legal objective is to ensure that the board of trustees abides by applicable laws, makes certain that the organization's activities are directed toward the purposes stated in the articles of incorporation, and protects the organization and its assets through oversight activities.

Most statutes of nonprofit incorporation deal with boards of trustees as legal entities (as "artificial persons"), not as individual persons. When directors are acting in their capacities as members of a board, for the most part, they are not "persons" in the eyes of the law, but rather parts of a corporation board—unless they individually violate provisions of laws, bylaws, or articles. The *corporate veil* is the legal assumption that the actions of a corporation are not the actions of its owners and directors; thus, its owners and directors usually cannot be held responsible for corporate actions. Also, a nonprofit board of trustees and its members are protected from undue personal liability when the nonprofit is incorporated under the laws of a state.[8] In the past few decades, however, the courts have been more inclined to hold individual board members co-responsible for the collective actions of a board; thus, service on a board of trustees involves a degree of exposure to legal liability.

Governance Defined

Merriam-Webster's Dictionary defines *govern* as:

> 1. To direct and control; rule. 2. To regulate; restrain. 3. To be a rule of law for; to determine. Syn. Govern, rule means to exercise power or authority in controlling others. Govern connotes as its end a keeping in a straight course or smooth operation for the good of the individual and the whole.

Governance is the function of oversight that a group of people assume when they incorporate under the laws of a state for an organizational purpose that qualifies for nonprofit status. For most observers of nonprofit organizations, governance is "a general term referring to the collective actions of a board of directors or board of trustees in its governing of a tax-exempt organization."[9] Governance includes serving on a board of trustees and exercising and expressing one's attitudes, beliefs, and values on matters pertaining to the organization. Some writers disagree with this narrow construction of governance and believe that the definition should be broader: for example, the term *governance* may be defined to mean the strategic leadership of nonprofit organizations. In current parlance, the term has taken on a more specific meaning as a process for making certain types of management decisions. These are commonly referred to as *strategic decisions*.[10]

The scope and depth of the influence of the board of directors on a nonprofit organization are, to say the least, substantial.

Most people would agree with these ideals: boards should know who they work for; they should require their organizations to be effective and efficient; they should be in control of their organizations; the control they exercise should be of a type that empowers rather than strangling; they should be fair in judging but unafraid to judge, rigorously holding delegates accountable; they should be disciplined as to their roles and their behavior; they should require discipline with regard to the roles and behavior of their individual members; as the highest authority in enterprise, they should be predictable and trustworthy.[11]

Who Governs?

Virtually everyone agrees that a nonprofit organization's board of trustees is—and should be—the final authority on governance decisions.[12] The term *board of directors*, or *board of trustees*, refers to a governing board. A *governing board* is a group of individuals who have assumed a legal responsibility for an organization's existence. These individuals make policy and are responsible for how money is generated and spent toward the accomplishment of a mission that can be beneficial to the general public or to a segment of the population.[13]

Not all boards of directors, however, live up to their potential. "Many nonprofit boards, probably the great majority, do not come close to realizing their leadership potential in practice and as a consequence have become increasingly frustrated, dissatisfied, and often angry."[14] Likewise, the composition of the board may not allow all board members to be proactive in "expressing one's attitudes, beliefs, and values on matters pertaining to the organization." This may occur if care is not taken to ensure that an inclusive environment is built: one where respect for others exists and a diversity of opinions may be shared. In practice, many boards also fail to live up to their potential by paying too much attention to nongoverning activities rather than shouldering their primary mission.[15]

Most discussions of governance in nonprofit organizations emphasize the roles and functions not only of the board but also of the executive director—usually the top-paid staff person responsible for the day-to-day operations of the organization.[16]

> In the voluntary sector context, *governance* generally refers to the arena of action in which boards of directors *and* executive staff are key players . . . . In most nonprofit organizations supported in part by public funds . . . the governance challenge is met by both executive staff and board members."[17]

Governing as a set of shared functions also extends to the consideration of input from client and stakeholder groups.[18] Nonprofit governance has also been conceptualized as *traditional* or *contemporary*.

> The traditional framework views nonprofit governance at the organizational level where the board of directors and trustees are considered responsible for higher-level policy decisions, the accomplishment of the agency's goals, and conformance to all the legal requirements. In contrast, the contemporary framework views nonprofit governance as moving beyond the internal scope of responsibility to addressing the community or public interest.[19]

An organizational life cycle approach to governing has also been proposed.[20]

Why Governance Is Needed

Nonprofit governance may sound like an unnecessary complication. After all, the presence of multiple actors practically guarantees that there will be multiple headaches. Why is governance even needed in nonprofit organizations, which provide services or engage in other activities that are not for the personal gain of the people who volunteer with or are employed by them or serve on their boards? Only in modern times have legal structures and formal rules seriously affected the efforts of people to help their neighbors. The complexities of our society, the force of law (notably laws that involve licensure and tax-exempt status), and citizens' growing concerns about potential abuses, fraud, and violations of expectations (implied social contracts) by nonprofit organizations, government, small businesses, and communities have all changed the environment for nonprofits and, with it, the "ground rules."[21]

A well-functioning, mission-focused, informed, and perhaps influential board of trustees is essential for long-term organizational effectiveness and survival. Networks of information, interorganizational linkages, and knowledge come together through the connections between executive directors and boards of trustees.[22]

Nonprofit organizations also need the benefit of free (or nearly free) advice. Executive directors must be able to turn to board members for counsel and support. The day-to-day time and energy needed to manage the dynamics of a nonprofit's mission, goals, programs, personnel, volunteers, board officers, and external constituencies do not permit an executive director to stay current on all important laws, court rulings, and regulations. Without rapid access to accurate information from experts who are sympathetic board members and who, therefore, also know the organization and its programs, a nonprofit organization may sometimes be at considerable risk. This *advice and counsel* function of trustees is only one vital piece, however, of their larger set of responsibilities and accountabilities. Not only do board members have responsibilities as part of the organization's formal internal control and oversight mechanism, but they also fill important boundary-spanning roles that connect the organization with segments of its environment.[23]

Board members are the primary links between a nonprofit organization and its community. Trustees thus function as information channels, interorganizational intermediaries, and sources of legitimacy who buffer an organization from pressures in its environment.[24] They also seek and attract external resources and information through their established networks of relationships.

Thus, governance is both the "steering" and the overseeing of organizational activities, assets, and relationships by boards of trustees and executives, within a framework of law and ethics. From this perspective, governing is a form of philanthropy: "voluntary giving, voluntary serving, and voluntary association to achieve some vision of the public good."[25] Governing is a form of philanthropy because it represents individuals giving their time, effort, and influence to help improve an aspect of the quality of life or to prevent it from deteriorating.[26]

The challenges facing the nonprofit sector related to governance and boards of trustees are great. The findings from a 2007 survey conducted by Francie Ostrower of over 5,100 public charities in the United States showed that a large percentage of nonprofit boards were racially and ethnically homogeneous, raising questions about their ability to be responsive to a diverse public. The Ostrower report, *Nonprofit Governance in the United States*, also showed that a substantial percentage of nonprofit board members were not actively engaged in basic governance activities such as fundraising, monitoring of programs, and community relations. Likewise, 70 percent of nonprofit organizations reported having some difficulty finding board members.[27]

Readings Reprinted in Part I

In his 1998 classic definition of "board of directors," Stephen R. Block emphasizes the unequivocal governance responsibilities of boards:

> Accountability for any nonprofit organization ultimately rests with its board of directors . . . .
> Although the board may delegate management authority to a paid staff person . . . the board

can never be relieved of its legal and fiduciary responsibilities. Governing board members are stewards of the public interest."[28]

Block addresses many board-related issues, including board purposes, relationships between a board and an executive director, important board responsibilities, the functions of specific board officers, the board's role in development, board diversity, the desirable size of a board, board liability, the dismissal of board members who are not performing, and fundamental differences between governing, advisory, and honorary boards.

"Ethno-racial Diversity on Nonprofit Boards: A Critical Mass Perspective" by Christopher Fredette and Ruth Sessler Bernstein posits that although there is wide agreement among scholars that diversity and inclusion in the composition of a board are essential, studies consistently find homogeneity within board membership. Diversifying boards is a key goal for nonprofits—to be representative, inclusive of diverse perspectives, and in tune with their constituents and communities. Fredette and Sessler Bernstein's research is designed to "disentangle and clarify the relationship between board diversity and governance outcomes by testing a 'critical mass' or 'tipping point' explanation for the observed variability for this relationship" (p. 932). Their study focuses on the composition and governance of 247 nonprofit boards of directors in the greater Toronto, Canada, area. The authors investigate levels of diversity in board composition and identify implications for fiduciary performance, stakeholder engagement, and organizational responsiveness. What, they ask, is the tipping point for minority voices to really be heard?

Case Studies in Part I

The two case studies in Part I, "Welcome to the Board of Directors" and "Leadership and Growth Challenges in Nonprofit Organizations," provide readers with an opportunity to consider the decisions and activities that fall under the purview of a member of a board of directors. In "Welcome to the Board of Directors," a new member of a national board is elated to become a part of the governing body. As often happens, however, she must soon confront a preexisting board culture that creates a less-than-ideal state of affairs.

In "Leadership and Growth Challenges in Nonprofit Organizations," the actions of a board of directors, issues of leadership, and aspects of vision and mission drift raise questions about past obligations and new governance responsibilities. Readers are asked to consider the overarching idea of governance and the role of a board of directors and their obligations to constituents amid the ever-changing composition of stakeholders. What is the role of the governing board when confronted with new visions and opportunities that call for change? In what ways does the composition of a board of directors affect potential governing priorities and activities?

Notes

1. Robert D. Herman and David O. Renz, "Multiple Constituencies and the Social Construction of Nonprofit Organization Effectiveness" (reprinted in Part X of *Understanding Nonprofit Organizations,* 2nd ed., 2012).

2. In some states, the term *charter* or *articles of association* is used instead of *articles of incorporation.*

3. Although nonprofit organizations and for-profit corporations share many similarities, they also have important differences. From a legal perspective, however, both may be corporations.

4. For a more extensive discussion, see Part II, "The Legal Framework."

5. *Sibley Hospital* is the popular name for *Stern v. Lucy Webb Hayes National Training School* (381 F. Supp. 1003 [D. DC, 1974]).

6. BoardSource and Independent Sector, "The Sarbanes-Oxley Act and Implications for Nonprofit Organizations," 2003 (revised January 2006), www.independentsector.org/uploads/Accountability_Documents/sarbanes_oxley_implications.pdf

7. Rick Cohen, "Sarbanes-Oxley: Ten Years After," *Nonprofit Quarterly* (December 30, 2012), https://nonprofitquarterly.org/governancevoice/21563-sarbanes-oxley-ten-years-later.html

8. Statutes vary widely among states, however, and court interpretations of liability statutes have changed considerably in recent decades. Staying abreast of legal rulings and interpretations is an ongoing responsibility for nonprofit boards.

9. J. Steven Ott and Jay M. Shafritz, "Governance," in J. Steven Ott and Jay M. Shafritz, *The Facts on File Dictionary of Nonprofit Organization Management* (New York: Facts on File, 1986), 172.

10. Vic Murray, "Governance of Nonprofit Organizations," in *The International Encyclopedia of Public Policy and Administration*, edited by Jay M. Shafritz (Boulder, CO: Westview Press, 1998), 993.

11. John Carver and Miriam Carver, *The Policy Governance Model and the Role of the Board Member* (San Francisco: Jossey-Bass/Wiley, 2009), 2.

12. See, for example, John Carver, *Boards That Make a Difference*, 3rd ed. (San Francisco: Jossey-Bass/Wiley, 2006); and Cyril O. Houle, *Governing Boards: Their Nature and Nurture*, 2nd ed. (San Francisco: Jossey-Bass, 1997).

13. Stephen R. Block, *Perfect Nonprofit Boards: Myths, Paradoxes, and Paradigms* (Needham Heights, MA: Simon & Schuster Custom Publishing, 1998), 30.

14. Doug Eadie, *Extraordinary Board Leadership: The Keys to High-Impact Governing*, 2nd ed. (Sudbury, MA: Jones and Bartlett, 2009), 9.

15. See, for example, ibid., 1–34.

16. See Vic Murray, "Governance of Nonprofit Organizations," 993–997, and Judith R. Saidel, "Expanding the Governance Construct: Functions and Contributions of Nonprofit Advisory Groups," *Nonprofit and Voluntary Sector Quarterly* 27, no. 4 (December 1998): 421, 422.

17. Judith R. Saidel. "Expanding the Governance Construct," 421, 422. Saidel argues that advisory groups and committees also fill important governance roles in many nonprofit organizations with government grants or contracts. 1998, *Nonprofit and Voluntary Sector Quarterly*, 27.

18. Kelly LeRoux, "Paternalistic or Participatory Governance? Examining Opportunities for Client Participation in Nonprofit Social Service Organizations," *Public Administration Review* (May-June 2009): 504–517.

19. Shamima Ahmed, "Nonprofit Governance," in Shamima Ahmed, *Effective Non-Profit Management: Context, Concepts, and Competencies* (Boca Raton, FL: CRC Press, 2012), 95–131, 95.

20. *Mike Burns, "Act Your Age! Organizational Life Cycles: How They Impact Your Board" (Branford, CT: BWB Solutions, 2010)*

21. See Part IX in our companion book *The Nature of the Nonprofit Sector*, 4th ed., edited by J. Steven Ott and Lisa A. Dicke (New York: Routledge. 2021).

22. Melissa Middleton-Stone, "Nonprofit Boards of Directors: Beyond the Governance Function," in *The Nonprofit Sector: A Research Handbook*, edited by W. W. Powell (New Haven: Yale University Press, 1987), 141–153.

23. See Part VII, "Community and Civil Society Theories of the Nonprofit Sector," in Ott and Dicke, *The Nature of the Nonprofit Sector*, 4th ed.

24. Pamela A. Popielarz and J. Miller McPherson, "On the Edge or In Between: Niche Position, Niche Overlap, and the Duration of Voluntary Association Memberships," *American Journal of Sociology* 101, no. 3 (November 1995): 698–720.

25. *Warren F. Ilchman, "Philanthropy," in Shafritz, The International Encyclopedia of Public Policy and Administration, 1654–1661.*

26. See Part VIII, "Theories of Giving and Philanthropy," in Ott and Dicke, *The Nature of the Nonprofit Sector,* 4th ed.

27. Francie Ostrower, "Nonprofit Governance in the United States: Findings on Performance and Accountability from the First National Representative Study," Urban Institute, 2007, www.urban.org/UploadedPDF/411479_ Nonprofit_Governance.pdf; see also "Five Questions for Francie Ostrower," Urban Institute: Elevate the Debate, July 19, 2007, www.urban.org/toolkit/fivequestions/FOstrower.cfm?renderforprint=1

28. Stephen R. Block, "Board of Directors," in Shafritz, *The International Encyclopedia of Public Policy and Administration,* 201–209, 201.

CHAPTER 1

Board of Directors

Stephen R. Block

Originally published in *The International Encyclopedia of Public Policy and Administration*, edited by Jay M. Shafritz, copyright © 1998. Reprinted by permission of Westview Press, a member of The Perseus Books Group.

[B]oards of directors are] vested with the legal responsibility to govern and control the affairs of organizations. Accountability for any nonprofit organization ultimately rests with its board of directors (sometimes called board of trustees). Although the board may delegate management authority to a paid staff person, known as the executive director, the board can never be relieved of its legal and fiduciary responsibilities. Governing board members are stewards of the public interest and have a burden of responsibility to use and preserve the organization's assets for advancing a beneficial mission.

Board membership is an admirable act of citizenship for those who are willing to accept a significant amount of volunteering. These special people are generally not compensated for their board service, and they must balance their board obligations with personal demands of work, family responsibilities, and other community activities. This commitment to community service is tied to a long history of voluntary action, with roots that precede the founding of the United States. The innate desire to help is said to be a unique quality in America, a democratic attribute that influences the modern nonprofit board of directors.

Because of the board's legal responsibilities, personal limitations on directors' time, and the daily involvement of the executive director, there is often confusion between the board and staff over roles, responsibilities, turf, and expectations for performance. The board and executive director must clearly understand their mutual expectations if they are to develop a healthy governing body.

Why Have a Board?

Of the many reasons for having a board of directors, legal necessity is primary. In some states, only one board member is required for incorporating an organization, but most states require at least three or more individuals to serve as directors of a governing board. The Internal Revenue Service also requires nonprofit organizations seeking or maintaining recognition for tax-exempt purposes to have governing boards of directors. Members of governing boards are expected to engage willingly in board activities,

DOI: 10.4324/9781003387800-2

without receiving any benefit of the organization's assets or earnings.

Aside from the legal necessities, the most practical reasons for having a board of directors are to ensure that the organization is effectively managed and is working toward the achievement of a mission that has a public purpose. Few nonprofit organizations have the resources to employ the personnel with the expertise that is necessary to accomplish their organizational activities. The collective wisdom of the board of directors can serve as a bank of skilled and knowledgeable resources to provide support, advice, and counsel. It has been widely proposed that board members should comprise the three Ws; individuals who are willing to "work," some with "wisdom," and others with "wealth."

Why Would Someone Want to Serve on a Board?

Each person has his or her own reason for voluntary board service; however, one of the most often-stated is to serve one's community. Volunteering as a board member is an honor and a fundamental privilege of a free people.

There are many reasons for joining or for staying on a board. For example, board participation may be an expectation of one's employer. It may provide an opportunity for gaining or maintaining social status in the community, satisfy socializing needs, lead to new knowledge and skills, and enhance one's résumé. For some people, voluntary board service satisfies religious convictions based on a belief in the organization's cause or mission; or is based on personal experience of a problem (such as a disease or tragedy) that is addressed by the work and mission of the organization.

The Board's Relationship with its Executive Director

Various authors have described their ideas about the ideal working relationship between the board

and executive director. Two governance models prevail. One model builds on the traditional view that the executive director is employed as a subordinate to the board. The working relationship is characterized by distinct and separate roles for the board and executive director, with the board directing, supervising, and limiting the director's activities as the board sees fit.

The other governance model builds on ideas of partnership and collegiality between the executive director and board of directors. This model acknowledges that the board of directors has clearly defined legal responsibilities. However, the model differs from traditional approaches in a fundamental way: The executive director takes an active role in assisting with or coordinating the participation of board members in fulfilling their governance commitment. This form of board management makes full use of the executive director's distinctive management and leadership skills. Consequently, the quality of the board's performance is a direct result of the executive director's ability to steer and promote productive interaction among board members. The executive director can call upon board managers to intervene when necessary in either the internal or external environment of the organization.

Who is in Charge of Making Policy?

Prescriptions for effective board practice often state that the board is legally responsible for making policy and the staff is responsible for carrying it out. Though this division of labor is technically correct, it is inaccurate in its practice. The staffs of nonprofit organizations have a significant level of influence on the creation of policy. Since they are closest to the operations and programs of the agency, they may know when a new policy would provide the guidance needed to get the job done. Thus, staff input is almost always required to create new policies. In addition, the staff often shapes the policy by drafting proposed policy statements.

In effective nonprofit organizations, the staff's point of view on matters of policy development is considered an integral part of governance. Often, effective organizations are those in which the board adopts policy with input of the staff, and the staff implement policy with the advice, counsel, and support of the board.

What are the Major Areas of Board Responsibility?

There are at least nine major areas of board responsibility; namely, to

1. determine the organization's mission;
2. set policies and adopt plans for the organization's operations;
3. approve the budget, establish fiscal policies and financial controls, and monitor the financial position of the organization;
4. provide adequate resources for the organization through establishment of resource- development goals and commitment to fundraising through giving and soliciting;
5. develop organizational visibility through networking and linkage to the community;
6. ensure that the organization's corporate and governance documents are updated and secured, and all reports are filed as required;
7. recruit and select new board members and provide them with an orientation to the board's business;
8. recruit, hire, evaluate, reward, or terminate, if necessary, the executive director of the organization; and
9. protect and preserve the organization's nonprofit tax-exempt status.

The Role of Board Officers

The officers of the board of directors have a responsibility to set the tone for organizational leadership. The duties of the president (chairperson), vice president, treasurer, and secretary are described in the organization's bylaws.

President

In most nonprofit organizations the title and position of president refers to the highest-level volunteer who also serves as chairperson of the organization. However, in some nonprofit organizations a corporate model of governance is followed; therefore, the title of "president" replaces the more commonly used title of "executive director." If the president is also the paid chief executive, the position usually allows for participation as a board member. In this instance, the role of chairperson is handled by the chief volunteer.

The volunteer president or chairperson is responsible for the activities of the board and for assigning board committee chairs, unless assignments are automatically spelled out in the bylaws. The chair is responsible for monitoring the work of the board and evaluating the board's performance. The chair presides at and calls special meetings of the board and sets the direction for organizational goal setting. This volunteer position requires a great deal of time commitment and responsibility.

Vice President

In the absence of the volunteer president, the vice president usually assumes the duties of president and the responsibility for chairing board meetings. Often, the role of vice president entails chairing a major committee of the board. In some organizations, the vice president automatically becomes president-elect, a succession plan that may not be effective in all organizations.

Secretary

The board secretary has the obligation to protect the organization's corporate documents, such as the bylaws, the articles of incorporation, board and committee minutes, and important correspondence.

Many individuals try to avoid election to the office of secretary because of the myth that the board secretary must take the minutes of the board and executive committee meetings. The board secretary does not have to write the minutes, but he or she is responsible for ensuring that the minutes are taken and accurately reflect the business meetings of the board and executive committee. Upon becoming official annals of the organization, the board minutes should be signed and dated by the board secretary. In organizations that rely on parliamentary rules and procedures (such as *Robert's Rules of Order Newly Revised)*, the board secretary is required to become familiar with the meeting procedures and may have to make procedural rulings.

Treasurer

The treasurer should not be expected to do the bookkeeping and accounting for the organization. Instead, the treasurer is responsible for making sure that the organization's finances are properly accounted for and excess revenues are wisely invested. If a finance committee exists, the treasurer often serves as its chairperson. On behalf of the board, the treasurer ensures that financial controls are in place and tested on a periodic basis. The treasurer also participates in the selection and recommendation of an auditing firm. The treasurer reports on the financial statements at board meetings, executive committee meetings, and, if applicable, at annual meetings of the organization.

The Board's Role in Fundraising

The board must play a fundamental role in raising money and resources. Board members also have the personal responsibility of making financial contributions in addition to giving their voluntary time to the organization. Instituting a policy that requires board members to contribute is sometimes employed.

Unanimous giving among the board sets the right tone for fundraising. It enhances the

credibility of the organization when it seeks contributions from others. Unanimous-board-giving practices have even become an expectation among many funders.

Giving is only one part of the board member's obligation; the other part is to assist in planning and solicitation activities. Collectively, the board can identify a pool of potential contributors. Friends, business associates, relatives, and vendors are among likely prospects. Some board members shy away from verbally asking for money, but they may be able to write letters or at least sign letters that have been drafted for them by staff.

Board Composition

Determining the composition of a board of directors is claimed by some to be a blend of science and art.

Board composition should not be the result of opening the door to just anyone who is willing to serve but should result from purposeful recruitment strategies. Prospective board members, for example, should be familiarized with the organization's purpose, mission, vision, goals, and objectives, as well as board duties, responsibilities, and the organization's expectations.

The task of filling vacancies on the board should be approached carefully and should result in a board composition that is able to advance the organization's mission. There are two preparatory steps to actively recruiting the right person. The initial step is to acknowledge that organizations go through different stages of development similar to the various life cycles experienced by individuals. Various maturational stages lead to differing organizational issues and needs. Assessing which phase an organization is in is useful not only to prepare the organization for change but also to determine the leadership qualities required of potential board members. Matching an organization's life cycle to the requisite skills of a board member could lead to more effective and purposeful organizational outcomes.

A second step is to conduct a thorough demographic inventory of board composition, which will reveal the board's weakest representational areas. Inventory results will show a compositional balance or imbalance in such variables as gender, age range, ethnicity, socioeconomic status, political party affiliation, educational level, professional or vocational interests, knowledge of consumer issues, and location of primary residence. Information of this type can be valuable to organizations especially seeking to create a diverse board.

As suggested, the composition of a board can contribute to the level of ease or difficulty with which an organization is governed and managed. A board composed of individuals with similar socioeconomic backgrounds or other familiar traits may reach consensus more often, but it is less likely to formulate challenging ideas or seek out policy reforms. Compared to homogeneous boards, those that reflect diversity among their members are likely to experience greater participatory challenges. Even though diversity is an enriching quality in a board, its members must contend with differing values, mores, and interpretations of community information and beliefs.

The Executive Director as Board Member

Some nonprofit organizations use a corporate model of governance structure in which the position of executive director is transformed from staff to member of the board as its president/chief executive officer (CEO).

The model of corporate governance may not be an appropriate structure for all nonprofit organizations. It is used by larger and more complex institutions that rely on a strong CEO. Regardless of size, the CEO as staff and board member must be wary of conflicts of interest and must avoid participating in discussions or decision making that will lead to personal benefits. Critics of nonprofit organizations using corporate models suggest that the CEOs have no choice but to use the knowledge they have acquired in managing the day-to-day operations. This knowledge is often used to influence the direction of the board and organization . . . .

Board Recruitment and Orientation

Preconditions of board recruitment include identifying the governance needs of organizations in (life-cycle) transition and discovering the characteristics and qualities to be found in new board members. There are many variables to consider in sizing up a board prospect, including:

1. an individual's ability to create a vision, problem-solve, and facilitate conflict resolution;
2. an individual's commitment of time to participate fully;
3. enthusiasm for the organization's mission, vision, goals, and values;
4. a person's skills and experience in such areas as public policy analysis and fundraising, or expertise in program service delivery; and
5. diversity factors.

Once a profile is developed that describes the ideal board member, the recruitment task can formally begin. On the basis of expediency, many nonprofit organizations make the mistake of ignoring the profile and recruiting the friends of board members. Sometimes, individuals are invited to become prospective board members for the simple reason that they are alive and seem agreeable to serving! Serious problems may occur when attempts have not been made to match the needs of the organization with the ideal board member. Locating someone who matches the profile and agrees to serve, however, is not a guarantee of board success. In fact, most governance problems seem to stem from the recruitment process. Though using a profile can increase the likelihood of finding the right person, a perfect match does not guarantee that problems will not arise, such as, nonattendance at board meetings, lack of participation in board committees, an unwillingness to contribute financially, or interfering with or trying to micromanage the day-to-day operations of the organization.

Finding a board prospect who fits the profile is, indeed, a critical part of the assignment, as is fully informing the prospect about specific board duties. The lack of knowledge about the expectations for board member role and governance responsibilities will directly contribute to organizational confusion, ineffectiveness, and a breach in a board member's commitment. Since each organization's board of directors has a different mission and focus for its work, even the seasoned board member who joins a new board should receive a briefing on the organization, its expectations of board members, and board responsibilities. It is imperative to seek an agreement to serve only after the board prospect understands the parameters of board service.

Organizations sometimes give prospects a board-prospecting packet, which may contain some or all of the following: a history of the organization; board job descriptions; a copy of the articles of incorporation and bylaws; a copy of the organization's purpose or mission statement; an organizational chart; and a description of program services, with a list of committees and duties of each. This packet may also include a roster of the current board, with work affiliations, addresses, and phone numbers; dates of future meetings and special events; an annual report and organization brochures, newsletters, or related materials; and a copy of a recent auditor's financial report, annual budget, and financial statements.

It may also be helpful for the organization's board to assign a veteran member to assist the prospect in "learning the ropes." The availability of a support person may encourage the board prospect to join a concerned board of directors. The veteran could serve as a resource person during the recruitment phase and then as a mentor or helper during the transition period following induction.

How Many Board Members?

There is no formula for determining the appropriate size of an organization's board of directors. The size of the board must be tailored to suit the needs of the organization.

One helpful way to determine board size is an organizational life-cycle analysis, referred to previously as a prerequisite to board recruitment. Organizations and their boards experience various developmental stages, all of which can influence the number and type of skilled board members that are needed.

Large- and small-sized boards have both advantages and disadvantages. The number of people on a board can be a factor that influences how board members comport themselves. Large boards are generally unwieldy because it is difficult to pay attention to so many people. Because the larger group will find it more difficult to become cohesive and familiar with the cohort, it may tend to be more formal in its board conduct and meetings. Organizations that are just starting out, or those in need of a boost in financial resources, may be better served by a larger board of 20 to 25 individuals. In this case, the larger the number of board members the greater the chances of reaching out to potential donors.

On one hand, smaller boards are limited in accomplishing supportive activities such as fundraising. On the other hand, a smaller group may have to rely on its creativity, such as developing a fundraising plan for implementation by a committee of staff, board members, and other community volunteers. Organizations that do not rely heavily on the board alone for fundraising or other supportive activities might be better served by a board of no more than ten members. The smaller group would have more of an opportunity to become cohesive; learn experientially how to mesh effectively their collective wisdom, advice, and counsel; reach decisions through consensus; and it would have no need to use controlling, parliamentary procedures for conducting board meetings.

Board Liability

Though nonprofit boards of directors are infrequently sued, the risk of liability is nevertheless a legitimate concern for volunteer board members. Financial losses associated with a lawsuit can be devastating to an organization and its board members. The quality and manner in which boards make decisions or fail to make decisions can result in a legal challenge that tests whether they have met or failed in their responsibilities as stewards of the public interest.

Board members and prospective members are often comforted by the knowledge that the nonprofit organization has purchased a director's and officers' (D&O) liability insurance policy. Concerns about lawsuits have caused a rising demand for this type of insurance, and consequently, premium costs vary widely.

A factor that affects the cost of D&O insurance is the nature of the organization's work, whether it is, for example, a direct service health care agency or an organization that promotes the arts. Features and exclusions may also differ greatly from one policy to another and affect the price and value of the policy.

Indemnification refers to the organization ensuring that it will pay the reasonable costs associated with liability suits, such as judgments and settlements against its board members. This practice is sometimes compelled by state law. In other situations it may be an optional practice of the board. In either event,

the organization's bylaws outline the extent of indemnification. Indemnification cannot, however, be exercised when the organization brings a suit against its own board members. In practice, indemnification is a form of self-insurance and assumes that the organization has the funds to pay legal costs. Given the resources of some nonprofit organizations, this assumption may not be valid.

In addition to indemnification and D&O liability insurance coverage, a board of directors can purchase various liability insurance policies, including, but not limited to, the following specialty policies: general liability, employees' liability, malpractice, automobile, and fiduciary.

To encourage board and other voluntary service in community organizations, all 50 states have passed volunteer protection laws. The extent of protection varies among the states, and this form of legislation has largely been untested in the courts.[1]

Volunteer protection laws and the varieties of liability insurance premiums are not the only ways boards can protect themselves. The most effective form of protection is limiting risk by adhering to effective governance practices. There are three standards of conduct that should guide the board member, as follows:

- *Duty of care:* Imposes an obligation that all board members discharge their duties with the care that an ordinarily prudent person would exercise under similar circumstances. This includes being diligent, attending meetings, and becoming acquainted with issues before reaching a decision.
- *Duty of loyalty:* Requires that each board member act primarily in the best interest of the organization and not in his or her own personal best interest or in the interest of individuals at the expense of the organization.
- *Duty of obedience:* Imposes an obligation that board members will act in conformity with all laws in addition to acting in accordance with the organization's mission.

For the voluntary members of boards of directors, acting prudently, lawfully, and in the best interests of the organization can, in part, be achieved by adhering to the following six responsible board practices:

1. *Becoming an active board member:* Board members who are familiar with the organization's mission and purpose are generally able to make better decisions for the organization. Members may wish to review the mission annually to serve as a reminder that the board uses the mission statement as its guide in decisionmaking.
2. *Attending all meetings:* Being absent from meetings will not necessarily excuse a board member from responsibilities for decisions reached by those in attendance. In fact, a member's absence from meetings increases potential risks for the entire board because it is making decisions without the benefit of the views of all of its members.
3. *Insisting on having sound financial management tools and control systems:* Board members need to learn how to read and use financial statements and audit reports to understand and monitor the organization's fiscal health. They also need to understand that their decisions have a financial impact on the organization.
4. *Speaking up:* Members should not remain silent when they disagree with a decision or an opinion expressed by others. Additionally, board members should ask questions when the organization's goals and objectives are not being met.
5. *Identifying conflicts of interest:* Board members need to avoid participating in discussions or decisionmaking when they have conflicts of interest. Even the perception of a conflict of interest must be avoided, if possible. If they are faced with an actual conflict or even the perception of one, board members must inform the other directors of the situation and excuse themselves from participation in related areas of decisionmaking or transactions.
6. *Staffing:* In addition to its having personnel policy guidelines for the executive director, the board must be certain that these personnel policies are adequate and updated to reflect all applicable mandates of law.

In summary, minimizing the risk of board liability requires an active and involved board of directors.

Dismissal of Board Members

Terminating a member from the board of directors for nonattendance at board meetings or lack of follow-through on assignments that are required for the board's decisionmaking purposes, for example, is a delicate procedure. Unfortunately, there are times when it becomes necessary to discharge board members because their actions create liability risks.

The chairperson of the board has the responsibility to request resignations from board members. The executive director plays a supportive role to the board chair and board member in what for all can be emotionally trying and embarrassing.

Confidence and sensitivity should be used when approaching the board member with the idea of resignation. A board member should be given every consideration to effect a smooth departure. Ultimately, the member's "saving face" is important for maintaining relationships at this level of community involvement.

To prevent the need for board dismissals or to support the actions of the board chair when a dismissal is called for, the board should adopt a principle stating that its work and organizational mission are too important to allow for unnecessary liability risks associated with uncommitted board members. The board can do some prevention work by adopting a bylaw passage and job description that reflect standards for board member conduct and participation. Of course, some organizations have rules of this type but choose not to enforce them. For a member to violate or ignore such bylaw provisions suggests poor judgment and raises the liability risks of the board.

How Often Should the Board Meet?

A board is generally required to meet at least once a year. In practice, some hold meetings once a month, every other month, or once each calendar quarter. Frequency of board meetings and the duration of each meeting should reflect the culture of the organization and the type of strategic issues requiring board attention. Dealing with planning and policy issues, threats of litigation or bad publicity, and concerns of financial obligations are reasons for a board to meet more frequently. Organizations that are new in their development, or in process of managing significant changes, as compared with an organization in a steady state, would also benefit from meeting more frequently.

Effective meetings are focused, to the point, and stick to the agenda. Meetings can be effective when board members come prepared, having studied the agenda and the issues prior to the meeting. The agenda should be mailed out at least a week to ten days in advance. Agenda items should be allocated realistic time frames for discussion and taking action, in addition to time designated for the routine review of minutes, financial reports, and progress reports on the implementation of the organization's strategic plans.

Newly identified obstacles are not always solved during board meetings. Instead of reacting to unfinished issues and business with more board meetings, attempts should first be made to streamline the review of issues by assigning the task to an appropriate standing or ad hoc committee. In this way, the committees can try to remedy issues or bring their findings and recommendations back to the board or executive committee without monopolizing the board's time and agenda.

How Long Should a Board Member Serve?

The solution to a member's length of service that is practiced by many organizations is to stagger the expiring terms of office. Rotations of three-year terms, for example, would mean that each member serves for three years, but, at the end of each year, obligations would end for one-third of the members. This system gives the board ample time to evaluate the performance of board members, to determine whether they should be invited back for another term. Additionally, the experience base accumulated by outgoing board members is information these members use to decide whether they would like to be reelected for another three-year term.

Some organizations also place a limit on the number of consecutive terms a person may serve. After reaching the maximum number of consecutive terms of service, the board member would automatically leave the board. A board member who rotated off could be elected again after a year or more, when consecutive service would not be an issue. After reaching the allowable service limit, an individual could also continue to support the organization's cause in some other capacity, such as on a committee or advisory board.

It is important that all board member terms do not expire at the same time. Without some overlapping representation from members of the board, the organization would lose its important history and continuity of policy development and strategic direction. Veteran board members bring a maturity and depth of understanding about the issues the organization faces, and when the board adds a group of newer members it brings enthusiasm and fresh ideas to the board's governing role.

How are Governing Boards, Advisory Boards, and Honorary Boards Different?

When one is referring to the term "board of directors" or "board of trustees," the reference is to a *governing board*, a grouping of individuals who have assumed a legal responsibility for an organization's existence. These people make policy and are responsible for how money is generated and spent, toward the accomplishment of a mission that can be beneficial to the general public or to a segment of the population.

Advisory boards, however, do not bear the legal burdens of governing boards. An advisory board exists to assist the governing board or the executive director in examining issues and recommendations. Recommendations that result from the work of an advisory board do not have to be accepted or followed by the governing board.

Honorary boards are usually composed of individuals who are well known because of some measure of celebrity or prominence in the community. Honorary boards do not necessarily meet. In fact, some individuals agree to serve as honorary members because they do not have the time or inclination to attend meetings. Individuals serving in this honorary capacity lend credibility to an organization by allowing the use of their prominent names in brochures and on letterheads.

Sometimes, members of honorary boards and advisory boards are enlisted to assist in organizational fundraising activities. The visibility and credibility of the honorary or advisory member sends a signal to the community that the organization is worthy of financial support.

Types of Committees

Committees are categorized as either standing committees or ad hoc committees. *Ad hoc (or special) committees*, on one hand, have a life span equal to the completion of the committee's assignment. *Standing committees*, on the other hand, are part of the permanent governance structure of an organization with duties and responsibilities described in bylaws. Standing committees may include executive, finance, bylaws, fundraising, public relations, nominating, personnel, planning, and policy committees, or any other committee that the organization believes should exist indefinitely to aid in governance. Seven of the most

common standing committees are described as follows:

1. The *executive committee* functions in place of the full board and handles routine and crisis matters between full board meetings. Empowered to make decisions for the organization, the executive committee is usually composed of the organization's officers. Depending on the size of the organization's board of directors, composition of the executive committee could include committee chairs or other selected leaders among the board. The executive committee is usually chaired by the board's volunteer president or chairperson.

2. The *finance committee* is responsible for monitoring the organization's finances and financial controls and attending to audit requirements. Typical functions for the finance committee are to oversee organizational investments and to work with the executive director to develop an annual budget.

3. The *nominations committee* is responsible for identifying and recruiting appropriate candidates for board positions and bringing forward its recommendations to the full board. This committee sometimes has the responsibility for planning board development activities and board retreats.

4. The *personnel committee* is usually responsible for recommending policies to guide the supervision of staff. In some organizations, this committee may have the responsibility for overseeing the search for an executive director and then for her or his performance evaluation. Members of this committee may need to acquaint themselves with personnel laws and regulations that regulate labor practices.

5. The *program committee* is responsible for monitoring the organization's service delivery system and may assist in evaluating client services. This committee is often responsible for keeping track of community trends that might affect the organization's short-term and long-term objectives. In complex organizations with

multiple services, there may be subcommittees that are responsible for monitoring each of the organization's program services.

6. The *resource development committee* is responsible for examining alternate methods of fundraising and for establishing annual fundraising goals. This committee often is active in the solicitation of gifts or participation in special events. In addition to raising money, it may solicit in-kind contributions.

7. The *public relations* or *community relations committee* has the responsibility for developing good relations with the larger community and with important community groups. The committee examines opportunities to participate in community events that will bring visibility to the organization. It may oversee the writing of press releases and may develop relationships with media professionals.

Participants appointed to standing or ad hoc committees do not need to be members of the board of directors. Committee members may include staff, volunteers, representatives from community agencies, and consumers of services. Committee chairs are usually appointed by the board's chairperson.

Note

1. *Note from the editors:* State laws and court decisions may change over time. Consultation is recommended to assess changes in any particular situation.

References

Block, Stephen R., and Jeffrey W Pryor. 1991. *Improving Nonprofit Management Practice: A Handbook for Community-Based Organizations.* Rockville, MD: OSAP/Public Health Service, US Department of Health and Human Services.

Carver, John. 1990. *Boards That Make a Difference.* San Francisco: Jossey-Bass.

Chait, Richard P, and Barbara E. Taylor. 1989. "Charting the Territory of Nonprofit Boards." *Harvard Business Review* (January–February): 44–54.

Conrad, William, and William E. Glenn. 1976. *The Effective Voluntary Board of Directors.* Chicago: Swallow Press.

Drucker, Peter F. 1989. "What Business Can Learn from Nonprofits." *Harvard Business Review* (September–October): 88–93.

———. 1990. "Lessons for Successful Nonprofit Governance." *Nonprofit Management and Leadership* 1, no. 1 (Fall): 7–14.

Hadden, Elaine M., and Blaire A. French. 1987. *Nonprofit Organizations: Rights and Liabilities for Members, Directors and Officers.* Wilmette, IL: Callaghan & Co.

Herman, Robert Dean, and Stephen R. Block. 1990. "The Board's Crucial Role in Fund Raising," in Jon Van Til et al., *Critical Issues in American Philanthropy,* 222–241. San Francisco: Jossey-Bass.

Herman, Robert Dean, and Richard D. Heimovics, 1991. *Executive Leadership in Nonprofit Organizations.* San Francisco: Jossey-Bass.

Herman, Robert Dean, and Jon Van Til, eds. 1989. *Nonprofit Boards of Directors: Analyses and Applications.* New Brunswick, NJ: Transaction Publishers.

Houle, Cyril O. 1989. *Governing Boards.* San Francisco: Jossey-Bass.

Kurtz, Daniel L. 1988. *Board Liability.* New York: Moyer Bell.

Middleton, Melissa. 1987. "Nonprofit Boards of Directors: Beyond the Governance Function," in Walter W. Powell, ed., *The Nonprofit Sector: A Research Handbook,* 141–153. New Haven, CT: Yale University Press.

O'Connell, Brian. 1985. *The Board Members Book.* New York: The Foundation Center.

Saidel, Judith R. 1993. "The Board Role in Relation to Government: Alternative Models," in Dennis R. Young, Robert M. Hollister, and Virginia A. Hodgkinson, eds., *Governing, Leading, and Managing Nonprofit Organizations,* 32–51. San Francisco: Jossey-Bass.

► CHAPTER 2

Ethno-racial Diversity on Nonprofit Boards

A Critical Mass Perspective

CHRISTOPHER FREDETTE AND RUTH SESSLER BERNSTEIN

University of Windsor, Windsor, Ontario, Canada
University of Washington Tacoma, Tacoma, Washington, USA

Corresponding Author:
Christopher Fredette, Odette School of Business, University of Windsor, 401 Sunset Avenue, OB 449, Windsor, Ontario, Canada N9B 3P4. Email: fredette@uwindsor.ca

Organizations in the third sector, and beyond, have recognized and continue to wrestle with the significant implications of the current diversity gap, which threatens to undermine the relevance, the legitimacy, and the ability of organizations to fulfill their mandates (Moore, 2000). Persistently, the nonprofit governance and leadership literature has focused on the relationship between board diversity and performance outcomes by examining how intervening processes (Fredette, Bradshaw, & Krause, 2016), practices (W. A. Brown, 2002; Buse, Bernstein, & Bilimoria, 2016), or contextual characteristics (Bradshaw & Fredette, 2013) might shape these relationships. Advocacy for greater leadership diversity is built on the premise that a broader and more diversely composed group, team, or organization improves the richness of decision-making outcomes and the ability to engage otherwise out-of-reach

stakeholders and enhances understanding of market opportunities (W. A. Brown, 2005; Jaskyte, 2012). However, activating these benefits, we suggest, is an uncertain proposition as is the pacing under which these diversity-derived performance benefits are received.

Our work seeks to disentangle and clarify the relationship between board diversity and governance outcomes by testing a critical mass or tipping point explanation for the observed variability of this relationship. Our intuition, drawing on our work in the field, is that boards often struggle with their initial attempts at increasing the diversity of their members. That is, moving from a board composed solely of one racial or ethnic group (i.e., a homogeneous board) to one that includes a first diverse or demographically different member sometimes results in performance decline, perhaps due to the slowing of governing processes or extending debate and decision-making activities, with boards finding that they do not achieve the anticipated performance improvement often prescribed by proponents of diversity. However, in our experience, boards that persist in efforts to transform their composition to better reflect their constituents and community members do frequently achieve a breakthrough, reaching a tipping point or critical mass threshold that seems to unlock performance improvements that seemingly exceed previous expectation, suggesting that diverse boards perform beyond the sum of their parts. Oliver, Marwell, and Teixeira (1985), exploring the nature and dynamics of social change, suggest that collective action "entails the development of a *critical mass*—a small segment of the population that chooses to make big contributions to the collective action while the majority do little or nothing" (p. 524). The presence of a *critical mass* lies at the heart of our thinking as an important determinant in understanding how and when diversity influences board performance, as well as a significant factor in explaining the inconsistent impact of diversity. To test this idea, we examine three important aspects—fiduciary performance, stakeholder engagement, and organizational responsiveness—of effective board performance, testing for the impact of increasing board diversity on these relationships, and whether effects of increasing board diversity are linearly distributed (equal to the sum of their parts), or whether these effects are nonlinear, demonstrating uneven accelerating and decelerating benefit (exceeding and failing to meet sum of their parts estimates) as threshold theories predict, thereby illustrating when and why ethno-racially diverse boards under- and overwhelm performance expectations.

We examine the impact of board diversity, more specifically defined here as the percentage of ethno-racial diversity within the membership of a board of directors, on board performance to shed new light on the complicated effect of diversity on governance capabilities. We suspect that diversity is neither constant nor linear in its impact on collective decision-making outcomes, such as board-level resource allocation choices or approaches to performance monitoring or in developing stakeholder engagement strategies. We anticipate that moving from homogeneity to low levels of ethno-racial diversity will likely not generate anticipated gains and may, in some cases, generate adverse impact relative to what a linear approach would predict, just as the change in composition from near-complete to complete heterogeneity will likely do the same (Kanter, 1977). For this, and the reasons expressed above, we explore the association of ethno-racial diversity and board performance, examining cubic (S-shaped) models of the pattern of relationships, as well as underlying first-order linear (straight-line) and second-order quadratic (U- or inverted U-shaped) patterns. Our contributions lie in identifying whether a critical mass logic better specifies the board diversity–performance relationship than conventional approaches and whether a critical mass explanation can add nuance to the leadership and governance diversity literature.

Understanding the Business Case for Ethno-racial Diversity and Board Performance

Tapping the benefits that group diversity—by combining and recombining varied perspectives, experiences, understandings, and beliefs—brings to bear on the complex problems facing today's boards and organizations forms the basis of what has been called the business case for diversity (Jayne & Dipboye, 2004; Litvin, 2006). To us, the challenge posed by governing is best reflected in the fundamental need for an organization to achieve its goals, for which equifinality reigns in the absence of singular or clear paths forward. These are strategic challenges embodying dilemma, contradiction, uncertainty, and paradox, in which a plurality of directions, approaches, choices, and opinions are equally (although uncertainly) deployable. These are not the incremental, day-to-day, routine managerial decisions faced frequently and resolved by habit, but rather those which exemplify the functional aspects of governance, including the building and sustaining of stakeholder relationships, the development and maintenance of the board's strategic direction, the protection and mitigation of the organization's financial risk profile, and the decision to deploy, withdraw, and redeploy organizational resources and assets (W. A. Brown, 2005; Cornforth, 2012; Gazley & Nicholson-Crotty, 2017). Diversity, and its embodied varieties of intellectual tradition and experiential understanding, contribute meaningfully to functional decision-making central to fiduciary performance (Fredette et al., 2016), as well as cultural familiarity needed for responsiveness (Buse et al., 2016).

We examine the effect of ethno-racial diversity on three aspects of governance activity for which boards of directors are responsible— fiduciary performance, stakeholder engagement, and organizational responsiveness—which are important indicators of organizational health, to examine whether our data support a critical mass pattern in which increased board diversity coincides with increased board performance in each of our constructs of interest.

Fiduciary Performance

Studies have highlighted the benefits to board performance, demonstrating financial and social implications, of greater diversity in the presence of inclusion-focused policies and practices (Ali et al., 2014; Torchia, Calabro, & Huse, 2011). Frequently, fiduciary activities—including the oversight of legal and financial decision-making, adherence to governing bylaws and procedures, as well as the evaluation of senior organizational executives—are cited as among the principal

responsibilities of nonprofit boards of directors (Bradshaw, Murray, & Wolpin, 1992; Fredette & Bradshaw, 2012). A primary reason for this is that boards act as a mechanism for collecting and integrating information to reduce uncertainty (Miller & del Carmen Triana, 2009), bringing together multidisciplinary perspectives (e.g., legal, financial, strategic, and contextual) to reconcile competing interests that impact where and how the organization secures, controls, and deploys its resources (W. A. Brown, 2005; Gazley & Nicholson-Crotty, 2017). These challenges are urgently encountered among the members of today's nonprofit boards of directors, and in this regard, diversity of thought, insight, and perspective are impactful to the people tasked with collectively addressing these activities (Jehn et al., 1999). Indeed, this is the domain in which the promise of diversity holds the greatest potential, particularly because inclusion in these processes tends to slow the pace of activity and trigger additional consideration of past practices (Buse et al., 2016; Fredette et al., 2016).

Stakeholder Engagement

The capacity to engage diverse and traditionally marginalized community members and constituents for the purposes of fundraising (Ostrower, 2007), or expanding relevance and legitimacy through the enlargement of the organization's client-base (Abzug & Galaskiewicz, 2001), are domains in which greater board diversity have shown value. Bradshaw and Fredette (2013) found that the demographic diversity of the community in which the organization is situated is a significant driver of board diversity, but did not find significant linkages to other aspects of the external environment. Indeed, the application of stakeholder theories to the governance of nonprofit organizations has served to further highlight the important signaling effect of leadership diversity as being representative of community interests (W. A. Brown, 2002; Cornforth, 2003), but also the ability to attract resources and demonstrate a tacit awareness market opportunities and limitations.

Organizational Responsiveness

Adapting to changing needs and updating programming to better serve the interests of current and potential clients improves an organization's fitness and long-term sustainability (Voss, Sirdeshmukh, & Voss, 2008). Organizations attempt to do so by updating, refining, revising, reinventing, or innovating current programming and offerings to better meet the needs and interests of current and potential client communities. In this regard, many communities may have noticed football and baseball fields repurposed to accommodate growing interests in soccer (also known as football) and cricket leagues, or perhaps as urban gardens in some cases, which are largely driven by changing tastes often brought on by, but not exclusive to, greater concentrations of demographic diversity in larger urban communities. Identifying and responding to external or market-driven pressures is aided by greater familiarity with an organization's constituents, which allows for a better understanding and incorporation of the needs and interests of diverse and traditionally marginalized community members which are often tacitly-held and who would otherwise remain underserved (Foldy, 2004).

Applying a Critical Mass Lens to the Diversity–performance Relationship

We believe that prior specifications of the diversity–performance relationship, including our own, have been limited in their approach to understanding the implications of interdependence among board members in decision-making, particularly as it relates to the nonsequential nature of governance work, which is subject to the exercise of majority–minority voting control.

One of the critical factors in understanding how and when board diversity impacts performance is a matter of the relative degree or proportion of diversity within a given composition as it is frequently the minority—whether in terms of diverse identity or in terms of voting proportion—who alter the conditions of the majority (Oliver & Marwell, 1993); that is, numbers matter in understanding how and when diversity generates negative, neutral, or positive outcomes. Blalock (1967), for example, contended that while the minority group made gains, the majority group members suffered a commensurate loss, because the majority group perceived the threat by the proportionate size of the minority group as undermining their established positions. In contrast, Kanter (1977) argued that both the minority and majority benefit from the resources the minority members bring to the organization, but that these gains became realized once there were enough minority group members to overcome dynamics of tokenism and dismissiveness. Building a "critical mass" is an important determinant in understanding how and when diversity influences board performance, as well as a significant factor in explaining the uneven impact of diversity. The intuition is that the benefits of diversity exist within a range of group variety, outside of which, too little or too much variety undershoots linear estimates. That is, that the first addition of diversity into a group does little to benefit group performance due to the limited influence in vote and marginalization of voice (Kanter, 1977). However, with the addition of each subsequent ethno-racially diverse member, these restraints diminish, and vote and voice become more influential, building to a critical mass, tipping the group or board from inertia to action, providing an accelerating benefit for performance that is underestimated by conventional modelling (Oliver & Marwell, 1993). Some have suggested that a change in the nature of the relationship occurs at three members (Konrad, Kramer, & Erkut, 2008), others say at compositions above 35% (Kanter, 1977).

We believe that there is both an early period of deceleration in the diversity–performance relationship and a subsequent period of acceleration, in which the impact of critical mass diversity is realized. We add to this, the belief that the acceleration of the board diversity–performance relationship has an upper bound in which saturation occurs and diminishing returns from additional diversity precede a final period of deceleration when the minority become a dominant majority, reverting to a new homogeneity or alternatively to fragmentation, where the difficulties of integration exceed the benefits of diversity.

D. A. H. Brown, Brown, D. L., and Anastasopoulos (2002) determined that Canadian boards in the private, public, and nonprofit sectors with three or more women are different from all-male boards when it comes to identifying criteria for measuring strategy, demonstrating that 94% of boards with a critical mass of gender monitor the implementation of their corporate strategy. Torchia and colleagues (2011), drawing on the work of others (Konrad et al., 2008), tested boards with one, two, and three women directors to determine whether reaching a critical mass enhanced firm innovation, finding that increasing from one to two women did not have an impact on the level of firm innovation. However, when the number of female directors was increased to a critical mass of three women, they saw a positive and significant increase in the level of firm organizational innovation. The value in achieving a critical mass of women on corporate boards is the ability to provide alternative perspectives, expand board discussions, and enable a greater stakeholder focus, raising more difficult questions about tough issues, and positively influencing board processes that enhance the overall quality of governance (Konrad et al., 2008). Other studies show that women impact corporate ethical, strategic, and social-responsibility practices (Nielsen & Huse, 2010), tending to be responsive to a broader spectrum of stakeholder concerns.

More recently, Joecks and colleagues (2013) found evidence that gender diversity initially negatively affects performance and then, only after a critical mass of about 30% women (or in their study, about 3 women) has been reached, does firm performance increase, suggesting a U-shaped relationship between gender diversity and firm performance; finding, in accordance with critical mass logic, more diverse boards outperformed uniform and less diverse boards. Here, we hypothesize that the impact of board diversity on board performance is amplified by the presence of a critical mass of ethno-racially diverse members.

Hypotheses 1 (H1): The benefits (effects) of increasing the percentage of ethno-racial diversity on boards of directors are unevenly distributed (curvilinearly related) in an S-shaped curve in effects on (i) fiduciary performance, (ii) stakeholder engagement, and (iii) organizational responsiveness, with accelerating effect between the inflection points.

Research Design, Method, and Analysis

We test our hypotheses with hierarchical regression techniques using survey data collected as part of an outreach initiative exploring ethno-racial diversity among boards of directors in organizations spanning the arts, sports, and environment. The Greater Toronto Area (GTA) is composed of slightly more than 6.5 million residents, with approximately 51.5% self-identifying as a member of a visible minority community (Statistics Canada, 2016). The term "visible minority" is defined in Canadian employment law, used in the collection of census information, and is a term in common usage and understanding among our respondents. Visible minority members are defined as "persons, other than Aboriginal peoples, who are non-Caucasian in race or non-white in colour" distinguishing among ethno-racial categories including Aboriginal, Arab, Black, Chinese, Filipino, Japanese, Korean, Latin American, South Asian, Southeast Asian, West Asian, and White (Statistics Canada, 2016). Respondents identified only 16.2% of the board members included in this study as visible minority members, slightly better than found in other research conducted in this regional context (Cukier, Yap, Aspevig, & Lejasisaks, 2011), but lower than what would be anticipated relative to the underlying demographics of the surrounding population. This is indicative of a gap between organization leadership and the constituencies these organizations serve.

Data were collected using a brief online survey focused on developing an understanding of the participation and perceived contribution of visible minority members to the leadership and governance of nonprofit organizations engaged in the sectors of arts, sports, and the environment. Our approach to sampling was purposive in the selection of arts, sports, and environmental dimensions of the nonprofit sector, domains in which we had limited understanding of the state of leadership diversity (Kalton, 1983). A leading civic rights and a social justice foundation aided by identifying and contacting 903 organizations, with 269 organizations responding, of which 247 provided enough data to be considered complete (response rate = 27.4%).

Participants and Procedures

For this study, 247 boards in the Greater Toronto Area were surveyed, representing 2,789 board members, 83.8% of whom respondents identified as White. Of the nonprofits, 55.5% had at least one visible minority member, but only 25.5% of the boards surveyed had at least three. The United States has a similar majority–minority board member divide with 16% of board seats filled by those who identified as racial or ethnic minorities; however, 27% of boards identify as having all White members

(BoardSource, 2016). Organizations represented in this survey were primarily well-established with an average budget of CAD$1,437,122 ($SD$ = CAD$3,633,148) and an average number of 12.5 full-time staff. The organizations had an average age of 30 years (SD = 25 years). Of the three broad organization types, 57.1% were involved in arts and culture, 26.3% sports and recreation, 6.5% environmental, and 10.1% fell into other sector categories. Only senior leaders in the organizations, which included Chief Executives, Executive Directors, Board Chairpersons, and Directors, participated in the survey. These respondents identified as being with their organizations for an average of 10.4 years and having served in their current roles for an average of 7 years. The respondents were 56.7% White and 59.3% female.

Variables and Measurement

Diversity

Diversity was derived from a board-level measure of the membership composition based on Canadian census categories of ethnic origin and visible minority status. The proportion of majority–minority members was reported as a percentage score (the number of visible minorities as a percentage of the total number of board members). This percentage score forms the basis for nonlinear quadratic and cubic testing (board diversity-squared and board diversity-cubed). The composition of board membership was dominantly White, with boards having an average of 1.79 ethno-racial groups represented (SD = 1.53). According to Ostrower and Stone (2005), contemporary nonprofit organizations continue to find ethno-racial diversity a challenge. In our view, the leadership and governance of nonprofit organizations is also an important societal linkage, providing communities with unique opportunities to share decision-making power and participate in the shaping and expression of community values and priorities.

Fiduciary Performance

We examine the capacity of the board to execute its fiduciary responsibilities, a core aspect of governance which centers around ensuring the organization's legal, financial, and competitive health into the future (Green & Griesinger, 1996; Ostrower & Stone, 2005). We operationalized effectiveness by asking the informants to assess the contribution of diversity to board performance in terms of their perception of the effectiveness of the board's ability to improve governance processes, understand and address legal obligations, evaluate senior executives, and monitor financial health. Fiduciary performance was measured with four items on a 5-point Likert-type scale (Cronbach's α = .922).

Stakeholder Engagement

Our interest in stakeholder engagement largely stems from opportunities and concerns related to the acquisition of resources and funding. We operationalized stakeholder engagement by asking respondents to assess the contribution of diversity to their board's ability to shape strategic direction, enhance fundraising efforts, and contribute to the management of stakeholder relationships. The stakeholder engagement scale was comprised of the three items on a 5-point Likert-type scale (Cronbach's α = .906).

Organizational Responsiveness

Identifying and meeting the evolving programming needs to better serve the interest of current potential clients improves an organization's ability to achieve long-term viability (Voss et al., 2008). We assessed the contribution of diversity by asking informants to assess their board's capacity to advance and improve service levels. Measurement items focused on areas such as community responsiveness, changing service design and delivery methods, ideation and decision-making, and progress toward a more inclusive organization. Organizational responsiveness was measured with six items on a 5-point Likert-type scale (Cronbach's α = 962).

Controls

This sample was drawn from nonprofit organizations in the well-documented ethno-racially diverse Greater Toronto Area (Statistics Canada, 2016). We included in our analysis three organizational characteristics considered significant to our analysis as control variables. The first control variable draws from the type of nonprofit organizations surveyed, coding the *sector* of activity in terms of artistic, sports, or environmental. The second variable measures *organization age* by number of years in existence. The age of an organization has been shown to influence how organizations approach diversity (Bradshaw & Fredette, 2013; Bradshaw, Murray, & Wolpin, 1996). The final control variable we included is the organization's *budget*, as budget size might well (de)prioritize diversity in light of other challenges. Boards that are predominantly White have been found to be most frequently local or regional in geographic scope, and smaller in terms of budget and size (Ostrower, 2007). By including these control variables, we aim to mitigate confounding factors while improving our model's accuracy and practical significance.

Data Analysis and Hypothesis Testing

The means, standard deviations, and zero-order correlations among the variables are presented in Table 2.1. The correlations demonstrate that moderate, significant correlations were found between our dependent variables fiduciary performance, stakeholder engagement, and organizational responsiveness. Correlations are also present between organization age and board diversity as well as between organization age and budget. All variables apart from organization annual budget had skew statistics smaller than ±2, and all are within acceptable levels for multiple regressions (not surprisingly, squared and cubed terms presented skew statistics of 2.188 and 2.543, slightly above the ±2 threshold). In our modelling, the variable

TABLE 2.1 Descriptive Statistics and Correlations of Measures

	M	SD	1	2	3	4	5	6
1. Sector	1.44	0.63						
2. Organization age (years)	30.06	24.98	.162*					
3. Annual budget (CAD$)	1,437,122.34	3,633,148.32	–.019	.243**				
4. Fiduciary performance	2.01	1.31	–.113	.077	.028			
5. Stakeholder engagement	2.92	1.37	–.130	.026	.078	.718**		
6. Organizational responsiveness	3.36	1.37	–.085	.009	.109	.619**	.709**	
7. % Board diversity	0.21	0.29	–.019	–.134*	–.959	.168*	.099	.101

*Correlation is significant at the .05 level (two-tailed). **Correlation is significant at the .01 level (two-tailed).

most skewed are included as predictors and controls, where higher levels of nonnormality are expected for regression, with our errors meeting the assumption of normality (McClelland & Judd, 1993).

Results

To examine our hypotheses, we first entered the control variables, followed sequentially by our main effects, producing a series of hierarchical multiple regression models in what Cohen, Cohen, Aiken, and West (2003, p. 210) describe as a build-up approach to modelling curvilinear relationships. Recognizing that we would be creating higher-order terms from our predictor variable and the meaningfulness of interpreting a zero or "no board diversity" condition, we chose not to mean-center our diversity predictor, recognizing the potential for multicollinearity (Cohen et al., 2003). To test the linear, quadratic, and cubic effects of board diversity on each of our dependent variables, quadratic and cubic terms derived from the diversity predictor were introduced sequentially to our modelling with the final model including each of the lower-order variables to partial out variance and improve interpretability of our analysis (Cohen et al., 2003, p. 200). Each step was repeated for each of the board-level dependent variables as Cohen and colleagues suggest (Table 2.2), with relationships illustrated in Figure 2.1. All three S-shaped curves demonstrated some consistency with respect to inflection points, with critical points occurring with minima of approximately 9% and maxima of approximately 70% diversity (8.95% and 70.46% for fiduciary performance, 8.65% and 69.87% for stakeholder engagement, 11.86% and 72.38% for organizational responsiveness, respectively). This means that on average, the low point in the independent variable/dependent variable relationships occur around the addition of the first ethno-racially diverse board member (assuming a 12-member board), with the peak occurring just after the addition of the eighth ethno-racially diverse

TABLE 2.2 Results of Hierarchical Multiple Regressions

| | Dimensions of governance performance | | | | | | | | | | | |
| | Fiduciary performance | | | | Stakeholder engagement | | | | Organizational responsiveness | | | |
Predictor	B	SE B	P value	Total R²	B	SE B	P value	Total R²	B	SE B	P value	Total R²
Step 1	$F_{(3,132)} = 0.821$, $P = .484$			1.80%	$F_{(3,134)} = 1.518$, $P = .213$			3.30%	$F_{(3,133)} = 0.726$, $P = .538$			1.60%
Controls												
Sector	-0.239	0.193	.217		-0.307	0.197	.122		-0.168	0.195	.389	
Organization age	0.005	0.005	.291		0.003	0.005	.502		0.000	0.005	.939	
Annual budget	0.000	0.000	.856		0.000	0.000	.239		0.000	0.000	.266	
Step 2	$F_{(4,131)} = 1.878$, $P = .118$			5.40%	$F_{(4,133)} = 1.807$, $P = .131$			5.20%	$F_{(4,132)} = 1.190$, $P = .318$			3.50%
Controls												
Sector	-0.203	1.191	.289		-0.303	0.196	.124		-0.163	0.193	.401	
Organization age	0.006	0.005	.165		0.004	0.005	.352		0.002	0.005	.714	
Annual budget	0.000	0.000	.995		0.000	0.000	.295		0.000	0.000	.322	
% Board diversity (linear)	0.854	0.383	.027		0.623	0.385	.108		0.613	0.383	.112	
Step 3	$F_{(5,130)} = 2.418$, $P = .039$			8.50%	$F_{(5,132)} = 2.211$, $P = .057$			7.70%	$F_{(5,131)} = 1.240$, $P = .294$			4.50%
Controls												
Sector	-0.218	0.188	.250		-0.305	0.194	.118		-0.156	0.193	.420	
Organization age	0.007	0.005	.158		0.005	0.005	.338		0.002	0.005	.727	
Annual budget	0.000	0.000	.879		0.000	0.000	.233		0.000	0.000	.284	

% Board diversity (linear)	3.209	1.187	.008	2.844	1.219	.021	2.028	1.246	.106
% Board diversity (quadratic)	−2.626	1.255	.038	−2.443	1.273	.057	−1.542	1.292	.235
Step 4	$F(6,129) = 3.346$, $P = .004$		13.50%	$F(6,131) = 2.711$, $P = .016$		11.00%	$F(6,130) = 1.832$, $P = .098$		7.80%
Controls									
Sector	0.276	0.185	.138	−0.339	0.192	.080	−0.192	0.191	.318
Organization age	0.008	0.004	.089	0.005	0.005	.250	0.003	0.005	.584
Annual budget	0.000	0.000	.709	0.000	0.000	.170	0.000	0.000	.215
% Board diversity (linear)	−2.600	2.430	.287	−2.095	2.537	.410	−2.979	2.634	.260
% Board diversity (quadratic)	16.366	7.090	.023	13.604	7.368	.067	14.617	7.623	.057
% Board diversity (cubic)	−13.740	5.052	.007	−11.550	5.226	.029	−11.568	5.381	.033

FIGURE 2.1 Relationships Among Ethno-racial Diversity and Dependent Variables

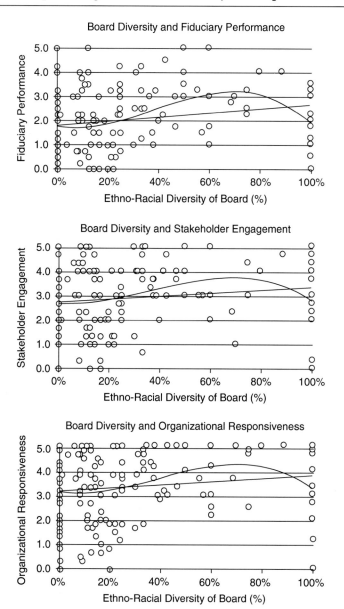

member, but of course, board size varies some-what among organizations.

We test H1 using a four-step build-up model with the fourth model containing our hypothesized critical mass or third-order cubic term and each subordinate lower-order term. We began by introducing our control variables

in Step 1 of our modelling (Table 2.2), follow-ing which we examined our linear predictor, the percentage of ethno-racial board diversity, for a positive association with (i) fiduciary performance, (ii) stakeholder engagement, and (iii) organizational responsiveness in Step 2. We find partial evidence supporting a linear relationship with (i) fiduciary performance, as neither of the other models reached statistical significance and are therefore uninterpretable. In Step 3, the quadratic or second-order predictor was introduced. Here, statistically significant relationships were revealed for (i) fiduciary performance and (ii) stakeholder engagement (model reached marginal significance with $p = .057$), with (iii) organizational responsiveness remaining nonsignificant and therefore uninterpretable. In Step 4, we test the hypothesized critical mass relationships among the criterion variables (i) fiduciary performance, (ii) stakeholder engagement, and (iii) organizational responsiveness and percentage of board diversity, such that each relationship reflects a third-order or cubic function with an S-shaped curve accelerating between the inflection points. Here, we find statistically significant results supporting the predicted cubic relationship between board diversity and each of our criterion variables, H1: (i) $B = -13.740$, $p = .007$; (ii) $B = -11.550$, $p = .029$; (iii) $B = -11.568$, $p = .033$, although the model for (iii) reached marginal significance with $p = .098$. Consistent with the interpretation of interaction terms, higher-order effects override the interpretability of lower-order effects (Cohen et al., 2003), illustrating the predicted patterns of acceleration between the inflection points as well as a waning or deceleration at very high levels of boards diversity. The presence of significant higher-order terms, even in the absence of linear ones, is particularly interesting as they reveal otherwise unobserved or overlooked associations in the data, as we discuss below.

Discussion of Findings

Our findings highlight a number of important dynamics associated with increasing relative board diversity as it pertains to governing toward solutions in the nonprofit sector. First, governance is not simply one set of activities requiring one set of capabilities (Gazley &

Nicholson-Crotty, 2017); it is instead rather open-ended, at times paradoxical, and frequently facing crises which are both abrupt and discontinuous. In our study, having greater ethno-racial diversity—with its commensurate variety of experience, thought, and perspective—was imminently helpful in some domains (fiduciary performance), while less-obviously so in others (stakeholder engagement and organizational responsiveness). This is somewhat surprising, in that stakeholder-based arguments tend to suggest that diversity should help organizations better reach otherwise unrepresented constituencies and to better adapt to the interest and concerns of these clients (W. A. Brown, 2002; Cornforth, 2003). Equally curious, however, are the strength and dynamics of building toward a critical mass of board diversity, even in the absence of first-order effects. Noteworthy is the regularity with which the criterion–predictor relationships reach inflection points relative to changes in board diversity, demonstrating a change in the strength and direction of the criterion–predictor association.

Our results speak to the difficulties in recognizing when diversity might improve governing outcomes and how much organizations should invest in the development of their own business case for diversity to avoid the potential pitfalls and activate the potential benefits that leadership diversity offers. We aimed to confront some of the resistance impeding greater participation of members of diverse and traditionally marginalized communities in the leadership and governance of nonprofit organizations. Indeed, even in a major North American metropolis where visible minority groups compose nearly half of the population, only about 16% of the board members in our study were of visible minority status. Our intuition is that achieving a critical mass is a precursor to creating more inclusive and ultimately more equitable boardrooms, because it affords opportunities to exercise collective influence and motivate change. Our findings are not simply about the business case for diversity and the role of difference in assumption or experience but speak to shifts in control that stem from the balance of power held in check by majority–minority composition. Understanding boards as centers of power provides insight into the benefits of greater diversity beyond what other perspectives of the business case would suggest across considerable portions of the diversity–performance curve.

This examination of visible minority members of nonprofit boards allows us to recognize the need for greater numbers of participants, bringing into the foreground the impact that increases in board diversity hold for governance effectiveness, which to date has largely been thought of in terms of discontinuous steps or as categorical dichotomies in their impact (Kanter, 1977; Konrad et al., 2008). Our approach to understanding the impact of board diversity on governance outcomes offers insight by demonstrating the bandwidth of effect that increasing diversity to a critical mass provides (Oliver & Marwell, 1993). In our modeling, early performance losses give way to a period of accelerated gains, which later decelerate with an apparent diminishing return from further diversity. This study holds potential for understanding the need for a critical mass of visible minority members to serve on nonprofit boards to positively impact board governance and performance. Achieving critical mass may offer the opportunity for transformational change, legitimization of critical mass leadership, and may be seen as critical to nonprofit sector success. Achieving these benefits might begin with increasing visible minority representation in nonprofit leadership positions but depends on evolving into an organization that values leading and governing together, an outcome which might well emerge as boards of directors accelerate toward critical mass diversity.

Limitations

Our study is prone to the concerns found in many cross-sectional surveys, including single method and perceptual biases in which a single informant per organization, at a single point in time, responds to questions that are subject to desirability biases such as self-rating performance. For example, respondents may perceive more or less diverse boards as contributing to higher or lower performing based on beliefs about their composition. Alternatively, informants may make judgments about performance outcomes and attribute them to the composition of the group-based implicit or explicit biases. In addition, our measure of board diversity is an imperfect one because it could be seen to assume equivalence among visible minority board members and may be sensitive to the effects of board size. Similarly, it does not distinguish between compositions that are multicultural and it fails to capture the intersectional effects of multiple facets of diversity.

Some may comment that our study is limited to narrow subsectors of nonprofits and grounded in contextual and temporal influences that may limit the generalizability of our findings. As we have noted, our sample was drawn from a significantly multicultural community, and while cities across North America tend to be more diverse than rural communities, the GTA has frequently been noted for its acceptance of multiculturalism, which may be different than in other jurisdictions.

Directions for the Future

Our sense is that there is a need for greater exploration of the underlying dynamics of change through the lens of "critical mass" thinking, and with respect to leadership diversity and inclusion, we need to better understand the mechanisms underlying change as a function of critical mass. Is it simply a numbers game with respect to majority voting or is there an accompanying cultural change component? Further investigation is warranted and revisiting past results would be a welcome first step, given the "messier reality" of diversity (Klein & Harrison, 2007). Attempts to replicate our results across a variety of settings and groups, inside the boardroom setting and beyond, would clarify the generalizability of our findings, both as it relates to our measurement approach (i.e., the third-order cubic specification), and to our pattern of results within and across sectors of the nonprofit community. We encourage others to return to the deeply held assumptions in our field to push our understanding forward.

Achieving critical mass diversity may offer the opportunity for transformational change, impact board governance and performance, and aid in nonprofit sector success. These benefits begin with increasing visible minority representation in nonprofit leadership positions but depend on evolving into an inclusive organization that values leading and governing together.

References

Abzug, R., & Galaskiewicz, J. (2001). Nonprofit boards: Crucibles of expertise or symbols of local identities? *Nonprofit and Voluntary Sector Quarterly, 30*, 51–73.

ALi, M., Ng, Y. L., & Kulik, C. T. (2014). Board age and gender diversity: A test of competing linear and curvilinear predictions. *Journal of Business Ethics, 125*, 497–512.

Anthias, F. (2013). Hierarchies of social location, class and intersectionality: Towards a translocational frame. *International Sociology, 28*, 121–138.

Baruch, Y., & Holtom, B. C. (2008). Survey response rate levels and trends in organizational research. *Human Relations, 61*, 1139–1160.

Bear, S., Rahman, N., & Post, C. (2010). The impact of board diversity and gender composition on corporate social responsibility and firm reputation. *Journal of Business Ethics, 97*, 207–221.

Blalock, H.M. (1967). *Toward a theory of minority-group relations*. New York, NY: Wiley.

BoardSource. (2016). *Leading with intent*. Washington, DC: Author.

Bøhren, Ø., & Strøm, R. Ø. (2010). Governance and politics: Regulating independence and diversity in the board room. *Journal of Business Finance and Accounting, 37*, 1281–1308.

Bradshaw, P., & Fredette, C. (2013). Determinants of the range of ethnocultural diversity on nonprofit boards: A study of large Canadian nonprofit organizations. *Nonprofit and Voluntary Sector Quarterly, 42*, 1111–1133.

Bradshaw, P., Murray, V., & Wolpin, J. (1996). Women on boards of nonprofits: What difference do they make? *Nonprofit Management and Leadership, 6*, 241–254.

Bradshaw, P., Murray, V. V., & Wolpin, J. (1992). Do nonprofit boards make a difference? An exploration of the relationships among board structure, process, and effectiveness. *Nonprofit and Voluntary Sector Quarterly, 21*, 227–249.

Brown, D. A. H., Brown, D. L., & Anastasopoulos, V. (2002). *Women on boards: Not just the right thing . . . But the "Bright" Thing*. Ottawa, Ontario: The Conference Board of Canada.

Brown, W. A. (2002). Inclusive governance practices in nonprofit organizations and implications for practice. *Nonprofit Management & Leadership, 12*, 369–385.

Brown, W. A. (2005). Exploring the association between board and organizational performance in nonprofit organizations. *Nonprofit Management and Leadership, 15*, 317–339.

Buse, K., Bernstein, R. S., & Bilimoria, D. (2016). The influence of board diversity, board diversity policies and practices, and board inclusion behaviors on nonprofit governance practices. *Journal of Business Ethics, 133*, 179–191.

Campbell, K., & Minguez-Vera, A. (2008). Gender diversity in the boardroom and firm financial performance. *Journal of Business Ethics, 83*, 435–451.

Carter, D. A., D'Souza, F., Simkins, B. J., & Simpson, W. G. (2010). The gender and ethnic diversity of US Boards and board committees and firm financial performance. *Corporate Governance: An International Review, 18*, 396–414.

Cohen, P., Cohen, J., Aiken, L. S., & West, S. G. (2003). *Applied multiple regression/correlation analysis for the behavioral sciences* (3rd ed.). Mahwah, NJ: Lawrence Erlbaum.

Cook, C., Heath, F., & Thompson, R. L. (2000). A meta-analysis of response rates in web- or internet-based surveys. *Educational and Psychological Measurement, 60*, 821–836.

Cornforth, C. (2003). *The governance of public and non-profit organizations: What do boards do?* London, England: Routledge.

Cornforth, C. (2012). Nonprofit governance research: Limitations of the focus on boards and suggestions for new directions. *Nonprofit and Voluntary Sector Quarterly, 41,* 1117–1136.

Cukier, W., Yap, M., Aspevig, K., & Lejasisaks, L. (2011). *DiverseCity Counts 3: A snapshot of diverse leadership in the GTA.* Toronto, Ontario, Canada: Diversity Institute, Ryerson University.

Dobbin, F., & Jung, J. (2011). Corporate board gender diversity and stock performance: The competence gap or institutional investor bias? *North Carolina Law Review, 89,* 809–839.

Ely, R. J., & Thomas, D. A. (2001). Cultural diversity at work: The effects of diversity perspectives on work group processes and outcomes. *Administrative Science Quarterly, 46,* 229–273.

Fan, W., & Yan, Z. (2010). Factors affecting response rates of the web survey: A systematic review. *Computers in Human Behavior, 26,* 132–139.

Foldy, E. G. (2004). Learning from diversity: A theoretical exploration. *Public Administration Review, 64,* 529–538.

Fredette, C., & Bradshaw, P. (2012). Social capital and nonprofit governance effectiveness. *Nonprofit Management and Leadership, 22,* 391–409.

Fredette, C., Bradshaw, P., & Krause, H. (2016). From diversity to inclusion: A multimethod study of diverse governing groups. *Nonprofit and Voluntary Sector Quarterly, 45*(1, Suppl.), 28S–51S.

Gazley, B., & Nicholson-Crotty, J. (2018). What drives good governance? A structural equation model of nonprofit board performance. *Nonprofit and Voluntary Sector Quarterly, 47,* 262–285.

Green, J. C., & Griesinger, D. W. (1996). Board performance and organizational effectiveness in nonprofit social services organizations. *Nonprofit Management and Leadership, 6,* 381–402.

Harris, E. E. (2014). The impact of board diversity and expertise on nonprofit performance. *Nonprofit Management & Leadership, 25,* 113–130.

Haslam, S. A., Ryan, M. K., Kulich, C., Trojanowski, G., & Atkins, C. (2010). Investing with prejudice: The relationship between women's presence on company boards and objective and subjective measures of company performance. *British Journal of Management, 21,* 484–497.

Jaskyte, K. (2012). Boards of directors and innovation in nonprofit organizations. *Nonprofit Management and Leadership, 22,* 439–459.

Jayne, M. E. A., & Dipboye, R. L. (2004). Leveraging diversity to improve business performance: Research findings and recommendations for organizations. *Human Resource Management, 43,* 409–424.

Jehn, K. A., Northcraft, G. B., & Neale, M. A. (1999). Why differences make a difference: A field study of diversity, conflict and performance in workgroups. *Administrative Science Quarterly, 44,* 741–763.

Jia, M., & Zhang, Z. (2013). Critical mass of women on BODs, multiple identities, and corporate philanthropic disaster response: Evidence from privately owned Chinese firms. *Journal of Business Ethics, 118,* 303–317.

Joecks, J., Pull, K., & Vetter, K. (2013). Gender diversity in the boardroom and firm performance: What exactly constitutes a "critical mass?" *Journal of Business Ethics, 118,* 61–72.

Kalton, G. (1983). *Introduction to survey sampling.* Newbury Park, CA: SAGE.

Kanter, R. M. (1977). Some effects of proportions on group life: Skewed sex ratios and responses to token women. *American Journal of Sociology, 82,* 965–990.

Klein, K. J., & Harrison, D. A. (2007). On the diversity of diversity: Tidy logic, messier realities. *Academy of Management Perspectives, 21,* 26–33.

Kochan, T., Bezrukova. K., Ely, R., Jackson, S., Joshi, A., Jehn, K., . . . Thomas, D. (2003). The effects of diversity on business performance: Report of the diversity research network. *Human Resource Management, 42,* 3–21.

Kogut, B., Colomer, J., & Belinky, M. (2014). Structural equality at the top of the corporation: Mandated quotas for women directors. *Strategic Management Journal, 35,* 891–902.

Konrad, A. M., Kramer, V. W., & Erkut, S. (2008). Critical mass: The impact of three or more women on corporate boards. *Organizational Dynamics, 37,* 145–164.

Litvin, D. R. (2006). Making space for a better case. In A. M. Konrad, P. Prasad, & J. Pringle (Eds.),

Handbook of workplace diversity (pp. 75–94). London, England: SAGE.

Lortie-Lussier, M., & Rinfret, N. (2002). The proportion of women managers: Where is the critical mass? *Journal of Applied Social Psychology, 32,* 1974–1991.

Mahadeo, J., Soobaroyen, T., & Hanuman, V. (2012). Board composition and financial performance: Uncovering the effects of diversity in an emerging economy. *Journal of Business Ethics, 105,* 375–388.

McClelland, G. H., & Judd, C. M. (1993). Statistical difficulties of detecting interactions and moderator effects. *Psychological Bulletin, 114,* 376–390.

Meier, K. J. (1993). Latinos and representative bureaucracy testing the Thompson and Henderson hypotheses. *Journal of Public Administration Research and Theory, 3,* 393–414.

Meier, K. J., Wrinkle, R. D., & Polinard, J. L. (1999). Representative bureaucracy and distributional equity: Addressing the hard question. *Journal of Politics, 61,* 1025–1039.

Miller, T., & del Carmen Triana, M. (2009). Demographic diversity in the boardroom: Mediators of the board diversity–firm performance relationship. *Journal of Management Studies, 46,* 755–786.

Moore, M. H. (2000). Managing for value: Organizational strategy in for-profit, nonprofit, and governmental organizations. *Nonprofit and Voluntary Sector Quarterly,* 29(Suppl. 1), 183–208.

Nielsen, S., & Huse, M. (2010). The contribution of women on boards of directors: Going beyond the surface. *Corporate Governance: An International Review, 18,* 136–148.

Oliver, P., & Marwell, G. (1993). *The critical mass in collective action: A micro-social theory.* Cambridge, UK: Cambridge University Press.

Oliver, P., Marwell, G., & Teixeira, R. (1985). A theory of the critical mass. I. Interdependence, group heterogeneity, and the production of collective action. *American Journal of Sociology, 91,* 522–556.

Ostrower, F. (2007). *Nonprofit governance in the United States: Findings on performance and accountability from the first national representative study.* Washington, DC: Center on Nonprofits and Philanthropy.

Ostrower, F., & Stone, M. (2005). Governance: Research trends, gaps and future prospects. In W. W. Powell & R. Steinberg (Eds.), *The nonprofit sector: A research handbook* (pp. 612–628). New Haven, CT: Yale University Press.

Shih, T.-H., & Fan, X. (2008). Comparing response rates from web and mail surveys: A meta analysis. *Field Methods, 20,* 249–271.

Siciliano, J. I. (1996). The relationship of board member diversity to organizational performance. *Journal of Business Ethics, 15,* 1313–1320.

Statistics Canada. (2016). *Population estimates and projections.* Ottawa, Ontario: Government of Canada.

Torchia, M., Calabro, A., & Huse, M. (2011). Women directors on corporate boards: From tokenism to critical mass. *Journal of Business Ethics, 102,* 299–317.

van Knippenberg, D., & Schippers, M. C. (2007). Work group diversity. *Annual Review of Psychology, 58,* 515–541.

Voss, G. B., Sirdeshmukh, D., & Voss, Z. G. (2008). The effects of slack resources and environmental threat on product exploration and exploitation. *Academy of Management Journal, 51,* 147–164.

Wang, Y., & Clift, B. (2009). Is there a "business case" for board diversity? *Pacific Accounting Review, 21,* 88–103.

Williams, K. Y., & O'Reilly, C. A. (1998). Demography and diversity in organizations: A review of 40 years of research. In B. M. Staw & L. L. Cummings (Eds.), *Research in organizational behavior* (Vol. 20, pp. 77–140). Greenwich, CT: JAI Press.

Welcome to the Board of Directors

C. Kenneth Meyer and Alison Lemke

Bethany Brown was elated when she learned that, by popular vote of other members of her professional health care society, she was elected to its board of directors at the national level. It had been a long road to navigate. Since she had become a member of the society nearly twenty years earlier, she had held several positions on the executive committee of the association at the state level and had volunteered extensively with the national association.

Over the years she had never refused to lend a helping hand, even if the committee assignment was more "work horse" than "show horse." She had contributed her energies and talents to the association because she agreed with its mission and value statements and felt that it had done a respectable job in meeting what she later termed "the needs, wants, desires, expectations, and demands of its nearly 50,000 state, national and international members." She could clearly recall her graduate studies adviser, and major professor, insisting that all graduate students become members of their professional associations because it would be an excellent way to pursue continual lifelong learning and professional development. And if they met the academic qualifications for membership, they should also respond positively, he suggested, to any invitation to join their discipline's national honorary society. Minimally, such memberships would look great, he said, on the "office bragging wall."

Bethany started her term on the national board of directors with zeal and optimism. She looked forward to the challenge and felt well prepared for the responsibility she knew she would be given. She had many years of experience in her health-related profession, having worked as a practitioner/provider and also in various management roles. She also had a lengthy history of volunteer service with the association at both the state and national levels. The various capacities in which she had worked and volunteered had prepared her well, she hoped, to be an effective board member and leader at the national level.

Bethany was not naive about the presence of some tension and divisiveness within the national association: there had been a history over the years of many troublesome turf battles between management and volunteer governance members. These skirmishes seemed to focus on issues of power and control between members of the board of directors and the executive director (both past and current) and national office staff. There had also been a protracted history of governance changes within the association. For a number of years, the requirement that major policy decisions be passed by a legislative body composed of representatives from every state in the nation had led to policy gridlock. Important motions and policy decisions died amid debate and disagreement in the legislative body, and confidence had diminished in the ability of the

DOI: 10.4324/9781003387800-4

national board to act resolutely on anything, especially any important national problem.

Several years earlier, a governance restructure movement had succeeded, perhaps against all odds, and the legislative body had voted to eliminate itself. Many in the association thought that this was a move in the right direction. Now the association was governed by a single, twenty-member board of directors, with members elected by vote of all association members from a national slate of candidates. As a student of organizational theory, Bethany knew the pros and cons associated with the size of this board. Larger boards give voice to a wider range of constituent interests, but they can also lead to "grandstanding" by some members and result, literally, in a "runaway" board of directors.

After the governance restructuring had been implemented, many volunteer association leaders, including Bethany, assumed that the turf battles and tension between the elected volunteer leadership and the association management staff would end. Unfortunately, Bethany discovered during her first year on the board of directors that a great deal of tension and distrust persisted. To Bethany, a newly elected board member, it appeared that both sides were culpable. During board meetings, she observed an insatiable pursuit of power plays that were identifiable even to the most inexperienced board member. As she told another board member in confidence at a luncheon meeting, the power exuded by the executive director and "Mahogany Row" was palpable!

To better understand the working relations that evolved between the board of directors and the executive suite, a historical note is in order. As is common for most national boards of directors associated with academic disciplines, whether in the health sciences, business, public administration, or the arts and natural sciences, the elected board members were often professionals who had extensive managerial and/or academic teaching and research backgrounds. They were accomplished and often came from

work settings in which they had wielded considerable influence, if not power. If they came to the board with extensive management experience, they were accustomed to being in charge of staff, managing day-to-day operations, dealing with budgets and financial accountings, and leading work units. If they came from academic teaching and research positions, they were accustomed to being immersed in the study of the clinical or subject areas pertinent to the profession, thereby earning great respect and enhancing the reputation of their department and parent university, but they often had little formal knowledge of association management and of the pedestrian, but salient, issues that regularly appeared on the board of directors' agenda.

After a year of being on the board of directors, Bethany saw that those from either background faced significant challenges in becoming effective board members. Those from managerial backgrounds tended to delve deeply into how policies and objectives would be implemented within the association's office, and they often became preoccupied with budget questions related to how much money should be allotted to particular activities. On the other hand, those from academic backgrounds tended, in Bethany's view, to debate various aspects of issues and policy decisions endlessly without ever reaching conclusions about how to move forward on them. The academics were used to reaching decisions by consensus—after lengthy, tedious debates.

On the other hand, Bethany could see that the paid management staff of the association also, and quite often, raised the tensions between board and staff. The association was large enough that it employed a staff of more than 175 people. For the past five years its executive director had been Henry Gray, who had risen through the ranks and was a veteran of previous governance structures and turf battles between staff and association leaders. Some members felt that he personally benefited from the "bar stool syndrome" and that it served his rise to a position of national prominence. He had great name recognition, was a person of some presence when he addressed the board, and could "wine and dine," "lift a few," and tell stories with the best of them. He was no stranger to conflict, but he was a weak leader in the area of conflict resolution and compromise.

Bethany's impression was that Henry, although personable and competent in many areas of management, was highly selective of the information he chose to share with members of the board; as a result, not all relevant or pertinent information was available to the board regarding the progress being made on some of the association's strategic objectives. Board members, particularly when they were new to the board of directors, did not always feel comfortable asking for information because, through word and deed, he seemed to convey the message that questions and concerns were unwelcome.

As Bethany often stated under her breath, "Yours is not to question why; yours is but to do or die." She knew her expected place, but as a seasoned professional, she was not ready to accept her newly assigned status and role—at least not as envisioned by Henry.

Although Bethany could understand why the executive director tended to erect a wall between the board of directors and the paid staff, it also seemed that his lack of openness and candor exacerbated the tensions that bubbled up and served as a barrier between board members and staff that impeded effective and constructive communication.

After one of the national meetings, she spoke briefly with her old graduate studies adviser about her board experience, and to her surprise, he shared with her a similar set of recollections. Years earlier, he too had been nominated and then elected by the organization membership to a prestigious executive board that also turned out to have several undesirable attributes. He had observed a "clique" mentality among the board members from prestigious colleges and universities. This group often succeeded in setting the guidelines and standards of the organization to mirror their own curricular direction—but not the national direction. Successive executive directors did not come from the academic discipline represented by the association, but instead were drawn from the ranks of career public appointees in Washington, DC. These people developed a network of friends, especially among nonprofit professional organizations, and prospered professionally because of the "entitlements of cronyism."

Year after year, the agenda for this association was developed by the executive director with only limited and highly selective input from those board members who were most compliant with the executive's lead. Important issues within the association related to ethics, discrimination, environmental and global trends, and civil and human rights received scant consideration or attention by the largely older, white, male executive board. Finally, Bethany's professor recalled, precious little input was solicited from the rank-and-file practitioners on the board or in the field.

Bethany's professor went on to say that, in his opinion, the main problem had rested in an elitism in the national office, coupled with the arrogance of a seemingly "untouchable and unaccountable" management cadre who had never distinguished themselves as practitioners or academics but were able to survive on "K Street" as sycophant bureaucrats. He chuckled as he recalled that the executive board meetings were largely centered on accepting the financial and budgetary audit reports prepared by one or another of the "Big Six" accounting firms, approving the two-year budget recommendations that would ensure the continuity of administrative services and making sure the association was actuarially sound insofar as it covered executive salaries, pensions and retirements, health benefits, and other perks. This board gave little attention to expanding the membership rostrum or providing meaningful technical, professional, and curriculum advice to its membership institutions and individual members.

Bethany left this conversation in a state of renewed perplexity: was she dealing with a similar set of issues? She wondered if she would be able to carve out a legacy of service that truly met the needs of the nearly 50,000 academic and practitioner members in her health field niche. Or would she end up disgruntled and alienated instead, like her mentor, after her service to the national board had been rendered?

Bethany reminisced about her many years of volunteer service and how she had prepared herself to meet earlier challenges. She had delved into the existing literature on association governance, issues with boards of directors, strategic planning, and collaborative leadership. After reflecting on her study of these topics, she had felt that it served her well in her various roles at the state level of the association. Now, she wondered, would her knowledge and leadership skills be enough to improve the working relationship between the national association staff and the board of directors as well? She remembered that she had often been a voice of moderation and reason on the state board of directors, and she was also aware that she was increasingly being looked to as a source of knowledge concerning association governance.

Bethany could see, without being too vain, that she had the knowledge to make a difference in how the board of directors conducted its business. How could she communicate that, she wondered, and start to make a difference?

Questions and Instructions

1. What information should be available to new members of a board of directors? How might some of the issues discussed in the case have been handled through information supplied at a board orientation for new members? Should seasoned board members be expected to attend orientations for new members? Offer justifications for your responses.

2. Should an executive director get involved in board-of-directors relationship dynamics including any cliques that may form or elitism that may develop? Should the views of the organization's staff members or the views of practitioners outside of the organization affect the decisions of members of a board of directors? Please explain your answers.

3. Bethany Brown appears to be a thoughtful new recruit to her professional association's board of directors. What is she doing well to prepare herself to serve in this role? What strategies might she also wish to consider?

Leadership and Growth Challenges in Nonprofit Organizations

JULIE ANN O'CONNELL, BENJAMIN S. BINGLE AND C. KENNETH MEYER

A well-housed electorate is paramount to a civil society, and housing security is often part of a larger discussion regarding health, education, and mental wellness. Snow Country Home Help is a local chapter of a larger international nonprofit organization; the 'home' organization, Home Help International (HHI), is a highly regarded nonprofit with a household name and far reach around the world. The mission of HHI is purposefully broad, centered on rehabbing current housing stock to ensure safe shelter for all, and the organization has traditionally focused on projects for senior citizens. As an umbrella organization, HHI focuses on marketing, fundraising, and supporting local affiliates to work in ways that make sense for their geographic and economic location.

Snow Country Home Help (SCHH) was chartered over 30 years ago, starting as an outreach ministry of a local church. Church members noticed that many elderly congregation members were having difficulty maintaining their homes in a safe manner, causing distress for the elderly church members and consternation for local officials who were intent enforcing housing codes and reducing 'sore spots' in the village. SCHH is located in one of the most affluent areas in the state. One might assume that there is no need for help maintaining homes in such an well-off area, but a downward national economy coupled with a growing population of older civil servants and white collar workers has kept SCHH busy in the past couple decades.

When SNHH moved from being an all-volunteer organization to being a chapter of a larger affiliate, the first Executive Director was hired. For the next 15 years, the ED along with a solid team of volunteers grew the chapter to the point where additional paid staff members were added to the payroll. The original ED retired, and over the next 10 years two different executives took the helm. The ED position opened up again, and the Board was ecstatic when Nancy applied. Nancy was a veteran of the Home Help organization, having been with a large urban affiliate for eight years. She was moving back to the Snow Country area to be near family, and to raise her high school aged children. Nancy had big ideas for how SCHH could build capacity to serve more people, and she had an infectious personality that made people want to join the organization and be a part of moving the mission forward.

Nancy found that Snow Country Home Helpers was perfectly situated to grow, and she inherited a small staff to help her do so.

DOI: 10.4324/9781003387800-5

SCHH was able to work with the local housing authority and county government to help senior citizens maintain and stay in their homes, and to identify other homes that were in danger of becoming code violations. An increasing local population coupled with growing needs spurred Nancy and her staff to dream of what *could be* if the organization grew beyond helping rehab homes for senior citizens and into rehabbing homes for the growing low-income population. She and her staff started meeting with other potential partners—local churches, county officials, and nonprofit organizations that served low income populations—to discuss what needs the locale was experiencing, and what an expansion of Home Help might look like. With a development manager, a construction manager, a volunteer manager, and an administrative assistant, Nancy found that in order to grow, she would need to grow the staff as well.

The Board of Directors had moved past being a 'working board' but was not yet a purely governing board. Board members were surprised and intrigued (and a little wary) when Nancy brought up the issue of affiliate expansion during the Executive Director report of the Board of Directors meeting, and asked for board approval to begin the process in earnest to consider expansion.

Discussion Questions

1. Discuss issues of a Board of Directors moving from a working board to a governing board.
2. Discuss organizational vision. Whose job is it to vision for an organization? What should go into the visioning process?
3. Define mission drift. Analyze this case looking for signs of mission drift. If you were a member of the SCHH Board of Directors, what would be your official stance with regard to possible expansion and the potential for mission drift?
4. What happens when an Executive Director has a big, bold, or new vision; but, the board is unsure about the vision or resistant? Putting yourself in the role of Board President, how should an effective leader navigate this tension?

PART II

The Legal Framework

Jared C. Bennett[1]

For the past three days, the executive director of a nonprofit organization could not sleep, eat, or focus on work. Her acute agitation stemmed from knowing that for three days, a jury of 12 strangers had been deliberating her future and that of the nonprofit organization she founded and worked so hard to build for the past decade.

As she was yet again allowing her mind to wander to what the jurors might be thinking, she received the call that she desperately wanted but also greatly feared. The voice of her attorney—with which she had become all too familiar over the past three years of litigation—somberly said, "The court just called. The jury has finally reached a verdict. I need you to meet me at the courthouse right away."

A nervous "Okay, I'll be right there" was all the executive could stammer in response.

From the moment she hung up the phone until she arrived at the courthouse parking lot, the executive director's mind replayed the three years of litigation, starting from the time she was served with the board of trustees' civil complaint alleging that she had breached her fiduciary duties. The executive director's mind first pondered the extensive amount of time that she had spent responding to seemingly endless interrogatories, requests for admission, and document requests that the board's attorneys had made, seeking her personal financial records as well as those of the nonprofit. As if providing this information to her adversaries wasn't bad enough, she thought, the board had also communicated its accusations against her to the Internal Revenue Service (IRS), the United States Department of Justice, and the state attorney general. In response to the board's accusations, the IRS issued an administrative summons that required the executive director to produce her financial documents and answer questions under oath about them to an IRS revenue officer. Likewise, she received a federal grand jury subpoena for her nonprofit's financial records, including payments that the nonprofit had made to some foreign charities in two developing nations. Additionally, investigators from the state attorney general's office sent over investigators to question her as to whether she had complied with state tax laws.

Along with this, she reflected on the grueling hours she had spent in depositions, during which her adversaries' attorney peppered her with questions about her private life, her personal finances,

DOI: 10.4324/9781003387800-6

and her decisions as executive director of her nonprofit organization. She thought about how every question from the opposing attorney seemed to insinuate that she had been both dishonest and incompetent. Although these memories made her blood simmer, it came to a full boil as she recalled the several hours of depositions that she had attended with trustees who repeatedly accused her of wrongdoing. She fumed as she remembered how helpless she felt having to silently observe as her attorney asked questions to which her adversaries gave their accusatory answers.

"How could the government and the trustees think I would do such a thing when I am the one who started this operation and sacrificed so much to make this place what it is today?" she muttered to herself while driving.

Her anger quickly changed to bewilderment as she recalled the stream of letters that the attorneys had exchanged, the numerous motions that the attorneys had drafted and argued before the court, the court hearings and scheduling conferences that had preceded the trial, the failed settlement negotiations, and finally, the hard-fought three-week trial that required her to relive everything that had happened over the past three years. After all this, she hated litigation.

Her hate of litigation quickly changed to tears as she thought about the cost of producing all those documents, the $400 an hour that the nonprofit had been paying her attorney for his work, and the incalculable amount of time she had wanted to spend fulfilling the mission of the nonprofit but, instead, was wasting on litigation. "How could it have come to this?" she asked herself as she exited the car and walked toward the courthouse doors. After going through security, she saw the all-too-familiar face of her attorney in the hallway.

"Are you nervous?" the attorney asked.

"What do you think?" she curtly replied. "What if the jury comes back and finds me liable?"

"Well, we can always appeal," the attorney replied.

"How much does that cost, and how long does that take?" the executive director inquired.

"For my firm to prepare an appellate brief for a case this complicated and to argue it before an appellate court, you can expect the cost to be around $10,000, and the case may last another year or two," the attorney dryly replied. "Even then, you may not win. In fact, if we prevail on appeal, the appellate court may simply order a new trial."

"But what if I win the trial?" the executive director asked, trying to sound positive.

"Then the board of trustees can appeal, and we would have to respond by filing an appellate brief and by arguing the matter before the appellate court," the attorney said.

"So, no matter what, I may be in this for another two years and $10,000? And even after all that, we may be back here for more proceedings and possibly *another* trial?" the executive director asked incredulously.

"I'm afraid so," the attorney said. "We had better get into the courtroom. I see that the other side has arrived."

A few minutes after they entered the courtroom, the bailiff entered and declared, "All rise!" The judge entered through one door and the jurors through another. As the jury entered, some jurors looked right at the executive director, but others look elsewhere and avoided eye contact with her. Without any preliminary comments, the judge cut to the chase: "Please be seated. Has the jury reached a verdict?"

"Yes, Your Honor," the jury foreperson replied.

"Then let's hear it," said the judge.

"As to the first cause of action, whether the defendant breached her fiduciary duties, we the jury find . . . "

"Who won?" you ask. The sad fact is that regardless of the verdict the jury reached, the executive director, the board of trustees, and the nonprofit organization have all lost. Litigation is extremely costly in both time and money, neither of which is an abundant resource for most nonprofit organizations. Moreover, litigation permanently damages trust and the interpersonal relationships on which all nonprofit organizations rely to effectively fund and accomplish their important societal missions. Worse yet, if the state and/or the federal government brings a civil action or seeks criminal charges against the executive director, she will be doing this all over again. Therefore, those who lead and manage nonprofit organization simply cannot afford to be unaware of or indifferent to the many laws that govern the activities of the organization and those who lead it.

For example, nonprofit organization managers and trustees need to be aware of the laws governing taxes, torts (e.g., personal injury), contracts, foreign transactions, securities, antitrust, property, labor, employment discrimination, and bankruptcy, to name only a few. However, we cannot present an exhaustive analysis of all laws that apply to nonprofit organizations in this part. Therefore, this introduction and the three reprinted readings that follow seek to familiarize nonprofit leaders with three basic areas of law that are universal to nonprofit organizations: (1) tax exemption, (2) nonprofit leader liability (including international concerns), and (3) tort liability.

Tax Exemption

The tax exemptions that federal and state governments provide to qualifying nonprofit organizations recognize the vital role that nonprofits play in society. Without these tax advantages, few, if any, organizations would be able to survive the financial burden of providing the services on which so many vulnerable people rely. After all, who could possibly make a successful for-profit business when the business model is to distribute as much food as possible to the homeless without receiving anything in return?

Nevertheless, recent fraud scandals—too numerous and notorious to discuss here—have shown that these tax incentives can be abused. Thus, federal and most state governments have passed laws that attempt to ensure that organizations availing themselves of the favorable tax treatment are actually engaging in the types of activities that society has deemed worthy of special tax concessions. To achieve the dual purpose of incentivizing worthy nonprofit activities while protecting against waste, fraud, and abuse, Congress has enacted Internal Revenue Code provisions that apply specifically to nonprofit organizations (Title 26 of the United States Code). For example, 26 U.S.C. § 501(c)(3) provides that the following types of organizations are exempt from federal taxation:

> Corporations, and any community chest, fund, or foundation, organized and operated exclusively for religious, charitable, scientific, testing for public safety, literary, or educational purposes, or to foster national or international amateur sports competition (but only if no part of its activities involve the provision of athletic facilities or equipment), or for the prevention of cruelty to children or animals, no part of the net earnings of which inures to the benefit of any private shareholder or individual, no substantial part of the activities of which is carrying on propaganda, or otherwise attempting, to influence legislation (except as otherwise provided in subsection (h)), and which does not participate in, or intervene in (including the publishing or distributing of statements), any political campaign on behalf of (or in opposition to) any candidate for public office.

In addition to exempting these organizations from federal taxation, section 501(c)(3) allows individuals and other entities that donate to qualifying 501(c)(3) organizations to deduct these donations from their own tax liability. Consequently, Congress has provided many attractive incentives for organizations that qualify for preferential tax treatment under section 501(c)(3).

Even though Congress created these incentives for qualifying organizations, it did not enact the requirements or tests that an organization would need to qualify for 501(c)(3) status. It delegated the promulgation of the 501(c)(3) qualification rules to the secretary of the treasury through the Administrative Procedure Act.[2] The IRS promulgated rules mandating that every would-be 501(c)(3) organization must meet the following tests: the Organizational Test and the Operational Test.[3] "If an organization fails to meet either the organizational test or the operational test, it is not exempt."[4] The US Supreme Court and the IRS also apply a third test that is not expressly stated in IRS regulations or section 501(c)(3): "the community conscience test." Because all three of these tests are necessary to attain and maintain tax-exempt status, each is briefly discussed next.

The Organizational Test

For a would-be 501(c)(3) entity to meet the Organizational Test, the IRS must determine that the entity is "organized exclusively for one or more exempt purposes" as listed in section 501(c)(3).[5] To make this determination, the IRS relies primarily on two sources: the statement of purpose in the documents creating the organization (usually called "articles of organization" or something similar) and the organization's plan to dispose of its assets when it eventually dissolves.[6]

Statement of purpose. An entity's articles of organization must contain a statement of purpose that shows the entity will engage in activities exempted from taxation in section 501(c)(3). The statement of purpose in the articles of organization does not have to be highly detailed or elaborate to pass muster. As an illustration, if the statement of purpose in the articles of organization simply says that the entity "is formed for charitable purposes," then, according to the IRS, "such articles ordinarily shall be sufficient for purposes of the organizational test."[7] Even though the statement of purpose portion of the Organizational Test tolerates great generality (e.g., "for charitable purposes"), it also accommodates more specific statements of purpose.[8]

However, the Organizational Test will not accommodate statements of purpose that authorize the entity (1) to devote anything more than an insubstantial part of its operations to purposes that are not exempt under section 501(c)(3),[9] (2) to engage in political activities in which the organization devotes more than an insubstantial part of its activities to influence legislation "by propaganda or otherwise,"[10] or (3) to wage a political campaign for or against any particular candidate for election.[11] Thus, if the articles of organization contain a 501(c)(3)–compliant statement of purpose, the IRS will determine that the organization has cleared this portion of the Organizational Test.

Dissolution. To ensure that the statement of purpose in the articles of organization does more than pay mere lip service to the exempt purposes in section 501(c)(3), the IRS has included a requirement in the Organizational Test compelling entities to show that their assets will continue to be used for 501(c)(3)–exempt purposes even after the entity is dissolved.[12] For example, the articles of incorporation could say that if the entity should dissolve, all of its assets will be distributed by court order to either a government agency for a public purpose or another organization with an exempt primary purpose under 501(c)(3). "However, an organization does not meet the organizational test if its articles [of organization] or the law of the State in which it was created to provide that its assets would, upon dissolution, be distributed to its members or shareholders."[13] Indeed, knowledge of state law is very important when it comes to the Organizational Test. If the entity satisfies the statement of purpose and the dissolution portions of the Organizational Test, the IRS will determine that the entity has met the first requirement for 501(c)(3) status.

The Operational Test

Even if the entity passes the Organizational Test, the IRS will not grant 501(c)(3) status unless its operations are also consistent with section 501(c)(3)'s purposes. To make this determination, the IRS relies on three criteria: (1) the entity's primary activities, (2) the entity's distribution of earnings, and (3) whether the entity is an action organization.[14]

Primary activities. To meet the Operational Test, the entity must show that its primary activities fall within an exempt purpose mentioned in section 501(c)(3). Recall that section 501(c)(3) applies only to organizations that are "operated exclusively" for the purposes mentioned therein. However, if this phrase were interpreted literally, then no organization could engage in any business activity outside the section 501(c)(3) boundaries. Indeed, if nonprofit organizations were not allowed to engage in at least some activities that are outside section 501(c)(3), many nonprofits would lose significant revenue sources on which they have come to rely over recent decades. Given the high cost of a literal interpretation of section 501(c)(3), the IRS has interpreted "exclusively" to mean "primarily." For example, IRS regulations state:

> An organization will be regarded as operated exclusively for one or more exempt purposes only if it engages primarily in activities which accomplish one or more of such exempt purposes specified in section 501(c)(3). An organization will not be so regarded if more than an insubstantial part of its activities is not in furtherance of an exempt purpose.[15]

Thus, an organization can engage in profit-making enterprises and still comply with the Operational Test as long as it can demonstrate that its profit-making enterprises are only "an insubstantial part of its activities" and advance "an exempt purpose."[16]

Unfortunately (or fortunately, depending on your point of view), neither the IRS nor the courts have defined what percentage of an organization's activities is "insubstantial." Whether nonexempt activities under 501(c)(3) constitute a "substantial" or an "insubstantial" portion of an organization's operations is decided on a case-by-case basis. Because judicial approaches to this issue differ throughout the country, leaders of a nonprofit organization must become familiar with court rulings in the jurisdiction(s) where their organization operates.

Distribution of earnings. Many people believe that nonprofit organizations are precluded from earning more than their total expenditures (i.e., generating a profit). This belief is mistaken. Nonprofit organizations may indeed earn profits. What they may not do, however, is distribute profits to trustees, directors, or board members for their personal benefit and still pass the Operational Test.[17] To this end, IRS regulations state that an organization will not meet the Operational Test if "its net earnings inure in whole or in part to the benefit of private shareholders or individuals."[18] Instead, the organization must show that its earnings are distributed in ways that further its 501(c)(3)–exempt purposes.

Action organizations. Designation as an "action organization" means that an entity has failed to meet the Operational Test and, consequently, has failed to attain 501(c)(3) status.[19] An action organization devotes more than an "insubstantial" portion of its activities to "attempting to influence legislation by propaganda or otherwise."[20] The IRS will deem an entity to be in the business of influencing legislation—and therefore an action organization—if it engages in at least one of three activities. First, an organization that "(a) contacts, or urges the public to contact, members of the legislative body for the purpose of proposing, supporting, or opposing legislation; or (b) advocates the adoption or rejection of legislation" will be deemed an action organization.[21] The IRS defines *legislation* as "action by the Congress, by any State legislature, by any local council or similar governing body, or by the public in a referendum, initiative, constitutional amendment, or similar procedure."[22] Thus, if an organization spends a "substantial part" of its time, effort, and money advocating for or against legislation, then the IRS will deem it in action organization that fails the Operational Test and, consequently, will not be afforded 501(c)(3) status.[23]

Second, if an entity "participates or intervenes, directly or indirectly, in any political campaign or be on behalf of or in opposition to any candidate for public office," then it is an action organization.[24]

The IRS has defined the phrase *candidate for public office* as "an individual who offers himself, or is proposed by others, as a contestant for an elective public office, whether such office be national, state, or local."[25]

Finally, the IRS will deem an entity to be an action organization if its primary objectives could only be achieved through the adoption or failure of proposed legislation and if the entity advocates or campaigns more than insubstantial amount for its political ends.[26] Note that the entity must advocate or campaign for a cause. Merely providing information about candidates or an analysis of specific legislation does not constitute "advocacy" or "campaigning" and, therefore, does not make an entity an action organization.[27]

If the IRS determines that an entity is an action organization, it's tax-free status is not necessarily in jeopardy because the entity may still qualify for tax-exempt status under 501(c)(4).[28] Entities that are tax exempt under 501(c)(4) are known as civic or social welfare organizations.[29] However, donors to 501(c)(4) organizations cannot write off their donations on their personal or corporate income taxes, which takes away a significant revenue-generating incentive. Once the IRS is satisfied that a nonprofit organization's primary activities are truly devoted to an exempt purpose under 501(c)(3), its earnings are properly distributed, and it is not a national organization, then it is deemed to have passed the Operational Test.

The Community Conscience Test

Organizations that satisfy both the Organizational and Operational Tests still may not qualify for 501(c)(3) status if their primary purpose is contrary to the community conscience. Although this requirement is not expressly stated in section 501(c)(3) or other IRS regulations, the IRS introduced it in 1971 through Revenue Ruling 71–447.[30] An IRS Revenue Ruling notifies the public about how the IRS will interpret and apply laws, rules, and regulations. Revenue Ruling 71–447 provides that organizations that discriminate based on race are not the types of "charities" that 501(c)(3) was intended to foster and, therefore, cannot receive 501(c)(3) status.[31] The best-known community conscience case occurred in 1974, when Bob Jones University, a South Carolina private nonprofit religious university that engaged in racial discrimination, challenged Revenue Ruling 71–447. The plaintiff-university claimed that its discriminatory policies were an integral part of its religious beliefs.[32] Because of these racially discriminatory policies, the IRS revoked the 501(c)(3) status the university had previously enjoyed.[33] The university sought judicial review of the IRS's determination, which eventually reached the United States Supreme Court. The Court affirmed the IRS's determination:

> When the Government grants exemptions or allows deductions all taxpayers are affected; the very fact of the exemption or deduction for the donor means that other taxpayers can be said to be indirect and vicarious "donors." Charitable exemptions are justified on the basis that the exempt entity confers a public benefit—a benefit which the society or the community may not itself choose or be able to provide, or which supplements and advances the work of public institutions already supported by tax revenues. History buttresses logic to make clear that, to warrant exemption under § 501(c)(3), an institution must fall within a category specified in that section and must demonstrably serve and be in harmony with the public interest. The institution's purpose must not be so at odds with the common community conscience as to undermine any public benefit that might otherwise be conferred.[34]

As the IRS's Revenue Ruling and the Supreme Court's endorsement thereof show, 501(c)(3) status is a symbol of public support for that which a nonprofit organization does. Consequently, the IRS will not grant 501(c)(3) status to an organization whose conduct is repugnant to the community conscience.[35]

Many questions surround the community conscience doctrine, however. How does the IRS or a court determine what the community conscience is? How large is the "community" whose conscience the IRS will attempt to determine? If, for example, a charitable nonprofit organization provides condoms and other informational materials on safe sex for teens in an area in which the vast majority of voters would like to shut down the nonprofit and run it out of town, is the nonprofit's activity so contrary to the community conscience to warrant revocation of its 501(c)(3) status? Surely the community conscience test will be litigated. Be that as it may, a nonprofit organization that meets the Organizational Test and the Operational Test and works within the community conscience—whatever that means—will be eligible for 501(c)(3) status.

The Liability of Nonprofit Leaders

Recent scandals involving the nonprofit sector have brought increased scrutiny of the leaders of nonprofit organizations. Accordingly, nonprofit leaders may face criminal and civil liability under federal and state law for the decisions they make. This introduction does not focus on the criminal sanctions that may be imposed against leaders of nonprofits. This topic is addressed in Part I, where the Sarbanes-Oxley Act of 2002 was introduced.[36] Therefore, this introduction briefly presents the civil aspects of liability that will help nonprofit leaders know how to avoid difficult litigation situations like the one presented at the beginning of this introduction.

The executive directors and governing boards of nonprofit organizations may be subject to civil liability under federal and state law. On the federal side, Congress prohibits any person from engaging in excess benefit transactions with a 501(c)(3) organization. If a person runs afoul of this prohibition, the IRS may impose heavy penalties against that person, including, among other things, a tax of 200 percent of the improper benefit the person obtained from the prohibited transaction with the nonprofit organization.[37] Thus, nonprofit leaders who engage in self-dealing may pay dearly.

In addition to facing federal civil liability for their actions, nonprofit leaders must also protect themselves from civil liability under state law. Although state laws governing nonprofit organizations vary, there are certain fiduciary duties that every state imposes on nonprofit directors and governing boards. For example, courts in many states require nonprofit leaders to abide by a duty of care, a duty of loyalty, and a duty of obedience.[38] Because state laws regarding the duties imposed on nonprofit directors vary somewhat, we rely here on the American Bar Association's Revised Model Nonprofit Corporation Act, which concisely sums up the duties under which nonprofit leaders must operate. The Model Act stipulates that

An officer with discretionary authority shall discharge his or her duties under that authority:

(1) in good faith;
(2) with the care an ordinarily prudent person in a like position would exercise under similar circumstances; and
(3) in a manner the officer reasonably believes to be in the best interests of the corporation and its members, if any.[39]

Under the Model Act, "good faith" means the directors rely on the competent advice of others such as staff, legal counsel, and other professionals in making decisions they reasonably believe to be in the best interest of the organization.[40] The Model Act also provides a liability shield for leaders who comply with their duty of good faith.[41] Conversely, the breach of any of these duties may subject nonprofit leaders to civil litigation, which can ruin careers, reputations, the organization itself, and priceless personal relationships, no matter who "wins" the litigation.

Additionally, as more nonprofit organizations start working in other countries, nonprofit leadership must be cognizant of two sets of possibly conflicting laws: those of the nonprofit's home country and those of the nonprofit's foreign host country. First, the nonprofit's home country will likely impose obligations on the nonprofit organization's financial transactions in foreign nations, with foreign governments, and with foreign nonprofit entities. In the United States, domestic nonprofits' foreign activities are governed by the Foreign Corrupt Practices Act of 1977,[42] and, in the United Kingdom, those same activities are governed by Bribery Act of 2010.[43] These acts are examples of how the nonprofit's host country can punish a nonprofit and its leaders for foreign activities that violate the host nation's laws against corruption. Second, the nonprofit's foreign host nation may have its own laws (taxation, labor, employment, anti-bribery, etc.), all of which may greatly differ from those of the nonprofit's home country. The responsible nonprofit leader must learn to successfully navigate both sets of laws and not assume that the laws of the foreign host are the same as those of the nonprofit's home country.

General Tort Liability

Besides facing legal liability for their decisions, leaders of nonprofit organizations may also be subject to suit for personal injuries that are allegedly caused by the nonprofit's actions or occur on the nonprofit's property. Historically, courts developed the doctrine of charitable immunity, which barred all suits against nonprofit organizations.[44] The reasons for according nonprofit organizations favored treatment for tort liability are self-evident. Nonprofit organizations provide benefits to the public and often rely heavily on volunteers. If legislatures put too much liability on nonprofit organizations, their leaders, and the volunteers, nonprofits would be reluctant to provide the services on which so many rely, for fear of being sued. Therefore, the burden of providing these services would shift to the government, thereby increasing the size and cost of government or resulting in the loss of services that vulnerable individuals need. Courts and legislatures therefore historically exempted nonprofits from suits or greatly limited their liability.

Over time, however, that immunity has eroded. Now, nonprofits and their leaders are exposed to more potential liability, even though they are still accorded more favorable treatment than for-profit corporations.[45] Many scholars would like to see nonprofit liability expand even further because they do not believe that the historic policy reasons for according nonprofits greater protection from tort litigation are valid in the 21st century. For example, some scholars argue that, in a modern world where some nonprofit organizations are extremely wealthy and liability insurance is readily available, they should not continue to receive heightened protection from tort liability.[46] Given this debate, nonprofit leaders should carefully watch for future legislation and litigation regarding nonprofit tort immunity in their states.

In addition to tort liability for the nonprofit's own acts or omissions, nonprofit volunteers often wonder whether the service they render for a nonprofit could subject them to civil liability. Prior to 1997, the answer to that question greatly differed from state to state. To bring national uniformity to volunteer tort liability, Congress enacted the Volunteer Protection Act of 1997 (VPA).[47] In the VPA, Congress expressly preempted any state law that is inconsistent with the VPA so that volunteers of a large national nonprofit are as protected as those of a local nonprofit anywhere in the United States.[48] The VPA provides that "no volunteer of a nonprofit organization . . . shall be liable for harm caused by an act or omission of the volunteer on behalf of the [nonprofit] organization or entity" if four criteria are met.[49] First, the volunteer must act "within the scope of the volunteer's responsibilities in the nonprofit organization."[50] Second, the volunteer must be appropriately licensed to perform the allegedly tortious act if the law in the state requires a license to perform that act (e.g., medical or dental services).[51] Third, the volunteer cannot act against the rights or safety of the "individual harmed by the volunteer" in a manner that is willful, reckless, or criminal.[52] Finally, the volunteer cannot have caused the harm while operating a motor vehicle for which the state requires the volunteer to have an "operator's license" and "maintain insurance."[53] The VPA allows states to require nonprofits to train their volunteers, and, where the state requires training but the nonprofit fails to train, volunteers do not have the VPA's liability protections. Nonprofit leaders must know and understand how to avoid tort liability for themselves and their volunteers.

Readings Reprinted in Part II

The readings in this chapter begin with a selection from nonprofit legal expert Bruce R. Hopkins. In this selection, Hopkins discusses in a question-and-answer format the legal concerns that all nonprofits must address to become and remain tax-exempt organizations.

Next, attorneys Elena Helmer and Stuart H. Deming discuss the anticorruption perils that nonprofits encounter when engaging in international work. Nonprofits must beware of the risks of being prosecuted by their home nation for foreign corruption as well as the dangers to the operation from foreign corruption.

Notes

1. Jared C. Bennett is a United States Magistrate Judge in the United States District Court for the District of Utah and an adjunct professor at the S. J. Quinney College of Law at the University of Utah. Any opinions expressed in this introductory essay are his alone and do not necessarily reflect those of any governmental entity.
2. 5 U.S.C. § 556 (2012).
3. 26 C.F.R. § 1.501(c)(3)-1(a) (2013) amended by 79 Fed. Reg. 37,631 (July 2, 2014).
4. Id.
5. Id. § 1.501(c)(3)-(1)(b).
6. Id. § 1.501(c)(3)-(1)(b)(1), (4).
7. Id. § 1.501(c)(3)-(1)(b)(1)(ii).
8. Id.
9. Id. § 1.501(c)(3)-(1)(b)(1)(i).
10. Id. § 1.501(c)(3)-(1)(b)(3)(i).
11. Id. § 1.501(c)(3)-(1)(b)(3)(ii).
12. Id. § 1.501(c)(3)-(1)(b)(4).
13. Id.
14. Id. § 1.501(c)(3)-(1)(c).
15. Id. § 1.501(c)(3)-(1)(c)(1).
16. Id.
17. Id. § 1.501(c)(3)-(1)(c)(2).
18. Id.
19. Id. § 1.501(c)(3)-(1)(c)(3)(i).
20. Id. § 1.501(c)(3)-(1)(c)(3)(ii).
21. Id. § 1.501(c)(3)-(1)(c)(3)(ii)(a), (b).
22. Id. § 1.501(c)(3)-(1)(c)(3)(ii).

23. *Id.*

24. *Id.* § 1.501(c)(3)-1(c)(3)(iii).

25. *Id.*

26. *Id.* § 1.501(c)(3)-1(c)(3)(iv).

27. *Id.*

28. 26 U.S.C. § 501(c)(4).

29. 26 C.F.R. § 501(c)(4)-1(a) (2013).

30. Rev. Rul 71–447, 1971–2 C.B. 230 (Jan. 1, 1971); *Bob Jones Univ. v. United States*, 461 U.S. 574, 592 (1974).

31. *Bob Jones Univ.*, 461 U.S. at 579.

32. *Id.* at 580–81 (discussing the university's racially discriminatory policies).

33. *Id.* at 581.

34. *Id.* at 591–92 (footnotes omitted).

35. *Id.* at 592.

36. Pub.L.No. 107–204.

37. 26 U.S.C. § 4958(b).

38. See, e.g., Jaclyn A. Cherry, "Update: The Current State of Nonprofit Director Liability," 37 Duq.L.Rev. 557, 560–62 (1999).

39. Revised Model Nonprofit Corporation Act § 8.42(a).

40. *Id.* § 8.42(b).

41. *Id.* § 8.42(d).

42. 15 U.S.C. §§ 78dd-1 to 78dd-3.

43. Bribery Act 2010, c. 23 (Eng.).

44. "Developments in the Law—Nonprofit Corporations," 105 Harv.L.Rev. 1578, 1679–1680 (1992).

45. *Id.* at 1680.

46. *Id.* at 1680–99.

47. 42 U.S.C. §§ 14501 to 14505.

48. 42 U.S.C. § 14502(a).

49. 42 U.S.C. § 14503(a).

50. *Id.* § 14503(a)(1).

51. *Id.* § 14503(a)(2).

52. *Id.* § 14503(a)(3).

53. *Id.* § 14503(a)(4).

CHAPTER 3

Nonprofit Organizations Law Generally

BRUCE R. HOPKINS

Nonprofit law basics

1.1 What is a nonprofit organization?

The term *nonprofit organization* is somewhat misleading; regrettably, the English language lacks a better one. It does not mean an organization that cannot earn a profit. Many nonprofit organizations are realizing profits, in the sense of revenues exceeding expenses. Colleges and universities exemplify this point. Using data for institutions' tax years ending in 2006, the average amount of net revenue received by small colleges and universities was $11 million, by medium-size institutions was $33 million, and by large institutions was $87 million. An entity of any type cannot long exist without revenues that at least equal expenses.

The easiest way to define a nonprofit organization is to first define its counterpart, the for-profit organization. A *for-profit organization* exists to operate a business and to generate profits (revenue in excess of costs) from that business for those who own the enterprise. As an example, the owners of a for-profit corporation are stockholders, who take their profits in the form of dividends. Thus, when the term *for-profit* is used, it refers to profits acquired by the owners of the business, not by the business itself. The law, therefore, differentiates between profits at the entity level and profits at the ownership level.

Both for-profit and nonprofit organizations are allowed by the law to earn profits at the entity level. But only for-profit organizations are permitted profits at the ownership level. Nonprofit organizations rarely have owners; these organizations are not permitted to pass along profits (net earnings) to those who control them.

Profits permitted to for-profit entities but not nonprofit entities are forms of private inurement. That is, private inurement refers to ways of transferring an organization's net earnings to persons in their private capacity. The purpose of a for-profit organization is to engage in private inurement. By contrast, nonprofit organizations are forbidden to engage in acts of private inurement. (Economists call this fundamental standard the *nondistribution constraint.*) Nonprofit organizations are required to use their profits for their program activities. In the case

DOI: 10.4324/9781003387800-7

of tax-exempt nonprofit organizations, these activities are termed their *exempt functions*.

Consequently, the doctrine of private inurement is the essential dividing line, in the law, between nonprofit and for-profit organizations.

The definition in the federal tax law of a nonprofit organization focuses largely on what this type of entity may not do. The law as to tax-exempt status includes rules as to what an exempt organization must do. Not all nonprofit organizations are tax-exempt organizations, however. State law may add to the requirements as to what a nonprofit organization is expected to do programmatically.

. . .

1.2 Is the term nonprofit organization *defined in the federal case law?*

The courts have not paid much attention to this definition. For example, throughout the nation's history, the U.S. Supreme Court has had only one occasion to define the term (in a non-tax-law case). The Court wrote that a "nonprofit entity is ordinarily understood to differ from a for-profit corporation principally because it is barred from distributing its net earnings, if any, to individuals who exercise control over it, such as members, officers, directors, or trustees."

The Supreme Court's definition of the term *nonprofit organization* is not far off the mark. The matter of *control*, however, is not confined to *individuals* (although ultimately a transaction or arrangement involving private inurement always entails something done by one or more individuals); control of a nonprofit organization can also be exercised by *organizations* (such as corporations, partnerships, and trusts). Additionally, the Court's definition of *nonprofit organization* is somewhat too narrow in that the requisite insider can be a person who is *in a position to* exercise control over the entity (that is, actual control is not necessary to cause a person to be an insider).

. . .

1.3 Sometimes the term not-for-profit organization *is used instead of* nonprofit organization. Are the terms synonymous?

As a matter of law, the terms *not-for-profit* and *nonprofit* do not mean the same. The two terms are often used interchangeably, but the proper legal term in this context is nonprofit organization (1.1).

The law employs the term *not-for-profit* to apply to an activity rather than to an entity. For example, the federal tax law denies business expense deductions for expenditures that are for a not-for-profit activity. Basically, this type of activity is not engaged in with a business or commercial motive; a not-for-profit activity is essentially a hobby.

The term *not-for-profit* often is applied in the nonprofit context by those who do not understand or appreciate the difference between profit at the entity level and profit at the ownership level (*id.*).

1.4 What are the types of nonprofit organizations?

The principal type of nonprofit organization is the nonprofit corporation. The other types of nonprofit organizations are trusts, unincorporated associations, and limited liability companies.

Some nonprofit organizations are chartered pursuant to state law. A fewer number of them are chartered by federal law.

. . .

1.5 How is a nonprofit organization started?

Generally, a nonprofit organization is formed in adherence with the law of the appropriate state (or District of Columbia).

Thus, if the organization is to be a corporation, it commences its existence by filing articles of incorporation with a state (1.6). If the entity is a trust, it is formed by executing a declaration of trust or a trust agreement. An unincorporated association is established by execution of a constitution. A limited liability company is formed by execution of articles of organization (followed by adoption of an operating agreement governing operations, relationships among members, distributions, sharing of income and losses, and the like).

The federal tax law also will, assuming the nonprofit organization is to become a tax-exempt organization, require and encourage various provisions of the articles of organization. The law in this context is termed the *organizational test* (1.27).

Most nonprofit organizations also have a set of bylaws—the rules by which they are operated. Some organizations have additional rules, such as codes of ethics, manuals of operation, and employee handbooks as well as a variety of policies and procedures.

Following the creation (and, if necessary, the filing) of the articles of organization, the newly formed entity should have an organizational meeting of the initial board of directors. At that meeting, the directors should adopt a set of bylaws, elect the officers, pass one or more resolutions to open bank and investment accounts, and attend to whatever other initial business there may be.

1.6 How does a nonprofit organization incorporate?

A nonprofit organization incorporates by filing a document with the appropriate state, usually termed *articles of incorporation*. State law likely will dictate some of the contents of these articles. At a minimum, the articles of incorporation will state the corporation's name, describe its corporate purposes, list the names and addresses of the directors, name a registered agent (1.7), and recite the names and perhaps the addresses of the incorporators (1.10).

The articles of incorporation likely will be filed with the secretary of state's office in the state. If that office determines that the articles qualify under the law, the state will issue a certificate of incorporation. The entity becomes a corporation as of the date on the certificate.

1.7 What is a registered agent?

Typically, the *registered agent* must be either an individual who is a resident of the state or a company that is licensed by the state to be a commercial registered agent.

1.8 What does the registered agent do?

The registered agent functions as the corporation's point of communication to the outside world. Any formal communication for the corporation as a whole is sent to the registered agent. Thus, if the state authorities want to communicate with the corporation, they do so by contacting the agent. If someone wants to sue the corporation, the agent is served with the papers.

1.9 Does the registered agent have any liability for the corporation's affairs?

No. The registered agent, as such, is not a director or officer of the corporation. Thus, the agent has no exposure to liability for the corporation's activities. The agent would be held liable for his or her own offenses, such as breach of contract.

1.10 Who are the incorporators?

The *incorporators* are the individuals who technically create a corporation. (They may or may not be the corporation's true founders.) They execute the articles of incorporation. Under the typical legal requirement around the country, anyone who is 18 years of age and a U.S. citizen can incorporate a nonprofit corporation. Each state's law should be confirmed on this point, however. Many states require at least three incorporators.

An incorporator, as such, does not have a subsequent role with respect to the corporation. Once the corporation comes into being, the function of the incorporators terminates. An individual who serves as an incorporator can, and often does, serve as a trustee, director, officer, and/or employee of the corporation.

Some entities are quite sensitive to the matter of who is listed as an incorporator. They see the articles of incorporation as being of great significance to the organization—a document to be preserved and treasured for posterity. Thus, often, the initial board members are the incorporators. Others prefer to let the lawyers working on the case be the incorporators. No particular legal significance is attached to service as an incorporator.

. . .

1.11 Who owns a nonprofit organization?

For the most part, a nonprofit organization does not have owners who would be comparable to stockholders of a for-profit corporation or general partners in a partnership. There are some exceptions; a few states allow nonprofit corporations to be established with the authority to issue stock.

Stock in a nonprofit organization is used solely for purposes of ownership. Any person (an individual, a business entity, or another nonprofit organization) can be a shareholder under this arrangement.

1.12 Who controls a nonprofit organization?

The nature of control of a nonprofit organization depends on the nature of the entity. Usually control of a nonprofit organization is vested in its governing body, frequently termed a *board of directors* or *board of trustees*. Actual control may

lie elsewhere—with the officers or key employees, for example. It is unlikely that control of a large-membership organization would be with the membership, because that element of power is too dissipated. In a small-membership entity, such as a coalition, control may well be with the membership. The foregoing is particularly the case with respect to corporations and unincorporated associations. Control of a trust lies with its trustees.

1.13 How many directors must a nonprofit organization have?

The number of directors (or trustees) a nonprofit organization must have is generally a matter of state law. This is particularly the case for corporations, where state law generally mandates at least three directors. In a few states, however, it is permissible for a nonprofit corporation to have only one director. By dint of the nature of an unincorporated association, it is likely to have several directors. By contrast, it is common for a trust to have only one trustee.

For some nonprofit organizations, the size (and composition) of the board is dictated not by law but by other considerations, such as a range of expertise, a need to be reflective of the community, diversity, or concentration of a particular profession or other field on the board. Certainly, for example, a tax-exempt college or university is not likely to have a mere smattering of directors or trustees; these institutions tend to be guided by a much larger governing board, in the range of 20–40 individuals. In the case of some governmental colleges and universities, the members of the board of regents of a university system are elected by the public.

With the advent of federal law and regulation focusing on governance, however, the size of a nonprofit organization's board of directors is becoming a federal law factor. This is particularly the case for public charities. The IRS is issuing private letter rulings holding that an organization cannot qualify as a public charity, at least in part, where it has only one or two directors; this entails an application (albeit strained) of the private benefit doctrine. Indeed, one court decision holds that a corporation with only one director (even if allowable under state law) cannot qualify under the federal tax law as a public charity.

1.14 Can the same individuals serve as the directors, officers, and incorporators?

Generally, an individual can serve as a director (or trustee), officer, and incorporator of a corporation. For example, the chancellor or president of a private, incorporated college can serve simultaneously on the institution's board of trustees. The law of the appropriate state should be reviewed as to this point. For example, under the laws of some states, the same individual cannot simultaneously be president and secretary of a corporation; this is because other state law may require that a document must be executed by two individuals, the entity's president and secretary.

1.15 Can the same individual serve as a director, officer, incorporator, and registered agent?

Yes, with respect to a corporation, an individual may serve as a director, officer, incorporator, and registered agent, unless state law forbids such a multirole status, which is unlikely. The registered agent—if an individual—must be a resident of the state in which the entity is functioning, but the requirement of residency is not applicable to the other roles.

1.16 What is the legal standard by which a nonprofit organization should be operated?

The legal standard by which a nonprofit organization should be operated depends on the type of organization. If the nonprofit organization is not tax-exempt, the standard is nearly the same as that for a for-profit entity. If the nonprofit organization is tax-exempt but is not a charitable organization,

the standard is somewhat higher. The legal standard is highest for a tax-exempt charitable organization (1.32). In general, the standard is easy to articulate but often difficult to implement.

. . .

1.17 What is the legal standard for an organization that is tax-exempt and charitable?

The legal standard by which all aspects of operations of the organization should be tested requires reasonableness and prudence. Everything the organization does should be undertaken in a reasonable manner and to a reasonable end. Also, those working for or otherwise serving the charitable organization should act in a way that is prudent. Tax-exempt charitable organizations are required to satisfy an operational test (1.28).

The federal tax exemption granted to charitable and certain other forms of tax-exempt organizations can be revoked if the organization makes an expenditure or engages in some other activity that is deemed to be not reasonable. The same is likely true at the state level: Unreasonable behavior may cause the attorney general to investigate the organization.

. . .

1.18 What does the term fiduciary mean?

A *fiduciary* is a person who has special responsibilities in connection with the administration, investment, and distribution of property, where the property belongs to someone else. This range of duties is termed *fiduciary responsibility*. For example, guardians, executors, receivers, and the like are fiduciaries. Trustees of charitable trusts are fiduciaries. Today, a director or officer of a charitable organization is a fiduciary.

Indeed, the law can make anyone a fiduciary. As an illustration of the broad reach of this term, in a few states, professional fundraisers are deemed, by statute, fiduciaries of the charitable gifts raised during the campaigns in which they are involved.

1.19 What is the legal standard underlying fiduciary responsibility?

In a word, prudence; a fiduciary is expected to act, with respect to the income and assets involved, in a way that is prudent. This standard of behavior is known as the prudent person rule. This rule means that fiduciaries are charged with acting with the same degree of judgment—prudence—in administering the affairs of the organization as they would in their personal affairs. Originally devised to apply in the context of investments, this rule today applies to all categories of behavior—both commissions and omissions—undertaken in relation to the organization being served.

1.20 What is the meaning of the term reasonable?

The word *reasonable* is much more difficult to define than prudence. A judge, attorney general, IRS agent, and the like will say that the word is applied on a case-by-case basis. In other words, the term describes one of those things that one "knows when one sees it."

The term *reasonable* is basically synonymous with *rational*. A faculty of the mind enables individuals to distinguish truth from falsehood and good from evil by deducing inferences from facts. Other words that often can be substituted for *reasonable* are *appropriate, proper, suitable, equitable,* and *moderate*. Whatever term is used, an individual in this setting is expected to use this faculty and act in an appropriate and rational manner.

1.21 Who are the fiduciaries of a charitable organization?

The principal fiduciaries of a charitable organization are the directors. The officers are also fiduciaries. Other fiduciaries may include an employee who has responsibilities similar to those of an officer, such as a chief executive officer or a chief financial officer who is not officially a director or officer. Outsiders, such as people who are hired to administer an endowment fund or pension plan, are fiduciaries with respect to the organization. Each of these individuals has what is known as fiduciary responsibility (1.18), which includes the responsibility of acting reasonably (1.19) under the circumstances.

. . .

1.22 What is the law as to board management responsibilities?

One of the bedrock principles in the law is that trustees of charitable trusts are deemed to have the same obligation (duty of care) toward the assets of the trust as they do their personal resources. Their responsibility is to act *prudently* in their handling of the nonprofit organization's income and assets. The trustees are *fiduciaries*; the law (for now, largely state law) imposes on them standards of conduct and management that together comprise principles of *fiduciary responsibility*. Most state law, whether statutory or court opinions, imposes the standards of fiduciary responsibility on directors of nonprofit organizations, whether or not the organizations are trusts and whether or not they are charitable.

The contemporaneous general standard is that a member of the board of a nonprofit organization is required to perform his or her duties in good faith, with the care an ordinary prudent person in a like position would exercise under similar circumstances, and in a manner the director reasonably believes to be in the best interests of the mission, goals, and purposes of the organization.

Thus, one of the main responsibilities of nonprofit board members is to maintain financial accountability and effective oversight of the organizations they serve. Fiduciary duty requires board members to remain objective, unselfish, responsible, honest, and trustworthy in relation to the organization. Board members are stewards of the entity, and are expected to act for the good of the organization rather than for their personal aggrandizement. They need to exercise reasonable care in all decision making, without placing the nonprofit organization at unnecessary risk.

. . .

Basic nonprofit organizations documents

1.23 What are the articles of incorporation/articles of organization?

Generically, the document by which a tax-exempt organization is created is known, in the parlance of the federal tax law, as *articles of organization.* There usually is a separate document containing rules by which the organization conducts its affairs; this document is most often termed *bylaws.* The organization may develop other documents governing its operations, such as an employee handbook, a conflict-of-interest policy (although that may be part of the bylaws), code of ethics, code of conduct, an investment policy, a document retention policy, a whistleblower policy, and/or various other policies and procedures.

There are several types of articles of organization for each of the principal types of tax-exempt, nonprofit organizations:

- Corporation: articles of incorporation (or certificate of formation)
- Unincorporated association: constitution
- Trust: declaration of trust or trust agreement

The contents of a set of articles of organization should include the following:

- The name of the organization
- A statement of its purpose

- The name(s) and address(es) of its initial directors or trustees
- The name and address of the registered agent (if a corporation)
- The name(s) and address(es) of its incorporator(s)(if a corporation)
- A statement as to whether the entity has members
- A statement as to whether the entity can issue stock (if a corporation)
- Provisions reflecting any other state law requirements
- A dissolution clause

The *articles of incorporation* is in fact a single document, filed with the state in which incorporation is sought, that formally begins an entity's existence as a corporation and sets forth such matters as would be included in *articles of organization*, including but not limited to the organization's name, corporate purposes, the identity of its directors, the identity of its registered agent, and the identity of its incorporators.

1.24 What is a constitution?

An unincorporated association, like a corporation or trust, also has articles of organization, which are referred to as a *constitution* in the context of an unincorporated association. The form and contents of such a document are not prescribed by law and are rarely filed with the state, and often an informal organization may set forth its basic guiding principles and manner of operation in a constitution before the decision to incorporate has been made. Thus, the same entity at different times may have and refer to both documents. The constitution will likely be the only document that memorializes the consent to promote a common objective shared by the group of persons comprising the unincorporated association.

1.25 What are bylaws?

Bylaws contain the rules of internal governance an entity has chosen to adopt, or in some cases, is required to follow by statute. It is contemplated by state law governing corporations in most states that bylaws will be adopted, though unlike articles of incorporation, bylaws are rarely filed with the state. The bylaws of a nonprofit organization will usually include provisions with respect to the following:

- The organization's purposes
- The origins (e.g., election) and duties of its directors
- The origins and duties of its officers
- The role of its members (if any)
- Meetings of members and directors, including dates, notice, quorum, and voting
- The role of executive and other committees
- The role of its chapters (if any)
- The organization's fiscal year
- A conflict-of-interest policy (if not separately stated)
- Reference to (any) affiliated entities
- Restatement of the federal tax law requirements

1.26 What is a statement of purpose?

One of the fundamental first steps a nonprofit organization must necessarily take is recitation of its purposes. This is not just dictated by the law; an organization simply, as a practical matter, must state its purpose or purposes for existence in writing. An organization's purposes are different from the organization's activities. Activities are undertaken to effectuate purposes (mission).

An organization's statement of purpose must first be written to comport with the applicable state's nonprofit law. This usually is not too difficult to achieve, as long as the statement does not empower the organization to engage in substantial commercial activities.

Second, the statement of purpose needs to be prepared properly to enable the organization

to qualify for tax-exempt status (assuming that classification is available and desired). This statement must be in the organization's *articles of organization*, which is, as noted, the document creating the entity. The contents of this aspect of the statement are dependent on the type of tax-exempt organization the nonprofit entity intends to be.

The types of tax-exempt organizations are, generally, the following:

- Charitable (religious, educational, or scientific) organization
- Social welfare (e.g., advocacy) organization
- Labor organization
- Business league (association)
- Social club
- Employee benefit fund
- Fraternal society
- Political society
- Political organization

The wording of the statement of purpose, even independent of the actual purposes pursued, is reviewed and becomes important when tax exemption is sought. The organization's statement of purpose needs to be written so as to bring the entity into conformity with the appropriate category of exempt organization; thus, it should expressly make reference to the specific Internal Revenue Code section that is or will be the basis for the exemption where the statement of purpose is confined to those purposes that are inherently exempt. Otherwise, the statement of purpose must state that the organization will not engage in any activities outside the scope of the selected category of exemption.

Federal tax law basics

1.27 What is the organizational test?

The two most significant aspects of the organizational test are the requirements for a suitable statement of purposes and a dissolution clause that determines where the organization's net income and assets will be distributed should the organization dissolve or liquidate. It is also common practice to recite the organization's compliance with the applicable tax law rules. For example, the articles of organization of a public charity, which includes colleges and universities, often will state that the organization will not violate the private inurement doctrine, will not engage in significant attempts to influence legislation, and will not participate or intervene in political campaigns involving candidates for public office. The federal tax law includes additional organizational tests for supporting organizations and private foundations.

1.28 What is the operational test?

Basically, the operational test requires a tax-exempt charitable organization to, if it is to remain exempt, engage primarily (1.30) in activities that accomplish one or more of its exempt purposes. For example, exempt charitable organizations are not permitted to distribute their net earnings for the benefit of persons in their private capacity or function as advocacy—or action—organizations.

1.29 What does the term primarily mean?

The word *primarily* does not mean *exclusively*. Thus, a tax-exempt charitable organization may engage in some nonexempt activity as long as it is insubstantial. Thus, if nonexempt activities exceed this threshold of insubstantiality, the organization cannot be exempt as a charitable, educational, or like entity. As the U.S. Supreme Court wrote, the "presence of a single . . . [non-exempt] purpose, if substantial in nature, will destroy the exemption regardless of the number or importance of truly . . . [exempt] purposes." A federal court of appeals held that nonexempt activity will not result in loss or denial of exemption where it is "only incidental and less than

substantial" and that a "slight and comparatively unimportant deviation from the narrow furrow of tax approved activity is not fatal." In the words of the IRS, the rules applicable to charitable organizations in general have been "construed as requiring all the resources of the organization [other than an insubstantial part] to be applied to the pursuit of one or more of the exempt purposes therein specified." Consequently, the existence of one or more authentic exempt purposes of an organization will not be productive of tax exemption as a charitable or other entity if a substantial nonexempt purpose is present in its operations.

It is the use of the term *primarily* rather than *exclusively* (in its literal sense) that, among other aspects of the law, enables tax-exempt organizations to engage in unrelated business activity and remain exempt.

1.30 What is the commensurate test?

The commensurate test, which is somewhat related to the operational test (1.27), is applied by the IRS to assess whether a charitable organization is maintaining program activities that are commensurate in scope with its financial resources. The IRS wrote (in an unnumbered technical advice memorandum published in 1991) that this test "requires that organizations have a charitable program that is both real and, taking the organization's circumstances and financial resources into account, substantial." Therefore, the IRS added, an organization that "raises funds for charitable purposes but consistently uses virtually all its income for administrative and promotional expenses with little or no direct charitable accomplishments cannot reasonably argue that its charitable program is commensurate with its financial resources and capabilities."

Few instances of application of this test are recorded. It was first applied in connection with an organization that derived most of its financial support in the form of rental income, yet successfully preserved its tax-exempt status because it satisfied the test, in that it was engaging in an adequate amount of charitable activity. In the case of the organization that was the subject of the foregoing technical advice memorandum, the IRS concluded that the test was transgressed because of its finding that the charity involved expended, during the years examined, only about 1 percent of its revenue for charitable purposes; the rest was allegedly spent for fundraising and administration.

The commensurate test and the primary purpose test (1.30) have an awkward coexistence. For example, a charitable organization was allowed to retain its tax-exempt status while receiving 98 percent of its financial support from passive unrelated business income inasmuch as 41 percent of the organization's activities were charitable programs. Another organization remained an exempt charitable entity, even though two-thirds of its activities were unrelated business, because the net unrelated revenue was used in furtherance of its charitable activity. Yet a public charity had its tax exemption revoked, by application of this test, where, in the two years under examination, although its bingo game gross income was 73 percent and 92 percent of its total gross income, only a small amount of this money was distributed for charitable purposes.

Despite infrequent application of the commensurate test by the IRS (and never by a court), the IRS recently reincarnated the test as the *charitable spending initiative*, making the use of it one of the agency's top priorities in the exempt organizations area. In 2009, the IRS announced this initiative, characterizing it as a "long-range study to learn more about sources and uses of funds in the charitable sector and their impact on the accomplishment of charitable purposes." In late 2010, the IRS announced that it is examining exempt charitable organizations with high levels of fundraising expenses, organizations reporting unrelated business activity with relatively low levels of program service expenditures, organizations with high levels of officer compensation in comparison with program service expenditures, and organizations with low levels of program service expenditures in comparison to their total revenue.

1.31 What is the commerciality doctrine?

The *commerciality doctrine*, which is a body of law the courts have grafted onto the statutory and regulatory rules for tax exemption for charitable entities, posits that an organization is engaged in a nonexempt activity when that activity is undertaken in a manner that is commercial in nature. An activity is considered to be *commercial* if it has a direct counterpart in, or is conducted in the same manner as is the case in, the realm of for-profit organizations.

Thus, this matter of commerciality surfaces where there are similar organizations in the for-profit sector, as is the case, for example, with tax-exempt hospitals and credit unions and organizations providing food services and conference facilities. It is beginning to manifest itself in the higher education setting, with the emergence of for-profit colleges and universities. Other fields with counterpart functions are publishing, consulting, and retreat facilities. As an illustration, a nonprofit adoption agency was denied exemption as a charitable entity, being cast as operating in a manner not "distinguishable from a commercial adoption agency," because it generated substantial profits, accumulated capital, was funded entirely by fees, lacked plans to solicit contributions, and had a paid staff.

A federal court of appeals stated the factors to be applied in determining commerciality: (1) the organization sells goods and/or services to the public (this element alone was said to make the operations "presumptively commercial"), (2) the organization is in "direct competition" with for-profit counterparts, (3) the prices set by the organization are based on pricing formulas common in the comparable for-profit industry, (4) the organization utilizes promotional materials and "commercial catch phrases" to enhance sales, (5) the organization is advertising its services and/or goods, (6) the organization's hours of operation are basically the same as for-profit enterprises, (7) the guidelines by which the organization operates require that its management have "business ability" and training, (8) the organization does not utilize volunteers but pays salaries, and (9) the organization does not engage in charitable fundraising. These criteria are being applied by other courts, such as denial of exemption to an organization the principal purpose of which was operation of a conference center, and by the IRS, such as denial of exemption to a non-profit restaurant.

In addition to its impact on tax exemption issues, the commerciality doctrine is emerging as a significant force in determining what is an unrelated trade or business.

1.32 What are the categories of charitable organizations?

The federal tax regulations reference nine categories of charitable entities—those that:

1. Provide relief for the poor
2. Provide relief for the distressed
3. Provide relief for the underprivileged
4. Advance religion
5. Advance education
6. Advance science
7. Erect or maintain public buildings, monuments, or works
8. Lessen the burdens of government
9. Promote social welfare

In addition, the federal tax statutory law provides tax exemption as charitable entities for:

1. Cooperative hospital service organizations
2. Cooperative educational service organizations
3. Charitable risk pools

Also, court opinions and IRS rulings identify ten other categories of charitable organizations—those that:

1. Promote health
2. Promote the arts
3. Promote sports for youth
4. Protect the environment
5. Promote patriotism
6. Engage in local economic development
7. Provide care for orphans
8. Facilitate cultural exchanges
9. Improve the administration of justice
10. Engage in the practice of law in the public interest

1.33 What are the other categories of tax-exempt organizations?

There are seven categories of organizations that are tax-exempt pursuant to the same provision for exemption as charitable entities:

1. Educational organizations
2. Religious organizations
3. Scientific organizations
4. Literary organizations
5. Organizations that foster national or international sports competition
6. Organizations that prevent cruelty to children or animals
7. Organizations that test for public safety

The federal tax law provides tax exemption for many other categories of non-profit organizations, including these ten:

1. Social welfare organizations
2. Business leagues (associations)
3. Labor unions and similar organizations
4. Social clubs
5. Political organizations
6. Title-holding companies (single-parent and multiparent)
7. Fraternal organizations
8. Credit unions

9. Veterans' organizations
10. Prepaid tuition plans

1.34 What is a governmental unit?

An entity is a *governmental unit* if it is (1) a state or local governmental unit as defined in the rules providing an exclusion from gross income for interest earned on bonds issued by these units, (2) entitled to receive deductible charitable contributions as a unit of government, or (3) an Indian tribal government or a political subdivision of this type of government. The second of these categories encompasses the states, possessions of the United States, political subdivisions of the foregoing, the United States, and the District of Columbia.

1.35 Can a nonprofit organization be affiliated with a governmental unit?

Yes. The federal tax law recognizes the concept of an *affiliate of a governmental unit*. This type of entity is a tax-exempt organization that meets one of two sets of requirements (1.36).

1.36 How is this type of affiliation established?

As noted (1.35), there are two ways in which an entity may be treated as an affiliate of a governmental unit. One of these sets of requirements is that the organization has a ruling or a determination letter from the IRS that (1) its income, derived from activities constituting the basis for its exemption, is excluded from gross income under the rules for political subdivisions and the like, (2) it is entitled to receive deductible charitable contributions on the basis that contributions to it are for the use of governmental units, or (3) it is a wholly owned instrumentality of a state or political subdivision of a state for employment tax purposes.

The other set of requirements is available for an entity that does not have a ruling or a

determination letter from the IRS but (1) it is either operated, supervised, or controlled by governmental units, or by organizations that are affiliates of governmental units, or the members of the organization's governing body are elected by the public, pursuant to local statute or ordinance; (2) it possesses two or more of certain affiliation factors; and (3) its filing of an annual information return is not otherwise necessary to the efficient administration of the internal revenue laws.

An organization can (but is not required to) request a determination letter or ruling from the IRS that it is an affiliate of a governmental unit.

1.37 What are the federal tax law consequences for a nonprofit organization that is affiliated with a governmental unit?

The federal tax law consequences for a nonprofit that is affiliated with a governmental unit can be significant. It depends on the basis for the tax exemption. For example, in the case of an organization that is "tax-exempt" solely by reason of the fact that its revenue is excluded from gross income—the situation for most governmentally owned colleges and universities—most of the federal tax law that applies to conventional exempt organizations is inapplicable. That is, these bodies of law, otherwise applicable to public charities, do not apply: the private inurement doctrine, the private benefit doctrine, the intermediate sanctions rules, the limitations on allowable lobbying, the prohibition on political campaign activity, and the requirement that annual information returns be filed with the IRS (except for supporting organizations).

Some organizations and institutions that have their tax exemption rested on the gross income exclusion rule also have a ruling from the IRS that they are exempt by reason of being charitable, educational, and the like. This dual status can pose special problems, such as for governmentally owned colleges, universities, and hospitals.

1.38 How is the IRS structured in connection with its oversight of tax-exempt organizations?

The IRS is a component of the Department of the Treasury, which has as two of its functions the assessment and collection of federal income and other taxes. This department is authorized to conduct examinations, serve summonses, and generally enforce the internal revenue laws. The tax assessment and collection functions largely have been assigned to the IRS, which is an agency of the department. The mission of the IRS, according to its website, is to "provide America's taxpayers with top quality service by helping them understand and meet their tax responsibilities and by applying the tax law with integrity and fairness to all."

The IRS is headquartered in Washington, D.C.; its operations there are housed in its National Office. An Internal Revenue Service Oversight Board is responsible for overseeing the agency in its administration, conduct, direction, and supervision of the execution and application of the nation's internal revenue laws. The head of the IRS is the Commissioner of Internal Revenue. . . .

1.39 Does the IRS communicate what its efforts and priorities are in connection with its administration of the law of tax-exempt organizations?

Yes. The IRS provides this type of disclosure in many ways. The IRS Exempt Organizations Division (1.38) publishes an annual report, including a work plan, summarizing its efforts for the fiscal year involved and sketching its enforcement and regulatory priorities for the following fiscal year. The division maintains a website and has a monthly newsletter. The IRS publishes many "plain-language" publications concerning tax-exempt organizations law topics, and its personnel participate in a variety of exempt organizations law seminars and conferences.

1.40 What is the role of a lawyer who represents one or more nonprofit organizations?

Overall, the role of a lawyer for a nonprofit organization—sometimes termed a *nonprofit lawyer*—is no different from that of a lawyer for any other type of client. The tasks are to know the law (and avoid malpractice), represent the client in legal matters to the fullest extent of one's capabilities and energy, and otherwise zealously perform legal services without violating the law or breaching professional ethics.

The typical lawyer today is a specialist, and the nonprofit lawyer is no exception. Nonprofit law is unique and complex; the lawyer who dabbles in it does so at peril. A lawyer may be the best of experts on labor or securities law and know nothing about nonprofit law. The reverse is, of course, also true: The nonprofit lawyer is likely to know nothing about admiralty or domestic relations law.

The first task listed is "to know the law." That is literally impossible: No lawyer can know all of the law. The nonprofit lawyer, like any other lawyer, needs to be just as aware of what he or she does not know as of what is known. The nonprofit lawyer may be called in as a specialist to assist another lawyer, or, occasionally, a nonprofit lawyer may turn to a specialist in other fields that can pertain to nonprofit entities, such as environmental or bankruptcy law.

Some lawyers represent nonprofit organizations that have a significant involvement in a field that entails a considerable amount of federal and/or state regulation. This is particularly the case with trade, business, and professional organizations.

. . .

AMERICAN BAR ASSOCIATION
Defending Liberty
Pursuing Justice

Non-Governmental Organizations: Anticorruption Compliance Challenges and Risks Author(s): Elena Helmer and Stuart H. Deming

Source: *The International Lawyer*, Vol. 45, No. 2 (SUMMER 2011), pp. 597–624 Published by: American Bar Association

Stable URL: www.jstor.org/stable/23824630 Accessed: 06–06–2020 19:56 UTC

JSTOR

CHAPTER 4

Non-Governmental Organizations
Anticorruption Compliance Challenges and Risks

ELENA HELMER AND STUART H. DEMING

Originally published as "Non-Governmental Organizations: Anticorruption Compliance Challenges and Risks," in *The International Lawyer* (2011): 597–624. Reprinted with permission.

Introduction

Over the course of the past decade, enforcement of the anti-bribery provisions of the Foreign Corrupt Practices Act (FCPA),[1] prohibiting the bribery of foreign officials,[2] has experienced tremendous growth.[3] The growth of foreign bribery prosecutions under the FCPA has been exponential in nature[4] when consideration is also given to the use of the FCPA's accounting and record-keeping provisions as an alternative means of prosecuting behavior prohibited by the anti-bribery provisions.[5]

As Lanny Breuer, the Assistant Attorney General for the Criminal Division of the U.S. Department of Justice (DOJ) has stated, "we are in a new era of FCPA enforcement; and we are here to stay."[6] This statement accords with the recent record of the DOJ and the Securities and Exchange Commission (SEC), the government agencies charged with enforcement of the FCPA. In 2010 alone, the DOJ and SEC resolved twenty-three FCPA enforcement cases with

$1.8 billion in fines and disgorged profits.[7] Over fifty individuals were indicted, tried, or sentenced for FCPA violations during the same period of time—a record number since the FCPA's adoption in 1977.[8] In 2009–2010, the DOJ alone collected nearly $2 billion from FCPA cases.[9]

Even though the United States and much of the developed world are home to many nonprofit and non-governmental organizations (NGOs) that operate in countries where corruption is rife, this large sector has yet to be the special focus of enforcement activity. But NGOs and nonprofits suffer many of the same corruption-related risks as traditional business organizations. Are NGOs and nonprofits subject to the FCPA, and can they and their officers, employees, and agents be held liable for FCPA violations? Could the NGO and nonprofit sector be the next frontier in FCPA enforcement?

Related questions include: What are the implications for NGOs and nonprofits as a result of the other anti-bribery legal regimes being implemented and increasingly enforced by other countries? What special provisions are made for NGOs

 DOI: 10.4324/9781003387800-8

or nonprofits? Are they in any way exempted from the prohibitions on foreign bribery? If not, what are the implications? How else can corruption affect the activities of international NGOs? What proactive steps are they taking? What steps should they be taking? What considerations are unique to NGOs and nonprofits?

In addressing these and related issues, the acronym "NGO" will be used to refer to both non-governmental organizations and nonprofit or not-for-profit organizations. In the United States, and elsewhere, these terms are often used interchangeably to refer to organizations that pursue some wider social aim; that do not distribute surplus funds to owners or shareholders; and that are normally exempt from income and property taxation. Unless the context dictates otherwise, the term "NGO" will be used throughout this article.

I. NGOs and International Assistance

The most recent edition of the *Yearbook of International Organizations* lists 64,523 international "civil society organizations" in 300 countries and territories.[10] The United States and much of the developed world are home to many NGOs involved in an immense variety of activities domestically and abroad. These activities include education and cultural development, conservation and preservation, fighting poverty and disease, humanitarian assistance, and other forms of foreign aid and disaster relief. Geographically, many of the larger NGOs operate in scores of countries all over the world. For example, among U.S.-based NGOs in 2010 alone, the American Red Cross assisted more than sixty-eight million people in sixty-six countries;[11] AmeriCares Foundation was active in ninety-seven countries;[12] and CARE USA worked in eighty-seven countries, reaching more than eighty-two million people.[13] Faith-based organizations are not far behind, and some even surpass secular NGOs in the reach of

their overseas activities. World Vision, a Christian humanitarian relief and development organization, works in nearly 100 countries[14] while the Catholic Relief Services' activities spread to more than 100 countries on five continents.[15]

The geographic extension of these NGOs is matched by their hefty budgets. According to the *Chronicle of Philanthropy*, in fiscal year 2009, the latest year for which complete data is available, each of the four largest U.S.-based NGOs focusing on international charitable work, AmeriCares Foundation, Feed The Children, Food For The Poor, and World Vision, had a total revenue of over $1 billion.[16] Even during the recent economic downturn when charitable giving was down by eleven percent,[17] Food for the Poor and World Vision reported that their net income in 2010 stayed above $1 billion, at $1.047 billion and $1.014 billion respectively.[18] The revenue of the American Red Cross for 2010 was almost $3.6 billion, with over $252 million spent on programs outside the United States.[19]

Significant parts of the budgets of many NGOs are financed by the U.S. government through the U.S. Agency for International Development (USAID), the U.S. State Department, the Millennium Challenge Corporation, and other government entities, as well as by international government and other organizations, such as the United Nations and the World Bank.[20] The traditional U.S. government of foreign aid model, as represented by USAID,[21] relies on private-sector contractors, including NGOs, for the vast majority of program implementation.[22] In 2008, eighty-five percent of USAID's budget was committed to contracting organizations through direct grants, cooperative agreements, or contracts.[23] NGOs routinely compete for USAID grants and contracts along with for-profit entities. NGOs may also sub-contract for other organizations receiving government funding.[24]

A well-developed network of regular USAID contractors and subcontractors includes both for-profit and not-for-profit organizations. Some of them have been working with USAID for decades, administering projects worth hundreds of millions of dollars and encompassing scores of countries.[25] A number of large NGOs, such as CARE, Catholic Relief Services, and Save the Children, are major USAID contractors. Among the top twenty "vendors" that USAID lists for 2010 are eight U.S.-based nonprofits, with the amounts of money awarded to them ranging from $165 million to over $432 million.[26]

The World Bank also recognizes NGOs as "important actors in the development process" and frequently relies on them in the delivery of its programs.[27] Projects supported by the World Bank often involve national and international NGOs[28] because of the "skills and resources they bring to emergency relief and development activities and because they foster participatory development processes."[29] The World Bank also uses NGOs as contractors and grantees.[30] Thirty-three large international NGOs are listed on the World Bank's website as those "with whom the Bank maintains ongoing relations through policy dialogue, training, and/or [sic] operational collaboration."[31] At least a dozen of them are based in the United States or have U.S. branches.[32]

Acknowledging the role played by NGOs and other nonprofits, the World Bank calls civil society organizations—the term that includes such diverse entities as "community groups, non-governmental organizations, . . . labor unions, indigenous groups, charitable organizations, faith-based organizations, professional associations, and foundations"[33]—"significant players in global development assistance."[34] The World Bank estimated that, as of 2006, civil society organizations "provided approximately . . . $15 billion in international assistance."[35]

II. NGOs and Corruption Risks

Many NGOs, especially those providing humanitarian assistance and engaged in development projects, operate in developing countries where they face the same risks as traditional business organizations. One of those risks is corruption. NGOs face two kinds of corruption-related risks. One is the risk of becoming an offender by paying a bribe to a government official, violating the FCPA or other anti-bribery laws. The other risk is becoming a victim of corruption, such as when the funds or assets of an NGO are misappropriated or otherwise misused.

A. The Risk of Violating Foreign Bribery Laws

Under the FCPA, mere status as an NGO does not exempt an entity from being subject to the anti-bribery provisions.[36] NGOs fall into the category of "domestic concerns" subject to the anti-bribery provisions.[37] No legal basis exists for distinguishing between a traditional commercial enterprise and an NGO in determining what qualifies as a "domestic concern."[38] No "carve out," "safe harbor," or other express exception exists, nor does an exception exist for an NGO that is strictly charitable in nature.[39]

The definition of what constitutes a "domestic concern" is broad. In addition to "any individual who is a citizen, national, or resident of the United States,"[40] a "domestic concern" includes "any corporation, partnership, association, joint stock company, business trust, unincorporated organization, or sole proprietorship which has its principal place of business in the United States, or which is organized under the laws of States of the United States or a territory, possession, or commonwealth of the United States."[41]

Though not binding as precedent, the DOJ explicitly found a nonprofit organization to be a "domestic concern" subject to the terms of the FCPA's anti-bribery provisions.[42] It involved "a non-profit, U.S.-based microfinance institution . . . whose mission is to provide loans and other basic financial services to the world's lowest-income entrepreneurs."[43] To support its mission, the microfinance institution received grants and investments from the "United States government, other governmental . . . aid agencies and development banks, nongovernmental organizations . . . and private investors."[44]

Arguably, the only categorical exception may relate to whether the business of the NGO falls within the prohibitions of the FCPA's anti-bribery provisions. No clarity is provided as to whether the business that is sought to be obtained or retained must be commercial in nature or whether it extends more generally to the business of an individual or entity. What constitutes "business" under the anti-bribery provisions has yet to be clearly defined.[45] Neither the language of the statute nor the legislative history provides clear guidance as to whether activities of an NGO constitute "business" as that term is used within the context of the anti-bribery provisions.

While the legislative history of the anti-bribery provisions focuses on business in the classic commercial sense,[46] the legislative history also demonstrates that "the business nexus requirement [was] not to be interpreted unduly narrowly."[47] "When the FCPA is read as a whole, its core of criminality is seen to be bribery of a foreign official to induce him to perform an official duty in a corrupt manner."[48] The FCPA was enacted not only because foreign bribery was "morally and economically suspect, but also because it was causing foreign policy problems for the United States."[49]

Like the FCPA, none of the international anti-bribery conventions provides an express exception for NGOs. Of the three that the United States has ratified, the Organization for Economic Co-operation and Development Convention on Combating Bribery of Foreign Public Officials in International Business Transactions (OECD Convention),[50] the Inter-American Convention Against Corruption (OAS Convention)[51] and the United Nations Convention against Corruption (UN Convention),[52] all make reference to there being a need for a business or commercial nexus in order for the conduct to be prohibited. The OECD Convention and the UN Convention make specific reference to the prohibition applying to "the conduct of international business."[53] The OAS Convention refers to the prohibition applying "in connection with any economic or commercial transaction."[54]

But the business nexus requirements of the most important of the international antibribery conventions, the UN and OECD Conventions,[55] are not narrow in scope. The UN Convention expands on what may be viewed as a more customary definition of "international business" to include "the provision of international aid" within the meaning of "the conduct of international business."[56] The Interpretative Notes for the Official Records, *Travaux Preparatoires*, of the Negotiations of the UN Convention (Interpretative Notes to the UN Convention), state that the "phrase 'the conduct of international business' is intended to include the provision of international aid."[57] By its very nature, the provision of international aid includes the work of NGOs in foreign settings.

The Council of Europe Criminal Law Convention (CoE Convention),[58] one of the other major international anti-bribery conventions, contains no business nexus requirement. It requires parties to the CoE Convention to adopt "legislation and other measures as may be necessary to establish as criminal offences under its domestic law . . . [the bribery of] a public official of any other State."[59] The Explanatory Report to the CoE Convention emphasizes that there is "no restriction as to the context in which the bribery of the foreign official occurs."[60] Significantly, most Western and Eastern European countries, including the United Kingdom, France, Switzerland, and Spain, have ratified the CoE Convention.[61]

In general, mere status as an NGO or a nonprofit organization is not likely to insulate an entity from the prohibitions of the FCPA and other foreign bribery laws. Moreover, many

NGOs and nonprofit organizations compete directly against traditional for-profit organizations for USAID, World Bank, UNDP, and other entities' contracts and grants. Indeed, activities of nonprofit organizations are often similar to or interchangeable with those of for-profit organizations.[62] As a result, NGOs and nonprofit organizations should be presumed to be fully subject to the anti-bribery provisions of the FCPA and other foreign bribery laws.

1. Risk Factors

How often do NGOs face corruption risks associated with violating foreign bribery laws and what factors determine these risks? In a limited survey of international NGOs (the survey),[63] the answers to the first question ranged from "never" to "all the time."[64]

The factors that were determinative of an NGO's exposure to bribery risks include the nature of its activities, the countries it operates in, the structure of the organization, the pattern of communication with its field offices, and the level of internal reporting and other internal controls.[65]

The nature of an NGO's activities is the most important factor in determining whether it will face significant bribery risks. An NGO that conducts, for example, environmental or conservation programs, provides education and vocational training, or organizes camps for children would be at a lower risk of violating the FCPA and its counterparts than an NGO involved with providing humanitarian aid or relief and development services. It matters little that both NGOs might be operating in the same high-corruption country. In contrast to a situation where an NGO sends experts, volunteers, and others to do the work and provide services, much greater opportunities are afforded to local government officials to demand improper payments when an NGO is distributing or awarding certain assets or funds.

The general level of corruption in a country raises a red flag.[66] In countries where corruption is a way of life, local culture may be highly tolerant of graft, even tacitly approving of it as a means of survival. An NGO's indigenous staff or its local partners may not see a problem with paying bribes, especially small ones, like facilitating payments, to "keep things moving."[67] As one survey participant noted, "[b]ribes may be paid on our behalf by local partners but we do not have an ability to monitor them."[68] Local employees and partners may also be highly susceptible to conflicts of interests. They may be subject to influence by family members, by tribal or ethnic groups, or by other relationships that may not be easy to discern. This may lead to the second type of corruption risks: the misappropriation or misuse of the funds and resources of an NGO.[69]

The structure of the organization also plays a role in determining the level of risk of violating foreign bribery laws. More centralized NGOs with reasonable oversight by their headquarters appear to have lower risks than NGOs with a highly decentralized structure.[70] This is particularly so where the NGO has a multitude of foreign offices with significant autonomy that are staffed, for the most part, with local employees.[71] Similarly, NGOs relying heavily on indigenous NGOs to carry out their activities face greater chances of violating foreign bribery laws than NGOs that employ expatriates, at least in management positions.[72]

Moreover, organizational structure influences patterns of communication between the headquarters and field offices. To reduce their risk, some NGOs actively pursue collecting compliance-related information and investigate complaints.[73] But in highly decentralized NGOs, local offices have significant autonomy which extends, among other things, to what issues are reported to headquarters. Most problems are supposed to be addressed at the local level. As a result, headquarters may rarely hear compliance-related concerns from the field offices.[74] If they do learn of them, it is several months later and often too late for headquarters to intervene.[75] No common practice appears to exist among NGOs on the related issues of internal reporting and internal controls.

2. Types of Risks

The types of risks of violating foreign bribery laws faced by international NGOs vary according to the country and activities involved. Some organizations have to deal mostly with requests for what are often referred to as facilitating or expediting payments for such things as having documents approved, goods released by customs, or a license for a vehicle issued or renewed.[76] Facilitating payments, typically relatively small in amount, are bribes "the purpose of which is to expedite or to secure the performance of a routine governmental action by a foreign official."[77] Under the FCPA, such payments are not prohibited.[78] But other foreign bribery laws, such as the Bribery Act 2010 adopted by the United Kingdom (UK Bribery Act), do not contain exceptions for facilitating payments.[79] Thus, authorities in the United Kingdom may prosecute a U.S.-based NGO with a U.K. branch for facilitating payments in a third country.[80]

Other NGOs may see more serious extortionist demands, for example, from police or military at road checkpoints for the right to proceed further into the territory with humanitarian assistance or from local officials or tribal leaders eager to receive "their" share of food or other assistance.[81] While some checkpoint demands may be satisfied with a payment as small as a twenty-dollar bill,[82] other bribery requests may involve significant amounts of goods or money.[83]

B. The Risk of Becoming a Victim of Corruption

Despite the general unease among international NGOs regarding possible FCPA violations, outright requests for bribes do not appear to be their main corruption-related concern.[84] Most NGOs' primary compliance concerns

are related to corruption in their programs and activities, such as diversion of aid,[85] misuse of funds,[86] fraud in procurement,[87] fraud in reporting documents, and accounting irregularities.[88] The consequences of corruption in these areas can be even more daunting for NGOs than the prospect of an enforcement action for an FCPA or other foreign bribery law violation.

Diversion and misuse of aid, when food, medicines, construction materials, and other items are sold for cash or otherwise embezzled or misused, occur frequently in international assistance programs. For example, the Global Fund to Fight AIDS, Tuberculosis and Malaria (Global Fund), financed by the United Nations, many national governments and private organizations,[89] came to the spotlight in January 2011 after the Global Fund Inspector General's report revealed that "as much as two thirds" of the Global Funds grants in Djibouti, Mali, Mauritania, and Zambia had been "eaten up by corruption."[90] The Associated Press story that broke the news cited forged or non-existing receipts for "training events," forged signatures on travel and lodging claims, questionable bookkeeping, and outright theft.[91] Subsequent audits uncovered more violations in other Global Fund programs. To date, the total amount of money lost to corruption stands at nearly $53 million.[92] In a recent case involving World Vision, a large California-based NGO subcontracting for a USAID project in Liberia, two of the organization's Liberian managers diverted ninety-one percent of USAID-funded humanitarian aid for their personal benefit.[93] As a result, USAID was defrauded of $1.9 million.[94] An anonymous tip prompted an internal audit that uncovered the problem; both managers were later charged and convicted of fraud.[95] World Vision had to reimburse USAID for the misappropriated funds.[96]

According to one survey participant, fraud in reporting and accounting irregularities may range in scope from several hundred dollars to much greater amounts involving well-coordinated and systemic fraud schemes.[97] The same is true about corruption and fraud in procurement, which may include collusion, favoritism, lack of transparency, fictitious bidders, bogus vendors, fake tender processes, overpricing, conflicts of interest, and lack of competition.[98] Not infrequently, fraud is committed by the local employees or partners in collusion with local government officials. An example is the Academy for Educational Development (AED) programs in Afghanistan and Pakistan that caused USAID to suspend AED and the Global Fund's projects in several African countries where local nonprofits fared no better, in terms of corruption and fraud, than government entities.[99]

The consequences of this kind of corruption for NGOs are difficult to overstate. In December 2010, USAID suspended AED after uncovering "serious corporate misconduct, mismanagement, and a lack of internal controls that raise [d] serious concerns of corporate integrity."[100] USAID undertook a review of every program associated with AED.[101] AED's suspension prevented it from bidding on or receiving any further awards from the U.S. government.[102] As a result, on March 3, 2011, after nearly fifty years in existence, thousands of development projects, and hundreds of millions of dollars in USAID funds, AED announced that it would sell its assets and dissolve itself.[103] A single program termination was sufficient to bring the organization down.[104]

III. NGO Anticorruption Compliance Programs

Since NGOs face many of the same corruption risks as traditional business organizations, the remedy is also similar: putting in place a robust compliance program. A number of large, well-established NGOs now have, or are in the process of establishing, anticorruption compliance measures as part of their broader compliance programs. But unlike compliance programs at many large publicly held companies,

anticorruption compliance programs at NGOs are generally a relatively new development.[105]

Most of the major NGOs have policies that govern all their operations, including fundraising, delivering programs, meeting donor requirements, employment, finance, legal, and other issues. In addition, many of them have adopted codes of ethics or codes of conduct that govern conflicts of interest, whistleblower policies, and other corruption-related concerns.[106] Global hotlines, both telephone and internet, are becoming more routine.[107] Due diligence practices, however, seem to be at an early stage of development, with some NGOs only recently turning their attention to this aspect of compliance.[108] Putting in place policies and procedures and other components of a compliance program are less challenging than conducting due diligence and actively monitoring and enforcing a compliance program.[109] A whole range of extremely challenging and often-controversial decisions can be anticipated.

For some NGOs, the move towards instituting more formal compliance programs was driven by public revelations of questionable practices, pressure from major donors, or the prospect of losing USAID funding. "Compliance was a condition for improvement, for resolving critical issues," said one survey participant referring to the problems his organization has encountered with one of the U.S. government agencies.[110] Losing government funds can be deadly, as demonstrated by the recent demise of AED, one of the largest and oldest NGO contractors for USAID.[111] Another major NGO, Oklahoma-based Feed The Children, was recently engulfed in a scandal that drew media attention due to its $1 billion budget and the global scope of its activities.[112] Feed The Children's board of directors, after ousting its charismatic president and facing a significant decline in donor support, put in place elements of a compliance program, including a new ethics policy, a nepotism policy, and a fraternization policy.[113]

A. Anticorruption Compliance Programs for NGOs: General Considerations

The same general principles that apply to compliance programs of issuers and other companies that are subject to the FCPA and to the UK Bribery Act should apply to NGOs. Consideration also needs to be given to harmonizing compliance policies governed by the FCPA and the UK Bribery Act.[114] The basic contours of an effective internal compliance program should resemble those set forth in the U.S. Federal Sentencing Guidelines for organizations and the U.K.'s Ministry of Justice's Guidance issued in conjunction with the UK Bribery Act.[115]

1. Critical Components of an Effective Compliance Program

In implementing a compliance program, the DOJ's policy guidance must always be kept in mind. "[T]he critical factors in evaluating any program are whether the program is adequately designed for maximum effectiveness in preventing and detecting wrongdoing by employees and whether . . . management is enforcing the program or is tacitly encouraging or pressuring employees to engage in misconduct to achieve business objectives."[116] It must determine whether a "compliance program is merely a 'paper program' or whether it was designed, implemented, reviewed, and revised, as appropriate, in an effective manner."[117]

The considerations for an anticorruption compliance program are essentially the same whether a traditional business organization or NGO is involved.[118] A separate anticorruption compliance program is not required if an entity has in place an effective compliance program for other legal or policy concerns.[119] An anticorruption compliance program can serve as an adjunct or a supplement to existing compliance programs.

A. PROPORTIONATE PROCEDURES

An "organisation's procedures to prevent bribery by persons associated with it" must be "proportionate to the . . . risks [of corruption] it faces and to the nature, scale, and complexity of the organisation's activities."[120] The procedures must be tailored to meet the organization's needs. They must be clear, practical, and relevant. Sufficient staff should be in place "to audit, document, analyze, and utilize the results of the [entity's] compliance efforts."[121]

B. COMMITMENT FROM THE TOP

An organization's top management must be committed to preventing the prohibited conduct by individuals and entities associated with it.[122] A "culture" of anticorruption compliance must be "fostered" throughout the organization and extend to its agents, consultants, and representatives.[123] An effective compliance program must be more than a series of policies and procedures. Employees must be "adequately informed about the compliance program and [be] convinced of the [entity's] commitment to it."[124] Sanctions must be enforced against senior and lower-level official as well as employees, agents, and other intermediaries.[125]

Genuine efforts also need to be made to ensure that anyone seeking, in good faith, to secure guidance or to make appropriate disclosures is not subject to retaliation.[126] Procedures need to be put in places to that knowledgeable officials can quickly answer questions and respond to concerns.[127] The procedures must not be cumbersome or perceived as being punitive in nature. Otherwise, guidance will not be sought and corrective action will not be taken.

C. RISK ASSESSMENT

The organization must assess the nature and extent of its exposure to potential external and internal risks of corruption of persons associated with it.[128] "The assessment must be periodic, informed, and documented." Factors and considerations can change over time.[129]

D. DUE DILIGENCE

The organization must undertake due diligence procedures, taking a proportionate and risk-based approach.[130] In each situation, the extent of the inquiry should be governed by the circumstances. But regardless of the context, due diligence must always be conducted in good faith. It cannot be perfunctory. "It requires a dispassionate consideration of all relevant factors."[131]

Due diligence "also entails determining whether the basis for concern is unfounded and, if not, whether effective means are available to avoid the risks associated with the concerns raised."[132] For example, written agreements by themselves seldom suffice, but they may deter prohibited conduct by incorporating a series of compliance measures and providing a basis for termination.

E. COMMUNICATION AND TRAINING

An organization must ensure that its anticorruption policies and procedures are understood throughout the organization.[133] Ongoing education and training must be proportionate to the organization's risks.[134] Compliance policies and procedures must be simple, clear, and readily available to individuals acting on behalf of the organization.[135] To be effective, the policies and procedures must be understandable to a person unsophisticated or unfamiliar with the issues.

F. MONITORING AND REVIEW

"On an ongoing basis, [a] compliance program must be monitored, regularly reviewed, and modified as necessary to address weaknesses and to be made more effective."[136] The challenge is to develop a compliance program that effectively addresses areas of concern without becoming unduly burdensome, unresponsive, and unable to adjust to ever-changing needs.

IV. Conclusion

The dangers of corruption in NGO projects and the consequences of such corruption are ever-present and may cost NGOs their reputation, funding sources, and donors. International

NGOs also increasingly fear the risks of violating foreign bribery and other anticorruption laws.[137]

Yet the mood in the international nonprofit circles appears to be that of general concern and cautious waiting. One survey participant reported that "[e]verybody in our space is concerned . . . It is a matter of time before the attention [of the Department of Justice] will be turned to NGOs."[138] Another noted, "[w]e are watching the UK Bribery Act closely as perhaps it applies to NGOs."[139] Still another survey participant is sure that "USAID will keep pressure on the NGOs it works with," demanding greater accountability.[140] But there also seems to be a consensus that "without a lawsuit, an indictment, or debarment, nonprofits will do little in this area."[141] Some NGOs are simply relying on the nature of their activities for some protection: "The Department of Justice is less likely to target NGOs than businesses, which gives us a little more comfort."[142]

Special protective legislation is not suggested for NGOs.[143] Unlike most industries, NGOs with a truly charitable nature are unlikely to be targeted by enforcement authorities for foreign bribery violations. A public backlash and considerable political fallout from such an agenda can be expected. Practical considerations such as the receptivity of juries and judges are also likely to discourage the targeting of NGOs in general. But in egregious situations, enforcement authorities will not, and cannot be expected to, overlook clear violations, even for NGOs that undertake the most laudable of missions.

For NGOs that are not fundamentally of a charitable nature, and that compete with more traditional business organizations, the DOJ can be expected to be aggressive in its enforcement efforts when warranted by the facts and circumstances. While it is less clear what enforcement officials will do in other jurisdictions, over time NGOs can and should be expected to be fully subject to investigations and enforcement actions. In general, NGOs can expect to face increasingly greater scrutiny. Despite the lack of resources and an assortment of challenges, NGOs must find efficient and cost-effective ways to implement and enforce compliance programs that adequately address their corruption risks. The key for the international NGO community is to be proactive and not reactive.

Notes

1. Foreign Corrupt Practices Act (FCPA), 15 U.S.C. §§ 78m (2010), 78dd-1,2,3 (1998), 78ff (2002).

2. *Id.* §78dd-l,2,3.

3. Thomas R. Fox, *FCPA Enforcement: Why the Increase Between the First 25 Years and the Last 5?* FCPA COMPLIANCE AND ETHICS BLOG (Mar. 11, 2011, 6:48 AM), http://tfoxlaw.wordpress. com/2011/03/ll/fcpaenforcement-why-the-increase-between-the-first-25-years-and-thelast-5/.

4. *Id.*

5. Often overlooked in the dramatic increase in FCPA enforcement is the critical role of the FCPA's accounting and record-keeping provisions. *See* FCPA §78m. In addition to prohibiting improper inducements to foreign officials, the FCPA placed new and significant obligations on issuers to maintain records that accurately reflect transactions and dispositions of assets and to maintain systems of internal accounting controls. *Id.* They apply to foreign and domestic issuers of securities as defined by Section 3 of the Securities Exchange Act of 1934 as entities required to register under Section 12 or file reports under Section 15(d). *See id.* §78a-c, 78o(d), 78l. Issuers can include foreign entities with American Depository Receipts (ADRs). Unlike the FCPA's anti-bribery provisions, the accounting and record-keeping provisions also apply to majority-owned foreign subsidiaries of an issuer. *Id.* §78m(b)(6). The anti-bribery provisions and accounting and record-keeping provisions "were intended to work in 'tandem' and thereby complement one another." Stuart H. Deming, *The Potent and Broad-Ranging Implications of the Accounting and Record-Keeping Provisions of the Foreign Corrupt Practices Act*, 96 J. CRIM. L. &CRIMINOLOGY 465, 468 (2006) (citing S. Rep. No. 95–114, at 7 (1977)), reprinted in 1977 U.S.C.C.A.N 4098. "For example,

the Senate Report associated with the FCPA's passage stated that 'a U.S. company "which looks the other way" in order to be able to raise the defense that they were ignorant of bribes made by a foreign, subsidiary, could be in violation of [the accounting and record-keeping provisions] requiring companies to devise and maintain adequate accounting controls.'" *Id.* at 468, n.14 (citing S. Rep. No. 95–114, at 11).

6. Press Release, Dep't of Justice, Assistant Att'y Gen. Lanny A. Breuer Speaks at the 24th Nat'l Conference on the FCPA (Nov. 16, 2010), *available at* http://www.justice.gov/criminal/pr/speeches/2010/crmspeech-101116.html

7. The FCPA Blog, 2010 FCPA Enforcement Index (Jan. 3, 2011, 7:02 AM), http://www.fcpablog. com/blog/2011/1/3/2010-fcpa-enforcement-index. html.

8. *Id.*

9. *See* Press Release, Dep't of Justice, *supra* note 6.

10. Union of Int'l Ass'ns, Yearbook of International Organizations Online, http://www.uia.be/yearbook (last visited Jul. 10, 2011).

11. American Red Cross, Global Impact Report, Fiscal Year 2010, *available at* http://www.redcross.org/www-files/Documents/pdf/international/10ISDreport.pdf.

12. Americares Found, 2010 Annual Report, *available at* http://www.americares.org/newsroom/publications/.

13. CARE USA CARE's Work, http://www.care. org/careswork/index.asp (last visited Jun. 5, 2011).

14. World Vision, Our International Work, http://www.worldvision.org/content.nsf/learn/our-international-work (last visited Jun. 5, 2011).

15. Catholic Relief Services, About Catholic Relief Services, http://crs.org/about/ (last visited Jun. 5, 2011).

16. The Chronicle of Philanthropy, Philanthropy 400 Data, *available at* http://philanthropy. com/premium/stats/philanthropy400/index. php?search=Search&category= International&year= 2010&sort=income_total (last visited Jun. 26, 2011).

17. William P. Barrett, *America's Biggest Charities*, FORBES.COM, Dec. 6, 2010, http://www.forbes. com/forbes/2010/12 06/investment-guide-charity-americares-united-way-ymca-biggest-charities.html.

18. Food For The Poor, 2010 Annual Report, *available at* http://www.foodforthepoor.org/about/finances/annual_report_2010b.pdf; Larry Probus,

World Vision CFO, Financial Assessment of 2010 and Outlook for 2011, *available at* http://www.worldvision.org/resources.nsf/Main/annual-review-2010-resources/$FILE/AR_2010LetterFromCFO.pdf.

19. Bryan Rhoa, American Red Cross CFO, FY10 Financial Results, *available at* http://www.redcross.org/portal/site/en/menuitem.d229a5f06620c6052ble cfbf43181aa0/?vgnextoid=666bl3eb7d83e210VgnV CM10000089f0870aRCRD8cvgnextchannel=0bf26 a5e61dcell0VgnVCM10000089f0870aRCRD

20. Though many U.S. government agencies are involved in international development and foreign assistance, in the interest of brevity this article will largely focus on USAID as the primary source of funding.

21. In 2010, USAID administered about $22 billion in programs. Curt Tarnoff & Marian Leonardo Lawson, Foreign Aid: An Introduction to U.S. Programs and Policy, Cong. Research Serv. R40213, at 21 (2011), *available at* http://assets.opencrs.com/rpts/R40213_20110210.pdf.

22. *Id.* at 26; *see also* Save The Children, Supporting Local Ownership & Building National Capacity: Applying a Flexible and Country-Based Approach to Aid Instruments (May 2010), http://www.savethechildren.org/atf/cf/%7B9def2ebe-10ae-432c-9bd0-df91d2eba74a%7D/Save-the-Children-Aidmodalities-forcountry-ownership-May-2 0 1 0.pdf.

23. Save The Children, *supra* note 22, at 1.

24. For example, USAID awarded a two-year grant to Catholic Relief Services for the Community Reset dement and Rehabilitation Project in post-civil war Liberia. The latter selected World Vision as a subgrantee to conduct food distribution and food-for-work projects, parts of the USAID grant. *See* World Vision, World Vision Statement Regarding Alleged Fraud in Liberia, http://www.worldvision.org/content.nsf/about/2 0090604-liberia (last visited Jun. 5, 2011).

25. For example, Chemonics International Inc., a USAID contractor since 1975, worked in almost 140 countries managing more than 900 projects in all key development areas. USAID, About Chemonics Int'l, http://ghiqc.usaid.gov/hpi/contractor/chemonics.html (last visited Jun. 5, 2011). It "currently manages more than 105 contracts for USAID in some 70 countries." *Id.*

26. USAID, USAID Budget: Where Does USAID's Money Go?, http://www.usaid.gov/policy/budget/money/ (last visited Jun. 5, 2011) (listing the following nonprofits: Partnership for Supply Chain Mgmt., Int'l Relief and Dev., Academy for Educational Dev., Catholic Relief Services, Family Health Int'l, Mgmt. Sciences for Health, Research Triangle Institute, and Mercy Corps).

27. The World Bank, Civil Society—Involving Nongovernmental Organizations in Bank-Supported Activities, http://web.worldbank.org/WBSITE/EXTERNAL/TOPICS/CSO/0"print:Y~isCURL:Y ~contentMDK:22511723~pagePK:220503~piPK:2 20476~theSitePK:228717,00.html (last visited Aug. 8, 2011).

28. Christopher Gibbs, Claudia Fumo & Thomas Kuby, Nongovernmental Organizations In World Bank-Supported Projects: A Review 1 (The World Bank 1999), *available at* http://lnweb90.worldbank.org/oed/oeddoclib.nsf/DocUNIDViewF orJavaSearch/167F2AAEA498DBC185256817004 C81BE/$file/NGO_Book.pdf.

29. *Id.* At vii.

30. *See* The World Bank, Civil Society—Frequently Asked Questions, http://go.worldbank.org/Q4JHC82S80 (last visited Jun. 26, 2011); The World Bank, Civil Society—Civil Society Organizations, http://go.worldbank.org/KK5KGT24X0 (last visited Jun. 26, 2011); The World Bank, Projects-Contract Awards Search, http://go.worldbank.org/GM7GBOVGS0 (last visited Jun. 26, 2011).

31. Civil Society Organizations, *supra* note 30.

32. *See, e.g.,* Action Aid Int'l, Where We Work, http://www.actionaid.org/where-we-work (last visited Jun. 26, 2011); The Access Initiative, TAI Countries, http://www.accessinitiative.org/countries (last visited Jun. 26, 2011); Environmental Defense Fund, Our Offices, http://www.edf.org/page. cfm?tagid=361 (last visited Jun. 26, 2011).

33. The World Bank, Civil Society—Defining Civil Society, http://go.worldbank.org/4CE7W046K0 (last visited Jun. 26, 2011).

34. *Id.*

35. *Id.*

36. *See* Foreign Corrupt Practices Act (FCPA), 15 U.S.C. §78dd-2(h)(l) (1998).

37. *Id.*

38. *Id.*

39. *See* generally *id.* §78dd-2.

40. *Id.* §78dd-2(h)(l)(A).

41. *Id.* §78-2(h)(l)(B).

42. FCPA Review, 10-02 Op. Dep't of Justice 5 (2010), *available at* http://www.justice.gov/criminal/fraud/fcpa/opinion/2010/1002.pdf In two other opinion procedure releases, the DOJ implicitly found the nonprofit entities to be domestic concerns subject to the FCPA. *See* FCPA Review, 08-03 Op. Dep't of Justice 1 (2008), *available at* http://www.justice.gov/criminal/fraud/fcpa/opinion/2008/0803.pdf; FCPA Review, 96-01 Op. Dep't of Justice 1 (1996), *available at* http://www.justice.gov/criminal/fraud/fcpa/opinion/1996/9601.pdf. In the more recent of the two releases, the entity seeking the opinion was found to be a domestic concern. 08-03 Op. Dep't of Justice, at 1. But no reference was made to it being a non-profit. *See id.* Yet it is a matter of public record that the entity, TRACE International, Inc., is a non-profit organization. *See* Trace Int'l, About Us, https://secure.traceinternational.org/about (last visited Jun. 26, 2011). The older opinion procedure release made no express finding that the entity seeking the opinion was a domestic concern. *See* 96-01 Op. Dep't of Justice, at 1. However, only issuers and domestic concerns are eligible to obtain an opinion pursuant to the opinion procedure release. 28 C.F.R. §80.1 (1992).

43. 10-02 Op. Dep't of Justice, *supra* note 42, at 1.

44. *Id.*

45. *See* FCPA §78dd-2(a).

46. Reference was made to "corporate bribery." S. Rep. No. 95-114, at 4 (1977), *reprinted in* 1977 US.C.C.A.N 4098, 4101.

47. United States v. Kay (*Kay II*), 359 F.3d 738, 754 (5th Cir. 2004).

48. *Id.* at 761.

49. *Id.* at 746.

50. Convention on Combating Bribery of Foreign Public Officials in International Business Transactions, Dec. 18, 1997, 37 I.L.M. 1 [hereinafter OECD Convention].

51. Organization of American States, Inter-American Convention Against Corruption, Mar. 29, 1996, 35 I.L.M. 724 [hereinafter OAS Convention].

52. United Nations Convention Against Corruption, Oct. 31, 2003, 43 I.L.M. 37 [hereinafter UN Convention].

53. OECD Convention, *supra* note 50, art. 1; UN Convention, *supra* note 52, art. 16.

54. OAS Convention, *supra* note 51, art. VIII.

55. The basis for giving primacy to the OECD and UN Conventions is summarized in the following:

> The OECD Convention is narrowly tailored to focus specifically on bribery of foreign officials in the context of obtaining or retaining business. Given its narrow focus and its effective follow-up mechanism for ensuring active and uniform enforcement, the OECD Convention has already had a dramatic impact in a relatively short period on the number of countries actively investigating and prosecuting individuals and entities for improper inducements to foreign officials. As enforcement activity increases and as more countries accede to the OECD Convention, the body of law associated with the OECD Convention will become a principal resource for defining the international norms.
>
> Due to its global nature, and the vast number of ratifications that have already taken place, the UN Convention . . . will play the critical role in the globalization of the international norms. Initially, the UN Convention will serve to expand the scope of cooperation and prompt the adoption of domestic legislation in parts of the world less inclined to participate in the other international and anti-bribery conventions. Over time, with the exception of the OECD Convention, the UN Convention will surpass many of the regional anti-bribery conventions in becoming the focus of [future] developments.
>
> STUART H. DEMING, THE FOREIGN CORRUPT PRACTICES ACT AND THE NEW INTERNATIONAL NORMS 306 (2d ed. 2010) (footnotes omitted).

56. Ad Hoc Committee for the Negotiation of a Convention Against Corruption, *Report on the Work of Its First to Seventh Sessions*, Addendum, art. 16, U.N. Doc. A/58/422/Add.l (Oct. 7, 2003), *available at* https://www.unodc.org/pdf/crime/convention_corruption/session_7/42 2addl.pdf

57. *Id.*

58. Criminal Law Convention on Corruption, Jan. 27, 1999, Europ. TS. No. 173, 38 I.L.M. 505.

59. *Id.* art. 5.

60. Criminal Law Convention on Corruption Explanatory Rep., art. 5, Jan. 27, 1999, ET.S. No. 173, *available at* http://conventions.coe.int/treaty/en/Reports/Html/173.htm.

61. Criminal Law Convention on Corruption, *supra* note 60 (charting signatures and ratifications). Though the United States has not ratified the CoE Convention, it is a signatory. *Id.*

62. For example, the work of medical organizations, educational institutions, and adoption agencies is performed by both for-profit and nonprofit organizations. Nonprofits and NGOs with high pay scales for senior officials are also less likely to be perceived as being entirely charitable or humanitarian in nature. According to a USA TODAY review, "[f]our chief executives whose government-funded non-profit corporations are paid to deliver U.S. foreign assistance earned more that half a million dollars in 2007." Ken Dilanian, *Review: High Salaries for Aid Group CEOs*, USA Today, Sep. 1, 2009, http://www.usatoday.com/news/world/200908-3 1-us-aid-groups_N.htm; *see also* Barrett, *supra* note 17 (listing salaries of the CEOs of the ten largest U.S. charitable organizations). The highest paid CEOs on the list are the President of American Cancer Society, at $1.3 million, and of United Way, at $715,000. In 2010, President of the American Red Cross received $995,718 in pay while the CEO of AED in 2009 was paid over $870,000 in total compensation. *See* Charity Navigator, American Red Cross Rating, http://www.charitynavigator.org/index.cfm?bay=search.summary&orgid=3277 (last visited Jun. 22, 2011); CEO Update, 2011 Executive Compensation in Associations, http://www.ceoupdate.com/articles/articleDetails.htm?articleid=1720 (last visited Jun. 22, 2011).

63. Survey of NGOs and Other Nonprofit Organizations on the Issue of Corruption and Anticorruption Compliance (January 2011–February 2011) [hereinafter Survey] (data on file with the authors). The survey was conducted by one of the authors on the condition that the information provided, as well as its source, would remain confidential. For the purpose of anonymity, survey participants will be referenced hereinafter as "Participant 1," "Participant 2,"

etc. when information obtained from a participant is referenced.

64. *Id.*

65. *Id.*

66. "[I]n general, a red flag is a set of facts that, in a given context, would prompt a reasonable person to have a basis for concern as to whether prohibited conduct took place or is intended or likely to occur." Deming, *supra* note 55, at 654.

67. Survey, *supra* note 63, Participants 1 & 2.

68. *Id.* Participant 2.

69. *See infra* Part II.2.

70. Survey, *supra* note 63, Participant 2.

71. *Id.*

72. *Id.* Participant 3.

73. *Id.*

74. *Id.* Participants 1 & 3.

75. *Id.*

76. *Id.* Participant 1.

77. Foreign Corrupt Practices Act (FCPA), 15 U.S.C. §78dd-l(b), 2(b), 3(b) (1998). The FCPA further defines "routine governmental action" as: an action which is ordinarily and commonly performed by a foreign official in—

   (i) obtaining permits, licenses, or other official documents to qualify a person to do business in a foreign country;

   (ii) processing governmental papers, such as visas and work orders;

   (iii) providing police protection, mail pick-up and delivery, or scheduling inspections associated with contract performance or inspections related to transit of goods across country;

   (iv) providing phone service, power and water supply, loading and unloading cargo, or protecting perishable products or commodities from deterioration; or

   (v) actions of a similar nature.

   Id. §78dd-2(h)(4)(A).

78. *Id.* §78dd-l(a), 2(a), 3(a).

79. Bribery Act 2010, c. 23 (U.K.), *available at* http://www.legislation.gov.uk/ukpga/2010/23/contents.

80. Aside from the compliance concerns, practical reasons may justify the need to ensure that even facilitating payments are prohibited. Keep in mind that a host country considers a facilitating payment a

bribe. In many countries, NGOs can become the focal point of threats and various forms of retaliation by the host government or groups that may resent or fear their presence. *See, e.g.*, Center for the Development of Democracy and Human Rights, Report Prepared for the 4th Round of EU-Russia Consultations on Human Rights, Deteriorating Situation of NGOs and Infringement of the Right to Association in Russia (November 2006), *available at* http://www.europarl. europa.eu/meetdocs/2004_2009/documents/ dv/centerfordevelopment_/centerfor development_ en.pdf; *Uzbek N.G.O.S Under Threat*, VOANEws. com, Jul. 28, 2006, http://www.voanews.com/policy/ editorials/a-41-2006-07-3 l-voal-83 105557.html.

81. Survey, *supra* note 63, Participant 1.

82. *Id.* Participant 2.

83. Theoretically, even a twenty-dollar payment can get an NGO in trouble. It would be a legal viola- tion in the host country. For many countries, like the United Kingdom, that do not allow facilitating payments, it would also be a violation. The circum- stances of the road checkpoint situation may also not fall within the FCPA's exception for facilitating pay- ments. *See* FCPA 15 U.S.C. §78dd-2(b) (1998). The particular facts will dictate whether the circumstances fall within the category of expediting or securing "the performance of a routine governmental action." *Id.* §78dd-2(b), (f)(3).

84. Survey, *supra* note 63, Participant 3.

85. *Id.* Participants 2 & 3.

86. *Id.*

87. *Id.* Participants 3 & 4.

88. *Id.* Participants 2, 3 & 4.

89. "The Global Fund is a unique, public-private partnership and international financing institution dedicated to attracting and disbursing additional resources to prevent and treat [several diseases]." The Global Fund, About the Global Fund, http:// www.theglobalfund.org/en/about/ (last visited Jun. 5, 2011). The Global Fund provides billions of dollars in assistance to developing countries. *Id.*

90. *AP: Fraud Plagues Global Health Fund*, CBS NEws, Jan. 24, 2011, http://www.cbsnews.com/ stories/2011/01/24/world/main7277776.shtml.

91. *Id.*

92. John Heilprin, *Global Fund Rethinks Transparency Policy after Corruption Scandal*, HUFFINGTON POST, May 10, 2011, http://www. huffingtonpost.com/2011/05/10/global-fund- transparency_n_860004.html

93. Press Release, Dep't of Justice, Former Humanitarian Workers Convicted for International Fraud Scheme (Nov. 16, 2010), *available at* http:// www.justice.gov/opa/pr/2010/November/10- crm-1305.html; Nedra Pickler, *Workers Charged with Stealing US Aid to Liberia*, NEWSVINE. com, Jun. 4, 2009, http://www.newsvine.com/_ news/2009/06/04/2895439-workers-charged-with- stealing-us-aid-to-liberia.

94. Press Release, Dep't of Justice, *supra* note 93.

95. Press Release, Dep't of Justice, Former Humanitarian Workers Each Sentenced to 142 Months in Prison for Defrauding USAID of $1.9 Mil- lion (Apr. 26, 2011), *available at* http://www.justice. gov/opa/pr/2011/April/l l-crm-525.html.

96. *Id.*

97. Survey, *supra* note 63, Participant 2.

98. Robert Appleton, Office of the Inspec- tor General, Presentation on Fraud, Misappro- priation and Financial Abuse in Global Fund Grant Programs and the Role of the LFA (Novem- ber 2010), *available at* http://www.theglobalfund. org/documents/lfa/workshops/2010november/ LFA_FraudAbuseInGFGrants_Presentation_en.pdf.

99. Dana Hedgpeth & Josh Boak, *USAID Sus- pends District-Based Nonprofit AED from Contracts amid Investigation*, WASHINGTON POST, Dec. 8, 2010, http://www.washingtonpost.com/wp-dyn/ content/article/2010/12/08/AR2010120807665. html; Office of the Inspector General, Country Audit of Global Fund Grants to Zambia, Audit Report No: GF-OIG-09-15 (Oct. 5, 2010), *avail- able at* http://www.theglobalfund.org/documents/ oig/GF_CountryAudit-GF-Grants-Zambia_Report- GF-OIG-09-015.pdf. The audit focused on three government agencies and one nonprofit organiza- tion, the Christian Health Association of Zambia, and identified "significant financial management and control weaknesses, episodes of misappropriation and fraud, and losses of grant funds" in all four recipients of the Global Fund's grants in Zambia. *Id.*

100. Press Release, USAID, USAID Suspends Academy for Educational Development from Receiving New U.S. Government Awards (Dec. 8, 2010), *available at* http://www.usaid.gov/press/ releases/2010/prl01208.html.

101. *Id.*

102. *Id.*

103. Press Release, AED, Statement from the AED Chairman of the Board, Edward W. 'Peter' Russell to AED Staff (Mar. 3, 2011), *available at* http://www.aed.org/News/AED-to-Seek-Orderly-Acquisition-andTransfer-of-its-Programs-and-Assets.cfm. AED sought a single purchaser and in early June 2011, it was announced that "FHI and AED have signed an asset purchase agreement for FHI to acquire the programs, expertise, and other assets of AED," with the acquisition to be completed "within the next month, ensuring that projects continue uninterrupted." Press Release, AED, FHI and AED Sign Asset Purchase Agreement (Jun. 8, 2011), *available at* http://www.aed.org/News/Releases/asset-purchase-agreement.cfm. FHI is a "global health and development organization." FHI, Who We Are, http://www.fhi.org/en/AboutFHI/index.htm (last visited Jun. 13, 2011).

104. Press Release, AED, AED Pursuing Orderly Transfer and Sale of Its Programs and Assets to a Single Acquirer (Mar. 10, 2011), *available at* http://www.aed.org/News/Releases/aed-pursuing-orderly-transfer-andsale.cfm.

105. Survey, *supra* note 63, Participants 1, 3, & 4.

106. Charity Navigator specifically includes this information in the "Accountability" section for each NGO it rates. *See, e.g.,* Charity Navigator, Compassion International, http://www.charitynavigator.org/index.cfrn?bay=search.accountability&orgid=3555 (last visited Jun. 27, 2011).

107. *See, e.g.,* American Red Cross, Concern Connection Line, https://www.integrity-helpline.com/RedCross.jsp (last visited Jun. 13, 2011); Feed The Children, Report Fraud or Abuse, http://www.feedthechildren.org/site/PageServer?pagename=org_report_fraud (last visited Jun. 5, 2011); IRD, Who We Are: Compliance, http://www.ird.org/who/compliance.html (last visited Jun. 13, 2011).

108. Survey, *supra* note 63, Participant 3.

109. *See* discussion *infra* pp. 138–39.

110. Survey, *supra* note 63, Participant 2.

111. *See* discussion, *supra* pp. 130–31.

112. *See, e.g.,* Ken Miller, *Feed The Children Charily Under Criminal Investigation By Oklahoma Attorney General*, Huffington Post, Jan. 26, 2011, http://www.huffingtonpost.com/2011/01/26/feed-thechildrenfounder_n_814537.html; Debra Blum, *A Beleaguered Charity Giant Turns to a Veteran Leader to Restore Its Reputation*, Philanthropy, Dec. 16, 2010, http://philanthropy.com/article/Scandal-Ridden-Charity-Seeks/125728/.

113. Nolan Clay, *Feed The Children No Longer Billion-Dollar Charity*, NewsOK, Apr. 23, 2011, http://newsok.com/feed-the-children-no-longer-billion-dollar-charity/article/3 561299.

114. For example, since the UK Bribery Act provides no exception, facilitating payments will need to be prohibited throughout an organization. Similarly, the UK Bribery Act's prohibitions on improper inducements to private individuals or entities often described as "private bribery," will also need to be implemented throughout an NGO. Bribery Act 2010, §1 (U.K.), *available at* http://www.legislation.gov.uk/ukpga/2010/23/contents. On the other hand since the definition of a foreign official is broader under the FCPA, prohibitions on the payment of improper inducements to foreign officials will need to include candidates as well as political parties and party officials. See Foreign Corrupt Practices Act (FCPA), 15 U.S.C. % 78dd-2(a)(2)(1998).

115. U.S. SENTENCING GUIDELINES MANUAL § 8A1.1 (2011); UK Ministry of Justice, *The Bribery act 2010-Guidance about Procedures Which Relevant Commercial Organisations Can Put into Place to Prevent Persons Associated with Them from Bribing*, www. justice.gov.uk/guidance/docs/bribery-act-2010-guidance.pdf (last visited Aug.8,2011) [hereinafter Bribery Act 2010 Guidance).

116. U.S. Attorneys Manual §9-28.800 (2008).

117. *Id.*

118. As was evident from the analysis in the opinion procedure release previously discussed regarding nonprofit involvement with micro-financing in developing countries, many of the proactive measures discussed and recommended were essentially similar to those employed by more traditional business organizations. FCPA Review, 10-02 Op. Dep't of Justice 5 (2010), *available at* http://www.justice.gov/criminal/fraud/fcpa/opinion/2010/1002.pdf, *see also supra* note 42 and accompanying text.

119. An organization's compliance program should not necessarily be separate from its system of internal accounting controls. An effective system

of internal accounting controls includes a range of review and approval guidelines designed to detect and deter questionable conduct. Indeed, the planning, implementation, and monitoring of a compliance program should be closely linked to, if not intertwined with, an entity's system of internal accounting controls. DEMING, *supra* note 55, at 49–50.

120. Bribery Act 2010—Guidance, *supra* note 139, Principle 1; *see also* U.S. Sentencing Guidelines Manual §8B2.1 (2011), Applications Notes, §2(A) (2011).

121. U.S. Attorneys Manual, *supra* note 114, §9–28.800.

122. UK Ministry of Justice, The Bribery Act 2010-Guidance about Procedures Which Relevant Commercial Organisations Can Put into Place to Prevent Persons Associated with Them from Bribing, www.justice.gov.uk/guidance/docs/bribery-act-2010-guidance.pdf (last visited Aug. 8, 2011), Principle 2 [hereinafter Bribery Act 2010–Guidance]; U.S. Sentencing Guidelines Manual, *supra* note 118 §8B2. 1(b)(2)(B).

123. Bribery Act 2010—Guidance, *supra* note 120, Principle 2.

124. U.S. Attorneys Manual, *supra* note 114, §9–28.800.

125. *See* U.S. Sentencing Guidelines Manual, *supra* note 118, §8B2.1 (b)(6).

126. *Id.*

127. DEMING, *supra* note 55, at 650–51.

128. Bribery Act 2010–Guidance, *supra* note 120, Principle 3; U.S. Sentencing Guidelines Manual, *supra* note 118, §8B2.1(c), Applications Notes, §6.

129. Bribery Act 2010—Guidance, *supra* note 120, Principle 3.

130. *Id.* Principle 4; *see also* U.S. Sentencing Guidelines Manual, *supra* note 118 §8B2. 1(a)(1), (b).

131. DEMING, *supra* note 55, at 653.

132. *Id.*

133. Bribery Act 2010–Guidance, *supra* note 120, Principle 5; DEMING, *supra* note 55, at 648.

134. DEMING, *supra* note 55, at 648.

135. *Id.*

136. *Id.*; *see* Bribery Act 2010—Guidance, *supra* note 120, Principle 6; U.S. Sentencing Guidelines Manual, *supra* note 120 §8B2. 1(b)(5), (c), Applications Notes, §6.

137. As an indicator that the time for anticorruption compliance at NGOs has arrived, the roundtable on the FPCA and anticorruption good practices in the NGO sector, organized last November by Inside NGO, an umbrella organization for the international relief and development nonprofit community, attracted representatives from about two dozen NGOs. Survey, *supra* note 63, Participant 1

138. *Id.*

139. *Id.* Participant 3.

140. *Id.* Participant 2.

141. *Id.* Participant 3.

142. *Id.* Participant 1.

143. The underlying basis for the FCPA and other anti-bribery legislation should apply equally to NGOs. If the NGOs objectives are truly laudable in nature, no basis should exist for the payment of a bribe. Whether it is in the form of exercise of prosecutorial discretion, an absence of the requisite elements to establish a violation, or the duress or necessity exceptions, sufficient flexibility currently exists to address extraordinary situations. Moreover, NGOs have not been subjected to a history of unwarranted prosecutions. To the contrary, an NGO has not been charged to date with a violation of the FCPA. If any special legislation or regulations were to be considered, they would relate to requiring that sufficient resources be dedicated to addressing compliance needs.

Daughter Dearest
Nonprofit Nepotism

BENJAMIN S. BINGLE AND C. KENNETH MEYER

Dan Grayson felt physically and emotionally spent and was ready for a time-out from his daily office routines. He was a self-identified workaholic with broad experience and knew the responsibilities of his position. He was never given a project that he did not relish doing, but this orientation would soon become problematic. Accordingly, as the number of projects under his purview grew, he became stretched and stressed. Thus, it came as no surprise that he would be waiting with hurried anticipation for the Christmas–New Year break, a week of paid time off.

Generally, Dan enjoyed his position as program director for the Credit Builders Association (CBA), a national 501(c)(3) nonprofit organization that provided training and resources for low-income clients with credit problems. He loved being able to help vulnerable people establish creditworthiness and have a lasting impact on the lives of others in this way. Although national in scope, CBA had a staff of only ten employees—a tight-knit group that Tina Murphy, the CBA executive director, often referred to as "a family."

Dan Grayson did not consider his associates part of his own family, but he did enjoy the cordial and caring working relationships he had established with them. He found the organizational culture of CBA to be inviting, warm,

and flexible, but he was not terribly comfortable with its lack of structure and standardization; he preferred organizational formality. For example, although organizational policies governing hiring and procurement (purchasing) were in place, they were essentially "copy-and-pasted" from examples downloaded from the Internet. Though elementary, these policies had been sufficient to pass muster for a national audit that CBA had undergone several years earlier.

The audit required mandatory written policies for the different functions and phases of human resources management, budgeting, and financial administration. However, the executive director and the board of directors did not look at these policies as amounting to much more than "window dressing." In short, as one director quipped, "CBA will comply until we die." It was also noteworthy that organizational decisions were rarely made on the substance of these "boiler-plated" policies.

Dan had five years of experience with the national organization in CBA's Prairie Island office and was the most tenured staff member other than Tina Murphy. The executive director relied on him completely as a trusted and valued coworker and sought out his advice and assistance when making hiring decisions, developing strategic partnership, and confronting organizational difficulties.

 DOI: 10.4324/9781003387800-9

Even though he would have preferred a more structured work environment, Dan often laughed to himself about CBA not being policy-bound. When asked for his advice on important matters by Tina, Dan would sometimes say jokingly, "This isn't in my job description, and it certainly is above my pay level!"

Dan had a few projects to finish before he left for the holidays. First and foremost, he had to prepare the agenda for the upcoming staff meeting at the end of the week. He would be meeting with staff from CBA's other branch offices, and they would present their quarterly progress reports. Then they would have a "holiday lunch," exchange some gifts, and head back to their offices to prepare for the anticipated break. Dan especially was looking forward to "putting his feet up" and taking off some well-deserved time.

The time finally came for the staff meeting, which "went off without a hitch." As Dan and his colleagues were gathering their materials and placing their laptops in the carrying cases inscribed with the CBA acronym, Tina Murphy nervously cleared her throat.

She said, "Excuse me, I have a couple of things I would like to cover that were not on the agenda."

Taken aback, all eyes and attention turned to her as she slowly rose from her chair and began to speak in an authoritative voice. She informed her associates about a commitment she had entered into with Banker's Loan and Trust (BLT) and how excited she was about the new partnership.

She said, "CBA would gain access to new revenue sources and much-needed credit lines. This will enable CBA to help qualified clients get reasonably low interest rates on their loans without meeting the 'normally' expected higher credit scores." Tina did not appear to be conversant with all of the details surrounding the newly formed agreement and did not itemize any of its positive or negative implications. However, she indicated that CBA would be moving ahead with the project because it would open some doors that had been closed and ultimately serve as a good source of unrestricted revenue. Her eyes darting around the conference table, she added that they would need to immediately staff up for the new venture and make a new hire.

Then, to everyone's astonishment, she told the group that she had already made the hiring decision: Mandy Murphy would be joining the staff and heading up the new initiative. While she elaborated, her staff responded with blank stares and stony silence; no words were exchanged, and no one made eye contact. She intoned with a raised voice, "I realize that the decision to hire my daughter may raise questions, but please know that I have thoroughly discussed this appointment with Mandy, and I guarantee you that there will be no conflict of interest. Initially I had some reservations about this hire, but as I talked it over with Mandy it became obvious she was a great candidate and a good fit for the organization. Also, time is a factor if we want to capitalize on the BLT project. To reiterate, and I can't say this more emphatically, there will be no conflict of interest or preferential treatment. As you get acquainted with Mandy, you will come to know that she is a perfect fit with our culture and staff."

As she wound down her remarks, the staff began to fidget nervously with the paperwork they had received during the staff meeting. Tina then asked if there were any thoughts or concerns on the matter. Of course, how could anyone express their concerns or reservations at this juncture? After all, the issue at hand was the hiring of the boss's daughter!

After a period of uncomfortable silence—a quietude that seemed to last for an eternity—Tina thanked them for their attention, wished them a joyful holiday season, and then gleefully closed the matter: "Okay, I just wanted to make sure that everyone was aware of what we have going on. I know Mandy looks forward to working with you. Who's ready for lunch? I'm excited that we will have the opportunity to share some quality time together before we go our separate ways."

Dan carpooled to the restaurant with two of his closest associates, in stark silence. As they waited to be seated, it was obvious that everyone was trying to erase from their minds what they had just heard at the staff meeting. Accordingly, they began to chitchat about their holiday plans and upcoming schedules.

As Dan sat down at the long table set by the restaurant staff, arranging his napkin and adjusting his tie, Tina came over and whispered in his ear, "Just give Mandy a week and she will show you why I hired her for the job. She'll be great!"

Once more, Dan could not believe his ears. Tina had singled him out in front of the entire staff in order to inform him of her daughter's greatness. Dan wondered if Tina actually thought that he was the only staff member who would question Mandy's hiring; if so, she had totally lost her footing in reality.

"What a way to begin a vacation," Dan muttered to himself as he drove back to the office. As he reflected on what had just transpired, he began to feel nauseated. Dan knew that there were no specific state laws against nepotism, but he could not fathom why Tina had approached this hire so differently from past CBA hiring decisions. Tina usually never made a hire without first consulting him. This time the position had not been advertised to ensure a large candidate pool, it had been filled before the funding had been established, and a detailed recruitment and selection process had not been satisfied.

The more Dan assessed what Tina had done the more his nausea turned into psychological disgust. He had a déjà vu moment as he recalled a conversation initiated by Tina six months earlier: she had told him that Mandy had been actively looking for a job the past year, without much luck. Obviously, Dan reasoned further, Tina knew this decision would reverberate throughout the organization. Why else would

she have asked him to give Mandy a chance? Had Tina sprung this on the CBA staff right before the holiday lunch and their week off from work as a premeditated strategy? Or was the timing purely coincidental? Would any ill feeling, as Tina presumed, actually subside over time? Then Dan found himself wondering whether Mandy had submitted a resume. Was she qualified for the task at hand when a position description had not yet been written? And what would happen if the partnership with BLT failed?

Dan knew that all of these questions needed to be probed, but who would risk jeopardizing their relationship with Tina by asking them?

As Dan entered the city limits of his hometown, he thought about the awkwardness of the next staff meeting. He knew that Mandy lived in a city on the East Coast: would she relocate or telecommunicate from a remote office located in her home? Would she be provided with a subsidy for a residential office with a computer, printer, Internet connection, and office supplies? Would CBA authorize air travel for her to attend staff meetings at the home base? Dan thought about the first staff meeting with both Tina and Mandy present. Would this "mother-daughter banquet" have other, possibly even greater, repercussions on the CBA staff, organizational culture, and balance sheet? These questions would eventually be answered, but meanwhile Dan was not only tired but had just had the "wind taken out of his sails."

One last idea occurred to Dan as he pulled into his garage: with the holidays coming up, was there any better way to show love for a daughter than to hire her?

• • •

Dan Grayson enjoyed his vacation despite all that had transpired earlier in the CBA office, and despite the fact that, as much as he wanted to put the nepotism issue to rest, it seemed to arise as his conversations with visiting friends and family members drifted toward work. When Dan told them about the recent CBA hiring decision, the most common reactions were shock and disbelief. The circumstances surrounding the hiring and the blatant disregard for both the spirit and the letter of Equal Employment Opportunity Act regulations would surely have to be dealt with later.

After the holiday, Dan returned to his office and everything again seemed normal: mountains of paperwork to process, dozens of phone calls and hundreds of emails to answer—some important and some that should have been blocked. One of those emails came from a close colleague with the subject line "Get a load of this!" Attached to the email was a document entitled "Credit Builders Association Conflict of Interest Policy" (as displayed in Exhibit 1).

CS Exhibit 3.1: Credit Builders Association Conflict of Interest Policy

Definition: Organizational Conflict of Interest

A conflict of interest arises when a director or employee involved in a decision-making capacity is in the position to benefit, directly or indirectly, from his/her dealings with CBA or entities and/or individuals conducting business with CBA.

Examples of conflicts of interest include, but are not limited to, situations in which a director or employee of CBA:

1. Negotiates or approves a contract, purchase, lease, or other legally binding agreement on behalf of CBA and has a direct or indirect interest in, or receives personal benefit from CBA or the individual providing or receiving the goods or services;

2. Employs, endorses the employment of, or approves the employment of, on behalf of CBA, a person who is an immediate family member of the director or employee; and,

3. Sells products and/or services offered by CBA in competition with CBA.

Conflict of Interest Violations

Violations of this policy, including failure to disclose conflicts of interest, may result in termination of a director, executive director, or member of senior management (at the direction of the audit committee) or employee (at the direction of the executive director or chair of the audit committee).

Pressed for time, given the backlog of communication he had on his desk, Dan read the attachment quickly and gathered that Tina Murphy's decision to hire her daughter was a direct violation of the CBA policy and was "punishable" with termination. Yet he felt charitable toward his director, since she had never referenced this policy in discussing organizational decisions and might not have known that her new hire violated CBA policy. More problematic and troublesome to Dan was the revelation that the concern over nepotism had spread throughout the office. He knew this was not a good thing.

Fighting the urge, Dan finally opened his Internet browser and typed the words "workplace nepotism" into the search field. He wanted to become more informed about the consequences, legalities, and pros and cons of nepotism. He knew that nepotism had both proponents and detractors in industry and commerce. It was considered one of the many ways in which prospective employees were given preparation to join an organization; along with education, training, internships, apprenticeships, and other means of enhancing vocational aptitude. Nepotism was considered by some an "effective" way to socialize and assimilate prospective employees. Whatever the case, push had come to shove, and Dan and others would have to come to terms with CBA's newest employee.

Questions and Instructions

1. Is there any substance to Dan Grayson's questioning of Tina Murphy's hiring decision and the way it was done?

2. Identify and elaborate on the implications of nepotism, both positive and negative.

3. Assess the manner in which Tina Murphy announced the new hire. Was her timing premeditated, or was it coincidental that she announced her decision at the holiday staff meeting before a weeklong break?

4. In consideration of the CBA conflict of interest policy, what responsibilities, if any, do the members of the CBA board of directors share in this case of nepotism?

5. Did the conflict of interest policy preclude the hiring of Mandy Murphy? Please explain.

6. What are some of the considerations that the executive director should have weighed before hiring an immediate family member? Please elaborate. Would you have made a similar decision had you been in Tina Murphy's position? Why or why not?

Conflicting Values

CAROL SIPFLE AND C. KENNETH MEYER

On With Living (OWL) is a nonprofit organization dedicated to improving the physical and mental health of individuals age sixty-five and older. It is a local chapter of a national organization, the OWL Association, which had been in existence for nearly thirty years. Both the local chapter and the national organizational offer programs and services to help seniors stay healthy and fund research to find ways to prevent, treat, and cure diseases that affect people over sixty-five, such as Alzheimer's disease, diabetes, and heart disease.

Each local chapter is obligated to adhere to the positions of the national organization, and any modification or rejection of the national position is prohibited according to the "statement of relationship" signed by both parties. Any violation of this relationship agreement would result in "disaffiliation from the national organization," which local chapters attempt to avoid at all costs.

One position statement of the national organization took a firm position on stem cell research: "In keeping with our mission, we oppose any restriction or limitation on human stem cell research, provided that appropriate scientific review and ethical and oversight guidelines are in place." Without differentiating between embryonic and adult stem cell research, the position further asserted that the federal government was responsible for defining

and monitoring scientific review and ethical and oversight guidelines.

Cora Shipman is the executive director of a local OWL chapter. Her responsibilities are typical for an executive director of a nonprofit organization—strategic planning, financial oversight, selecting and managing staff, fundraising, community relations, and board development. Her work with the organization's board of directors included identifying potential new board members. Upon their appointment to the board, Shipman would orient them to the organization and provide a general overview of the many tasks and responsibilities assumed by board members.

Cora was excited when she learned that Andres Vasquez wanted to serve on the chapter's board of directors. Andres worked as a banker and had the financial acumen that she sought on the board. He was viewed as an up-and-coming leader in the community and was passionate about accomplishing the mission of the organization. Also, he taught a public relations class at a local university and had access to students who could serve as interns or volunteers in supporting the organization's programs. His previous volunteer experience with the chapter made him a qualified candidate for the board of directors.

Andres was quickly nominated and elected to the board of directors. Within six months, he

DOI: 10.4324/9781003387800-10

was asked to assume the role of vice president, putting him in line to be the board's next president. Although he was new to the board, things were going well and he has provided many valuable services to the organization. His energy and passion were contagious, and other board members became more involved.

OWL traditionally held several fundraising walks each spring, including one in Andres's community. Andres volunteered to serve on the event planning committee and assist in securing corporate sponsorships. He volunteered to visit a local insurance company and solicit sponsorship for the walk—a solicitation he felt comfortable making because his neighbor, John McNamara, served on the company's charitable giving committee.

Andres and John met over lunch and enjoyed the pleasantries of catching up with each other. When the subject switched to Andres's involvement with OWL and the upcoming walk, John was surprised to learn of Andres's involvement.

John said, "How can you volunteer for an organization that supports stem cell research?" Jokingly, he added, "I thought all good Christian men like you believe life begins with conception. Aren't those stem cells they use for research a human life? Are you comfortable in supporting an organization that destroys those cells for research purposes? And isn't it true that stem cells come from aborted fetuses?"

Andres was shocked and embarrassed and felt ill prepared to respond to John's comments. During his orientation, he had not inquired about the organization's position on stem cell research, nor had Cora mentioned it. In fact, the issue of stem cell research had not crossed his mind.

After ending the lunch hurriedly, he rushed to his office and called Cora. He told her about his conversation with his neighbor and his embarrassment in not being able to provide an informed and definitive response. Cora expressed concern for his embarrassment and

provided the clarification that he sought. She once more stated the position of OWL and reminded him that the chapter was bound to the positions of the national office. She further explained that OWL had not actually funded research involving stem cells. She also explained that the policy was in support of its mission and that it allowed the organization to keep all options open for research, both now and in the future. She assured him that no organization obtained stem cells from aborted fetuses. At least for the short term, Andres was satisfied with her response.

However, Andres struggled with this new knowledge over the next week. His personal belief was that life indeed began at the moment of conception. According to his beliefs, stem cells were not simply a collection of cells but a living human being, and to destroy those cells for the purpose of research—even if that research was designed to save lives—was immoral. While he was proud of his association with OWL, he felt like a hypocrite. His personal beliefs were incongruent with the position of an organization he publicly supported and on whose board he gave direction.

The situation intensified over the weekend when a letter to the editor about OWL appeared in the local newspaper. Written by the president of a right-to-life organization, the letter called for a boycott of OWL's upcoming walk. It cited the organization's position on stem cell research and called on the public to stop contributing to OWL and other organizations that approved of this kind of research. After Andres attended church on Sunday, several members of the congregation approached him and asked for his reactions to the letter to the editor.

On Monday morning, Andres called Cora and discussed his beliefs, but also assured her of his commitment to the organization. He proposed a compromise—a solution that he believed would reconcile the conflict between his personal beliefs and the organizational position. He proposed that the OWL board of directors pass a resolution to reject the national position and develop its own position to oppose stem cell research. He envisioned using his public relations knowledge to make this rejection a newsworthy event. He acknowledged that the local chapter would be viewed as a "maverick" in the community by standing up to the more powerful national organization. Andres was also convinced that the maverick position would raise public awareness about the organization and actually increase participation in the upcoming walk.

Cora knew that rejecting a national position statement was both futile and foolhardy and would result in disaffiliation from the national office. It would also mean a loss of valuable national and local support and access to important resources—a price she was not willing to pay because of one board member's personal beliefs. She believed that Andres's opposition to stem cell research was a minority view and that, in reality, "most people" supported this kind of research, which might lead to cures for devastating diseases. She looked to other board members for counsel and learned that most of them rejected Andres's position and proposal. The board cautioned Cora about the consequences of aligning the organization's positions with those of a particular religious group or political party.

Andres soon realized that his compromise would not be supported by the executive director and his fellow board members and withdrew the proposal. Ultimately, he realized the impossibility of reconciling his personal beliefs with the organization's position on stem cell research. He called Cora and resigned from the board of directors. Cora accepted the resignation with

mixed feelings. OWL had lost one of its most vocal advocates and promising leaders. Yet she was relieved that her organization would avoid a confrontation with its national office and the serious consequences of disaffiliation. Similarly, she was relieved that the organization's limited human and financial resources could be devoted to serving its mission rather than engaging in a conflict that would result in a no-win outcome.

Questions and Instructions

1. What criteria should a nonprofit organization utilize in the identification, selection, and appointment of members of the board of directors? Please explain.

2. Contact at least three nonprofit organizations and secure their requirements for membership on their board of directors, trustees, or governors. Present to the class the attributes and characteristics that these organizations use in the appointment process.

3. In OWL's applications for employment, would you recommend that Cora have the human resources department spell out OWL's position on stem cell research on the form? Would opposition to stem cell research be sufficient for disqualification for a position in the organization? Please elaborate.

4. Would it be advisable for Cora to write a rebuttal to the letter to the editor and clarify OWL's position on stem cell research, as well as on attendant issues related to euthanasia and death and dying? If so, please provide an example of what you would write. Alternatively, delineate other actions you would deem appropriate for the executive director to take.

PART III

STRATEGIC LEADERSHIP[1]

Interest in leadership has been expressed for centuries. Philosophers, religious figures, politicians, and scientists have all contributed treatises on leadership. In addition, a plethora of do-it-yourself volumes abound. Truly, there are thousands of books on leadership that seemingly offer something for everyone. A short list of titles includes *Leadership A to Z: A Guide for the Appropriately Ambitious, Ultimate Leadership, Leadership Passion, Leadership with a Feminine Cast, Why Leaders Can't Lead, Leadership Is an Art, Leadership: When the Heat's On*, and even, for the deeply discouraged, *Leadership for the Disillusioned*. Some authors have written biographies of famous leaders, while others offer step-by-step approaches that provide the faithful follower with a road map to leadership success. Oh, if it were only that easy!

There is no shortcut to becoming an effective leader. For all that has been written and said, the struggle to recruit, grow, establish, and maintain effective leadership remains a constant concern for all types of organizations, including nonprofits. Chief among these concerns is the ability to recruit good people. Leadership in nonprofit organizations is vested in both a voluntary board of directors (see Part I) and compensated officers, including the executive director[2] and, in larger agencies, a development director, chief financial officer, program managers, and others.

A conservative assumption is that the sector will need "330,000 new senior executives over the next decade."[3] Finding and attracting people to serve in these high-level positions will be a challenge. For example, a survey conducted in 2007 with over 6,000 potential nonprofit leaders showed that although the charity world is expected to require "tens of thousands of new leaders within the next decade," two-thirds of those surveyed said that they did not want to be an executive director or were unsure whether the top spot at a nonprofit organization would be among their goals.[4]

Likewise, the Urban Institute's National Survey of Nonprofit Governance found that the recruitment of new members was a key leadership challenge for nonprofit boards. "Seventy percent of leaders surveyed reported at least some difficulty attracting new members and 20 percent had a lot of difficulty."[5] Part of the problem is that nonprofit compensation levels have lagged behind those of similarly situated executives in businesses and government agencies. Therefore, turnover is a constant concern. "It is one thing to take a low paying job just out of college to follow your bliss, and another thing entirely to support a family or face retirement on a $40,000 salary, particularly in more urban areas."[6]

Leadership and Management

The study of leadership has typically followed one of two paths. One focuses on the individuals who practice leadership while the other analyzes the systems that need leaders.[7]

DOI: 10.4324/9781003387800-11

In the first approach, leaders commonly conduct assessments of their organizations and their environments that provide the context, note their constraints and priorities, take stock of their abilities and ultimately act concretely (behaviors) and in patterns (styles). In the second approach, a network or system is analyzed, its needs are diagnosed and ideal leaders styles and behaviors are deduced from that analysis.[8]

Many have sought to distinguish between leadership and management. Although these two functions and roles overlap substantially, the term *manager* connotes that authority has been formally granted to an individual by an organization. Management involves power—legitimate formal authority—that is granted to the occupant of a position by a higher organizational authority. Responsibility and accountability for the use of organizational resources accompany the power accorded to a manager or director.

In contrast, the term *leader* implies effective use of influence that is independent of the formal authority granted to an individual because of position. Leadership cannot be granted to a person by a higher authority; rather, those who decide to follow bestow it on an individual. Whereas managers and directors have formal authority, leaders have the informal ability to get things done by attracting and influencing followers. Today, most believe that effective managers in nonprofit organizations must also be leaders.

Until about 1950, the field of leadership research studied the personal traits and skills of leaders in attempts to determine which were most important. Since then, most of the research has looked at leadership styles, the roles of organizational leaders and other contextual factors, leadership competencies, gender, leader-follower relations, leaders as visionaries, ethical leadership, integrity and stewardship, leadership as collaboration, and the list goes on.[9] Although many unanswered questions remain about leadership, two important practical points stand virtually uncontested: (1) leadership involves a relationship between people in which influence and power are unevenly distributed, formally or informally; and (2) a leader cannot function in isolation. For there to be a leader, there must be followers.[10]

Ethical Leadership

In "Ethics in Nonprofit Management: Creating a Culture of Integrity," Thomas Jeavons explores the importance of an ethical organizational culture and concludes that responsibility for creating an ethical culture lies at the feet of organizational leaders.[11] Lack of an ethical base ultimately destroys a nonprofit organization—and other organizations around it.

Unfortunately, the problem of unethical behavior has not dwindled since Jeavons's piece first appeared in 1994, and when one nonprofit organization is discovered to be dishonest, other non-profits suffer: the level of public and regulatory scrutiny of nonprofits has never been higher. Concern about the ethical leadership (or the lack thereof) of nonprofit organizations has moved onto the front pages of newspapers, trade magazines, and professional journals. It is desirable to have an ethical organizational culture not only to avoid legal problems but also as a good business strategy. The study of leadership ethics is thus of high practical importance for nonprofit executives and trustees.

All students of the nonprofit sector are familiar with at least one or two scandals that have hit the front pages and have shaken their heads at the lines that were crossed and the social contracts that were violated. One of these, EduCap Inc., a multibillion-dollar student loan charity, was found by the Internal Revenue Service to have abused its tax-exempt status by charging excessive interest on loans and providing millions in compensation and lavish perks to its CEO and her husband, including use of the organization's $31 million private jet for family and friends.[12] Yet other difficult but less blatantly unethical situations are also likely to cross the path of a nonprofit leader sooner or later. For example, is it acceptable—ethical—for a nonprofit organization that serves victims of hunger and poverty to create a news story using a composite victim? Do the photographs used in a news story or brochure need to show the real victims or recipients of services? Should a leader of a nonprofit accept large donations for the organization from a polluter if the organization's mission is environmental protection? Most nonprofit organization leaders must eventually deal with and ultimately resolve this type of ethical problem.

Who Leads a Nonprofit Organization?

Historically, the nonprofit organization literature has placed responsibility for leadership squarely on the board officers, usually the president or chair of the board.[13] Under the traditional leadership model, the executive director or CEO is the chief implementer of board policies. From this perspective, to the extent that an executive director plays a central leadership role, it is for purposes of garnering and mobilizing the support necessary to accomplish the board's plans. This traditional model of how nonprofit organization leadership should work faded in the 1980s. For example, Terry McAdam and David Gies argued for "leadership partnerships" between board officers and executive directors, with explicit understandings about mutual expectations.[14] Using a model of organizational life-cycle stages, Michael Ostrowski explained that leadership needs and relationships between a board of trustees and staff are dynamic.[15]

In more current models, leadership in the nonprofit organization is grounded in the executive director. Although the traditional model argued that leadership should reside with the board of directors, in practice, it has been shown repeatedly that leadership is exercised significantly by executive directors.[16] In a study of nonprofit organizations in the Kansas City area, Robert Herman and Richard Heimovics concluded:

> We believe that in most established, staffed nonprofit organizations chief executives come to be expected by board members, other staff, and themselves to be finally responsible for the successes and failures of the organization. . . . We discovered that . . . effective executives provided substantially more leadership for their boards than those in the comparison group; that is, they took responsibility for providing board-centered leadership.[17]

Although a handful of authors continue to debate where ultimate leadership resides in a nonprofit organization, most observers today have moved on to an understanding that leadership is usually shared between a few individuals on the board of directors and the executive director. Their newer collaborative models reflect the view that "governance is a team sport."[18] In *Forces for Good: The Six Practices of High-Impact Nonprofits*, Leslie Crutchfield and Heather McLeod Grant assert:

> Strong leadership doesn't only exist at the very top of high-impact nonprofits; rather it extends throughout the organization. CEOs of high-impact nonprofits . . . use their leadership to empower others. And . . . they almost all have large, enduring and engaged boards. They have distributed leadership throughout their organization, and others throughout their larger network of allies and affiliates as well.[19]

The hierarchical organization model with leadership at the top charting the course of action does not capture the complexity of leadership given the preponderance of "wicked problems" that seep across organizational boundaries. Today, a nonprofit executive director is but one of many policy actors, and the nonprofit organization is but one of many in a jointly inhabited sea of public problems and concerns. Nonprofit executive directors and managers must be able to navigate convoluted seas and recognize the myriad actors, places, and points where opportunities or dangers may lie at any given time. They also must strive to use shared power to become connected to other effective leaders who can guide their organizations responsibly through those seas.

Conclusions

Executive directors are managers and—hopefully—organizational leaders who are appointed by the board of trustees, whereas board members are elected to their seats. A board's power to hire and fire the executive director implies that the board is the hierarchical superior, and the logical conclusion is that the board—especially the board president—is the rightful leader in a nonprofit organization. Although it is true that leadership rests in part on the authority that laws give to the board and through it to other positions in an organization, this is not the whole story. Leadership emerges when others willingly follow a person's vision, suggestions, requests, and directives. Leadership can transcend hierarchical superiority and even position-based legal authority. Leadership is created by followers, whereas management is created by authority. Leadership is transitory and fragile since what is created separate from authority can also leave or be destroyed.

All leaders have a responsibility to help ensure an ethical organizational culture.[20] Lack of an ethical base ultimately destroys a nonprofit organization—and other organizations around it. Unfortunately, the problem of unethical behavior has not dwindled, and the level of public and regulatory scrutiny of nonprofits has never been higher. Concern about ethical leadership (or the lack thereof) in nonprofit organizations has moved onto the front pages of newspapers, trade magazines, and professional journals. Besides the obvious desirability of an ethical organizational culture to avoid legal problems, it also is good business strategy. The study of leadership ethics is thus of high practical importance for nonprofit executives and trustees.

In nonprofit organizations, effective management depends on effective leadership. Newer models of leadership recognize the importance of collaboration, and some models locate leadership in network relationships rather than organizational positions. The primary purposes of leadership in nonprofit organizations have always been to help followers engage in activities that advance organizational missions and ensure survival while at the same time creating an organizational culture that respects employees and is centered on ethical values. Any serious attempt to understand the nature of managerial responsibility in the nonprofit sector must consider not only what the manager owes the organization but also what the organization, the sector, and the society owe the manager. "It is a pledge, a promise, a moral pact; and the pact goes both ways."[21]

Readings Reprinted in Part III

The first reading reprinted in Part III has been retained from the very first edition of *Understanding Nonprofit Organizations* because it continues to stand the test of time. Stephen R. Block's essay "Executive Director" examines the differences between leaders and managers in for-profit and nonprofit organizations and asks, "How does a person become an executive director?"[22] Block's finding that "executive director applicants comprise candidates with varied backgrounds" continues to hold true today. In a recent study, David Suarez examined the career paths of nonprofit executives and found that "leaders with applied credentials are common in the nonprofit sector including those with advanced degrees in, for example, social work, the arts, counseling, education and a wide variety of others."[23]

Block also explores the competencies required of an effective executive director. Using Henry Mintzberg's model, he explores the ten roles of an executive director within the framework of three sets of behavior: *informational* (monitor, disseminator, spokesperson), *interpersonal* (figurehead, leader, liaison), and *decisional* (entrepreneur, disturbance handler, resource allocator, negotiator).[24] Each role comports with the expectations for executive directors under both old and new models of leadership.

In the second reading, "Critical Standpoint: Leaders of Color Advancing Racial Equality in Predominately White Organizations,"[25] Fulton, Oyakawa, and Wood examine the association between an organization and its leaders of color and its likelihood of addressing issues of racial inequality and policies that may be negatively affecting people of color and/or other minority groups. The leadership examined in the study includes paid community organizers and the board of directors. The analyses are useful for thinking beyond general questions of board composition to the dynamics of leadership and its impacts on the organization and its members. Qualitative data add richness to the piece.

Fulton et al. assert that leadership in nonprofit community organizations shares power in fields of networked organizations. The methods and resources for sharing may include information, informal or formal coordination, shared power, and shared authority. Networks of actors may comprise units, departments, individuals, or organizations, and organizations are part of a variety of external networks that are fluid and chaotic. These organizational and environmental realities affect leadership strategies and require leaders to share space and work collectively with others for common but sometimes conflicting goals.

Planning is a key leadership activity that has changed with the shared power paradigm. Strategic planning has become a popular means for nonprofit leaders working with networked stakeholders to clarify common values, establish priorities, and seek to have an impact on the community. The change has been from long-range planning, which is depicted as "generally considered to assume that current knowledge about future conditions is sufficiently reliable to ensure the plan's reliability over the duration of its implementation," to strategic planning, which "assumes that an organization must respond to an environment that is dynamic and hard to predict."[26]

As with strategic planning (a staple in the nonprofit leadership toolbox for the past three decades), effective leadership today is concerned with building on strengths and tending to weaknesses, as well as with exploiting opportunities and minimizing threats. Leadership includes the responsibility to oversee the internal management of an organization's resources and mission-related goals, but it also requires joint efforts toward outcomes that a cadre of nonprofit leaders (among others) may be pursuing. Taken together, the readings reprinted in Part III shed light on the roles and responsibilities of leaders, including executive directors and others involved in significant leadership activities. Among the leadership goals worth pursuing are equity and diversity not only in the executive and board roles but also in high-level decision making and representation in leadership strategies and goals embedded in strategic planning.

Case Studies in Part III

The first case study, "Organizational Stability in the Midst of Turnover and Leadership Change," provides an account of the "revolving door" of executive directors at the Black Diamond Foundation. Readers are asked to identify factors that may be contributing to the many changes in leadership.

In "Best Laid Plans: Challenges in Strategic Planning," readers are asked to consider the many stakeholders involved in strategic planning and the implications of turnover during a strategic planning process. A SWOT analysis of the Southeast Illinois University College of Education's Literacy

Clinic's is included that considers the many views and goals of those participating in the processes. Disagreements and dilemmas arise over time, however, and the case illustrates how decisions approved at one point in time can be undone almost at a moment's notice. Readers are asked to provide their own analysis of how to implement strategic planning more effectively.

Notes

1. Peter M. Nelson contributed substantially to drafting this introductory essay.

2. Typically compensated but in many smaller organizations, not compensated.

3. Thomas J. Tierney, "Understanding the Nonprofit Sector's Leadership Deficit," in *The Jossey-Bass Reader on Nonprofit and Public Leadership,* edited by James L. Perry (San Francisco: Jossey-Bass, 2010), 551–560.

4. Survey participants were drawn from two groups: members of Idealist.org and individuals who participated in workshops and conferences sponsored by CompassPoint. Each group comprised people who had demonstrated an interest in a nonprofit career. See Jennifer C. Berkshire, "Potential Charity Leaders See Top Job as Unappealing, New Survey Reveals," *Chronicle of Philanthropy,* March 6, 2008.

5. Francie Ostrower, "A Better Way to Deal with the Leadership Crisis," *Chronicle of Philanthropy,* May 29, 2008.

6. Leslie Crutchfield and Heather McLeod Grant, "Sustaining Impact," in Perry, *The Jossey-Bass Reader on Nonprofit and Public Leadership,* 451–478.

7. Montgomery Van Wart, "Two Approaches to Leadership," *Public Administration Review* 70, no. 4 (July–August 2010): 650–652.

8. Ibid., 650.

9. Montgomery Van Wart and Lisa A. Dicke, eds., *Administrative Leadership in the Public Sector* (Armonk, NY: M. E. Sharpe, 2008).

10. Fred E. Fiedler and Martin M. Chemers, *Leadership Styles and Effective Management* (Glenview, IL: Scott Foresman, 1974).

11. Thomas H. Jeavons, "Ethics in Nonprofit Management: Creating a Culture of Integrity," in *The Jossey-Bass Handbook of Nonprofit Leadership and Management,* edited by Robert D. Herman (San Francisco: Jossey-Bass, 1994), 184–207.

12. Deborah L. Rhode and Amanda K. Packel, "Ethics and Nonprofits," *Stanford Social Innovation Review* (Summer 2009): 28; Sharyl Attkisson, "Student Loan Charity Under Fire: Is One Education Charity Abusing Their Status with Lavish Travel and Huge Salaries?" *CBS News,* March 2, 2009; Sharyl Attkisson, "Loan Charity's High-Flying Guests Exposed: Educational Nonprofit Under Fire for Transporting Politicians with Money That Could Have Gone to Students," *CBS News,* March 3, 2009.

13. Alfred R. Stern, "Instilling Activism in Trustees," *Harvard Business Review* (January–February 1980): 24–32.

14. Terry W. McAdam and David L. Gies, "Managing Expectations: What Effective Board Members Ought to Expect from Nonprofit Organizations," *Journal of Voluntary Action Research* 14, no. 4 (October–December 1985): 77–88.

15. Michael Ostrowski, "Nonprofit Boards of Directors," in *The Nonprofit Organization: Essential Readings,* edited by David L. Gies, J. Steven Ott, and Jay M. Shafritz (Fort Worth, TX: Harcourt Brace, 1990), 182–189.

16. E. G. Knauft, Renee A. Berger, and Sandra T. Gray, *Profiles of Excellence: Achieving Success in the Nonprofit Sector* (San Francisco: Jossey-Bass, 1991), 9.

17. Robert D. Herman and Richard D. Heimovics, *Executive Leadership in Nonprofit Organizations* (San Francisco: Jossey-Bass, 1991), 55, 57; see also Robert D. Herman and Richard D. Heimovics, "Critical Events in the Management of Nonprofit Organizations: Initial Evidence," *Nonprofit and Voluntary Sector Quarterly* 18, no. 2 (Summer 1989): 119–131.

18. Doug Eadie, *Extraordinary Board Leadership* (Sudbury, MA: Jones and Bartlett, 2009), 21.

19. Leslie Crutchfield and Heather McLeod Grant, *Forces for Good: The Six Practices of High-Impact Nonprofits* (San Francisco: Jossey-Bass/Wiley, 2008), 156.

20. Thomas H. Jeavons, "Ethics in Nonprofit Management: Creating a Culture of Integrity," in Herman, *The Jossey-Bass Handbook of Nonprofit Leadership and Management,* 184–207; see also James H. Svara, *The Ethics Primer for Public Administrators in Government and Nonprofit Organizations* (Burlington, MA: Jones & Bartlett, 2014), 12.

21. Michael O'Neill, "Responsible Management in the Nonprofit Sector," in *The Future of the Nonprofit Sector,* edited by Virginia A. Hodgkinson and Richard W. Lyman (San Francisco: Jossey-Bass, 1989), 272.

22. Stephen R. Block, "Executive Director," in *The International Encyclopedia of Public Policy and Administration,* edited by Jay M. Shafritz (Boulder, CO: Westview Press, 1998), 832–837.

23. David F. Suarez, "Street Credentials and Management Backgrounds: Careers of Nonprofit Executives in an Evolving Sector," *Nonprofit and Voluntary Sector Quarterly* 39, no. 4 (August 2010): 696–716, 702.

24. Henry Mintzberg, *The Nature of Managerial Work* (New York: Harper & Row, 1973).

25. Brad. R. Fulton, Michelle Oyakawa, and Richard L. Wood, "Critical Standpoint: Leaders of Color Advancing Racial Equality in Predominately White Organizations," *Nonprofit Management and Leadership* Nonprofit Management and Leadership 30 no. 4 (August 2019), DOI:10.1002/nml.21387

26. Michael Allison and Jude Kaye, *Strategic Planning for Nonprofit Organizations: A Practical Guide and Workbook,* 2nd ed. (San Francisco: Wiley, 2005), 7.

CHAPTER 5

Executive Director

STEPHEN R. BLOCK

Originally published in *The International Encyclopedia of Public Policy and Administration*, edited by Jay M. Shafritz. Copyright © 1998 by Jay Shafritz. Reprinted by permission of Westview Press, a member of Perseus Books Group.

[E xecutive director" is] a title that accompanies the management role for the highest-ranking staff position in a private nonprofit organization. In some states, the heads of public agencies are also referred to as executive directors.

Early developments in commerce, followed by improved manufacturing technologies during the Industrial Revolution, led to stronger interests in management techniques during the late 1800s and into the twentieth century. During the same time period that scientific management principles were being advanced, Congress in 1894 created public policy that formally supported tax exemptions for charitable organizations. The development of management as a field of professional practice began to flourish during the first 20 years of the twentieth century. As attention to university programs developed and societies concerned with management practices formed, the importance of senior management positions became significant, not only in business but also in public administration and organizations of the private nonprofit sector.

The title and position of executive director is equivalent to chief executive officer (CEO) or president, both of which are executive management titles generally used in for-profit organizations to designate the foremost decision maker who is in charge of operations.

Among private nonprofit organizations, the title of president is often reserved for the highest-ranking volunteer (sometimes called the chief volunteer officer or otherwise known as chairperson of the board of directors). In some nonprofit organizations, however, the corporate title of president is substituted for the title of executive director. In such situations, the highest-ranking volunteer will be referred to as the chairperson of the board of directors.

The relationship between the chairperson, the board of directors, and the executive director position is initially forged through the process of hiring the executive director. In fact, the board of directors has ultimate responsibility for hiring and establishing the compensation of the executive director. The board is also responsible for evaluating the performance of the executive director and rewarding (or terminating, if required) him or her.

Once hired, the executive director may assume many governance and management roles and responsibilities. Though boards of directors

 DOI: 10.4324/9781003387800-12

can never truly delegate their legal obligations and fiduciary responsibilities, they are known to assign (or expect) their executive directors to help them fulfill their roles as effective board members. In some organizations, the role of the executive director is not shaped through the board's articulation of expectations, but rather the position is shaped by the executive director's experiences and know-how. In public sector organizations, the executive director has a responsibility to manage a department. Above all, the focus of the position is to support the policies and direction of the elected official who appointed the executive director.

How Does a Person Become an Executive Director?

How a person becomes an executive director of a private nonprofit organization may not always follow a clear and logical career path. There is much anecdotal evidence to suggest that many executive directors have been hired on the basis of their programmatic skills and not on their qualifications as executive managers. Laurence J. Peter coined the phrase "the Peter Principle," to identify this type of organizational ascendency into positions beyond one's competency. For example, competent social workers known for outstanding family counseling skills can find themselves hired into executive director positions on the basis of their proven clinical activities. In this example, the social worker may have no training or education in management, no experience with policy implementation, or no other competencies usually required of the executive director position. Consequently, the person is promoted into the highest of management level positions and removed from the one position in which he or she excelled.

More recently, hiring pools of executive director applications comprise candidates with varied backgrounds. Some include individuals with program expertise along with a mix of

individuals who have been trained or educated in nonprofit management. Many management oriented candidates seek management expertise through nonprofit management workshops, conferences, and continuing education opportunities, some of which lead to a certificate in nonprofit management from a host college or university. In more recent years, executive director position applicants may include individuals who have earned graduate degrees in nonprofit management or degrees from other disciplines that offer a concentration in nonprofit management, such as those degrees or areas of academic concentration available in the fields of human services, business, or public administration.

Whether individuals have backgrounds emphasizing program capabilities, management skills, or a combination of the two, there does not appear to be a shortage of candidates who willingly express their interest in vacant executive director positions, for a variety of reasons. The size of a nonprofit organization's budget and the complexity of the operations can be factors in attracting an executive director. Salary range and fringe benefits for the executive director position may influence both the size of an applicant pool and the characteristics and competencies of the candidates. For example, one would expect an executive director hired at US$20,000 a year to have competencies different from those of an individual who is paid US$100,000 a year. One might also expect that the larger, more-established nonprofit organization will be able to attract the most experienced and seasoned of executive directors, but the smaller-budgeted organization might be a valuable training ground for the newer and emerging executive manager.

Other important factors that have a bearing on the interest level of qualified applicants include the organization's mission, beliefs, and values; the geographical location of the organization; the reputation of the organization; the status of the board members in the community; the extent of (under-, over-, or balanced) involvement of board members in the organization; and the clarity of the board's expectations of the executive director.

When an organization is searching for a new executive director, it is important to identify clearly the skills and characteristics necessary for leading the organization toward the achievement of its mission and vision. When the board is clear about its organization's direction and purpose, the board has a higher probability of selecting the right person. The most critical factors are a candidate's knowledge about the role of executive director, proven management and human resource skills, and solid (and candid) references.

What Are Required Competencies for an Executive Director?

The executive director position comprises many multifaceted roles and responsibilities. The effective executive director possesses a range of qualifications that take into account personal characteristics, skills, knowledge, and abilities. Management expert Henry Mintzberg (1973) suggested that the position of an executive manager is organized around ten roles within three sets of behaviors: (1) four decisional roles (entrepreneur, disturbance handler, resource allocator, negotiator); (2) three informational roles (monitor, disseminator, spokesperson); and (3) three interpersonal roles (figurehead, leader, liaison). Mintzberg's concepts have also been applied to managing nonprofit organizations.

Daily work experiences of the nonprofit executive director illustrate the continuum of skills and abilities that are required of the position. Since executive directors tend to be involved in many activities simultaneously, their management focus must continually shift. This shifting can cause a blurring of the boundaries among the various roles categorized as either informational, decisional, or interpersonal, as illustrated in the following scenarios.

1. *Informational.* The executive director monitors the opinions of local stakeholders to determine if there will be any impact on the organization's reputation and its ability to raise private funds. This information is shared (as disseminator) in different formats with key staff and board members in order to plan appropriate responses and fundraising activities. The executive director speaks (spokesperson) before civic groups and corporate funders to explain the mission and direction of the organization.

2. *Interpersonal.* The executive director represents the organization and its board of directors (as figurehead) at important community meetings. At a monthly meeting the executive director (as leader) encourages the staff to work on improving its skills and offers guidance for exploring individual beliefs in comparison with the organization's mission and purpose. The executive director (as liaison) meets with the staff of the mayor's office to determine (as entrepreneur) if local community development funds exist to help finance a volunteer youth program.

3. *Decisional.* In response to a negative article in the local newspaper, the executive director (as disturbance handler) reacts to the external pressures to fend off a public relations crisis. In preparation for drafting the coming year's budget for the board's consideration, the executive director studies the agency's finances (as resource allocator) to shift the revenues among the key priorities and programs of the organization. The executive director also plays a negotiating role among department managers and board members with regard to establishing funding priorities and eliminating some favorite but underfunded projects.

Demands of the executive director position will vary among nonprofit organizations. Regardless of the organizational complexity of the position, the job generally requires some functional ability to shift attention back and forth between internal and external issues.

Executive directors are expected to have the skill to assess their organizations' strengths and weaknesses and to analyze the results of the information. The results can be used to develop a purposeful and strategic course of action, such as designing activities to improve or maintain the capability of staff or to protect or enhance the quality of the organization's service delivery system.

The ability to project how current events or emerging trends in the community will positively or adversely impact the nonprofit organization is another critical management trait that is necessary for controlling or influencing outcomes and for planning thoughtful strategic reactions. The executive director is also expected to respond to the pressures of the external environment by developing a network of community supports and collaborative working relationships.

Paying attention to the organization's internal and external environments is just one of many important components of the executive director's job. In fact, there are several essential management tasks in which the results-oriented executive director will participate, lead, or carry out explicitly or implicitly.

The tasks are as follows: *mission development, visioning, goal setting.* The executive director will have an opportunity to assist the board, staff, and other community members in the creation of an organizational mission statement or to annually review and, if necessary, revise the organization's mission statement. The mission statement is a reflection of the needs of the community and represents a collective vision of what the community could strive to become as a result of the efforts of the organization. By exerting leadership, the executive director is in a position to interpret the significance of the mission statements for establishing operational goals and objectives, recommending policy changes, and for motivating staff, volunteers, and others to believe in the importance of the mission.

Planning

The executive director plays an instrumental role in working with the board and staff to use the mission statement as a guide for establishing short-term and long-term goals and objectives of the organization and for developing action steps for implementation. The executive director is positioned to communicate to staff the purpose, time lines, and strategies of the plan. Managing the resources of money and people to accomplish the organization's plan and monitoring and developing strategies when obstacles impede progress are also major responsibilities of the executive director. The executive director assists the board of directors with its duties by assuring an evaluation of the plan's progress and reporting its results and, likewise, communicating the need to revise aspects of the plan on an ongoing basis.

Organizing

In practice, the executive director is responsible for determining what monetary resources and people are needed to accomplish an organization's plan, projects, and program services. Structuring the staffing patterns of the organization and establishing performance standards are other management responsibilities of the executive director.

Motivating

It is sometimes said that an effective manager is one who is able to get things accomplished through the work of other people. The complexity of motivating individuals either through intrinsic or extrinsic rewards requires an understanding of basic human nature. The effective executive director is one who understands the varying needs of individuals and responds by providing enriching opportunities, which build a sense of spirit and belief in the organization. If the director stimulates an interest in the work of the organization, the staff, board members, and other volunteers will use their energies, knowledge, and skills to achieve accomplishments for the organization and to enhance its service capacity.

Decisionmaking

Herbert A. Simon once suggested that decisionmaking is synonymous with managing. Decisionmaking is a pervasive management task of the executive director and includes making a choice among varying alternatives and weighing the likely consequences and risks of choosing one alternative over another. The effective executive director is one who uses a model or framework for approaching complex and far-reaching organizational decisions. Of particular importance is the recurring task of seeking and analyzing information through informal and formal communication channels that are internal and external to the organization. Information is a necessary ingredient for recognizing the need to make a decision and for serving as a pertinent database for developing a decision. Savvy executive directors also monitor reactions to their decisions and use the feedback as additional critical bits of data for ongoing decisionmaking.

Delegating

To be efficient and effective, the executive director must be able to recognize which aspects of his or her work can be scheduled or reorganized for attention during another time period. Also, it is important to identify which portions of the job can be accomplished by assigning responsibility to others within the organization or by making temporary assignments to outside consultants. Appropriate delegation of the executive director's work assignments to staff requires an understanding of staff's skills and abilities; a sensitivity to its workload demands; a level of trust in staff's ability and willingness to accomplish tasks at a level that will meet or exceed

the executive director's own standards; and the capacity to thank staff for helping out, either on temporary or permanently assigned tasks. Even though executive directors can never truly delegate away their organizational management responsibilities, their uses of delegation can help to alleviate the stresses of work overload, which can adversely impact outcomes.

Coordinating

Executive directors of moderate to large organizations have a management challenge of coordinating the variety of tasks and activities that take place among different specialized departments within an organization. In addition, they need to assure the coordination of work activities that occur up and down the organizational hierarchy. Almost thirty years ago, the term "integration" was introduced, referring to the process of managing the linkages across the formal structures of the organization. Without attending to the function of coordination, departments and staff may work at cross-purposes and thereby waste resources and adversely impact the opportunity for organizational success. The coordination of tasks and activities is also at play in smaller nonprofit organizations; due to smaller size and fewer staff, the executive director may have a greater level of participation in the different activities, thus minimizing the coordination challenges.

Reporting

The accountability concept of reporting is tied to the idea of lines of responsibilities and a chain of command. Different individuals in the organization are responsible for a variety of outcomes and are responsible to their supervisor for reporting on the progress of achieving assignments, goals, and objectives. The aggregate of all of this information is eventually reported by senior management staff to the executive director, who similarly must report on the organization's progress to the board of directors. The executive director's responsibility is to assure that there is no confusion in the lines of reporting, and that staff have available to them the proper supports and supervision that enable them to do their work and report their outcomes.

Supervising

The executive director must rely heavily on the capabilities of staff to accomplish the organization's plans; therefore, human resource management is central to an effective organization. In addition to the ability to motivate staff, coordinate activities, and delegate to other personnel, the executive director must have a mechanism of identifying performance outcomes and an acceptable process of supporting or promoting change among staff. The process of supervision is an interactive approach that is centered on developing the abilities of the employee by reflecting on work performance, jointly searching for solutions to work problems, clarifying expectations of the position, clarifying the direction of the organization, assessing the employee's progress in achieving performance objectives, and modeling the values and beliefs of the organization. Supervisors will typically style their supervision of staff based on how executive directors comport themselves in supervisory conferences with senior management staff.

Managing Finances

All management decisions have some level of impact on an organization's allocation of resources, expenditure of funds, or the need for securing additional money. Technically, a board of directors has a fiduciary responsibility as representatives of the public to assure that there is an annual budget and a plan to acquire an adequate amount of financial resources for stabilizing the organization and implementing its services. Practically speaking, the management of the daily operations requires that the

executive director be the one to provide the oversight for carefully monitoring the level of available cash, the organization's current debt, and its outstanding liabilities and receivables.

Complex or simple managerial decisions require that the executive director be fully aware of the organization's fiscal health. Most responsible executive directors rely on the use of financial management tools and the information they produce for making decisions. The tools include: financial statements, functional expense reports, and cash flow statements. An effective executive director knows how to interpret the financial reports and understands the implications of analysis on the stewardship of the organization's budget and resources. In addition, the executive director analyzes the organization's fiscal health by paying close attention to the effects of rising costs, increased or decreased activities, and the variable impacts from planned or unplanned changes in the organization's internal or external environment—including the organization's available working capital, current ratio, and debt-to-equity ratio.

The executive director also plays an important role in the organization's investment strategies. The executive director advises and supports the board after seeking expert advice on the development investment policy and its execution by locating reasonable investment risks. The executive director can also help the board to be prudent in its decisionmaking by watching the returns on investments and forecasting both the current and future needs of the organization.

Fund-Raising

Although many fund-raising experts claim that a primary leadership role of the board of directors is to raise sufficient capital for the operations and program, in reality, fund-raising becomes a management responsibility. The executive director should be as concerned, if not more so, for the organization to be financially sound and have the necessary funding to operate programs and pay staff wages and salary.

The executive director may take on a varying level of direct involvement for raising funds or see to it that the fund-raising activities are shared or carried out by specific staff, consultants, or volunteers. An executive director, for example, might secure appointments with community funders and solicit funding, but be accompanied by board members who bring credibility with their volunteer concerns and as examples for other volunteers like themselves who commit unpaid time and energy to the organization's cause.

Though the support and participation of board members is undeniably a critical factor to fund-raising success, the board's ability to be successful is often dependent on the management expertise and involvement of the executive director. The basis for successful fund-raising, for example, is to build off the needs, achievements, and plans of the organization. The short-term or long-term capability of an organization's fund-raising program requires that the organization be in good working order, operating productively and efficiently, both of which are results of effective management. The executive director assures the soundness of the organization's operations and programs through the controls, processes, and systems that he or she manages, making certain they are supported by skillful and knowledgeable staff and, if applicable, a cadre of committed and dedicated volunteers, all of whom are knowledgeable about the organization's mission, vision, and direction.

The basic characteristics of volunteer support require the involvement of the executive director, providing oversight and assurances that the tools of fund-raising are in place. Necessary fund-raising tools include a well-crafted "case statement," a donor or prospect list, an annual report or other significant brochures that illustrate the achievements of the organization, and a plan that has realistic goals with a time frame that is also reasonable. With regard to the implementation of a fund-raising plan,

the executive director must also be up-to-date about the efforts of the staff, volunteers, or resource development committee members so that people are working together and not inadvertently at cross-purposes.

Volunteers are very important to fundraising success; however, if volunteers do not follow through on important assignments or find that their personal lives and occupational demands are interfering with their volunteer commitment, the executive director must be ready to step in. More than one executive director has found him- or herself "jumping in" to salvage a fund-raising project, while publicly giving the credit for the project's success to the volunteers, board, and staff.

Executive Director's Leadership Role in Relation to the Board's Governance Role

Clarifying the differences between the responsibilities of the board and those of the executive director, Kenneth Dayton stated simply that governance is governance, and not management. It is largely an indisputable custom that the executive director's role is to oversee the day-to-day operations of the organization, as well as to share jointly with the board in matters critical to the strategic direction and survival of the organization. Because the organizational stakes are high, there is good reason to have concern over the ambiguity that sometimes exists between what board members should actually do and what executive directors are expected to do on behalf of the board.

Some authors have suggested that the board–executive director relationship would be more productive if it were conceptualized as a partnership. Research investigations into what constitutes effective governance and executive leadership have led some researchers to suggest that an especially effective executive director is one who takes active responsibility for the accomplishment of the organizational mission and its stewardship by providing substantial "board-centered" leadership for steering the efforts of the board of directors.

This view also asserts that there are several flaws in the traditional governance model. In the traditional model, the executive director is ranked in a subordinate position to the board. The hierarchical relationship would suggest that the executive director's daily work activities are being directed and supervised by the board of directors. Robert Herman and Richard Heimovics (1991) affirm through their research findings what many executive directors have come to believe through practical experience: that the board may legally be in charge, but the work of the organization is accomplished by the leadership demonstrated by the executive director. In this alternative "board-centered" model of governance, the executive director's distinctive leadership skills, information base, and management expertise are used for leading the organization toward the accomplishment of its mission. Furthermore, this model acknowledges that board performance is reliant on the leadership and management skills of the executive director. In this way, the executive director works to promote board participation and to facilitate decision-making. In addition, the executive director uses his or her interpersonal skills to craft respectful and productive interaction among the board members. With this approach, the executive director is (justifiably) credited with successful or unsuccessful organizational outcomes.

References

Bennis, Warren, and Burt Nanus. 1985. *Leaders: The Strategies for Taking Charge*. New York: Harper & Row.

Block, Peter. 1989. *The Empowered Manager: Positive Political Skills at Work*. San Francisco: Jossey-Bass.

Boyatzis, Richard E. 1982. *The Competent Manager: A Model for Effective Performance*. New York: John Wiley & Sons.

Drucker, Peter F. 1990. *Managing the Non-Profit Organization*. Oxford, England: Butterworth Heinemann.

Heimovics, Richard D., and Robert D. Herman. 1989. "The Salient Management Skills: A Conceptual Framework for a Curriculum for Managers in Nonprofit Organizations." *American Review of Public Administration* 18, no. 2, 119–132.

Herman, Robert D. Herman, and Richard D. Heimovics. 1991. *Executive Leadership in Nonprofit Organizations*. San Francisco: Jossey-Bass.

McCauley, Cynthia D., and Martha W. Hughes, 1993. In Dennis R. Young, Robert M. Hollister, and Virginia A. Hodgkinson, eds., *Governing, Leading, and Managing Nonprofit Organizations*. San Francisco: Jossey-Bass, 155–169.

Mintzberg, Henry. 1973. *The Nature of Managerial Work*. New York: Harper & Row.

Young, Dennis R. 1987. "Executive Leadership in Nonprofit Organizations." In Walter W. Powell, ed., *The Nonprofit Sector: A Research Handbook*. New Haven: Yale University Press, 167–179.

CHAPTER 6

Critical Standpoint
Leaders of Color Advancing Racial Equality in Predominantly White Organizations

BRAD R. FULTON[1] , MICHELLE OYAKAWA[2] AND RICHARD L. WOOD[3]

[1]O'Neill School of Public and Environmental Affairs. Indiana University, Bloomington, Indiana
[2]Sociology, Ohio State University Columbus, Ohio
[3]Sociology, University of New Mexico, Albuquerque, New Mexico

Originally published as "Critical standpoint: Leaders of color advancing racial equality in predominantly white organizations," in *Nonprofit Management and Leadership* (2019): 255–276. Copyright © Wiley Periodicals, Inc (2019). Reprinted with permission.

1 Introduction

Throughout U.S. history, racial and ethnic minorities have led movements for racial equality—albeit often with involvement from white allies (Morris, 1984). Given the continuing predominance of white organizational elites, many scholars argue that people of color need white allies in the contemporary struggle for racial equality (Warren, 2010). Moreover, the literature on "white anti-racism" argues on moral grounds that this struggle ought to be primarily the burden of white people (Ignatiev & Garvey, 1996). However, many white people prefer to adopt a "colorblind" posture, which often serves to mask structural racism and perpetuate racial inequality (Bonilla-Silva, 2003; DiAngelo, 2018; Foldy & Buckley, 2014).

Given that people of color have historically led efforts to achieve racial equality, we examine whether and how leaders of color within predominantly white organizations can help their organization do this work. We argue that some people of color bring into predominantly white contexts a "critical standpoint" developed through living as a racial minority in a white-dominated society. When such people are empowered within predominantly white organizations, they can use their position and critical standpoint to promote racial equality through institutional work to challenge and change the organization's white-dominated perspectives and practices. While this article focuses on the role of leaders of color, it does not absolve white people from their responsibility to address racial inequality nor does it diminish the importance of white people empowering leaders of color in transforming such organizations.

To better understand whether and how leaders of color can help predominantly white organizations address racial inequality, this study uses a multi-method approach to examine

 DOI: 10.4324/9781003387800-13

the leadership and activities of politically oriented civic organizations that are predominantly white. The quantitative analysis indicates that having leaders of color is associated with predominantly white organizations addressing racial issues both internally and within the public sphere. The qualitative analysis shows how leaders of color can use their position and critical standpoint to help predominantly white organizations address race internally by (a) providing alternatives to white-dominated perspectives, (b) developing tools to educate white members about racial inequality, and (c) identifying and addressing barriers to becoming a more racially diverse organization. The qualitative analysis also shows how leaders of color help their organization address race externally by (a) sharing personal narratives about living in a white-dominated society and (b) brokering collaborations with organizations led by people of color.

These findings contribute to research on organizations and inequality by demonstrating how leaders of color can help predominantly white organizations promote racial equality. This research also has implications for organizations seeking to promote social equality more broadly (Ospina & Foldy, 2010). Our findings suggest that when members of marginalized groups are empowered within organizations (e.g., given autonomy, authority, resources, and support, and not undermined), they can use their position and critical standpoint to engage in institutional work that disrupts exclusionary dynamics and promotes greater equality.

2 Inequality in Organizations, Institutional Work, and Leaders

Organizations are often core sites where social inequality is produced and perpetuated (Acker, 2006). While extensive research details how organizations increase inequality (Stainback, Tomaskovic Devey, & Skaggs, 2010), less is

known about how organizations can reduce it (DiTomaso, Post, & Parks-Yancy, 2007; Zanoni, Janssens, Benschop, & Nkomo, 2010). Particularly understudied is how racial inequality is addressed in predominantly white organizations (Winefield & Alston, 2014).

This study addresses these gaps by focusing on organizational leaders engaged in disruptive institutional work. By analyzing how leaders of color address racial inequality, this study links critical and institutional perspectives on organizational change. We posit that leaders' positions within racialized power structures can influence their ability to engage in institutional work to promote racial equality. Furthermore, we contend that a key condition for advancing racial equality within an organization is having leaders of color and empowering them to do institutional work.

Our analysis focuses on two prominent ways predominantly white organizations can advance racial equality: (a) by addressing racial inequality *within* the organization, such as educating members about structural racism, countering assumptions that privilege white members, and empowering racial minorities in the organization and (b) by addressing racial inequality in the public sphere, including educating the public about racial discrimination, advocating for policies that reduce segregation, and promoting initiatives that direct resources to racially marginalized neighborhoods.

3 Critical Whiteness Theory and the Outsider-Within Concept

To better understand how leaders of color might help predominantly white organizations promote racial equality, we draw on critical whiteness theory—the study of whiteness within the sociology of race/ethnicity—and the outsider-within concept. Critical whiteness theory argues that white privilege looks "normal and natural" to many people (Delgado & Stefancic, 2013;

Hatch, 2007). The theory asserts that most white people do not "see" the racial benefits they accrue (Garner, 2007; McIntosh, 1990). This blindness to white privilege impairs white people's ability to recognize racism operating within organizations and society at large (Bonilla Silva, 2003; Staiger, 2004). Even white people who are committed to reducing racial inequality can hold colorblind perceptions of self and society that deemphasize racialized structures (McCorkel & Rodriquez, 2009). Furthermore, many white people see themselves as "culture-less" (Perry, 2001) and view people of color as having a culture that is outside the (white) norm (Frankenberg, 1993). Indeed, "when people of color are not present, often whites believe that 'race' itself is absent" (McKinney, 2005, p. 43). These (mis)perceptions can inhibit white people's ability to recognize racialized dynamics within organizations.

A long tradition of scholarship in race/ethnicity asserts that people of color have a distinct perspective that enables them to see the workings of race-based entitlement and prejudice (Collins, 1986; DuBois, 1903; Fanon, 1967; hooks, 1998). DuBois (1903) explains that black people possess a "double consciousness" from functioning in a white dominant society: black people internalize white narratives about blackness and have firsthand experience of how racial power structures devalue their perspectives. Contemporary scholars explain that people of color often have "special knowledge of whiteness" (Hooks, 1998, p. 38), largely due to their experiences of racial marginalization in a white-dominated society. As such, racial minorities in the United States often experience cultural dynamics in which they are racialized as "Other" and excluded from power centers in society (Ahmed, 2004). Because of these experiences, people of color can more readily identify perspectives and practices that are racially biased (Carbado & Gulati, 2000). Although this literature is probabilistic rather than deterministic (e.g., not every person of color is aware and

critical of factors contributing to racial inequality and there are white people who disavow colorblindness and critique white privilege), most research supports the claim that people of color are more likely than white people to recognize and critique racial inequality (Ahmed, 2004; Bonila-Silva, 2003).

These aspects of critical whiteness theory are closely related to the outsider-within concept. Outsider-within are members of marginalized social groups who live and work in settings controlled by dominant group members (Collins, 1986). The outsider-within concept posits that people's perceptions of a situation depend greatly on their positions within embedded social relations that are structured by power (Collins, 1997). While dominant perspectives are often presented as the only perspectives, there are multiple vantage points from which social situations can be understood (Collins, 1986). Moreover, the outsider-within concept highlights how marginalized members of society can provide valuable alternative perspectives that are often unrecognized (Bell, 2009; Jang, 2017).

Applying this concept, members of historically privileged or dominant groups are likely to see situations refracted through their privileged view, regardless of their intentions. For example, some men might be blind to the disempowering effects that traditional gender roles can have on women. In contrast, members of subordinated groups are likely to see situations through the lens of living in a society dominated by another group (Collins, 2006; DuBois, 1903; Wylie, 2003). For example. women of color in academia can offer distinct perspectives on issues of race and gender because of their status as outsider within white- and (at times) male-dominated academic cultures (Collins, 1986). Similarly, feminist scholars argue that philosophy and science prioritize male perspectives and that a woman's standpoint can add significant insight (Harding, 2004; Hartsock, 1983; Smith, 1987). This outsider-within status enables subordinated group members to generate unique insights about that setting (Schilt, 2006) and to critique and contest social inequality (Kwon, 2015).

The outsider-within concept need not assume that one perspective holds "the truth" in any pure sense. Rather, it contends that assessments that rely only on dominant group perspectives produce a limited view of reality that can obscure inequitable practices and undermine efforts to promote equality. For instance, research on law firms finds that male attorneys are less conscious of gender bias and inequality than female attorneys (Martin, Reynolds, & Keith, 2002). By extension, predominantly white organizations that draw only from white perspectives are likely to underestimate their racial bias (Ward, 2008). In contrast, predominantly white organizations that draw also from the perspectives of leaders of color can have a more comprehensive understanding of their organization's racial dynamics. These leaders, who are better positioned to critique their organization's white-dominated perspectives and practices, are consequently better positioned to advance institutional work that promotes racial equality.

Combining critical whiteness theory and the outsider-within concept, we argue that leaders of color can help predominantly white organizations work for racial equality by providing a "critical standpoint"—an outsider-within perspective that allows them to see and critique racialized dimensions of organizational life. This theoretical framework, along with the authors' ethnographic research presented next, leads us to explore the role of leaders of color within predominantly white organizations. Our quantitative analysis examines *whether* having leaders of color is associated with predominantly white organizations having an internal and external focus on race. The qualitative analysis examines *how* leaders of color who possess a critical standpoint help predominantly white organizations work for racial equality.

Overview of Community Organizing Organizations

To examine whether and how leaders of color can help predominantly white organizations address racial inequality, we analyze a sample of predominantly white organizations engaged in community organizing (Wood, Fulton, & Partridge, 2012). These organizations are best understood as politically oriented civic organizations, as they have characteristics of both social movements and civic organizations (Wood & Fulton, 2015). Similar to social movement organizations, they mobilize constituents to address issues through the public exercise of political power (Morris, 1984; Tarrow, 1994). Similar to civic organizations, their most common forms of public engagement are collective civic actions (Sampson, McAdam, MacIndoe, & Weffer-Elizondo, 2005). Given their social justice mission, community organizing organizations often engage in issue work associated with racial inequality, which makes them a useful case to analyze for this study.

Historically, although most of these organizations addressed issues that disproportionately affect racial minorities in the United States, many pursued this work while avoiding discussions focused explicitly on race (Hart, 2001; Wood, 2002). While many community organizing leaders believed that such discussions would be divisive, others, mostly leaders of color, criticized "race-blind" organizing. Addressing poverty in the United States while neglecting the pernicious influence of racism, they argued, ignored the experience of communities of color and could not succeed (Sen, 2003). Nevertheless, the bulk of work in this field continued to address issues that disproportionately affect racial minorities *without* explicitly focusing on race.

Over the past decade, while some of these organizations have continued this pattern of addressing race only indirectly, others have moved to systematically incorporate an explicit focus on race into their work (Braunstein, Fulton, & Wood, 2014; Fulton & Wood, 2017). This bifurcated response to race among these organizations is reflected in 2011 data from the National Study of Community Organizing Organizations (NSCOO) (described next). Among the predominantly white organizations, over 60% indicated that they are addressing issues related to poverty, while less than 30% indicated that they are addressing race-related issues. Similarly, approximately one third of the predominantly white organizations regularly discuss racial differences in their planning meetings.

Quantitative Data and Analysis

To examine the association between an organization having leaders of color and its likelihood of addressing racial inequality, we analyze data from the NSCOO (Fulton, Wood, & Interfaith Funders, 2011). Although the organizations in this study are situated in different community contexts, they share a similar structure and mission. They operate as community-based organizations that bring together individuals from their member institutions to address social, economic, and political issues that affect poor, low-income, and middle-class sectors of U.S. society. Each organization has two types of leaders: paid community organizers and a board of directors consisting of representatives from its member institutions, which include religious congregations, nonprofit organizations, schools, unions, and other civic associations. Because the organizations tend to have a relatively flat hierarchy and a culture of empowering their leaders, the paid organizers have substantial autonomy to develop strategies and direct organizational activities. These commonalities enable our analysis to hold the organizations' form relatively constant, while allowing their social composition and organizational activities to vary.

The national study surveyed the entire field of these organizations by asking the director of each organization to complete a survey. This study achieved a response rate of 94%, gathering data on 178 of the 189 organizations in the country and demographic information on the 4,145 member institutions, 2,939 board members, and 506 paid organizers affiliated with these organizations (Fulton, 2018). Because this article focuses on predominantly white organizations, we restrict the sample to organizations in which at least two thirds of their active institutional members are majority-white organizations. The resulting sample contains 41 organizations and their 803 member institutions, 631 board members, and 100 paid organizers.

The analysis incorporates five dependent variables related to an organization's focus on race. The first three variables are ordered categorical variables, which measure an organization's internal focus on race: (a) how often the organization explicitly discussed racial differences in its planning meetings, (b) the extent to which racial differences prolonged its planning meetings, and (c) the extent to which racial differences complicated its planning meetings. The development of the corresponding survey items was based on ethnographic observations of organizations addressing racial issues (Fulton, 2019). These survey items were designed to identify an organization's level of engagement with racial issues, while limiting social desirability bias (Blanton & Jaccard, 2008). To measure an organization's external focus on race, we use the following binary variables: (d) whether the organization actively organizes people of color and (e) whether it actively addresses race-related issues.

We measure the presence of leaders of color in each organization using a binary variable indicating whether the organization has at least one organizer of color on staff and another variable indicating the proportion of people of color on the organization's board. The analysis also controls for the age of the

TABLE 6.1 Descriptive Statistics for ELIJAH and the Field of Predominantly White Community Organizing Organizations

Variable	ELIJAH	Mean	SD	Min	Max
Internal focus on race					
Frequency of discussing racial differences	4.00	2.93	.88	1.00	4.00
Extent racial differences prolong meetings	4.00	1.73	1.05	1.00	5.00
Extent racial differences complicate meetings	4.00	2.00	1.05	1.00	5.00
External focus on race					
Actively organizing people of color	1.00	.46	.50	.00	1.00
Actively addressing race-related issues	1.00	.29	.46	.00	1.00
Characteristics of the organization					
Organization has at least one organizer of color on staff	1.00	.44	.50	.00	1.00
Proportion of board members who are people of color	.55	.22	.17	.00	.67
Age of the organization	12.00	11.41	7.07	2.00	30.00
Male director	.00	.46	.50	.00	1.00
Age of director	35.00	46.71	14.12	25.00	75.00
Director has an advanced degree	1.00	.51	.51	.00	1.00
Proportion of male board members	.36	.44	.16	.18	.73
Mean age of board members	56.82	55.04	4.41	44.38	63.46
Proportion of board members with an advanced degree	.91	.43	.21	.09	.91
Proportion of board members who are clergy	.36	.23	.17	.00	.67
Proportion of people of color in the organization's county	.28	.24	.16	.05	.65

Note: N = 41.

Source: 2011 National Study of Community Organizing Organizations.

organization; the gender, age, and educational level of the organization's director; the gender, age, education level, and religious composition of the organization's board; and the proportion of people of color in the organization's county. Table 6.1 displays the descriptive statistics for the variables used in the quantitative analysis.

The analysis performs ordered logistic regressions for the ordered categorical dependent variables and logistic regressions for the binary dependent variables. Each model uses maximum likelihood methods to estimate the change in the log odds of focusing on race associated with a change in the independent variable.[1] Table 6.2 displays the results of the

TABLE 6.2 Logistic and Ordered Logistic Regression Models Estimating Whether and the Extent to Which an Organization has an Internal and External Focus on Race

	Internal focus on race			External focus on race	
	Frequency of discussing racial differences	*Extent racial differences prolong meetings*	*Extent racial differences complicate meetings*	*Actively organizes people of color*	*Actively addresses race-related issues*
Organization has at least one organizer of color on staff	.257*(2.058)	.380***(2.685)	.273*(1.698)	.261**(2.062)	.468**(2.520)
Proportion of board members who are people of color	-.245(-1.312)	.335(1.111)	.087(.455)	.053(.385)	.069(.529)
Age of the organization	-.159(-1.374)	.145(1.027)	.325*(1.874)	.195(1.304)	-.401*(-1.955)
Male director	.287**(2.082)	-.172(-1.101)	-.002(-.011)	-.083(-.626)	-.077(-.404)
Age of director	-.117(-.720)	.378*(1.727)	.096(.623)	.147(.872)	.014(.086)
Director has an advanced degree	.121(.865)	.190(.702)	-.049(-.316)	.309***(2.683)	.142(1.013)
Proportion of male board members	.123(.944)	-.289*(-1.672)	-.175(-.830)	-.229(-1.474)	-.030(-.175)
Mean age of board members	-.251(-1.561)	-.069(=.601)	-.016(-.110)	-.078(-.677)	-.473***(-2.764)
Proportion of board members with an advanced degree	.285(1.037)	-.067(-397)	.162(.912)	.081(.428)	.244*(1.660)
Proportion of board members who are clergy	.069(.310)	-.026(-.141)	.037(.186)	.147(.857)	-.447**(-2.024)
Proportion of people of color in the organization's county[a]	.484***(3.042)	.085(.301)	.243(1.240)	.419**(2.226)	.081(.605)

Note: $N = 41$. Coefficients are fully standardized; z-statistics in parentheses.

[a]Logged values

$= p < .10;$ ** $p < .05;$ *** $p < .01.$

five multivariate analyses. The first three models indicate that having at least one organizer of color on staff is positively associated with the organization having an internal focus on race. Having at least one organizer of color is associated with a fourfold increase in the likelihood of an organization discussing racial differences, and with a ninefold increase in the odds of racial differences prolonging planning meetings. However, these models do not indicate a significant relationship between the proportion of people of color on the organization's board and the organization having an internal focus on race.

The final two models indicate that having at least one organizer of color on staff is positively associated with the organization having an external focus on race. Having an organizer of color is associated with increasing the odds of organizing people of color by a factor of almost 5, and with increasing the odds of addressing race-related issues by a factor of 19. Again, however, these models do not indicate a significance between the racial makeup of the organization's board and having an external focus on race.

This analysis provides strong evidence that among predominantly white organizations, having at least one organizer of color on staff is associated with having both an internal and external focus on race. Having organizers of color within predominantly white organizations thus matters for efforts to promote racial equality. The analysis, however, fails to provide evidence that the proportion of people of color on the organization's board is associated with having an internal or external focus on race. This null finding may be driven by variance in board members' levels of involvement and power within organizations. For example, in two organizations with the same proportion of board members of color, the members' effects on activities may differ widely depending on their level of involvement and how much power they or the board wield. In contrast, most paid organizers are deeply involved in the day-to-day

work of their organizations. In summary, the analysis indicates that a predominantly white organization's likelihood of addressing racial issues—both internally and externally—is associated with having people of color represented among its leaders. However, this association holds only for the paid organizers, not the board members. While the quantitative analysis indicates a relationship between having leaders of color and addressing racial inequality, it cannot explain the organizational dynamics underlying this relationship; for that, we turn to the qualitative analysis.

ELIJAH: A Case Study of a Predominantly White Community Organizing Organization

To better understand the relationship between leaders of color and work for racial equality, we draw on qualitative data from an in-depth case study of one predominantly white community organizing organization located in the Midwest—ELIJAH.[2] Data from the NSCOO indicate that ELIJAH has 93 institutional members, 85% of which are majority-white organizations. and three organizers of color on staff. The director of ELIJAH reported that they "often" discuss racial differences in their planning meetings and that racial differences "somewhat" complicate and prolong their meetings. She also indicated that ELIJAH is "very involved" in organizing people of color and "very involved" in addressing race-related issues (see Table 6.1 for ELIJAH's descriptive statistics). Like many other organizations in the NSCOO, ELIJAH has a relatively flat organizational structure and a culture of empowering its leaders (e.g., giving them autonomy, authority, resources, and support). Furthermore, we selected ELIJAH for close analysis not because it is "typical" of all community organizing organizations, but because it is a predominantly white organization where organizational efforts to address racial inequality are visible. While these organizational conditions likely enhanced the ability of ELIJAH's leaders of color to engage in institutional work to promote racial equality, the conditions did not eliminate the challenges and personal costs associated with expressing and acting on a critical standpoint.

The ethnographic fieldwork within ELIJAH was conducted by the second author during the summer of 2011, simultaneous with the NSCOO data collection.[3] The ethnographic data include participant observations of organizational activities and 30 semi-structured interviews which lasted 45–90 min and focused on a respondents' participation in ELIJAH and their experience with leadership development in the organization.[4] Table 6.3 displays the characteristics of ELIJAH's leaders who participated in the interviews.[5] Although the ethnographic study was not designed specifically to reveal how leaders of color can help predominantly white organizations address racial inequality,

analysis of the observational and interview data provided extensive insight into how ELIJAH's leaders of color helped their organization promote racial equality.

Leaders of Color Addressing Racial Inequality Internally

Leaders of color advanced ELIJAH's efforts to address racial inequality within their organization by (a) challenging and providing alternatives to ELIJAH'S white-dominated perspectives; (b) developing and implementing tools to educate ELIJAH's white members about racial inequality; and (c) identifying and addressing barriers to becoming a more racially diverse organization.

The experiences and perspectives of ELIJAH's leaders of color differed substantially from those of ELIJAH's white leaders and members. During the period in which interviews were

TABLE 6.3 Characteristics of ELIJAH's Leaders Who Participated in the Qualitative Interview

Characteristic	N (%)
Paid organizers/staff leaders	10 (33)
Volunteer leaders	20 (67)
White leaders	24 (80)
Leaders of color	6 (20)
African-American leaders	3 (10)
Asian-American leaders	2 (7)
Latinx leaders	1 (3)
Male leaders	10 (33)
Female leaders	20 (67)
White male leaders	8 (27)
White female leaders	16 (53)
Male leaders of color	2 (7)
Female leaders of color	4 (13)

Note: Total number of ELIJAH's leaders interviewed = 30.

conducted, ELIJAH had three organizers of color on staff, the most influential of which was Ruby—a charismatic African-American woman in her early 30s whom ELIJAH hired in 2008.[6] At the time of her interview, Ruby reported directly to ELIJAH's executive director and held the title of "Lead Organizer," making her the most senior organizer on ELIJAH's staff. Ruby's critical standpoint was evident in her stated motivations for involvement in organizing:

> There's a silent genocide going on with the African-American community. We lead in death and destruction, you know what I mean? We lead in certain cancer rates, HIV, we go to the penitentiary system quicker than anyone else, our infant mortality rate is off the chart. So it's kind of hard to get in the world, it's easy to get yo' ass out, you know what I mean? Even if you live, it seems like you have a freakin' prolonged existence full of depression and heartache. And . . . as an organizer, [I am] trying to figure out what the hell to do about that.

Ruby's piercing account of the oppression experienced by African-American people reveals how her worldview is shaped by the material realities she has seen and lived in black communities. Knowing that her people lead in "death and destruction" leads to "depression and heartache" in her own life. Ruby's personal experience and knowledge underpinned the critical standpoint that she brought to bear on organizational life. During ELIJAH's meetings and events, Ruby would often speak about racism with vulnerability and great passion, sharing a perspective that many of ELIJAH's white leaders otherwise would be less likely to encounter given that most of their social networks are comprised predominantly of white people.

ELIJAH's leaders of color brought race to the forefront of their organization by challenging its white-dominated assumptions and providing alternative perspectives. When asked about her accomplishments as an organizer,

Ruby's response supports the second author's ethnographic observations indicating the central role she played in increasing ELIJAH's focus on race both internally and externally:

> I think probably the number one thing I feel proud of is being a part of and in some ways being at the center of moving [ELIJAH] to be multiracial and to focus on racial justice. For the three and a half years I've been here, that's been the majority of my work. . . . Whether that's being a part of [a coalition of mostly black community leaders] or looking at our programs or our campaigns or curriculum with [an] infusion or infiltration of racial justice, calling into question a lot of things. I just feel like I've been kind of an institutional builder. I think that's my biggest accomplishment.

Throughout the process of developing ELIJAH's training curriculums (i.e., internal work) and organizing campaigns (i.e., external work), Ruby incorporated a distinct focus on race. Ruby's African-American identity and life experiences—her critical standpoint—enabled her to see the bias in ELIJAH's perspectives and practices. Furthermore, Ruby's influential position within ELIJAH gave her the authority to call into question her white colleagues' assumptions and challenge them to consider alternative perspectives.

The dynamic that Ruby described in her interview was also apparent in the observation data. When ELIJAH's leaders evaluated its training sessions, they often asked whether race had come up in the session. During one evaluation, Ruby suggested that ELIJAH could be more effective at addressing race if it incorporated race into the *structure* of the training. She provided innovative ideas to accomplish this, for example proposing that the trainers could "pit African-Americans against whites" or "throw blacks out of the room" as provocative ways to prompt discussion about racialized power dynamics.

Ruby's suggestions reflected her sense that many of ELIJAH's white members lacked awareness of racial issues, which inhibited the organization's ability to practice racial equity internally. In response to this problem, ELIJAH's leaders created tools to help its white members see white privilege and understand structural racism. Ruby played a key role in developing and implementing those tools. In particular. she developed a training module that explained individual, institutional, and structural racism. Ruby trained ELIJAH's paid organizers, who then used this knowledge in their organizing work. In doing so, she provided an alternative perspective on the dynamics of a white-dominated organization and society, and challenged participants to adopt this perspective. Ruby used her position to ensure that ELIJAH's leadership development process explicitly acknowledged racism and involved all participants in learning about rather than eliding racism.

In another effort to address the white members' limited awareness of white privilege, a multiracial team of ELIJAH's paid organizers and volunteer leaders trained organizational participants to craft and share personalized "opportunity stories." ELIJAH used this tool to help its white leaders recognize and articulate the opportunities they had been given that may not have been offered to people of color. ELIJAH introduced this tool at a training session where Brynn (ELIJAH's white executive director) and Ruby each shared their opportunity stories, emphasizing where their race had played a role in opening or closing doors. This exercise required both speakers to inhabit a critical standpoint and view their lives through a lens of racialized mechanisms of advantage and disadvantage. Most of the trainees were white people who lived in predominantly white settings, largely disconnected from the experiences of people of color. In telling her story, Ruby exposed them to a viewpoint and a set of experiences they otherwise might not have encountered. Furthermore, having Ruby tell her story alongside a white leader provided a contrast that underscored the role of race in structuring people's lives and opportunities.

A third component of ELIJAH's efforts to address race internally involved identifying and addressing barriers to becoming a more racially diverse organization. Hope is an African-American woman who had multiple leadership roles in ELIJAH. She illustrated her critical standpoint when expressing concerns about ELIJAH's outreach toward people of color:

> I don't know that we do as good of a job as we can thinking about how we bring people of color into this work. There are fundamental obstacles in the lives of people of color that are going to be very different than addressing someone who's white. Part of what stands in the way of [ELIJAH involving people of color] is . . . the people making decisions about where we're going aren't people of color . . . I don't know that [race] is necessarily on the radar of [ELIJAH's white leaders] . . .

Hope recognized that because most of ELIJAH's members were white, its trainings and meetings were tailored to white participants. For example, the "opportunity stories" exercise was designed primarily to educate white people. She noted that most people of color do not need to be educated about racial inequality: they often already have a critical standpoint about racial inequality because they "live in it every single day." Hope understood that in order to become more diverse, ELIJAH had to both develop its white members' critical consciousness *and* effectively engage and empower people of color. Furthermore, as a top leader in the organization, Hope was well positioned to recognize that ELIJAH's white leaders were not always aware of the need to prioritize race. With these insights,

Hope was able to help ELIJAH identify where its organizational culture inhibited people of color from becoming involved.

In addition to identifying cultural barriers to participation, ELIJAH's leaders of color developed strategies to help address those barriers. Another leader of color, Diana, played a role in helping ELIJAH address barriers to becoming more racially diverse. A Mexican-American woman in her 50s, Diana was formerly a paid organizer with ELIJAH and was a board member at the time of her interview. When describing her experience as an organizer with ELIJAH, Diana shared how she translated ELIJAH's organizing methodology for the Latinx community:

> Among all the organizers back then, I was the only person of color. And the only one bicultural and bilingual. . . . I was working with a community that mostly didn't speak English, so all the documentation had to be translated into Spanish. Second, we [could not effectively] develop [Latinx] leaders in the [context of ELIJAH's] white culture. . . . So my [Latinx] leaders were constantly way behind. [Their] immigration status, education, and their understanding of English were issues for them.

Diana recognized how language and cultural barriers inhibited her community members from integrating into ELIJAH's leadership development programs. Moreover, because she was ELIJAH's only bicultural and bilingual organizer, she was the only paid organizer sufficiently equipped to recruit and train ELIJAH's Latinx constituents. Consequently, she translated ELIJAH's training materials from English to Spanish and developed curricula to help Latinx leaders understand approaches to political advocacy in the United States, thereby working to address ELIJAH's challenges with recruiting and developing Latinx leaders.

Several of ELIJAH's white leaders emphasized the critical role people of color play in helping their organization bridge racial divides. Pastor Ken, a white leader involved with ELIJAH for nearly 20 years, illustrated this dynamic when he shared about his experience working in the Latinx community:

> It's important to have people of color being organizers . . . The only reason that I can work in the Latino community and [be effective] was [by] simply walking with and listening for years [to leaders in the Latinx community]. I needed guides. We're not going to be successful working cross-culturally while we're still dominated by European American leaders and congregations.

Pastor Ken's experience illustrates how people of color can serve as mentors, guides, and cultural translators to white organizers working in a multiracial context. Methods of organizing that have been developed by white organizers and implemented in white communities often need to be adapted to work effectively in a multiracial context. Although white people could do this translation work, people of color tend to be more adept at translating because they are more aware of cultural and linguistic barriers and are more likely to have experience navigating multiple cultural terrains (Giorgi, Bartunek, & King, 2017).

In summary, the qualitative analysis reveals three ways leaders of color within predominantly white organizations can use their positions and critical standpoints to help their organizations address racial inequality internally. First, they can call into question white-dominated assumptions and provide alternative perspectives. Second, leaders of color can develop and implement tools to educate white people about racial inequality. Third, they can expose aspects of their organizations' cultures and practices that might inhibit people of color from becoming involved, and help their organization address those barriers.

Leaders of Color Addressing Racial Inequality Externally

Leaders of color can also help organizations address race externally. The quantitative analysis indicates that having leaders of color is associated with having an external focus on race. This section draws on the qualitative data to examine the mechanisms underlying this relationship. The analysis reveals that leaders of color advanced ELIJAH's efforts to address racial inequality in the public sphere by (a) publicly sharing personal narratives regarding the impact of structural racism and (b) brokering collaborations with organizations and communities of color.

To personalize the consequences of structural racism, ELIJAH's leaders of color often shared how they had been impacted by racial inequality. Part of the power of narratives in social change work lies in their capacity to make concrete how abstract social forces, such as structural racism, affect real people (Nepstad, 2001; Polletta, 2006). While leading a session at a training conference, Ruby opened with anger and pain in her voice, sharing a series of statements partly echoing the earlier quotation. "There is a silent genocide against African Americans in this country. African Americans lead in death and destruction. . . ." She proceeded to describe how racism and racial inequality personally impacted her and caused her to question the presumed race-blindness of public institutions and policies. Ruby's personalized and emotionally intense presentation illustrated her critical standpoint and made the impact of structural racism more concrete for the white participants.

ELIJAH's leaders of color also advanced ELIJAH's external racial justice work by brokering collaborations with organizations and communities of color. These collaborations enabled

ELIJAH to work closely with people adversely affected by racial inequality, which helped to widen its base and increase its political legitimacy. Ruby described her role in building such organizational relationships:

> What I do is make sure I have a continuing relationship, a blossoming one with [a predominantly African-American neighborhood association], getting to know them from their executive director all the way down to their leadership. We just had three people from [the neighborhood association] go to [our] weeklong training [conference].

Ruby helped ELIJAH develop connections with this and other African-American organizations by building personal relationships and inviting people to participate in ELIJAH's activities.

Similarly, Diana, the Mexican-American woman introduced above, led ELIJAH's efforts to mobilize the Latinx community for immigrant rights:

> 2005 and 6 was the peak of the immigration issue and I can say that I'm really proud of the job that I did in [that] 6 month period. [I was] constantly bringing many people . . . I did an event on immigration [in front of] two mayors and a state representative, and 300 people turned out at that event . . . I was able to be part of the big march that we had with thousands of people, organizing through ELIJAH. I was able to pull 15,000 people from different Catholic churches.

By building relationships with Latinx individuals and organizations, Diana mobilized large numbers of people around the issue of immigration.[7] As described above, she also translated ELIJAH's organizing language and culture so that Latinxs could understand and participate in ELIJAH's public actions. In addition, by working through Latinx institutions Diana was able to recruit many Latinxs from

Catholic congregations to participate in ELI-JAH's racial justice work. Interestingly, following Diana's resignation, ELIJAH was unable to sustain its relationships with the Latinx community. Although Diana resigned because of family medical issues, her departure and ELIJAH's subsequent loss of connection to the Latinx community nonetheless underscore the critical role leaders of color can play in predominantly white organizations and the importance for such organizations to develop comprehensive processes for recruiting and retaining leaders of color (Yukich et al., forthcoming).

In summary, the analysis reveals two ways leaders of color within predominantly white organizations can use their position and critical standpoint to enhance their organization's efforts to address racial inequality in the public sphere. First, they can help mobilize a predominantly white base for involvement in racial justice issues by sharing stories about the personal impact of structural racism. Second, they can increase their organization's mobilizing capacity and credibility by brokering collaborations with organizations rooted in communities of color. Both of these activities represent ways that leaders of color can engage in intentional, practical, and purposeful action in order to help their organizations address its habitual adherence to colorblind ideology. Noteworthy, however, is that under the model for organizational change analyzed here, the burden of helping predominantly white organizations advance racial equality falls significantly on people of color (those who generally have been beneficiaries of racial inequality).

Conclusion

Although extensive research details how organizations propagate social inequality (Acker, 2006; Stainback et al., 2010), less is known about how organizations can reduce inequality (DiTomaso et al., 2007; Zanoni et al., 2010). Particularly

thin is research on organizations reducing *racial* inequality (Cook & Glass, 2013). Given that racial inequality is one of the most pressing and persistent issues facing U.S. society, this knowledge gap warrants greater analytical attention. Reducing racial inequality in the United States has been difficult, in part because of the concentration of social and political power among white organizational elites (Gillis, 2017; Ostrower, 2007) and because many organizational practices of predominantly white organizations serve to maintain racial hierarchies (Wingfield & Alston, 2014). Thus, understanding racial dynamics within predominantly white organizations remains particularly important.

Rather than assuming that predominantly white organizations always contribute to racial inequality, we explored how racial equality work can occur within such organizations. Our study draws on institutional work research and combines the outsider-within concept with insights from critical whiteness theory to provide a novel theoretical framework for analyzing organizational dynamics. We argue that some people of color possess a critical standpoint born out of living as a racial minority in a white-dominated society, which enables them to see and critique racialized dimensions of organizational life that others may miss. When such people are empowered within predominantly white organizations, they can use their position and critical standpoint to challenge and change organizational perspectives and practices that perpetuate racial inequality.

Predominantly white organizations, however, have been criticized for leaning too heavily on people of color to represent their racial/ethnic group and lead diversity-related initiatives (Joseph & Hirshfield, 2011; Padilla, 1994). Leaders of color in predominantly white contexts often do extra work to educate white people about racial dynamics, and this role can involve significant emotional labor (Moore, Acosta, Perry, & Edwards, 2010). Importantly, such work is generally not compensated nor associated with increased prestige (Harris, 2012). This study seeks to highlight the contributions leaders of color can bring to predominantly white organizations and the need to recognize the value that these leaders provide as well as the burdens that they incur.

Notes

1. Because the quantitative analysis uses cross-sectional data, causal order cannot be determined nor the impact of exogenous shocks. Consequently, the interpretations of the results avoids using language that implies causality. However, the qualitative analysis provides an initial look at the kinds of causal dynamics that may underlie the relationship.

2. ELIJAH and all individuals' names are pseudonyms. ELIJAH is not an acronym.

3. The second author, who is a woman of color, was on ELIJAH's staff as an organizer from August 2009 until August 2010. The other two authors are white men who have extensive experience engaging race-related dynamics within community-based organizations.

4. The full list of interview questions is available upon request.

5. During the period in which the ethnographic data were collected and the survey was completed, ELIJAH had 11 paid organizers on staff: three of whom were people of color.

6. The racial/ethnic and gender categorizations of the interviewees are based on self-identification.

7. Although the exact number of people that Diana mobilized in the mid-2000s is not known, multiple sources confirmed that ELIJAH had a significant presence of Latinxs at the immigration march that Diana referenced.

References

Acker, J. (2006). Inequality regimes: Gender. class, and race in organizations. *Gender & Society, 20*(4), 441–464.

Ahmed, S. (2004). Declaration of whiteness: The non-performativity of anti-racism. *Borderlands, 3*(2), 1–15.

Battilana, J., & D'aunno, T. (2009). Institutional work and the paradox of embedded agency. In T. Lawrence, R. Suddaby, & B. Leca (Eds.). *Institutional work: Actors and agency in institutional studies of organizations* (pp. 31–58). New York, NY: Cambridge University Press.

Bell. A. (2009). "It's way out of my league": Low-income women's experiences of medicalized infertility. *Gender and Society. 23*(5), 688–709.

Blanton, H., & Jaccard, J. (2008). Unconscious racism: A concept in pursuit of a measure. *Annual Review of Sociology, 34*(1), 277–297.

Bonilla Silva, E. (2003). *Racism without racists.* Lanham, MD: Rowman & Littlefield.

Braunstein. R., Fulton. B. R. & Wood. R. L. (2014). The role of bridging cultural practices in racially and socioeconomically diverse civic organizations. *American Sociological Review, 79*, 705–725.

Brimhall. K. C. (2019). Inclusion and commitment as key pathways between leadership and nonprofit performance. *Nonprofit Management & Leadership.* https://doi.org/10.1002/nml.21368

Carbado, D., & Gulati, M. (2000). Working identity. *Cornell Law Review, 85*, 1259–1308.

Clarke, M. (2006). A study of the role of "representative" leadership in stimulating organization democracy. *Leadership, 2*(4), 427–450.

Collins, P. H. (1986). Learning from the outsider within: The sociological significance of black feminist thought. *Social Problems, 33*(6), S14–S32.

Collins, P. H. (1997). Comment on Hekman's "Truth and method: Feminist standpoint theory revisited": Where's the power? *Signs, 22*(2), 375–381.

Collins, P. H. (2006). Some group matters: Intersectionality, situated standpoints, and black feminist thought. *A Companion to African-American Philosophy, 12*, 205–229.

Cook, A., & Glass, C. (2013). Glass cliffs and organizational saviors: Barriers to minority leadership in work organizations? *Social Problems, 60*(2), 168–187.

Delgado, R., & Stefancic, J. (2013). *Critical race theory: An Introduction.* Philadelphia, PA: Temple University Press.

DiAngelo, R. (2018). *White fragility: Why it's so hard for white people to talk about racism*. Boston, MA: Beacon Press.

Dimaggio, P., & Powell, W. (1983). The iron cage revisited: Institutional isomorphism and collective rationality in organizational fields. *American Sociological Review*, *48*(2), 147–160.

DiTomaso, N., Post, C., & Parks-Yancy, R. (2007). Workforce diversity and inequality: Power, status, and numbers. *Annual Review of Sociology*, *33*(1), 473–501.

DuBois, W. E. B. (1903). *The souls of black folk*. New York, NY: Bantam.

Edwards, K. (2008). *The elusive dream: The power of race in interracial churches*. New York, NY: Oxford University Press.

Fanon, F. (1967). *Black skin white masks*. New York, NY: Grove Press.

Foldy, E., & Buckley, T. (2014). *The color bind: Talking (and not talking) about race at work*. New York, NY: Russell Sage.

Frankenberg, R. (1993). *The social construction of whiteness: White women, race matters*. New York, NY: Routledge.

Fulton, B. R. (2018). Organizations and survey research: Implementing response enhancing strategies and conducting nonresponse analyses. *Sociological Methods & Research*, *47*, 240–276.

Fulton, B. R. (2019). Engaging differences: How socially diverse organizations can mobilize their resources more effectively. *Academy of Management Proceedings*, *2019*, 19133.

Fulton, B. R., & Wood, R. L (2017). Achieving and leveraging diversity through faith-based organizing. In R. Brunstein, T. N. Fuist, & R. H. Williams (Eds.), *Religion and progressive activism* (pp. 29–55). New York, NY: New York University Press.

Fulton, B. R., Wood, R. L., & Interfaith Funders. (2011). *National study of community organizing organizations: Data file*. Durham, NC: Duke University.

Ganz, M. (2009). *Why David sometimes wins: Leadership, organization, and strategy in the California farm worker movement*. New York, NY: Oxford University Press.

Garner, S. (2007). *Whiteness: An introduction*. New York, NY: Routledge.

Gillis, D. (2017). *Missing pieces report*. New York, NY: Catalyst.

Giorgi, S., Bartunck, J., & King, B. (2017). A Saul Alinsky primer for the 21st century. *Research in Organizational Behavior*, *37*, 125–142.

Hajnal, Z., Lajevardi, N., & Nielson, L. (2017). Voter identification laws and the suppression of minority votes. *Journal of Politics*, *79*(2), 363–379.

Harding, S. (2004). *The feminist standpoint theory reader: Intellectual and political controversies*. New York, NY: Routledge.

Harris, G. (2012). Multiple marginality: How the disproportionate assignment of women and minorities to manage diversity programs reinforces and multiplies their marginality. *Administration & Society*, *45*(7), 775–808.

Hart, S. (2001). *Cultural dilemmas of progressive politics: Style of engagement among grassroots activists*. Chicago, IL: University of Chicago Press.

Hartsock, N. (1983). *The feminist standpoint: Developing the ground for a specifically feminist historical materialism*. New York, NY: Routledge.

Hatch, A. (2007). Critical race theory. *Blackwell encyclopedia of sociology*.

Hebert, J., & Jenkins, M. (2010). The need for state redistricting reform to rein in partisan gerrymandering. *Yale Law & Policy Review*, *29*, 543–558.

hooks. b. (1998). Representations of whiteness in the black imagination. In D. Roediger (Ed.). *Black on white: Black writers on what it means to be white* (pp. 38–53). New York, NY: Schocken Books.

Hughey, M. (2010). A paradox of participation: Nonwhites in white sororities and fraternities. *Social Problems*, *57*(4), 653–679.

Ignatiev, N., & Garvey, J. (1996). *Race traitor*. New York, NY: Routledge.

Jang, S. (2017). Cultural brokerage and creative performance in multicultural teams. *Organization Science*, *28*(6), 993–1009.

Joseph, T., & Hirshfield, L. (2011). "Why don't you get somebody new to do it?" Race and cultural taxation in the academy. *Ethnic and Racial Studies*, *34*(1), 121–141.

Kellogg, K. (2011). *Challenging operations: Medical reform and resistance in surgery*. Chicago, IL: University of Chicago Press.

Kraatz, M. S. (2009). Leadership as institutional work: A bridge to the other side. In T. B. Lawrence, R. Suddaby, & B. Leca (Eds.). *Institutional work* (pp. 59–91). New York, NY: Cambridge University Press.

Kwon, H. (2015). Intersectionality in interaction: Immigrant youth doing American from an outsider-within position. *Social Problems, 62*(4), 623–641.

Lawrence, T., Leca, B., & Zilber, T. (2013). Institutional work: Current research, new directions and overlooked issues. *Organization Studies. 34*(8), 1023–1033.

Lawrence. T., & Suddaby, R. (2006). *Institutions and institutional work.* New York, NY: Sage.

Martin, P., Reynolds, J., & Keith, S. (2002). Gender bias and feminist consciousness among judges and attorneys: A standpoint theory analysis. *Signs, 27*(3), 665–701.

McAdam, D., & Scott, W. R. (2012). Organizations and movements. In J. Ott & L. Dicke (Eds.), *Nature of the non-profit sector* (pp. 257–272). Boulder, CO: Westview Press.

McAdam, D., Tarrow, S., & Tilly, C. (2001). *Dynamics of contention.* New York, NY: Cambridge University Press.

McCorkel, J., & Rodriquez, J. (2009). "Are you an African?" The politics of self-construction in status-based social movements. *Social Problems, 56*(2), 357–384.

McIntosh, P. (1990). White privilege: Unpacking the invisible knapsack. *Independent School, 49*(2), 31–35.

McKinney, K. (2005). *Being white: Stories of race and racism.* New York, NY: Routledge.

Meyer, J. W., & Rowan, B. (1977). Institutionalized organization: Formal structure as myth and ceremony. *American Journal of Sociology, 83*(2), 340–363.

Moore, H., Acosta, K., Perry, G., & Edwards, C. (2010). Splitting the academy: The emotions of intersectionality at work. *Sociological Quarterly, 51*(2), 179–204.

Morris, A. (1984). *The origins of the civil rights movement: Black communities organizing for change.* New York, NY: Free Press.

Nepstad, S. (2001). Creating transnational solidarity: The use of narrative in the US-Central America peace movement. *Mobilization, 6*(1), 21–36.

Oliver, C. (1991). Strategic responses to institutional processes. *Academy of Management Review, 16*(1), 145–179.

Omi, M., & Winant, H. (2014). *Racial formation in the United States.* New York, NY: Routledge.

Ospina, S., & Foldy, E. (2010). Building bridges from the margin: The work of leadership in social change organizations. *The Leadership Quarterly, 21*(2), 292–307.

Ostrower, F. (2007). *Nonprofit governance in the United States: Findings on performance and accountability from the first national representative study.* Washington, DC: Urban Institute.

Padilla, A. (1994). Ethnic minority scholars, research, and mentoring: Current and future issues. *Educational Researcher, 23*(4), 24–27.

Parker, P. (2001). African-American women executives within dominant culture organizations. *Management Communication Quarterly, 15*(1), 42–82.

Perry, P. (2001). White means never having to say you're ethnic: White youth and the construction of "cultureless" identities. *Journal of Contemporary Ethnography, 30*(1), 56–91.

Perry, S. (2012). Racial habitus, moral conflict, and white moral hegemony within interracial evangelical organizations. *Qualitative Sociology, 35*(1), 89–108.

Polletta, F. (2006). *It was like a fever: Storytelling in protest and politics.* Chicago, IL: University of Chicago Press.

Sampson, R., McAdam, D., MacIndoe, H., & Weffer-Elizondo, S. (2005). Civil society reconsidered: The durable nature and community structure of collective civic action. American *Journal of Sociology, 111*(3), 673–714.

Schilt, K. (2006). Just one of the guys? How transmen make gender visible at work. *Gender & Society, 20*(4), 465–490.

Sen, R. (2003). *Stir it up: Lessons in community and advocacy.* San Francisco, CA: Jossey-Bass.

Shapiro, T., Meschede, T., & Sullivan, L. (2010). *The racial wealth gap increases fourfold.* Waltham, MA: Institute on Assets and Social Policy.

Slocum, R. (2006). Anti-racist practice and the work of community food organizations. *Antipode, 38*(2), 327–349.

Smith, D. (1987). *The everyday world as problematic: A feminist sociology.* Toronto, Canada: University of Toronto Press.

Srivastava, S. (2006). Tears, fears and careers: Anti-racism and emotion in social movement organizations. *Canadian Journal of Sociology, 31*(1), 55–90.

Staiger. A. (2004). Whiteness as giftedness: Racial formation at an urban high school. *Social Problems, 51*(2), 161–181.

Stainback, K., Tomaskovic-Devey, D., & Skaggs, S. (2010). Organizational approaches to inequality: Inertia, relative power, and environments. *Annual Review of Sociology, 36*(1), 225–247.

Tarrow, S. (1994). *Power in movement: Social movement, collective action, and politics.* New York, NY: Cambridge University Press.

Verba, S., Schlozman, K., & Brady, H. (1995). *Voice and equality: Civic volumarism in American politics.* Cambridge: Harvard University Press.

Ward, J. (2008). White normativity: The cultural dimensions of whiteness in a radically diverse LGBT organization. *Sociological Perspectives, 51*(3), 563–586.

Warren, M. (2010). *Fire in the heart: How white activists embrace racial justice.* New York, NY: Oxford University Press.

Wingfield, A., & Alston, R. (2014). Maintaining hierarchies in predominantly white organizations. *American Behavioral Scientist, 58*(2), 274–287.

Wood, R. L. (2002). *Faith in action: Religion, race, and democratic organizing in America.* Chicago, IL: University of Chicago Press.

Wood, R. L., & Fulton, B. R. (2015). *A shared future: Faith-based organizing for racial equity and ethical democracy.* Chicago, IL: University of Chicago Press.

Wood, R. L., Fulton, B. R., & Partridge, K. (2012). *Building bridges, building power: Development in institution-based community organizing.* Denver: Interfaith Funders.

Wylie, A. (2003). Why standpoint matters. In R. Figueroa & S. Harding (Eds.). *Science and other cultures* (pp. 26–48). New York, NY: Routledge.

Yukich, G., Fulton, B. R., & Wood, R. L. (forthcoming). Representative group styles: How ally immigrant rights organizations promote immigrant involvement. *Social Problems.*

Zanoni, P., Janssens, M., Benschop, Y., & Nkomo, S. (2010). Unpacking diversity, grasping inequality. Rethinking difference through critical perspectives. *Organization, 17*(1), 9–29.

Author Biographies

Brad R. Fulton is an assistant professor in the O'Neill School of Public and Environmental Affairs at Indiana University. His research draws on organizational theory and network analysis to examine the social, political, and economic impact of community-based organizations.

Michelle Oyakawa is a lecturer in sociology at The Ohio State University. Her research examines culture and strategy in social movement and religious organizations and explores how these organizations can both ameliorate and perpetuate racial inequality.

Richard L. Wood serves as professor of sociology at the University of New Mexico. His research focuses on the cultural and institutional dynamics underlying democratic life, particularly those tied to faith communities. He recently stepped down as interim provost and senior vice provost at UNM.

How to cite this article: Fulton BR. Oyakawa M, Wood RL. Critical standpoint: Leaders of color advancing racial equality in predominantly white organizations. *Nonprofit Management and Leadership.* 2019;30:255–276. https://doi.org/10.1002/nml.21387

Organizational Stability in the Midst of Turnover and Leadership Change

Julie Ann O'Connell, Benjamin S. Bingle and C. Kenneth Meyer

Change can be difficult. Frequent change, in a nonprofit leadership position, can be disastrous.

The Black Diamond Foundation was about to celebrate its tenth year in existence. Located in a small, peri-urban area, the Foundation was the culmination of several years of work by local philanthropists and thought leaders interested in supporting not only the local and regional community, but the international community as well. When the groundwork had been set and it was time to launch the Foundation, a steering committee conducted an international search for an Executive Director that landed a well-seasoned professional with extensive experience in both domestic and international program development who was excited about the challenge to build a new organization from the ground up.

This inaugural Executive Director (ED) brought prestige to the infant organization; having lived and traveled abroad for years, she was an exciting hire. The first years of the Foundation were heady, building a three-person staff and creating a structure in which the Foundation could move forward. Branding efforts were launched, relationships with local nonprofits and donors were forged, and new initiatives were developed.

Two and a half years into the venture, the ED was recruited back into the international development arena and left the Black Diamond Foundation with fairly short notice. Surprised and unprepared for this sudden departure, the Board of Directors decided to move an existing senior staff member into the leadership role on an interim basis, giving the organization time to consider their next move.

While the Interim Director was also a seasoned professional, the Board felt it necessary to initiate a search for a permanent ED with more international contacts and experience. Although several qualified professionals applied for the position, none of them were willing to relocate and the search failed. As a result, the Interim Director was moved permanently into the position as ED, becoming the second chief executive of the Black Diamond Foundation.

Things went well under the guidance of this new ED. With deep ties to the local and regional nonprofit community and a keen sense of how best to blend local and international interests, she excelled and so did the Foundation. Funding was secured to bring in a new experienced senior staff member to help the ED expand capacity. The three current staff members were happy with the new hire and

 DOI: 10.4324/9781003387800-14

the direction of the organization, the Board was happy, and donors were happy to fund the solid programming coming out of the Foundation. All was well until the ED needed to take early retirement due to circumstances beyond her control. The Foundation's Board found itself in the unenviable position of looking for another Executive Director—the third in its five short years of existence.

Determined to take their time to make sure the next ED would have longevity and durability, the Board hired an Interim Director to buy the time necessary to search for the 'right' person. This new Interim Director, accepted the role with the clear understanding that she was temporary—hopefully one year, but no longer than 18 months—and she would be keeping the organization afloat, but not tackling any new initiatives. She had phenomenal administrative skills and an abiding respect for the core work done by the Foundation, but she had no practical experience developing relationships or ties to the community doing the work. The senior staff member stepped up to take on some of the relationship-building duties the Interim Director was unable to fulfill, and between the two along with the remaining two staff members, the Foundation was able to remain on autopilot and even make some small gains while the Board contemplated its next move. Little did they know that just months later, the senior staff member would be offered a position at a regional nonprofit organization, giving him a large salary bump as well as the opportunity to take the helm of several groundbreaking initiatives. It was a job he could not pass up, and the Black Diamond Foundation found itself with an Interim Director and two experienced, but junior level, staff members running the organization while the Board searched for the next ED.

During this time, one of the junior staffers was moved up to the recently vacated senior staff position, and a new part-time position was added bringing the staff total to 3.5 alongside

the Interim Director. The staff worked hard to keep the organization on track, continuing to maintain the already established relationships and programs and trying to inch the organization forward. The Board had not given up on its dream of acquiring a seasoned, international professional in the Executive Director position, so a new international search was initiated for the ED of the Black Diamond Foundation. The first search failed to turn up a qualified applicant, so the Board rewrote the job description and adjusted the salary level, and another search was initiated. This search was successful, and after 18 months, the fourth Executive Director was hired during the Black Diamond Foundation's eighth year of existence.

This ED came onboard with great promise. The Foundation's Board had been unable to find the international professional they sought, instead deciding between two candidates: a local experienced female and a regionally experienced male with *some* international experience. Two Board members had very strong opinions on the candidates; they liked the female candidate, but wanted to bring in someone who wasn't 'home-grown'—they felt they needed an 'outsider' to build on the prestige they sought for the Foundation. They were insistent on this, and bullied other Board members to vote their way.

This ED was the first male Director of the Foundation, bringing with him a solid reputation in the domestic field and some work internationally. While he did not live locally, he did live in the region. The new ED had a decidedly hands-off approach to running the organization and he had some issues warming up to the community. Staff was hopeful that they had a solid new leader, but community members and donors were unsure—what was happening at the Foundation that made the ED position look like a game of musical chairs?

As the first year of his Directorship concluded, both staff and the organization's primary constituents realized that a mistake had been made. This ED was struggling to lead the organization. Stakeholder relationships faltered, there were few new initiatives and little enthusiasm. The staff became despondent and approached the Board with issues they thought needed to be addressed.

The Board, hopeful that the ED just needed a little more time to adjust, signaled to staff that no changes would be made. One by one, the three remaining staff members made plans to leave the organization. By the time one staff member had departed for a new job and the other two staff members (including the senior staff member) were job hunting, the Board recognized that the leadership of the ED was not working out as planned. The ED saw the writing on the wall and resigned. Now, the Black Diamond Foundation would be looking for its fifth ED in only nine years.

The Board slowly came to consensus that it was unlikely that they would find a seasoned professional with international experience, willing to move to their small, peri-urban community. The two Board members who had been insistent on hiring an 'outsider' admitted the damage that befell the organization by insisting on such narrow parameters. Instead of launching an international search, they agreed to conduct a local search, and named an Interim Director to lead the organization while a search was conducted.

This new Interim Director—technically the fifth ED—was the 'home-grown' candidate they had passed up during the previous search. She was respected by the community, admired by the two remaining (but job hunting) staff, lived locally, and had a solid plan to finally move the organization forward. This local professional had a mix of administrative skills and a deep passion for the mission of the Foundation. She

also made it clear that while she was happy to be the interim leader, she would be applying to become the 'real' Director in time. She had a clear understanding of the damage that had been done in the past years with revolving leadership, and cast a vivid plan of how she would get the Black Diamond Foundation back on track and thriving. Remaining staff were ecstatic; they abandoned their own job searches in order to support the Interim Director and be part of the team implementing new initiatives. The Board promised to have a new search conducted within the year, and while other candidates did make it to the final round it was apparent that the 'home-grown' candidate who was doing an excellent job as Interim Director was clearly the best candidate for the job.

The Black Diamond Foundation welcomed the sixth ED just in time to celebrate the organization's tenth anniversary. Had the many leadership changes over the years permanently damaged their reputation and ability to serve, or could the Foundation move forward and build capacity to fulfill its mission?

Discussion Questions

1. Reviewing the timeline, is there a clear sense of why the Foundation's Executive Director position was such a revolving door? Please discuss.
2. Could the Board have done anything to prevent such frequent changes, or were those unavoidable?
3. Describe and discuss the ways in which frequent leadership changes can hinder the progress of an organization.
4. Could the work of a community organizer be useful for affecting the stability of a local Foundation's leadership?

Best Laid Plans
Challenges in Strategic Planning

BETSY HULL, BENJAMIN S. BINGLE AND C. KENNETH MEYER

The Southeast Illinois University College of Education's Literacy Clinic provides reading support services for K-12 students, high quality practicum experiences for graduate students, continuing education, and professional development opportunities for reading specialists. Established 60 years ago, the clinic also supports university courses leading to the reading teacher endorsement and reading specialist licensure. The clinic is primarily funded with appropriated College of Education funds, which are diminishing. Revenue is also earned through fee-for-service programming, literacy grant funds, and via contracts with a local elementary school. The College has voiced its hope for a more self-sustaining funding model.

Over time, the clinic's services have evolved and leadership duties have been assigned to tenured faculty in the College of Education's Department of Instruction. For many years, the clinic director was Dr. Lisa Smith, a well-respected professor of literacy. Dr. Smith worked tirelessly to sustain programming to the community while providing clinical opportunities for Southeast Illinois University students. In 2014, when Dr. Smith was promoted to Dean of the College of Education, her clinic director position was filled with several interim directors who struggled to provide the same service level without the institutional knowledge that Dr. Smith possessed.

In 2017, Sheila—the third interim director in as many years—approached Annie, the department chair, with concerns. She voiced apprehension about the static level of programming, the need for additional revenue, as well as her desire to see more engagement with the department and college faculty.

Together, they asked Becky, a Master of Public Administration graduate student, for suggestions. After hearing their concerns and researching the clinic's recent client and program data, Becky proposed that the clinic embark on its first strategic plan. Working as a team, the three established four objectives of the plan:

1. To describe the clinic's current condition and operating environment.
2. To define the clinic's mission, mandates, and vision.
3. To identify strategic directions and tools to assess future opportunities.
4. To identify measurements of success toward the clinic's strategic goals.

Over the next six months, the team worked through a strategic planning process with Becky's assistance. First, they compiled community client data, identified courses that engaged with the clinic, and researched the clinic's programming since its inception. They also identified the following stakeholder groups, group members, and actions they would take to engage each group in the process:

Stakeholder Group	Group Members	Action
Faculty	Literacy/Reading Faculty, Bilingual/ESL Faculty, Special Education Faculty	Focus Groups
Professional Advisory Committee	Internal (University) and External (In-Service) Committee Members	Online Survey
Local Educators	Teachers and Administrators from District #421 and District #422	Online Survey (random sample)
Clinic Staff	Office Support Specialist, Graduate Assistants, Tutors, Reading Specialists	Online Survey
Local Public Library Staff	Executive and/or Youth Directors	On-site Interviews at Library Locations
Parents of Clinic Clients	Parents	Written Survey (random sample)
College of Education Dean	Dr. Lisa Smith	Interview

All seven stakeholder groups were engaged with interesting and often robust results. Using various methods of engagement brought many opinions to the surface and Becky was excited that the strategic planning process was moving along. In fact, she found herself able to incorporate many of the lessons she learned during a strategic planning course she had taken the previous semester via her MPA program.

As Becky was summarizing these results to report to the team and to various university leaders, Annie—the department chair—announced her resignation. While Becky and Sheila were disappointed, they decided it was best to continue with the report and prepared a SWOT analysis (see Appendix A) and the following summary.

Overall, the clinic has an excellent reputation. Its location, design, content area experts, and most importantly, its purpose to assist youth in developing literary skills, are all strengths to

be recognized. However, feedback from both internal and external stakeholders revealed the need for identifying a clear mission of the clinic before acting on collaboration ideas. Additionally, marketing efforts must accompany the mission to gain exposure for the clinic.

Phase 1 produced a great deal of positive feedback when looking to the clinic's future. In the original process plan, Phase 1 included development of the clinic's mission, vision, and values. Yet, in light of recent personnel changes, it was decided to delay the mission, vision, and values discussions until Phase 2 when clinic leadership can be determined.

An updated strategic plan team will be assembled in Phase 2 under new leadership and will be responsible for assessing the feedback presented here in Phase 1 and ultimately will be establishing goals and objectives and an action plan for implementation. It is recommended that the team be comprised of several internal and external stakeholders to be fully representative.

Under the new interim department chair, Carrie, Phase 2 continued. Becky and Sheila asked five more individuals (faculty and clinic tutors) to help evaluate the newly developed College of Education Strategic Action Planning Framework. They also asked a few others to join the planning team: a community school district representative, the assistant clinic director/graduate assistant, and the college finance director to assist in a productive collaborative goal-setting session.

The strategic objectives and goal-setting sessions were productive. With diverse team members at the table, ideas surfaced to address the findings of the stakeholder engagement. With Becky's assistance, the group brainstormed and continued to narrow down the goals and objectives.

While Becky was summarizing the results of Phase 2, several more employee changes surfaced. Sheila decided to retire and a former graduate assistant was named new interim director. Carrie's interim chair appointment came to an end and was she was replaced with a new permanent department chair.

After several unsuccessful attempts to convene new leadership and report the progress on the clinic's strategic planning process, Becky decided to take a permanent position with a nonprofit organization in the area. Since that time, she often thinks about how the process could have been different and led to a successful strategic plan.

Discussion Questions

1. Was the clinic ready to engage in strategic planning? What do you believe to be essential elements to consider before an organization begins a strategic planning process? Discuss why the elements you identified are so vital.

2. Are there aspects of the strategic planning process that you would have changed? If so, what would you have done differently and why?

3. Evaluate the SWOT analysis in Appendix A and discuss. Given what the case reveals about programming, revenue, and staffing, do you agree with what is outlined in the SWOT analysis?

4. Discuss organizational leadership turnover and how it impacted the clinic's strategic planning process.

5. In this case, the clinic never finished the development of their strategic plan. What recommendations do you have for organizations that do complete their plans? How can organizations successfully implement a strategic plan?

Appendix A—SWOT Analysis

	Opportunities	*Threats*
Strengths	EXTERNAL: ✓ Local educators want to be engaged ✓ Local libraries have collaboration ideas ✓ Centrally located; public transportation available ✓ Strong donor base ✓ Reputable naming donor INTERNAL: ✓ Faculty expertise in content area and grant writing; research, teaching, and professional service opportunities ✓ Spacious floor plan ✓ Abundant resources in student employees and graduate assistants	EXTERNAL: ✓ Local competitors ✓ Mission confusion among local nonprofits INTERNAL: ✓ Change in department/clinic leadership ✓ Changing higher-education environment ✓ Faculty groups not aligned
Weaknesses	EXTERNAL: ✓ Small number of clinic staff to address rising bilingual population ✓ Mission not clear to public ✓ Lack of collaboration with schools/nonprofits INTERNAL: ✓ Multiple objectives ✓ No strategic plan ✓ Lack of marketing/ communication staff ✓ Lack of budget analysis staff ✓ Lack of fundraising staff	EXTERNAL: ✓ Fee for service/socioeconomic demographics ✓ Financial base is not guaranteed INTERNAL: ✓ Change in department/clinic leadership ✓ Competing demands for philanthropy ✓ Resource constraints

PART IV

INNOVATION, CAPACITY, AND COLLABORATIONS

Whether innovations originate in the nonprofit sector or as part of the larger environment is rather unimportant. In this country, the free-market business sector, with profits as its driving force, has thrived on innovation arguably more than in any other country in history. Government agencies, too, have sought to be innovative in order to find solutions to complex "wicked problems"; to effectively address political, economic, and social needs; and to save taxpayers money. Nonprofit organizations do not exist separate from their environment: the existence, roles, functions, and revenues of nonprofits are affected by changes in these other two sectors as well as by technology and ideology, and the nonprofit culture has always had innovation as one of its guiding goals.[1]

Facebook, Twitter, YouTube, Tumblr, TikTok, SharePoint, and myriad others are part and parcel of today's vernacular, and there are thousands of other examples of how technology has changed the way nonprofits have built their capacity to get their message out and to collaborate with others. For example, the National Marrow Donor Program's "Be the Match" registry uses database and communication technology to gather information about volunteers willing to donate bone marrow and connects them with patients, doctors, and researchers on a scale hard to imagine a few years ago. Caring Bridge provides free websites that connect people experiencing significant health challenges to family and friends. The Generation Project sends gifts from young donors to teachers and students in need. Obviously, technological advances are changing the type of work in which nonprofit organizations are engaged and how they accomplish the work they have been doing all along.[2]

Innovation—an integral part of capacity building—has been defined as a multistage process involving leaders, coworkers, and components including organizational culture and climate.[3] It also refers to a process of turning opportunities into new ideas and putting these into widely used practices.[4] Nonprofits that are creative strive to be close to and in tune with the needs of their service recipients. At the same time, they must also be innovative in order to successfully build the capacity to meet the needs and wishes of funders and other stakeholders. As an example, nonprofits have been viewed as innovative contracting partners for government agencies seeking to save money. Their flexible service delivery models are attractive, but they also must find ways to produce the accountability reports required by government agencies and other funders. In a 2012 survey conducted by the Urban Institute, the most frequently cited problems with contracting with government "involved governments' complicated and time consuming application and reporting requirements."[5] Paradoxically, the amount of US government money flowing to the human services, the arts, and environmental protection prior to the pandemic had declined steadily and sometimes dramatically.[6]

 DOI: 10.4324/9781003387800-16

Moreover, states, counties, and municipalities have not been eager to replace declining federal funds when tax and deficit reductions continue to command high public support.[7]

Innovation and Leadership

The leadership arrangements in most nonprofits are ideal for creating and supporting innovation. Leadership is a chief factor that influences or stifles creativity and innovation.[8] A nonprofit's board of directors should bring together people from a variety of backgrounds in order to ensure a diversity of talents and perspectives for generating innovative ideas. And board leadership is shared with the executive director who has their own distinctive perspectives and talents. Nonprofit staff members and a solid volunteer base can also bring a variety of backgrounds and interests together to help innovation grow and thrive.

> In the organizational context, innovation can occur in products, processes, or services. It can be incremental or radical and it can occur at various levels in an organization, from management groups and departments to project teams and even individuals.[9]

Of course, the number of people involved an organization does not ensure innovation. Nonprofits must be on guard against groupthink and other potentially stultifying scenarios. "In the management of the innovation process, destroying poor ideas often is as important as nurturing good ones; in this way, scarce resources can be released and good ideas spotlighted."[10]

Innovation and Social Entrepreneurship

Nonprofits face a never-ending struggle to find new sources of revenue (see Part V). Many have faced the funding challenge by becoming more entrepreneurial. They pursue businesses and businesslike ventures. *Nonprofit entrepreneurship* is "a proactive style of management through which leaders of nonprofit organizations seek to implement change through new organizational and programmatic initiatives."[11] Dennis Young offers three indicators of the importance of entrepreneurship to nonprofit organizations: (1) the rapid growth of the nonprofit sector signals the presence of considerable entrepreneurial activity; (2) many nonprofits have been in existence for only a short period of time, a trend that "reflects the classic mode of nonprofit entrepreneurship—individuals or groups motivated to address a social, health, environmental, or other issue, unsatisfied with existing services and aware of potential resources to support their interests, forming their own organizations"; and (3) many nonprofits were established for the specific purpose of introducing change in society. Entrepreneurship thus has been a factor in "the sector's ability to transform concern over social issues . . . into new operating programs and services."[12]

In response to Young's indicators, many nonprofit organizations have increased the level of professionalism of their staff and management and have recruited individuals with business backgrounds for their boards. As a result, many nonprofits have become aggressively commercial, often competing with for-profit firms for the same business.[13] Changing from an organization focused on operations to an entrepreneurial organization is exciting, but it also can be frustrating for board and staff and can cause "mission creep," which can easily lead to the loss of identity, purpose, and "spirit."

> On the one hand, [an entrepreneurial organization] offers the excitement of breakthrough thinking, compelling life stories, and potentially dramatic progress against daunting global problems

such as hunger, poverty, and disease. . . . On the other hand, the field offers fewer evidence-based insights on how social entrepreneurs can improve the odds of impact. Given few tools for separating the wheat from the chaff, social entrepreneurs are left with long menus of advice. As a result, they often reinvent the wheel as they struggle to discern lessons from a relatively small number of exemplary peers.[14]

Commercialization: Blurring the Line Between Businesses and Nonprofits

Nonprofit organizations in many subsectors have ventured into a variety of commercial markets.[15] Figures and percentages differ according to definitions and sources of information, but in 2020, public charities in the US reported total revenues of $2.04 trillion.[16] Fees from the sale of services and goods, which include tuition payments, hospital patient revenues, and ticket sales, are estimated to represent approximately 70 percent of their revenues. This number includes large charitable nonprofits such as hospitals and higher education institutions. When these larger institutions are excluded, sources of revenue distributions change substantially. Smaller nonprofit organizations are less dependent on fees for services and more dependent on private contributions and government contracts and grants.

Some are critical of government contracts being awarded to large, politically astute nonprofits that are subsequently portrayed as models of entrepreneurial success, which smaller and less politically connected nonprofits cannot hope to emulate. The *Nonprofit Quarterly* cites nonprofit social entrepreneurialism as just one more example of government largesse paid to large, influential, politically connected nonprofits.

To most small local nonprofits, the concept of social entrepreneurialism that they hear touted by their funders implies earning income from business-related activities. But some of the most highly publicized nonprofit social entrepreneurs that have been held up as models for the nonprofit sector have achieved part of their entrepreneurialism by success at the public trough. For example, due to its size, entrepreneurial aggressiveness, and solid political contacts, a significant part of the funding success of Teach for America (TFA) is attributable to attracting juicy government earmarks, not simply successful competitive grantsmanship.[17]

Despite the concerns, many nonprofits are engaging in entrepreneurial activities and often are successfully competing directly with for-profit businesses. Nonprofits in the health care subsector, for example, have been competing directly and aggressively with for-profit businesses since the 1970s.[18] Many nonprofit hospitals and clinics own for-profit subsidiaries that provide corporate wellness programs, manage condominium physicians' offices, and operate private health clubs.[19] Nonprofits in the mental health, intellectual challenges, and other fields that serve mostly low-income populations regularly buy and manage companies that operate apartment houses, pet stores, laundries, and other historically low-wage service businesses.

> Major museums, such as Chicago's Art Institute, Shedd Aquarium, and the Field Museum of Natural History . . . have begun holding afterhours cocktail parties that compete with local taverns. . . . Revenue is produced through admission fees and drink sales.[20]

Although the unrelated business income tax (UBIT) limits nonprofit activity that competes with market-based firms, many commercial ventures have proven enormously successful for nonprofits.

Commercial entrepreneurial-type ventures can contribute to the financial health of a nonprofit and provide benefits for clients. Many entrepreneurial nonprofits have generated revenues that have been "plowed back" into more or better services, thereby benefiting clients and advancing their mission.

They also can create employment opportunities for current and former clients that otherwise would not have existed.[21] It is easy to understand why the commercial activities of nonprofit organizations have occasionally caused loud cries of "unfair competition," particularly from small businesses.[22]

Other developments have contributed to the commercialization of the nonprofit sector. First, for-profit businesses have been "invading turf" that historically has "belonged" to the nonprofit sector.[23] For-profit chains have replaced nonprofits as the primary providers of hospital care in the United States. Private emergency medical services (EMS) companies have all but driven nonprofit ambulance squads out of urban and suburban markets and made major inroads in many rural areas. Businesses also have aggressively entered the mental health and substance abuse fields, as well as day care centers, trade and technical schools, and youth and adult corrections. Nonprofits and for-profits thus are competing with each other in fields that used to be each other's "turf." To compete successfully, nonprofits have had to become more businesslike.

Second, the professionalism of nonprofit organization managers has increased dramatically in recent decades. Master's degree programs and concentrations in nonprofit organization management have proliferated at a dizzying pace over the past decades, with correspondingly dramatic increases in the number of students and graduates.[24] And many larger nonprofit organizations recruit business executives who, in a few subsectors, are receiving "Fortune 500" wages.[25]

Third, more business executives and fewer government and nonprofit organization managers sit on boards of trustees than was the case 30 years ago. Overall, boards of trustees have tended to become more business oriented.[26]

Finally, mutually beneficial venture partnerships between businesses and nonprofits have become commonplace in recent decades. Planned giving programs, cause-related marketing ventures, loaned executives, and businesses using higher education research facilities and faculty (rather than investing in their own) are a few examples of the array of these partnerships.

When nonprofits enter commercial ventures, they must carefully follow regulations to avoid or limit unrelated business income taxes (UBIT) and to preserve their tax-exempt status with the IRS and state taxing authorities. The stakes are higher, however, than worries about UBIT.

> The greatest peril is not that nonprofits may ultimately be driven out of the social service market-place. Rather, the danger is that in their struggle to become more viable competitors in the short term, nonprofit organizations will be forced to compromise the very assets that made them so vital to society in the first place.[27]

Lester Salamon asserts that the nonprofit sector is facing four challenges "of crisis proportions."[28] Each of these challenges by itself represents a serious danger to the sector's ability to survive in its current form. Of Salamon's four categories of challenges—fiscal challenges, economic challenges, effectiveness challenges, and legitimacy challenges—the crisis of legitimacy is the most problematic. The single greatest force behind this crisis is the sector's inability to find or successfully define its role in between the government and business sectors. Citizens and elected officials alike are questioning whether the "commercialized" nonprofit sector should continue to receive favorable tax treatment and preferred contracting status with government. William Ryan asks, "Is the common interest best served when nonprofits aim to compete on for-profit terms?"[29] In the United States, we still have a mental image of a nonprofit as a community-based organization that organizes volunteers to administer to local people in need—not as a multi-state conglomerate with a director who earns a six-or seven-digit salary.[30] Unless the nonprofit sector is able to (re)define its role in the minds and perceptions of citizens and elected officials, the crisis of legitimacy eventually may disable it. According to one scholar:

> Because government funding has declined precipitously and the reporting requirements have become increasingly onerous, it appears that many nonprofits are abandoning their mission in

order to gain revenues through the market. This could cause nonprofits to win and lose simultaneously. Can nonprofits win contracts and still be responsive to their clients and communities? Can they really compete long-term in markets dominated by for-profit firms? Unlike their for-profit counterparts, if faced with compromising their social missions, nonprofits may conclude that winning isn't everything.[31]

Readings Reprinted in Part IV

The readings reprinted in Part IV address a variety of innovations, opportunities, and problems that most nonprofit managers and board members face when becoming part of a network or a collaboration. Although there are many hurdles to cross, managing joint efforts is necessary for solving complex community problems.

"A Manager's Guide to Choosing and Using Collaborative Networks" by H. Brinton Milward and Keith Provan presents findings from a report funded through the IBM Center for the Business of Government. Although the reading is targeted at government managers, we include it here because nonprofits are actors—and often the primary actors—in these networks.

Milward and Provan provide a glossary for "networking newcomers" that includes terms such as *networks*, *nodes*, and *linkages*. For example, they present Agranoff's definition of networks as "formal and informal structures, composed of representatives, from governmental and nongovernmental agencies working interdependently to exchange information and/or jointly formulate and implement policies that are usually designed for action through their respective organizations."[32] Milward and Provan identify the characteristics of four types of networks—service implementation, information diffusion, problem solving, and community capacity building—and how the tasks associated with managing each of these vary. "Public managers must understand what type of network they are managing and what its purpose is before they can manage it effectively."

The second reading in Part IV is "Effective Leadership in Network Collaboration: Lessons Learned from Continuum of Care Homeless Programs," by Hee Soun Jang, Jesus N. Valero, and Kyujin Jung. As with the Milward and Provan reading, this research report was funded by the IBM Center for the Business of Government. The authors ask two primary questions: (1) What does effective collaboration look like—and does leadership matter? And (2) If leadership is important, what specific skills and qualities are valuable for leaders to possess and/or develop in order to lead successful collaborative efforts? In answering these questions, the authors provide the reader with insightful "lessons learned" and offer some action steps for leaders in collaborative networks.

The final reading in Part IV is "How Does a Board of Directors Influence Within- and Cross-Sector Nonprofit Collaboration?" by Jennifer Ihm and Michelle Shumate. The authors examine and discuss the significant yet largely unexamined roles that board members play in nonprofit collaborations. "Processes, such as finding prospective partners, creating common ground with a partner, and establishing appropriate collaborative governance implicate nonprofit board members" and examines "the role of board members' social and human capital on nonprofit collaboration with other nonprofits, businesses, and government agencies."

Case Studies in Part IV

In the first case study in Part IV, "Fostering Growth Through Capacity Building," the authors place the reader in the scenario of a struggling but highly regarded nonprofit in Anguilla that is seeking to build capacity with the help of consultants at J&M Consultancy. The reader is situated at a bird's eye level to evaluate the actors and perspectives offered and to evaluate existing areas of capacity building in need of attention at the small, respected arts academy presented in the case. A performance evaluation assessment tool is offered by J&M Consultancy for the reader's consideration.

The final case, "Show Me the Money" by C. Kenneth Meyer and Stacy Gibbs, asks the reader to analyze the privacy and accountability issues that are raised in enacting a comprehensive medical record system. In reviewing the case and responding to the managerial questions asked, the reader must decide how to balance the needs of a variety of stakeholders when a new technology is introduced.

Notes

1. See, for example, Jay M. Shafritz, J. Steven Ott, and Yong Suk Jang, "Theories of Organizations and Environments" and "Theories of Organizations and Society," in Jay M. Shafritz, J. Steven Ott, and Yong Suk Jang, eds., *Classics of Organization Theory*, 8th ed. (Boston: Cengage/Wadsworth, 2016).

2. Kelly M. Hannum, Jennifer Deal, Liz Livingston Howard, Linshuang Lu, Marian N. Ruderman, Sarah Stawiski, Nancie Zane, and Rick Price, *Emerging Leadership in Nonprofit Organizations: Myths, Meaning, and Motivations* (Greensboro, NC: Center for Creative Leadership, 2011).

3. Susanne G. Scott and Reginald A. Bruce, "Determinants of Innovative Behaviour: A Path Model of Individual Innovation in the Workplace," *Academy of Management Journal* 37 (1994): 580–607.

4. Joe Tidd, John Bessant, and Keith Pavitt, *Managing Innovation: Integrating Technological, Market, and Organizational Change*, 2nd ed. (Chichester, UK: Wiley, 2001); also, Adela J. McMurray, Md. Mazharul Islam, James C. Sarros, and Andrew Pirola-Merlo, "Workplace Innovation in a Nonprofit Organization," *Nonprofit Management and Leadership* 23 no. 3 (Spring 2013): 367–388.

5. Sarah L. Pettijohn and Elizabeth T. Boris, "Contracts and Grants Between Human Service Nonprofits and Government: Comparative Analysis," Urban Institute Brief 4, July 2014, www.urban.org/UploadedPDF/413189-Contracts-and-Grants-between-Human-Service-Nonprofits-and-Government.pdf

6. Lester M. Salamon, "Trends and Challenges," in Lester M. Salamon, *America's Nonprofit Sector: A Primer*, 3rd ed. (New York: Foundation Center, 2012): 245–269; see also Virginia A. Hodgkinson and Murray S. Weitzman, *Nonprofit Almanac, 1996–1997: Dimensions of the Independent Sector* (San Francisco: Bass, 1996).

7. Heather R. McLeod, "The Devolution Revolution—Are Nonprofits Ready?" *WhoCares* (Fall 1995): 36–42.

8. McMurray et al., "Workplace Innovation in a Nonprofit Organization," 370.

9. David O'Sullivan and Lawrence Dooley, *Applying Innovation* (Thousand Oaks, CA: Sage Publications, 2009): 4.

10. Ibid.

11. Dennis R. Young, "Nonprofit Entrepreneurship," in *The International Encyclopedia of Public Policy and Administration*, Jay M. Shafritz, ed. (Boulder, CO: Westview Press, 1998): 1506–1509.

12. Ibid. 1507.

13. Salamon, "Trends and Challenges."

14. Paul C. Light, "Searching for Social Entrepreneurs: Who They Might Be, Where They Might Be Found, What They Do," in Rachel Mosher-Williams, *Research on Entrepreneurship: Understanding and Contributing to An Emerging Field*, Association for Research on Nonprofit Organizations and Voluntary Action (ARNOVA) Occasional Paper Series 1, no. 3 (Washington, DC: Aspen Institute, 2006): 13–37.

15. Burton A. Weisbrod, "The Future of the Nonprofit Sector: Its Entwining with Private Enterprise and Government," *Journal of Policy Analysis and Management* 16 no. 4 (1997): 541–555.

16. Urban Institute. The Nonprofit Sector in Brief 2019, https://nccs.urban.org/publication/nonprofit-sector-brief-2019#the-nonprofit-sector-in-brief-2019

17. Rick Cohen, "Social Entrepreneurship at the Public Trough," *Nonprofit Quarterly*, February 13, 2009, accessed March 15, 2011, https://nonprofitquarterly.org/policysocial-context/1539-social-entrepreneurialism-at-the-public-trough.html

18. Since the 1990s, however, nonprofit hospitals have been "losing" in the competition.

19. Montague Brown, "Commentary: The Commercialization of America's Voluntary Health Care System," *Health Care Management Review* 21 no. 3 (1996): 13–18; see also Malik Hasan, "Let's End the Nonprofit Charade," *New England Journal of Medicine* 334 no. 16 (April 18, 1996): 1055–1058.

20. Burton A. Weisbrod, "Commercialism and the Road Ahead," in Burton A. Weisbrod, *To Profit or Not to Profit: The Commercial Transformation of the Nonprofit Sector* (Cambridge: Cambridge University Press, 1998): 288.

21. Robert Egger, *Begging for Change: The Dollars and Sense of Making Nonprofits Responsive, Efficient, and Rewarding for All* (New York: HarperCollins, 2004).

22. US Small Business Administration, *Unfair Competition by Nonprofit Organizations with Small Business: An Issue for the 1980s,* 3rd ed. (Washington, DC: US Government Printing Office, June 1984); see also James T. Bennett and Thomas J. DiLorenzo, *Unfair Competition: The Profits of Nonprofits* (Lanham, MD: Hamilton Press, 1989).

23. William P. Ryan, "The New Landscape for Nonprofits," *Harvard Business Review* (January-February 1999): 127–136.

24. Roseanne M. Mirabella, "Education Director of Nonprofit Management Education, *The Nonprofit Quarterly,* Spring Issues (2009, 2008, 2007, 2006).

25. For example, *US News and World Report'*s October 2, 1995, cover story exclaimed: "Tax Exempt! Many nonprofits look and act like normal companies—running businesses, making money. So why aren't they paying Uncle Sam?"

26. Melissa Middleton Stone, "Competing Contexts: The Evolution of a Nonprofit Organization's Governance System in Multiple Environments," *Administration and Society* 28 no. 1 (May 1996): 61–89.

27. Ryan, "The New Landscape for Nonprofits," 128.

28. Salamon, "Trends and Challenges."

29. Ryan, "The New Landscape for Nonprofits," 128.

30. Edward T. Pound, Gary Cohen, and Penny Loeb, "Tax Exempt! Many Nonprofits Look and Act Like Normal Companies—Running Businesses, Making Money. So Why Aren't They Paying Uncle Sam?" *US News & World Report* (October 2, 1995): 36–39, 42–46, 51.

31. Ryan, "The New Landscape for Nonprofits," 136.

32. Robert Agranoff, "Leveraging Networks: A Guide for Public Managers Working Across Organizations," in *Collaboration: Using Networks and Partnerships,* edited by John M. Kamensky and Thomas J. Burlin (Lanham, MD: Rowman & Littlefield, 2004): 63.

CHAPTER 7

A Manager's Guide to Choosing and Using Collaborative Networks

H. Brinton Milward and Keith G. Provan

Originally published online by IBM Center for the Business of Government, 2006 (www.businessof government.org). Reprinted with permission.

In what he calls the "global public management revolution," Don Kettl has identified six common ideas behind the public management revolution: "the search for greater productivity; more public reliance on private markets; a stronger orientation toward service; more decentralization from national to subnational governments; increased capacity to devise and track public policy; and tactics to enhance accountability for results" (Kettl 2005).

Instead of organizing, providing, and managing services on its own, government has increasingly turned to contracting out these services, most often to nonprofit, but sometimes to for-profit, organizations. This increased contracting out of services has meant that public managers at all levels have had to coordinate and oversee the activities of the many organizations that government funds to ensure the smooth provision of multiple services to clients. Thus, government must not only manage its own internal operations but it must also manage multi-organization networks (Goldsmith and Eggers 2004).

These core ideas in the revolution in public management have led public managers to seek alternatives to traditional bureaucratic organizations to provide services to citizens in innovative ways. Two of these ways are *contracting out* services to third parties and relying on *networks of* public, nonprofit, and for-profit organizations, instead of a bureaucratic hierarchy. Contracts may be a way in which two or more organizations are linked, but a set of contractual relationships is not the same as a network (Johnston and Romzek 2000). Networks may be funded by grants, contracts, or fee-for-service arrangements (or a mixture of all three), but they use collaboration as a way of dealing with problems in a coordinated fashion that would be impossible for just one organization. The idea behind contracting is exactly the opposite of collaboration—competition, where two or more organizations are forced to compete for the contract. The network logic is that collaboration is needed to deal with problems that don't fit neatly within the boundaries of a single organization.[1]

Collaborative networks are seen as appropriate devices to tackle public management problems like homelessness, child welfare, and terrorism. Since the problem is bigger than any

DOI: 10.4324/9781003387800-17

organization, collaborating with other organizations is necessary if there is any hope of making progress in effectively managing the problem.

There are many kinds of networks in the world. Each individual is part of a social network that links one to others in a variety of ways—friends, relatives, work colleagues, and so on. Each person is called a "node" in network terminology. Relationships, or linkages, among a group of individuals are commonly referred to as a social network, and the network as a whole is the pattern of linkages among the individuals.[2] In this report, we examine networks of organizations—or what scholars call interorganizational networks—and discuss how managing a network or managing in a network differs from managing an organization.

Like a social network, an interorganizational network consists of linkages among a set of nodes, but instead of people, the nodes are organizations. The term organizational network has many different definitions. Most note that they consist of multiple organizations that are legally autonomous. Relationships (linkages) are based on cooperation and collaboration and, in the public sector, law and funding holds them together:

> [N]etworks of public organizations . . . [involve] formal and informal structures, composed of representatives from governmental and nongovernmental agencies working interdependently to exchange information and/or jointly formulate and implement policies that are usually designed for action through their respective organizations.
>
> (Agranoff 2004, 63)

Public Management Networks: Types and Purpose

The currency of a network is the trust and reciprocity that exist among its members. As Robert Axelrod (1984) famously said, trust and reciprocity "lengthen the shadow of the future" and reward those who choose to cooperate, because people want to work with them again; therefore, the more trust and reciprocity in the network, the greater the ability of the network to accomplish shared goals. The task of network managers is to increase the stock of trust and reciprocity by creating incentives (using resources) and to increase their collaborative skills to build relationships within the network to accomplish network goals, whether it is environmental cleanup, alleviating homelessness, reducing teen pregnancy, or responding to a natural disaster.

Although much is now known about public networks, there is still a great deal of confusion about how they should be managed. One of the main problems is that most of the work on the topic has drawn few distinctions among the types of public networks that exist or the purposes they serve, while assuming that issues of network management are similar for all networks. From our own fieldwork and from our analysis of the literature on networks, however, we have identified four distinct types of public sector networks. Our argument is a contingent one—public managers must understand what type of network they are managing and what its purpose is before they can manage it effectively. The four types of public networks we discuss here are *service implementation networks, information diffusion networks, problem-solving networks,* and *community-capacity-building networks.* The key characteristics of each type of network are summarized in table 7.1.

Service Implementation Networks

Service implementation networks consist of intergovernmental programs like Temporary Assistance for Needy Families (TANF) and services for those who are seriously mentally ill, the aged, abused and neglected children, and the developmentally disabled, which are often funded by federal grants to the states. From the federal and often the state perspective, the task

TABLE 7.1 Public Management Networks—Types and Key Characteristics

Network Type	Key Characteristics
Service Implementation Networks	• Government funds the service under contract but doesn't directly provide it (frequently health and human services). • Services are jointly produced by two or more organizations. • Collaboration is often between programs of larger organizations. • Horizontal management of service providers is a key task. These can be firms, nonprofits, or government agencies. • A fiscal agent acts as the sole buyer of services. • Key management tasks include encouraging cooperation, negotiating contracts, planning network expansion, etc.
Information Diffusion Networks	• Horizontal and vertical ties between interdependent government agencies. • Primary focus is sharing information across departmental boundaries. • Commonly used for disaster preparedness and other "high uncertainty" problems. • Key network goal is to shape government responses to problems through better communication and collaboration. • May be either designed or emergent.
Problem-Solving Networks	• Primary purpose is to help organizational managers set the agenda for policy related to a critical national or regional problem. • Focus is on solving existing complex problems rather than building relationships for future problems. • Often emerges from information diffusion networks. • Relationships may be temporary, to address a specific problem, and then become dormant after the problem is resolved. • May be either designed or emergent.
Community-Capacity-Building Networks	• Primary goal is to build social capital in community-based settings. • Network purpose is both current and future oriented (i.e., to build the capacity to address future community needs as they arise). • May be created by participants (bottom-up) or by private and government funders (top-down). • Often involves a wide range of agencies with many emergent sub-networks to address different community needs that may arise.

is to manage programs that are lodged in public, private, and nonprofit organizations that actually deliver services directly to clients. The tools in the hands of federal and state managers consist of grants, contracts, rules, and training opportunities that, over time, can help to shape the way a given program is delivered at the local level. For services like this, government effectively becomes the sole buyer of services. Economists refer to this type of market as a *monopsony*.

At the local or state level, managing a service implementation network that actually delivers services is a horizontal management problem involving both assembly and joint production. Using some type of contract or fee-for-service arrangement, the network manager must assemble a set of largely nongovernmental third parties to jointly produce a service like community trauma care or drug and alcohol prevention. The money from each federal or state program usually flows to a lead agency or a network administrative organization, like a mental health authority, whose job it is to arrange for a set of services to be delivered to clients who qualify for the program. Horizontal network management requires a government-designated fiscal agent (like a mental health authority) that issues contracts (sometimes competitively) to specific organizations while urging them to collaborate with one another. Since no one organization delivers all of the services a client is likely to need, collaboration is essential if a client's needs are to be met. Managers of horizontal networks view service integration as their major task as they try to overcome the tendency of networks to fragment, which is why many of the managers we have interviewed think competitive contracting (often in a thin market with few sellers) is an impediment to collaboration. This may be the reason that studies of contracting for social services find that contracting is done no more frequently than required by higher levels of government, and that the same agencies often get the contracts year after year (Smith and Smyth 1996).

Information Diffusion Networks

Information diffusion networks are a common form of network within any level of government. Whether it is a joint task force on intelligence sharing in the wake of 9/11 or a state task force created in the wake of a child protective services

horror story, the job is the same: Interdependent government organizations need to develop the means to share information across departmental boundaries so that disasters have a better chance of being avoided. Unlike the service implementation network, the product of an interagency task force is to shape government's response to problems through better communication and collaboration rather than more effective service provision, as with the service implementation network. It is the shared information that should lead to improved services produced by each agency. A terrorist watch list that combines the resources of the CIA, FBI, and foreign intelligence agencies allows the State Department consular officer to do a better job of screening out threats to the United States who may apply for a visa in a foreign country.

The National Institutes of Health and some medical foundations have managers whose task it is to manage knowledge that flows from the research that they fund, diffusing information among a set of researchers so that everyone in the program is informed of problems, protocols, and findings. The government of Canada has created networks of excellence in many different areas of health to improve information sharing among networks of doctors, researchers, and healthcare professionals. One of the newest networks is called AllerGen, which brings together allergists, geneticists, and immunologists around the funding of a set of research issues that the government of Canada has deemed critical after seeking advice from the community of practice (Snyder and de Souza Briggs 2004) that has coalesced around the study of the genetic basis of allergic disease.

While AllerGen is a *designed* information diffusion network, there are *emergent* information diffusion networks. Big-city police chiefs in cities like Los Angeles, Washington, DC, Chicago, and Las Vegas have banded together out of frustration with the "slow and sometimes grudging way that federal officials share information about terrorist incidents" (Broder 2005,

A12). Spearheaded by William J. Bratton, the [then] Los Angeles police chief, a number of big-city chiefs have instituted their own network to share information about terrorist threats. While acknowledging that the information they receive from the FBI and the Department of Homeland Security is generally of high quality, it is received so slowly that it is rarely actionable. Police chiefs have to deploy officers and cordon off areas in real time if a threat emerges like the London subway or Madrid train bombings, and they view the federal information as more analytical in nature. Federal officials admit that the information they share has to be vetted before it is sent out, which takes time, and the police chiefs want raw, unfiltered information, even if it is later proved to be wrong, since good information received after a terrorist event is worthless.

What is so interesting about this case is that there is a formal, designed network in place where local police chiefs have a place at the table in the Homeland Security Operations Center, whose job is to diffuse information on terrorist threats to police departments all over the country. Chief Bratton is attempting to organize an emergent network in response to perceived weaknesses in this designed network. Bratton is working with the police departments in 10 to 15 US and Canadian cities to share raw data on rapidly emerging terrorist threats. In a twist of irony, the actions of one network serve to create another to remedy the designed network's flaws. Out of this conflict comes a new type of network with a different purpose—a problem-solving network.

Problem-Solving Networks

Problem-solving networks have several different purposes. When an information diffusion network reaches a certain point, it can morph into a problem-solving network that can help managers set the agenda in regard to policy toward a critical national or regional problem.

In a decentralized and devolved political system like the United States has, it can help to shape the implementation of a new policy. After most states deinstitutionalized their mentally ill clients, the Community Support Program of the National Institute of Mental Health proved to be a very effective way of providing information and training to many public and nonprofit mental health managers about how to run a decentralized, community-based mental health system (Weiss 1990).

Problem-solving networks are also used in the case of disasters as a way to quickly solve the ensuing crisis. It can either be designed prior to a problem occurring, like a wildfire incident command system that can be adapted to a variety of settings, or it can emerge in the aftermath of an unanticipated problem. Emergencies of any magnitude are rarely contained within the boundaries of one organization, and public managers have struggled over many years to try to prepare for what [former] Secretary of Defense Donald Rumsfeld calls "known unknowns." This characterization refers to events that we *know* will happen, the only *unknown* being when and where they will happen. Wildfires are an example of a known unknown. In the western United States, generally arid conditions and periodic drought create perfect conditions for seasonal wildfires. Whether started by lightning, a lit cigarette, or a campfire, every summer thousands of acres across the West go up in flames, sometimes threatening major cities like Los Angeles and San Diego.

Given the predictability of wildfires, it makes sense to plan for these occurrences. What has come to be known as the Incident Command System (ICS) was born out of the frustration of the lack of collaboration among agencies and levels of government in the face of these periodic wildfires. Congress required the US Forest Service to design a system to alleviate these problems, and in the 1970s the Forest Service worked with the California Department of Forestry and Fire Protection,

Office of Emergency Services, and local police and fire departments in California to coordinate their firefighting efforts. The ICS has proved so successful in fighting wildfires that all federal agencies are required to use it for managing emergencies.

Community-Capacity-Building Networks

Community-capacity-building networks have become very important in recent years. In the wake of Robert Putnam's pioneering work on social capital, a variety of federal agencies have challenged communities to create partnerships in areas like economic development or the prevention of drug and alcohol abuse (Putnam 1993, 2000). The goal of the network is to build social capital so that communities will be better able to deal with a variety of problems related to education, economic development, crime, and so on. Federal agencies like the Center for Substance Abuse Prevention, which is part of the Substance Abuse and Mental Health Services Administration (SAMHSA) in the Department of Health and Human Services, have given grants to many communities if they will create a prevention partnership organization that will serve as a fiscal agent to coordinate drug and alcohol abuse prevention for youth.

We were involved in one of these grants that created a partnership agency whose job it was to weave together all of the prevention resources in an urban county with a population of just under a million people (Milward and Provan 1998). At the very beginning of the grant, we were hired to map the network of potential partners who were interested in substance abuse prevention. The number of agencies was quite large and included police, school systems, parks and recreation departments, Boys and Girls Clubs, the YMCA, and the YWCA as well as many specific drug and alcohol prevention agencies, some governmental, some nonprofit, and some for-profit. The goal was clear—to increase the

level of community awareness of substance abuse and increase the capacity of the county to decrease the level of youth substance abuse.

This network was both emergent and designed. There had been prior prevention efforts that involved voluntary cooperation, and a group of organizations came together to write the grant proposal, but the Center for Substance Abuse Prevention grant award required that one organization serve as fiscal agent and assume responsibility for network coordination. As an aside, it should be noted that while network researchers often exhibit a bias in favor of emergent networks (Jones, Hesterly, and Borgatti 1997), there is very little evidence to support the assertion that emergent networks are more effective than networks that have been designed or mandated. In this case, a condition of the grant was that the set of substance abuse agencies that submitted the grant would have to create a fiscal agent to receive the funds, promote the cause, manage the network, and monitor its progress through periodic evaluations.

We began our work with the network by conducting meetings with representatives of all of the agencies and getting them to talk about who worked together in regard to substance abuse prevention. We soon found that there were major gaps in the network. The substance abuse agencies operated in one world, the after-school-based programs operated in another, and the police became involved in a crisis or very episodically through programs like DARE in the schools. At a series of meetings with agency representatives, we gave out network questionnaires and asked that the representatives indicate who they had relationships with and the nature of these relationships. Using a network analysis software program,[3] we graphed the relationships so that anyone looking at the results could clearly see which agencies were connected to which other agencies in several different ways—information sharing, referrals, contracts, and joint programming. The response to the analysis was quite interesting.

When the network maps were presented, it verified what leaders of the prevention partnership had been saying—that there were a number of independent networks of substance abuse prevention with little connection between them. In addition, there were some agencies, particularly in the more rural parts of the county, that were completely isolated.

The response to these "network snapshots" was to create a strategic plan to weave the elements of the substance abuse prevention community together much more closely. There was a great deal of discussion about how to bring the isolated agencies to the table and how to bridge the different worlds of substance abuse prevention to create a more coordinated approach to what was clearly a community-wide problem. Seeing the gaps in the networks created a movement to bring the community together around this problem.

Essential Tasks for Network Managers

No doubt there are countless small things that managers can do to enhance the effectiveness of their network. Rather than getting into these details, we propose what we have found to be five broad and essential tasks that managers must perform if their networks are to be successful. The importance of each task is based both on network research and on our extensive consulting experience. A critical point is that each network management task has both network- and organization-level implications. That is, each task is essential both to the role of the managers/networks and to the role of managers operating *in* networks. Effective networks must have both. Managers/networks are concerned with the network as a whole. These are typically individuals who are charged with the task of coordinating overall network activities and, in general, ensuring that network-level goals are set, addressed, and attained. The goals and success

of organizational members become secondary to the network as a whole. Managers *in* networks are individuals who represent their organization within the network. They are managers whose primary loyalty is to their organization, but who must work within a network context, addressing both organization- and network-level goals and objectives. These managers have split missions and, sometimes, split loyalties. The essential tasks of both types of managers are explained below and summarized in table 7.2.

Conclusion

While each type of network (based on purpose) has its own unique characteristics and challenges, all must be managed effectively. To do that, network managers need to accomplish an interrelated series of tasks. Likewise, managers in networks have a challenging set of tasks as well.

To date, most of the literature on networks has focused on discussing their value for addressing complex public problems. Networks have been considered as unique multi-organizational forms that are different from either informal market-based arrangements or formal hierarchy-based organizations. Although the difficulties of networking are often discussed, networks are often thought of as panaceas for problems that cannot be solved by traditional governmental organizations. While networks can be extremely useful for addressing public problems, the reality, of course, is far more complex. In particular, networks are often difficult to form and sustain, and outcomes are not always positive.

What we have argued here is that addressing complex public sector problems effectively is not simply dependent on whether the problem is managed through a hierarchy versus a network. While networks have many advantages over hierarchies, networks can certainly be ineffective and fail. As with organizational hierarchies, effectiveness depends heavily on good management. However, organizational and network

Table 7.2 Management Tasks in Public Networks

Essential Network Management Tasks	Management of Networks	Management in Networks
Management of Accountability	• Determining who is responsible for which outcomes. • Rewarding and reinforcing compliance with network goals. • Monitoring and responding to network "free riders."	• Monitoring your organization's involvement in the network. • Ensuring that dedicated resources are actually used for network activities. • Ensuring that your organization gets credit for network contributions. • Resisting efforts to "free ride."
Management of Legitimacy	• Building and maintaining legitimacy of the network concept, network structures, and network involvement. • Attracting positive publicity, resources, new members, tangible successes, etc.	• Demonstrating to others (members, stakeholders) the value of network participation. • Legitimizing the role of the organization among other network members.
Management of Conflict	• Setting up mechanisms for conflict and dispute resolution. • Acting as a "good faith" broker. • Making decisions that reflect network-level goals and not the specific interests of members.	• Working at the dyad level to avoid and resolve problems with individual network members. • Working inside your organization to act as a "linking pin" to balance organization versus network demands and needs.
Management of Design (Governance Structure)	• Determining which structural governance forms would be most appropriate for network success. • Implementing and managing the structure. • Recognizing when structure should change based on network and participant needs.	• Working effectively with other network participants and with network-level management, based on the governance structure in place. • Accepting some loss of control over network-level decisions.
Management of Commitment	• Getting the "buy-in" of participants. • Working with participants to ensure they understand how network success can contribute to the organization's effectiveness. • Ensuring that network resources are distributed equitably to network participants based on network needs. • Ensuring that participants are well informed about network activities.	• Building commitment within the organization to network-level goals. • Institutionalizing network involvement so that support of network goals and participation goes beyond a single person in the organization.

management are quite different, and the success of networks in addressing public problems depends on effective network management.

Notes

1. In the real world, hard and fast distinctions tend to blur at certain points. Collaboration and contracting come together with what economists call "relational contracting," which is contracting that is based on trust and reciprocity (just like networks) rather than a written contract that specifies what both parties' obligations are in great detail. Relational contracts are typically kept in place as long as they serve the interests of both parties rather than being competitively bid with some frequency. They tend to be used for goods and services where price is less important than quality.

2. For an excellent layman's guide to social network analysis, see Duncan J. Watts, *Six Degrees: The Science of a Connected Age* (New York: W. W. Norton and Company, 2003).

3. The network analysis program we used for mapping the network was UCINET, which is available from Analytic Technologies at www.analytictech.com.

References

Agranoff, Robert. 2004. "Leveraging Networks: A Guide for Public Managers Working Across Organizations." In *Collaboration: Using Networks and Partnerships,* edited by John M. Kamensky and Thomas J. Burlin, 61–102. Lanham, MD: Rowman & Littlefield Publishers.

Axelrod, Robert. 1984. *The Evolution of Cooperation.* New York: Basic Books.

Broder, John M. 2005. "Police Chiefs Moving to Share Terror Data." *New York Times,* July 28, A12.

Goldsmith, Stephen, and William D. Eggers. 2004. *Government by Network: The New Shape of the Public Sector.* Washington, DC: The Brookings Institution.

Johnston, Jocelyn M., and Barbara S. Romzek. 2000. *Implementing State Contracts for Social Services: An Assessment of the Kansas Experience.* Washington, DC: IBM Center for the Business of Government.

Jones, Candace, William Hesterly, and Stephen Borgatti. 1997. "A General Theory of Network Governance: Exchange Conditions and Social Mechanisms." *Academy of Management Review* 22: 911–945.

Kettl, Donald F. 2005. *The Global Public Management Revolution,* 2nd ed. Washington, DC: The Brookings Institution.

Milward, H. Brinton, and Keith G. Provan. 1998. "Measuring Network Structure." *Public Administration* 76: 387–407.

Putnam, Robert D. 1993. *Making Democracy Work.* Princeton, NJ: Princeton University Press.

———. 2000. *Bowling Alone.* New York: Touchstone.

Smith, Steven Rathgeb, and Judith Smyth. 1996. "Contracting for Services in a Decentralized System." *Journal of Public Administration Research and Theory* 6, no. 2, 277–296.

Snyder, William M., and Xavier de Souza Briggs. 2004. "Communities of Practice: A New Tool for Government Managers." In *Collaboration: Using Networks and Partnerships,* edited by John M. Kamensky and Thomas J. Burlin, 171–272. Lanham, MD: Rowman & Littlefield Publishers.

Weiss, Janet A. 1990. "Ideas and Inducements in Mental Health Policy." *Journal of Policy Analysis and Management* 9: 178–200.

CHAPTER 8

Effective Leadership in Network Collaboration

Lessons Learned from Continuum of Care Homeless Programs

HEE SOUN JANG, JESUS N. VALERO AND KYUJIN JUNG

Originally published as "Effective Leadership in Network Collaboration: Lessons Learned from Continuum of Care Homeless Programs," by IBM Center for the Business of Government (2016). Reprinted with permission.

Cross-sector collaboration has the potential to become a highly useful form of governance to effectively resolve difficult problems that cannot be addressed by a single organization or sector. While scholars and practitioners alike have a solid understanding of why organizations collaborate with one another, more research is needed about what effective collaboration looks like and the role that leadership style plays in the process.

In order to answer these questions, this report examines collaboration within the context of homeless policy networks, an area receiving significant policy attention in recent years. This report specifically investigates the role of managers leading continuum of care (CoC) homeless programs and the leadership behaviors that matter in achieving successful collaborative outcomes.

According to the U.S. Department of Housing and Urban Development (HUD), a CoC homeless program is "a community plan to organize and deliver housing and services to meet the specific needs of people who are homeless as they move to stable housing and maximize self-sufficiency. It includes action steps to end homelessness and prevent a return to homelessness." HUD identifies four necessary parts of a homeless continuum:

- Outreach, intake, and assessment to identify service and housing needs and provide a link to the appropriate level of both
- Emergency shelter to provide an immediate and safe alternative to sleeping on the streets, especially for homeless families with children
- Transitional housing with supportive services to allow for the development of skills that will be needed in permanent housing
- Permanent supportive housing with services to provide individuals and families with an affordable place to live, if needed

Based on research for this report, we found the following about the impact of leadership on effective collaboration:

- **Finding One**: CoC networks have positive impacts
- **Finding Two**: CoC networks raise awareness of homelessness
- **Finding Three**: CoC leaders enhance internal capacity of the network
- **Finding Four**: CoC leaders foster idea sharing and information sharing

The report concludes with six recommendations:

- **Recommendation One**: Develop expertise
- **Recommendation Two**: Cultivate a collaborative culture
- **Recommendation Three**: Take risks
- **Recommendation Four**: Be an inclusive leader
- **Recommendation Five**: Be agile and adaptive
- **Recommendation Six**: Use performance indicators effectively

Cross-sector collaboration has become a prevalent form of governance for effectively tackling difficult problems that cannot be addressed by a single organization or sector. A scarcity of resources and efforts to reinvent the way government functions has also conditioned many public managers to pursue new approaches beyond organizational boundaries.

Leaders have choices in how they engage with member agencies and in how they achieve the mission and objectives of collaboration. Different styles of leadership will show different activities that either enhance or reduce effective collaborations. This is because a public manager who leads a collaborative network plays an incredibly important role in the process. Among other responsibilities, they are commonly tasked with bringing organizations together to participate, securing the necessary

resources to achieve the goals of the network, and articulating a common vision and mission. Scholarly research has usually treated network leaders as agents of underlying organizational decisions driving the management of collaborations. But public managers leading collaborative efforts are real people who possess leadership qualities and skills that will influence effective collaboration in predictable ways.

This report, therefore, focuses on answering two practical questions:

- What does effective collaboration look like and does leadership matter?
- If leadership is important, what specific skills and qualities are valuable for leaders to possess and/or develop in order to lead successful collaborative efforts?

CoC Homeless Networks Examined

We conducted in-depth reviews of four CoC homeless networks in the states of Utah, Texas (two networks), and New York to develop a deeper understanding about the different approaches to collaboration and the role of leadership.

Metro Dallas Homeless Alliance (Texas)

This CoC homeless network has been in existence since 2002 and has approximately 50 active member organizations serving Dallas and Collin counties, Texas. The CoC established itself as a 501(c)(3) public charity and is named Metro Dallas Homeless Alliance (MDHA). MDHA manages the network's daily operations (e.g., managing HUD grants and funding), but a board comprised of community stakeholders provides the overall direction, service priorities, and vision. MDHA is also the designated administrator of the network's HMIS (Homeless Management Information System). MDHA's current goal is to ensure that all organizations provide homelessness services report data (e.g., number of people served, etc.) back to the network—including for shelters that are not funded by HUD—and to understand the homeless service demand and sheltering resources available in real time. About half of its member organizations are HUD-funded.[1]

Denton County Homeless Coalition/ Texas Homeless Network (Texas)

This homeless coalition was originally formed as its own CoC in 2007 to serve Denton County, Texas. In 2013, the CoC made the decision to merge with the statewide network known as the Texas Homeless Network.[2]

The decision to merge was predicated on the fact that the network was not as competitive for HUD funding as a stand-alone CoC and lacked administrative capacity. As a member of the statewide network, the coalition benefits from technical support and increased access to funding. The coalition reports its minutes to the statewide network to ensure efficient operation but still enjoys some autonomy. For example, the coalition—comprised of 40 member agencies—has its own governance system, made up of a steering committee and a general body membership, which provides direction for the network. The steering committee chair serves as the coalition's leader while the daily operations are shared between HUD-funded agencies within the coalition.

Salt Lake City and County CoC (Utah)

The Salt Lake City and County CoC has been in existence for over 20 years. Unlike previously discussed CoCs, this network is led by a local government entity—the Salt Lake County

government. The county provides staffing and administrative assistance to the CoC to ensure that the network is able to maintain its daily operations and functions. As the lead agency, the county is also responsible for overseeing the organizations funded by HUD and evaluating their performance. The 25 member agencies elect a board that is representative of the membership, and the board is responsible for ensuring that all stakeholders fulfill their duties and responsibilities via memoranda of understanding.[3]

Cattaraugus County CoC (New York)

The Cattaraugus County CoC network was formally established in 2006 to be compliant with HUD funding requirements. Before its creation as a CoC, there had been informal meetings among agencies that served the homeless community. The network is comprised of 20 agencies, but HUD only funds four of them. The CoC describes its governance structure as led by a board of directors, but recently it has struggled to maintain an active board membership. While the CoC network prefers to maintain its own identity and autonomy, the loss of HUD funding and the absence of active board leadership has led the CoC to rethink its strategy and independence. Because the state of New York does not have a statewide network, Cattaraugus is considering merging with one of its neighboring CoC networks.

Understanding Leadership in Effective Public Service Collaboration

What Does Effective Collaboration Mean for CoC Homeless Networks?

- If 20 organizations are working together to address a complex social issue within their community, how should they measure effectiveness?

TABLE 8.1 Examples of CoC Homeless Networks in Three States

CoC Network	Homeless Population	Stand-Alone CoC Network	HUD Funding in 2013	HUD-Funded Agencies
Salt Lake City & County	2,463	Yes	$5,678,852	11
Dallas City & County	3,447	Yes	$15,663,757	24
Denton County	216	No (part of "Balance of State" system)	$638,374	3
Cattaraugus County	38	Yes, but seeking merger	$417,058	4

- How do these organizations know that they are making a positive impact toward agreed policy goals?

Because a collaboration effort has multiple stakeholders, including network member agencies and the community it serves, we consider what network effectiveness would mean for the two key stakeholder groups. Thus, we measure effective public service collaboration at two levels:

- Network
- Community

Managers can use measures of network effectiveness to assess the performance of their collaboration efforts at two levels. Using a five-point scale ranging from "did not experience success at all" to "experienced success to a very great extent," public managers can take a close look at how well they are doing in achieving success during a set time period that varies from network to network, depending on the needs and preferences of key stakeholders (e.g., board of directors, funding agencies, and/or HUD). In doing so, it is important that public managers be candid about how well they are doing in the various effectiveness measures in order to strategize ways to improve their collaboration.

Measuring Network-Level Effectiveness

At the network level, effectiveness is measured by considering the degree to which the network as a whole is able to achieve collective benefits. Here, the interest is not on individual organizational benefits but on the extent to which the network, as a whole body, achieves outcomes that benefit everyone.

Measures of network-level effectiveness include:

- **Increasing Membership**. By increasing membership, the network is showing signs of being able to convey a collective vision and mission. It also indicates that members work well with each other, which encourages others to become interested in joining the collaboration efforts.
- **Increasing Member Commitment**. In the process of growing a network's membership, or when it has achieved the desired level of membership, an effective network is able to maintain and increase the membership's commitment to the collaboration efforts. Without an increasingly committed group of organizations, the network will struggle to achieve its goals and objectives.
- **Increasing Range of Services**. The network is working well when it is not only adding new members, but also increasing the scope

of services that it offers. This is indicative of a network that is conscientious of what it is currently capable of doing, understands the extent of community needs, and works to add to its line of services to address unmet needs.

- **Reducing Duplication of Services.** An efficient and effective network is also able to assess its current scope of services and eliminate any service overlap or duplication. This then allows for limited resources to be allocated to new ideas and solutions.

Measuring Community-Level Effectiveness

At the community level, the focus is on assessing whether the network is able to contribute value to the community it serves. Here, the network must think carefully about what being effective would mean for those members of the community that have a stake in the collaboration. The general question that public managers should be asking themselves is: Are we making a difference in the community we serve?

Measures of community-level effectiveness include:

- **Building Greater Awareness About Homelessness.** A CoC homeless network contributes value to the community it serves when it is able to build awareness of the problem. Do citizens, local elected officials, and community organizations understand the severity of the problem and what it is going to take as a community to eradicate homelessness?
- **Decreasing the Rate of Homelessness.** Homeless networks are primarily created to reduce the rate of homelessness within the geography they serve. Thus, to contribute value to the community means to reduce the severity of the problem. The same would be true of other types of networks created, for instance, to eliminate the number of students dropping out of high school or reducing the

incidence of crime among young people in the community.

- **Lowering Service Cost.** A network achieves community-level effectiveness when it pools resources and community program coordination and is able to reduce the cost of homeless service, including housing, case management, and other needed services.

Elements of Effective Leadership in a CoC Homeless Collaboration

There are two types of behaviors seen in cross-sector collaboration:

- **Task-oriented behaviors** are focused on facilitating network goal achievement, such as identifying roles and responsibilities, holding network members accountable for performance, and putting plans into action.
- **Relationship-oriented behaviors** place a greater focus on building positive social relations, such as motivating and inspiring network members and ensuring that the individual needs of members are carefully addressed.

Both task and relationship behaviors are important for the effective management of a CoC homeless network. Network managers who engage in both types of behaviors will be more effective than others in achieving successful collaborative outcomes.

Study Findings

The findings presented below are generated from the analyses of a survey of 259 CoC networks nationwide.

Our findings discuss the degree to which networks perceive that they are being effective, the key leadership behaviors in networked collaboration, and the impact of leadership on effective collaboration.

FIGURE 8.1 Performance of CoC Networks at the Network Level

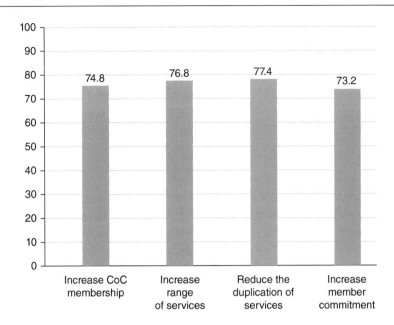

Note: Survey respondents were asked to assess the extent to which their CoC has been able to achieve success in the various dimensions by using a scale from 1 (did not experience success at all) to 5 (experienced success to a very great extent). The average was calculated and then multiplied by 20 to achieve a scale ranging from 0 to 100.

Finding One: CoC Networks Have Positive Impacts

We asked network leaders to assess the performance of their CoC homeless networks in the various indicators of both network- and community-level effectiveness.[4][5] These results are recorded in Figure 8.1.

With regards to the network level, leaders report that they are successful in all four indicators of effectiveness:

- Increasing CoC membership
- Increasing range of services
- Reducing duplication of services
- Increasing member commitment

This finding suggests that public managers can realize important benefits through networked collaboration—namely, reducing the duplication of services by pooling resources, coordinating efforts in the community to increase the range

of services, and increasing member agencies of the CoC. A leader of a small CoC network in New York, for example, defines network level effectiveness as follows:

> Being an effective CoC is having an effective service delivery system to address the needs of those that are homeless or at risk of homelessness. It is about collaboration and working together and thinking outside of the box to address those needs.

Of the four network level measures, "increasing member commitment" was ranked lowest. A CoC leader discussed the challenges of building member commitment:

> One big part of effectiveness is that everybody is working together. It is important that the HUD-funded agencies recognize that they are getting a gift from the government

and they have to participate in the committee in an active manner that is required by HUD because of the funding. There is a lot more to funding than just filling out a grant application in my opinion. I want the HUD-funded agencies to take ownership.

CoC leaders need to think carefully about ways of capturing and maintaining the interest of organizations to be active network members:

- Are members being consulted and engaged in the decision-making process?
- Are members involved in brainstorming new ideas and solutions?

These kinds of activities may prove useful in increasing network members' commitment.

Finding Two: CoC Networks Raise Awareness of Homelessness

Network leaders report successes and challenges in contributing value to the communities they serve. In general, networks are most successful in increasing awareness about homelessness in their community.

A CoC leader highlighted the key role played by city officials in letting the community know what the city is doing and what the city cares about. The city also offers data assistance to better understand the multi-dimensional nature of homelessness.

We found that CoC networks make good use of social media outlets to raise awareness about the incidence of homelessness and the service needs that homeless people may have. Recent research has found that social media outlets such as Facebook can be helpful in raising awareness about homelessness, engaging stakeholders, and increasing the profile of the network in the community.[6]

Networks struggle most in reducing service costs. Here, public managers need to engage not only their membership but also community stakeholders in pooling resources and identifying a community plan by which to create more affordable access to services for their homeless population.

FIGURE 8.2 Performance of CoC Networks at the Community Level

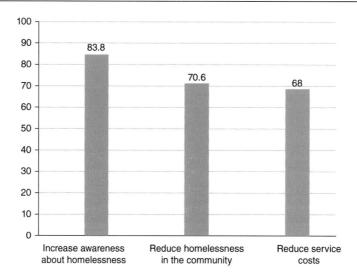

Note: Survey respondents were asked to assess the extent to which their CoC has been able to achieve success in the various dimensions by using a scale from 1 (did not experience success at all) to 5 (experienced success to a very great extent). The average was calculated and then multiplied by 20 to achieve a scale ranging from 0 to 100.

Finding Three: CoC Leaders Enhance Internal Capacities of the Network

We asked CoC leaders to report the degree to which they engage in task-oriented leadership behaviors, and the results are presented in Table 8.2. Here, we show the behaviors that occur in greater frequency and the specific tasks that public managers pay the most attention to.

In general, these findings suggest that public managers emphasize establishing and building the capacity of the CoC homeless network by ensuring that it has the necessary resources and involves the right people (e.g., potential leaders and members) in the collaboration efforts.

TABLE 8.2 Rating of Task-Oriented Leadership Behaviors

Task-Oriented Leadership Behaviors	Mean	Rank
Treating all network members as equals (activation)	4.6	1
Freely sharing information among network members (synthesizing)	4.5	2
Identifying resources (activation)	4.4	3
Identifying stakeholders (activation)	4.2	4
Sharing leadership role with other network members (framing)	4.1	5

Note: Survey respondents were asked as follows: "How often do you engage in the following behaviors?" Respondents then used a scale from 1 (never) to 5 (very often). The mean for each survey item was a calculated to understand the degree to which public managers (on average) engaged in these leadership behaviors.

Finding Four: CoC Leaders Foster Idea Sharing and Information Exchange

Table 8.3 lists the most highly-rated relationship-oriented dimensions and activities. Creating this

TABLE 8.3 Rating of Relationship-Orientated Leadership Behaviors

Relationship-Oriented Leadership Behaviors	Mean	Rank
Seeking the counsel of key network stakeholders (intellectual stimulation)	4.4	1
Being open to the ideas and suggestions of network members (intellectual stimulation)	4.3	2
Instilling fairness in the process of managing resources in the network (idealized influence)	4.2	3
Inspiring network members to work cohesively for a common purpose (inspirational motivation)	4.1	4
Helping network members look at issues from different perspectives (intellectual stimulation)	4.0	5
Considering the needs of network members before those of my own organization (idealized influence)	4.0	5
Expressing the need to adhere to ethical standards among members of the network (idealized influence)	4.0	5

Note: Survey respondents were asked as follows: "How often do you engage in the following behaviors?" Respondents then used a scale from 1 (never) to 5 (very often). The mean for each survey item was a calculated to understand the degree to which public managers (on average) engaged in these leadership behaviors.

type of environment may prove to be rewarding during the yearly competition for HUD funding, as networks with the most innovative approaches to ending homelessness are likely to score more points. In addition, allowing network members to contribute to the discussion of ending homelessness may strengthen ties to the effort of solving the problem as a collective unit as opposed to through individualized efforts. One interviewee indicated that: "People show up to the member meetings just because they care about homelessness."

In discussing the need for cultivating an environment of exchange, she explained:

> I need to let members decide what the focus of the CoC network should be. I ask them if there are any new projects that they think we need to be working on. I take the proposals to the steering committee and the steering committee votes on the top one that they really want to look at.

Cultivating a culture of sharing ideas and solutions can prove to be rewarding for networks that are looking for new ways to eradicate homelessness. In addition, including the voice of network members will send a clear message to members that their thoughts and values matter—which encourages member commitment and support for the efforts of the network.

Implications for Practice: Recommendations for Leaders in Collaborative Networks

Recommendation One: Develop Expertise

Managing networks requires the development of expertise in a subject matter policy area. This recommendation is centered on the idea that managers need to be equipped with extensive knowledge, expertise, and best practices in order to be an effective network leader.

Leaders of policy networks can gain knowledge of policy priorities and funding by becoming well connected to local stakeholders and existing national associations. For example, it may be useful for homeless networks to connect to the National Alliance to End Homelessness, which provides technical support, research, and hosts a yearly conference. A network leader has to have access to rich information and resources in order to lead the network effectively. Leaders lacking policy understanding or expertise in homelessness must rely on longtime homelessness serving leaders, both local and national, to be connected to the network of experts.

Recommendation Two: Cultivate a Collaborative Culture

The collaborative process is about constant communication, building trust among network members, and just as importantly, cultivating a culture that welcomes both competition and collaboration. Traditional notions consider competition to be at the opposite end of the spectrum from collaboration, but we suggest that encouraging competition in the collaborative process can be a healthy exercise.

In the context of federal homeless policy, networks compete for federal funding on a yearly basis. As such, homeless networks have to submit an application that is innovative, results-driven, and collaborative in nature to score high points and achieve funding. Each network is only able to submit one application to HUD, comprised of various program proposals to be carried out by member organizations. Because not all proposals by member organizations can be chosen as part of the single application, network leaders are presented with an opportunity to cultivate a sense of competition among network members to see who is able to produce the most innovative and impactful project. Creating competition, therefore, can result in the stimulation of new ideas and solutions.

While some member organizations may not be funded through HUD during one funding cycle, the network leader should continue encouraging collaboration by reminding members that there are other benefits to be enjoyed through the process of working together, including tackling homelessness as community partners as opposed to in silos. In addition, network leaders should be careful to continue communicating a common vision and how selecting certain projects to be included in the application will help the network be one step closer to achieving its goals and objectives as a collective.

Recommendation Three: Take Risks

Previous research on the management of networks indicates that establishing ground rules and holding members accountable are important responsibilities of a network leader.[7] In our research, we find that network leaders should not be afraid to risk relationships with other members of the network when necessary— particularly when enforcing shared norms, rules, and expectations. Risking relationships means being a bold leader and communicating expectations to network members, whether some members may like hearing those expectations or not. This may be particularly germane to individuals who are new to the leadership role and are interested in taking the collaborative efforts in a new direction.

Taking risks should be exercised by taking actions such as:

- Reminding members of their responsibilities
- Providing the members with options (e.g., actively participate or allow someone else to take that role)

Recommendation Four: Be an Inclusive Leader

Research shows that homelessness is a multidimensional problem requiring a cross-sector strategy that engages a wide array of supportive programs and services.[8] As a result, any intervention to eradicate homelessness will take real coordination and a diverse group of stakeholders. The same is likely true for other types of public services in response to difficult social problems.

This reality requires network leaders to be inclusive of community stakeholders such as local governments, nonprofit shelters, food pantries, church-operated soup kitchens, school districts, and others. Community leaders should be invited to take an active role within the network, as well as in the network's governance, by participating in working groups, task forces, steering committees, and so on. This allows local stakeholders to have a voice in the homeless services in their community. In addition, by being an inclusive leader, the network may benefit from new and fresh perspectives. One network leader described the importance of being an inclusive leader. She reflected, "In this collaboration, every person that comes to a meeting is important." Here is the one example of being an inclusive leader and its benefit to the effective network:

> We have chronically homeless persons that regularly attend our general meetings and they have a voice. Their input is very useful because sometimes we will be talking about something and they will shake their heads and say that on the streets this is what it looks like. I didn't realize how big an impact that would have. What I love is the fact that they are welcomed like any other member of the community. I'm real proud of our general membership because each of the members is just like anybody else regardless of if they are HUD-funded or not.

Local stakeholders also will be an invaluable resource, especially for CoCs with little to no paid staff capacity. Member agencies with strong capacities may offer technical or administrate support for CoC network operations. A significant proportion of the networks that responded to our national survey reported that they have a governance structure that is shared among member agencies. Only a few networks were established as a stand-alone 501(c)(3) public charity. From this finding we learned that the daily management of the network will be left to the member organizations without designated personnel for the administration of grant applications and management of funding. Thus, the inclusion of community stakeholders and affording them an opportunity to serve can help the network overcome challenges from lack of administrative capacity and help them advance the mission and vision.

Recommendation Five: Be Agile and Adaptive

Leadership is critical in balancing the reality and interests of the local community while maintaining team spirit valued by network members including policy makers, government managers, nonprofit service providers, religious communities, advocacy groups, and so on. Like an organization, networks evolve over time—sometimes the network evolves for good and other times it does not. In this process, network leaders must stand ready to accept the reality of their network's status and adapt as necessary. Effective leaders must understand reality and adapt quickly to the new normal for the best interest of the community.

Recommendation Six: Use Performance Indicators Effectively

Network leaders must realize the advantage in having access to data and information, and they must use them properly. Funding agencies, community stakeholders, and others come to expect data in order to understand the severity of a problem, allocate funding, and develop objective metrics of success in implementing local homeless programs. Securing new and unique data on the homeless population certainly

creates an advantage. For instance, the Metro Dallas Homeless Alliance has developed a coordinated assessment tool and a comprehensive and up-to-date HMIS (Homeless Management Information System) to track homeless services in the area. This allows the network to make a stronger case for why funding is needed and important for a new area of service.

We suggest that CoC networks use an inventory of currently available data sources that may aid their data efforts. The HUD Exchange website[9] makes data on all of the CoC networks—such as homelessness estimates and funding allocations readily available. The HUD website allows users to generate reports for each homeless network in spreadsheet format. It also provides access to the contact information of regional offices and other network leaders. Smart use of the data will help CoCs develop comparative analyses to understand where each network stands in the national standards. These data sources can be used to create an advantage when applying for funding or making a case for new programs.

Notes

1. MDHA'S website is www.mdhadallas.org.

2. The Texas Homeless Network website is www.thn.org.

3. The Salt Lake City and County CoC website is http://sico.org/homeless-services.

4. The survey was sent to 382 CoC networks. From that, 259 networks responded, for a response rate of 68 percent.

5. Leaders were also provided with the opportunity to identify instances where they did not focus efforts in an area, which allows us to obtain a clearer picture of how networks are doing.

6. Jung, Kyujin, and Jesus N. Valero. "Assessing the Evolutionary Structure of Homeless Network: Social Media Use, Keywords, and Influential Stakeholders," *Technological Forecasting and Social Change* (2015).

7. Anseil, Chris, and Alison Gash. "Collaborative Governance in Theory and Practice." *Journal of Public Administration Research and Theory* 18, no. 4 (2007):

543–71. Milward. H. Brinton, and Keith G. Provan "A Manager's Guide to Choosing and Using Collaborative Networks," IBM Center for the Business of Government (2006).

8. Cunningham. Maiy "Preventing and Ending Homelessness: Next Steps " Washington, D.C.: Urban Institute, 2009; Fargo, et al. "Community-Level Characteristics Associated with Variation in Rates of Homelessness among Families and Single Adults." *American journal of Public Health* 103, no. Suppl 2 (2013): S340–S47.

9. www.hudexchange.info/

How Does a Board of Directors Influence within- and Cross-sector Nonprofit Collaboration?

JENNIFER IHM[1] ⓘ AND MICHELLE SHUMATE[2] ⓘ
[1]School of Communications, Kwangwoon University, Seoul, Republic of Korea
[2]Communication Studies, Northwestern University, Evanston, Illinois

Collaboration among governmental, private, and nonprofit organizations has become a significant mechanism to achieve collective goals that cannot be accomplished by a single party (Chen, 2010; Kenis & Provan, 2006). While solving complex social problems is an important objective of nonprofit collaboration, organizational resources (Grønbjerg, 1993; Pfeffer & Salancik, 1978), institutional forces (DiMaggio & Powell, 1983; Oliver, 1990), and interlocking directorates (Austin, 2000; Guo & Acar, 2005; Osborne, 2000) may be the actual catalysts of nonprofit collaboration to serve each partner's needs.

The purpose of this study is to examine the role of board members and their resources in three types of nonprofit collaboration.

Nonprofit organizations collaborate with three different types of partners: other nonprofits, corporations, and governmental organizations (Austin & Seitanidi, 2012; Gazley &

Brudney, 2007; Guo & Acar, 2005; Provan & Lemaire, 2012). Nonprofits collaborate with other nonprofits to collectively solve communal problems (Milward & Provan, 2006) and improve service delivery to the community through joint effort, resources, and decision-making (Blau & Rabrenovic, 1991). These partnerships are described in this paper as within-sector collaboration. Although the intensity of within-sector collaboration may vary (Keast, Brown, & Mandell, 2007), this paper regarded within-sector collaboration as relationships among nonprofit organizations in a broad sense including less intense, informal relationships as well as more integrative collaboration.

Nonprofit-business collaboration is a strategic alliance between two sectors to exchange resources and achieve social and economic missions (Austin & Seitanidi, 2012). It differs

DOI: 10.4324/9781003387800-19

from other types of collaboration because the businesses and nonprofits have different goals in cross-sector partnerships (Shumate, Hsieh, & O'Connor, 2018). As such, these partnerships often have different processes, challenges, and opportunities (Austin & Seitanidi, 2012), in comparison to within-sector collaboration.

Because of an increasing emphasis on effective social change (Fabig & Boele, 1999), innovation (Sanzo, Álvarez, Rey, & García, 2015) and the limited nature of philanthropic relationships (Austin & Seitanidi, 2012), nonprofits have broadened the scope of activities and resources and extended "philanthropic relationships" to more "transformational" ones (see collaboration continuum in Austin & Seitanidi, 2012). As such, this paper focuses on nonprofit and business partnerships that are more integrative than philanthropic relationships, referred to hereafter as nonprofit-business collaboration.

Nonprofit-government collaboration is the last type of nonprofit collaboration. It differs from the other two types, because it has emerged as the welfare state necessitated and provided opportunities for nonprofits to deliver public services as a substitution for governmental organizations; nonprofits secured the resources and funding from the government in turn (Gazley & Brudney, 2007). Governmental organizations do not need to fulfill CSR or manage their reputation, but their objectives and resources may be more fixed and clear than other types of collaboration (Osborne, 2000).

Contracting is common in nonprofit-government relations, but the two sectors also collaborate more intimately in order to solve local issues, strengthen community relations, and ultimately fulfill their missions more effectively (Gazley & Brudney, 2007; Jing & Chen, 2012). This paper focuses on nonprofit-government collaboration that is more integrative than contracting relationships, because it involves responsibility, formality, and interaction among the partners (Gazley & Brudney, 2007; Jing & Chen, 2012).

Previous studies have not focused on different types of nonprofit collaboration based on the different partners. Distinguishing different types of nonprofit collaboration is important, because each type of partner has disparate objectives in the relationship, which may lead to different decision-making process and different role of boards in collaboration. The next section introduces role of boards and their resources in nonprofit collaboration and asks how boards may influence the three types of nonprofit collaboration.

Board social capital and human capital in nonprofit collaboration

Board members are a governing body of individuals responsible for the affairs and conduct of the organization (Herman & Renz, 2000). They make strategic decisions for better organizational performance when confronted with financial, institutional, or environmental difficulties (Brown, 2005; Hwang & Bromley, 2015; Miller-Millesen, 2003). They are the top decision makers for nonprofits. Nonprofit collaboration is a significant strategy for organizational survival and legitimacy (Guo & Acar, 2005; Sowa, 2009). Considering the influential role of board members on organizational strategic decision-making (Herman & Renz, 2000), board members may also affect decisions about nonprofit collaboration.

The predominant explanation of the role of boards in interorganizational collaboration has been interlocking directorates. In this explanation, board members serve as conduits for the development of relationships between the organizations with which they have affiliations (Austin, 2000; Burt, 1980; Gulati & Westphal, 1999; Guo & Acar, 2005; Osborne, 2000).

Board members do not always develop their multiple organizational affiliations into interorganizational collaborations. Instead, they may bring resources that facilitate nonprofit collaboration. Focusing on board resources may broaden the understanding of diverse board roles in nonprofit collaboration beyond those of matchmaker (Austin, 2000; Guo & Acar, 2005; Osborne, 2000) and emphasize the role of individuals in nonprofit collaboration in comparison to the organizational and environmental predictors (DiMaggio & Powell, 1983; Grønbjerg, 1993; Pfeffer & Salancik, 1978). Therefore, we focus on board social and human capital as two dimensions that may explain differences in the degree of nonprofit interorganizational collaboration.

Board social capital

Board social capital refers to board members' connections to other organizations (Barroso-Castro, Villegas-Periñan, & Casillas-Bueno, 2015). As boundaries between sectors are blurred, board social capital arising from ties outside the organization (e.g., interlocking directorates or board members with multiple organizational affiliations) has become more prevalent and important (Cornforth, 2012; Vidovich & Currie, 2012). By taking advantage of social connections in other organizations, board members can access critical resources and information and enhance administrative innovation, financial success, and organizational performance and survival (Chait, Ryan, & Taylor, 2011; Fu & Shumate, 2017).

Board social capital can also be an effective means for initiating and maintaining nonprofit collaboration. First, board social capital allows board members to access reliable information and necessary resources for nonprofit collaboration (Austin, 2000; Fu & Shumate, 2017; Rondinelli & London, 2003). Nonprofit collaboration requires significant effort, time, and resources among the partners; finding appropriate partners with compatible goals, culture, and

needs is imperative for the network benefits to outweigh the costs (Provan & Milward, 1995). Initiating nonprofit collaboration carries risks, including freeriding and behaving opportunistically (Fu & Shumate, 2017). However, information about organizational reliability and compatibility is often not easily accessible. Board members with greater social capital have easier access to internal information and broader knowledge about future partners through their direct or indirect ties with other organizations. For instance, research suggests that board members' affiliations with multiple nonprofits or corporations can facilitate information acquisition about partners (Austin, 2000; Guo & Acar, 2005; Rondinelli & London, 2003). In nonprofit-government collaboration, board social capital can be leveraged to secure government funding and provide useful information about collaborative opportunities with governmental organizations.

Second, board social capital enhances organizations' legitimacy in the field and makes the nonprofit a more attractive interorganizational partner. Forming more ties with other organizations can enhance the focal organization's structural position in the field. Drawing from functions board social capital may play, this paper hypothesizes positive relationships between board social capital and the number of three types of nonprofit collaboration:

> H1: Board social capital is positively related to the number of (a) within-sector, (b) nonprofit-business, and (c) nonprofit-government nonprofit collaborators.

Board human capital

Board social capital may contribute to nonprofit collaboration, but board human capital is required for decision-making about nonprofit collaboration. Human capital refers to an "individual's set of knowledge and skills, which are typically developed through investments in education, training, and various experiences" (Kor & Sundaramurthy, 2009, p. 982). At the board level, human capital refers to both the sum of the knowledge and skills possessed by board members and the joint fulfillment of their duties from that capital (Chait et al., 2011; Ostrower, 2007).

Board governance literature notes the importance of knowledgeable, responsible, and expert boards in making strategic decisions for the organizations (Brown, 2005; Brown & Guo, 2010; Chait et al., 2011; Herman & Renz, 2000, 2008). Board human capital may also play an integral role in organizational strategies for nonprofit collaboration. On the one hand, knowledgeable, professional, and committed boards can lead to effective board performance and decision-making as the number of partners grows (Fredette & Bradshaw, 2012) and support an effective collaborative process. On the other hand, boards with high human capital may use their knowledge and skills in attentive assessment of conditions and risk factors and make more conservative decisions about nonprofit collaboration. They may be more critical about whether collaboration is "really worth pursuing," being aware that collaborative advantage is "a seriously resource-consuming activity" (Huxham & Vangen, 2013, p. 13).

Second, board human capital may influence nonprofit collaboration by improving organizational performance (Brown, 2005; Herman & Renz, 2000, 2008). Organizations are more likely to partner with better performing organizations in order to reduce the risks of collaborating with unreliable partners (Fu & Shumate, 2017) and increase their competencies (Atouba, 2016; Bryson, Ackermann, & Eden, 2007). However, board with high human capital may rather decide to concentrate on their own organization as their capacity may lead to high organizational performance by themselves (Brown, 2005; Herman & Renz, 2000, 2008) without other partners. Board with low human capital may be more desperate

to turn to collaboration to supplement their lack of capacity. Thus, we ask:

> RQ1: How will board human capital influence the number of (a) within-sector, (b) nonprofit-business, and (c) nonprofit-government collaborators?

Further, board social and human capital, when combined, may influence the number of nonprofit collaboration differently from either factor independently. First, when board members possess appropriate expertise, the influence of board social capital on nonprofit collaboration may be enhanced. For instance, as board social capital provides information and connections to potential partners (Austin, 2000; Guo & Acar, 2005; Rondinelli & London, 2003), board human capital can enhance the exploration of that information, helping the nonprofit make the best strategic collaborative choices (Ingram, 2009). Second, despite information and connections to other organizations, board members' high competencies and expertise may discourage pursuing collaboration. Being well aware of collaborative challenges (Huxham & Vangen, 2013), they may refrain from unnecessary collaboration unless they find the perfect match from their organizational connections. Therefore, we ask:

> RQ2: How will board human capital interact with board social capital and influence the number of (a) within-sector, (b) nonprofit-business, and (c) nonprofit-government collaborators?

Method

For our study, nonprofit executive directors or their equivalents were surveyed from October 2013 to June 2015 about board of directors in their organizations. We invited 1,159 executive directors to complete an online survey through email, and we sent an additional 4,825 postcards inviting participation in the study (N = 5,984). Asking executive directors about their board members has been widely used in research to assess nonprofit governance including the first national survey conducted by the Urban Institute (Ostrower, 2007) as a way to overcome the limitation of reaching out to every board member individually for each organization. The list of potential participants was drawn from the Yearbook of International Organizations (Union of International Associations, 2013) and from the Urban Institute's 2013 list of active 501(c)(3) organizations with revenues greater than $100,000 from B (education), C (environment), and S (community improvement and capacity building) National Taxonomy of Exempt Entities (NTEE) categories. We chose these categories to maximize diversity and because each has been areas of cross-sector social partnership research (see Milward & Provan, 2006; Rondinelli & London, 2003; Simo & Bies, 2007; Sowa, 2009). There were 1,168 English-speaking nongovernmental organizations (NGOs) that began the survey (20%), and a total of 776 NGOs that completed the survey (13%). Most of the NGOs were located in the United States (n = 747), with 12 additional countries having limited representation (e.g., United Kingdom, Canada, South Africa, and China).

To gauge the representativeness of our sample, we compared our sample with the population of nonprofit organizations in the Urban Institute database (2013), because most of our nonprofits were from the United States.

To validate survey responses of nonprofit collaboration, we conducted follow-up interviews with nonprofit organizations that reported no ties to other organizations via phone. Of the 68 identified, one organization was permanently closed during the study period. In total, we contacted 67 valid organizations, and 31 responded (response rate = 46.27%). However, eight organizations declined to participate, leaving 23 organizations interviewed. Among these

23 organizations, 13 organizations (56.52%) indicated they did collaborate; eight organizations (34.78%) said they did not collaborate. In addition, two organizations (8.70%) did not have collaborations at the time of the survey participation, but had formed collaborations at the time of the interview. Due to the inaccuracy of these survey responses, we treated their data as missing data instead of zero collaboration (n = 42). Additionally, 97 surveys were excluded from the final analysis because of missing data. This left us with an effective sample size of 636.

Measures
Nonprofit collaboration

In order to measure whether board members develop their organizational affiliations into nonprofit collaboration and the role of board capital in nonprofit collaboration, we asked the participants to provide the names of up to 20 organizations (e.g., nonprofit, business, and governmental organizations) with which their "organization have relationships with" at the present. Specifically, for cross-sector collaboration, the study asked about "relationships that extend beyond funder-recipient." The participants reported the number of collaborators they have with other nonprofits (n = 528; M = 6.99; SD = 5.60), private organizations (n = 560; M = 0.76; SD = 2.24), and governmental organizations (n = 590; M = 0.98; SD = 2.33). Twenty-nine nonprofits reported to have no relationship with other nonprofits. For nonprofit-business collaboration, 458 nonprofits reported to have no relationship with other private organizations and only 77 organizations reported having more than one nonprofit-business collaboration. For nonprofit-government collaboration, 426 nonprofits reported to have relationships with other governmental organizations and only 129 organizations reported having more than one nonprofit-government collaboration. Because of the lack of variance, only the presence of the relationship was measured for nonprofit-business

TABLE 9.1 Correlation Matrix of Variables

			(1)	(2)	(3)	(4)	(5)	(6)
(1)	Budget		–					
(2)	Social capital		–.02	–				
(3)	Human capital		.02	–.00	–			
(4)	Within-sector	Number	.09	.33*	–.02	–		
(5)	Nonprofit-business	Presence	.04	.23*	–.06	.36	–	
(6)	Nonprofit-government	Presence	.08	.24*	–.06	.28	.22	–

*$p < 0.05$.

($n = 632$; $M = 0.28$; $SD = 0.45$) and nonprofit-government collaboration ($n = 632$, $M = 0.33$; $SD = 0.47$) (Table 9.1).

Board social capital

In order to measure the relationship between board members' social capital with other organizations and nonprofit collaboration, we asked the names of affiliations board members had. The survey participants were asked to list as many (up to 20) organizational affiliations of their board as possible. We then counted the number of organizations that the respondents entered. Each board in surveyed organizations had about four board affiliations with other organizations on the average ($n = 662$; $M = 4.16$; $SD = 4.38$).

Board human capital

We used a measure of board capacity to capture their human capital (Shumate et al., 2017). Seven items in the measure were first drawn from previous studies and were classified as board capacity after exploratory factor analysis and confirmatory factor analysis; the items were validated by criterion validity of examining the correlation with peer-rated and self-reported nonprofit effectiveness (Shumate et al., 2017, see endnote for actual items).[1] This measure asked participants to rate the boards' knowledge,

commitment, accessibility, and relationships to the staff using statement which they indicated their agreement (1 = *strongly disagree*, 2 = *disagree*, 3 = *agree*, 4 = *strongly agree*).

Control variables

In order to examine the unique role of board capital on nonprofit collaboration, this study controlled for effects of organizational resources and institutional forces, budgets and organizational resources.

Second, we controlled for mission in order to control the influence of setting institutional norms or pressures related to being in a common industry. Guo and Acar (2005) addressed organizational mission as institutional forces that may influence nonprofits' propensity to collaborate. For instance, organizations such as hospitals and universities are less likely to collaborate with other organizations because their participants believe that their own profession should be controlled by themselves, not by others (Guo & Acar, 2005). Participants selected the best description of their organizational mission from 12 categories, using the International Classification of Nonprofit Organizations (Salamon & Anheier, 1996). These values were entered to control for the influence of nonprofit organization missions.

Analysis

Name match

We examined whether board members' multiple organizational affiliations develop into actual nonprofit collaboration. We identified matches between the names of the nonprofit partners and board affiliations by using string matching in R (R Core Team, 2016). This analysis was completed to examine two alternative explanations for the relationships between board social capital and collaboration: the interlocking directorates explanation and that board members were appointed from current interorganizational partners.

The results suggest that although there are some overlaps between the names of nonprofit partners and board affiliations, the proportion is very small (see Table 9.2 for proportions). The low percentage suggests that organizations that nonprofits collaborate with are not typically the organizations with which their board members have affiliations. Thus, we have evidence that any relationships between board social capital and nonprofit collaboration is unlikely to be due to these two alternative explanations.

Results

In this section, we report the influence of board social capital, board human capital, and their interaction terms on within- and cross-sector nonprofit collaboration.

Within-sector nonprofit collaboration

Hypotheses 1a predicted that board social capital would have a positive relationship to the number of within-sector nonprofit collaborators. RQ1 and RQ2 asked about the role of board human capital and an interaction effect between board human capital and board social capital in the number of within-sector nonprofit collaboration. The final regression model did not have a significant difference; the interaction effect does not have a significant influence on the number of within-sector nonprofit collaborators. Board social capital was the only significant predictor of the number of within-sector nonprofit collaboration (social capital: $\beta = .26$, $p < 0.001$). Therefore, H1a was supported (see Table 9.3 for full results).

Nonprofit-business collaboration

Hypotheses 1b predicted that board social capital would be positively related to the presence of nonprofit-business collaboration. RQ1 and RQ2 asked about the role of board human capital and an interaction effect between board

TABLE 9.2 Overlap of Names Between Nonprofit Partners and Board Affiliations

Organization A	Organization that was tested for the name match with Organization A	Overlap proportion
NPO partners	Board affiliations	0.05
Business partners	Board affiliations	0.03
Governmental partners	Board affiliations	0.03
Board affiliations	NPO partners	0.09
Board affiliations	Business partners	0.01
Board affiliations	Governmental partners	0.00

Note. NPO: nonprofit organization

TABLE 9.3 The Impact of Board Capital and Organizational Characteristics on the Number of Within-Sector Collaborators

	Model 1		Model 2		Final model	
	β	*(SE)*	*β*	*(SE)*	*β*	*(SE)*
Budget	.06	(.17)	.06	(.16)	.06	(.16)
Culture and Recreation	.05	(.91)	.05	(.94)	.05	(.93)
Education and Research	−.14	(.62)	−.15	(.72)	−.15	(.72)
Environment	.10	(.71)	.05	(.77)	.05	(.77)
Health	−.03	(.68)	−.03	(.76)	−.03	(.76)
Social services	.14	(.69)	.15	(.78)	.15	(.78)
Law, advocacy, and politics	.03	(.22)	.02	(.20)	.03	(.20)
Religion	−.04	(.98)	−.01	(.05)	−.01	(.05)
Business and professional associations, unions	−.05	(.86)	−.05	(.91)	−.05	(.91)
Not elsewhere classified	.09	(.80)	.07	(.86)	.07	(.86)
International	−.02	(.85)	−.01	(.94)	−.01	(.94)
Development and housing	.06	(.32)	.03	(.32)	.03	(.32)
Social capital			$.26^{***}$	(.06)	$.26^{***}$	(.06)
Human capital			−.04	(.53)	−.10	(.53)
(Social capital) * (Human capital)					.07	(.15)
n	525		525		525	
R^2	.08		.14		.15	
∇R^2	.08		.06		.002	
F	6.43^{***}		16.63^{***}		1.09	

Note. Robust *SEs* are reported.

$^*p < 0.05$, $^{**}p < 0.01$, $^{***}p < 0.001$.

human capital and social capital on the presence of nonprofit-business collaboration. Both board social capital and human capital were significant predictors of the presence of nonprofit-business collaborations (social capital: $b = .09$, $p < 0.001$; human capital: $b = -.56$, $p < 0.001$). Therefore, H1b was supported (see Table 9.4 for full results).

Nonprofit-government collaboration

Hypotheses 1c predicted that board social capital was positively related to nonprofit-government collaboration. RQ1 and RQ2 asked about the role of board human capital and an interaction effect between board human and social capital in the presence of nonprofit-government collaboration. Board social capital *(b = .13, p < 0.01)*,

TABLE 9.4 The Impact of Board Capital and Organizational Characteristics on the Presence of Nonprofit-Business Collaboration

	Model 1		Model 2		Final model	
	b	(SE)	b	(SE)	b	(SE)
Budget	−.00	(.00)	.00	(.00)	.001	(.00)
Culture and recreation	.16	(.63)	.02	(.61)	.01	(.61)
Education and research	−.93	(.58)	−.05	(.57)	−.04	(.57)
Environment	.29	(.48)	.02	(.47)	.02	(.47)
Health	.10	(.50)	−.01	(.48)	−.01	(.48)
Social services	.15	(.48)	.09	(.47)	.10	(.47)
Law, advocacy, and politics	.18	(.74)	−.08	(.74)	−.09	(.74)
Religion	−.20	(.86)	−.92	(.86)	−.93	(.86)
Business and professional associations, unions	−.06	(.67)	−.08	(.65)	−.07	(.65)
Not elsewhere classified	.57	(.51)	.38	(.49)	.38	(.49)
International	−.08	(.56)	−.15	(.55)	−.14	(.55)
Development and housing	.95**	(.66)	.72**	(.66)	.73**	(.66)
Social capital			.09***	(.02)	.09***	(.03)
Human capital			−.56**	(.22)	−.50	(.33)
(Social capital) * (Human capital)					−.01	(.06)
n	626		626		626	
Wald χ^2	28.95		42.78		42.83	
∇ Wald χ^2	28.95***		19.66***		0.05	
df	12		2		1	

Note. Robust SEs are reported.

$^*p < 0.05$, $^{**}p < 0.01$, $^{***}p < 0.001$.

human capital ($b = -.87$, $p < 0.05$), and their interaction term ($b = .14$, $p < 0.05$) were significant predictors of the presence of the nonprofit-government collaboration. Therefore, H1c was supported (Table 9.5).

Discussion

This study examines the role of board social capital and human capital in nonprofit collaboration

with other nonprofits, businesses, and government agencies. The results from this study suggest that both board social capital and human capital play an important role in within- and cross-sector nonprofit collaboration. First, board social capital is positively related to every type of nonprofit collaboration in this study, above and beyond the influence of organizational budget and service sector. Board size alone is not enough (Kim & Peng, 2018). Boards vary in their composition, with some boards

TABLE 9.5 The Impact of Board Capital and Organizational Characteristics on the Presence of Nonprofit-Government Collaboration

	Model 1		Model 2		Final model	
	b	*(SE)*	*b*	*(SE)*	*b*	*(SE)*
Budget	−.00	(.00)	−.00	(.00)	−.00	(.00)
Culture and recreation	.35	(.61)	.28	(.63)	.30	(.63)
Education and research	−.27	(.53)	−.34	(.54)	−.37	(.55)
Environment	.26**	(.48)	.06*	(.49)	.05*	(.49)
Health	−.46	(.52)	−.50	(.53)	−.49	(.53)
Social services	.19	(.48)	.21	(.50)	.13	(.50)
Law, advocacy, and politics	.94	(.71)	.85	(.74)	.92	(.73)
Religion	−.94	(.11)	−.60	(.12)	−.55	(.12)
Business and professional associations, unions	.19	(.65)	.19	(.66)	.16	(.67)
Not elsewhere classified	.84	(.51)	.69	(.52)	.68	(.52)
International	−.05	(.56)	−.003	(.57)	−.02	(.58)
Development and housing	.95*	(.66)	.74**	(.67)	.69**	(.67)
Social capital			.13***	(.03)	.13***	(.03)
Human capital			−.27	(.22)	−.87*	(.35)
(Social capital) * (Human capital)					−.14*	(.06)
n	626		626		626	
Wald χ^2	67.89		96.76		101.82	
∇ *Wald* χ^2	67.89***		26.52***		4.74*	
df	12		2		1	

Note. Robust *SEs* are reported.

*$p < 0.05$, **$p < 0.01$, ***$p < 0.001$.

having more connections to other organizations through their board members than others. That variation explains the degree to which nonprofits participate in interorganizational collaboration with other nonprofits, businesses, and government agencies. Thus, the results indicate that board members' social networks play an important role not only in enhancing administrative innovation, financial success, and organizational performance and survival (Chait et al., 2011; Fu & Shumate, 2017), but also in enabling nonprofits to find appropriate partners, enhancing organizational legitimacy, and initiating relationships with the partners (Austin, 2000; Guo & Acar, 2005; Rondinelli & London, 2003).

Second, board human capital plays an important, but more complex role in nonprofit collaboration even when the alternative explanations are controlled. Specifically, the role of board human capital differed across the three types of collaboration. Board human capital was unrelated to within-sector collaboration. It was negatively related to business-nonprofit collaboration. For government-nonprofit collaboration, the relationship was positive in the presence of high levels of board social capital. Making sense of these varied relationships is difficult because previous research has not examined the role of board characteristics on collaboration and has not examined these three types of collaboration simultaneously. We discuss each of these finding briefly, noting that each provides an area in need of additional research.

First, although many studies on nonprofit governance have discussed how board capacity and effectiveness are related to organizational behaviors and strategies (Cornforth, 2012), the current study suggests that within-sector collaboration may not result from an independent role of board human capital. Because nonprofit collaborations cross organizational boundaries, it may fundamentally require more than effective and competent boards of one organization. Insider-information and broader knowledge for future partners or collaborative opportunities (Guo & Acar, 2005; Rondinelli & London, 2003) based on boards' social connections across organization may have to come first to form within-sector collaboration.

Second, board human capital had a negative effect on nonprofit-business collaboration, regardless of board social capital. Previous research suggests that nonprofit-business collaboration often initiates as an extension of business executives' personal relationships (Austin, 2000). In other words, nonprofit-business collaboration may not necessarily result from boards with high human capital. Because boards with high human capital are better aware of challenges in nonprofit-business collaboration

(Austin, 2000; Onishi, 2015), they may make more conservative decisions for the organization based on attentive assessment of conditions and risk factors; they may rather decide to concentrate on their own organizations by taking advantage of their board capacity. On the other hand, boards with low human capital may be more likely to turn to collaboration, because they lack internal board capacity to achieve organizational goals. By forming alliances with other organizations, they may enhance nonprofit capacity and competency (Atouba, 2016; Bryson et al., 2007) beyond the limited board capabilities.

Third, board human capital had a negative role in nonprofit-government collaboration only when board social capital was considered. This result suggests that after controlling for board social capital, boards with high human capital may focus internally on their own organizations, while boards with low human capital may look beyond the organizational boundary to leverage their capacity. When high human capital was combined with high social capital, however, there seemed to be a synergistic effect on forming nonprofit-government collaboration: the interaction term between human capital and social capital was positively related to the presence of nonprofit-government collaboration. As board social capital supports to find better partners and resolves the uncertainty of the partners (Fu & Shumate, 2017), board human capital may function effectively (Fredette & Bradshaw, 2012) to initiate and buttress collaboration as a strategic decision for the organization (Brown, 2005; Brown & Guo, 2010; Chait et al., 2011; Herman & Renz, 2000, 2008).

In sum, the results suggest that board capital plays a powerful and active role in nonprofit collaboration; it is more than a proxy for budget or service sector. This research extends the attention to the individual level where actual decisions for nonprofit collaboration are made.

Conclusion

The purpose of this study was to examine the role of board social and human capital in three types of nonprofit collaboration. Nonprofit board capital may have an important role in nonprofit collaboration. Board social capital positively contributes to every type of nonprofit collaboration. In contrast, nonprofits with less board human capital are more likely to have a business-nonprofit collaborator. Finally, board human capital enhances the probability that nonprofits will have a government partnership in the presence of high social capital, but decrease the probability of independent social capital.

This study examined the role of board social capital and human capital in nonprofit within- and cross-sector collaboration. Collaboration among governmental, private, and nonprofit organizations has become a significant strategy to achieve collective goals in response to complex social problems and fewer resources (Chen, 2010; Kenis & Provan, 2006). The results from this study suggest the crucial role of board members in forging collective solutions to such complex social problems. Based on their social connections, sometimes in appropriate combination with their organizational knowledge and skills, board members may enact an active mechanism of supporting nonprofit collaboration and achieving collective goals.

Note

1. The actual items are: 1) Board members are committed to the vision of this organization; 2) The board members are accessible to employees; 3) This organization's board has a good working relationship with staff; 4) The board takes regular steps to stay informed about the important trends in the larger environment that might affect the organization; 5) The board explicitly examines the "downside" or possible pitfalls of any important decision it is about to make; 6) The board periodically sets aside time to learn more about important issues facing organizations like this one; 7) The board learns from its mistakes.

References

Atouba, Y. C. (2016). Let's start from the beginning: Examining the connections between partner selection, trust, and communicative effectiveness in voluntary partnerships among human services nonprofits. *Communication Research*. First published February 3, 2016, https://doi.org/10.1177/0093650215626982

Austin, J. E. (2000). *The collaboration challenge: How nonprofits and businesses succeed through strategic alliances*. San Francisco, CA: Jossey-Bass.

Austin, J. E., & Seitanidi, M. M. (2012). Collaborative value creation: A review of partnering between nonprofits and businesses: Part 1. Value creation spectrum and collaboration stages. *Nonprofit and Voluntary Sector Quarterly*, *41*(5), 726–758.

Barroso-Castro, C., Villegas-Periñan, M., & Casillas-Bueno, J. C. (2015). How boards' internal and external social capital interact to affect firm performance. *Strategic Organization*, *14*(1), 6–31, https://doi.org/10.1177/1476127015604799

Bluu, J. R., & Rabrenovic, G. (1991). Interorganizational relations of nonprofit organizations: An exploratory study. *Sociological Forum*, *6*(2), 327–347.

Bollen, K. A. (1989*). Structural equations with latent variables*. New York, NY: Wiley-Interscience Publication.

Brown, W. A. (2005). Exploring the association between board und organizational performance in nonprofit organizations. *Nonprofit Management and Leadership*, *15*(3), 317–339, https://doi org/10.1002/nml.71

Brown, W. A., & Guo, C. (2010). Exploring the key roles for nonprofit boards. *Nonprofit and Voluntary Sector Quarterly*, *39*(3), 536–546, https://doi.org/10.1177/0899764009334588

Bryson, J. M., Ackermann, F., & Eden, C. (2007). Putting the resource-based view of strategy and distinctive competencies to work in public organizations. *Public Administration Review*, *67*(4), 702–717.

Chait, R. P., Ryan, W. P., & Taylor, B. E. (2011). *Governance as leadership: Reframing the work of nonprofit boards*. Hoboken, NJ: John Wiley & Sons.

Chen, B. (2010). Antecedents or processes? Determinants of perceived effectiveness of interorganizational collaborations for public service delivery. *International Public Management Journal, 13*(4), 381–407.

Cooper, K. R., & Shumate M. (2012). Interorganizational collaboration explored through the bona fide network perspective. *Management Communication Quarterly, 26*(4), 623–654.

Cornforth, C. (2012). Nonprofit governance research: Limitations of the focus on boards and suggestions for new directions. *Nonprofit and Voluntary Sector Quarterly, 41*(6), 1116–1135, https://doi.org/10.1177/0899764011427959

DiMaggio, P. J., & Powell, W. W. (1983). The iron case revisited: Institutional isomorphism and collective rationality in organizational fields. *American Sociological Review, 48*, 147–160, https://doi.org/10.2307/2095101

Fabig, H., & Boele, R. (1999). The changing nature of NGO activity in a globalising world: Pushing the corporate responsibility agenda. *IDS Bulletin, 30*(3), 58–67, https://doi.org/10.1111/j.1759-5436.1999 mp30003008.x

Fredette, C., & Bradshaw, P. (2012). Social capital and nonprofit governance effectiveness. *Nonprofit Management and Leadership, 22*(4), 391–409, https://doi.org/10.1002/nml.21037

Fu, J. S., & Shumate, M (2017). Understanding the size and spread of Chinese NGO networks: Capacity and board affiliations. *Chinese Journal of Communication, 10*(1), 72–88.

Gazley, B., & Brudney, J. L. (2007). The purpose (and perils) of government-nonprofit partnership. *Nonprofit and Voluntary Sector Quarterly, 36*(3), 389–415, https://doi.org/10.1177/0899764006295997

Gazley, B., & Guo, C. (2015). What do we know about nonprofit collaboration? A comprehensive systematic review of the literature. *Academy of Management Proceedings, 2015*(1), 15409.

Ghosh, D., & Vogt, A. (2012). Outliers: An evaluation of methodologies. In *Joint statistical meetings* (pp. 3455–3460). San Diego, CA: American Statistical Association.

Gray, B. (2000). Assessing inter-organizational collaboration: Multiple conceptions and multiple methods. In D. Faulkner & M de Rond (Eds.), *Cooperative strategy: Economic, business, and organizational issues* (pp. 243–260), New York, NY: Oxford University Press.

Grønbjerg, K. A. (1993). *Understanding nonprofit funding*. San Francisco, CA: Jossey-Bass.

Gulati, R., & Westphal, J. D. (1999). Cooperative or controlling? The effects of CEO-board relations and the content of interlocks on the formation of joint ventures. *Administrative Science Quarterly, 44*(3), 473–506.

Guo, C., & Acar, M. (2005). Understanding collaboration among nonprofit organizations: Combining resource dependency institutional and network perspectives. *Nonprofit and Voluntary Sector Quarterly, 34*(3), 340–361, https://doi.org/10.1177/0899764005275411

Herman, R. D., & Renz, D. O. (2000). Board practices of especially effective and less effective local nonprofit organizations. *The American Review of Public Administration, 30*(2), 146–160, https://doi.org/10.1177/02750740022064605

Herman, R. D., & Renz, D. O. (2008). Advancing nonprofit organizational effectiveness research and theory: Nine theses. *Nonprofit Management and Leadership, 18*(4), 399–415, https://doi.org/10.1002/nml.195

Human, S. E., & Provan, K. G. (2000). Legitimacy building in the evolution of small-firm multilateral networks: A comparative study of success and demise. *Administrative Science Quarterly, 45*(2), 327–365.

Huxham, C., & Vangen, S. (2013). *Managing to collaborate: The theory and practice of collaborative advantage*. New York, NY: Routledge.

Hwang, H., & Bromley, P. (2015). Internal and external determinants of formal plants in the nonprofit sector. *International Public Management Journal, 18*(4), 568–588.

Ingram, R. T. (2009). *Ten basic responsibilities of nonprofit boards*. Washington, DC: National Center for Nonprofit Boards.

Jing, Y., & Chen, B. (2012). Is competitive contracting really competitive? Exploring government-nonprofit collaboration in China. *International Public Management Journal, 15*(4), 405–428.

Keast, R., Brown, K., & Mandell, M. (2007). Getting the right mix: Unpacking integration and strategies. *International Public Management Journal*, *10*(1), 9–33, https://doi.org/10.1080/10967 490601185716

Kenis, P., & Provan, K. G. (2006). The control of public networks. *International Public Management Journal*, *9*(3), 227–247.

Kim, M., & Peng, S. (2018). The dilemma for small human service nonprofits: Engaging in collaborations with limited human resource capacity. *Nonprofit Management and Leadership*, *29*, 83–103.

Lewis, L. K. (2006). Collaborative interaction: Review of communication scholarship and a research agenda. In C. S. Beck (Ed.). *Communication yearbook* (Vol. 30. pp. 197–247), Mahwah, NJ: Lawrence Erlbaum.

Miller-Millesen, J. L. (2003). Understanding the behavior of nonprofit boards of directors: A theory-based approach. *Nonprofit and Voluntary Sector Quarterly*, *32*(4), 521–547, https://doi.org/10.1177/0899764003257463

Milward, H. B., & Provan, K. G. (2006). *A manager's guide to choosing and using nonprofit collaboration.* Washington, DC: IBM Center for the Business of Government.

Oliver, C. (1990). Determinants of interorganizational relationships: Integration and future directions. *Academy of Management Review*, *15*(2), 241–265.

Onishi, T. (2015). Influences of venture philanthropy on nonprofits' funding: The current state of practices, challenges, and lessons. *The Foundation Review*, *7*(4), 8, https://doi.org/10.9707/1944-5660.1267

Osborne, S. P. (2000). *Public-private partnerships: Theory and practice in international perspective.* London, England: Routledge.

Ostrower, F. (2007). *Nonprofit governance in the United States: Findings on performance and accountability from the first national representative study.* Washington, DC: The Urban Institute.

Pfeffer, J., & Salancik, G. R. (1978). *The external control of organizations: A resource dependence perspective.* New York, NY: HarperCollins.

Pilny, A., & Shumate, M. (2012). Hyperlinks as extensions of offline instrumental collective action. *Information Communication & Society*, *15*(2), 260–286.

Provan, K. G., & Kenis, P. (2008). Modes of network governance: Structure, management, and effectiveness. *Journal of Public Administration Research and Theory*, *18*(2), 229–252, https://doi.org/10.1093/jopart/mum015

Provan, K. G., & Lemaire, R. H. (2012). Core concepts and key ideas for understanding public sector organizational networks: Using research to inform scholarship and practice. *Public Administration Review*, *72*(5), 638–648.

Provan, K. G., & Milward, H. B. (1995). A preliminary theory of interorganizational network effectiveness: A comparative study of four community mental health systems. *Administrative Science Quarterly*, *40*(1), 1–33.

R Core Team, (2016). *R: A language and environment for statistical computing.* Vienna, Austria: R Foundation for Statistical Computing. Retrieved from www.R-project.org/

Rondinelli, D. A. & London, T. (2003). How corporations and environmental groups cooperate: Assessing cross-sector alliances and collaborations. *The Academy of Management Executive*, *17*(1), 61–76, https://doi.org/10.5465/AME.2003.9474812

Rowley, T. J. (1997). Moving beyond dyadic ties: A network theory of stakeholder influences. *Academy of Management Review*, *22*(4), 887–910.

Salamon, L. M., & Anheier, H. K. (1996). *The international classification of non-profit organizations—ICNPO-revision 1.* Baltimore, MD: The Johns Hopkins University Institute for Policy Studies.

Sanzo, M. J., Álvarez L.I., Rey, M., & García, N. (2015). Business–nonprofit partnerships: A new form of collaboration in a corporate responsibility and social innovation context. *Service Business*, *9*(4), 611–636, https://doi.org/10.1007/s11628-014-0242-1

Schneider, J. A. (2009). Organizational social capital and nonprofits. *Nonprofit and Voluntary Sector Quarterly*, *38*(4), 643–662, https://doi.org/10.1177/0899764009333956

Shumate, M., Cooper, K. R., Pilny, A., & Peña-y-Lillo, M. (2017). The nonprofit capacities instrument. *Nonprofit Management & Leadership*, *28*(2), 155–174, https://doi.org/10.1002/nml.21276

Shumate, M., Hsieh, Y. P., & O'Connor. A. (2018). A nonprofit perspective on business–nonprofit partnerships: Extending the symbiotic sustainability model. *Business & Society*, *57*(7), 1337–1373.

Simo, G., & Bies, A. L. (2007). The role of nonprofits in disaster response: An expanded model of cross-sector collaboration. *Public Administration Review*, *67*(s1), 125–142.

Sowa, J. E. (2009). The collaboration decision in nonprofit organizations: Views from the front line. *Nonprofit and Voluntary Sector Quarterly*, *38*(6), 1003–1025, https://doi.org/10.1177/0899764008325247

Union of International Associations. (2013). *Yearbook of international organizations online: Guide to global civil society networks*. Brussels, Belgium: Union of International Associations.

Urban Institute Database. (2013). *Nonprofits and philanthropy*. Retrieved from www.urban.org/research-area/nonprofits-and-philanthropy/all

Vidovich, L., & Currie, J. (2012) Governance networks: Interlocking directorships of corporate and nonprofit boards. *Nonprofit Management and Leadership*, *22*(4), 507–523, https://doi.org/10.1002/nml.21042

Fostering Growth Through Capacity Building

Valencia Prentice and Mohamed Bamanie

Jack Sedman and Mary Evans recently graduated from Capacitia University with Master's in Public Administration degrees. Because both concentrated in Nonprofit Management and were excited to run their own consultancy business, they established J&M Consultancy to offer consulting services to nonprofit organizations. J&M Consultancy's vision is to specialize in helping nonprofits build capacity in organizational development including program evaluation, strategic planning, board development, volunteer management, and fund development.

As Mary began promoting J&M on social media and by reaching out to her professional network of nonprofits, she was pleased to reconnect with Asher Andrews, a former undergraduate classmate. Over lunch, Mary learned that Asher was the current CEO and Managing Director of the Opportunity Arts Academy of Anguilla (OAAA) and was interested in engaging J&M Consultancy for an organizational capacity audit. Asher had become the Managing Director in 2018.

OAAA is a nonprofit arts academy that has offered a number of arts programs since its inception in 2007, including arts exhibits and dance and theatre performances. OAAA is located in Anguilla, a British overseas territory island in the Caribbean. Although Mary knew little about the nonprofit environment in Anguilla, she was not surprised to learn that he was having trouble with board recruitment and financial challenges which are perennial concerns for almost all small nonprofits. Mary talked with Jack about Asher's concerns and both felt capable of helping strengthen OAAA, and they were determined to help a friend like Asher turn the organization around. J&M Consultancy, therefore, accepted OAAA as their client at a very modest fee with a contract to provide a tool that could be used to perform a capacity assessment for the organization.

Background on Anguilla and its Nonprofit Environment

Anguilla has a population of about 17,000. The average family income of Anguilla households is low. Given the island's small size, Anguillans have developed a close-knit community culture. The economy is heavily dependent on tourism and financial services. Many tourists are from the United States which contributes to many similarities between Anguillan and North American institutions. The influence of American fashion, music, television, and media also contribute to North America's influence on Anguilla's culture. Additionally, the United States currency is widely circulated in Anguilla.

 DOI: 10.4324/9781003387800-20

Anguilla is a tax-free jurisdiction with no sales tax or income tax. Government revenues consist mostly of import duties, property taxes, taxes on services, and service fees. Government services are primarily provided internally or outsourced to the private sector. Nonprofit organizations have minimal involvement in the production of public goods. The limited involvement of nonprofits in public service delivery probably can be attributed mostly to the lack of the sector's robustness.

The sluggishness of the Anguillan nonprofit sector is largely because of the limited wealth of citizens and because there are few tax laws in Anguilla that help nonprofits secure the resources required to support their missions. In contrast, nonprofit organizations in the United States are able to enjoy tax exemptions from federal, state, and local governments on their income. U.S. donors to charitable 501(c)(3) organizations can deduct their contributions from their federal income tax which provides a strong incentive to donate. U.S. Nonprofits also receive tax exemptions from federal income, and state and local property taxes, sales taxes, and hotel occupancy taxes. Without tax incentives available in Anguilla, individuals are not as motivated to start nonprofit ventures or to contribute financially to nonprofits.

Opportunity Arts Academy Anguilla (OAAA)

OAAA was established in October 2007 as an arts organization with the mission to build and develop well-rounded, confident individuals by providing a safe and nurturing environment where creativity and arts programming are able to thrive. OAAA developed a creed based on excellence, service, and molding the lives of young people. Although OAAA is highly regarded in Anguilla, it has become stagnant with individual memberships plateauing for the past decade at about 90 members annually.

As the CEO and Managing Director of this highly regarded but seemingly stalled nonprofit organization, Asher explained that he is most concerned that the organization is losing relevance in the community and is lacking a solid plan to move the organization forward with more financial support and expanded membership. Asher's relationship with the OAAA's board is solid, and he is hopeful that J&M Consultancy can help him invigorate the current members of the board of directors and elevate OAAA's visibility and presence in the community. In his discussion with Mary Evans, she assured him that OAAA could benefit from an organizational analysis using J&M's Organizational Capacity Assessment tool.

OAAA has undergone a series of organizational changes since its establishment in 2007 when it was staffed by a handful of volunteers. The board of directors is comprised of five members each holding an office:

- President
- Manager
- Secretary
- Treasurer
- Public Relations Officer

OAAA's by-laws stipulate that the members of the board of directors serve in their positions for two years. The directors are responsible for setting the organization's strategic priorities and overseeing the implementation of its strategic and financial operations. In recent years, OAAA has been unable to attract enough interested persons from the community to serve on its board. Therefore, two of the current board members have been serving in their roles for multiple years.

Back in 2008, OAAA had a simple organization structure which used all volunteers—including hands-on board members—in the day to day operations. In 2011, OAAA decided to expand its staff by adding a few positions including a dance director, a theatre director and the full-time managing director. In order to expand its programming, volunteers and

CS Figure 7.1: OAAA's 2008 Organizational Structure

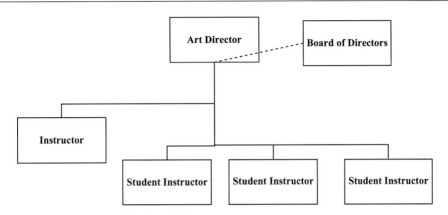

CS Figure 7.2: OAAA's 2011 Organizational Structure

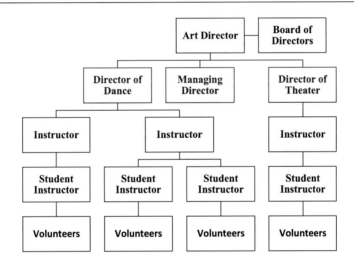

student interns were enticed to serve as program instructors in both the dance and theatre classes. Two grants were secured to provide funding for these programs. However, by 2020, OAAA had dropped its theatre program due to a lack of volunteers, and the staff was downsized to stay afloat. That same year, Asher was hired as the new CEO and managing director.

Despite the many changes over the years, OAAA has not changed its mission since its inception in 2007. The mission was created as an exercise while developing the organization's first strategic plan in 2007. OAAA has not updated its old strategic plan or created a new one since then, however, and the directors have not reviewed OAAA's mission since the organization was founded.

Asher is concerned that the mission is not communicated well to the organization's members, instructors, volunteers, or to the Anguillan community. The board has not focused on

CS Figure 7.3 OAAA's 2020 Organizational Structure

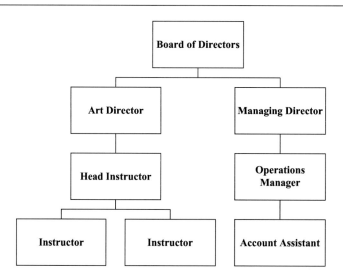

strategic planning because it has been preoccupied with operational activities. The lack of resources has made it impossible to hire trained staff for the operational and program functions. Thus, OAAA still has board members performing many operational and program related duties. OAAA relies on membership dues and a few grants for its revenue. The organization also raises some funding by charging for dance performances.

OAAA has also been struggling with volunteer recruitment. Two dedicated volunteers have been assisting with administrative duties such as keeping the membership records up to date and scheduling classes and workshops. However, there are no job descriptions for the volunteers, no guidelines about required weekly volunteer hours, or policies about oversight of the volunteers. OAAA mainly recruits volunteers by sending emails to parents of its youth members asking for their involvement, and board members occasionally ask close friends to volunteer. Neither of these strategies has been successful; hence, the organization has steadily reduced its recruitment efforts. In addition, the organization does not have a website where potential volunteers can find information about the organization. More broadly, OAAA's lack of resources and energy make it difficult for the organization to consistently engage and communicate with the community.

Although the board of directors is responsible for fund development, it is not a customary practice in Anguilla for nonprofit board members to donate personal funds to nonprofits on whose boards they serve. OAAA's board members spend most of their time communicating with youth members' parents, collecting and recording dues, and sending billing notices and reminders. Board meetings often are used to plan organizational events, such as art exhibits, recitals and dance trips. Meetings that focus on governing or capacity building have been put on the back burner.

OAAA does not have a strategy to deal with rising overhead costs. In 2019, a sponsorship proposal was sent to the Anguilla Tourist Board outlining sponsorship categories and benefits associated with each category. Sponsor benefits might include company logos on print materials disseminated through social media or on billboards, event naming rights, VIP seating at recitals, and dedicated performances at recitals. OAAA has not been successful at securing these targeted sponsorships using this approach.

The organization's annual budget for fiscal year 2020 is presented in Table 7.1.

CS TABLE 7.1 OAAA's Annual Budget for Fiscal Year 2020

Opportunity Arts Academy Anguilla
Annual Budget
For the period ending December 31st, 2020

Revenues			
	Program Activities		
	Regular dance tuition	40,800	
	Opportunity Edge	1,440	
	Opportunity Diamonds	300	
	Registration	1,575	
	Additional Classes	1,200	
	Subtotal		*45,315*
	Merchandise		
	T-Shirt	1,440	
	Leotard	1,800	
	Other Items	600	
	Subtotal		*3,840*
	Donations		
	Corporations	500	
	Individuals	100	
	Subtotal		*600*
	Performances		*3,800*
Total Revenues			**53,555**
Operating Expenses			
	Salaries and wages	24,000	
	Administrative	6,600	
	Employee benefits	6,000	
	Payroll taxes	1,152	
	Rent	10,800	
	Utilities	3,000	
	Travel	700	
	Telephone	480	
	Office supplies	450	
	Advertising	2,400	
	Marketing/promotion	3,600	
	Depreciation	1,080	
	Miscellaneous	1,200	
Total Expenses			**61,462**
Net Income (Loss)			**(7,907)**

With this organizational and financial information, J&M consulting began working with Asher on building OAAA's capacity. Jack and Mary recommended an organizational capacity assessment using the Nonprofit Organizational Capacity Assessment tool. (See Exhibit 1). The tool was created by J&M Consultancy to help its clients assess their organizations' capacity on four capacity dimensions: Governance and Leadership, Management, Resource Development, and Service. J&M believes that this tool and the resulting analysis will enable OAAA to have a much better understanding of what is needed to build its capacity in the short- and long-term. Asher has agreed to bring the idea to the board including using the capacity assessment tool to help the board set priorities. The board reluctantly agreed with Asher that J&M Consultancy should be retained. Afterall, the cost would be modest and the time frame of one month to conduct the assessment was seen as a reasonable.

CS Exhibit 7.1

Nonprofit Organizational Capacity Self-Assessment Tool

Instructions

Please check "yes" if the answer to the question is yes for your nonprofit and "no" if otherwise. Total the number of questions for which the answer is "yes" at the end of each dimension. Next, use the rubric at the end to determine the strength of your nonprofit for each dimension

Governance and Leadership Capacity

		Yes	No
1.	Does your organization's vision reflect its long-term aspirations?		
2.	Does your board review the organization's mission annually?		
3.	Does your organization set strategic goals annually?		
4.	Does the board evaluate the CEO's performance regularly?		
5.	Does the board evaluate its own performance regularly?		
6.	Is the board composed of individuals with the right mix of expertise?		
7.	Is the board composed of the diversified members in terms of gender, age and race?		
8.	Is the board well informed about the current issues faced by the organization?		
9.	Does the board meet regularly?		
10.	Does the board adopt an annual budget		

Management Capacity

		Yes	No
1.	Does your organization effectively manage its finances?		
2.	Does your organization regularly assess the workload of staff members?		

Management Capacity

		Yes	*No*
3.	Does your organization prepare a budget variance report each month?		
4.	Does your organization prepare cash flow forecasts to guide decision making?		
5.	Does your organization have job descriptions for staff and volunteers?		
6.	Does your organization have written performance objectives for staff and volunteers?		
7.	Does your organization have difficulty recruiting volunteers with the right skills mix?		
8.	Does your organization train staff and volunteers to do their jobs?		
9.	Does your organization regularly review performance of staff and volunteers		
10.	Does your organization have appropriate database with important information?		

Resource Development

		Yes	*No*
1.	Does your organization have an annual fundraising plan?		
2.	Does your organization have savings?		
3.	Does your organization attain new funders annually?		
4.	Can your organization comfortably cover all of its expenses?		
5.	Does your organization have a diversified revenue portfolio?		
6.	Does your organization have a plan to grow its revenues over time?		
7.	Does your organization have short term and long-term financial targets?		
8.	Does your organization keep a registry of past donors?		
9.	Does your organization maintain strong relationships with past donors?		
10.	Does your organization have aggressive campaigns to find new donors?		

Service Capacity

		Yes	*No*
1.	Does your organization engage in partnership with other organizations?		
2.	Does your organization regularly interact with community members and leaders?		

(Continued)

CS Exhibit 7.1 (Continued)

		Yes	*No*
3.	Does your organization regularly engage its members?		
4.	Does your organization design its programs in line with industry standards?		
5.	Does your organization have the appropriate facility and equipment to deliver programs?		
6.	Does the organization regularly compare its program quality with similar organizations?		
7.	Does the organization increase its program participants annually?		
8.	Does the organization adjust its programs to keep up with community needs?		
9.	Does the organization evaluate the effectiveness of its program?		
10.	Does the organization encourage participants to provide feedback on its service quality?		

Dimension	*Total Number of Yeses*	*Percentage*
Governance		
Management Capacity		
Resource Development		
Service Capacity		

Interpreting the Results

Below 40%—Low Nonprofit Capacity
41% to 79%—Medium Nonprofit Capacity
80% to 100%—High Nonprofit Capacity

After conducting the audit, J&M and Asher learned that OAAA had a "Low Nonprofit Capacity" score in the capacity areas of governance and leadership, management, and resource development. The organization had a ranking of "Medium Nonprofit Capacity" in service.

Questions:

1. Does the J&M Nonprofit Capacity Assessment tool measure all of the important areas of organizational capacity? If not, what areas would you add?

2. Who in and around OAAA should be asked to complete the Nonprofit Capacity Assessment tool?

3. Are the findings of the Nonprofit Capacity Assessment tool useful for providing OAAA with the information needed to address the problems identified in the case? If not, what else would you recommend?

4. What advice would you give to Asher to help him more effectively work with the board of directors in moving the organization forward?

5. What advice would you give to J&M Consultancy about their consulting business?

6. What advice would you give to JYM Consultancy about conducting business with nonprofits outside of the U.S.?

7. Do you believe that tools such as this one created to help U.S. nonprofits are useful for assessing capacity in other countries where nonprofit laws or customs are different?

Show Me the Money

C. KENNETH MEYER AND STACY GIBBS

Gertrude "Gerty" Madison was astonished when she learned about the demographic statistics of Garmin County and its low per capita income, high unemployment, and high school dropout rate. She was aghast to find that Garmin had an out-county migration rate that was among the state's highest. The county's health indicators, such as its maternal mortality rate (MMR) and infant mortality rate (IMR), were similar to those of many countries in the developing world. Further, she was beginning to develop an intimate knowledge of the county's food security issues as she traveled around and learned that there were no food stores in the county at the scale of a Kroger, a Hy-Vee, or an Aldi grocery store.

Gerty had loved to return from college to visit her relatives who lived in Garmin and spend blissful weekends on the century-old farm that had been homesteaded by her great-grandparents—one that she had often romanticized as characteristic of rural life in general. But as a mature adult, her perspective had shifted and she wondered why Garmin had fallen so far behind adjacent counties on basic indicators of social well-being and quality-of-life measurements. In particular, why did such a low percentage of Garmin's high school graduates go to college and gain higher degrees?

Gerty couldn't believe that her own upper-middle-class upbringing had sheltered her from the plight of her family friends and a large segment of the county. She was ashamed to tell others about her belief that poverty, and its accompanying disarray, is but a mental abstraction. She told her friends at work that rural poverty is no disgrace, but it is inconvenient. And she chuckled with her colleagues about her belief in the variation on the golden rule: those who have the gold, rule.

She also remembered talking to a friend while she was once visiting relatives. Gerty had tried to get a "dipstick reading" on the prevailing economic conditions in Garmin County. Her friend, a trust officer at the community bank, had said, "Gerty, you can't improve on the biblical injunction—the poor will always be with us."

Seeing the concern on Gerty's face, the trust officer of the bank leaned back in her overstuffed burgundy executive chair and explained: "I have been in the banking business for nearly twenty years and have been through some good times and some bad times. I prefer the good times. The economy is really in the dumps right now, and we have tightened our terms for loans to farmers, ranchers, and small businesses. In fact, if you don't need a loan because your balance sheet looks good, we are happy to provide one. On the other hand, if you are in a financial pinch, forget it. We are running a bank, not a charitable foundation."

As Gerty reflected on her impressions of modern-day Garmin County—the robust

 DOI: 10.4324/9781003387800-21

flurry of anecdotes she had heard as well as the statistics she had consulted—she wondered if she had made the right decision in applying for the executive director position of the Garmin County Development Corporation (GCDC), a small, nonprofit organization. Gerty had been reserved and tentative when she was actually offered the position, but taking on the executive director responsibilities would be a big step up for her in terms of responsibility and pay. Although a seasoned program manager, she would now have her leadership and administrative skills tested as she worked for an active seventeen-member board of directors.

The GCDC had applied to the state for a gaming license and was granted one for a newly opened riverboat casino. This meant that the Corporation would receive a large portion of the casino's profit each month, thus incurring a considerable fiduciary responsibility that would require careful daily management. As a condition of the licensure, as set forth by state code, GCDC was obligated to distribute this money or return it to the public in the form of grants. Gerty would be in charge of the "whole guacamole," as she told others, and she would have to create policies and procedures for the implementation of the grant program.

Her board of directors was composed entirely of men and was drawn from across the county; it included the mayor and a city council member of Arbor Lake, the largest city in the county; three bank presidents; three owners of real estate agencies; owners of two local insurance agencies; the owners of the two car dealerships; the owner of the local newspaper; two members of the water board; and the manager of the rural electric cooperative. The average tenure on the board was fifteen years. As she sized up the board, Gerty understood that it was a close-knit group and that she was going to have her first experience with a politically savvy and cohesive "good old boys' club."

The board members were very proud of the fact that they were mostly responsible for

bringing the casino to the county. They bragged about the projected revenues that might be as high as $40 million a year. Because of their negotiations, the GCDC would receive 1.5 percent of these revenues per year—25 percent of which could be applied toward operations and 75 percent of which the GDCD was required to return to other nonprofit entities in the form of grants.

Every member of the board had his own idea on how the money should be granted out and was very vocal about it. Most importantly, the board members felt a collective ownership and stewardship over the funds it would receive from the casino and wanted a grant process that would be under their close scrutiny and control.

Gerty started creating a grant process by reviewing what other casino license-holders did with their monies. She reasoned that there was no sense in reinventing the wheel. Gerty scouted around and found a model for spending such monies that had been used by a similar-sized group for five years. After several discussions with the executive director of this group, she decided that, with a few modifications, this model could work well for the GCDC. The board created a subcommittee to work with Gerty on a model plan and present it to the full board.

Under the model, grant applications would only be accepted from 501(c)(3) nonprofit organizations or governmental agencies serving a charitable purpose located in Garmin County. It would also require a dollar-for-dollar cash match from the applicant. In other words, for every dollar requested from the grant program, the applicant would have to match it with a dollar of its own funds. A scoring system would be used to rate each application based on selected factors such as projected community impact, contribution to economic development, innovativeness of the project, and the number of people affected. Additionally, there was a maximum award amount of $100,000, and projects awarded had to be completed within twelve months. Applicants who received an award could not apply for another project from GDGC until the awarded project was completed. If an application was denied, the applicant had to wait at least six months before reapplying. Lastly, a subcommittee of the board would review all applications on a monthly basis and make recommendations to the full board for final approval.

Gerty was pleased with the process that she and the subcommittee collectively worked out and excited to present it to the board and begin the grant implementation process. The reaction from the board members, for the most part, was very positive, although they did suggest a few changes to the methods and criteria used in scoring the applications. Finally, after a cordial, if lengthy, discussion, the subcommittee's report was approved by a unanimous vote. It was determined that the board would wait six months to implement the grant program in order to have sufficient funds in reserve for the approved applications.

A year later, with six months of grant applications and awards tucked under her belt, Gerty felt that the grant program was functioning fairly well, although it had needed tweaking in a number of places. The subcommittee was performing well, and the board seemed to accept recommendations without much question. Most applications were for smaller projects that funded youth programs, recreation and parks programs, and beautification projects. Then an application was received from the Arbor Lake Street Department to fund a large portion of a citywide street reconstruction project. The subcommittee, using the scoring system that was in place, scored the application very high. The Arbor Lake city administrator, who wrote the application, had justified the project by emphasizing its impact on Arbor Lake's economic development with the beautification of the city and an increase in property values.

Despite the application's high score, the subcommittee had several problems with approving it. First, they did not think it was appropriate to use grant funds for a tax-supported entity. They also argued that the city received casino revenues as well, so why did the city need GCDC money?

In response, Gerty pointed out that the application fit all of the requirements that had been set forth and published by the board. She also asked the subcommittee to consider that this project would probably not take place without grant funding. Her arguments and justification were not convincing, and the subcommittee sent the application to the full board and asked them to consider the dilemma.

This was Gerty's first setback since becoming the executive director, and she felt a sense of personal defeat as she forwarded the application to the full board with strict instructions to complete the scoring sheet and be prepared to discuss the application at their next meeting.

The intervening month passed rather slowly, and Arbor Lake representatives contacted Gerty several times inquiring on the final disposition of their application for grant money. She was ready to get this political issue behind her and move on to more productive ventures. When the full board convened, Gerty was disappointed and frustrated to learn that the majority of the board, surprisingly, had not completed the scoring sheets. Additionally, most of the discussion centered on opinions instead of the factual information provided by the city administrator in the application. The Arbor Lake mayor and city council member, who were members of the GCDC board, were very vocal about the need for the project and argued vociferously for the approval of the application. They reminded the board of the financial commitment that the Arbor Lake council made each year to the GCDC. The board discussed the many pros and cons associated with the application and went on to approve it with a small majority. Gerty knew that, for the most part, the public would view the board's decision as a good thing, but she also knew that the board had bent to the pressure from Arbor Lake officials and that the approval was not solely based on the merit of the project.

News of the approval quickly spread through the county grapevine and opened the door for an onslaught of similar applications from many of the smaller cities. For instance, the Garmin County Board of Supervisors requested money for road maintenance equipment. The county hospital asked for a new ambulance. One of the smaller city governments in the county requested funds for a city paving project. All of the applications would have to be considered, and the subcommittee once more felt that they had to take all of the requests to the full board and let them decide.

The routine became normal for Gerty, and once more she stressed the importance of following the grant guidelines and using the scoring sheets to justify the board's decisions on the grant applications. She reminded the board of how important it was that they read the proposals and complete the scoring cards on each application prior to meeting as a group. Gerty told the board that they would be held accountable to the public for their decisions on how the grants were approved and that their credibility would be jeopardized if they had no valid justifications for their decisions. She further explained that she would be placed in a delicate and compromised position if the criteria for grant funding were not consistently followed. After all, she stated, she had to explain to some applicants why their applications were denied. She mentioned these concerns to the board because she knew that inconsistent decisions by the board would be talked about and cause great turmoil in the many local jurisdictions.

The next time the full board met, about half of the board members had completed the scoring sheets, but as Gerty quickly discovered, their ratings did not matter. The board members revisited the issue of funding governmental jurisdictions, and the questions and arguments did not differ much from their

earlier reservations and concerns. In the end, the full board acted inconsistently in its funding decisions. The applications from the Board of Supervisors for equipment and from the smaller city government for paving funds were rejected. The request for a new ambulance for the county hospital was approved.

The board established a precedent of funding tax-supported entities when it approved the application for the Arbor Lake paving project and when it funded the new ambulance for the county hospital. Gerty knew that it would not take long for the public to figure out the reasoning behind the board's actions. Simply, two members of the GCDC board were from the city of Arbor Lake and three others were also on the county Board of Supervisors. To say that there was a conflict of interest was an understatement. Yet, Gerty was expected to make the board's decision fit the grant scoring and rating criteria.

CS Exhibit 8.1: Garmin County Development Corporation (GCDC) General Grant Background and Instructions

Garmin County Development Corporation (GCDC) Mission

The Garmin County Development Corporation (GCDC) is a donor-driven public foundation whose purpose is to improve the quality of life in our community through philanthropy.

The GCDC works to improve the quality of life for all by connecting donors with their passions, fostering links between community organizations, and convening local leaders to advance the common good. Increasing our community's connectedness includes building trust, civility, and volunteerism and encouraging informal socializing and civic engagement.

Making community connections builds on our remarkable tendency to reach out to one another and lend a hand to those in need . . . we're simply better together.

Leadership and Developmental Grants

Leadership and developmental grants are intended to advance GCDC's agenda and positively impact our communities in Garmin County. The GCDC's Grant- Making Committee is committed to strengthening our community by proactively responding to emerging community needs, trends, and opportunities. Therefore, GCDC allocates a significant portion of its discretionary dollars to fund grants.

Eligibility Requirements

Grants are made only to charitable organizations or causes with 501(c)(3) status or to governmental agencies serving a charitable purpose. Geographically, funding is limited to projects that will significantly improve communities in Garmin County. It is strongly recommended that organizations speak with GCDC staff prior to submitting a leadership grant letter of intent.

Grant Cycle Timeline

First cycle: The letter of intent is due on or before 4:00 PM on April 4 of the current year.

Second cycle: The letter of intent is due on or before 4:00 PM on October 3 of the current year.

The GCDC will notify applicants of the status of their proposals within ten business days after it is received. Proposals that advance in the process will receive further instructions at that time.

Documents Required

Please submit the letter of intent along with the documents listed below:

- A copy of the 501(c)(3) designation letter of organization or fiscal sponsor, unless the organization is a governmental entity

- A projected budget for the project
- A list of the director on the organization's board of directors with contact information and email addresses

Eligible Projects

The GCDC approves grant applications for projects that:

- Advance the initiatives included in the GCDC's leadership agenda (see the grant-making guidelines for more information).
- Include an opportunity for GCDC to participate in a "signature" program or project within the scope of the entire project.
- Demonstrate significant community impact, are broad and wide-reaching in nature, and are inclusive of the entire community.
- Include evidence of a strong statement of community need and broad-ranging community support and endorsement, demonstrated by a broad donor base and community buy-in.
- Show evidence of long-term community planning for the project and an organizational strategic plan that has been included in the project.
- Include a well-developed plan for evaluating success. Grant recipients may be asked to present project results to the GCDC Grant-Making Committee.
- Have an achievable plan to sustain the program well beyond the grant period.
- Recognize and celebrate our community's diversity and provide access for underserved populations. Show planning for outreach and accessibility to underserved populations.
- Demonstrate evidence of sufficient planning and organizational capacity to suggest a good opportunity for success.
- Show strong probability for leveraged funding from other sources.

In addition, funding will be most favorably considered for those organizations that:

- Build social capital
- Have not received a leadership grant in the prior year
- Have committed to meeting the "Principles and Practices for Charitable Nonprofit Excellence" identified by the State Nonprofit Resource Center

Specific examples of eligible projects include:

- New programs and projects that are the result of an expansion or building project (enhanced programming as a result of a capital project)
- Seed funding for a long-term community betterment project (annual festival)
- Projects that will enhance recreational or community economic development
- Programs or projects that will significantly impact emerging community needs, opportunities, and trends
- Projects that address a critical issue and build community connections and partnerships

The GCDC will not consider:

- Ongoing annual operating expenses
- Grants to individuals

- Sectarian religious programs
- Projects not serving residents of Garmin County

Questions and Instructions

1. What role, if any, should members of the board play in reviewing grant applications from their own organizations? Please identify two grant-making bodies and contact them to ask for a copy of their conflict of interest policy, if it exists.
2. Do you think the grant program was structured in the most effective manner to address the social capital issues that Gerty discusses at the beginning of the case? Please explain.
3. Should taxpayer-supported organizations be eligible for GCDC grant funding? Would you differentiate between taxpayer-supported nonprofit organizations and local governments? Please explain.
4. Would you suggest any changes in the grant application criteria or scoring process? If so, what changes and why?
5. Do you think the makeup of the GCDC board of directors is sufficient, or would you suggest changes to the makeup of the board?

PART V

FUND DEVELOPMENT
Generating Revenues

Nonprofit organizations raise funds in many ways and from many types of sources, but most limit their fundraising activities and sources of funds to those that "fit" their mission and the strengths and skills of their staff and volunteers. Many nonprofit organizations raise most of their funds from private sources—for example, private and corporate foundations, corporate gifts, and contracts for services.[1] Others appeal to the general public through special events, person-to-person and social media community fundraising drives, and direct-mail campaigns. Religious, fraternal, and professional membership organizations approach their members. Many organizations turn to government agencies for grants, contracts, and subsidies, while others raise funds from sales of goods and services to recipients or third-party payers such as private schools and colleges, museum gift shops, client-staffed pet stores, hospitals, and home health agencies.

Fundraising is both an art and a science. Six functions have been identified as essential for fundraising success: research, planning, cultivation, solicitation, stewardship, and evaluation. The implementation of each of these functions is an art form that "takes time, patience, and the motivation to succeed."[2] Research, for example, is needed to identify prospective donors, including individuals, foundations, corporations, and organizations, and to understand the motivations of each as well as the constraints of their environments. In an environment where many nonprofits compete for funds, research also contributes to an understanding of one's own organization and other organizations with similar missions.[3]

Types of Fundraising Strategies and Sources

Fundraising strategies and sources can be grouped into the following broad categories:

(1) Donations from:
    a. individuals and families and their trusts
    b. public and private foundations

(2) Grants from:
    a. corporations
    b. government agencies (for example, the National Institutes of Health)
    c. federated funding sources or intermediaries (for example, the United Way)
    d. foundations (which can be community, corporate, or family foundations)

DOI: 10.4324/9781003387800-22

(3) Sales of goods and services from:

    a. contracts with government agencies

        i. to provide services or goods to clients of government agencies (third-party payment arrangements)

       ii. to provide goods or services to government agencies

    b. contracts with corporations to provide services or goods

    c. sales to individuals

    d. sales to other nonprofit organizations

(4) Fees, dues, and pledges from members

(5) Interest and investment income

Although most of these broad categories of fundraising activities and sources are self-explanatory, the category titles mask an almost infinite variety of innovative fundraising tactics and arrangements. For example, there are many types of "sales of goods and services" to individuals, including cause-related marketing arrangements through which contractual "win-win partnerships" are formed with businesses. The business uses a nonprofit's name in promotional advertising, and the nonprofit receives a percentage of either the sales or the sales increase in exchange.[4] Although cause-related marketing usually generates needed revenues, some have argued that business-sector approaches to nonprofit management and fund development also may undercut the importance of promoting democratic values and philanthropy. As noted by Angela Eikenberry, increasing reliance on fees for services and entrepreneurial fundraising is causing changes across the nonprofit sector, with important social implications. For example, pursuing fee-based revenues as opposed to donor funds changes the skill sets of nonprofit executives and development staff members—and the curriculum in university nonprofit management programs. Likewise, the marketization of the nonprofit sector and the increasingly common depiction of human relations as "transactions" or "market exchanges" challenge the democratic values of discourse and shared decision making and undermine the notion of philanthropy as "love of mankind."[5]

There are also many varieties of donations. With a *charitable remainder trust*, for example, an individual or family makes a gift (usually a large gift); the gift assets are transferred to a trustee; the family receives income on the value of the assets for a number of years; and when the time arrives, the assets and the income they generate are transferred to a preselected nonprofit. In contrast, a *charitable lead trust* permits an individual or family to transfer income-yielding assets to a trust for a specified period during which the income flows to a chosen nonprofit organization. When the period is up, the assets and the income from them are returned to the family.

Special events usually combine donations and *sales of goods and services*. Individuals and corporations buy donated goods and services at the event, or they pay more than market value for them. Corporations and sometimes government agencies also may become *event sponsors*, which is another variety of donation.

Within the category "sales of goods and services," some sales are paid for by the recipient and others are paid for or reimbursed by a *third-party payer*, such as an insurance company or a government program.

All varieties of revenue-generating activities have advantages and disadvantages. They require different skills, time commitments, and types of efforts by board members and staff. They often involve multiple arrangements with government agencies or businesses. Different fundraising activities also have varying levels of expected payouts. Thus, some fundraising strategies fit better with different types of nonprofit organizations than others. Many larger nonprofits can devote considerable skilled staff effort to, for example, writing grants or organizing celebrity-studded gala events that smaller nonprofits are not staffed to handle. Nonprofits that serve sympathy-evoking clients and causes can employ fundraising strategies and tap sources that may not be available to nonprofits that serve unpopular causes or stigmatized populations. Nonprofits enjoying high status in a community can require their trustees to make large annual contributions and to solicit donations from their friends and associates. Many nonprofits are not as fortunate, however, and are happy just to fill all the vacant board positions. A request for these trustees to donate or solicit funds would not be well received and might even cause some trustees to resign.

Trustees and Fundraising

The trustees are at the heart of fundraising in most nonprofits. Numerous studies have shown that larger donations are made "people to people"—more so than "people to organizations" or to causes. When a respected peer who serves on a board asks for a major gift to an organization or cause, we are more likely to reach for our checkbook or credit card.

> To the extent that trustees are active in the community, are givers themselves, and are not afraid to ask for money, the organization will be more successful in the fundraising effort. Furthermore, the fiscal health of the organization depends on the extent to which the trustees feel that the income gap (the difference between what is earned and what is expended) is their responsibility.[6]

All Fundraising Strategies Have Advantages and Disadvantages

Almost all types of fundraising activities place some restrictions on the nonprofit organization. Corporate partnership arrangements, for example, may prevent the nonprofit from entering into arrangements with other corporations. Acceptance of United Way funding historically has required nonprofits to refrain from soliciting other funding from participating employers (for example, corporate sponsorships of special events). Government contracts to provide services often come with burdensome requirements and may require a nonprofit to accept clients it would not ordinarily serve or to limit the quantity of services provided to some individuals. A nonprofit organization's reliance on government contracts or a corporate marketing program may cause individual donors to divert their gifts to other causes in the belief that the organization does not need their money. Restricted gifts can commit a nonprofit to a long-term program or project that may decline in importance over the years or to a project that requires a substantial amount of additional funding—thereby possibly creating organizational rigidity or draining limited resources.

The decision to pursue a certain funding source also reduces options. Once a nonprofit has committed itself to one or two major fundraising activities in a year, it is locked in. Few nonprofits have enough staff members and volunteers to pursue multiple sources of funding simultaneously. It is important, therefore, to select carefully. Finally, no discussion of fundraising would be complete without a consideration of foundations. Elizabeth Boris describes foundations as a revenue source for nonprofit organizations and as nonprofit organizations themselves. *Foundations* are defined as

> nonprofit, nongovernmental organizations that promote charitable giving and other public purposes usually by giving grants of money to nonprofit organizations, qualified individuals, and other entities. Under US law, philanthropic foundations must serve the public by being organized and operated exclusively for religious, charitable, scientific, testing for public safety, literary, or educational purposes.[7]

The work of foundations has contributed to the growth in the sheer number of nonprofits through financial support for projects, programs, and at times, administrative support.

Recent Trends in Nonprofit Revenue Sources

In 2016, public charities accounted for just over three-quarters of revenue and expenses for the nonprofit sector as a whole ($2.04 trillion and $1.94 trillion, respectively) and just under two-thirds of the nonprofit sector's total assets ($3.79 trillion).[8] In 2018, private giving from individuals, foundations, and businesses totaled $427.71 billion,[9] a decrease of 1.7 percent from 2017 (after adjusting for inflation). According to Giving USA (2018), total charitable giving rose for consecutive years from 2014 to 2017, making 2017 the largest single year for private charitable giving, even after adjusting for inflation.[10]

The mix of revenues and the importance of each type of revenue vary by type of nonprofit organization. For example, for institutions of higher education and hospitals, fees for services—which include tuition payments, hospital patient revenues including Medicare and Medicaid, and ticket sales—accounted for 70.3 percent of all revenues, and public support—including private contributions at 12.3 percent and government grants at 9.0 percent—totaled only 21.3 percent. Investment income accounted for 5.4 percent of revenue, and all other income for 2.9 percent. When hospitals and institutions of higher education are excluded, however, the mix of revenues changes markedly. Without these two subsectors, fees for services in 2005 represented 53.6 percent of all revenue to public charities. Public support was 40.3 percent (with private contributions at 23.3 percent and government grants at 17 percent). Other income was 3.9 percent and investment income was 2.3 percent.[11]

During the past two decades, many nonprofits have increased their reliance on government contracts as steady sources of revenue, but at the same time, the total amount of US government money flowing into the human services, the arts, and environmental protection has declined steadily—and sometimes dramatically. Delays in government payments have also created difficult circumstances for nonprofits.[12].States, counties, and cities have not been anxious to replace the declining funds from Washington, DC, at a time when political pressures for tax reductions and control of deficits enjoy strong public support. Thus, many nonprofits have turned to fees for services and other entrepreneurial activities to support their activities.

The percentage of income that charitable nonprofit organizations receive from government grants varies by subsector, with human services receiving the lion's share. Despite the widespread cutbacks in government funding, government reliance on nonprofits—and thus government as a source of income—has continued to grow in some subsectors, particularly through contracts for services for persons with mental illness, disabilities (including developmental disabilities), chemical dependencies, youth (including gangs), the elderly, families, individuals who need job training, and victims of abuse (including legal services). Government funding also helps support and coordinate the arts and provide financial support, for example, to national parks, seashores, and rivers. Massachusetts and New Jersey, for example, provide almost no direct human services because virtually all such services have been contracted out to nonprofits.[13] This growing reliance—or dependence—on government contracts, unfortunately, comes at a time when government funding has been in a long-term decline. The government "downsizing, devolution, and diffusion movement" of the 1990s and early 2000s peaked at a time when individual and corporate donations to nonprofit organizations were stagnant and, by many measures, declining.[14]

Nonprofits have been under increasing pressure to be more *entrepreneurial*—to pursue alternative sources of revenue—and many have been doing much better at meeting this "charge" than expected. Some are selling services and products aggressively and often compete for business directly with for-profit firms. Others have become adept at *social entrepreneurship* and are engaging in a wide array of types of enterprises that were unknown in the sector less than a two decades ago.[15]

Readings Reprinted in Part V

The readings in Part V provide a framework for understanding fund development and a review of some of the "nuts and bolts" of managing fund development activities. In addition, a few philosophical concerns and the managerial realities associated with fluctuations and changes in organizations' fund portfolios are discussed.

In the first essay in Part V, "Capacity Building: Strategies for Successful Fundraising," Michele Cole introduces the wide variety of techniques and strategies used by nonprofits to raise funds and thereby build their capacity to remain viable organizations. Capacity-building includes the myriad "activities that nonprofits undertake to enhance their ability to meet mission goals. Fundraising . . . is a key element in capacity-building." The chapter walks us through a wide range of funding approaches, starting with the fundraising plan through potential sources of support, government fundraising, foundation fundraising, annual funds, special events, capital campaigns, legacy fundraising, endowments, and crowdfunding. Cole emphasizes that fundraising must be "an integral function in the management of any nonprofit relying on public support for a significant portion of its revenue."

In the second reading, "Analyzing the Dynamics of Funding: Reliability and Autonomy," Jon Pratt provides a useful framework for understanding the advantages and challenges associated with different revenue sources, including individual contributions, membership dues, government contracts, United Way allocations, earned income, third-party payers, foundation grants, and blended and diversified revenues. Each source of income has ramifications for autonomy and reliability. Pratt's framework nicely illustrates problems endemic to nonprofits as they seek to ease financial insecurities. For example, nonprofits that rely too heavily on any single type of revenue are at risk of becoming resource dependent, which can lead to unhealthy goals displacement whereby goals and activities are modified for the purpose of satisfying the preferences of key stakeholders—in particular, those of major donors.[16]

Too often, nonprofits will write grants for activities that foundations are likely to fund instead of seeking funds that fit well with their mission and the needs of their clients. A beggar's mentality, however, is shortsighted.

> Since foundations and corporations have varied priorities, we have often tried to be all things to all people, cutting and tailoring our interests and programs to fit those of the donors. In many cases, the result has been dismal. Either we undermined our mission or initiated programs for which we were ill suited.[17, 18, 19, 20]

To the extent that funded activities are not congruent with a nonprofit organization's mission, goals, or vision, mission creep may change the nature and character of the organization. Government contracts, for example, usually have a formalizing effect on nonprofits because they may require contracted nonprofits to professionalize their staffs and bureaucratize their organizations, which reduces administrative autonomy in the nonprofit organizations.

Case Studies in Part V

In the two case studies, "Ethical Considerations in Fundraising" and "The Selling of America," the perennial concerns about balancing financial need with image, continuity, and political support are raised. In "Ethical Considerations in Fundraising," the lure of "easy money" requires the executive director of a nonprofit serving the elderly to consider the relationship that her organization has formed with a longtime donor who has suddenly upped the financial stakes—along with the risks and ethical concerns. After analyzing the case, readers are asked to draft acceptance policies that are consistent with ethical obligations in fund development.

"The Selling of America" situates the reader in the role of a fire chief who must find ways to do more with less as dollars shrink. The chief is presented with an opportunity to pursue grant funding from an area casino, the Lucky Sevens, which is soliciting funding proposals from public and nonprofit organizations. The reader must consider the ramifications of applying for a potentially controversial source of funding and complying with the stipulations that will accompany the grant monies.

Notes

1. For an excellent overview of the different types of corporate foundations, see Elizabeth T. Boris, "Foundations," in *The International Encyclopedia of Public Policy and Administration,* edited by Jay M. Shafritz (Boulder, CO: Westview Press, 1998), 928–935.

2. Wesley E. Lindahl, *Principles of Fundraising: Theory and Practice* (Sudbury, MA: Jones and Bartlett, 2010), 129.

3. Ibid., 130.

4. Barbara L. Ciconte and Jeanne G. Jacob, *Fundraising Basics: A Complete Guide,* 3rd ed. (Sudbury, MA; Jones and Bartlett, 2009), 3.

5. Angela Eickenberry, "The Modernization and Marketization of Voluntarism," in Angela Eickenberry, *Giving Circles* (Bloomington: Indiana University Press, 2009), 29–43.

6. Thomas Wolf, *Managing a Nonprofit Organization*, updated 21st-century ed. (New York: Free Press, 2012), 242.

7. Boris, "Foundations," in Shafritz, *The International Encyclopedia of Public Policy and Administration.*

8. Urban Institute. The Nonprofit Sector in Brief 2019. https://nccs.urban.org/publication/nonprofit-sector-brief-2019#the-nonprofit-sector-in-brief-2019

9. Giving USA Foundation 2019. https://givingusa.org/giving-usa-2019-americans-gave-427-71-billion-to-charity-in-2018-amid-complex-year-for-charitable-giving/

10. Urban Institute. The Nonprofit Sector in Brief 2019. https://nccs.urban.org/publication/nonprofit-sector-brief-2019#the-nonprofit-sector-in-brief-2019

11. Steven R. Smith and Michael Lipsky, *Nonprofits for Hire* (Cambridge, MA: Harvard University Press, 1993).

12. NCCS Project, "The Nonprofit Sector in Brief, 2019" (June 2020). https://nccs.urban.org/publication/nonprofit-sector-brief-2019#the-nonprofit-sector-in-brief-2019

13. Ibid.

14. Kennard T. Wing, Thomas H. Pollak, and Amy Blackwood, *The Nonprofit Almanac 2008* (Washington, DC: Urban Institute, 2008), 144.

15. Lester M. Salamon, Stephanie L. Geller, and Kasey Spence, "Impact of the 2007–09 Economic Recession on Nonprofit Organizations," Listening Post Project Communique 14 (Baltimore, MD: Johns Hopkins Center for Civil Society Studies, 2009), 5.

16. J. Steven Ott and Lisa A. Dicke, "Challenges Facing Public Sector Management in an Era of Downsizing, Devolution, Diffusion, Empowerment—and Accountability?" *Public Organization Review* 1, no. 3 (September 2002), 321–339.

17. See, for example, Jay M. Shafritz, J. Steven Ott, and Yong Suk Jang, "Theories of Organizations and Society," in *Classics of Organization Theory*, 8th ed., edited by Jay M. Shafritz, J. Steven Ott, and Yong Suk Jang (Boston: Wadsworth/Cengage, 2016).

18. See, for example, Karen A. Froelich, "Diversification of Revenue Strategies: Evolving Resource Dependence in Nonprofit Organizations," *Nonprofit and Voluntary Sector Quarterly* 28, no. 3 (September 1999), 246–268.

19. Pablo Eisenberg, "Penetrating the Mystique of Philanthropy: Relations Between Fund Raisers and Grant Makers," in *Challenges for Nonprofits and Philanthropy: The Courage to Change*, edited by Stacy Palmer (Medford, MA: Tufts University Press, 2005), 64.

20. Boris, "Foundations," in Shafritz, *The International Encyclopedia of Public Policy and Administration.*

► CHAPTER 10

Capacity Building
Strategies for Successful Fundraising

MICHELE T. COLE

First published in *Understanding Nonprofit Organizations: Governance, Leadership, and Management*, 3rd ed., edited by J. Steven Ott and Lisa A. Dicke (Boulder, CO: Westview Press, 2016).

UNESCO's International Institute for Educational Planning (IIEP) has defined *capacity-building* as "the process by which individuals, groups, organizations, institutions and societies increase their abilities to: (a) perform core functions, solve problems, define and achieve objectives; and (b) understand and deal with their development needs in a broad context and in a sustainable manner" (IIEP 2006, 1). Although UNESCO's IIEP context is educational planning, the definition embraces activities that nonprofits undertake to enhance their ability to meet mission goals. Fundraising as part of the overall development effort is a key element in capacity-building. Unlike its counterparts in the for-profit and public sectors, organizations in the nonprofit sector rely on fundraising to support their programs and pursue their missions.

Capacity-Building

Why is capacity-building important? Nonprofits, eleemosynary, nongovernmental, and voluntary organizations worldwide provide critical services to people and communities. These are organizations that, in Lester Salamon's words, seek "to alleviate want, deliver health care and education, provide social services, and give voice to a multitude of cultural, artistic, religious, ethnic, social, and environmental concerns" (Salamon, Sokolowski, and Associates 2004, xxi). To be effective, organizations need adequate managerial, financial, and relationship-building skills to be able to deliver services and to serve their purposes. Healthy nonprofits contribute to a vibrant third sector and further advance a global civil society. As an investment in sustainability, capacity-building is about the future of these organizations.

McKinsey & Company (2001) presents the seven key elements of effective capacitybuilding for nonprofits as a pyramid, not unlike the giving pyramid used in describing the gradual progression of successful donor cultivation. In their framework, capacity-building depends on human resources, systems and infrastructure, and organizational structure. On this foundation, organizational skills are built, strategies developed, and aspirations set. The seventh and final element, culture, surrounds the pyramid,

DOI: 10.4324/9781003387800-23

providing the framework for capacity-building (McKinsey & Company 2001, 36).

As in the capacity-building framework, successful fundraising also depends on appropriate staffing, adequate technical support, and a recognized position within the organizational structure. Upon that foundation, fundraising skills for staff and board may be developed, a fundraising strategy adopted, and goals set. The organization's culture facilitates successful development efforts.

Fundraising

Fundraising involves building relationships with individuals, with private and public funders, and with the community. As a key element in the organization's development program, fundraising supports and is critical to realizing the goals and objectives of the organization's strategic plan. Kent Dove explains the relationship this way: "No development program can succeed without an effective fundraising operation to provide the necessary resources. But development in the broadest sense includes much more than fundraising" (Dove 2001, 5). A nonprofit's development program is concerned with "institution-raising." Fundraising is concerned with enabling development efforts.

Different fundraising activities are designed to serve different specific purposes and may require specialized staffing and volunteers. For example, special events, particularly for new or small organizations, are thought of more as "friend-raisers" than fundraisers. Organizing charity balls, golf outings, awards dinners, and marathons, among others, is time-intensive, and these events, unless otherwise funded, often cost more than can be recovered by the ticket revenue. Annual funds, on the other hand, can be managed by a small staff supported by adequate record-keeping and marketing tools, but they may take years to mature. Capital campaigns need board leadership and often require professional fundraising counsel to support staff and board efforts.

All fundraising involves (1) understanding and appreciating the organization that is the subject of the fundraising effort—its culture, as well as the external and internal forces that impact it; (2) possessing or having access to the research skills necessary to identify potential funding sources; (3) cultivating the relationships that are essential to soliciting support; (4) planning and implementing a fundraising strategy that meets the organization's needs; and (5) having systems in place to ensure stewardship of the funds received.

It has been said that fundraising is more an art than a science. Most often, it is a combination of the two. Relationship-building and stewardship require organizational support. Without an underlying management and governance infrastructure, stewardship is difficult at best. Donors, grantors, and regulators expect it. Stewardship is about transparency, accountability, and ethics (Ciconte 2007).

Some Fundraising Requirements

Who can fundraise? The short answer is that anyone can solicit funding for any cause or purpose. However, a nonprofit organization in the United States cannot ask for donations in support of its programs and mission without meeting certain legal requirements. At this writing, thirty-nine states and the District of Columbia require charitable nonprofits—those classified as 501(c)(3) organizations under the Internal Revenue Code (26 U.S.C. § 501(c))—to register with the state prior to beginning any solicitation. Many states exempt religious entities, nonprofit hospitals, educational institutions, and very small nonprofit organizations from this requirement.

Organizations engaged in Internet and social media fundraising face additional challenges when soliciting in multiple states. Several states require that the solicitation (as well as the acknowledgment) contain a disclosure statement.

If the organization contracts with a professional fundraising consultant, some jurisdictions require that the person be registered with that state as well. Note that certain types of fundraising vehicles, such as bingos and raffles, require a license from the municipality in which the activity takes place. In some instances, joint fundraisers, including onetime or recurring solicitations, special events, and campaigns, among others, are considered commercial co-ventures. Commercial co-ventures have additional requirements (National Council of Nonprofits 2014).

Donations to organizations designated as charitable nonprofits qualify for special treatment under the federal income tax code. However, for the taxpayer/donor to be able to deduct the contribution, the charity must comply with the regulations governing receipt and acknowledgment of gifts.

The Fundraising Process

Most would agree with Wesley Lindahl (2012) that effective fundraising requires research, planning, cultivation, solicitation, stewardship, and evaluation. As noted earlier, an organization's ability to raise sufficient funding to support its programs rests on its ability to identify, cultivate, and solicit appropriate funding. Research helps to identify those sources of support that are most likely to fund the organization and facilitates profiling the potential donor pool for individual gifts. Throughout the fundraising process, it is helpful to remember that the fundraising function is as affected by staff-board relationships as it is by the capacity of the organization to secure the necessary resources.

Steps to Successful Fundraising

Fundraising is about building relationships and following a process:

1. Know your nonprofit—its long-range plan, mission, goals, and objectives.

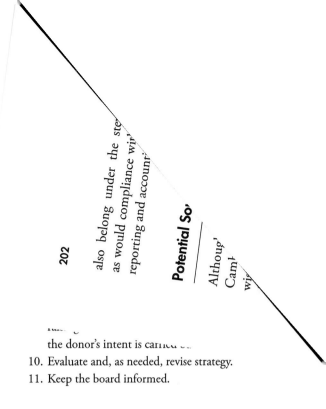

also belong under the ste
as would compliance wi
reporting and accoun

Potential So

Althoug
Cam
wi

the donor's intent is carried

10. Evaluate and, as needed, revise strategy.
11. Keep the board informed.

The Fundraising Plan

Fundraising plans are meant to support an organization's strategic initiatives and are best developed in consort with board, senior staff, and key stakeholders. Here a development audit can be valuable to identify the organization's strengths and weaknesses, as well as its threats and opportunities (similar to an organizational SWOT analysis). The development audit should include a review of the nonprofit's organizational structure, business processes, communication and marketing programs, reputation, donor base and sources of funding, and staff and board competencies. It can be conducted by staff or by outside counsel and is generally recommended before an organization undertakes a major campaign or begins a significant fundraising program. A development audit can point to shortfalls that need to be addressed before proceeding as well as identify unrecognized strengths.

Fundraising plans should also identify who is responsible for which initiative and who will solicit which donors, when, and how. Evaluation is the final piece in the plan. How successful were the solicitation efforts? How well did the funding meet the needs of the organization? Was the donor's intent fulfilled? The last may

wardship function,
.n the various funders'
.ng requirements.

.rces of Support

,n there has been some dissent (Mc-
.oridge 2014), the generally accepted
.sdom is that nonprofit organizations should
diversify their funding to guard against changes
in government support, economic downturns,
and fickle donors. However, for a small nonprofit with limited staff and a singular mission,
diversification may be as difficult as it can be
for controversial nonprofits, such as Planned
Parenthood. Nor is diversification automatically
the response to an organization's need to grow
(Foster and Fine 2007). As Paul Lagasse notes,
finding new sources of support "is not a turmoil-
free proposition" (Lagasse 2013, 25). That said,
identifying and cultivating as many appropriate
funding streams as possible helps the nonprofit
to build capacity—to provide services and fulfill
its mission.

What might a diversified portfolio look like?
Charitable nonprofits are supported directly by
individuals, corporations, foundations, and
government agencies and indirectly by the
taxpayer by way of local, state, and federal tax
exemptions. Nonprofits may charge fees for
services, may operate a profit-making entity
(and declare the income), and may partner with
other nonprofits or with for-profits to operate
an enterprise in which they share revenue. Thus,
the nonprofit might be 38 percent government-
supported. One half of that might be in the
form of a sustaining grant that requires annual
grant applications and annual reports. The other
half might be a mix of county and city funding
that requires periodic proposal presentations to
the relevant council or decisionmaking body. In
these cases, the endorsement of a local official
may be important in securing the funding. Other
nonprofit scenarios include perhaps 20 percent

funding through a fee-for-service contract with
the region's area office on aging. The original
contract (if a reimbursement contract) may
only require timely expenditure reports for the
funding to continue. The remaining 42 percent
could be made up of the annual fund (10 percent), annual and multiyear foundation grants
(20 percent), corporate support (5 percent), an
annual special event (2 percent), and 5 percent
from endowment.

Different fundraising strategies are required
for each of these monetary streams. All require a
match between the interests and purposes of the
funding source and the mission and services of
the nonprofit. Fortunately, there are a number
of resources available to those seeking support
for their nonprofit organizations. At the end of
this chapter is an appendix listing the websites
of selected fundraising resources. In the next
few sections, common sources of funding are
discussed.

Government Fundraising

Grant funding available from federal agencies
can be found in the Catalog of Federal Domestic
Assistance (CFDA) and the *Federal Register* (for
RFPs). Grant opportunities may also be found
in newsletters and on websites of organizations
that belong to a network of providers or that
fall under the umbrella of a national organization. Staff and board members may be sources
of information on local grant opportunities.
Once a source is identified and its objectives are
shown to align with your nonprofits goals and
objectives, it is important to assess your capacity
to perform and follow the guidelines for submission. Grant-writing is about demonstrating that
what your organization is prepared to do is what
the government program needs to have done for
the specified amount.

Contracts are often awarded in response to
a publicized *request for proposal* (RFP) and are
negotiated based on the funder's specifications
and the organization's qualifications. In general,

the terms and conditions are specific, and a timeline is imposed. If the RFP is biddable, it is important that the nonprofit not underestimate its costs. Most government grants and contracts allow for indirect costs related to the project, such as a percentage of support services (management, accounting, fundraising), overhead, salaries, space, equipment, and utilities. Indirect rates may be set by various government agencies (US Department of Labor 2012). For a research institution, a rate exceeding 50 percent of the grant is not unusual.

Foundation Fundraising

There are two types of foundations, *private and public*. In the private category, there are *family foundations* such as the Bill and Melinda Gates Foundation, in which the donor-family is often directly involved in grant-making; *corporate foundations*, such as the Bank of America Charitable Foundation, Inc., which, while legally separate from the Bank of America, does receive its income from the bank's operations; and *operating foundations*, such as the Metropolitan Museum of New York, which funds its own programs.

Public foundations include *community foundations*, such as the Cleveland Foundation and the Pittsburgh Foundation. These are publicly supported to make grants to other nonprofits. Other public foundations include *field-specific funds*, such as those related to health care, and *population-specific funds*, such as the Ms. Foundation for Women.

The nonprofit's strategy for seeking foundation funds will depend on the size, location, and purposes of the foundation. Large foundations, including community foundations, generally have staff who serve as gatekeepers. Grant seekers will be expected to follow published guidelines that outline what types of organizations are eligible for funding, what sorts of projects are desired, and what levels of funding are appropriate. Guidelines will also prescribe how the foundation should be approached.

Some will ask for a letter of intent, to be followed by a discussion with the program officer before a formal proposal is invited. Others will set out the guidelines and due dates for proposal submission without the initial inquiry. It is a good idea to contact the foundation program officer before preparing a submission, as that person can provide valuable information and may become the nonprofit's advocate before the foundation's board of trustees. If the foundation is local, the nonprofit's board members or staff may have contacts on the foundation board. Board members and staff who are involved in the solicitation should be kept informed of the submission. Small foundations may have one staff person who handles all contact with potential grant seekers. Others may rely on a trustee to vet the proposals.

Corporate foundation giving is different from family or community foundation giving in the sense that the corporate foundation's interests are most often tied to the company's interests. Corporate foundations tend to focus on the geographic areas where they are located or have staff. In some cases, the corporate foundation's giving is also part of a marketing plan or community outreach program. Consequently, the nonprofit's proposed activity needs to be positioned in a way that clearly advances the company's interests.

In all cases, the first step is to determine if there is a good fit between the foundation and the nonprofit. The Foundation Center is a good source for information on foundations. Large foundations have websites that outline the components of a successful application. As important as foundation and corporate grant-making is for nonprofits, it should be noted that individuals constitute the bulk of private philanthropy. According to *Giving USA*, grants from foundations and corporations represented only 19 percent of total private giving in 2010. Individual gifts and bequests made up 81 percent (Foundation Center, "*Foundations Today* Tutorial").

The Annual Fund

The annual fund is critical for many nonprofits' development strategy. Typically, the annual fund is built on individual donors' sustained giving. Often presented as a pyramid, the gradual progression of individual cultivation is built on identifying prospects, soliciting first-time donors, transforming those donors into annual givers, and identifying potential major donors. The apex of the fundraising pyramid is planned giving. These last steps, toward major gifts and bequests, rely on personal cultivation. Moving from one level of the pyramid to the next relies on stewardship. How solicitation is managed depends on the type and size of the organization and its staff and board, as well as how valuable the nonprofit is perceived as being to the well-being of the community.

An annual solicitation may be a direct-mail piece and/or, increasingly, a web-based appeal. The annual fund may also include an annual special event as part of its revenue projections. Some nonprofits include recurring government grants in their annual fund strategy. Major donor cultivation that involves face-to-face interaction is not usually included in the annual fund budget.

Developing the annual fund is a gradual process, one that takes years of cultivation and stewardship. Depending on the organization and the contacts its board and staff may or may not have, identifying potential donors can take time. Data-mining companies supply, for a fee, lists of potential donors based on criteria that the nonprofit defines. This is similar to a university's admissions office purchasing lists of potential applicants. Once obtained, staff or volunteers then mail the prepared solicitation letter or card. The solicitation could also be emailed or placed on the organization's website. Email and Internet-based campaigns avoid one of the major disincentives of direct mail—cost. However, with the exception of disaster or special needs appeals, first-time direct-mail solicitations have a poor return. Citing JWM Business

Services, Julie Richards (n.d.) reports that direct mail yields a 0.5–2 percent return. Laurie Beasley (2013) puts the rate of return on direct-mail marketing at 4.4 percent. Direct-mail remains an expensive venture for small nonprofits.

Before soliciting others outside of the organization, major stakeholders (such as board members and other volunteers, staff, and, where appropriate, clients) should be asked to support the organization in which they are investing their time and care. Some funding sources, particularly foundations, require that board contributions be included in the annual fund budget.

As Kim Klein (2011, 21) points out, fundraising is about acquiring donors, not donations; it's about acquiring givers, not gifts. In other words, fundraising is about building relationships:

> Focusing on building a donor base rather than on simply raising money means that sometimes you will undertake a fundraising strategy that does not raise money in the first year, such as direct mail, or that may not raise money for several years, such as legacy giving. . . . You will relate to your donors as individual human beings rather than ATMs that you engage when you want money but whom you otherwise ignore. . . . Plan fundraising for both the short term and the long term.

Special Event Fundraising

Special events often play a significant role in the nonprofit's relationship-building campaign. As noted before, special events are time-intensive for both staff and volunteers and often do not raise much money. Before undertaking an event, whether it is a five-mile run, a golf outing, a charity ball, or an awards/recognition dinner, the nonprofit needs to determine what it hopes to achieve with the event and then to evaluate the time and resources needed to support it. Some typical steps in special event planning include identifying an oversight committee; assigning responsible staff; establishing a budget; setting a timeline; and recruiting volunteers. Post-event activities include acknowledging volunteers, evaluating the event's success at achieving the goals set, and reporting to the board.

Capital Campaign Fundraising

Capital campaigns are usually undertaken for major projects, such as building construction and renovation, or for seeding an endowment. They are intensive and time-limited, usually beginning with a silent phase in which the organization tries to raise at least 50 percent of its goal before going public. Capital campaigns are also viewed as vehicles for moving annual fund donors into the major donor category. Unlike the annual fund campaign, a capital campaign generally seeks large onetime gifts to finance a onetime project. Capital campaigns can include solicitations for assets, such as stocks and bonds, real estate, art, insurance policies, and so forth, as well as legacy gifts such as bequests, in addition to gifts of income.

Legacy Fundraising

Once referred to as deferred giving, *legacy giving* or *planned giving* is that element of the nonprofit's fundraising program that is built on promised future gifts that a donor provides for in his or her will. Legacy gifts are part of a person's estate plan. In most cases, legal counsel should be involved in the planning. It is not appropriate for the nonprofit's legal counsel to also act on behalf of the donor. Planned giving programs are well developed in the educational realm and for large nonprofits as well as religious institutions. Small nonprofits do not always have the expertise on staff or on the board to mount planned giving programs.

As with all fundraising, understanding the motivations of potential donors is key to a successful solicitation. Does the nonprofit have an established donor base? If so, is there enough information about the donor to determine if a legacy gift is possible? What is the donor's relationship with the nonprofit? Does the nonprofit have the tools in place to affect a legacy program, such as a gift acceptance policy, a will information kit, legal counsel, and other professional resources? Is the board engaged? Can the nonprofit provide the necessary follow-up once the potential donor is identified?

Fundraising for Endowments

An endowment may be thought of as a permanent savings account for an organization in which money is set aside as principal and a percentage of the income from it is designated for the organization's use on an annual basis (Klein 2011). While subject to market fluctuations, endowments are considered to be a hedge against changes in government support and declines in private giving. Endowments are often part of the organization's capital campaign. If organized as a separate endowment campaign, the fundraising process is similar to that for a capital campaign in that a goal is set, a giftrange table is developed, a realistic timeline is created, solicitation committees are established, and prospects are identified and assigned to volunteers for solicitation. Evaluation of the campaign's progress is ongoing and subject to modification as necessary.

It is important that the endowment be well managed. If the organization does not have the expertise on staff or on the board, it is advisable to contract with a professional manager. Most likely, the financial institution that holds the endowment's assets will have professional advisers. As part of its fiduciary duty to the organization, the board is responsible for the oversight of management of the endowment.

Crowdfunding

Crowdfunding is a relatively new tool for fundraising. Because its reach is broad and less costly than other fundraising vehicles, crowdfunding is being touted as a valuable resource for nonprofits. Crowdfunding happens because the organization is using an online website to solicit for a cause or a project, or because it has sponsored a "live" crowdfunding event designed to attract large numbers of potential donors. As Joe Garecht (2013) explains, crowdfunding websites allow the charity to set up an online fundraising campaign based around a fundraising page that enables the organization to receive donations directly from that page using the website's credit card processor. The same websites may also allow individuals outside the organization to set up fundraising pages on behalf of a charity and to tie those pages into the charity's campaign page. Note that the nonprofit organization remains responsible for fundraising activities conducted on its behalf.

Online services, such as Fundraise.com, CauseVox, and Fundly, are organized to help nonprofits raise funds. Others, such as Kickstarter and indiegogo, while not exclusively dedicated to nonprofit fundraising, are used by nonprofits to raise money (Garecht 2013). Live crowdfunding, on the other hand, features live events sponsored by the nonprofit itself or by third-party organizations, such as The Funding Network, which specializes in creating live crowdfunding events for charities (Woodruff 2014).

Nonprofits use crowdfunding to expand their reach and raise money and awareness for their causes. Empirical support for the efficacy of crowdfunding for nonprofit fundraising is lacking; nevertheless, as crowdfunding specialist Devin Thorpe puts it, "While crowdfunding does not constitute a complete development plan, no development plan is complete without crowdfunding" (Woodruff 2014).

At the present time it is unclear how states' fundraising regulations apply to crowdfunding.

Conclusion

Fundraising for nonprofit organizations is about building capacity in those organizations to secure the resources needed to fulfill their missions. In so doing, critical services are provided to the most vulnerable and art, music, and dance are made available to the public. Nonprofits enrich our lives, help make education more accessible to all, and hold a promise for building a better future. Fundraising is a process that, over time, develops relationships and helps secure for the nonprofit public awareness of its programs and services, thus building its capacity to provide those programs and services. Fundraising therefore is an integral function in the management of any nonprofit relying on public support for a significant portion of its revenue.

Appendix: Selected Fundraising Resources

There are a number of excellent resources for fundraising tips and techniques, such as the Association of Fundraising Professionals (AFP), The Grantsmanship Center, and The Foundation Center. Foundation Search enables the grant seeker to research foundations by location, type of grant, and average amount. GuideStar is an excellent resource for data on public charities (501[c][3] nonprofits), including foundations. The *Nonprofit Times* and the *Chronicle of Philanthropy* are both good sources for news on what is happening in the third sector. In addition to the CFDA and the *Federal Register*, Grants.gov provides information on federal grant opportunities. Grants.gov also enables the potential grantee to apply for grants online.

The Center on Philanthropy at Indiana University—Purdue University Indianapolis (IUPUI) publishes research on philanthropy-related issues. The Program on Nonprofit Organizations (PONPO) at Yale University is also a good resource for working papers on matters related to nonprofits. The Independent Sector (IS) is a forum for organizations interested in furthering a civil society. IS also advocates on behalf of organizations in the third sector.

Websites

Association of Fundraising Professionals (AFP): www.afpnet.org

Catalog of Federal Domestic Assistance (CFDA): www.cfda.gov/

Center on Philanthropy: www.philanthropy.iupui.edu/

Chronicle of Philanthropy: www.philanthropy.com/
Federal Register: www.federalregister.gov/

Foundation Search: www.foundationsearch.com

Foundation Center, Foundation Directory Online: fconline.foundationcenter.org/

Grants.gov: www.grants.gov/

Grantsmanship Center: www.tgci.com/about/our-mission

GuideStar: www.guidestar.org

Independent Sector (IS): www.independentsector.org

Nonprofit Times (NPT): www.thenonprofit-times.com/

Program on Nonprofit Organizations (PONPO) at Yale University: http://ponpo.som.yale.edu/

References

Beasley, Laurie. 2013. "Why Direct Mail Still Yields the Lowest Cost-per-Lead and Highest Conversion Rate." *Direct Marketing* (June 13). Available at: www.onlinemarketinginstitute.org/blog/2013/06/why-direct-mail-still-yields-the-lowest-cost-per-lead-and-highest-conversion-rate/.

Ciconte, Barbara L. 2007. *Developing Fundraising Policies and Procedures: Best Practices for Accountability and Transparency.* Arlington, VA: AFP Ready Reference Series.

Dove, Kent E. 2001. *Conducting a Successful Fundraising Program: A Comprehensive Guide and Resource.* San Francisco: Jossey-Bass.

Foster, William, and Gail Fine. 2007. "How Nonprofits Get Really Big." *Stanford Social Innovation Review* (Spring): 13–26. Available at: www.ssireview.org/articles/entry/how_nonprofits_get_really_big.

Foundation Center. "*Foundations Today* Tutorial." Available at: http://foundationcenter.org/getstarted/tutorials/ft_tutorial/compare.html.

Garecht, Joe. 2013. "How to Use Crowd-Funding Sites to Raise Money for Your Non-Profit." The Fundraising Authority (web log post), February 6. Available at: http://trust.guidestar.org/2013/02/06/how-to-use-crowd-funding-to-raise-money-for-your-non-profit/.

International Institute for Educational Planning (IIEP). 2006. "Capacity Building." Ch. 3 in IIEP, *Guidebook for Planning Education in Emergencies and Reconstruction.* Paris: IIEP.

Klein, Kim. 2011. *Fundraising for Social Change*, 6th ed. San Francisco: Jossey-Bass.

Lagasse, Paul. 2013. "The Right Mix." *Advancing Philanthropy* (Summer): 20–25. Available at: www.benevon.com/documents/press/The-Right-Mix--Advancing-Philanthropy-Summer-2013.pdf.

Lindahl, Wesley E. 2012. "The Fundraising Process." In *Understanding Nonprofit Organizations: Governance, Leadership, and Management*, 2nd ed., edited by J. Steven Ott and Lisa A. Dicke, 117–126. Boulder, CO: Westview Press.

McCambridge, Ruth. 2014. "To Diversify, or Not to Diversify Revenue—(It's Complicated)." *Nonprofit Quarterly* (July 14). Available at: https://nonprofitquarterly.org/policysocial-context/24501-to-diversify-or-not-to-diversify-that-is-the-question-but-it-s-complicated.html?utm_source=NPQ+New.

McKinsey & Company. 2001. *Effective Capacity Building in Nonprofit Organizations.* Washington, DC: Venture Philanthropy Partners.

National Council of Nonprofits. 2014. "Laws That Regulate Fundraising." Available at: www.councilofnonprofits.org/resources/resources-topic/fundraising/laws-regulate-fundraising.

Richards, Julie. N.d. "What Is the Average Rate of Return on a Direct Mail Campaign?" *Houston Chronicle.* Available at: http://smallbusiness.chron.com/average-rate-return-direct-mail-campaign-23974.html.

Salamon, Lester, S. Wojciech Sokolowski, and Associates. 2004. *Global Civil Society: Dimensions of the Nonprofit Sector.* Bloomfield, CT: Kumarian Press.

US Department of Labor. Division of Cost Determination. 2012. "A Guide for Indirect Cost Rate Determination: Based on the Cost Principles and

Procedures Required by OMB Circular A-122 (2 CFR Part 230) for Non-Profit Organizations and by the Federal Acquisition Regulation—Part 31.2 for Commercial Organizations." Washington, DC: US Department of Labor (July). Available at: www.dol.gov/oasam/programs/boc/costdeterminationguide/cdg.pdf.

Woodruff, Alexandra. 2014. "What Nonprofits Need to Know About Crowdfunding." New York: National Council on Nonprofits (July 9). Available at: www.councilofnonprofits.org/thought-leadership/what-nonprofits-need-know-about-crowdfunding.

CHAPTER 11

Analyzing the Dynamics of Funding
Reliability and Autonomy

Jon Pratt

Originally published as "Analyzing the Dynamics of Funding: Reliability and Autonomy," in Nonprofit Quarterly (2004): 8–13. Copyright © 2004 by Nonprofit Information Networking Association. Reprinted with permission.

Every nonprofit organization begins with high hopes and aspirations for public benefit, with a mission to make the world a better place. An immediate challenge is how to put these goals into action, and how to finance the organization.

Money is a limited and competitive resource; organizations without a permanent source of funds must do their best to accommodate the preferences and conditions of funding sources. Striking necessary bargains with devils and angels constitutes the defining struggle for nonprofit boards and managers. This existential dilemma is played out in every nonprofit budget and strategic plan: How does the organization raise funds to realize its long-range purpose while also scrambling for its existence?

The way an organization handles decisions about funding sources sets in motion an ongoing chain of consequences, further decisions, and compromises about what the organization will and will not agree to do. Throughout the history of nonprofits, major changes in size, direction, and strategy (and even new names and purposes) are more commonly due to shifts in revenue than to changed intent.

Among the funders of nonprofit activity, attaching conditions and targeted funding are considered valid methods for increasing the accountability and effectiveness of grantees. Whether it is a government agency or a private foundation, the allocators of funds have authority over a finite resource with many requests from the outside. They conclude from previous experience which types of activities are most likely to succeed and seek the "biggest bang for the buck" by focusing and restricting their money to this narrower range of activities.

For nonprofit organizations, not all funding has an equal effect on the bottom line. Complying with the conditions attached to funding—and coping with fluctuations in revenue—imposes direct and indirect costs and occupies the attention of managers and boards. The drawbacks of this situation are self-evident to anyone who has managed a nonprofit organization, but board meetings and financial reports can have the effect of simplifying the problem

DOI: 10.4324/9781003387800-24

down to "will we take in enough money to cover expenses?"

Board members, nonprofit employees, and clients (and even other funders) frequently believe that an organization has more latitude over how and when it spends its funds than is actually the case. This limited autonomy squeezes nonprofit managers by putting them in the onerous position of enforcing and defending compliance with funding conditions, sometimes in the face of solid arguments for an alternative course—all the while being criticized that "if they wanted to do it, they could." Or worse still, different parts of the organization disagree about the conditions that exist, the wisdom of compliance, or the likelihood and severity of sanctions, causing internal conflict or even misappropriation.

An organization-wide appreciation of these revenue-source issues is in the interest of the board and staff, informed by an examination of the two major variables: reliability and autonomy. This does not lessen the constraints—but can clear the air so that decision making is based on a common understanding of an organization's available degrees of freedom and the future implications for revenue changes.

Reliability of Funding

To what extent can an organization predict its revenues year-to-year for budgeting, staffing, and program planning? Is it reasonable to expect a particular funding source will be renewed? This information—projecting and tracking revenue and expenses—is key to managing any enterprise. Boards and nonprofit managers are under a legal mandate to exercise their best judgment concerning what revenue will be available, with serious consequences if they are wrong. The decisions they make will be based on their confidence level regarding the relative stability or volatility of each element of the organization's financial support.

The Reliability-Autonomy Matrix divides twelve common types of nonprofit funding into three levels of reliability: high, medium, and low. This necessarily gross categorization is useful to identify funding sources on a continuum from dependable to speculative, although an individual organization's experiences will vary. (The placement of any specific funding source on the reliability axis can vary considerably based on the organization's relationships, existing commitments, and other constraints influencing the funding source.) The three levels of reliability include:

- *High reliability:* Small to medium-sized individual contributions, endowments, memberships, United Way support, rental income, advertising
- *Medium reliability:* Fees for services, ongoing government contracts, third-party reimbursements, major individual contributions, corporate charitable contributions
- *Low reliability:* Government project grants, foundation grants, corporate sponsorships

Organizational Autonomy

Dependency theory indicates that the autonomy of nonprofit organizations is directly related to the extent of their reliance on suppliers of funds. From government contracts to foundation grants, organizations know they are signing on to a variety of conditions that are attached to funding, comparable to "if you take the King's shilling you do the King's bidding." These conditions can range from the general targeting of an activity to extremely detailed specifications dictating the ingredients, personnel, time, place, and manner of activity. For the donor, these conditions represent due-diligence assurances that funds will be effectively and responsibly expended, while for the recipient organization, a number of these conditions are unwelcome, burdensome, and counterproductive.

As with the reliability index, the matrix divides eight common types of nonprofit funding into three levels of autonomy: high, medium, and low. This similarly gross categorization distinguishes between conditional and unconditional sources, and an individual organization's situation will vary. (The location of any specific funding source on the autonomy axis can be adjusted based on the organization's relationships, existing commitments, and other constraints influencing the funding source.) The three levels of autonomy include:

- *High autonomy:* Small to medium-sized individual contributions, fees for services, foundation operating grants, endowments, memberships
- *Medium autonomy:* Major individual contributions, corporate charitable contributions
- *Low autonomy:* Third-party reimbursements, government project grants, ongoing government contracts, foundation project grants, United Way support

Understanding an Organization's Reliability/Autonomy Profile

The revenue situation for any particular organization will have special characteristics and could change over time. The eight revenue archetypes set out some typical situations and management responses (see table 11.1). A closer analysis of a single organization can reveal a greater level of detail and more options . . . based on a frank assessment of their own situation and relationships.

Management and Governance Implications

The Reliability-Autonomy Matrix is designed to reveal priority issues for board and management attention and indicate strategies needed to handle the relative reliability and independence of its revenues. The profiles and archetypes, themselves, are difficult to shift (e.g., dramatically increasing autonomy), since most mature organizations have an established mix of funding. Wherever a funding source falls within the matrix, it carries with it a variety of management options, many of which, in turn, increase the complexity of the management task. Increasing the number of sources and transactions is generally a useful strategy to increase organizational autonomy and security—though it demands more administration.

One critical additional variable is the sheer number of funding sources. Most organizations work hard to diversify their sources of funding, both in type and number of sources, in order to reduce funding volatility and lower their risk of catastrophic loss (such as when a major funding source withdraws its support).

Boards of directors expect to be involved in budget planning and monitoring, but in many organizations they are often not aware of the degree of volatility of their funding, or what the organization should do about it.

Organizations with funding that is low in reliability have a variety of possible actions to reduce the uncertainty in their environment:

- Maintain higher cash reserves to fill in gaps and reduce the roller-coaster-budget effect.
- Give greater management and board attention to cash management and financial systems, thus predicting shortfalls and allowing quick decisions.
- Use volunteers, consultants, and temporary employees to increase flexibility of the workforce, and thus reduce dislocation.
- Develop close relationships with organizations in the same subject area to track industry changes, and share information on funding source preferences and behavior.
- Submit multiple applications to offset low-response rates.

Organizations *low in autonomy* have a special set of problems, because although their funding sources are definitely willing to transfer funds to them, they want to do this in a particular way. An African proverb says that "if you want to give a man a goat you have to let go of the rope," but of course many funders have perfectly good reasons why they can't completely "let go of the rope."

TABLE 11.1 Eight Nonprofit Revenue Archetypes: A Guide for Managers and Boards

The ability to recognize patterns in any endeavor gives us a valuable leg up. Having those patterns explicitly laid out provides us with a greater capacity to make an informed decision about the course we wish to take in choosing the financing model for our work. Sometimes these models may appear to be predetermined by the field that we are in, but there is often some room for choice about balance and proportion.

COMMON REVENUE TYPES What is the dominant source of income?	EXAMPLES What kinds of organizations tend to rely on this revenue type as dominant?	REVENUE PROFILE Where does this leave you in terms of reliability and autonomy?
Individual contributions dominant	Small grassroots organizations working on local issues; Humane and animal-rights organizations; Faith-based programs; Environmental and other national advocacy organizations; Disease-specific organizations.	High reliability; High autonomy
Individual or organizational: membership dues dominant	Labor unions; Credit unions; Neighborhood associations.	Medium reliability; High autonomy
Government contract dominant	Charter schools; Workforce development groups; Human service agencies.	Medium reliability; Low autonomy
United Way dominant	YMCA/YWCA; Boys and Girls Clubs; Boy Scouts/Girl Scouts; Campfire Girls.	Medium reliability; Low autonomy
Earned Income dominant, Individual payors	Theaters; Private colleges or universities; Management support organizations.	Medium reliability; High autonomy
Third-party payor dominant	Community health centers; Hospitals; Nursing homes.	High reliability; Low autonomy
Foundation grant dominant	Advocacy groups; Public-policy centers; Start-up organizations; Arts organizations; Some organizing groups.	Low reliability; Low autonomy
Blended/diversified revenues	Advocacy organizations; Community-based organizations.	Medium reliability; Medium autonomy

The following easy-to-use chart begins a process of clearly and simply laying out some common patterns and the association between them including:

- the predominance of a particular revenue source in a nonprofit;
- the degree of autonomy the nonprofit has;
- the degree to which that source is reliable, and;
- the management challenges and tasks associated with that source.

MANAGEMENT CHALLENGES What are the special problems or demands associated with this revenue situation?	*MANAGEMENT FOCUS* *What appropriate responses are available to management to cope with these specific management challenges?*
Need for high recognition, good reputation; Management of multiple-donor relationships; List management; Monitoring of continuous changes in market and market reactions to various solicitation techniques.	Systematic research and analysis; Intensive, frequent communications; Excellent information systems; Storytelling; Development of volunteer base; Perpetual scanning for new donors.
High expectations for transparency; Member engagement and interactive communications; Leadership development; Collection of dues; Member politics.	Large representative, democratically elected board; Member interest tracking; Visible commitment to procedural rights of members; Pricing; Well-designed member benefits; Effective conflict-resolution mechanisms and skills.
Cash flow issues; Limited capital; Maintenance of political relationships; Compliance with reporting regimen and external standards of demonstrating results; Contracts often lag behind innovations; Tight eligibility requirements; Dependence on categorical, inflexible funding leads to political skewing of mission or programs; Underpriced services produce need for other subsidies; Requires ability to predict, track, and produce outcomes required by funders.	Closely monitor and educate authorizing environment; Negotiate optimal contract terms; Maintain cash reserves; Systems-focused to ensure compliance.
Often requires compliance with many conditions including those associated with measurement and reporting; May restrict own donor-development activities; May include fundraising blackout periods.	Close monitoring of changing United Way preferences and conditions; Support public relations of United Way; Responsiveness to information requests.

MANAGEMENT CHALLENGES *What are the special problems or demands associated with this revenue situation?*	MANAGEMENT FOCUS *What appropriate responses are available to management to cope with these specific management challenges?*
Need for visibility in primary and secondary markets; Maintenance of institutional reputation; Maintaining knowledge of market needs and preferences; Incentive to focus exclusively on "billable hours" or strictly marketable or self-paying activities.	Ethic of excellence; Innovation in products and services; Relentless marketing; Customer research; Competitor analysis; Seek charitable or government funds to subsidize and broaden user base.
Highly detailed transaction processing; Quality control; Certification, licensing, and regulatory compliance; Employee motivation and retention.	Tight management systems and chains of command; Standardized treatment, automated transaction; Cross-function employed communications.
Sponsor relations and education; Visibility in field; Project development and sequencing; Institutional reputation.	Development expertise; Innovation and anticipation of developments in field; Fundraising and negotiating skills to maximize revenue and minimize adverse grant conditions; Substantial cash reserves.
Complexity of revenue streams; Complexity of financial management and reporting; Cash flow; Variable combination of all of the above with specific sources driving management challenges.	Attentive board with understanding of budget; Financial protocols and tracking that makes sense of complexity; Strong strategic-planning processes keyed to financial planning.

Boards of directors are less aware of their role in monitoring the restrictions placed on the funds their organizations receive. Low-autonomy organizations must also develop a special set of skills to preserve sufficient maneuvering room:

- Emphasize negotiation skills and develop a persuasive case of what the organization brings to the table (local community knowledge, flexibility, reputation, track record, volunteers, leveraged money, etc.) to equalize exchange and offset unwanted conditions.

- Monitor (via the board) the consonance between the organization's mission and the nature of the projects it is asked to undertake.
- Be prepared to resist and reject incompatible conditions by having a gift-and-grant-acceptance policy.
- Maintain a robust financial system to track and comply with conditions and restrictions on funding and effective segregation of funds. Monitor conditions on funding. Discuss as a board the purpose of funding and contract monitoring.

- Increase the total number of funding sources, even if they are low autonomy, to reduce the degree of control of any one source. An organization with a dozen or more low-autonomy funding sources can mitigate the lack of flexibility by diversifying.
- Take part in policy networks and coalitions to resist or reduce excessive conditions by government funding sources.

One of the easiest types of organizations to manage, and the most satisfying for a board experience, is a high-reliability/high-autonomy organization. These organizations are better able to chart their own course and stay flexible, and have the time and freedom to ask the big questions and make long-term plans. More complex are high-reliability/low-autonomy organizations, which are often large institutions enjoying tight relationships with government or the United Way; they are generally long-term relationships in which funding conditions are accommodated over a long period of time.

The most difficult organizations of all to manage are low-reliability/low-autonomy (a.k.a., Dante's Seventh Circle of Hell). These organizations are stuck in an ongoing loop of project creation, submission, and approval, and have a high need for both negotiation and earnings management, which sometimes are in conflict.

Many organizations are so steeped in their existing funding patterns and relationships that they no longer recognize or think about the nature and limits of their situation. The Reliability-Autonomy Matrix enables boards and managers to take a systemic view of their revenues by providing a framework for examining them in a relevant, strategic context. The value of the Matrix is its ability to help nonprofits easily identify funding limitations and flexibility within their organizations, which is central to effective strategic and financial planning.

Ethical Considerations in Fundraising

CAROL SIPFLE AND C. KENNETH MEYER

Nan Brownstone was excited about a meeting she had just finished with the CEO and chief financial officer of Loving Care, a large statewide nursing home corporation. The purpose of the meeting was to discuss possible funding for Seniors United for Healthy Living and Dignity, Inc. (SUHLD), a nonprofit organization for which Nan worked as executive director. Upon completion of the meeting, one sentence stood out in her mind.

"We'll write you a big check," said Mike Donaldson, CFO, about their potential partnership. As she returned to her car, this statement replayed in Nan's mind as if it were on her iPod's automatic replay.

Once back in her office, Nan reviewed the history between the two organizations and her notes of the meeting. SUHLD had previously solicited Loving Care to sponsor its fundraising events, including golf outings and walkathons. These solicitations were usually for small amounts and were made periodically throughout the year. Now, however, Loving Care was agreeable to receiving one sponsorship proposal per year for a much larger amount, and it was up to Nan to determine the best project. In the final analysis, the type of proposal would determine the amount of the "big check." Nan felt up to the challenge and solicited her staff to work with her to develop a winning proposal.

However, Mr. Donaldson's comment "We'll write you a big check," as it was later revealed,

had included three contingencies that caused Nan to feel uneasy. First, Loving Care requested that SUHLD make referrals to its nursing facilities throughout the state in exchange for its financial support. This was problematic, of course, since SUHLD was prohibited by its charter from making endorsements of or direct referrals to nursing facilities. Second, Loving Care requested that, when possible, Nan would advocate for its facilities in the event that it received negative publicity, particularly publicity about poor care of nursing home residents. Third, Nan was asked to continue to promote Loving Care as a sponsor of the golf outings and walkathons even though it would no longer provide financial support for these fundraising events.

Nan had nagging doubts about the appropriateness of such requests and whether they fell outside the boundaries of ethical fundraising. However, she took them under consideration and began developing a proposal for funding, not sure how she would address the three contingencies outlined by Mr. Donaldson. Her efforts came to an abrupt stop one morning after she read in the newspaper an article headlined "Nursing Home CEO Accused of Sexual Abuse." Her worst fears were realized when she read the article and learned that the CEO of Loving Care was accused of sexual harassment by a female employee in the corporate office.

DOI: 10.4324/9781003387800-25

Nan's concerns were now elevated to a new level, and the threefold request from Loving Care began to fall into place and make sense. The allegations blemished the reputation of Loving Care, but Nan wondered if her organization's reputation would also be at risk if the proposal was funded. Perhaps she was making a "mountain out of a molehill," or reading more into the news of the allegations than was justified. After all, these were only allegations and the case involved two individuals, not the entire company. She wondered if the general public would remember the allegations months later, when the proposed sponsorship would be publicized.

In considering the ethics of fundraising in this situation, Nan asked herself whether nonprofit organizations should have guidelines on the types of companies they solicited for sponsorships and contributions. Should SUHLD develop guidelines similar to those religiously followed by funds investing in only socially responsible ventures or organizations? And, she mused, at what point did "a big check" carry too high a price tag for an organization to bear?

Questions and Instructions

1. Should nonprofit organizations have guidelines on what types of companies they solicit for sponsorships and contributions? Please explain your answer. If yes, provide at least five general examples of guidelines you think nonprofit organizations could use related to seeking sponsorships and contributions.

2. Please check with at least three nonprofit organizations to determine if they have any specific guidelines for investment of resources. Report on these guidelines to the class.

3. Would you still submit a proposal to Loving Care in an effort to receive the "big check"? Please explain the reasoning for your answer.

4. What guidelines would you put in place concerning quid pro quo exchanges like the one proposed by Mr. Donaldson?

5. Once an organization's reputation has been tarnished or called into question, how does the organization, whether guilty or not, restore its rightful image and reputation? Please research and provide examples of organizations whose images have been tarnished and how their positive image has been restored.

The Selling of America

GARRY L. FRANK AND C. KENNETH MEYER

Elwood James became a volunteer fire-fighter when he turned eighteen. This was a momentous time for Elwood, since he had always been fascinated with fire trucks, ladders, pike poles, and hoses, and he was especially intrigued by the ear-busting sirens that blazed when the big red trucks left the fire barn located across the street from his childhood home. Of course he knew that this youthful dream of being fitted for a helmet and the lettered and numbered turnout gear would have to be set aside for the realities that he now faced as an adult. Now he was properly dressed in a uniform, and he was trained to assist individuals, families, and even animals who faced the terror of fire, accidents, and other adversities.

The image of his local fire department was further emblazoned in his mind by the high respect he felt, like his parents and neighbors, for those who placed their lives in harm's way so that the public might be served. He also enjoyed the pancake feed that the firefighters cooked up each year to raise money so that they could give new toys to children who had lost their possessions in household fires.

Elwood chuckled to himself at the pleasant memory of the wonderment, imagination, and fantasy that characterized the days of his youth when his basic character and attitude toward community service were being formed. But that was then and this was now, and time had changed everything. It was nice to reminisce,

but as fire chief in Johnsonville, he had to shoulder the responsibility of managing the fire department that had been the focus of his childhood dreams.

Not unlike other urban municipalities, Johnsonville had almost tapped out the various sources of revenue generation, including a sales tax, users' fees, water and utility usage rates, hotel and motel excise taxes, and the ever-unpopular rise in property taxes. These traditional sources of local funding had been fully exploited, and the residents of Johnsonville wanted to "hold the line" on any added taxation efforts. The city had also gambled on the future and taken on the daunting challenge of attracting new industries and businesses to provide good-paying and secure jobs. To achieve this goal, the city had used tax increment financing (TIF) schemes and tax abatement policies for new construction in underutilized and undeveloped areas of Johnsonville, and it had also reduced water and utility rates for new businesses it succeeded in attracting to the town. However, the revenue generated was not keeping up with the escalating costs of providing government services as the city's infrastructure continued to deteriorate, the existing housing stock aged, and the population became increasingly diverse.

Times were especially challenging for the department as the personnel costs of its small core of full-time firefighters ratcheted upward and the cost of health care increased in double-digit,

DOI: 10.4324/9781003387800-26

inflationary jumps. Union negotiators were also determined to see that union members were treated fairly in the upcoming labor-management negotiations. As chief, Elwood also had to cope with the continuing saga of aging equipment, an old and deteriorating stock of houses, and the expensive maintenance associated with a fleet of older ambulances, pumper engines, and ladder trucks. He also had to replace the dated protective clothing and safety masks and the equipment required for the safe handling of hazardous materials and accidents.

Elwood presented his customarily well prepared budget before the city council, whose members, in turn, allocated the usual 2 percent increase in funding for the fire department. He spoke to the council about the state of his department and the rising costs associated with providing fire inspection, fire reduction, and fire suppression in a city where the houses were aging, the population was growing, and the fire risk, as his statistics indicated, was increasing. He knew that he sounded like other department heads and that he would not be able to get money from a "stone." At the end of the council meeting, he returned to the fire station and retreated to his office. It was, he thought, the "worst of times." What novel ideas could he come up with that might liberate his department from its financial exigencies?

As Elwood thumbed through the *New Reporter*—the city's only daily newspaper—he noticed an advertisement from the local gambling facility, Lucky Sevens Resort and Casino, claiming to have had a "bumper" year, with its 98 percent payoff rate for the tables and slots. He laughed about the absurdity of gambling and wondered whether this ad was just an unusual ploy to pay back an average of $98 for every $100 dropped into the machines or laid on the green felt tables. Yet, the advertisement touted that it had paid out over $300 million in winnings during the last fiscal year—a figure that Elwood felt was astonishingly high.

The feature story on Lucky Sevens was soliciting funding proposals from public and community nonprofit organizations that would help address recognized community needs. Elwood remembered the added equipment and training that was required in his department when Lucky Sevens came on-line and thought perhaps this was a chance to get some needed funding for the equipment and training needs he had prioritized and just presented to Johnsonville's city council. The article indicated that all inquiries should be directed to the attention of Marietta Hughes, the chair of the board of directors of Lucky Sevens. He would contact her tomorrow, Elwood thought, and she certainly would be receptive to his department, especially given the good relationship he had with the casino and its recognition that Johnsonville's fire department was encumbered with new expenses associated with the largest gaming facility in the state.

When Elwood called the next day, Marietta Hughes seemed most anxious to inform him about their request for proposal (RFP) and told him that they would be happy to talk about the prospect of granting the department up to $600,000. She added, however, that with funding at a level that high, Lucky Sevens would require that the money be used to purchase a piece of equipment such as a first responders' hazmat truck; fortunately, Elwood had just received a low competitive bid of $550,000 for a fire/hazmat vehicle. Hughes also stated that the new truck would be required to bear the logo of Lucky Sevens Resort and Casino on each door of the cab and on the back of the truck. She said that the logo would be shown with a picture that displayed a winning slot machine—all red sevens—and the accompanying statement, "Sponsored by the Lucky Sevens Resort and Casino." Elwood thanked her for her courtesy, time, and information and said that he would examine the ramifications, if any, of their discussion.

Elwood was anxious to get the financing that would enable him to upgrade his department, but the idea of the gaudy logo and the accompanying statement on a department vehicle bothered him. Not being a novice to the budgetary process, he realized that added funding from the city would not be forthcoming. He also knew that the city council had given all department heads the authorization to pursue outside funding at their discretion, whether from companies, philanthropic organizations, private donations and grants, or governmental sources. At a fall meeting of the International City Managers Associations (ICMA), the topic of extramural funding had been addressed during a panel session, and the overall response had been very positive—especially from the city managers. Elwood knew that a gift from the casino was not prohibited under applicable state and local laws. Yet the idea of an advertisement on a city-owned vehicle was deeply troubling to him, especially since, having grown up seeing only the city logo on the sides of city vehicles, it seemed to him that the city logo should be the only allowable logo.

As he faced this dilemma, he thought of many examples of city public space and equipment being used for advertising—some were corporate ads and others were from nonprofit organizations. He reflected on the appropriateness of corporate advertisements being posted on the parking meters, like miniature billboards, but had to concede that revenue was being generated.

He had seen the advertisements posted on public buses, trams, and commuter cars and thought that the buses wrapped in their colorful "vinyl advertisements" were actually attractive. Of course, he had learned early on in his civics courses that speech is protected by the First Amendment, but should Johnsonville's public property—fire trucks, water towers, city vehicles, police cars, traffic control signals, public parks, civic centers and arenas, ballparks, swimming pools, and schools—become the billboards of the future?

Enumerating examples of such advertising did not ease his decision-making dilemma, for the list seemed to be endless. He wondered if the trend toward advertisement on public property was merely a new type of blight seductively taking over urban spaces. If so, was the Lucky Sevens proposal any different from the commercial advertisements that already appeared on park benches and bus stands? Or even more dramatically, was it any different from the public university's advertisements printed in the media and shown on television? Additionally, what about the advertisements that states and cities used to attract business to enhance their chances for economic development?

Elwood thought about the overall implications of commercial advertising, and particularly of advertisements on his fire equipment. He wondered if it was truly worth it to get a new hazmat truck that also sported the casino's "graffiti." What message would his department be giving to the city, and especially to those who were most adversely affected by gambling—those least able to afford to gamble responsibly?

Questions and Instructions

1. If you were faced with Chief Elwood James's dilemma, what would you do? What would you find alluring about Marietta Hughes's offer? Or do you find Hughes's proposal repugnant? Please elaborate.

2. Explain why you would either accept or reject the offer from Lucky Sevens. How would you justify your decision? Would your justification be the same if you were making it before the city council or the citizenry? Please explain.

3. Although this case involves a local government entity, nonprofit organizations have also used commercial advertisements as a means to generate revenue. What are the implications of using or featuring commercial messages or logos on a nonprofit organization's printed educational materials, social media, or websites? Justify your answers.

4. Please develop a policy statement that could guide a board of directors in its thinking about the appropriateness of an affiliation with commercial advertising and in its use of such advertising.

PART VI

PHILANTHROPY AND ADVOCACY

The number and demographics of people who are interested in and passionate about social issues has grown rapidly in recent years. For example, the work of community organizers and activists for social justice is demonstrated in the Black Lives Matter movement as voices have been heard and nonprofit organizations established to address social equity concerns.[1] The impact of the coronavirus outbreak in underserved communities also has revealed pervasive inequities in health care, educational outcomes, and access to technology. The high profile #MeToo movement has received significant attention in media outlets as well-known Hollywood actors have blown the whistle on cultures of violence and exploitation in the movie and television industries and beyond. In universities, concerns about justice, diversity, equity, and inclusion have been widely embraced and are being institutionalized. At the same time, rhetoric about critical race theory has been deeply embedded in political circles, resulting in demonstrations at school board meetings across the US.

Nonprofits have a lot of work to do to help communities engage in frank but respectful conversations and to cultivate forums that are open to diverse ideas and opinions. Social media outlets provide avenues for various publics to be active in advocating for or against causes. Advocates may seek to educate while others attempt to change minds, promote action, and seek financial resources for furthering or blocking attempts at rational discourse. Regardless of the issue, change is a fundamental feature of the circumstances facing organizations in the nonprofit sector.[2]

The world of philanthropy is also ever changing: for example, in the ways that messages are able to gain public attention and send out calls to action. It is easy to recall the activities in the summer of 2014 when the ALS Ice Bucket Challenge went viral after celebrities and high-profile corporate leaders joined in.[3] The premise was simple: if someone challenged you, you had 24 hours to videotape yourself dumping a bucket of ice water over your head or donate to a charity benefiting research into amyotrophic lateral sclerosis (ALS), commonly known as Lou Gehrig's disease. Many participants did both. The August 29, 2014, headline on the national ALS Association website shouted the results: "The ALS Association Expresses Sincere Gratitude to Over Three Million Donors. Ice Bucket Challenge Donations Top $100 million in 30 days."[4]

Most charitable organizations can only dream about a windfall of unrestricted revenue. Put into perspective, from July 29 to August 29, 2014, the ALS Association received $100.9 million in donations, compared to $2.8 million during the same time period in 2013. The ALS Association's

 DOI: 10.4324/9781003387800-27

president and CEO, Barbara Newhouse, said, "The word gratitude doesn't do enough to express what we are feeling right now."[5]

"Going viral" is a chain reaction. When original content is posted on an internet platform, such as Facebook, Instagram, or the like, and people find the content compelling, many of the original poster's friends reshare the photo or video, many of their friends see it and reshare it, and the resharing goes on and on until thousands or millions of people have seen it—the vast majority of whom are total strangers to the original poster.[6] Donations from the Ice Bucket Challenge were made by individuals, corporations, and foundations; the ALS Association reported gifts ranging from under $1 to $200,000. Individual gifts were made by celebrities, including the actors Leonardo DiCaprio and David Spade, and by corporate leaders such as the president and CEO of T-Mobile US and the chairman of the Carnival Cruise Lines. Corporations contributing included Wells Fargo, Sprint, the Parsons Foundation, and the New York Yankees.[7]

In 30 days, donations through the Ice Bucket Challenge put the ALS Association's cash budget over five times the amount that it had available in the entire 2014 fiscal year. The organization's financial bonanza from the Ice Bucket Challenge had huge implications for its board of directors and management teams, who had to make solid financial decisions about how to use and invest the money. It also reinvigorated a spontaneous nationwide discussion about how philanthropy has been conceptualized and pursued across the nonprofit sector.

The visibility raised through the Ice Bucket Challenge placed the ALS Association on the radar of CharityWatch (formerly the American Institute of Philanthropy [AIP]) and Charity Navigator, two "charity watchdogs" that provide charitable donors with information to help them make informed giving decisions.[8] Each uses a scoring system to assign a rating that largely reflects a charity's business acumen and fiscal transparency as reported on its annual IRS Form 990-PF. CharityWatch noted on its website that it "will be monitoring the ALS Association to make sure that it has a reasonable plan or budget to spend the Ice Bucket windfall."[9] Ken Berger, president and CEO of Charity Navigator, said: "There is a concern that gimmicky fundraising appeals perpetuate a lack of discussion around what should be a core issue—a charity's impact and true worthiness of support."[10]

The reasons specific content goes viral currently elude precise understanding, but almost all conscious efforts to intentionally make something go viral fail.[11] The "lottery stories" of philanthropy-gone-viral are rare.[12] Nonetheless, with Facebook reporting over 38 million URLs linked to it, people and nonprofit organizations will keep trying.[13] Although online giving accounted for just 6.4 percent of all charitable giving in 2013, by 2020, the percentage of online giving rose to 13 percent.[14] In 2006, $6.8 billion was raised online, and this figure rose to over $22 billion in 2011.[15]

What makes a charity "worthy" often depends on how well it is able to demonstrate its business capabilities, not simply its philanthropic purpose. The perception of a charity's worthiness has generated concerns that extend far beyond the management of philanthropic activities because it challenges what it means to be a nonprofit. Almost 25 years ago, Richard Bush expressed his fear that by focusing on private-sector methods, nonprofit organizations were underappreciating the value of what has made them distinctive: participation and membership.[16] Jon Van Til suggested that many professional nonprofits should be removed from the tax-exempt rolls because they look and act more like businesses than voluntary organizations: "A lean third sector, consisting only of organizations true to principles of voluntary citizen-driven service and advocacy, would merit both the public privileges and the reputation it must continue to earn."[17] As Lori Brainard and Patricia Siplon wrote: "The soul of the nonprofit sector seems to be up for grabs."[18] More about the contested notion of "worthy philanthropy" is found in Holona LeAnne Ochs's article reprinted here as Chapter 12 in this part. As she argues, worthiness resting on business acumen or measurable results does not necessarily take into consideration human need.

Philanthropy

Philanthropy has a long history in the United States.[19] The word *philanthropy* is derived from the Greek for "love of mankind."[20] The Association of Fundraising Professionals defines *philanthropy* as:

> (1) the love of humankind, usually expressed by an effort to enhance the well-being of humanity through personal acts of practical kindness or by financial support of a cause or causes, such as a charity (e.g., the American Red Cross), mutual aid or assistance (e.g., service clubs and youth groups), quality of life (e.g., arts, education, and the environment), and religion; and (2) any effort to relieve human misery or suffering, improve the quality of life, encourage aid or assistance, or foster the preservation of values through gifts, service or other voluntary activity, and all of which are external to government involvement or marketplace exchange.[21]

Charity is "relieving or alleviating specific instances of suffering, aiding the individual victims of specific social ills. Charity is acts of mercy and compassion."[22]

Philanthropy differs from charity in that philanthropy is "the giving of money or self to solve social problems. Philanthropy is developmental, an investment in the future, an effort to prevent future occurrences or recurrence of socials ills." The work of philanthropists is exemplified by the late Paul Farmer, a global health champion[23] who died in 2022. Farmer dedicated his life's work to helping the poor receive health care. Farmer co-founded the nonprofit health organization Partners in Health (PIH), a social justice organization with the mission to "provide a preferential option for the poor in health care.[24] PIH works to make changes at the systems levels when possible. When systems have not existed, Farmer and PIH worked to build them, providing an example of "philanthropy in action."

Multiple perspectives have been offered to explain motivations for giving, including self-interest, altruism, and social relations, as well as government and market failures.[25] Gift giving has also been conceptualized as a component of social obligation. "The gift is the initiator of reciprocity and finds its purpose neither in self-interest nor in altruism, but rather in creating a system of social relations."[26]

Research is showing that the meaning and practices of philanthropy and cultural and moral choices about giving are in flux. In the foreword to this volume, David Renz identifies five converging central trends affecting nonprofits: demographic shifts that redefine participation; technological advances; growing networks; rising interest in civic engagement and volunteerism; and a blurring of sectoral boundaries among nonprofit organizations, for-profit organizations, and government. In the United States, an unprecedented $45 trillion to $150 trillion in wealth will be transferred over the next five decades, with 50 to 65 percent of this amount coming from households with $1 million or more in net worth. Not surprisingly, this is changing the way fundraisers, charities, and financial professionals should perceive, articulate, and implement their endeavors.[27]

There is work to be done, however. A 2013 study of financial planners and affluent donors conducted by Bank of America's US Trust and the Philanthropic Initiative found that nearly three-quarters of financial advisers initiate conversations about charitable giving with clients from a technical perspective. Only 35 percent focus on their clients' philanthropic goals or passions.[28] Not surprisingly, only 41 percent of the donors reported being fully satisfied with these conversations.[29] Donors want to choose how they become who they want to become and accomplish what they want to do for themselves, their families, and the world around them.[30]

Giving Practices

In *The 2021 Bank of America Study of High Net Worth Philanthropy*, wealthy donors reported becoming more intentional about their giving—they gave to support specific issues and causes. The majority of these donors relied on an impact strategy and focused on particular causes or geographical areas.[31] This intentionality is based in the belief that their gift can make a difference. A rise in media attention to celebrity philanthropy and high-profile business entrepreneurs also reflects keen interest in creating measurable impact. The 2022 Forbes 400 Summit on Philanthropy included approximately 150 billionaires or near-billionaires and social entrepreneurs. Forum participants considered topics such as disruptive business models and entrepreneurial solutions to global poverty. According to Mike Perlis, CEO and president of Forbes Media, previous Forbes 400 Summits have concluded "that transparency will be critical in driving growth in impoverished countries and ending corruption."[32]

Although philanthropy is often associated with the very wealthy, corporations, and foundations, the vast predominance of offerings come from average citizens, many of moderate income. Estimated giving by individuals in 2020 rose 2.2 percent over 2019 to $324.10 billion, out of total 2020 charitable giving of $471.44 billion.[33]

Demonstrating Philanthropy

The ways in which philanthropic action and caring can be done include individual cash donations, corporate sponsorships, social entrepreneurship and enterprises, and investments of time and talents through volunteering. The type or level of one's donations of cash or property may be influenced by a desire to promote a positive public or corporate image, or it may be based on individual or business-related tax incentives (see Part II). Social characteristics, including personal wealth, education level, age, and gender, affect philanthropic behavior as well. Data from the US Bureau of Labor Statistics show that education level is the best predictor of volunteering, along with female gender.[34] Generational differences also affect philanthropic behaviors such as volunteering (see Part VIII). Economic upturns, recessions, and political mistrust of government or business corporations can alter philanthropic attitudes. Media attention to charitable causes or disasters, religious teachings, social mores, family values, and professional skill sets may also affect one's participation in philanthropic activities.

The Transmission of Philanthropic Values

The 2021 Bank of America Study of High Net Worth Philanthropy showed that most high net worth households depend on their own family's efforts to educate younger relatives about charitable giving, but this practice has been decreasing. Likewise, a significant percent of high net worth households indicated that they relied on their church, synagogue, mosque, or other place of worship to transmit charitable values to their children, but this trend is also headed downward.[35] These declines raise a question: from what sources are younger professionals—say, millennials (those born in 1982 or later)—receiving their philanthropic cues? Technology is clearly transforming philanthropy—changing the ways people engage with nonprofit organizations. Now, it is crucial to understand how organizations market and manage information. Mobile technology is also growing. Nearly half of all emails are now read on mobile devices, and this is changing how organizations use data to drive mission delivery.[36]

Some research evidence shows that young people are more apt to ask, "What is in it for me?" than, "How can I give?"[37] Yet young people who are not actively involved in donating to charities may not have been asked.[38] Countless studies show that young people *are* philanthropically engaged through volunteering. The Nonprofit Source reports that although people aged 20 to 24 are less likely to volunteer than middle-aged people, 18.4 percent of this population volunteered in 2016.[39] These numbers may reflect family values and a commitment to meeting human needs, but they are also likely to reflect a community service opportunity or requirement in high school or college.

The Bureau of Labor Statistics has reported dips, however, in millennial volunteering in recent years, and this has some worried.[40] Unfortunately, there is evidence to suggest that young people may not sustain their volunteering activities.[41] Short-term project volunteering and episodic volunteering are on the rise, which may present managerial challenges for nonprofits that need ongoing or long-term support.[42]

Influences on Philanthropy

The past several decades have seen a sharp rise in social and corporate philanthropy. Cause marketing is a strategy whereby a promotional partnership between a nonprofit and a for-profit corporation is created. Ochs identifies governance partnerships along a spectrum that ranges from those based on civic logic to those that use market logic.[43] The spectrum includes traditional nonprofits, nonprofits engaged in income-generating activities, social enterprises, socially responsible businesses, corporate social responsibility, and traditional private entities. These organizations may be involved in governance partnerships that include or exclude activities typical of each type.[44] Technology has shaped the ways in which philanthropy is carried out, with volunteering recruitment and online activities serving as ways for organizations to build relations. Professional associations, even those whose mission is primarily business oriented, are using their networks, connections, expertise, and skills to encourage their memberships and staff members to contribute to the welfare of others through volunteering.[45]

Advocacy

Advocacy and philanthropy share the common purpose of furthering the achievement of nonprofit mission-related outcomes and shared visions. Citing the Free Online Dictionary, *advocacy* means "the act of pleading or arguing in favour of something, such as a cause, idea, or policy; active support."[46] Very simply, advocacy is aiding, protection, and support to individuals or groups of people. Broader definitions expand this to include activities in political arenas and attempts to change policies or influence the decisions of elite government and state institutions through civic participation.[47] Effective advocacy today requires access to information technology in order to communicate quickly with various stakeholders, mobilize broad public support, and monitor government and industry activity.[48]

Advocacy is pursued for a variety of reasons that include influencing policy, building social capital, seeking social justice and healing, strengthening communities, conducting listening tours, or enhancing the public voice, among others. In the review article, "Nonprofit Advocacy Tactics: Thinking Inside the Box?", Clear, Paull, and Holloway find that a variety of advocacy forms exist. These include administrative, legislative, direct and indirect strategies, institutional and radical approaches, and insider and outsider strategies.[49] Examples of these approaches in action include nonprofit personnel working on government committees; meeting with policy makers engaging in confrontations at public hearings, conducting lobbying activities, writing letters to the editor, issuing press releases, mobilization through campaigns, strikes, research including media advocacy, grassroots lobbying, public events and direct action, public education, and expert testimony, to name only a few!

Policy advocacy is an eminent feature of nonprofit organizations' activities that includes engaging and representing their constituencies; giving voice to diverse views and demands; promoting economic and social justice; contributing to a more vital, active civil society; and strengthening democracy and equality of opportunity.[50] Paradoxically, research findings indicate that the scope of advocacy activities in charitable 501(c)(3) nonprofits is limited and that advocacy does not play a major role in nonprofit human service organizations that provide social services.[51]

Conclusion

As the fields of philanthropy and nonprofit advocacy continue to undergo changes, one constant remains—there are many reasons people give or come to the aid of others. Some donors create and give their fortunes to foundations because of deeply held religious beliefs or a tradition of family social responsibility and concern for the poor, while others have political or ideological beliefs they wish to advance. Some give to foundations because they want to try to improve the human condition around the world, and others feel a commitment to give back to a local community or a cause. Some seek to create a memorial to themselves or their families, and others are feeling pressure from their peers to be philanthropic.[52] People in all times and places have felt the need and the desire to help others. Developing strong relationships and trust, however, takes time.[53]

Returning to where we began, a BBC News Magazine article asked the question "How Much Has the Ice Bucket Challenge Achieved?" Nonprofit managers today are pressed to respond to a similar question: philanthropically, what did we achieve? From an economic perspective, the Ice Bucket Challenge resulted in a large sum of money being raised in a short time. As that money is used for research, the hope is that the challenge will pay off with the development of ALS prevention strategies and cures and that it will improve the quality of life for people afflicted with ALS conditions. The visibility of the ALS Association's charitable activity also raised public visibility for the disease. Google searches for both "ALS" and "Lou Gehrig's disease" in the United States rose sharply during the Ice Bucket Challenge. In August 2014, the ALS Wikipedia page had close to 2.8 million views, compared with 1.7 million people who had visited it during the entire preceding 12 months.[54] These outcomes are encouraging, but as we have shown, they do not tell the whole story.

Philanthropic activities require money, but money is a means to an end. The value of caring for its own sake can be lost in chasing Facebook "shares" in an effort to get a message to go viral. There is another lesson to be learned from the ALS Ice Bucket Challenge: although widespread interest in ALS was generated in August 2014, the number of "hits" has not been sustained. It is unlikely that the ALS Association will be able to maintain a relationship with all of those three million donors.

Nonetheless, we do not want to be perceived as naysayers. All nonprofits must compete to find ways to increase their resources in order to carry out their mission-related activities, and the internet is one tool for doing so. Relationships are built through many channels, however, and we all have a vested interest in advocacy and in promoting the values of caring, sharing, and love of humankind on which philanthropy is based.

Readings Reprinted in Part VI

The first reading in this part is "Philanthropic Social Ventures: A Framework and Profile of the Emerging Field." Holona LeAnne Ochs offers an analysis and discussion of philanthropic social ventures. Ochs begins with the assertion that "modern philanthropy is infused with the notion that promoting social wealth yields self-sustaining benefits through innovative practices that create value and maintain their worth. The consequence of which may enhance investments among the underserved." As nonprofits adopt strategies and innovative partnerships that hinge on market strategies, they also have "the potential to further marginalize the interests of those who continue to be undervalued in the market context." Ochs's piece provides a useful continuum for understanding the many forms that may be created through philanthropic partnerships. Her key argument is a reminder to all that philanthropy is based on love of mankind, not market metrics.

The second reading in Part VI is "Political Advocacy by Nonprofit Organizations: A Strategic Management Explanation," by Kelly LeRoux and Holly T. Goerdel.[55] The authors discuss implications for nonprofit management of engaging in political advocacy. The authors note: "Nonprofit organizations serve as a voice for their constituent publics in the policy arena, even though advocacy practices remain outside of their core mission" (p. 514 of original article). Experience with collaborative networking, productive exchange relations with funding principals, representation of lobbying skills at the managerial level, dependence on government resources, and competition in the resource environment all shape nonprofits' advocacy practice in important ways.[56]

Hopefully, this introduction and these readings will encourage our readers to engage in discussions about philanthropy, professionalism, and advocacy in the nonprofit sector. They reflect the philanthropic challenges and opportunities that organizations face when addressing mission-related needs. Nonprofit board members, executive directors, officers, staff, and volunteers comprise a large set of actors, each working with others in an attempt to make a difference in the world. These networks of people and organizations cross all boundaries and sectors, and they introduce new and competing values for those engaged in philanthropy and advocacy. Traditional values of caring and giving for the sake of others, as foundational values of philanthropy, must remain strong if they are to be the legacy for philanthropy in the decades to come.

Case Studies in Part VI

The first case in Part VI, "Southwest County Foodbank: Nonprofit Board Advocacy," prepares the reader for a discussion about social media and how an organization, the Soup Bowl, is trying to use social media to build its base of philanthropic and financial supporters. Readers are asked to analyze the data that the Soup Bowl is gathering via Facebook and offer conclusions about its usefulness. Social media is only one of many avenues that nonprofit organizations are using to encourage engagement and inspire people to support their missions.

In the second case, "Volunteer and Donor Recruitment on Social Media," a nonprofit organization recognizes that generational differences may affect how it does outreach. One of its strategies is to use social media to sponsor a contest and encourage potential supporters to interact with the organization through fun activities and games. As this nonprofit seeks to be innovative and "in touch" with potential volunteers, the reader is asked to consider whether its tactics are working and also whether they constitute the best use of the nonprofit's time.

Notes

1. Rashawn Ray, "Black Lives Matter at 10 Years: 8 Ways the Movement Has Been Highly Effective," The Brookings Institution, October 12, 2022, https://www.brookings.edu/blog/how-we-rise/2022/10/12/black-lives-matter-at-10-years-what-impact-has-it-had-on-policing/

2. Peri H. Pakroo, *Starting and Building a Nonprofit: A Practical Guide,* 9th ed. (Berkley: NOLO: 2021), 2.

3. Eddie Scarry, "Ice Bucket Challenge Leads to $100 Million in Donations," Mediate, August 29, 2014, www.mediaite.com/online/ice-bucket-challenge-leads-to-100-million-in-donations/ (accessed October 21, 2014).

4. "The ALS Association Expresses Sincere Gratitude to Over Three Million Donors: Ice Bucket Challenge Donations Top $100 Million in 30 Days," ALS Association, August 29, 2014, www.alsa.org/news/media/press-releases/ice-bucket-challenge-082914.html. The ALS Association is a 501(c)(3) charitable nonprofit organization.

5. Ibid.

6. Josh Fredman, "What Does 'Goes Viral' on Facebook Mean?" Demand Media, http://science.opposingviews.com/goes-viral-facebook-mean-3009.html (accessed October 21, 2014).

7. "Individuals, Organizations, and Corporations Respond with Immense Generosity to Ice Bucket Challenge," ALS Association, August 29, 2014, www.alsa.org/news/media/press-releases/ice-bucket-challenge-generosity.html

8. See CharityWatch, "About Us," http://charitywatch.org/aboutaip.html, and Charity Navigator, "Mission," www.charitynavigator.org/index.cfm?bay=content.view&cpid=17#.VMk76JUtDIU. "Charity Navigator works to guide intelligent giving. By guiding intelligent giving, we aim to advance a more efficient and responsive philanthropic marketplace, in which givers and the charities they support work in tandem to overcome our nation's and the world's most persistent challenges."

9. CharityWatch, "Ice Bucket Donations Pour into ALS Association," September 2014, http://charitywatch.org/articles/alsicebucketchallenge.html

10. Ken Berger discussed the ALS Association receiving a large influx of cash in a short period of time on *CBS This Morning,* September 19, 2014, www.cbsnews.com/news/ice-bucket-challenge-als-association-how-to-spend-money/

11. Fredman, "What Does 'Goes Viral' on Facebook Mean?"

12. Mashable, "Crowdsourced Philanthropy—Making Your Cause Go Viral." *The Nonprofit Quarterly,* July 12, 2012, https://nonprofitquarterly.org/philanthropy/20647-crowdsourced-philanthropymaking-your-cause-go-viral.html

13. Alexa, "facebook.com," www.alexa.com/siteinfo/facebook.com (accessed October 21, 2014).

14. https://institute.blackbaud.com/charitable-giving-report/online-giving-trends/#:~:text=In%202020%2C%2012.9%25%20of%20total,the%20year%20it%20finally%20happened

15. Blackbaud, "Most Generous Online Cities" (2012) www.blackbaud.com/files/resources/downloads/2012MostGenerousOnlineCities.pdf

16. Richard Bush, "Survival of the Nonprofit Spirit in a For-Profit World," *Nonprofit and Voluntary Sector Quarterly,* 21 (1992): 391–410. See also Lori A. Brainard and Patricia D. Siplon, "Toward Nonprofit Organization Reform in the Voluntary Spirit: Lessons from the Internet," *Nonprofit and Voluntary Sector Quarterly* 33 (2004), 435.

17. Jon Van Til, *Growing Civil Society: From Nonprofit Sector to Third Space* (Bloomington: Indiana University Press, 2000), 203.

18. Brainard and Siplon, "Toward Nonprofit Organization Reform in the Voluntary Spirit," 436.

19. This introductory essay discusses issues in philanthropy and advocacy. For more focused discussions, see the introductory essays for Part V ("Fund Development: Generating Revenues") and Part VIII ("Managing Volunteers"). For a more complete discussion of philanthropy and its historical roots, see *The Nature of the*

Nonprofit Sector, 4th ed., edited by J. Steven Ott and Lisa A. Dicke (Boulder, CO: Westview Press, 2016): Part II, "The History, Values, and Activities of Nonprofit Organizations in the United States," and Part III, "The Nonprofit Sector Internationally: The Global Context." See also Peter Dobkin Hall, "A Historical Overview of Philanthropy, Voluntary Associations, and Nonprofit Organizations in the United States, 1600–2002," in *The Nonprofit Sector,* edited by Walter W. Powell and Richard Steinberg (New Haven: Yale University Press, 2006).

20. Barbara L. Ciconte and Jeanne G. Jacob, *Fundraising Basics: A Complete Guide* (Sudbury, MA: Jones and Bartlett, 2009), 2.

21. From the AFP's online dictionary, cited in ibid., 2.

22. Ott and Dicke, *The Nature of the Nonprofit Sector,* 4th ed., Part VIII, "Theories of Giving and Philanthropy."

23. Malaka Garib, "Global health champion Dr. Paul Farmer has died," NPR, February 21, 2022; "Dr. Paul Farmer, global health champion, has died," NPR, Goats and Soda.

24. www.pih.org/our-mission#:~:text=We%20are%20a%20social%20justice,other%20key%20 components%20of%20healing

25. See "Economic Theories of the Nonprofit Sector," in *The Nature of the Nonprofit Sector,* 4th ed., edited by Ott and Dicke (New York: Routledge, 2021).

26. Marcel Mauss, *The Gift: Forms and Functions of Exchange in Archaic Societies* (1925; reprint, London: Cohen and West, 1966); reprinted in Helmut K. Anheier, *Nonprofit Organizations,* 2nd ed. (New York: Routledge, 2014), 228.

27. Paul G. Schervish, "The Cultural Horizons of Charitable Giving in an Age of Affluence: The Leading Questions of the 21st Century," Boston College Center on Wealth and Philanthropy, www.wealthandgiving.org/ uploads/Cultural_Horizons.pdf

28. Doug Donovan, "Wealthy Donors Don't Get Giving Advice They Want," *Chronicle of Philanthropy,* October 9, 2013, http://philanthropy.com/article/Wealthy-Donors-Don-t-Get/142221/. For the study, see The Philanthropic Initiative, "The US Trust Study of the Philanthropic Conversation: Understanding Advisor Approaches and Client Expectations," October 2013, http://newsroom.bankofamerica.com/sites/bankofamerica.newshq. businesswire.com/files/press_kit/additional/US_Trust_Study_of_the_Philanthropic_Conversation_2013.pdf

29. Donovan, "Wealthy Donors Don't Get Giving Advice They Want," 2.

30. Schervish, "The Cultural Horizons of Charitable Giving in an Age of Affluence."

31. Bank of America. *2021 Bank of America Study of Philanthropy: Charitable Giving by Affluent Households.* www.privatebank.bankofamerica.com/articles/2021-bank-of-america-study-how-affluent-households-gave-back-in-2020.html (accessed February 26, 2022).

32. "Forbes Hosts Second Annual Forbes 400 Summit on Philanthropy," *Forbes,* June 6, 2013, www.forbes. com/sites/forbespr/2013/06/06/forbes-host-second-annual-forbes-400-summit-on-philanthropy/print/. The 2022 Forbes Philanthropy Summit on Philanthropy, was held in June 2022.

33. *Giving USA 2021: The Annual Report on Philanthropy for the year 2020.* Reported by the Lilly Family School of Philanthropy, "Giving USA 2021: In a Year of Unprecedented Events and Challenges, Charitable Giving Reached a Record $471.44 billion in 2020," June 15, 2021. https://philanthropy.iupui.edu/news-events/news-item/giving-usa-2021:-in-a-year-of-unprecedented-events-and-challenges,-charitable-giving-reached-a-record-%24471.44-billion-in-2020.html?id=361#:~:text=Giving%20USA%202021%3A%20The%20 Annual,to%20U.S.%20charities%20in%202020 (accessed February 25, 2022).

34. US Department of Labor, Bureau of Labor Statistics, "Volunteering in the United States, 2015," February 25, 2016, www.bls.gov/news.release/volun.nr0.htm (accessed February 26, 2022).

35. Bank of America, *2021 Bank of America Study of High Net Worth Philanthropy.*

36. Jordie van Rijn, "The Ultimate Mobile Email Stats Overview." Emailmonday, February 2022, www. emailmonday.com/mobile-email-usage-statistics/ (accessed February 26, 2022).

37. "The Connecticut Story: Millennials Are Leading the Way in Charitable Giving and Volunteering," *Connecticut Magazine,* November 19, 2020, www.connecticutmag.com/the-connecticut-story/

millennials-are-leading-the-way-in-charitable-giving-and-volunteering/article_d2d13ec2-2903-11eb-9de4-d348d4082f84.html (accessed February 26, 2022).

38. "The Connecticut Story."

39. Nonprofit Source, "Volunteering Statistics and Trends for Nonprofits," from https://nonprofitssource.com/online-giving-statistics/volunteering-statistics/ (accessed February 26, 2022).

40. US Department of Labor, Bureau of Labor Statistics, "Volunteering in the United States," (2015).

41. Theresa Wu, "2021 Volunteering Trends and How to Optimize the Relaunch of Your Volunteer Program." Civic Champs, November 18, 2021. www.civicchamps.com/post/2021-volunteering-trends-and-how-to-optimize-the-relaunch-of-your-volunteer-program (accessed February 26, 2022).

42. Lesley Hustinx and Lucas C. P. M. Meijs, "Re-Embedding Volunteering: In Search of a New Collective Ground," *Voluntary Sector Review* 2 (2011): 5–21; Richard A. Sundeen, Cristina Garcia, and Sally A. Raskoff, "Ethnicity, Acculturation, and Volunteering to Organizations: A Comparison of Africans, Asians, Hispanics, and Whites," *Nonprofit and Voluntary Sector Quarterly* 38 (2009): 929–955.

43. Holona LeAnne Ochs, "Philanthropic Social Ventures: A Framework and Profile of the Emerging Field," *Journal of Public Management and Social Policy*, 18 no. 1 (Spring 2012): 3–26. Reprinted in this part as Chapter 12.

44. Ibid., 9.

45. Marina Saitgalina and Lisa A. Dicke, "The Role of Professional Associations in Strengthening Civil Society Through Membership Engagement." Paper presented at the annual conference of the Association for Research on Nonprofit and Voluntary Associations, Hartford, CT, November 2013.

46. Michel Almog-Bar and Hillel Schmid, "Advocacy Activities of Nonprofit Human Service Organizations: A Critical Review," *Nonprofit and Voluntary Sector Quarterly*, 43 no. 1 (2014): 11–35.

47. Ibid, 15.

48. Kirsten Gronbjerg and Curtis D. Child, "Nonprofit Advocacy Organizations: Their Characteristics and Activities," *Social Science Quarterly*, 88 no. 1 (March 2007).

49. Anne Clear, Megan Paull, and David Holloway, "Nonprofit Advocacy Tactics: Thinking Inside the Box?" *Voluntas* 29 (2018): 857–869.

50. Michel Almog-Bar and Hillel Schmid, "Advocacy Activities of Nonprofit Human Service Organizations: A Critical Review, *Nonprofit and Voluntary Sector Quarterly*, 43, no. 1 (2014): 11–35, 12.

51. Ibid, 15.

52. See Part II, "The History, Values, and Activities of Nonprofit Organizations in the United States," in Ott and Dicke, *The Nature of the Nonprofit Sector,* 4th ed. (New York: Routledge, 2021).

53. Ruth McCambridge, "Naomi Levine: Insights from a Master of Fundraising," *Nonprofit Quarterly* 70 (Summer 2013).

54. Lucy Townsend, "How Much Has the Ice Bucket Challenge Achieved?" *BBC News Magazine,* September 1, 2014, www.bbc.com/news/magazine-29013707

55. Kelly LeRoux and Holly T. Goerdel, "Political Advocacy by Nonprofit Organizations: A Strategic Management Explanation," *Public Performance & Management Review* 32 no. 4 (2009): 514–536. Reprinted in this part as Chapter 13.

56. Ibid.

CHAPTER 12

Philanthropic Social Ventures
A Framework and Profile of the Emerging Field

HOLONA LEANNE OCHS

Originally published as "Philanthropic Social Ventures: A Framework and Profile of the Emerging Field" by Holona LeAnne Ochs, *Journal of Public Management and Social Policy* 18, no. 1 (Spring 2012). Reprinted with permission.

Recent attention has turned to how to best conceptualize and implement philanthropy in the public interest. Defining who deserves assistance, what kind, and how much is influenced by the charitable. The capacity to differentiate a public and direct the corresponding interest has tremendous potential to affect the opportunities available and shape the access to those opportunities. Moreover, the devolved, contractual nature of the provision of public goods within the current governance context results in increasingly blurry boundaries between the public, private, and nonprofit sectors in social service delivery systems. As a result, the intentions, functions, and enactment of social objectives are expressed in a complex, competitive, and highly variable display of civic engagement. Some describe the shift in public interest orientation in pluralist terms, suggesting a socialization of the private sector; while others are concerned that the shift is essentially a colonization of the public and nonprofit sectors by the private sector that may enhance wealth inequalities.

Where traditional philanthropy has served those who tend to be undervalued, modern philanthropy insists upon assigning economic value to social ends or reconstructing economic value as a means to a social end rather than an end in itself. Modern philanthropy is infused with the notion that promoting social wealth yields self-sustaining benefits through innovative practices that create value and maintain their worth. The consequence of which may enhance investments among the underserved but also has the potential to further marginalize the interests of those who continue to be undervalued in the market context.

In many ways, philanthropic innovation is a developing arena in which the public interest is increasingly contested and entrepreneurial processes are transforming the field. Venture philanthropy refers to the financing of innovative social investments; whereas social entrepreneurship encompasses "the activities and processes undertaken to discover, define, and exploit opportunities in order to enhance social wealth by creating new ventures or managing existing organizations in an innovative manner" (Zahra et al. 2009, 522). Venture philanthropy is a form of social entrepreneurship in itself,

 DOI: 10.4324/9781003387800-28

and alternatively, social entrepreneurs may be funded by foundations using the venture philanthropy model. The evolution of these innovative social investments and the social entrepreneurs implementing them characterize the worth and consequence of the social wealth created by these endeavors. . . .

Development of the Practice of Philanthropy in the United States

Traditional Philanthropy

Charitable institutions in the United States emerged in a context in which there was initially a considerable degree of hostility toward private philanthropy. Yet, the progressive realignment of the party system early in the 20th century paved the way for the establishment of the first modern grant making institutions (Hall 2006). The various foundations established by Carnegie and Rockefeller did demonstrate to the American public that wealth may be more than simply predatory and self-serving, but the resistance of political officials during that period suggests concerns regarding the influence of foundations persisted (Hall 2006). And, the threat of the potential for political, economic, and social reform originating outside the democratic process was to some extent perceived as a threat to the legitimacy of government. Shifts in influence and sector boundaries between the public, private, and nonprofit sector continue to be a source of tension over the legitimacy of collective, private, and voluntary action in matters described as the "public interest" in the United States.

Historically, traditional philanthropy was conceived of as serving the following functions in ways that were thought to be consistent with the public interest as it was defined at the time (Prewitt 2006): (1) a redistributive function; (2) a more cost-effective distribution of public goods than the public sector could (or would not) provide and that the private sector had

no incentive to provide; (3) a liberal function in which public goods provision through foundations was seen as imposing the least cost on economic liberty; and/or (4) a pluralist function that afforded the opportunity for the expression of benevolence with the potential to inspire social change. These boundaries began to blur with the first reference associating venture capital and philanthropy by F. Emerson Andrews, who described foundations as the "venture capital of philanthropy" (Andrews 1950). It was again political reform and wealth accumulation that eventually led to a shift in influence and the convergence of practices in philanthropy that are now described as venture philanthropy.

"New" Philanthropy

Broadly speaking, two factors help explain the rise of social entrepreneurship and venture philanthropy: the challenges of the welfare state in the modern global context and increased competition within the nonprofit sector (Perrini and Vurro 2006; Robinson 2006). Nonprofits face the pressures of lower financial reserves, increased competition, and increased pressure to perform. Financial support fell as policy was privatized and decentralized in the welfare state (Perrini and Vurro 2006), resulting in reduced government financial support for nonprofits (Wei-Skillern et al. 2007). Lower marginal tax rates in the Bush era also reduced tax savings and the incentive to give to charities, philanthropies, and other nonprofits; the recent recession also contributes to this trend. At the same time, nonprofits face increased public scrutiny and pressure (Boschee 2006). Greater demands for professionalized services and an increasing emphasis on accountability along with escalating competitive pressure among nonprofits for diminishing sources of funding, particularly where there are service redundancies, place tremendous pressure on the nonprofit sector (Alter 2006). Nonprofit organizations are expected to strengthen their evaluation methods, enhance performance, and broaden strategic alliances with increasingly lower levels of financial support. The broad societal trend toward consumerism and moral individualism in conjunction with the rapidly changing market forces of the new global economy dominated by neoliberal managerial ideals have produced a social economy in which welfare demands are not met by the state but may be met by social entrepreneurs (see Mayo and Moore 2001). Yet, meeting these social expectations relies on exploiting opportunities to create social wealth through mutually beneficial exchange in contexts that have been traditionally undervalued.

Venture philanthropy differs from traditional philanthropy in the following ways:

1. The foundation, philanthropreneur(s), partners, investors, and/or consultants are "highly engaged" with the organizations that they support (Pepin 2005; Raymond 2004) in a relationship conceived of as long-term (Frumkin 2003), usually lasting between 4–7 years, beginning with a one-year planning stage (WeiSkillern et al. 2007).
2. The outcomes and effectiveness are defined by the foundation's business metric and are often referred to as impact (Frumkin 2003; Nicholls 2006).
3. The focus is on strategic management for the sustainability of the organization (Frumkin 2003), dominated by aggressive revenue generation strategies (Bornstein and Davis 2010).
4. Philanthropic social ventures operate within business models that define an "exit strategy" at the outset (Walker 2004).
5. Venture philanthropy tends to involve a wider range of investments and engage in risk management rather than mitigating risk (Osberg 2006).

It is a relationship presumed to be built on mutually beneficial partnerships as well as one recognizing that social investments are maintained through relationships in which all parties are committed to and accountable for turning problems into opportunities. Venture philanthropy is an approach to philanthropy that borrows heavily from private sector concepts, based on the assumption that development models, efficiency, microfinance techniques, and professionalism are optimal in the private sector and that applying these concepts to traditional philanthropic approaches may enhance the social impact (Raymond 2004). Venture philanthropy attempts to improve the strength and sustainability of nonprofit organizations by facilitating sector collaboration through diversified investments, conferences and networking opportunities, fellowships, technology, and advocacy . . .

Measuring performance is a critical component of venture philanthropy. Many qualitative performance measures are available for social ventures, such as Triple Bottom Line accounting and the Balanced Score Card . . . Venture philanthropy often utilizes benchmarking to enhance mission-driven performance by comparing the social enterprise to the best in the chosen social arena (Raymond 2004) . . .

Many venture philanthropists pick out social enterprises based on performance, not need (Walker 2004). Unlike traditional philanthropies in which applications are open or invited, venture philanthropies take a proactive approach and seek out partners (Osberg 2006). The nonprofits that demonstrate a willingness to engage in the venture philanthropy model and have high potential for social impact are the most likely candidates for philanthropic investments . . .

Critics argue that the venture philanthropy model is structurally inappropriate (Shakely 2003), over-extended (Kramer 1999), does not apply after the dot-com boom (Sievers 1997), or that it tries to impose an economic model on an ethical or moral discipline (DiMaggio 1997). Sievers (2001) raises concerns about the potential for venture philanthropy to redefine the frame of reference of civil society in ways that may not benefit society, resulting from a narrow emphasis on performance indicators, the trade-offs inherent in scalability that contribute to the conceptualization of the community and its corresponding responsibilities, the potential for inordinate influence by highly engaged investors, and the fact that commercializing nonprofit organizations is likely to distort the mission. Venture philanthropists themselves contend that there are several factors a foundation should consider when evaluating whether venture philanthropy is suitable. The following have been outlined in several reports and speeches provided by the Chair of Venture Philanthropy Partners, Mario Morino:

1. The mission of the organization needs to be conducive to leveraging financial resources to foster innovation without compromising the organizational principles.
2. The intellectual resources of the staff and board must be sufficiently diverse, given the financial, technical, experiential, and methodological demands of the issue at hand.
3. The funding capacity needs to be large enough to generate innovation on a scale that is proportionate to the mission over the long-term . . .

. . . The various claims and concerns about venture philanthropy are based on assumptions about the character of the market rather than direct evidence. Understanding the extent to which venture philanthropy might improve performance and the circumstances within which such performance enhancement might result in a greater social impact requires a framework for mapping the emerging philanthropic landscape (see Frumkin 2003; Moody 2008) . . .

Theoretical Framework

. . . The following section outlines a typology of the organizations that might receive investments

or support from venture philanthropists and illustrates the spectrum of organizational motives. This section also defines the various strategies utilized for leveraging impact in order to understand the different components of the venture philanthropy movement.

The Hybrid Spectrum of Funding

The venture philanthropy movement diversifies the types of investments that philanthropists might make by expanding the types of organizations that are conceived of as contributing to the development of social wealth. Venture philanthropists may invest in the following types of entities: (1) traditional nonprofits; (2) nonprofits engaged in income generating activities; (3) social enterprises; (4) socially responsible businesses; (5) corporate social responsibility; and/or (6) traditional private entities. Social entrepreneurship refers to the hybrid spectrum of organizations that attempt to balance civic motives and market logic. Because philanthropic social ventures may also involve cross-sector collaborations, public-private partnerships, and/or contracts for social service delivery implemented by the public, private, and/or nonprofit sectors, some venture philanthropists further their objectives by engaging the full spectrum of governance partnerships. These relationships are illustrated in Figure 13.1.

The hybrid spectrum includes nonprofits engaged in income generating activities. Those activities include, but are not necessarily limited to, the following:

- cost recovery mechanisms such as special events, conferences, seminars, and fee-for-service; and/or
- earned income revenue streams such as membership dues, sales of publications and products, and consulting programs.

Social enterprise, social entrepreneurship, *and* social entrepreneurs *are often used to refer*

FIGURE 12.1 Hybrid Spectrum of Governance Partnerships

HYBRID SPECTRUM					
CIVIC LOGIC					
	MARKET LOGIC				
Traditional Nonprofit	Nonprofit Engaged in Income Generating Activities	Social Enterprise	Socially Responsible Business	Corporate Social Responsibility	Traditional Private Entity
GOVERNANCE PARTNERSHIPS					

to a field of research despite the fact that the concepts are distinct and suggest different levels of analysis. In terms of the types of entities that might receive venture philanthropy investments, the social enterprise is the level of focus. The social enterprise is characterized by having a social purpose, an entrepreneurial approach, and an emphasis on stewardship (Fayolle and Matlay 2010). Social enterprises may be structured as departments or affiliates within an organization or as a separate legal entity—either nonprofit or for-profit. Social enterprise is distinct from the socially responsible business in that the latter operates with the dual purpose of generating shareholder profits while contributing to a social good. In the socially responsible business, every decision is anchored in the company's core values. This is distinct from corporate social responsibility in that for-profit businesses operating under the profit motive and also engaging in philanthropy make business decisions apart from the social values supported by their philanthropy.

Strategies for Leveraging Impact

Zahra et al. (2009) outline a typology of social entrepreneurship, focusing on identifying different types of social entrepreneurs. They propose the following three categories: (1) the social bricoleur; (2) the social constructionist; and (3) the social engineer. Each of these types employs distinct strategic repertoires.

Bricolage is an idea developed by Levi-Straus (1967) that refers to the process of combining and transforming existing resources to innovate and add value. Baker and Nelson (2005) refine this concept by specifying the following conditions: (1) focus on the resources at hand; (2) utilization of existing resources for new purposes; and (3) recombining existing resources for the creation of new economic and social value. The processes, relationships, and interconnections among these networks are the focus of evaluation and the genesis of solution-focused intervention. Bricolage assumes that path creation is possible for rational individuals or firms in interaction with the environment or context in which the individual or firm operates. Generating novel solutions and targeting underserved markets is a part of the process of innovation sometimes referred to as intrapreneurship (see Mair and Martí 2006). Intrapreneurship patterns are theorized to occur in episodes that Corner and Ho (2010) characterize in the following manner: (1) opportunity development; (2) collective action; (3) experience corridors; and (4) spark. These innovative episodes are the critical components of entrepreneurship broadly.

Capitalizing on local markets with minimal or depleted resources that may be accessed at low cost by what is referred to as knowledge spillovers, economic regeneration, and proximity designs . . . describes how bricolage functions (see Fayolle and Matlay 2010). Knowledge spillover occurs when a non-rival mechanism for distributing facts, information, and/or skills that have not previously been accounted for are picked up, stimulating broader improvements (Arrow 1962). Economic regeneration is distinct from economic development in that economic regeneration refers to the reinvestment in industrial or business areas that have suffered decline (Stohr 1990), and proximity designs group related items to maximize gain (Lagendijk and Oinas 2005).

Social constructionists attempt to create social wealth by identifying the inadequacies in existing institutions or organizations and launching ventures to better address those social issues. Constructionists operate at the regional, national, or global level, and they design systemic solutions to address the perceived cause of a broader social problem. Constructionists may fund bricoleurs to build the infrastructure and/or code the operations for the systemic reform. The strategies that characterize the social constructionist are knowledge transfer and scalable solutions.

Social engineers find fundamental and irreparable flaws in the existing system and seek to undermine, deconstruct, and replace present practices in existing institutions. Social engineers require political capital to legitimize their projects. The strategies that characterize social engineers involve education and advocacy in addition to influencing the policy process through lobbying, resistance/protest, and the media. While all social entrepreneurs are likely to engage in these activities to some degree, social engineers rely on them to build the political capital necessary for collective, collaborative, or voluntary action.

Characteristics of Philanthropic Social Ventures

There are three distinct but not necessarily mutually exclusive models for engaging venture philanthropy: traditional foundations practicing high-engagement grant making; social value organizations funded by individuals and implemented by a professional staff; and the partnership model in which financial investors become highly engaged with the grantees. These philanthropic models reflect the structure and operations of the foundation as well as symbolize the role the philanthropists envision themselves playing in the generation of social wealth . . .

Venture philanthropists funding traditional nonprofits are likely to do so with the expectation that the nonprofit begin engaging in more income generating activities as a means to sustainability. This trend is likely to select from the nonprofit sector those "high performing nonprofits" with market potential . . . It does appear that philanthropic social ventures regularly utilize bricolage strategies. It is common for philanthropic social ventures utilizing constructionist strategies at the global level to also fund local bricoleurs, which is essential to implementing a scalable solution and potentially beneficial to local organizations. Engineering and promoting corporate social responsibility are uncommon strategies among philanthropic social ventures However, these strategies may be more common among other types of changemakers. It is also important to note that some philanthropic social ventures appear to position themselves as a hub for orchestrating change at multiple levels and/or coordinating action among like-minded individuals and organizations.

Understanding the Legal Environment

With the rapid growth in the number and size of foundations and the greater publicity given to the nonprofit sector, there is increased interest and focus on foundation activities . . .

The attention of government and the legal sector has resulted in changes along several dimensions as it relates to the practice of modern philanthropy. Supervisory legislation has appeared in many different states, and the IRS has started to police the exemption provisions of the tax laws that govern nonprofits (Fremont-Smith 1965) . . .

Government plays a large role in the realm of philanthropy as a major source of nonprofit revenue as well. Government grants, contracts, and reimbursement from public agencies account for about 36 percent of the sector's revenue (Raymond 2004). Government policy is pivotal in catalyzing new social ventures by defining the laws, regulations, and support given to social enterprises (Mulgan 2006). For example, organizations that solicit contributions nationwide can utilize the Unified Registration Statement, which allows such organizations in 34 states to file a single form in lieu of separate state registration statements.[1] Governments may utilize technology to minimize transaction costs for nonprofit accountability as well, such as the online charitable registration system available in Colorado, Hawaii, and New Mexico (among a handful of other states) or the e-Postcard required by the IRS. Legal environments that reduce barriers to entry facilitate social entrepreneurship (Mulgan 2006, 82) . . .

Many foundations are now encouraged to perform a voluntary legal audit. This is a decision made by the board to systematically review all legal processes and documents to ensure the minimization of legal risks (Andringa and Engstrom 2002). Because of the changing legal and financial landscape surrounding philanthropy, foundations are being held to higher legal standards and accountability demands. Federal law, IRS regulations, state statutes, and court decisions in recent years have started to remove the traditional hands-off approach. At the same time, donors and employees have become more demanding and litigious (Andringa and Engstrom 2002) . . .

Conclusion

Venture philanthropy developed within the broad conceptual umbrella of social entrepreneurship due to increasing competition for limited philanthropic dollars, entrepreneurial development, and public demands for greater accountability and efficiency within philanthropic foundations. As the legal environment surrounding philanthropy starts to change, venture philanthropy is in a position to influence this level of change. Venture philanthropy groups differ in number, motivations, characteristics, and pace of evolution by region. Venture philanthropy rapidly evolved and enjoys the most supportive environment within urban areas and California. However, as the venture philanthropy model continues to spread throughout the United States, these regional distinctions are likely to become less pronounced . . .

Note

1. This streamlined system developed from a collaborative effort on the part of the charitable community and the National Association of State Charity Officials (NASCO) and can be downloaded at www.nonprofits.org/library/gov/urs/.

References

Alter, Sutia Kim. 2006. "Social Enterprise Models and Their Mission and Money Relationships." In *Social Entrepreneurship: New Paradigms of Sustainable Social Change*, edited by Alex Nicholls. New York: Oxford University Press.

Andrews, F. Emerson. 1950. *Philanthropic Giving*. New York: Russell Sage Foundation.

Andringa, Robert C., and Ted W. Engstrom. 2002. *Nonprofit Board Answer Book*. Washington, DC: Board Source.

Arrow, Kenneth. 1962. "Economic Welfare and the Allocation of Resources for Invention." In *The Rate and Direction of Inventive Activity: Economic and Social Factors.* Universities-National Bureau (ed.), UMI (0–87014–304–2), 609–626.

Baker, T., and R. Nelson. 2005. "Creating Something from Nothing: Resource Construction Through Entrepreneurial Bricolage." *Administrative Science Quarterly* 50: 329–366.

Bornstein, David, and Susan Davis. 2010. *Social Entrepreneurship: What Everyone Needs to Know.* Oxford: Oxford University Press.

Boschee, Jerr. 2006. "Social Entrepreneurship: The Promise and the Perils." In *Social Entrepreneurship: New Paradigms of Sustainable Social Change,* edited by Alex Nicholls, 356–390. New York: Oxford University Press.

Corner, Patricia Doyle, and Marcus Ho. 2010. "How Opportunities Develop in Social Entrepreneurship." *Entrepreneurship Theory and Practice* 34: 635–659.

DiMaggio, P. 1997. "Culture and Cognition." *Annual Review of Sociology* 23: 263–287.

Fayolle, Alain, and Harry Matlay. 2010. *Handbook of Research on Social Entrepreneurship.* Northampton, MA: Elgar Publishing.

Fremont-Smith, Marion R. 1965. *Foundations and Government.* Hartford, CT: Connecticut Printers, Inc.

Frumkin, Peter. 2003. "Inside Venture Philanthropy." *Society* (May-June): 7–15.

Hall, Peter Dobkin. 2006. "A Historical Overview of Philanthropy, Voluntary Associations, and Nonprofit Organizations in the United States, 1600–2000." In *The Nonprofit Sector,* edited by Walter W. Powell and Richard Steinberg. New Haven, CT: Yale University Press.

Kramer, Mark R. 1999. "Venture Capital and Philanthropy: A Bad Fit." *The Chronicle of Philanthropy* (April 22): 72–73.

Lagendijk, Arnoud, and Paivi Oinas. 2005. Proximity, Distance, and *Diversity: Issues on Economic Interaction and Local Development.* New York: Ashgate.

Mair, J., and I. Martí. 2006. "Social Entrepreneurship Research: A Source of Explanation, Prediction, and Delight." *Journal of World Business* 41, no. 1, 36.

Mayo, E., and H. Moore. 2001. *The Mutual State.* London: New Economics Foundation.

Moody, Michael. 2008. "Building a Culture: The Construction and Evolution of Venture Philanthropy as a New Organizational Field." *Nonprofit*

and Voluntary Sector Quarterly 37, no. 2, 324–352.

Mulgan, Geoff. 2006. "Cultivating the Other Invisible Hand of Social Entrepreneurship: Comparative Advantage, Public Policy, and Future Research Priorities." In *Social Entrepreneurship: New Paradigms of Sustainable Social Change,* edited by Alex Nicholls, 74–98. New York: Oxford University Press.

Nicholls, Alex. 2006. "Introduction." In *Social Entrepreneurship: New Paradigms of Sustainable Social Change,* edited by Alex Nicholls, 1–38. New York: Oxford University Press.

Osberg, Sally. 2006. "Wayfinding Without a Compass: Philanthropy's Changing Landscape and Its Implications for Social Entrepreneurs." In *Social Entrepreneurship: New Paradigms of Sustainable Social Change,* edited by Alex Nicholls, 309328. New York: Oxford University Press.

Pepin, John. 2005. "Venture Capitalists and Entrepreneurs Become Venture Philanthropists." *International Journal of Nonprofit and Voluntary Sector Marketing* 10, no. 3, 165–173.

Perrini, Francesco, and Clodia Vurro. 2006. *The New Social Entrepreneurship: What Awaits Social Entrepreneurship Ventures,* edited by Francesco Perrini. Northampton, MA: Edward Elgar.

Raymond, Susan U. 2004. The Future of Philanthropy: Economics, Ethics, and Management. Hoboken, NJ: John Wiley & Sons, Inc.

Robinson, Jeffrey. 2006. "Navigating Social and Institutional Barriers to Markets: How Social Entrepreneurs Identify and Evaluate Opportunities." In *Social Entrepreneurship,* edited by Johanna Mair, Jeffrey Robinson, and Kai Hockerts, 95–120. New York: Palgrave Macmillan.

Shakely, J. 2003. "The Meta-Foundation: Venture Philanthropy Starts the Next Leg of Its Journey, with a Surprising New Pilot." In *From Grantmaker to Leader: Emerging Strategies for Twenty-First Century Foundations,* edited by F. L. Ellsworth and J. Lumarda, 119–138. New York: John Wiley.

Sievers, Bruce. 1997. "If Pigs Had Wings." *Foundation News and Commentary* (November-December): 44–46.

Stohr, Walter B. 1990. *Global Challenge and Local Response: Initiatives for Economic Regeneration in Contemporary Europe.* London: Mansell.

Walker, Lewis J. 2004. "The Growth of Venture Philanthropy." *On Wall Street* 14, no. 11, 107–108.

Wei-Skillern, Jane, James Austin, Herman Leonard, and Howard Stevenson. 2007. *Entrepreneurship in the Social Sector*. Los Angeles: Sage Publications.

Zahra, S., E. Gedajlovic, D. Neubaum, and J. Shulman. 2009. "A Typology of Social Entrepreneurs: Motives, Search Processes, and Ethical Challenges." *Journal of Business Venturing* 24, no. 5, 519–534.

CHAPTER 13

Political Advocacy by Nonprofit Organizations

A Strategic Management Explanation

KELLY LEROUX AND HOLLY T. GOERDEL

Originally published as "Political Advocacy by Nonprofit Organizations: A Strategic Management Explanation," in *Public Performance & Management Review*: 514–536. Copyright © M E Sharpe, Inc. (2009). Reprinted by permission of Taylor & Francis.

In the form of voluntary associations, civic organizations, and lobbying groups, nonprofit organizations are widely recognized as influential actors in American policymaking and politics. By raising money for social causes, sponsoring petition campaigns, increasing public awareness of salient issues, and linking citizens to political actors and institutions, nonprofits are an integral part of the policymaking process at all levels of government. As outlets for political dialogue, social networking, and volunteerism (Reid, 2004), scholars have recognized nonprofits as important vehicles for promoting civic engagement and furthering democratic ideals (Putnam, 2000; Skocpol, 2003).

Economic theories of the nonprofit sector suggest these organizations exist to give expression to preferences of groups whose needs have not or cannot be fulfilled by government (Weisbrod, 1977). Attempts to influence policy on behalf of clients represents a form of substantive representation, or what Guo and Musso

described as "an organization acting in the interest of its constituents, in a manner responsive to them" (2007, p. 312). Political advocacy in the forms of representation and mobilization are regarded as legitimate and important activities for nonprofits to undertake (Bass et al., 2007; Berry & Arons, 2003; Salamon & Lessans-Geller, 2008).

Despite the critical responsibility of representing the interests of groups they serve, evidence has shown that nonprofits engage in advocacy at highly variable rates (Salamon & Lessans-Geller, 2008). A lack of relevant staff expertise, combined with concerns about violating laws and fears of losing public funds, often keeps nonprofits out of the political arena altogether. Understanding which factors promote nonprofit advocacy is important for four reasons. First, nonprofits comprise the fastest growing sector of the U.S. economy (Independent Sector, 2002). And thus their presence in the political arena is likely to

DOI: 10.4324/9781003387800-29

increase in the future. Secondly, these organizations ae uniquely suited for representing the interests of economically disadvantaged and marginalized clientele groups in the policy process (Berry & Arons, 2003). Third, the increasing reliance of nonprofits on government funding over the last four decades has led to a pattern of complex exchange relationships and mutual dependence between government and nonprofits in the formation and implementation stages of public policy (Heimovics, Herman, & Jurkewicz-Coughlin, 1993; Knoke, 1990; Laumann & Knoke, 1987; Saidel, 1991). Finally, nonprofit funders have begun to encourage investment in nonprofits' advocacy, encouraging funders and the public to support advocacy capacity building (Atlantic Philanthropies, 2008).

Using survey data from a sample of 119 nonprofit organizations in the state of Michigan, we attempt to answer the question of why nonprofits pursue advocacy goals at such variable rates. Through our empirical study, we contribute to the literature on nonprofit advocacy by identifying specific organizational and management capacities that enable nonprofits to carry out their advocacy goals.

An Organizational-Level Explanation of Advocacy

The organizational activity we focus on is advocacy performed by nonprofits with the purpose of connecting organizational constituencies to political and policymaking process. Given legal restrictions imposed on public charities by the Internal Revenue Service (IRS) to limit their advocacy activities,[1] these practices are by definition peripheral to the primary mission of the organization. Despite this, nonprofits perform this role to varying degrees, often advantaging their own survival in the process. Within these circumstances, which factors promote nonprofit advocacy?

The interest group and organization-level advocacy literature identifies two prominent dimensions of advocacy: *grass-roots advocacy* (Goldstein, 1999; Kollman, 1989), and *standing in decision making* (Knoke, 1986; Sabatier, 1991). Grassroots advocacy occurs through efforts by the organization to mobilize their constituencies for political action. Standing in decision making occurs when organizations attempt to shape the agenda or outcomes of the political process through their participation in policy communities comprised of bureaucrats, legislators, civic group leaders, and other participants. The organization initiates action within both of these dimensions, rather than acting in response to some external form of influence. Therefore, we posit a model in which advocacy can be explained through a series of variables measuring organizational-level competencies and capacities. These are acquired through processes of organizational learning, structural characteristics, relevant management and governance capacities, and aspects of the resource environment.

Processes of Organizational Learning

Engaging in advocacy requires an organizational supply of skills for brokering consensus. Organizations can acquire these and other skills in two prominent ways. The first is through collaborative networking. Nonprofits commonly engage in collaborative networking for the propose of economizing transaction costs associated with service delivery. Some organizations rely on these external relationships to "stretch their dollar" to meet demands, or to facilitate partnerships in piloting new programs or services. In a world of increased network governance, many nonprofits are required to engage in collaboration as a contingency for funding. While these actions are typically directed toward increasing performance on core functions of the organization, they are also vehicles for learning about how to productively coordinate groups of stakeholders; specifically, how to balance and protect mutual and individual interests, build effective coalitions of support, establish commitments to action from those around the table, develop standards of trust, fairness and reciprocity, and finally cultivate protocol for handling conflict (Agranoff, 2003; Bingham & O'Leary, 2007).

These collaborative capacities can also serve to increase political advocacy on behalf of nonprofits. For example, in recent interviews and focus groups, nonprofit executives report that a primary challenge for participating in advocacy is how "to link advocacy to strengthening the organization's mission" (Bass et al., 2007, p. 39). Other challenges include developing skills for how to influence administrative decisions such as agency rulemaking, how to build effective coalitions to address policy problems, and how to build up technical skills like writing letters to elected officials (Bass et al., 2007, p. 37). As this example demonstrates, many of these reported challenges are likely to benefit from skills learned through networking and collaboration, as cited above.

As more nonprofits find themselves with networks of agencies with similar service missions, coalitions, and professional associations, they also find themselves becoming more aware of how networking and collaboration activities, typically outside of day-to-day affairs, are becoming central to accomplishing the organization's mission. This awareness is also spilling over into policy advocacy (Bass et al., 2007). For example, a nonprofit organization providing family counselling reports how the agency evolved from being insulated and focused on very specific service therapies to engaged in new efforts to network with state advisory panels and connect with various mental health policy initiatives, and that such advocacy proved "essential to strengthening service delivery" (Bass et al., 2007, p. 39). For all of these reasons, nonprofits are likely better positioned for advocacy when they have capacity for, and experience with, external collaboration or networking.

The second way nonprofits acquire these skills is through reciprocal exchange of information between themselves and the enacting environment. Reciprocal exchange during policy formulation or change provides a change for organizations to shape their own policy environment and can serve to promote their interdependence with others. For example, Berry and Arons (2003) found the most important factor predicting nonprofits' propensity to lobby is the level of contact initiated with nonprofit managers by those who work in government agencies. These interactions present unique opportunities for nonprofits to establish their relevance to those in the enacting environment, as well as create demand for their expertise and services. Political advocacy requires many of these same competencies to be successful, which is why many nonprofits encourage and train clients for participation in advisory groups, where key policymaking officials are present, or for providing influential testimony at public meetings where policy actions are decided. Therefore, advocacy may benefit from an organization's experience with exerting influence, and exchanging information, in other arenas. To avoid conceptual overlap with collaborative networking, we focus on an exchange relation in the policymaking environment most salient to these agencies: the relation between nonprofits and those who fund their activities.

Taken together, these organizational learning processes produce two testable hypotheses:

> H1: *Organizations with experience in external collaboration are better positioned to engage in advocacy, which requires similar skills in coordination, interest linkages, and coalition formation; therefore, more collaborative experience is associated with more advocacy.*
>
> H2: *Organizations having more frequent transactions with their funding principals to exchange information about the policy environment will engage in more advocacy.*

Organizational Structure

Two aspects of organizational structure, professionalism and bureaucratization, may influence the extent to which nonprofits participate in advocacy activities. The degree of organizational professionalization may have two disparate effects on ability to advocate. Professionalized staff tend to formalize organizations strategically for protection against threats and challenges, which have the ability to destabilize the system of core production. They are also more likely to use institutional tactics and display ineptness for coalition-building (Baumgartner & Leech, 1998; Jenkins & Halcli, 1999). While the latter may be a favorable condition for advocacy, the others are problematic. Paid staff may displace organizational goals in deference to system maintenance and career advancement, which may harm attention spent on other activities, such as advocacy or other secondary goals. Deference may also create a myopic view of organizational functioning on core production and personal progress at the expense of advocacy and other important nonprofit goals.

Highly professionalized organizations may also be ill suited to represent an array of interests of those served, because professionals may grow out of touch with the true needs of clientele (Piven & Cloward, 1979). Similarly, Salamon (1995) suggested that when nonprofits depend more heavily on voluntary labor as opposed to professional staff, organizational leaders are perceived as more accessible to clientele, and this connection enables them to more accurately represent clientele interests in the political arena. Either way, the underlying incentive structures for voluntary and professional staff may shape advocacy practices in different ways. Therefore, we test the following hypothesis:

> H3: *As public charities grow more dependent on professionalized staff (as opposed to volunteers), their advocacy suffers.*

Organizational bureaucratization is another dimension of structure that may shape advocacy practices. Bureaucratization is the extent to which the organization is managed through hierarchical authority, systems of rules, procedures, and disciplined chains of command. As with professionalism, organizational bureaucratization can two ways. On one hand, bureaucratization may help incorporate the advocacy function more fully into core organizational routines. For instance, some nonprofits have written statement of purposes for policy participation or have established formal positions or departments expressly for the purpose of liaising with government and policymakers (Berry & Arons, 2003). On the other hand, Piven and Cloward's (1979) study of social movement organizations suggests that bureaucratization constrains the actions of marginalized groups. Organizational action that is tightly structured around organizational procedures may signal clientele to conform to conventional norms of interest participation, rather than encourage client activities associated with grassroots action.

These aspects of organizational structure suggest competing hypotheses about the propensity for nonprofits to advocate. And, although it is reasonable for a bureaucratic personality to emerge where more paid professionals are present, the theoretical rationale suggests they have independent effects as well; we test these competing arguments empirically using the following hypotheses:

> H4a: *Features of bureaucratic structure within the organization may prevent public charities from engaging in activities secondary to the core mission; therefore, bureaucratization may decrease advocacy.*
>
> H4b: *Bureaucratic structures may provide a vehicle for increased advocacy by incorporating related activities into organizational routines; therefore, highly bureaucratized organizations will engage in more advocacy.*

Management and Governance Capacities

In "speaking for" "acting for" and "looking after the interests of their respective groups" (Pitkin, 1972, p. 117), nonprofit leaders engage institutionalized systems of decision making, transacting with both elected and administrative public officials in a variety of contexts. These encounters may serve the purpose of providing technical or substantive information to policy makers about their clientele group, engaging with elected officials or their staff in the process of linking clients to political institutions and processes, or through direct attempts by organizational leaders to influence policy in ways that favor the organization's objectives. By engaging in advocacy, nonprofit leaders simultaneously represent the interests of their organization as well as the interests of clientele groups who depend on the organization. Because of this, we want to examine more closely how internal management contributes to nonprofit advocacy.

We suggest that three types of intermediary competencies would better position a nonprofit to engage in advocacy: managerial experience with (a) legislative and other political processes, (b) legal expertise, and (c) lobbying within institutionalized arenas of decision making.

The first competency is straightforward: managerial experience with when, where, and how to engage influential policy makers on issues relevant to the organization and its clients improves overall situational awareness in two primary ways. First, it reduces uncertainty about pitfalls in the political process, and, second, it provides a roadmap for where alliances may emerge. On the other hand, managerial experience with the political process can harm advocacy objectives if negative interactions accumulate or interpersonal conflicts arise.

The second managerial competency relates to legal expertise. There is substantial ambiguity in the tax code language that provides the regulatory framework for nonprofit advocacy.

These ambiguities create confusion on the part of nonprofit directors about the type and amount of advocacy activities that are permissible under federal law. Berry and Arons (2003) tested nonprofit administrators' knowledge about activities their organizations could and could not perform under federal advocacy regulations. They found that many nonprofit leaders misinterpret laws in ways that disadvantage the organization in the advocacy process. Organizations with an attorney on the board are likely to engage in advocacy more frequently because they are expected to be more knowledgeable about the legality of efforts to influence government, as well as have more confidence in the positive rights of advocacy granted through the law, rather than solely negative rights. Overall, nonprofits' interest in legal parameters is reflected in Bass et al. (2007), where 57.4 percent of nonprofit managers reported consulting an attorney before reaching out to influence government policymakers in 2006.

The final intermediary competency is representation of managerial skills relevant to lobbying. Lobbying is another avenue for organizations to increase awareness of public issues while also identifying sources of political and financial support crucial for continued operation. Federal IRS regulations governing public charities prohibit organizations from spending a "substantial" amount of their annual revenues on lobbying. However, with growing resource interdependence between government funders and others, nonprofits are looking for ways to produce efficiencies in their limited lobbying activities. Having lobbying expertise at the managerial level is one way of enhancing this effort.

Taken together, we expect the presence of these three management competencies to better position nonprofits for advocacy:

> H5: *Public charitable organizations with an elected official, attorney, and lobbyist serving on their board will engage in more advocacy, because of associated benefits brought by each to successfully manage advocacy efforts.*

Resource Dependence

Resource dependency theories suggest organizational leaders strategically attempt to exert control over the environment in which they are embedded (Pfeffer & Salancik, 1978). Nonprofit theories suggest two major forms of resource dependence may affect the propensity of these organizations to advocate: dependence on government contract and grant revenues, and dependence on private charitable contributions. There are two different rationales for how government resource dependence influences advocacy, and both logics predict a higher propensity to advocate when the organization relies on government funding.

The first logic projects a rational-choice view of nonprofit organizational leaders. According to this perspective, organizational leaders strategically align their actions with objectives of organizational utility-maximization and self-perservation. Critics have argued that nonprofit grantees use their government funding to lobby for more money.[2] There is evidence to suggest that nonprofits lobby government and mobilize clients to protect or expand their public funding base, or otherwise achieve outcomes in the organization's interest. For example, Pawlak and Flynn (1990) found a majority of executive directors cited positive consequences for their agency as a result of their advocacy activities. Outcomes included favorable funding decisions over time, the ability to defend against budget cuts, adoption of desired legislation or ordinances, and passage of favorable administrative rules that pertain to their agencies or client populations (Pawlak & Flynn, 1990).

A second logic, although quite different from rational choice, also suggests nonprofits advocate more frequently when they are recipients of government funding. Salamon's (1995) partnership theory of government–nonprofit relations suggests government funding embeds public service values and norms, such as democratic participation, by imposing rules, restrictions, and obligations on the part of nonprofits that accept government funding (see Freeman

[2003], for an application to contracting out). For example, nonprofits that receive government funding are more likely to educate their constituents about their rights, particularly if the organization administers services through a federal entitlement program. Both logics lead us to one testable hypothesis:

> H6: *As organizational reliance on government funding increases, nonprofits will engage in advocacy at higher levels.*

On the other hand, Salamon's (1995) philanthropic-paternalism argument suggests that when organizations rely to a greater extent on the traditional nonprofit budget base (i.e., private charitable contributions), they will be less likely to advocate the interests of their clientele in the political sphere. Salamon argued:

> So long as private charity is the only support for the voluntary sector, those in control of charitable resources can determine what the sector does and whom it serves. . . . Not only is this situation undemocratic, but it can create a self-defeating sense of dependency on the part of the poor since it gives them no say over the resources that are used on their behalf.
>
> (p. 47)

This provides information for another resource hypothesis on private funding:

> H7: *Organizations that are more heavily dependent on private sources of funding will engage in less advocacy.*

Resource Environment

The level of competition in the resource environment also has consequences for advocacy practices: managerial decisions about when to engage in advocacy are likely conditioned by patters of competition in the service market. Under normal circumstances, managers concentrate on improving performance on primary services, often at the expense of non-required advocacy practices. Within a competitive environment, however, this approach can reach a point of diminishing returns for performance, especially when the resource environment begins posing threats to organizational survival. In this case, nonprofit managers can use advocacy to protect their funding base, which ultimately enables core functions. By increasing their frequency of advocacy, nonprofit managers may hope to defend against environmental uncertainties. Nonprofit managers' decisions to engage in advocacy in the context of very competitive resource environments are viewed as strategic actions to manage external contingencies (Pfeffer & Salancik, 1978). This argument suggests hypotheses that capture nonlinear aspects of competition and advocacy:

> H8a: *As the resource environment becomes more competitive, organizations will turn their attention inward to concentrate on their core mission, and thus advocacy will decrease.*
>
> H8b: *When competition within the resource environment reaches very high levels, nonprofit advocacy will increase.*

Data and Methods

To test our hypotheses, we use survey data from a sample of 501(c)(3) nonprofit organizations in the state of Michigan. Surveys were administered by mail in three waves during the summer of 2004, according to the total design method (Dillman, 2000). A total response rate of 60.4 percent was achieved, yielding a final sample of 119 organizations. The organizations were randomly selected from the Michigan attorney general's database of licensed charities, which is free to the public and offers up-to-date mailing addresses and contact information. Surveys were addressed to executive directors

TABLE 13.1 Types of Nonprofit Organizations Represented in Sample

Primary mission	n	%
Social services	64	53.7
Arts and culture	18	15.1
Youth development	9	7.6
Education	5	4.2
Recreation, sports, leisure	5	4.2
Science and technology	5	4.2
Animal welfare	4	3.4
Spiritual development	4	3.4
Environmental	3	2.5
Unknown	2	1.7
Total	119	100.0

by name, so it is assumed these persons or a delegate in close proximity completed the questionnaire.

Organizations represented in the sample are distributed evenly throughout the state among urban, suburban, and rural communities of various sizes, and they perform a wide range of functions. Table 13.1 provides a frequency distribution describing the types of nonprofit organizations represented in the sample.

We use ordinary least squares (OLS) regression to estimate two models of political advocacy by nonprofits. These models are based on two dependent variables capturing distinct dimensions of advocacy. The first dependent variable is political representation, and the second is political mobilization. Previous studies have measured advocacy as total lobbying expenditures reported on Schedule C of the 990 form nonprofit organizations are required to file annually with the IRS. Yet, less than 2 percent of all public charities report lobbying expenditures (Boris & Krehely, 2002; Independent Sector, 2002). Because this measure fails to capture the vast majority of advocacy carried out by nonprofits, we use measures designed to account for a more complete scope of advocacy activities actually performed by nonprofits. These two measures are drawn from the advocacy and interest group literature (Andrews & Edwards, 2004) and are conceptualized as political representation (standing in decision making) and mobilization (grassroots advocacy). A detailed description of the measurement for these two dependent variables is found in Table 13.2.[3]

We posit that these two types of advocacy (representation and mobilization) are a function of organization-level learning processes, organizational structures, management and governance capacities, and factors in the resource environment. Eleven independent variables are used to measure these concepts: collaborative networking, reciprocal exchange, professionalization, bureaucratization, government resource dependence, dependence on private charitable contributions, having a lobbyist, elected official, and attorney on board of directors, competition in the resource environment, and competition squared. Finally, we include in the model a dummy variable to control for organizations that provide social services, because these organizations represent the largest single group in our sample. Table 13.2 provides a detailed description of the measurement for each independent variable used in our models. Descriptive statistics for each measure are also reported in the table, along with scale reliability statistics for multi-item measures.

Findings

How well does an organizational-level model explain nonprofits' propensity for advocacy? More specifically, to what extent do organizational factors account for the frequency of political representation and mobilization? Tables 13.3 and 13.4 display results from the empirical analysis.

Our first two hypotheses stated that two different mechanisms of organizational-level learning would have a positive effect on an organization's level of advocacy. Both hypotheses are confirmed by our findings, for both the representation and mobilization dimensions of advocacy. For each increment of change in the level of *exchange relations* that public charities have with the enacting environment, there is a positive and statistically significant increase of 0.339 in the 8-point representation scale ($p < 0.01$), and a 0.384 increase in the 12-point mobilization scale ($p < 0.01$). The second mechanism of organizational learning, *collaborative networking*, also produces a statistically significant increase in both forms of advocacy. For each additional unit of collaboration between nonprofit organizations and their counterparts in the community, the organization acquires greater experience with collaboration processes that help to promote advocacy, producing a 0.570 increase in activities related to political representation ($p < 0.01$), and increasing nonprofits' shared commitment to mobilizing clientele ($b = 0.603$, $p < 0.01$).

How well do aspects of organizational structure and professionalism affect nonprofit advocacy? Specifically, does greater reliance on professional staff versus volunteers promote advocacy? Does a rule-oriented, bureaucratic structure depress representation and mobilization activities, or does it encourage them? Contrary to our hypotheses, neither variable is statistically significant in the two models, suggesting that staffing capacity and management structure have little influence on nonprofits' advocacy practices.

What effects do managerial skill and governance capacities have on advocacy activities? Nonprofits may strategically position their organizations to engage institutionalized systems of policymaking if they possess intermediary managerial competencies necessary to do so.

TABLE 13.2 Descriptive Statistics and Variable Measures

Variable	Variable Measurement[a]	Mean	Std. Dev.	Min.[b]	Max.
Dependent variables					
Political representation	Index created from two survey items measuring how frequently the organization engages in the following activities: (a) giving testimony or speaking during public comment at public meetings and (b) advocating before government for the needs of clients/members. Each item scaled 0–4, with 0 = none, 4 = high. Scale reliability = 0.867.	2.85	2.05	0	8
Political mobilization	Index created from three survey items measuring how frequently the organization engages in the following activities: (a) linking clients/members to legislative offices or elected officials, (b) encouraging clients/members to attend public agencies or meetings, and (c) providing clients with assistance in writing, phoning, or e-mailing legislators. Each item scaled 0–4, with 0 = none, 4 = high. Scale reliability = 0.895.	3.14	3.28	0	12
Independent variables					
Collaborative networking	Additive measure of four types of collaboration respondents engage in with other nonprofits: (a) piloting new programs or services, (b) collaborating to reduce costs, (c) collaboration as a requirement of funding, and (d) other type of collaboration. Each item measured as a dichotomous variable, 1 = organization collaborates with another nonprofit for the activity, 0 = does not collaborate for the activity. The four binary measures were then summed.	1.88	1.32	0	4
Reciprocal exchange	Constructed from two survey items measuring how often funding entities consult with the organization for input when it becomes necessary to create new policies, rules, or requirements that will affect the work of the organization. Question asked for (a) foundations and (b) public organizations. Each item scaled 0–4, with 0 = never and 4 = frequently.	2.20	1.77	0	8
Professionalization	Proportion of the organization's total workforce comprised of paid staff, as opposed to volunteers.	56.64	30.38	0	100

Variable	Description				
Bureaucratic structure	Index created from four survey items measuring how important the following aspects of structure are for managing the work of the organization: (a) clear chain of command. (b) division of labor according to staff expertise, (c) standard operating procedures, and (d) agency rules, policies, or bylaws. Each item scaled 0–4, 0 = none, 4 = high. Scale reliability = 0.810.				
Lobbyist	Organization has a lobbyist serving on the Board of Directors. Measured 1 = organizations has a lobbyist on the board, 0 = organization does not.	0.11	0.31	0	1
Elected official	Organization has an elected official serving on the Board. Measured 1 = organization has an elected official on the board, 0 = organization does not.	0.24	0.42	0	1
Attorney	Organization has an attorney serving on the Board of Directors. Measured 1 = organization has a attorney on the board, 0 = organization does not.	0.50	0.49	0	0
Government dependence	Percentage of the organization's total budget that comes from government.	26.17	33.81	0	100
Private charity dependence	Percentage of the organization's total budget that comes from private charity.	26.49	30.07	0	100
Competition	Additive measure of how much competition the organization faces from (a) other nonprofits in the area, (b) for-profit organizations. Each item is scaled 0–4, with 0 = none, 4 = high.	2.88	2.05	0	8
Competition squared	Competition variable squared.	12.61	13.86	0	64

[a]For variable measurement, additive scaling is preferred to certain factor analytic approaches because of the binary data structure of some survey items, as well as the limited number of indicators available to test more complex latent constructs.

[b]The range of survey response categories is modeled after two validated surveys of nonprofit advocacy in the field. Berry and Arons (2003) and Bass et al. (2007).

TABLE 13.3 Influence of Organization-Level Factors on Political Representation (Ordinary Least Squares)

Independent variables	Dependent variable: Scale of political representation practices		
	b	se	t-score
Organizational learning mechanisms			
Collaborative networking	.570***	.165	3.45
Reciprocal exchange	.339***	.106	3.19
Organizational structure			
Professionalization	−.004	.063	−0.79
Bureaucratic structure	.028	.006	0.44
Management (representation of)			
Lobbyist	2.04***	.631	3.23
Elected official	−.318	.452	−0.70
Attorney	.454	.381	1.19
Resource dependence			
Government resource dependence	.011*	.006	1.70
Private source revenue dependence	−.003	.007	−0.43
Resource environment			
Competition	−.430	.275	−1.56
Competition squared	.077*	.040	1.90
Control			
Social service organization	−.452	.395	−1.14
Constant	.854	.989	0.86
R^2	0.408		
F	6.09		
N	119		

***$p < 0.01$. **$p < 0.05$. *$p < 0.10$.

Our hypotheses suggest public charities will advocate more often when they possess relevant expertise on their boards. These substantive areas of expertise include lobbying, elected office holding, and legal advising. We find mixed support for our hypotheses, and some unexpected effects. First, public charities with a registered lobbyist serving on their board have a statistically significant increase in frequency of both representing as well as mobilizing their clients. The magnitude of this increase is substantial, producing an increase of 2.04 on the representation index ($p < 0.01$) and 3.40 on the mobilization index ($p < 0.001$). However our hypothesis about the positive effect of legal representation on the board of directors is not supported; having legal expertise on the board in the form of an attorney has no effect statistically on either form of advocacy.

TABLE 13.4 Influence of Organization-Level Factors on Political Mobilization Activities (Ordinary Least Squares)

Independent variables	*b*	*Se*	*t-score*
	Dependent variable: Scale of political representation practies		
Organizational learning mechanisms			
Collaborative networking	.603***	.238	2.53
Reciprocal exchange	.384***	.153	2.51
Organizational structuwre			
Professionalization	.002	.009	0.22
Bureaucratic structure	.056	.091	0.62
Management (representation of)			
Lobbyist	3.40***	.910	3.73
Elected official	−1.24*	.651	−1.91
Attorney	−.037	.550	−0.07
Resource dependence			
Government resource dependence	0.23**	.010	2.38
Private source revenue dependence	.007	.010	0.72
Resource environment			
Competition	−.786**	.397	−1.98
Competition squared	.119**	.059	2.02
Control			
Social service organization	−.512	.569	−0.90
Constant	.485	1.426	0.34
R^2	0.349		
F	4.75		
N	119		

***$p < 0.01$. **$p < 0.05$. *$p < 0.10$.

Finally, we anticipated that organizations with an elected official serving on their board of directors would engage in advocacy more frequently, because these individuals bring critical information inside the organization about the workings of the local governing regime and about issues on the local decision-making agenda. Therefore, having an elected official serve on the board should position the organization favorably for advocacy. Yet, we find just the opposite; elected officials' serving on nonprofit boards has a statistically significant negative effect on public charities' mobilization activities ($b = -1.246$, $p < 0.10$), but no statistically relevant effect on these organizations' political representation roles.

One possibility for this unexpected finding is that nonprofit leaders feel politically constrained by the presence of an elected official, rather than politically empowered. Nonprofit leaders wary of attracting negative publicity and jeopardizing future fundraising opportunities for their organization may go out of their way to avoid mobilizing clients for political action, particularly in the local arena. Nonprofit managers and board members alike are reluctant to advocate when they believe such action will anger local elected officials and bring negative consequences to bear on organizational funding. Systematic evidence by Berry and Arons (2003) and qualitative evidence provided by Bass et al. (2007) confirms this point. Reporting on the concerns of nonprofit directors and board members with regard to advocacy, these authors noted:

> A board member in Texas told us that lobbying was not a good thing for his organization to do. He echoed what other board members told us that "board members have a fiduciary responsibility. We would be violating that responsibility by taking a position on a policy issue that might anger an elected official." His reasoning was the organization is heavily dependent on local financial support, and he does not want to upset the relationship with an elected leader, which in turn might influence decisions to continue funding the organization.
>
> (Bass et al., 2007, p. 26)

What role does resource dependence play in nonprofit advocacy? When public charities are more dependent on government financially, do they increase advocacy practices, as our hypothesis suggests? We find that government funding has a positive and statistically significant effect on the frequency of both forms of advocacy. For each additional percentage increase in the organization's budget that comes from government revenues, there is 0.011 increase in representational activities ($p < 0.05$) and a 0.023 increase in mobilization activities ($p < 0.05$). Although the magnitude of this change may not seem large initially, the size of the effect is masked by the unit of measurement for the

independent variable. A 1 percent increase in the total budget from government produces an increase in the organization's total budget from government results in an increase of 0.11 on the representation advocacy scale, and so on. Although we find support for our proposition that government resource dependence increases nonprofit advocacy, we do not find support for our hypothesis that dependence on private source revenues significantly decease either form of advocacy by public charities.

To what extent does the resource environment shape nonprofit managers' decisions to engage in advocacy? Does the level of competition in the resource environment have consequences for representation and mobilization practices? We find some support for a nonlinear relation between the level of competition in the resource environment and the frequency of organizational advocacy. As the resource environment becomes more competitive, nonprofits mobilize their clients less frequently, as evidenced by the statistically significant relationship ($b = -0.786$, $p < 0.05$). Strategically prioritizing organizational tasks, nonprofits reduce their advocacy activities in the face of increasing competition as they turn their attention inward to focus on the core mission. However, the relation between competition squared and mobilization activities is positive and statistically significant ($b = 0.119$, $p < 0.05$). This means that when levels of competition in the resource environment approach extremely high levels, nonprofits begin to mobilize their clients for political action, most likely in an effort to help protect the organization's funding base.

Support for this hypothesis also bears out partially when nonprofits' representation roles are the activity in question. Although the coefficient for the competition variable is in the predicted direction (–), it falls short of statistical significance. However, the competition-squared term is positive and statistically significant, suggesting that hypercompetition in the resource environment will prompt an organization to increase representational activities. Taken together, these findings uncover an interesting strategy-based difference about the effects of environmental competition: nonprofit managers may delay representation and mobilization tactics until competition is high enough to justify costs, political or otherwise, of their use. This may explain why nonprofit managers are compelled to advocate only when the level of pressure in the resource environment begins to pose a threat to organizational survival. In this context, leaders may be engaging in advocacy in reaction to government funding cuts, which increases the level of competition in the resource environment. What is most interesting, and perhaps ironic, is that an extremely competitive resource environment engenders cooperation on the part of public charities: the persistent positive effects of the collaborative networking variable on advocacy suggests that public charities make individual choices to shore up their core mission in the face of increasing competition, but when the resource environment challenges organizational sustainability, nonprofits join forces to represent their shared interests before government.

How well does this constellation of organizational-learning mechanisms, structures, managerial competencies, resource dependencies, and the resource environment explain political representation and mobilization by public charities? In other words, how well does our organizational-level model of advocacy fit? We are able to explain approximately 40.8 percent of the variance in public charities' political representation activities through our model, and approximately 34.9 percent of the variance in nonprofits' mobilization rates using the same explanatory factors. The robust relations demonstrated by approximately half the variables in our models provide clear evidence that organizational factors play a critical role in shaping nonprofit advocacy practices.

These findings provide support for an organizational-level of advocacy, and should prompt scholars to take a closer look at organization-level determinants when studying public charities' participation in the policy process.

Conclusions

Our findings have important implications for nonprofit practitioners. Organizational leaders interested in increasing their advocacy activities, but wary of doing so because of perceived funding consequences, might consider seeking out individuals to serve on their board who can bring relevant expertise. Nonprofit leaders might especially find it useful to bring someone on the board who has experience with lobbying. Our study also suggests that nonprofits' advocacy agendas will benefit from joining forces and forming coalitions with other nonprofits in their area. Nonprofits can organize themselves for political action formally by joining a state or local nonprofit association, if one exists in their area, or informally by partnering to share the costs of a lobbyist, drafting joint letters to elected officials, adopting unified stances on administrative rules, and organizing joint mobilization campaigns. By spreading the perception of political risk among several organizations, nonprofits may be able to allay some of their fears about participating in the political process.

Notes

1. The federal IRS regulations governing 501(c)(3) organizations (those analyzed in this study) limit the amount of money that can be spent on activities designed to influence public policy. Under these regulations, 501(c)(3)s are restricted from spending more than 20 percent of their total annual budget on lobbying-related activities, up to a limit of $1 million for organizations with total revenues in excess of $17 million.

2. Beginning in 1994, a congressional coalition let by Ernest Istook (R-OK) organized an attempt to pass a bill that would prevent lobbying by nonprofits that receive government funding. Istook and his allies

argued that nonprofits grantees used their funding to lobby for more money at the expense of taxpayers. Although the bill was shelved, Istook was successful in generating support for this position, particularly among conservatives.

3. OLS estimates are also compared with ordered estimates due to the range of each dependent variable (e.g., 0–8 for representation. 0–12 for mobilization). Results are nearly identical, with explanatory variables showing significant relations. OLS results are presented for ease for substantive interpretation.

References

Agranoff, R. (2003). *Leveraging networks: A guide for public managers working across organizations.* Arlington, VA: IBM Endowment for the Business of Government.

Andrews, K.T., & Edwards, B. (2004). Advocacy organizations in the U.S. political process. *Annual Review of Sociology, 30,* 479–506.

Atlantic Philanthropies. (2008). *Investing in change: Why supporting advocacy makes sense for foundations.* http://atlantiephilanthropies.org/news/atlantic_reports, accessed March 12, 2009.

Bass, G.D., Arons, D.F., Guinane, K., & Carter, M.F. (2007). *Seen but not heard: Strengthening nonprofit advocacy.* Washington, DC: Aspen Institute.

Baumgartner, F.R., & Leech, B. (1998). *Basic interests: The importance of groups in politics and in political science.* Princeton, NJ: Princeton University Press.

Berry, J.M., & Arons, D.F. (2003). *A voice for nonprofits.* Washington, DC: Brookings Institution Press.

Bingham, L.B., & O'Leary, R. (2007). *A manager's guide to resolving conflicts in collaborative networks.* Washington, DC: IBM Center for the Business of Government.

Boris, E., & Krehely, J. (2002). Civic participation and advocacy. In L. M. Salamon (Ed.). *The state of nonprofit America* (pp. 299–330). Washington, DC: Brookings Institution Press.

Dillman, D. (2000). *Mail and electronic surveys: The tailored design method.* New York: Wiley.

Freeman, J. (2003). Extending public law norms through privatization. *Harvard Law Review, 116*(5), 1285–1352.

Goldstein, K.M. (1999). *Interest groups, lobbying and participation in America.* New York: Cambridge University Press.

Guo, C., & Musso, J.A. (2007). Representation in nonprofit and voluntary organizations: A conceptual framework. *Nonprofit and Voluntary Sector Quarterly, 36*(2), 308–326.

Heimovics, R.D., Herman, R., & Jurkewicz-Coughlin, C. (1993). Executive leadership and resource dependence in nonprofit organizations: A frame analysis. *Public Administration Review, 53*(5), 419–427.

Independent Sector. (2002). *The new nonprofit almanac and desk reference: The essential facts and figures for managers, researchers, and volunteers.* New York: Wiley.

Jenkins, J.C., & Halcli, A. (1999). Grassrooting the system? The development and impact of social movement philanthropy, 1953–1990. In E.C. Lagemann (Ed.). *Philanthropic foundations* (pp. 229–256). Bloomington: Indiana University Press.

Knoke, D. (1986). Associations and interest groups. *Annual Review of Sociology, 12,* 1–21.

Knoke, D. (1990). *Organizing for collective action.* New York: Aldine de Gruyter.

Kollman, K. (1989). *Outside lobbying.* Princeton, NJ: Princeton University Press.

Laumann, E.O., & Knoke, D. (1987). *The organizational state: Social choice in national policy domains.* Madison: University of Wisconsin Press.

Pawlak, E., & Flynn, J. (1990). Executive directors' political activities. *Social Work, 33*(4), 307–312.

Pfeffer, J., & Salancik, G. (1978). *The external control of organizations: A resource dependence perspective.* New York: Harper and Row.

Pitkin, H.F. (1972). *The concept of representation.* Berkeley: University of California Press.

Piven, F. & Cloward, R. (1979). *Poor people's movements: Why they succeed, how they fail.* New York: Vintage Books.

Putnam, R.D. (2000). *Bowling alone: The collapse and revival of community in America.* New York: Simon and Schuster.

Reid, E. (2004). Nonprofit advocacy and political participation. In E.T. Boris & C.E. Steuerle (Eds.), *Nonprofits and government, Collaboration and conflict* (2d ed., pp. 291–325). Washington, DC: Urban Institute Press.

Sabatier, P.A. (1991) Political science and public policy. *PS: Political Science & Politics, 24*(2), 144–173.

Saidel, J.R. (1991). Resource interdependence: The relationship between state agencies and nonprofit organizations. *Public Administration Review, 51*(6), 543–553.

Salamon, L.M. (1995). *Partners in public service. Government-nonprofit relations in the modern welfare state.* Baltimore: Johns Hopkins University Press.

Salamon, L.M. (2002). *The state of nonprofit America.* Washington, DC: Brookings Institution Press.

Salamon, L.M., & Lessans-Geller, S. (2008). *Nonprofit America: A force for democracy?* Communique no. 9. New York: Johns Hopkins University Center for Civil Society Studies.

Skocpol, T. (2003) *Diminished democracy: From membership to management in American civic life.* Norman: University of Oklahoma Press.

Weisbrod, B. (1977). *The voluntary nonprofit sector: An economic analysis.* Lexington, MA: D.C. Heath.

Author Biographies

Kelly LeRoux is an assistant professor in the Department of Public Administration at the University of Kansas. Her research interests include government-nonprofit relations, service contracting, and the role of nonprofits in elections and poleicymaking. She is the author of Service Contracting: *A Local Government Guide* (2007, ICMA Press).

Holly T. Goerdel is assistant professor of public administration, University of Kansas. In her research, she has examined contributions of strategic management to performance in the public sector, as well as in select nonprofit arenas. She also explores the need for restoring balance between neoclassical economic values and democratic values in providing effective public services. She is currently directing an expansive research program on domestic security and intelligence management across U.S. states.

Southwest County Foodbank
Nonprofit Board Advocacy

JULIE ANN O'CONNELL, BENJAMIN S. BINGLE AND
C. KENNETH MEYER

The Southwest County Foodbank was on a mission to make hunger obsolete; yet, the Foodbank was facing an uphill battle in convincing local authorities to amend policy to allow for food pickup and redistribution from local restaurants. After staff worked with local officials for nearly a year to no avail, the Foodbank's Executive Director decided it was time the Board of Directors got involved with the fight.

Board members were invited to attend local city and county meetings to listen to discussion and offer input, and they were eager to be involved and use their influence. After the first few months of board involvement, one thing became very clear: while the board members had a passion for eliminating hunger in the Southwest County's footprint, they did not have the skills or knowledge to match their enthusiasm when it came time for advocacy. Board members felt unprepared to speak at local meetings, and did not have a grasp of even the most basic local, regional, and national hunger statistics to help make their case.

The Executive Director strongly believed it was a core responsibility of the board to help the organization advocate for its mission, and the Directors themselves were eager to take on this role. Acknowledging that strong understanding of what board advocacy even means was the first step, the ED and the Board President took on the challenge of developing an action plan to help board members learn how to be good advocates for the Southwest County Foodbank.

The Executive Director decided there was no time to reinvent the wheel, and reached out to the local community foundation to see if training was available for board members. The foundation had a robust board training series, and so the first step of the action plan was to make the training session calendar available to board members, with strong encouragement for the board to attend an upcoming Essentials of Board Leadership training session. At the training, the board members who were able to attend learned that nationally, over 42% of Executive Directors involved in a national study name advocacy and outreach as one of three areas most in need of board improvement. (BoardSource/Stand for Your Mission)

The next step was to identify board members who were interested in being trained in the following areas:

- Hunger issues locally, regionally, and nationally. The board training program suggested that advocacy often was most effective when hard data was married to personal stories, so the ED worked with the Development Director to come up with important core statistics combined with stories of actual clients of the foodbank.

DOI: 10.4324/9781003387800-30

- Public policy related to hunger in general, and to policies specifically involved with the ability to rescue and redistribute food from local restaurants in particular.
- Public speaking and relationship building tactics.

Several board members threw themselves in to the advocacy project, and when the issue of food rescue/redistribution came up at the next quarterly county board meeting the Southwest County Foodbank board members were prepared, passionate, and articulate in explaining why amending public policy to allow for such rescue/redistribution was a worthwhile endeavor. By the end of the meeting, the county board members expressed positive interest in the issue and asked the Foodbank board members to come up with a proposal.

Ultimately, the rescue/redistribution food proposal was passed by the county board and became public policy. Foodbank board members were ecstatic that they played a hand in educating a local governing body about food and hunger issues, and the Executive Director was grateful for the new sense of engagement by the board. The Board President and Executive Director met to discuss next steps and to brainstorm in what other areas the board could be more involved.

Discussion Questions

1. Define and discuss advocacy. What are the opportunities and limitations for nonprofit organizations with regard to advocacy and lobbying?
2. Develop and discuss a basic action plan for the Southwest County Board of Directors Advocacy Project. In which areas could board members be involved, and what would need to happen for those members to be effective?
3. How might the Foodbank's board members work with staff to develop the proposal for the county board meeting? Putting yourself in the role of Executive Director, what tasks would you delegate to staff and what tasks would you request from the board?
4. Now that board members are energized and educated around the mission of the organization, how else might they be involved in the Foodbank?

Reference

BoardSource. (2017). *Stand for your mission.* www. boardsource.org

Volunteer and Donor Recruitment on Social Media

Julie Ann O'Connell, Benjamin S. Bingle and C. Kenneth Meyer

Sometimes things just do not end up as planned. This lesson was learned the hard way by Hope Center after it implemented a volunteer and donor recruitment campaign on social media.

As a relatively new nonprofit organization, Hope Center was fortunate to have wide-ranging support from a dedicated group of volunteers. Its small yet efficient staff—whose ages spanned from a new college graduate to a recently retired CEO—were well respected for their ability to maximize every single dollar received through donations.

Hope Center was interested in increasing its name recognition, not only in the city in which it was headquartered, but also throughout the broader region. Outreach in the form of volunteer drives, guest speaking engagements, and more had taken place at the local high schools, community colleges, and churches and the area chambers of commerce. The organization had staffed so many booths at festivals, at fairs, and in front of various retail establishments that it was unusual to *not* see the Hope Center logo around town. Unfortunately, all the exposure and dedicated outreach had not resulted in significantly more volunteers or donations. The organization needed a new way to connect with the community and the region.

Observations

As fate would have it, Bill Perkins, the oldest member of the staff, spent a long weekend with his young-adult grandchildren at a family wedding. The former CEO was floored by how much time his grandchildren devoted to mobile devices. At any given time over the weekend, all five grand-children could be found on smartphones, tablets, or laptops. As he watched how this generation of young adults interacted with each other and with their devices, he mused that, as connected as he had been to his computer and phone while in charge of his business, it was nothing compared to these "youngsters."

When Bill headed into Hope Center headquarters on Monday morning, he grabbed a cup of coffee and sat down at the desk of Ashley Simmons, the newly graduated college student, to talk about his observations. Ashley confirmed that his grandchildren's behavior was normal, and that her generation did tend to be quite attached to their electronic devices. The coworkers discussed the current trifecta of social media—Facebook, Instagram, and Twitter—and the constant competition inflamed by popular media outlets. As Ashley showed Bill various Facebook postings, Instagram pictures,

DOI: 10.4324/9781003387800-31

and tweets posted by her friends, Bill wondered aloud if perhaps Hope Center could capitalize on this by sponsoring a social media contest.

A Social Media Contest

On the spot, Bill and Ashley created a rough outline of the competition. It would be a two-month online contest where volunteers and friends would be rewarded for their social media posts and their volunteering and donating habits, earning points toward a large prize. A small prize would be awarded for each week's competition, and points would be accumulated for the grand prize. Both Bill and Ashley thought that if they could capture the natural competitiveness of human beings and throw in a great prize at the end, they might be able to garner new friends for the organization while strengthening name recognition in the social media community.

The executive director of Hope Center was impressed with the proposed online competition and was able to secure a promise from a valued donor to purchase a highly anticipated new tablet device as the grand prize for the competition. Local dining establishments donated $10 gift certificates for the weekly prizes. Staff knew that the rules for the competition needed to be short and uncomplicated, and that the competition itself needed to be fun and quirky enough to gain online interest.

The "design" of the competition was set—at different points during each week of the competition, Hope Center would post activities for competitors to complete and then display on social media. This would encourage engagement not only in the physical world but also in the virtual world. It was sure to enliven Hope Center's social media pages.

Up and Running

It was agreed that the competition would kick off just before registration opened for Hope Center's annual 5-K run. There were a variety of ways to earn points, such as being among the first ten people to register for the run, registering multiple people (bring a friend!), or submitting the funniest photo. Participants were encouraged to take "selfies" at events and post them to Facebook. Hope Center also took photos and posted them on social media so that participants could tag themselves in them. Of course, tagging a photo would earn points for that individual. The posts of the race attendees spiked an increase in new Facebook and Instagram connections. Hope Center staff were thrilled and excited about the possible ways to weave the contest into upcoming programs and events.

The staff was kept busy thinking up these weekly competitions, and Ashley was in charge of posting to social media outlets, tracking point winners, and monitoring content. Sometimes the contest would revolve around responding to a tweet or quiz question on Facebook. Other times it might be more challenging, requiring participants to attend an event and upload photos in order to get points. Each Friday morning the organization posted on all three media sites the name of the person who had won the most points that week, and the winner received one of the donated $10 restaurant certificates. Staff thought the weekly mini-prizes would keep interest in the competition high.

Flash, but Few Results

The campaign was fun and created a splash among those who participated. Unfortunately, most participants had already been engaged with Hope Center in some way before the contest; very few new people were drawn in. Additionally, tracking point winners each week became quite time-consuming for staff members, and there were instances of inappropriate photos being uploaded to Hope Center social media sites. Finally, most of the newly engaged people were quite young. They might be able to volunteer, but they hardly had the disposable income to be regular Hope Center donors.

At the end of the two-month competition, the number of Hope Center's Facebook "friends" had reached an all-time high, but staff had not noticed an increase in either new volunteers or new donations. As they met to analyze the campaign, they discussed whether the social media competition had been an effective volunteer and donation recruitment tool.

Was it a worthwhile project and a wise use of staff time? Would any of the new "friends" the organization had made on social media remain loyal and active now that the prizes were gone? These questions lingered as the Hope Center staff tried to determine their next move to engage volunteers and donors.

Questions and Instructions

1. Please discuss some of the positive aspects of Hope Center's social media campaign.
2. Discuss some of the drawbacks and limitations of the campaign.
3. Given what you know about philanthropy, was Hope Center realistic in expecting to see an immediate increase in volunteerism or monetary donations from this contest? Why or why not?
4. How might a social media campaign strengthen a connection to an organization's mission? Identify a nonprofit or public service organization that effectively uses social media to connect their users with their mission. Discuss how they do this and why you consider the selected organization to be effective in this area.
5. Put yourself in the role of a Hope Center staff member. The case ends with a staff meeting where some pressing questions are being discussed. You have been tasked with ensuring that the new "friends" attracted to Hope Center by the contest remain engaged with the organization. Please discuss your plan for cultivating these individuals as long-term volunteers and donors.

PART VII

BUDGETS, FINANCIAL REPORTS, AND MANAGEMENT CONTROL

Budgeting, accounting, financial reporting, and management control are the most essential tools for responsible governance, accountability, planning, and management in nonprofit organizations. The budget document is "foremost a tool for maintaining financial accountability . . . a forum for establishing strategic goals and performance expectations . . . [and] a tool for holding administrators accountable for performance expectations."[1]

> Budgeting is a process which matches resources and needs in an organized and repetitive way so those collective choices about what an entity needs to do are properly resourced. Most definitions also emphasize that a budget is an itemized estimate of expected income and operating expenses . . . over a set time period. Budgeting is the process of arriving at such a plan.[2]

A budget is a plan, and the budget process is a planning process about what should happen in the future. The process of preparing budgets has evolved into a forum for establishing strategic goals and performance expectations for an organization. Budgets often represent the most important and consequential policy statements that governments or nonprofit organizations make. Not all strategies and plans have budgetary significance, but enough of them do, and public and nonprofit leaders and managers should consider involving themselves deeply in the process of budget making.[3] Thus, "budgets serve as the public record of a community dialogue for improving organizational performance and management oversight. The budget is a tool for holding administrators accountable for performance expectations."[4]

Budgeting matches resources and needs in an organized and repetitive way so that collective choices about what an entity needs to do are properly resourced. "A budget is an itemized estimate of expected income and operating expenses . . . over a set period of time."[5] "In its most complete form, a budget is a compilation of the plans and objectives of management that covers all phases of operations for a specific period of time."[6] Budgets breathe life into mission statements and goals. Mission statements may speak about a wide variety of problems and opportunities that are of concern to the organization, but a budget divides an organization's finite resources among its competing needs and wants—its priorities. Budgets, therefore, transform an array of noble intentions and

DOI: 10.4324/9781003387800-32

high ideals into the ability to act on a select set of problems or opportunities. In this sense, budgeting is an energizing function as well as a definitive governance activity.[7]

Budgeting is the "instrument" that boards use to manage the numerous competing visions, requests, and often demands of client groups, patrons, donors, staff, trustees, government agencies, and community groups. Executives and boards give energy to their preferred policies and programs by allocating funds to them. Programs or initiatives may be the beneficiaries of increased funding, or they may have their funds reduced or eliminated.

A budget is also an organization's short-term financial road map, which identifies planned expenditures and expected revenues. It requires decisions such as whether the organization should borrow or draw down savings to finance a program expansion or whether it should eliminate a program that is proving less effective than hoped. In a balanced budget, revenues and expenditures are equal. A budget deficit identifies the need to borrow, draw down funds from savings, or increase fundraising. A budget surplus allows funds to be budgeted for new activities, to be set aside for future uses, or to be used to reduce a former year's deficit.

Budgets as Financial Operating Reports and Management Control

After a budget has been adopted by the board of trustees, it continues to serve two other vitally important purposes: (1) as a governance and accountability tool for the board and the executive director and (2) as a management tool that provides an executive director and the management staff with discretion—the freedom to run the organization with some flexibility, within the limits established in the budget.

Budgets as a Governance and Accountability Tool

Budgets are the basis for an organization's financial operating reports, which almost always contain at least two columns of numbers: budgeted income and expenditures and actual income and expenditures. When an executive director and the trustees know the shortages and surpluses (the over and under gaps) between budgeted and actual income and expenditures, they can exert management control over operations.

Most boards of trustees spend considerable time reviewing and stewing over financial operating reports because financial accountability is a fundamental governance function. All too often, however, trustees spend too much time on the details rather than on the organization's overall financial status and financial trends and warning signals.

Budgets as a Source of Management Flexibility

Budgets provide management with the ability to make many expenditure decisions without needing approval in advance. The board should leave "space" for the executive director and staff to make day-to-day management decisions without trustees second-guessing every move.[8] Micromanaging is inefficient, communicates distrust, creates an undesirable working environment for staff, and wastes time. Budgets and financial operating reports give managers the freedom they need to act responsibly within parameters set at the start of the year and accounted for as the year progresses. They establish the limits of a manager's discretion to spend certain amounts of money for different categories of expenditures without prior approval.

Accounting, Financial Reports, Management Control, and Accountability

The primary sources of revenue for nonprofit agencies are (1) private contributions in the form of individual donations, corporate gifts, and foundation grants; (2) public support (government grants); (3) membership fees; and (4) payments for services (commercial activity) in the form of user fees, government contracts, and the sale of products and services.[9] Each revenue source offers a different set of advantages and disadvantages.[10] Each also requires a nonprofit to be able to manage and account for the funds both legally and ethically.

Accounting is the process of recording the financial information that is in financial reports.

> Because nonprofit organizations enjoy numerous financially lucrative privileges and benefits . . . they must be able to demonstrate that their fiscal houses are in order. Board members are ultimately responsible for these organizations and must be able to read financial statements and be aware of reporting requirements and fiscal systems.[11]

In order to implement an effective budgeting program, an organization must have an efficient financial system in place. This includes accurate financial data, timely and understandable financial statements that meet the organization's needs for information, actual versus budget figures for the period, and an annual audit by an independent certified public accountant (CPA) firm.[12] Murray Dropkin and Allyson Hayden's "Types of Nonprofit Income: Financial and Cash Management Considerations" is reprinted in this part as Chapter 14 to help nonprofit officers become fiscally responsible stewards.

Financial reports also inform management and the board about the organization's financial status and the need for corrective actions. Without these, trustees and management cannot effectively govern. A single system that includes budgets, management decision making, accounting, and evaluation is essential for the health of a nonprofit organization. Despite the importance of such a system, however, "financial analysis and managerial control remain among the most difficult areas for managers and directors [trustees] of nonprofit organizations to conquer."[13] The plethora of new integrated financial systems offered by software firms helps, but they can "only lead a horse to the water."

Not many individuals are recruited to serve on boards because of their skills or experience with finances. Particularly in smaller nonprofits, few trustees are educated or experienced in financial analysis or management controls, and financially savvy executive directors are the exceptions. Individuals with this type of education and experience are often recruited onto boards and to CEO positions in hopes that they will take responsibility for financial information and decisions. If the recruitment is successful, the other trustees are too often inclined to leave all responsibility for budgets and finances to them, preferring to devote their time and energy instead to the organization's programs, clients, fundraising, or public relations. Yet this represents a violation of a fundamental board member responsibility. "Attaining a balance between sober financial management and the creation of enlightening services is far from easy."[14]

As we emphasized in Parts I and II, trustees are legally and ethically obliged to account for an organization's actions and assets. They cannot avoid these responsibilities without risking individual and collective liability. Thus, they do not have a choice. Trustees must have at least a rudimentary understanding of nonprofit financial management. Understanding the basics of accounting, budgeting, financial reporting, and management control procedures and systems is a primary and fundamental responsibility of governance and accountability.

Readings Reprinted in Part VII

In the first reading, Murray Dropkin and Allyson Hayden's "Types of Nonprofit Income: Financial and Cash Management Considerations" presents a basic but thorough discussion of the resource considerations that affect nonprofits and their cash flows. Although the academic and practitioner literature about grants, contracts, business ventures, and the like is plentiful, fiscal management issues are usually only touched upon, if they are mentioned at all. Yet contemporary nonprofit executives are expected to be accountable for the proper use of resources and for the results they achieve while using them. This is not possible without sufficient awareness of the many considerations that accompany various streams of funding. In addition, financial pressures create conditions that require nonprofits to become much more creative in their ability to expand their revenue portfolios and, in turn, much savvier in accounting for new revenue streams.

Dropkin and Hayden untangle the confusing array of income flows that may be received or earned by a nonprofit and discuss the impacts of each on budgeting and reporting obligations. Nonprofit executives must be able to recognize the implications of these impacts when pursuing various sources of income and consider how information will be documented in the organization's financial reports. The authors classify three types of income identified by the Financial Accounting Standards Board (FASB), the body responsible for issuing accounting standings in the United States for nongovernmental entities: unrestricted net assets, temporarily restricted net assets, and permanently restricted net assets. They then systematically consider the implications of the most common donated income and resources received by nonprofits, including grants, donations, gifts and contributions, membership dues, and special fundraising income.

For example, grant income may require matching funds, whether a cash match, an in-kind match, or a combined match. "To avoid violating the grant agreement, organizations must comply with all matching requirements."[15] "In addition, a nonprofit's agreement to provide a program matching share usually becomes an auditable compliance requirement."[16] The authors show that financial planning for grant funding and compliance requires forethought and should not be entered into without consideration of the sources from which matching funds will be obtained.

The authors also provide information about managing earned income, including trade or business activities, sales of assets, program service fees, income from fees paid by government agencies, and asset-generated income.

The second reading in Part VII is "Resiliency Tactics During Financial Crisis: The Nonprofit Resiliency Framework" by Elizabeth A. M. Searing, Kimberly K. Wiley, and Sarah L. Young. As we noted earlier, it would be folly to assume that everyone close to a nonprofit has a full understanding of budgets and finances or cash flow dynamics. Nonprofit managers must understand the risks of financial dependency, however, that arise from heavy reliance on a single source of revenue, especially, as is noted in the reading, when the nonprofit's primary source of revenue for service delivery is from government. When government cash flow is stopped, managers must not only find ways to survive but also demonstrate resiliency. Searing et al.'s study discusses the resiliency tactics of 31 nonprofit organizations that found themselves with significant financial problems when three years of Illinois government budget impasses led to halted cash flows to these nonprofit agencies. Yet, "the nonprofit organizations were contractually obligated to maintain services despite the lack of funding."[17] The authors' research explains how the 2015–2017 Illinois state government's budget impasses created conditions for nonprofits to have to pivot to "Plan B" resiliency measures. Students of nonprofit fundraising, budgeting, and financial planning for service delivery are well advised to brush up on a variety of fiscal-related tools, including budgets, budget terminology, financial cash flow processes, and a variety of budgetary formats to help get them up to speed on the revenue-related and budgetary concerns that face all nonprofits. Experienced nonprofit executive directors and other nonprofit professionals know that budgets are often at the heart of the matter when planning and executing programs. Thus, a solid understanding of budgets and finance and the impacts of cash flow stoppages when political, economic, and other factors affect government funding serves as a cautionary tale for students of nonprofit management. In essence, budgets are at the heart of management today, whether preparing or explaining them. Solid financial information is needed by decision makers and other stakeholders to effectively plan, carry out, and evaluate mission-related activities or services.

Case Studies in Part VII

In "Throwing the First E-Stone," a financial officer is embarrassed to find that his practice of "surfing the web" at the office has come to the attention of the board of directors. Is this retaliation for an across-the-board budget cut? The reader is asked to analyze the situation and offer suggestions for dealing with workplace activities that may be viewed as wasteful and inefficient.

In the second case, "When the Funding Stops," the reader is asked to consider a variety of options when confronted with an experience that many nonprofit managers will face—trying to manage an organization and "make payroll" when revenue streams do not flow according to plan. For many nonprofit organizations, the scenario presented in the case presents an all-too-familiar and frustrating set of budgetary circumstances.

Notes

1. Robert L. Bland and Michael Overton, *A Budgeting Guide for Local Government,* 4th ed., (Washington, DC: International City/County Management Association Press, 2019), 2.

2. Jerry L. McCaffery, "Budgeting," in *The International Encyclopedia of Public Policy and Administration,* edited by Jay M. Shafritz (Boulder, CO: Westview Press, 1998), 294.

3. *John M. Byson, Strategic Planning for Public and Nonprofit Organizations: A Guide to Strengthening and Sustaining Organizational Achievement,* 5th ed. (San Francisco: Jossey-Bass, 2018).

4. Bland, *A Budgeting Guide for Local Government,* 2.

5. McCaffery, "Budgeting," 294.

6. Blackbaud, "Financial Management of Not-for-Profit Organizations," *Financial Management White Papers* (Charleston, SC: Blackbaud, October 2011), 2.

7. See Part I, "Governance of Nonprofit Organizations."

8. Robert N. Anthony and David W. Young, "The Management Control Function," in *Management Control in Nonprofit Organizations,* 7th ed. (New York: McGraw-Hill/Irwin, 2002).

9. Matthew M. Hodge and Ronald F. Piccolo, "Funding Source, Board Involvement Techniques, and Financial Vulnerability in Nonprofit Organizations," *Nonprofit Management and Leadership,* 16 no. 2 (Winter 2005): 171–190.

10. A. C. Brooks, "Public Subsidies and Charitable Giving: Crowding Out, Crowding In, or Both?" *Journal of Policy Analysis and Management,* 19 no. 3 (2000): 451–464.

11. Thomas Wolf, "Financial Statements and Fiscal Procedures," in Thomas Wolf, *Managing a Nonprofit Organization,* updated 21st-century ed. (New York: Free Press, 2013), 207–233.

12. Edward J. McMillan, *Not-For-Profit Budgeting and Financial Management,* 4th ed. (Hoboken, NJ: Wiley, 2010), 1.

13. Regina E. Herzlinger and Denise Nitterhouse, "A View from the Top," in *Financial Accounting and Managerial Control for Nonprofit Organizations,* edited by Regina E. Herzlinger and Denise Nitterhouse (Cincinnati: South-Western, 1994), 8.

14. Ibid., 2.

15. Murray Dropkin and Allyson Hayden, "Types of Nonprofit Income: Financial and Cash Flow Management Considerations," in Murray Dropkin and Allyson Hayden, *The Cash Flow Management Book for Nonprofits* (San Francisco: Jossey-Bass, 2001), 7–20.

16. Ibid., 11.

17. Elizabeth A.M. Searing, Kimberly K. Wiley, and Sarah L. Young, "Resiliency Tactics During Financial Crisis: The Nonprofit Resiliency Framework, *Nonprofit Management and Leadership* 32 (2021), 179–196.

CHAPTER 14

Types of Nonprofit Income
Financial and Cash Management Considerations

MURRAY DROPKIN AND ALLYSON HAYDEN

The nature of a nonprofit's income is the single most important factor in determining its overall financial management. All organizations, for-profit and nonprofit alike, need cash to operate. The manner in which organizations obtain cash and the form in which cash is received determine how cash flow is managed. In this chapter we provide brief discussions of the different types of income that can be a part of cash flow in nonprofit organizations. It would be highly unusual for your nonprofit to have every type of income we have identified. Most often organizations count on income from one or several sources to support their operations.

Generally, nonprofits either earn income through charging for goods and services or receiving resources (cash and noncash) from government agencies, foundations, businesses, other nonprofits, and private individuals.

In this chapter we identify and discuss the following major topics related to income classification and cash flow:

- Classifying income
- Managing donated income and resources
- Managing earned income
- Managing asset-generated income

Classifying Income

The types of income received by organizations will determine the approaches that should be used in managing cash flow. The Financial Accounting Standards Board (FASB), which is responsible for issuing accounting standards in the United States for nongovernmental entities, has created three classifications for net assets applicable to nonprofit organizations:

- *Unrestricted Net Assets*. These are defined in FASB Statement of Financial Standards No. 116 as "neither permanently restricted nor temporarily restricted by donor-imposed stipulations."
- *Temporarily Restricted Net Assets*. These are assets for which use is limited to specific purposes or time periods, as specified in contracts, grant agreements, or other written or oral statements.

    DOI: 10.4324/9781003387800-33

- *Permanently Restricted Net Assets.* These are assets held in perpetuity for a specific purpose (for example, endowments[1]), although the nonprofit can classify income generated from the principal amount as temporarily restricted or unrestricted, depending on donor stipulations. Restrictions on the use of net assets may be conveyed either orally or in writing and may be made:

1. By the individual or organization providing the resources at the time they are given (known as *donor restrictions*)
2. As a result of specific statements or commitments made when the organization originally solicited the contribution

Donor restrictions can only be changed by the organization or individual that made the contribution. Similarly, restrictions placed on contributions by the organization at the time of solicitation may only be changed with the consent of the donor(s). In addition, a nonprofit's board can decide that unrestricted funds may be designated for specific purposes. However, restrictions placed by a board of directors do not change the FASB classification of these funds (termed *board-designated funds*) as unrestricted net assets because the board is free to remove the restrictions at its own discretion.

Contributions that are not specifically designated as temporarily or permanently restricted will be considered unrestricted. Also, the funds received as a result of fundraising campaigns or special events will be considered unrestricted unless the organization had stated that the contribution would be used for a specific purpose when it was solicited. Generally, funds obtained through selling donated or other goods or providing services will be unrestricted unless otherwise stated during sales or solicitation.

Funds provided by government agencies are far more likely to have specific performance requirements than those provided by private individuals or foundations. Although the government

has many rules that go along with its funding, such funds are still considered unrestricted net assets by the FASB.

Managing Donated Income and Resources

Tax-exempt organizations receive money and other resources in a number of ways and from a number of different sources. The characteristics of each of these income streams will require a somewhat different approach to cash flow planning and management. Several of the major categories of contributed income and resources are:

- Grants of various types and from various sources;
- Donations, gifts, and contributions;
- Membership dues, assessments, or other payments from members; and
- Payments made in exchange for the right to attend certain fundraising events (known as *special fundraising income*).

Grants

Conditions of Grant

Nonprofits can receive grants from both private and public sources; in either case, grants are often accompanied by written *grant agreements*, or contracts specifying what the recipient organization must do in return for the funding. The legally binding requirements in most grant agreements (usually known as *conditions of grant*) tend to fall into three broad categories:

1. *Restrictions* on how resources can be used.
2. *Compliance requirements*, which require organizations to comply with specific laws, regulations, and practices in any of a wide range of areas. (See the subsection titled "Government Grants" later in this chapter for some compliance examples.)

3. *Measurable goals or service requirements*, which require nonprofits to achieve specific results or to provide specific quantifiable levels of goods or services to particular groups of individuals (known as *target groups or charitable classes*).

Grant agreements can directly (or by reference) require nonprofits to meet a wide range of requirements, including:

- Eligibility standards defining the groups or individuals that must be served under the grant
- Kinds and levels of services or activities the nonprofit must provide
- Additional funds or other resources that must be provided as a matching share to qualify for the grant funds
- Allowable and unallowable expenditures
- Requirements and procedures for making changes in the specific amounts, categories, or line items contained in an approved budget
- Specific hiring, personnel, accounting, cash management, record-keeping, reporting, and auditing requirements
- A wide range of other legally binding requirements that can affect a nonprofit's financial management

Program Matching Shares

Some grants may be accompanied by grant agreements that require, as a condition of grant, that the recipient organization provide a *program matching share*. This type of grant requirement is also referred to as a *match*, a *program match*, or a *matching share*. (Program matching shares should not be confused with challenge grants, which are defined later in this chapter.) The amount of the program matching share required is usually defined as a percentage of the resources the nonprofit needs to operate the specific program or activity. For example, a funding source or donor that requires a 25 percent program

matching share is agreeing to provide 75 percent of the resources needed to support a particular program or activity. The organization is responsible for providing the remaining 25 percent.

Conditions of grant are usually subject to audit either by the specific funding source or as part of the organization's own annual audit. Obviously, specific conditions of grant can directly and indirectly affect almost every aspect of an organization's financial management system. Therefore, financial managers must carefully read all grant documents and identify all conditions of grant (especially those affecting financial management and flow).

Funding sources may require organizations to meet program matching requirements through one of three methods:

1. A *cash match*, in which the organization must actually provide a specified amount of matching funds (sometimes limited to funds from certain categories or sources)
2. An *in-kind match*, in which an organization can meet matching requirements by receiving in-kind contributions of rental space, equipment, materials, or services, as long as the fair market value of the in-kind goods or services equals the required matching amount
3. A combined cash and in-kind match

The matching requirements of some types of grants will allow organizations to provide program matching shares simply by allocating existing resources to the required purpose. However, some grant agreements will specify that the organization must acquire new funds or resources. In any event, a program matching share is a condition of grant—a contractual obligation—that the organization agrees to meet at the time it receives the support. To avoid violating the grant agreement, organizations must comply with all matching requirements.

In addition, a nonprofit's agreement to provide a program matching share usually becomes an auditable compliance requirement. This means the nonprofit's auditors must determine whether or not the organization actually met the promised program matching requirements and must cite in the audit report any material noncompliance they find.

Challenge Grants

Challenge grants are grants that have, as a condition of grant, special program matching requirements. In a challenge grant situation, a funding source promises to provide an organization with money once the organization has attracted a specific amount of new support from other outside sources. In other words, the funding source promises to "match" the contributions the organization acquires from other sources.

Government Grants

Organizations that receive federal funds are subject to requirements beyond those attached to other income streams. Such additional requirements can affect cash flow management, particularly in its reporting and analysis aspects. A number of states have specific rules governing the operation of nonprofit organizations that legally do business in the state or solicit contributions from the state's residents. Depending on the amount of the organization's revenues or assets, states may also require that organizations be audited according to generally accepted auditing standards (GAAS), as issued by the American Institute of Certified Public Accountants (AICPA). Specific funding sources can establish additional audit requirements, which is often the case with federal funds. Receiving federal, state, or local government funds can subject a nonprofit to three sets of auditing requirements in addition to GAAS:

1. The audit requirements set forth in the General Accounting Office's *Government Auditing Standards*

2. The audit requirements spelled out in Office of Management and Budget Circular A-133
3. Any applicable state, city, or local audit requirements

These three types of audit requirements can affect nonprofit financial and cash flow management in many ways. For example, failure to follow the detailed requirements for recordkeeping, auditing, and compliance with a wide range of laws and regulations can lead to sanctions, including discontinuation of cash inflow. In this case, cash flow will be restored only when the requirements set forth in . . . [the] . . . grant agreement are met.

. . .

Gifts and Contributions

Gifts and *contributions* are cash or other assets provided to an organization to support its exempt activities by donors who are eligible to receive little or nothing of direct value in exchange. Gifts and contributions can come from individual, corporate, foundation, or other sources, including bequests. However, if a *tangible benefit* (that is, goods or services) of more than nominal value is offered in return for a contribution, only the amount above the fair market value of the goods or services offered is considered to be a contribution.

Donors can place restrictions on how a nonprofit may use gifts or contributions. They can also make pledges of future support that obligate the nonprofit to do certain things within a specified time period in order to receive the resources pledged.

In order to properly manage cash flow for gift and contribution income, a nonprofit's financial management system must be able to:

*   Identify the fair market value of any goods or services offered in return for contributions, membership payments, or admission to special fundraising events;

- Identify the expenses involved in generating such payments and determine the total amount of income that qualifies as contributions and that is therefore tax deductible to the donor;
- Provide individual donors who make individual contributions of over $250 with written statements regarding the tax deductibility of their donations; and
- Identify and track individual donations, gifts, and contributions for which use is restricted.

Noncash Contributions

Organizations may receive two types of noncash contributions from individuals, corporations, or other nonprofits:

1. Property (for example, securities, land, facilities, equipment, materials, or supplies)
2. Services or use of equipment, facilities, or materials owned by others when the service or use is provided free or at reduced cost

Receiving noncash contributions in a form the organization can use to fulfill a purpose reduces the need for the organization to spend cash for that purpose. This will obviously help cash flow. When the contribution is of securities of a publicly traded company, the organization can usually sell the security rapidly and have cash available in a short period of time. Organizations need to have cash flow management policies to properly handle such types of contributions.

Nonprofits must be able to identify, track, and report on each of the various sorts of noncash contributions they receive. Information on income from contributions will be necessary for generating financial statements, documenting the contribution in preparation for the annual audit, completing and submitting the required annual IRS information return, and issuing any required state reports.

Pledges

Pledges are promises to provide future support in the form of cash, securities, land, buildings, use of facilities or utilities, materials, supplies, intangible assets, or services. Pledges can be either conditional or unconditional. *Unconditional pledges* are economic support that donors promise to give with no conditions. *Conditional pledges* are support promised to the nonprofit only if specific conditions are met or come to pass.

Nonprofits must be able to identify, track, and report on individual pledges as either conditional or unconditional. Organizations will have to decide how pledges will be incorporated into cash flow forecasts and make this part of the organization's cash flow policy. If $1 million is pledged for a particular purpose, that money should not go into cash flow projections until the date that the organization is actually working on planning or building that project.

Membership Dues and Assessments

Membership dues or *assessments* are payments that organizations receive from members in exchange for offering them membership privileges. In terms of cash flow management, organizations must be able to perform proper record-keeping and reporting when receiving membership dues.

Income from Special Fundraising Events

Specific nonprofit fundraising events or activities constitute a substantial portion of some nonprofits' income. Cash flow planning and management for special-event income will include taking the necessary steps to comply with required Internal Revenue Service and financial reporting. Organizations must have financial and cash flow management systems in place to prepare financial reports required to report fundraising event income by event and in total.

Managing Earned Income

Tax-exempt nonprofits can earn income by providing goods or services for a fee. "Selling" different kinds of goods and services can generate different kinds of *income*, such as:

- Income from trade or business activities
- Income from sales of assets
- Income from program service fees
- Income from fees paid by government agencies (as opposed to grants or awards)

Each of these ways of earning income is discussed in the following subsections.

Income from Trade or Business Activities

Nonprofits are allowed to generate income by carrying out trade or business activities. Such income falls into three basic categories:

1. *Related business income:* Tax-free income from trade or business activities that are "substantially related" to a nonprofit's exempt purpose
2. *Unrelated business income (UBI):* Income from trade or business activities that are "not substantially related" to a nonprofit's exempt purpose
3. Income that would appear to be UBI but that is actually tax-free because it is excluded from unrelated business income tax (UBIT) under the Internal Revenue Code or specific legislation

Nonprofits that conduct trade or business activities must be able to identify, track, and report on

all related, unrelated, and excluded income (as well as applicable expenses).

Income from Sales of Assets

Nonprofits must be able to track income gains or losses from assets they sell. However, different types of assets are subject to different UBIT treatment and IRS reporting requirements. For example, to complete IRS Form 990 (Return of Organization Exempt from Income Tax), a nonprofit must be able to identify, track, account for, and report separately on income from the sale of at least three different kinds of assets:

1. Income from selling property held as part of a trade or business activity
2. Capital gains from selling investments or other non-inventory property (that is, property not intended for sale as part of a trade or business)
3. Income from selling real or personal property that was donated within the prior two years and for which the donor claimed a federal income tax deduction

Income from Program Service Fees

A nonprofit can charge fees for services it provides—services that can be either related or unrelated to the organization's exempt purpose. Organizations may receive fees for services directly from the individuals or organizations they serve from third parties who agree to pay all or some of the fees, or from some combination of the two.

When an organization generates fees for services, its financial management system must be able to generate bills and record collections for individual accounts and to track associated income and expenses.

Program service income (also called *fee-for-service income*) is primarily income a nonprofit receives in exchange for providing goods or services that further its exempt purpose. Program service revenue can include income from related trade or business activities as well as fees for other services.

Program service income will require organizations to develop financial management systems that are capable of performing all of the necessary billing, collection, data management, reporting, and analysis functions. This type of income stream can be one of the most complex in terms of cash flow planning and management.

Income from Fees Paid by Government Agencies

A nonprofit can receive fees from a government agency for providing goods or services to the agency. Fees from government agencies only include payments for services, facilities, or products that primarily benefit the government agency, either economically or physically. They do not include government grants or other payments that help a nonprofit provide services or maintain facilities for direct public benefit.

Service Agreements

Nonprofits may enter into contracts with private and public entities, such as individuals, governmental units, or other nonprofits, to provide services in exchange for money. (These are known as *service agreements, service contracts, or performance contracts.*) Such agreements may supply a nonprofit with agreed-on resources either before or after the nonprofit has provided specified goods or services. Under such contracts, the resources supplied are often determined by the specific amount of services the nonprofit provides. For example, Universal Nonprofit has a program that offers comprehensive mental health counseling services to

the community. To derive the greatest benefit from the staff and structure of this program, Universal Nonprofit has also negotiated service contracts with other organizations to provide their staffs with employee assistance program services for a fee.

As with grant agreements, any contract can directly (or by reference) commit the nonprofit to meet a wide range of requirements, including standards for eligibility, levels of service, matching resources, accounting, auditing, reporting, and expenditures, as well as other legally binding requirements that can affect a nonprofit's financial management. Some of these legally binding requirements may be restrictions on how resources can be used. Other requirements (*compliance requirements*) may bind the organization to comply with specific laws, regulations, and practices governing hiring, accounting, record-keeping, cash management, and so on.

Managing Asset-Generated Income

Tax-exempt nonprofits can earn income by using existing assets to produce income, usually through investments. This is because nonprofits are generally allowed to invest money and engage in the same sorts of investment transactions as for-profit entities. In addition to cash investments, such as interest-bearing bank accounts and certificates of deposit (CDs), a nonprofit's investments can also include any noninventory property (that is, property not intended for sale as part of a trade or business), such as stocks, bonds, options to purchase or sell securities, and real estate.

Categories of asset-generated income that affect nonprofit financial management and therefore may require special cash flow management include

- Income from debt-financed assets,
- Interest income,

- Dividend income,
- Gains or losses on investment transactions,
- Gains or losses on disposition of assets,
- Endowment income,[2]
- Rental income from real or personal property,
- Royalty income, and
- Income a nonprofit "parent" receives from a "controlled" taxable subsidiary.

Asset-generated income from any of these sources will have financial and cash flow planning and management requirements that are specific to the source, amount, and restriction status of the assets involved. Also, there will be requirements based on whether or not the income is related to the organization's tax-exempt purpose.

Notes

1. State laws differ on the definition of an endowment.

2. Some state laws prohibit using endowment funds for certain investments.

CHAPTER 15

Resiliency Tactics During Financial Crisis
The Nonprofit Resiliency Framework

ELIZABETH A. M. SEARING, KIMBERLY K. WILEY
AND SARAH L. YOUNG

Originally published as "Resiliency tactics during financial crisis: The nonprofit resiliency framework," in *Nonprofit Management and Leadership* (2021): 179–196. Copyright © Elizabeth A. M. Searing, Kimberly K. Wiley and Sarah L. Young (2021). Reprinted by permission of John Wiley & Sons.

Introduction

The ability of nonprofits to weather hard times is a popular theme in the academic and practitioner literature . . . this study provides insights into resiliency tactics used by publicly funded nonprofits during a revenue crisis. First, we captured the lived experiences of 31 nonprofits—a mix of umbrella associations, large direct service providers, and small direct service providers—to map the portfolio of managerial responses during a state budget crisis. Second, we employ qualitative analysis to establish the Nonprofit Resiliency Framework, mapping tactics in five areas: financial, human resources, outreach, program and services, and management and leadership.

The 2015–2017 Illinois Budget Impasse provided an excellent, if unfortunate example of resiliency demonstrated by resource-dependent nonprofits during a fiscal starvation of their organizations. This crisis occurred when the General Assembly of the state of Illinois

in the United States failed to pass a budget for three consecutive Legislative Sessions (2015, 2016, and 2017). . . . In Illinois, the long-established Democrat Speaker of the House and new Republican Governor could not agree on annual spending and appropriations, which meant that an official budget could not be passed. The impasse held up payments to nearly all entities dependent on state funding and created turmoil throughout the state. Nonprofit organizations with state contracts or other state funding found themselves not knowing if or when they would receive payments for the services they provided. The nonprofit organizations were contractually obligated to maintain services despite the lack of funding and were forced to develop tactics that would help them survive the impasse while still serving their mission.

This study strives to provide answers on how to survive a government revenue shock. Though provoking a clear financial crisis for many, the 3 years of the Illinois budget impasse

DOI: 10.4324/9781003387800-34

also influenced other aspects of nonprofit operations from struggles to keep their communities engaged to feeling held hostage by the partisan political battles on the state level. An examination of the resilience of publicly funded nonprofit organizations in Illinois during the 3-year starvation is extremely important because an impasse is likely to recur; further, the challenges of surviving and continuing service delivery during extended revenue shocks can be a complex reality for all nonprofits, as seen in the recent COVID-19 crisis.

The Many Faces of Resiliency

The concept of resiliency describes an entity's ability to survive change, and the formal study of the term stems back to the bioecological systems work of Holling (1973). Holling's original work focused on natural complex systems such as predator–prey interactions, but it posed initial theoretical conditions. First, there is a difference between stability (which is a rapid return to the initial equilibrium following a quick shock) and resiliency (which is the ability to persist through adapting to change while still maintaining relationships between key components). Second, survival is a necessary but not sufficient condition for persistence, which also includes maintaining core processes and functionality. Finally, the study of resiliency requires a systemic approach that is often complex and qualitatively oriented (Holling, 1973).

In the 50 years since Holling's original work, the concept of resiliency has been applied to individuals (Kimhi & Eshel, 2009), organizations (Bowman, 2011; Kimberlin, Schwartz, & Austin, 2011), sectors (Salamon, 2015), and societies (Berke & Campanella, 2006; Gotham & Campanella, 2011). Authors pushed on original conceptualizations, such as advocating that a return to the status quo following a shock is evidence of resiliency rather than just stability (Wildavsky, 1988).

Holling and colleagues refined the definition of resiliency to better fit socioecological systems in 2004: "the capacity of a system to absorb disturbance and reorganize while undergoing change so as to still retain essentially the same function, structure, identity, and feedbacks" (Walker, Holling, Carpenter, & Kinzig, 2004, p. 5). Recently, the scholarship on organizational resilience increased, with studies often focused on how a specific discipline or approach is the key (such as human resource management in Lengnick-Hall, Beck, and Lengnick-Hall (2011) or sustainable business practices in Ortiz-de-Mandojana and Bansal (2016)). We also expect there will be an explosion of the literature following the COVID-19 epidemic. However, certain key features of the original conceptualization remain: complexity, a catastrophic external shock, and both continued survival and functioning.

Following these initial studies, and aligned with existing resiliency theory, we define *resiliency* as the ability to withstand adverse conditions while still delivering services. Our study focuses on the organizational resiliency of nonprofit organizations in a specific resource niche: human services nonprofits in Illinois that rely heavily on government revenues.

. . .

Resiliency is a more appropriate concept than either vulnerability or survival to study nonprofit operations during periods of crisis or change. Survival simply measures the persistence of the legal organization. Though important, this singular view toward survival is too simple; if a nonprofit was only interested in organizational persistence, then they could cease delivering services and sell popcorn. But nonprofits are caught between decisions that might optimize the chances of organizational persistence (such as stockpiling assets) versus those that allow continued delivery of human services. The need for nonprofit managers to balance these goals even (and perhaps especially) during times of crisis means that we need a theoretical framework for resiliency that is likely as complex as the managerial decisions that they face.

There has been some progress toward understanding resiliency in the nonprofit sector. Lune (2002) explored how community organizations persisted in the face of severe political hostility. Besel (2001) explored how nonprofits that are dependent on local government can adopt tactics designed to weather resource dependency issues. Mosley, Maronick, and Katz (2012) surveyed nonprofits in Los Angeles to verify and explore the determinants of their responses to an economic downturn. Soh, Searing, and Young (2016) used four traits of resiliency in systems to explain the strategic behavior of housing nonprofits in Atlanta, Georgia. Searing (2020) used comparative case studies to unpack reasons why some mental health nonprofits closed while others thrived.

. . .

Research Design and Methods

We captured the lived experiences of nonprofit leaders immediately following the Illinois budget impasse. Our sample was limited to 501(c)3 nonprofit organizations dependent upon government funding because we expected that these organizations would feel the swiftest and largest impact from the withholding of government dollars. We interviewed leaders in the organization over the 4 months following the final resolution of the impasse in July 2017 and then conducted qualitative content analysis on the interview data. The three authors manually coded the data in qualitative analysis software. We were able to include more organizations in the study because of this multiple coder approach. The sample size ($N = 31$) is fairly sizeable and consistent with large qualitative studies (M. Mason, 2010). The larger sample size deepened our understanding of the experience

for each and helped contextualize the experience to the greater Illinois nonprofit sector.

Data Collection

A purposeful sampling technique was applied to build a dataset of 31 nonprofit organizations (Suri, 2011). Three criteria were used as guideposts to identify those nonprofits that would be at high financial risk while also in high demand for service during the impasse:

- 501(c)3 nonprofit organization providing direct human services
- 50% or more of revenue sourced from state or federal dollars
- At least 10 years old in 2017

First, the authors identified membership associations with member organizations that would likely fit the three criteria were invited to participate in the study. The membership associations played a variety of roles for their members, such as professional development, administrative oversight, and serving as funding pass-through entities. The membership associations also served as the mouthpiece for their members' legislative advocacy and public relations functions (Wiley, Searing & Young, 2020). Their inclusion in the study represented a wider breadth of 1,100 501(c)3 organizations operating in Illinois. In the interviews, they were asked to specifically focus on the tactics of their members.

These first nine membership association interviewees served as gatekeepers (Andoh-Arthur, 2019) between the authors and their members, which were community-based nonprofit organizations. Each association's interviewee emailed our interview solicitation to their membership. All respondents who fulfilled the criterion of the study were invited to participate. Each direct service organization was connected to at least one of the membership organizations in the study. Though we began with criterion sampling, we captured a stratified purposeful sample (Suri, 2011) of statewide membership associations (or "umbrella" organizations) and direct service nonprofits. After the sample was assembled, two natural clusters of large and small direct service nonprofits emerged from the data as we mapped their revenue, employee, and volunteer sizes. Table 15.1 presents quantitative descriptive statistics of the organizations. The final sample was sorted into five subsectors based on organizational mission: child welfare, vulnerable adults, victim advocacy, poverty alleviation, and capacity building. This iterative approach to sample design distilled clusters of comparable organizations under similar pressures from the financial crisis. The variation in the sample size for each cluster is explained by the achievement of storyline saturation within the clusters and across the sample. When new codes stopped emerging while coding data within each cluster, the investigators ceased interviews for that cluster and built out the remaining clusters with additional interviews. This process brought the total sample to 8 umbrella, 12 small, and 10 large organizations (M. Mason, 2010).[1]

The investigators conducted long-form interviews (Spradley, 1979) via video chat or in person with at least one member of the senior leadership team for the participating organizations; most often this was the executive director, but a former executive director and a chief operating officer were also included. The executive director serves as a liaison between the board of directors and the staff and deals with day-to-day crisis management. It is the executive director who makes the human resource and line-item budget decisions. In two cases, the executive director was brand new and was not involved in decision-making during the crisis. In those cases, we chose to interview another member of the executive leadership team who was engaged in decision-making during the crisis.

The interviews lasted 50–70 min, were recorded, and transcribed. Interviews began with a grand tour question (Spradley, 1979) about the nonprofit leader's initial emotional reactions and organizational responses to each of the three General Assembly sessions ending in a budget impasse, 2015, 2016, and 2017. The questioning progressed to explore the nonprofit's survival tactics, advocacy efforts, and impacts on their organizations. The semistructured interviews followed the line of questioning in the instrument provided in the Appendix. Probing questions were used to tease out more detailed responses about their reactions and tactics for resilience. For example, if

TABLE 15.1 Sample Characteristics in 2014 (Pre-Budget Impasse)

Organization type (n)		Age in years	Annual total revenue	Number of employees	Number of volunteers
Statewide	Range	5–47	$140,328–$15,013,890	0–25	0–61
Associations (8)	Median	38	$3,860,621	11	14
Large direct	Range	35–86	$2,839,410–$66,817,200	126–1,354	0–481
Service (10)	Median	54	$11,771,059	486	226
Small direct	Range	29–48	$502,943–$3,550,481	15–200	0–500
Service (13)	Median	38	$2,109,850	64	163

the interviewee answered the question, "What has been the largest impact of this fiscal crisis on your position within this organization?" with human resource concerns, we would follow up with a probing question such as "How are you coping with fewer staff members? What tools for resiliency are at your disposal? What have these coping tools accomplished in terms of financial survival or mission fulfillment? How effective have they been?"

To triangulate evidence identified in the interview data, the investigators examined newspaper articles on a budget impasse, the nonprofits' annual reports, and the IRS Form 990s. The news articles clarified and confirmed timelines and tactics pursued by participants, particularly legal and outreach tactics. Annual reports confirmed messaging tactics from the organization to their communities, public funders, and the Illinois General Assembly. The IRS Form 990 data were interpreted to make sense of revenue stability, cash flow shifts and employee expenses during and immediately prior to the budget impasse.[2] Though there are widespread concerns about the accuracy of Form 990 data, we do not rely on the more problematic elements, such as functional expense reporting or managerial compensation (Thornton & Belski, 2010). If other evidence seemingly contradicted the interviewee, the authors revisited the interview data or discussed the differences in perceptions of budget crisis. Contradictions were resolved through research team consensus.

Methods

The authors interpreted the interview data by applying qualitative conventional content analysis (Hsieh & Shannon, 2005). Coding occurred in three stages. First, in open coding, interview utterances were coded inductively as actions, conditions, or consequences (Brower & Jeong, 2008). As patterns emerged (or in axial coding), code names were created thematically. Iterative coding occurred throughout each stage as authors added new codes and revisited earlier coding schema and interview data. Finally, in the third round of coding (or selective coding), categories of survival tactics emerged.

We provide an example of our coding approach. For example, interviewees discussed different options they employed when their cash reserves dwindled. Those utterances were coded to actions as "survival tactics" during the open coding process. As the interviews progressed and interviewees referenced similar survival tactics, such as selling real estate, those survival patterns were captured with thematic code names like "sell assets" during the axial stage. Finally, we captured contextualized nuances during the selective level coding and grouped subcategories into themes, such as financial tactics. Three examples of our interview utterance coding approach are presented in Table 15.2.

In addition to the interviews, several different information sources were added to complete

TABLE 15.2 Example of Coding Strategy

Interview utterance	1. Open code	2. Axial code	3. Selective code
"We have an apartment building that we're looking to sell . . . and we're going to sell it to help our cash position to continue to secure the financial security."	Action	Sell assets	Financial tactic

(Continued)

TABLE 15.2 (Continued)

Interview utterance	1. Open code	2. Axial code	3. Selective code
"[M]y mission is not to serve the state of Illinois. My mission is to serve struggling kids and families."	Condition	Mission-driven	Mission as motivator
"We're losing people who know how to do the jobs, who normally rise up to supervisory positions."	Consequence	Loss of capacity	Strategic concern

the organizational picture and answer the second research question. We analyzed websites and promotional materials, and the Forms 990 collected for years 2013 through 2016 (the most recent available at the time of the interviews and coding). Finally, the news reports, annual reports, and Form 990s supported corroboration of information provided by the interviewees.

The Nonprofit Resiliency Framework

The budget impasse had a significant impact on different parts of the social service delivery ecosystem in the state of Illinois. Since many organizations needed to continue providing services in the absence of government funding, traditional management techniques were adapted, reinvented, or abandoned. To answer our first research question on what tactics were used, we utilized the three coding phases described in the Methods section. The resulting framework of resiliency tactics employed by the nonprofits is provided in Table 15.3. The tactics were grouped into five functional categories based on the resources utilized: financial; human resource; outreach; programs and services; and management and leadership. Four to six resiliency tactics emerged in each category.

Financial

Nonprofit managers employed six distinct tactics when responding to the Illinois budget crisis. Some were treated as emergency measures (such as asset sales), while others were often used as a means of ensuring a better future (such as revenue diversification). Due to these different needs, most organizations employed at least half of the financial tactics in their responses.

Cashflow monitoring was an intensification of a practice that many nonprofits were doing anyway, but now became a critical component for the organizations' response frameworks. Many nonprofits need to watch cash flow, especially since government funding (even in ideal times) may come long after service delivery in the form of reimbursements. However, monitoring systems increased since there was now a much weaker inflow of cash (even though revenue was still being counted according to accrual accounting guidelines). Nonprofits also tapped into their lines of credit and reserves in order to have the cash necessary to continue programming. They also developed new funding sources, though this was not necessarily tied to new programming initiatives (unlike the Mosley et al. (2012) study).

As a step beyond cashflow monitoring, many nonprofits also *reduce ancillary costs* such as employee travel and professional development. They also sought to *diversify their revenue*

TABLE 15.3 Nonprofit Resiliency Framework: Themes and Tactics

Tactical themes	Resiliency tactics
Financial	Cashflow monitor
	Lines of credit or reserves
	New funding sources
	Reduce ancillary cost
	Revenue portfolio diversification
	Sell assets
Human resources	Addressing burnout
	Didn't pay staff
	Maintaining capacity
	Nonmoney staff reward
	Reduce staff
Outreach	Advocating
	Altering messaging
	Improving relations w external stakeholders
	Increase fundraising
	Reliance on parent NP
Programs and services	Increased wait-list
	Mergers (picking up programs)
	Protect core services
	Reduced service quantity or quality
Management and leadership	Leader as example
	Personal debt
	Planning
	Relationship with the board
	Strategic action w partners

portfolios, which is standard advice for government-dependent nonprofits (though many of those studies envisioned a gradual reduction in spending and not a sudden cessation). Organizations that specifically sought to diversify revenue streams often did so as a way to ensure service provision in the long term; we treat it as separate from the tactic of developing a new revenue source because the phrase is industry jargon, was not tied to a specific revenue type, and used defensively. Finally, a few nonprofits had to resort to the *liquidation of assets* in order to provide cash.

I feel like we are in such a hole right now that we continue to plan some further action that we haven't taken yet, but we have an apartment building that we're looking to sell. It's occupied by people that we're going to have to find alternatives for, but there's some interest in the property and we're going to sell it to help our cash position.

(~L8)

This crisis of cashflow brings into focus some of the tension between the survival and service continuation pieces of the resiliency concept. The financial tactics brought into focus the tension between survival and service continuation for nonprofit organizations. In the example presented above, the nonprofit weighed their need for the cash gained from liquidating the asset versus the benefit the asset provides in delivering services to meet their mission. If they sell the building, they could use the cash to help stay afloat longer; however, this could complicate or possibly eliminate critical services. If they keep the building, the organization may not be able to survive as long as it could have otherwise. Financial stewardship and sustainability were expressed as complex, intertwined priorities during the crises.

Human Resources

There were more mentions of human resource tactics than any other type. . . . We distilled the responses into five main tactics. Three of the tactics addressed the problem of monetarily compensating staff, while the remaining two were more proactive in describing ways to appreciate the staff which remained.

Above all, most nonprofits tried to avoid *reducing staff.* There were several strong patterns that motivated this approach: a close-knit team, decreased capacity, and fierce competition for workers. However, few nonprofits were at a comfortable level of staffing even before the impasse began.

> There isn't fat to cut or slack. So, what you're talking about in cutting jobs is saying like we're not going to have a case manager. So we're going to have one less case manager in this program. And people are going to have higher caseloads and that means people aren't going to get what they need as well. These are is the impacts that there have been.
>
> (~S5)

Since letting staff go was considered the final option, there were some creative ways to handle the pecuniary issue. Some simply *did not pay staff* or had staff working extra hours as unpaid volunteers. Others *rewarded staff in nonmonetary ways* such as flexible working hours and sharing the personal stories of staff to build camaraderie. The organization's ability to maintain capacity in delivering their services was key, which included taking interns and learning the jobs of others so that gaps could be filled.

For many nonprofit workers, these tactics created large amounts of stress and, eventually, disenchantment with being a service provider. Not only did the nonprofits need to fight to keep their employees at their organization, they also had to fight the battle to keep them in the sector. Years of stagnant wages in the social services meant that nonprofits also had to *address burnout* since, in many ways, this was a crisis in a long line of hardships for nonprofit employees in Illinois. This was particularly difficult since there had not been money for this during the pre-impasse years. Now, organizations needed to counter not only the immediate shock of the impasse, but also pent-up frustrations from over a decade of difficult working conditions. And this is in a state where the minimum wage had continued to increase, but the compensation rates for direct care services providers in government contracts had not. As one of the interviewees remarked, "You can make as much working for Target as you can for us. And you don't have that concern about losing your job because government is not going to pay you where would you rather work?" The fear that workers would leave not only the nonprofit but the sector as a whole was repeated throughout the data.

Outreach

Several tactics involved the cultivation of relationships. These approaches had more in common with each other than with the target of the effort; thus, outreach was a suitable category. However, the exact purpose and target of each of the five different outreach tactics varied.

Some tactics, like *advocating* and *altering messaging*, applied to many possible recipient audiences. Advocating appeared in two main guises: activism about the nonprofit's importance and education regarding the state budgeting process. Both types of advocacy involved members of the public and the legislators directly responsible for the budget impasse. In terms of communicating the nonprofit's importance, these tactics often involved mobilizing members of the community that had been occasionally engaged and then using them to reach out to other members of the public and legislators. Education regarding the state budgeting process was a bit more complex, both in terms of the subject matter and the approach since the first step was legislators admitting that there was a lack of understanding, before that lack could be remedied.

> [W]e really have a hard time helping the individual legislatures understand the complexities of that budgeting and what happens once it gets out of their hands. So once the legislature passes a budget they don't have a clue what happens over in the individual departments.
>
> (~C5)

Both types of outreach often entailed *altering messaging*, especially as the impasse wore on. Advocates and potential advocates became victims of what resembled "compassion fatigue," where the endless stories of hardship faced by nonprofit service recipients started to cause a numbness and avoidance in the message recipients (Adams, Boscarino, & Figley, 2006). Faced with an increasingly dire situation and an increasingly numb populace, several nonprofits switched tactics. Some changed the framing from the individual hardship narrative over to making a case for how much the impasse was

hurting the business community. Other nonprofits abandoned the hardship narrative altogether and began talking about the nonprofit sector's resilience. The key was changing the messaging so that the deviation from the norm would, itself, attract the attention of a weary populace.

For the remaining three tactics, each had a unique modality and target audience. For *improving relations with external stakeholders*, this meant reaching out to community members who may have been aware of the nonprofit previously, but not involved in advocacy on their behalf. For example, nonprofits got to know their local bankers very well when they increased their communication about delayed income and accessing assets.

Increasing fundraising is part outreach and part finance; however, since the money often followed a personal connection and appeal, we classified this as an outreach tactic rather than a financial one.

> [W]e did a fundraiser . . . and it was picked up by the news and then it was picked up by [elected official's] office who used it. And then [another elected official]'s office picked it up and used it on their website. And then . . . someone from Chicago drove out on the day of our garage sale and offered to help us in a lot of different ways with marketing and things like that. So those were really nice opportunities.
>
> (~S7)

This is not to say that fundraising did not come with internal changes. Several organizations did not have an existing development team and had to develop one, ad hoc. Others had boards, which recognized that fundraising was essential; some had the resources or experience to step in as fundraisers, but many nonprofits did not. A few nonprofits had a "parent" nonprofit or institutional arrangement where they could rely on a much larger institution for support. This could be a much larger nonprofit that could provide resources, or a state agency that provided reduced rent. In all of these instances, *reliance on a parent nonprofit* or benefactor agency provided a necessary lifeline.

This re-energizing of existing relationships also applied to media, legislators, community members, and previous service recipients. The latter were especially important because they were often more comfortable in advocating on behalf of the nonprofit compared to the nonprofit itself. Overall, continuity of services was the priority in outreach to each stakeholder group.

Program and Services

Unfortunately, reduced funding often had direct negative impacts on the programs and services offered by human services nonprofits to the citizens of Illinois. Several agencies reported an *increase in wait-lists* for services. This was especially problematic for those agencies that provided crisis services. Many of these organizations' service recipients included potential victims of violence who were often unable to find timely relief during their crisis.

The shortage of services was compounded through the many *mergers and picking up of programs* that nonprofits engaged in when a neighboring nonprofit closed its programs. Here, we saw evidence of two different narratives. The first was that mergers were occurring because smaller nonprofits lacked the capacity for infrastructure and economies of scale; therefore, "fragmentation" was bad, and consolidation was a good thing. However, there was also a counternarrative that consolidated markets meant that there was less choice and fewer services overall, even if some of them were being saved. The difference in narrative often depended on the size of the nonprofit, with the larger nonprofits viewing consolidations as a positive impact of the impasse.

Most nonprofits attempted to *protect core services*, which meant that some services that the organization did not view as core to their central mission were closed to provide a longer projected survival time to those with a higher priority. There were also changes to help sustain the programs, such as shifting from individual counseling to group counseling. Other times, staff heroics were responsible, such as the decision of one individual to live at the nonprofit's shelter in order to make sure it was staffed and able to remain open.

There were many situations, however, where service quality or quantity were reduced. Sometimes this was because staff had to be repurposed, or local staff had dwindled to the point that the program was no longer viable. Programs had to reduce hours or close satellite offices, which hit rural areas particularly hard. It also meant that resources were diverted away from preventative programs and toward crisis intervention—not because the latter was core, but because the situation was potentially lethal. Though this triage makes sense in the short run, fears exist that such decisions may lead to more interventions in the long run, especially since the education and preventative services were cut the most. Program reductions also meant that some service recipients were simply turned away. For instance, one criminal justice diversion program for youth served as the child's final intervention before entering the prison system.

> Well, I think the most difficult part was when I had to tell [my clients] that we were ending the programs. And some of them, I mean we're talking kids that had stolen cars, have guns, the whole thing, and had them put their heads down and some of the boys said, "You were our last chance".
>
> (-S6)

This interviewee expressed their deep reluctance and regret in turning children away from a program that would impact the trajectory of their lives.

Management and Leadership

Our final group of tactics involve the roles and actions taken by the leadership team of the nonprofit. For example, many leaders spoke about their responsibility to model the type of self-sacrificing behavior they expected from their staff. This potentially involved salary reduction, furloughs, additional unpaid time, or a return to direct service delivery for those in administrative roles. D. E. Mason (1996) considered the duty of building commitment to the nonprofit to be the responsibility of nonprofit managers, who have the ability to control the informal or "expressive dimension" of working at a nonprofit. Our study provides empirical evidence of this, with several leaders speaking of their most important role being a cheerleader or morale-provider for their staff.

> I think it's trying to believe and keep sharing that belief with your staff that things are going to be okay. That, hang in there, keep going. Keep doing your job. Don't worry about it. I got it. You're going to get your paycheck. Please don't leave . . . I think, it's that constant pressure in trying to keep being a cheerleader. Knowing that you have no idea when the wheels are going to come off.
>
> (~S13)

Nonprofit leaders also took on roles that only they would be able to provide. An example of this is *personal debt*: at least one nonprofit had leadership take out mortgages on their homes to make payroll.

Beyond these levels of personal sacrifice, however, there were many things that the leadership team could do in order to facilitate the resiliency of the organization. *Strategic planning* became very important, even beyond the increased tracking of financial resources.

> [T]he first thing that I had us go through in that strategic planning process was identifying what our core services were . . . if the agency went away, what would be the biggest holes in the community[?] [T]hankfully, by doing that when we did, [when] we had to look at cuts and becoming smaller we knew we [could] preserve the core services.
>
> (~S3)

Planning also helped increase stakeholder buy-in to the management responses. This was particularly true when leadership made concerted efforts to improve the *relationship with the board,* whether this was for fundraising, governance, or advocacy reasons. Even beyond access to board resources, several leaders remarked that just having the support of their boards made their lives much easier because they felt less alone in the struggle.

If boards provided the leadership team with an internal source of support, then taking *strategic action with partners* provided an external source of support. This is especially the case if the agency opted to join one of the legal actions against the State, which was perceived by many to be a risky venture. Despite its extreme nature, the plaintiffs felt that the lawsuit was the only option.

> [We] joined the lawsuit from the beginning because we felt like we need to, at that point it just felt so, a lawsuit I think sounded a little extreme because I think people are really concerned about the potential backlash that would happen from the state around that.
>
> (~S5)

The shifting of policy-making venues from the legislative to the judicial branch in pursuit of funds was a strategic action that different agencies took based on previous court opinion and the actions of their peers. Without the support of peer agencies, it is unlikely that any of these advocacy venue shifts would have moved forward (see Wiley et al., 2020 for more details).

Conclusion and Recommendations

Nonprofits are complex organizations, and their strategic responses to periods of financial stress are likewise complex. Our study allowed resiliency tactics used by Illinois nonprofits during the state budget impasse to emerge from their own thick narratives.

This nuance allows us to provide several practical takeaways. First, the underlying issues of the crisis were not addressed when the impasse was resolved. The fiscal issues of the state remain, the process that allowed for the impasse was not altered, and human services delivery remains heavily dependent on state funding. Therefore, this may not be an isolated budgetary incident and we may see other crises impact human service delivery in similar ways (Young, Wiley, & Searing, 2020).

Second, the significance of the human resource tactics may be indicative of underlying issues in the nonprofit labor market. As seen in the COVID-19 Pandemic, a person's physical work location is much more fluid than ever previously thought. It is easier than ever before for workers to move between states; nonprofit wages are not where they should be to attract and keep workers in the state or even in the sector. The fact that direct care providers were already underpaid (especially given increases in the cost of living) will likely get lost in the impasse recovery efforts. At all times, nonprofits should be mindful of hidden costs such as increased burnout and re-training, Often, government contracts do not cover the full cost even under normal budgetary conditions. This shortfall includes not only administrative costs for the organization such as fundraising, but also hidden costs such as emotional labor and capacity development.

This study does have limitations. First, while the study included 31 interviews and achieved storyline saturation, and despite the efforts of the research team to provide triangulation, there still may be challenges in generalizing to the Illinois nonprofit sector more broadly. Our insights should be most applicable to organizations in our focus area: publicly funded human service organizations that have a large portion of their income from government sources. Further, there may be elements in the Illinois context, which are not generalizable outside of the state. Illinois is unique in its large local government sector (1,299 municipalities) and progressive leanings at the state level. Second, only nonprofit organizations that were still operating were interviewed because of the availability to contact them. Since we did not interview any nonprofits that had closed directly (though we did hear tales indirectly), this study does not include their lived experience. Finally, the fact that the impasse has only recently ended means that the study is timely, but it also means that we are limited to analyzing short-term responses rather than long-term reactions and impacts.

We distill the experiences of Illinois nonprofits delivering human services during the Illinois budget impasse into the Nonprofit Resiliency Framework, which identifies trends in five tactical areas: financial, human resources, outreach, program and services, and management and leadership. The trends detailed provide a tried-and-true approach for other practitioners interested in keeping their nonprofits alive and delivering services through hard times. Perhaps more importantly, they also provide a needed optimistic element to the vulnerability literature by focusing on resiliency and recovery instead of predicting demise. An executive director of a large publicly funded nonprofit best articulates the path forward:

> And I hope this is a wake-up call to organizations to—to ask the hard questions of ourselves and what are we doing differently,

what are we going to do differently because quite frankly my confidence that the state is going to change is pretty slim. And so if we want a different outcome, we teach our kids you can't control what someone else is going to do, you can only control what you do. So how are we as a sector going to take control to make sure that if this happens again there's a different outcome. And I'm not saying don't do business with the state. I'm saying if you're only doing business with the state, I'm not sure how you expect there to be a different outcome.

(~L10)

The COVID-19 Pandemic has caused us to focus on the detrimental impact of crises on nonprofits and the broader economy. Yet, like the Illinois Budget Impasse, the Pandemic will likely not be the last extended crisis nonprofits face. Nonprofits need to dedicate resources to resiliency now. This includes mapping out their own organizational strengths and weaknesses, with special attention to the perceptions and insights of stakeholders outside of the management team. Though the impasse may have initially seemed like a financial crisis, the tactics to address the situation came from a variety of sources; knowing what the staff, service recipients, and members of the community think are important if you expect to rely on them for crisis response or continuation of service.

Notes

1. The sample originally contained 32 organizations. However, the only interview designed to represent two organizations did not achieve enough distinction between the organizations (same subsector, staff, mission, etc.). Therefore, these two umbrellas were combined for the sake of analysis. We also conducted an interview of a small direct service organization whose audio was lost due to technological issues. Therefore, though there were 31 interviews, the final sample contained 30 organizations.

2. Though ideally financial information for the entire budget impasse would be available, only 2013 through 2016 had complete records at the time of the study. Research involving the full financial trajectory and impact of the budget impasse will be a noteworthy future study.

References

Adams, R. E., Boscarino, J. A., & Figley, C. R. (2006). Compassion fatigue and psychological distress among social workers: A validation study. *American Journal of Orthopsychiatry*, *76*(1), 103–108.

Andoh-Arthur, J. (2019). Gatekeepers in qualitative research. In P. Atkinson, S. Delamont, A. Cernat, J. W. Sakshaug, & R. A. Williams (Eds.), *SAGE research methods foundations*. London: SAGE Publications Ltd. https://doi.org/10.4135/9781526421036854377

Berke, P. R., & Campanella, T. J. (2006). Planning for postdisaster resiliency. *The Annals of the American Academy of Political and Social Science*, *604*(1), 192–207.

Besel, K. (2001). The role of local governmental funding in nonprofit survival. *Advances in Social Work*, *2*(1), 39–51.

Bowman, W. (2011). Financial capacity and sustainability of ordinary nonprofits. *Nonprofit Management & Leadership*, *22*(1), 37–51.

Brower, R. S., & Jeong, H. (2008). Grounded analysis: Going beyond description to derive theory from qualitative data. In K. Yang & G. J. Miller (Eds.), *Handbook of research methods in public administration* (pp. 823–840). Boca Raton, FL: CRC Press.

Gotham, K. F., & Campanella, R. (2011). Coupled vulnerability and resilience: The dynamics of cross-scale interactions in post-Katrina New Orleans. *Ecology and Society*, *16*(3).

Holling, C. S. (1973). Resilience and stability of ecological systems. *Annual Review of Ecology and Systematics*, *4*(1), 1–23.

Hsieh, H.F., & Shannon, S. E. (2005). Three approaches to qualitative content analysis. *Qualitative Health Research*, *15*(9), 1277–1288.

Kimberlin, S. E., Schwartz, S, L., & Austin, M, J. (2011). Growth and resilience of pioneering nonprofit human service organizations: A cross-case analysis of organizational histories. *Journal of Evidence-Based Social Work, 8*(1–2), 4–28.

Kimhi, S., & Eshel, Y. (2009). Individual and public resilience and coping with long-term outcomes of war 1. *Journal of Applied Biobehavioral Research, 14*(2), 70–89.

Lengnick-Hall, C. A., Beck, T. E., & Lengnick-Hall, M. L. (2011). Developing a capacity for organizational resilience through strategic human resource management. *Human Resource Management Review, 21*(3), 243–255.

Lune, H. (2002). Weathering the storm: Nonprofit organization survival strategies in a hostile climate. *Nonprofit and Voluntary Sector Quarterly, 31*(4), 463–483.

Mason, D. E. (1996). Leading and managing the expressive dimension: Harnessing the hidden power source of the nonprofit sector. San Francisco: Jossey-Bass.

Mason, M. (2010). Sample size and saturation in PhD studies using qualitative interviews. *Forum: Qualitative Social Research, 11*(3). https://doi.org/10.17169/fqs-11.3.1428

Mosley, J. E., Maronick, M. P., & Katz, H. (2012). How organizational characteristics affect the adaptive tactics used by human service nonprofit managers confronting financial uncertainty. *Nonprofit Management & Leadership, 22*(3), 281–303. https://doi.org/10.1002/nml.20055

Ortiz-de-Mandojana, N., & Bansal, P. (2016). The long-term benefits of organizational resilience through sustainable business practices. *Strategic Management Journal, 37*(8), 1615–1631.

Salamon, L. M. (2015). *The resilient sector revisited: The new challenge to nonprofit America.* Washington, DC: Brookings Institution Press.

Searing, E. A. M. (2020). Life, death, and zombies: Revisiting traditional concepts of nonprofit demise. *Journal of Public and Nonprofit Administration, 6*(3), 354–376.

Soh, J. I., Searing, E. A. M., & Young, D. (2016). Resiliency and stability of the zoo animals. In D. Young, C. Brewer, & E. A. M. Searing (Eds.), *The social enterprise zoo: A guide for perplexed scholars, entrepreneurs, philanthropists, leaders, investors and policymakers.* Cheltenham, England: Edward Elgar.

Spradley, J. (1979). Asking descriptive questions. *The Ethnographic Interview, 1*, 44–61.

Suri, H. (2011). Purposeful sampling in qualitative research synthesis. *Qualitative Research Journal, 11*(2), 63–75.

Thornton, J. P., & Belski, W. H. (2010). Financial reporting quality and price competition among nonprofit firms. *Applied Economics, 42*(21), 2699–2713.

Walker, B., Holling, C. S., Carpenter, S. R., & Kinzig, A. (2004). Resilience, adaptability and transformability in social-ecological systems. *Ecology and Society, 9*(2).

Wildavsky, A. B. (1988). *Searching for safety.* New Brunswick, USA: Transaction Publishers.

Wiley, K., Searing, E. A., & Young, S. (2020). Utility of the advocacy coalition framework in a regional budget crisis. *Public Policy and Administration,* 0952076720905007. https://doi.org/10.1177/0952076720905007.

Young S. L., Wiley, K. K., & Searing, E. A. (2020). "Squandered in real time": How public management theory underestimated the public administration–politics dichotomy. *The American Review of Public Administration, 50*(6–7), 480–488.

How to cite this article: Searing, E. A. M., Wiley, K. K., & Young, S, L. (2021). Resiliency tactics during financial crisis: The nonprofit resiliency framework. *Nonprofit Management and Leadership, 32*(2), 179–196. https://doi.org/10.1002/nml.21478

Interview instrument for direct service organizations

1. Tell me about a time when you first felt the impact of the budget impasse within your organization.
2. What is the most difficult (complicated, burdensome, resource-consuming) part of the budget impasse on your organization?
3. What has been the largest impact of this fiscal crisis on your position within this organization? (Probing questions: Was it staffing, fiscal, organization structure?)
4. Who advocates on your behalf with the public funders?
5. How similar or dissimilar is your experience to other nonprofit organizations dependent on public dollars?
6. In what way has the budget impasse impacted your mission? How has your service to your clients changed?
7. What has been predictable and what has surprised you during the budget impasse?

Adjusted Wording in Interview Instrument for Statewide Associations

1. Tell me about a time when you first felt the impact of the budget impasse within your organization.
2. What is the most difficult (complicated, burdensome, resource-consuming) part of the budget impasse on the nonprofits you serve?
3. What has been the largest impact of this fiscal crisis on the nonprofits you serve within the organization? (Probing questions: Was it staffing, fiscal, organization structure?)
4. What is your role in supporting your member organizations through this budget impasse?
5. How similar or dissimilar is the experience of the nonprofits you serve to other nonprofit organizations dependent on public dollars?
6. In what way has the budget impasse impacted their mission? How has their service to your clients changed?
7. What has been predictable and what has surprised you during the budget impasse?

Throwing the First E-Stone

C. Kenneth Meyer

Dean Hall, the new CEO and finance and budget officer of the United Way of Benneville Oak, was shocked to receive an official written reprimand dealing with the "inappropriate use of United Way property." The reprimand noted that he had violated agency policy by using the Internet and email for personal purposes that were not related directly to agency business. Even more shocking and embarrassing was the companion memo that had mysteriously appeared as an attachment to the minutes of the quarterly meeting of the agency's board of directors: it listed the sites he visited, which included news, sports, weather, golf, casino, and travel sites. It also showed that he had ordered items from Amazon, Harry and David Fruit Baskets, Victoria's Secret, and Cabela's Sporting Goods in the previous year.

The memo quoted Butch Hunter, director of information technology and a five-year veteran with the organization: "I have a duty and responsibility to the people who support this agency to inform the board of directors when an employee is in violation of the Internet policy. The computers are not put on their desks for pleasure or self-interest. They are provided by the donors and United Way of Benneville Oak and our region for agency business exclusively. Anyone surfing the net for their own pleasure is using up valuable time and space on our system and wasting the public's money, and that type of activity will not be permitted on my watch!"

Dean suspected that this had something to do with the directive he had been hired to implement when he was taken on by the executive director, which was to cut costs wherever they could be made. The foundation of the directive was to implement a 15 percent across-the-board cut in program and administrative costs, including infrastructure. Butch's plan to purchase a state-of-the-art information system that would handle the increased volume of networking had been cut.

Despite the fact that the memo was true—he did have a habit of checking the news, weather, and sports during his workday—Dean felt outraged. Some of the sites contained information relative to agency business. For example, his time spent on the casino website was in direct response to a request from an area businessman to give him an update on the financial condition of the area's two casinos. Thus, Dean had brought up the website as a starting point. Also, during the crunch time at the end of the fiscal year, Dean did some holiday shopping online from work since he was staying late each evening trying to close the books for the year. At the time it had seemed okay, since he was burning the midnight oil for the agency's sake and there would be no compensatory time given. Now all he could think of was how lucky he was that he had not visited any risqué sites or downloaded "Suzie."

DOI: 10.4324/9781003387800-35

The next day Dean met with the executive director, Sheila Warren, to find out where he stood. By now Dean was angry. "Come on, Sheila, who here doesn't check out the weather or sports or send a personal email from work? This is all about my implementing your policy!"

Sheila was sympathetic, admitting "off the record" that no doubt other staff members had also used agency computers for private matters in an effort to balance their busy workdays and private family lives.

"I don't know what to say," Sheila responded. "Butch has the right to ask for information and monitor the use of the computers and report what he sees as inappropriate uses to a board member, although I would have preferred that he bring it to my attention first. Nonetheless, you were in violation of the policy. "My hands are tied," she said, adding with a chuckle, "well, at least you can bet that everyone was busy this morning erasing bookmarks and personal emails as a result of the memo."

Dean didn't grasp the humor that Sheila found in his dilemma.

Questions and Instructions

1. Experts report that over $1 billion is "wasted" by employees pursuing personal business on work computers. Is this a problem that needs to be addressed? If so, please indicate how you would begin to compile the information needed to write an effective policy.

2. Most firms have the technical ability and the legal authority to track employee actions on their office computers. Comment on the situation presented in the case from an ethical and financial perspective. Should budgetary or financial matters affect how an organization monitors its technology use?

3. All nonprofit agencies must deal with harsh budgetary restrictions from time to time. Do you believe that an across-the-board budget cut is the best way to implement cost-saving decisions? Please explain your answer.

When the Funding Stops

DON MUNKERS AND C. KENNETH MEYER

The United Operators Association (UOA) was a 501(c)(3) nonprofit organization funded through membership dues and contracts from the parent organization, the American United Operators Association (AUOA). AUOA received appropriated funding from the US government, and these monies were further administered by two national agencies of the federal government—the Environmental Protection Agency (EPA) and the US Department of Agriculture (USDA). In turn, the AUOA entered into contracts with the state chapter of UOA. Overall, the goal of UOA was to provide services in the world of environmental protection as a subcontractor to AUOA, EPA, and USDA. As such, it serviced small rural municipalities throughout the state, thereby not only protecting the environment but also enhancing public health.

The programs delivered by UOA were varied and included the protection of watersheds and aquifers and assistance in the development and implementation of source water protection plans. In total, there were seven programs that linked together services that ranged from providing technical assistance and operator training to actually protecting many sources of drinking water.

The cost reimbursement contracts were based on multiyear contracts and were annually reviewed for renewal purposes. In reality, the contracts were actually "sub-award agreements" between the parent AUOA and the state organization. As part and parcel of the communicated and reinforced organizational culture, employees were "indoctrinated" with the fact that they were employed at the state level. They were not to refer to their employment status at any other level—and it was especially important that they not represent themselves as members of the national organization.

To take care that the fiduciary responsibilities of the UOA were met, the organization required employees to maintain extensive monthly logs with detailed records of their activities as they provided contract-mandated services to the constituents of the state. These technical assistance and financial logs provided the basis or justification for all cost reimbursements made to the state up to, but not exceeding, the total amounted awarded. Expenditures in excess of the contractual agreement approved by the national AUOA were entered into at the expense of the state organization, and any underexpenditures were deducted from the contract for the next year. In addition, one important, but frequently overlooked, section of the contract stipulated that, "if for any reason" the national agency that administered the contract did not pay the parent organization, the state organization would likewise not be reimbursed. However, the state would have to continue to fulfill its work- and service-related obligations under the contract as if they were "fully funded." In essence, the state would have to fulfill its obligation to meet the contractual requirements and perform the necessary work even though, in the final analysis, it might not be entitled to reimbursement for expenses. This cumbersome and uncertain arrangement presented a major problem for the state agency, since the funding was based on the unknown vicissitudes surrounding federal funding of the administering agency. Recently, however, this funding arrangement had changed.

Presently, the state UOA had seven contracts totaling $900,000 under the agreement as previously detailed. This amount, coupled with membership fees, provided a total operating budget of $1.3 million. While each contract specifically outlined the purposes (functions, services, and activities) to which these federal monies might be applied, the regulations governing the utilization of membership dues were much more flexible and made the use of these funds largely subject to the personal judgment calls of the executive director of the state UOA—provided these uses complied with the bylaws of the organization.

For the present fiscal year, an unfortunate set of policies had been put into effect by the administering agencies. Although Congress had appropriated the funding for the programs, the national agencies, while knowing that the funds had been appropriated, failed to allocate them. Two of the programs began experiencing a funding lag at the beginning of the federal budget year. One was the Environmental Training Program (ETP), a program that provided environmental training to address compliance issues connected with national environmental regulation standards. To carry out its mandate of assisting small communities in protecting the environment and public health, this program was delivered through classes given to the municipal employees who had been charged with implementing these standards. The other program assisted small communities in the development of programs to protect watershed

areas by assessing and inventorying the potential sources of water contamination. In brief, the needed federal monies were not distributed to the state UOA for an eleven-month period—a long time to be faced with the turbulence of financial uncertainty.

During this period, other programs began to see their funding go into arrears, with delays of up to four months or more in allocation. As the fiscal year progressed, UOA began to experience serious shortfalls in cash flow. It remedied the situation initially by making arrangements with the financial institution that serviced the UOA account. First National Bank simply covered any drafts made on the account, apparently assured by the assumption that "lag-pay" would eventually be forthcoming and that the federal funding was covered by a contractual agreement. The financial officer at First National was fully aware, however, that the contracts could not be used as collateral, as specifically detailed in the terms of the contract.

The national AUOA organization offered to loan the state UOA the non-allocated shortfall at the prime interest rate, plus-1 percent. Detailed financials and authorizations from the UOA board were required monthly, but even though the board submitted these reports monthly, the AUOA always found a reason not to loan the money. Since operations were being covered by the local bank, Orangelo Baldwin, the executive director of the state UOA, upon receiving what she called "sage advice" from Beth Ausman, a veteran employee of the agency, decided to continue funding cash-flow shortages, unabated, through the local bank. While this arrangement presented a financial burden, the state UOA was able, with First National's assistance, to meet its obligations. This arrangement continued until the bulk of the other programs began to fall behind in contributions.

Ted Jacobs, comptroller for the state UOA, called Orangelo and voiced his concern about the basis for funding and reimbursement and wanted to know when the lag-pay would end.

He stated, "I find this lag-pay problem to be disruptive to the administration of our programs, especially if I am to convey the confidence normally associated with professional fiduciary responsibility."

Orangelo asked Beth to look into the matter, and she made several telephone calls and emailed her inquiries to the national AUOA asking for ending dates. As they had claimed several times before, they told her that the ending date would be the end of the current week. Beth dutifully passed this information on to Ted, who was patiently waiting for a response. But Ted became irritated when it turned out that his inquiries had once again been answered with false information: the communicated ending date came and went and the agency's claims for reimbursement had yet to be settled.

The problem was exacerbated when First National tired of getting what it called the "runaround" began to "bounce" checks written on the state UOA's account. In an attempt to balance the accounts for UOA, Orangelo had informed all the vendors that they would be paid, but when, through no fault of the UOA's, they were informed that UOA could not meet these obligations, chaos broke out in the organization. As could have been expected, insurance policies were canceled, ordered supplies were not delivered, and critical office equipment was threatened with repossession. Finally, employee payroll was jeopardized. The final threat in a long series of threats had arrived and immediate action was required.

Through the persistent efforts of Ted and Beth, who were in constant consultation with the bank, the payroll was financed. However, travel reimbursements were placed on the backburner and fringe benefit contributions were not placed in the retirement and pension accounts. For the time being, UOA was still in business. The state UOA staff continued in their efforts to secure an interim loan from the national AUOA to cover obligated expenses. They had sent the required documents via certified mail to the national office in Washington, DC, requesting the required signatures. Delays were more usual than exceptional in dealing with the national office, but this time the staff had tried to convey the real urgency behind its request that the paperwork be promptly processed.

After a week or so had transpired and no word had been received from First National regarding the interim loan, Ted called the principal at the national AUOA and inquired about the status of the loan documentation. The conversation went smoothly enough, but in the end he was told that the papers had not been received. Although Ted was typically cordial in his dealings with the national office, he had reached a point of frustration that was hard to control. He questioned the accuracy of this claim and said that he held a receipt certifying that the document package had been delivered and signed for nearly six days earlier. Three days later, the national AUOA principal called Ted and informed him that the envelope containing the application for the interim loan had been found, and he apologized for what was either the "apparent mix-up" in the US mail or a "misrouting" in the agency.

Completely turned off by the repeated delays in funding and the constant excuses he had received from AUOA over the years, Ted decided that it was time to seek political intervention. As someone who was familiar with the political process and knowledgeable about effective congressional communication, he contacted the office of the state's senior senator and requested that the national agencies responsible for administering the funds be investigated. About a week later, after a member of the senatorial staff contacted the principal parties at the national agencies, the funds began to flow again.

Temporarily, the problem had been fixed, but the state UOA had been severely affected and the damage had already been inflicted. Indeed, at one point in time the federal government owed the state UOA $365,000 for the work it had certified as completed. This represented nearly 40 percent of the total contribution from the contracts, an amount that the UOA could not easily absorb. With the approved and transmitted deposit, however, the state UOA felt that it was back in business and began to refurbish its "tarnished reputation" with its insurer and other service providers.

In discussing the matter with Orangelo, Ted told her what he had done to get the funding dilemma fixed and vowed that, should delays and postponements once again become the "order of the day" in the future, he would not hesitate to contact his congressional delegation and work through them to solve the problem. "It takes powerful people who know the system," he said, "to get the attention of national bureaucrats, and when they are heard, action results." He lamented having had to turn to the political process for action, but the state UOA could not function as a credible agency when it was in a constant state of budgetary crisis—a crisis not of its own making and one that could not be solved with the receipts for membership dues.

Clyde Crimson, chairperson of the UOA board, had been kept informed of the events that led to Ted's call for political help. As Ted reflected on what had transpired, he wondered if the board realized how close the UOA had come to closing its doors. In fact, he wondered, did the board members fully understand the importance of their position on the board during periods of crisis as well as normalcy? And should Orangelo have done a better job of informing them of their overall fiduciary duties and responsibilities, including assistance in identifying supplemental philanthropic, private, and public funding sources? Ted wondered if board members knew how important they were to the agency, especially "when the funding stops."

Questions and Instructions

1. How would you characterize the funding relationship that existed between the national AUOA and state UOA? Explain.

2. What could be done to resolve the myriad of problems presented in the case, especially the funding mechanism used by the administering agencies? Please elaborate.

3. Do you believe that this type of financial problem is commonly or uncommonly faced by agencies dependent on funding from the national level? Can you provide relevant examples of similar funding problems in your own state? Please discuss.

4. Considerably frustrated by the existing funding process, Ted Jacobs finally resorted to using the political process. What were the implications of his actions, both in the near term and the long term? What were the positive and negative effects of his actions?

5. What role, if any, should Orangelo Baldwin have played in the financial dilemma presented in this case study? What role should a board of directors play when faced with this type of financial exigency?

PART VIII

MANAGING VOLUNTEERS AND STAFF[*]

Volunteering is an important and distinguishing feature of civil society in countries around the globe. Volunteering and voluntarism represent a distinctive aspect of nonprofit organizations.[1] It is almost impossible to discuss the nonprofit sector without mentioning volunteers, and indeed, it is not uncommon to hear the nonprofit sector called the "voluntary sector." Because volunteers and nonprofits fit together so closely, many of us mentally connect voluntarism with the nonprofit sector only, even though many citizens also volunteer with government libraries, fire departments, emergency medical services systems, schools, veterans' hospitals, and numerous other public agencies and programs.[2] In 2016, 25 percent of Americans age 16 and older who were not disabled or serving on active duty in the military reported volunteering with an organization. The biggest gain in volunteer activity from the previous years involved collecting and distributing food.[3]

Volunteering and Voluntarism

Ram A. Cnaan, Femida Handy, and Margaret Wadsworth rightfully argue that *voluntarism* and *volunteer* are "rich concepts" that cannot be explained adequately in a single-sentence definition.[4] They observe that definitions of *volunteer* vary on four key dimensions: the voluntary nature of the act, the nature of the reward, the context or auspices under which the volunteer activity is performed, and who benefits. Each of these dimensions has "steps" that differentiate between volunteers and nonvolunteers. For example, in the dimension of free choice, three key categories emerge: (1) free will (the ability to voluntarily choose), (2) the relative lack of coercion, and (3) the obligation to volunteer. While all definitions would accept free will as relevant in defining a volunteer, pure definitions would not accept the relative lack of coercion, and only the broadest definition would include court-ordered "volunteers" or students in a required service program fulfilling their obligation as volunteers.[5]

Studies of volunteering have escalated over the past three decades, and a variety of theoretical frameworks have emerged to guide the studies. These include sociological theories that focus on individual sociodemographic characteristics such as race, gender, and social class and economic theories that treat volunteerism as a form of unpaid labor motivated by the promise of rewards.

Psychological studies of motivation may be embedded in a sociological framework that explores the origins of motives in social structures or the economic study of rewards and costs of volunteerism can be embedded in a psychological theory that subjective dispositions, such as empathy, condition

 DOI: 10.4324/9781003387800-37

the rationality of certain behaviors or in a sociology theory that factors in circles of friends or memberships in formal organizations as moderators of costs and benefits.[6]

Marc A. Musick and John Wilson offer five reasons for the growing interest in volunteerism research: (1) volunteers (and nonprofit organizations) are increasingly viewed by political actors as means for helping government agencies achieve important public policy goals; (2) the growth of identity politics has spawned a wide range of groups that draw heavily on volunteer labor; (3) old modes of civic engagement and associational life have changed and are seen as a threat to the fabric of civil society; (4) traditional notions about what counts as productive labor are being challenged, and volunteering has been absorbed into this broader investigation of how work is being restructured and redefined; and (5) the nonprofit sector is demanding science-based information about volunteering to use for more effective recruitment and retention.[7] Other scholars have been raising questions about the nature of volunteers, the phenomenon of voluntarism, and the cultural and ethnic aspects of volunteerism.[8] Answers to these questions will help unravel the complexities of the nonprofit sector and are vitally important to the trustees and managers of the thousands of nonprofit organizations that rely on volunteers to staff their programs, serve on their boards, and stuff their envelopes. There are, however, definitional complexities of what it means to use the word *volunteering*.[9] Although most of us have a general idea of what it means to volunteer and we seldom question the idea that volunteering is "unpaid work," where does volunteerism end and similar activities such as participating in a voluntary association, social activism, and or caring for an elderly relative begin? Do we want to consider helping one's elderly neighbor clear snow from their driveway a volunteer act? The concept of volunteering is paradoxical on many fronts. For example, depicting volunteerism as "unpaid labor" ignores the many volunteers who receive reimbursement for their time and travel or claim these as charitable gifts on their income tax returns. AmeriCorps is one of the best-known volunteer programs in the United States, and it pays workers. This is true of other stipend-based programs as well, including the foster grandparent program in the United States and the "Good Neighbors" initiative of the UK nonprofit Age Concern, among others.

Why People Volunteer

Volunteering provides a way to help others in the community and also offers a means for "gaining self-fulfillment, skills, confidence, and a social network."[10] The reasons people volunteer have long fascinated academic researchers.[11] Explanations include altruistic or values-based motives, social motives, and utilitarian motives. Altruistic or values-based motives include religious beliefs, support for causes, and a desire to help others. Indeed, in a recent study, almost all volunteers (96 percent) reported feeling compassion toward people in need.[12] Those whose motives are social may be looking to extend their social networks, volunteering because friends or colleagues do so, or responding to a variety of other social pressures to volunteer.[13] Utilitarian motives underlie voluntarism by those seeking to enhance their human capital by gaining work experience and job training, developing new skills, exploring career paths, enhancing their résumés, and making useful contacts.[14]

Successful nonprofit organizations must appeal to the motivational needs of volunteers and use their talents appropriately. In his classic piece on motivation, David McClelland identified three need-based motives that affect human activity: the needs for achievement, power, and affiliation.[15] Individuals have varying degrees of need in each of these three areas. In another seminal piece on motivation, Abraham Maslow offered a needs-based hierarchical model.[16] Here, individuals are initially motivated by lower-level needs, but once those are satisfied, they seek to satisfy higher-level needs. Thus, an individual who is struggling to meet the basic physiological needs for food, clothing, and shelter will not be "motivated" by higher-level, more abstract needs. Maslow believed that most people in our society move among different levels of the needs for safety and security, affiliation, and self-esteem. Recognizing the differences in these motives can assist nonprofit organizations in developing recruiting approaches and also in shaping volunteers' tasks.

Although managers in nonprofit organizations do not need to read McClelland or Maslow to know that people tend to behave in ways that help them satisfy their needs, their failure to understand the importance of tending to these needs may result in preventable turnover among volunteers. Today, volunteer managers work with a wide variety of people from all walks of life. The recruitment and retention of volunteer labor must be a priority for nonprofits as they seek to build and engage a dedicated volunteer workforce.

Managing Volunteers

Nonprofits that are thinking about using volunteers need to consider how volunteers would be used and managed. Volunteer labor is not free labor in that managing volunteers consumes considerable staff time, effort, and patience. Add to that the cost of supplies and training, volunteers' possible lack of clarity on organizational expectations, and the unpredictability of staff reactions to their presence. "Problems associated with volunteers' limited time, uncertain motives, and high degree of individual independence can result in debilitating levels of organizational uncertainty."[17] In addition, as is noted in the two readings included in Part VIII, tensions between and among staff and volunteers is not uncommon. Volunteers and staff wear many hats, and the reasons people choose to volunteer or take a paid position with a nonprofit vary significantly from person to person. Nonprofits may be significantly professionalized with clear roles and succinct job descriptions for volunteers, or these may be in short supply or absent altogether. Shifting sets of activities and new projects also require personnel to adjust their perspectives about the importance of the work that they do and how to carry out tasks. This then creates a need for adjustments in the amount of oversight necessary to ensure that staff and volunteers can successfully accomplish tasks and goals.

In a 2007–2008 study of volunteering and giving in the United Kingdom, the most common activities undertaken by regular formal volunteers were organizing or helping run an activity or event and raising or handling money.[18] A nonprofit organization's needs must be clearly identified for the volunteers, and activities should be assigned that meet the volunteers' primary needs. Which tasks are necessary, and what knowledge, skills, and abilities are required of volunteers to carry out these tasks? What time commitments are necessary? By differentiating among the skills needed and the investments of time required to carry out different types of useful activities, an organization can broaden its volunteer base to accommodate a wider variety of volunteers and target specialized interests and abilities. In recent years, for example, virtual volunteering via online technology and short-term episodic volunteering have both been on the rise.[19] Such opportunities have been especially popular with younger volunteers.

Differentiating among the types of tasks an organization needs to have done makes it easier to create successful matches with volunteers' needs, and it can also help identify areas in which existing volunteers may develop new skills and abilities. Developing volunteers requires that an organization (1) know what tasks it needs to have performed and the skills necessary to do so, (2) assess the needs of individual volunteers, and (3) create an organizational process that allows volunteers to grow through strategies such as job enrichment.

Risk Management and Other Concerns

Nonprofit organizations must consider the risks associated with using volunteers and the nature of the activities that volunteers will perform. Oversight, training, and feedback will be needed to successfully manage volunteers. Policies must be in place that anticipate potential high-risk situations. For example, will volunteers working with the public be able to make discretionary decisions about the type or level of services received? Will performance reviews be conducted and, if so, by whom? Will volunteers be working with vulnerable populations or operating motor vehicles? What background checks are necessary, and what licenses are required for volunteers to be able to legally perform their tasks? An organization's failure to protect vulnerable recipient populations can result in charges of negligent recruiting or negligent hiring.[20] Will volunteers be going into the homes of persons who are elderly or disabled? Should the volunteer be bonded? Will the volunteer be working in dangerous locations, working late at night, or working alone? Will staff members be overseeing the work of volunteers? Is it ever permissible for volunteers to supervise paid staff members? Nonprofit organizations must anticipate and conduct periodic organizational assessments to answer these types of questions. In the US, the Volunteer Protection Act of 1997 offers guidance to nonprofits for assessing their own organization's risks and understanding the extent to which liabilities may arise. The act helps protect volunteers and organizations with regard to liabilities that may arise during the scope of the volunteering activities performed.[21] Amendments to the act proposed by Congress in 2017 provide additional insight into the importance of understanding the liabilities and protections offered in the original legislation.

Many nonprofit organizations also carry liability insurance to protect volunteers (including the board of directors) and the organization. For example, volunteers in a local needle exchange program may be at risk of a needle stick from a dirty syringe. Who should pay for the HIV and hepatitis prevention treatment? Who should provide counseling for the volunteers whose lives will change dramatically? Who should pay to treat a volunteer driver who injures her back while assisting elderly patients in and out of an assisted living center's van? If a volunteer is sued while providing services, who will pay for the legal defense of the volunteer, the volunteer director, the executive director, and members of the board of trustees?

Indemnification for volunteers in some form is essential in this litigation-happy society. Often, legal action taken against a volunteer's actions is only a first step. The plaintiff may have little or no desire to take the volunteer's assets, but establishing the legal culpability of the volunteer is a first step toward also establishing the nonprofit organization's responsibility and culpability. This is the doctrine of deep pockets.

Legal liability is an unavoidable part of the volunteer environment in the United States today. The old adage is painfully true: "There are only two types of volunteers (and employees)—those who have been sued and those who are going to be sued." Nonprofit organizations are at least partially responsible for the actions of their volunteers. An attorney who is well versed in tort liability law can be an invaluable resource for an executive director and a board of trustees.

Recognizing Volunteers

Like paid employees, volunteers appreciate being recognized for their contributions. Many nonprofits and communities sponsor an annual celebration to formally recognize volunteers. Those recognized may be presented with a certificate, plaque, or other acknowledgment of appreciation. Many nonprofit organizations track the number of hours donated by volunteers and proudly announce to the media and the community the time and energy expended by its volunteers.

When a volunteer leaves an organization, it is wise to conduct an exit interview to learn what is working well and what could be changed to improve the experiences of current and future volunteers. Exit interviews can also help the director of volunteers and the executive director detect trends, become aware of general opportunities or problems, and identify problems that could adversely affect the organization if not remedied.

The Future of Volunteers and Voluntarism

Volunteers will become increasingly important for nonprofits over the upcoming decades for several reasons:

(1) Our population will live longer and have more productive years after retirement. Volunteering provides retirees with opportunities to use their skills and feel useful while making a difference.

(2) Many higher educational institutions now offer volunteer opportunities—through community service, service learning, internships, and outreach programs—as a way for students to learn to live more fulfilling lives, and some are requiring participation for graduation. Among young volunteers, 44 percent believe that "people working together" can make a great deal of difference in solving local problems.[22]

(3) A few government programs are providing a new variety of paid volunteers who may be available to nonprofit organizations. The Corporation for National and Community Service (CNCS) is a federal government agency that engages more than five million Americans in service through its core programs, which include Senior Corps, the Social Innovation Fund, and AmeriCorps. The best-known of these, AmeriCorps (founded in 1994), pays stipends and grants to qualified individuals that enable them to provide services through nonprofit organizations while also helping them finance their college education.[23]

(4) More services, skills, and energy from volunteers will be required in the upcoming years because we are in a long-term era of declining government funding for human services and the arts, increasing populations with service needs, and expanded service mandates.[24]

The last reason for increasing voluntarism over the coming years is perhaps the most important: if nonprofit organizations do not provide services for the many vulnerable populations, it is questionable whether other organizations will. More volunteers will be needed than perhaps at any other time in our nation's history. Recognizing this need, studies are on the rise to learn more about attracting various groups to volunteering and creating circumstances and environments that will attract and retain volunteers. To be more inclusive and to strive for more equitable outcomes are driving factors for continually evaluating our communities and the needs of our organization and for extending the reach of nonprofit services.

Special events such as the once-a-decade White House Conferences on Aging (WHCOA) issue calls for new and more meaningful volunteer opportunities for older Americans.[22] The 2015 WHCOA raised similar calls to ensure that older Americans remain engaged, active, and vital. In addition, the WHCOA 2015 recognized the need to work collaboratively with the HHS Administration for Community Living and Services and Advocacy for GLBT Seniors (SAGE) to host key stakeholders from state and local aging programs and the LGBT community to analyze available data and identify next steps for improving Older Americans Act outreach to older LGBT adults.[23]

To meet the rising needs for the services of volunteers, nonprofit organizations will need to continue to strengthen their ability to recruit and retain volunteers from all walks of life, match volunteer needs with organizational and community needs, manage volunteers well, develop and implement training programs, and reduce liability risks.

Readings Reprinted in Part VIII

The first reading in Part VIII is "Exploring the Dynamics of Volunteer and Staff Interactions" by Heather Rimes, Rebecca Nesbit, Robert K. Christensen, and the late Jeffrey L. Brudney. Here, the authors note that the quality of the relationships between volunteers and paid staff can have far-reaching consequences for organizations that utilize volunteer programs to support service delivery. As the authors show, conflict in interactions arise most often due to communication problems, behavioral or attitudinal issues, perception of job vulnerability and divergent expectations, lack of trust, and workflow integration hurdles. Training is recommended by the authors to help staff and volunteers work together successfully.

In the second reading, "Volunteers as Boundary Workers: Negotiating Tensions Between Volunteerism and Professionalism in Nonprofit Organizations", Kirstie McAllum uses a boundary work framework to analyze how volunteers from two nonprofit human services organizations navigated the tensions between volunteerism and professionalism. The study offers insights for nonprofit organizations wishing to professionalize their volunteer workforce by specifying how volunteer job types, organizational structure, and interactional partners' feedback impact volunteers' ability to engage in boundary crossing, passing, and spanning.

Volunteer labor is a relatively fragile shared resource. In essence, a community volunteer endowment must be carefully managed and cultivated. Stewardship is required of volunteer managers, and they must work closely with staff and with other organizations in the community to carefully cultivate a diversity of volunteers and volunteer experiences. Roger Lohmann expresses a similar sentiment in his well-known book on nonprofits, *The Commons*:

> The endowment of any commons ordinarily consists of its treasures of money, property and marketable goods; its collection of precious, priceless objects; and its repertories of routines, cults, skills, techniques and other meaningful behavior learned by participants in the commons . . . [and] . . . *passed on to others for the common good* [emphasis added].[24]

Case Studies in Part VIII

In the first case study, "Changing of the Guard: Leadership Change in Nonprofit Organizations" by Betsy Hull, Benjamin S. Bingle, and C. Kenneth Meyer, the challenges of acquiring new leadership after a tragic suicide are identified. The case asks the reader to consider the roles of volunteers such as the members of a board of directors and staff in selecting a new executive director. Staff members felt slighted when the new hire process did not include their input into the selection processes. Should staff have input into new hires? Should volunteers not serving on the board of directors be included? The case study challenges the reader to consider just how inclusive processes such as hiring should be. In addition, to what extent do current policies address succession planning and inclusive processes for staff and volunteers?

Managerial concerns also arise in "Turning the Tide: Transitioning from Volunteers to Paid Staff." In this case study, significant growing pains within an organization present a board of directors with some tough decisions that will directly affect the residents of a community in need.

Notes

* The authors would like to thank Peter M. Nelson for his contributions to this introduction.

1. Jeffrey L. Brudney and Lucas C. P. M. Meijs, "It Ain't Natural: Toward a New (Natural) Resource Conceptualization for Volunteer Management," *Nonprofit and Voluntary Sector Quarterly* 38, no. 4 (August 2009): 564–581.

2. Jeffrey L. Brudney, *Fostering Volunteer Programs in the Public Sector* (San Francisco: Jossey-Bass, 1990).

3. Thom Patterson, "Stats Reveal How Many Americans Volunteer and Where," CNN, updated July 20, 2018. Data are from a survey released by the US Bureau of Labor Statistics and sponsored by the Corporation of National and Community Service. www.cnn.com/2018/07/19/us/volunteering-statistics-cfc/index.html (accessed February 17, 2022).

4. Ram A. Cnaan, Femida Handy, and Margaret Wadsworth, "Defining Who Is a Volunteer: Conceptual and Empirical Considerations," *Nonprofit and Voluntary Sector Quarterly* 25, no. 3 (September 1996): 364–383.

5. Ibid., 370.

6. John Wilson, "Volunteerism Research: A Review Essay," *Nonprofit and Voluntary Sector Quarterly* 41, no. 2 (2012): 176–212.

7. Marc A. Musick and John Wilson, "What Is Volunteering?" in Marc A. Musick and John Wilson, *Volunteers: A Social Profile* (Indianapolis: Indiana University Press, 2008), 4–6.

8. Robert D. Putnam, *Bowling Alone: Revised and Updated: The Collapse and Revival of American Community* (New York: Simon and Schuster, 2020).

9. Op cit. Musick and Wilson (2008).

10. *Giving and Volunteering in the USA: Findings from a National Survey* (Washington, DC: Independent Sector, 2016).

11. Femida Handy, Ram A. Cnaan, Lesley Hustinx, Chulhee Kang, Jeffrey L. Brudney, Debbie Haski-Leventhal, Kirsten Holmes, Lucas C. P. M. Meijs, Anne Birgitta Pessi, Bhagyashree Ranade, Naoto Yamauchi, and Sinisa Zrinscak, "A Cross-Cultural Examination of Student Volunteering: Is It All About Resume Building?" *Nonprofit and Voluntary Sector Quarterly* 39, no. 3 (June 2010): 498–523.

12. Ibid., 20.

13. Lorenzo Cappellari and Gilberto Turati, "Volunteer Labour Supply: The Role of Workers' Motivations," *Annals of Public Cooperative Economics* 75 (2004): 619–643.

14. Ram A. Cnaan and Robin S. Goldberg-Glen, "Measuring Motivation to Volunteer in Human Services," *Journal of Applied Behavioral Science* 27 (1991): 269–284.

15. David C. McClelland, *Human Motivation* (New York: Cambridge University Press, 1987).

16. Abraham Maslow, *Motivation and Personality* (New York: Harper & Row, 1954).

17. Jone L. Pearce, "Volunteers at Work," in Jone L. Pearce, *Volunteers: The Organizational Behavior of Unpaid Workers* (London: Routledge, 1993), 3–14. See also Heather Rimes, Rebecca Nesbit, and Jeffrey L. Brudney, "Exploring the Dynamics of Volunteer and Staff Interactions." *Nonprofit Management and Leadership,* 28 no. 2 (Winter 2017): 195–213; and Kirstie McAllum, "Volunteers as Boundary Workers: Negotiating Tensions Between Volunteerism and Professionalism in Nonprofit Organizations." *Management Communication Quarterly,* 32 no. 4 (2019): 534–564.

18. *Communities and Local Government: 2007–08 Citizenship Survey: Volunteering and Charitable Giving Topic Report* (London: Communities and Local Government, 2008): 6.

19. Lesley Hustinx, "I Quit, Therefore I Am? Volunteer Turnover and the Politics of Self-Actualization," *Nonprofit and Voluntary Sector Quarterly* 39, no. 2 (2010): 236–255.

20. Negligent recruiting, hiring, retention, or supervision occurs when the organization knows its responsibility but fails to act to meet that responsibility. A variety of Circuit Court of Appeals and Supreme Court cases have upheld the responsibility of an organization to adhere to proper practices in these areas. See *Hartsell v. Duplex Products, Inc.* (4th Circuit, 1997); *SCI v. Hartford Fire Ins.* (11th Circuit, 1998); *Burlington Industries, Inc. v. Ellerth,* 524 U.S. 742, 754 (1998); and *Faragher v. Boca Raton,* 524 U.S. 775, 804, n. 4 (1998).

21. Volunteer Protection Act 1997, www.govinfo.gov/content/pkg/PLAW-105publ19/pdf/PLAW-105publ19.pdf

22. Center for Information and Research on Civic Learning and Engagement, 2006, *Civic and Political Health of the Nation* (Medford, MA: Tufts University Press, 2006), www.civicyouth.org(accessed June 25, 2010).

23. Corporation for National and Community Service, *AmeriCorps State and National*, www.nationalservice.gov/programs (accessed August 5, 2014).

24. Linda S. Hartenian, "Nonprofit Agency Dependence on Direct Service and Indirect Support Volunteers: An Empirical Investigation," *Nonprofit Management and Leadership* 17, no. 2 (Spring 2007): 319–334.

▶ CHAPTER 16

Exploring the Dynamics of Volunteer and Staff Interactions
From Satisfaction to Conflict

HEATHER RIMES, REBECCA NESBIT, ROBERT K. CHRISTENSEN AND
JEFFREY L. BRUDNEY

VOLUNTEERS SERVE AS key sources of human capital for many organizations in the public and nonprofit spheres, often working in conjunction with the paid staff in those organizations (Gidron 1985). Engaging volunteers requires investments of effort, time, training, and fiscal resources so that both organizations and volunteers benefit. Nancy Macduff (2012, 256) argues that "the relationship between volunteers and staff can influence the success or failure of a program . . . and the ability to make positive organizational changes." As such, a purposive volunteer-staff relationship is critical. Despite the importance of these working relationships, many organizations fall prey to the misperception that volunteers are a source of "free labor" (Handy and Mook 2011). Such organizations may inadequately invest in the management of these valuable human resources (Hager and Brudney 2004; Machin and Paine 2008). Too often, paid employees find themselves inadvertently directing and supervising volunteer labor, rather than being trained and prepared to take on this role (Nesbit et al. 2016). This situation can be particularly challenging when organizations increase their use of volunteers, such as during times of fiscal constraint when increased reliance on volunteers is often utilized as a strategy to reduce personnel costs (Brudney 1990, 1993; Dover 2010).

Notwithstanding the aforementioned challenges, organizations cannot ignore the dynamics of volunteer-staff interactions, because tension between volunteers and staff leads to dissatisfaction and costly turnover in both groups (Hobson and Heler 2007; Kulik 2006; Rogelberg et al. 2010). We argue that equipping staff to navigate daily interactions with volunteers is therefore a key component of successful volunteer involvement strategies specifically and of organizational effectiveness more generally.

DOI: 10.4324/9781003387800-38

We adopt a mixed-methods case study design to investigate several aspects of volunteer-staff interactions.

We consider the questions of how volunteers and paid staff view their mutual interactions and why some areas of interaction might be vulnerable to conflict.

Dynamics of Volunteer-Staff Interactions: From Satisfaction to Conflict

In order to investigate the dynamics of volunteer-staff interactions, we turn first to the relevant literature. Our review identifies two overarching, although not equally explored, themes: satisfaction and conflict.

Satisfaction

The importance of satisfaction in the volunteer-staff relationship context often builds on ideas and theories in the general management literature. Empirical management studies link employee relationships with supervisors and coworkers to job satisfaction (Hackman and Oldham 1975; Smith, Kendall, and Hulin 1969), and job satisfaction, in turn, has been connected to outcomes such as job performance and turnover intention (see Judge et al. 2001 for an overview). When volunteers experience positive social relationships in the host organization, they are more likely to indicate that they will continue volunteering (Galindo-Kuhn and Guzley 2002). Other empirical studies of volunteers in organizations find that negative interpersonal experiences or interactions with other volunteers or paid staff are one of the main reasons volunteers leave the organization (Brodie et al. 2011).

Rogelberg and colleagues (2010) explore similar assumptions from the perspective of the employee rather than the volunteer; they find that paid staff who report poor experiences

with volunteers are more likely to feel stressed and overworked and are more likely to express turnover intentions. Their study suggests that an organization's volunteer resource management practices are key for maintaining positive volunteer-staff relationships. Additionally, poor volunteer-staff relationships are associated with outcomes such as decreased job satisfaction and increased turnover intentions among both paid staff and volunteers (Hobson and Heler 2007; Kulik 2006; Rogelberg et al. 2010).

Conflict

Conflict is the second theme we find in the scholarly literature (Macduff 2012). Perhaps due to the altruism implied by the nature of volunteerism and the general feeling that organizations should be appreciative of unpaid labor (Brudney 1990), we note an apparent reluctance to acknowledge and address volunteer-staff conflict. Pearce (1993, 142) describes this situation as "one of the unpleasant secrets of nonprofit organizations." Conflict in these relationships is likely more widespread than observers realize. For example, Wandersman and Alderman (1993) report that in one organization 66 percent of staff have had some sort of conflict with volunteers. We argue that the literature related to volunteer-staff conflict may be categorized by discussions of four broad mechanisms leading to conflict in volunteer-staff relationships: divergent expectations, communication issues, behavioral or emotional discord, and perceptions of job vulnerability.

Divergent Expectations

Volunteers and paid staff have different relationships—contractually and often functionally—with their organization (Studer and von Schnurbein 2013). Conflict can arise when the nature of these relationships leads the two groups to have divergent expectations for their mutual work. For example, a 2006 study traces conflict within a community sport organization; the staff members in the study emphasize professional and legal standards, while volunteers demonstrate more concern for their social environment and the ability to work within their own time constraints (Taylor et al. 2006). Studies of volunteer use in public libraries echo these issues, particularly in describing the expectations of paid staff that certain aspects of their job are not appropriate for volunteers, and that the use of volunteers in these roles can undermine professional standards and represent a threat to confidentiality (Nicol and Johnson 2008; Roy 1984). Kreutzer and Jäger (2011) argue that another key factor underlying divergent expectations may be that volunteers and staff have opposing perceptions about organizational identity and thus the roles that each group should play. Ultimately, divergent expectations may lead to conflict around assertions that volunteers are not capable of performing certain tasks or beliefs that volunteers are not pulling their weight in various roles (Wandersman and Alderman 1993).

Communication Issues

Communication issues can also be a key source of volunteer-staff conflict. Wandersman and Alderman (1993) conduct a case study of a state division of the American Cancer Society in which they identify lack of communication as one of the most commonly reported conflicts described by interviewees. Other studies describe specific communication deficiencies that contribute to antagonistic relationships between volunteers and staff, such as insufficient acknowledgment of volunteer contributions and unclear definition of organizational goals (Studer and von Schnurbein 2013) as well as structural barriers due to lack of physical or organizational proximity (Macduff 2012). Garner and Garner (2011) utilize Hirschman's (1970) theory of exit, voice, and loyalty to examine connections between volunteers' ability to communicate feedback to their organization and indicators of

volunteer satisfaction and turnover. They suggest "the voluntary nature of their work may . . . place some volunteers on the periphery of the organization's communication" (Garner and Garner 2011, 814).

Behavioral/Emotional Discord

A third source of conflict pertains to behavioral or emotional discord between volunteers and paid staff members. These types of friction are typically ignited by interpersonal incompatibilities that may manifest in a variety of ways. Researchers in the *Pathways through Participation* project in England conducted 100 in-depth interviews with volunteers in which they asked volunteers about their current and past volunteering experiences. Interpersonal issues in the host organization were a primary factor leading to discontinuation of volunteering. Problems commonly reported included insular groups and cliques, backstabbing, infighting, personal politics and conflicts, power dynamics, hassle or pressure, and people just not getting along (Brodie et al. 2011).

Job Vulnerability

The mere perception of job vulnerability may have the potential to incite volunteer-staff conflict. Researchers observe that staff members often fear that volunteers may take jobs from paid employees or that use of volunteers will be cited as a reason for reducing an organization's budget (Brudney 1990; Scheier 2003). Similar concerns may be expressed from the volunteer perspective in situations where new staff is hired to take on duties that were formerly performed by volunteers.

Case Description

Our case is a large library system comprising twenty library locations in an urban area in a southeastern state. In 2010 the municipality reduced the library system's budget by

$15 million, a 39 percent decrease. As a result, the library laid off 35 percent of its total staff across all library locations (175 staff members out of 500) and was forced to close two of its smaller branch library locations and reduce hours of operation at several others. In the six months following the personnel reductions, the library system sought to double its volunteer use as a means of trying to maintain service levels and increase hours of operation at some library locations. Volunteers were used in a variety of tasks, but shelving books was crucial at all library locations. At the time this study commenced in 2012, the library system maintained about 350 paid staff and had expanded its volunteer program to include approximately 500 volunteers (up from about 250 volunteers in 2010 before the crisis).

Prior to the budget crisis, the library system had utilized smaller numbers of volunteers for many years and had an infrastructure already in place for managing library volunteers. The most recent precrisis change to the library's volunteer program structure had taken place in 2002, when the library system had hired a central volunteer coordinator to assist branches with managing volunteers. Under the volunteer coordinator's direction, branch managers selected employee(s) to serve as volunteer managers at each branch. The central coordinator provided support and training to the volunteer managers. In addition, the coordinator centralized some volunteer management tasks, such as posting volunteer job descriptions on the library system website and ensuring that incoming applications for volunteers were directed to the appropriate volunteer manager. This existing infrastructure for managing volunteers was instrumental to the success of the volunteer ramp-up.

Many employees who had previously served as volunteer managers were among those laid off in early 2010, which led the majority of library locations to shift volunteer management responsibilities to remaining employees, most of whom had little to no previous managerial

experience, with volunteers or otherwise. To ease this transition, the central library system volunteer coordinator provided a minimum level of training to these staff members (hereafter referred to as volunteer managers), including two workshops on the basics of volunteer management duties and direction to online resources about volunteer management. The central administration of the library system also expressed general expectations for the adoption of several volunteer management best practices at the branch locations, such as a standard volunteer application process, an interview screening process, and mechanisms for volunteer recognition.

Due to the underlying fiscal reasons for the volunteer ramp-up, concerns arose about potential negative consequences for volunteer-staff relationships. For instance, if staff felt that volunteers were taking their jobs, then library branches might experience turf battles or hostile working relationships between the two groups. Further, staff members might resent assumptions by library administrators that volunteers with only a modicum of training could carry out the professional duties usually performed by staff members, again exacerbating the potential for tension between the two groups.

Study Design

According to Small (2011) our study can be classified as a mixed methods case study that employs both mixed data collection (utilizing data from surveys, interviews, and a focus group) and mixed data analysis (utilizing multiple analytical techniques). It is also a complementary design, in which the "value in combining types of data lies in the ability of one type to compensate for weaknesses in the other" (Small 2011, 64). In our case, open-ended survey questions and qualitative information from interviews and a focus group enhance our interpretation of our quantitative survey data. The data are nested; that is, participants with specific roles (all volunteer managers and selected volunteers and general staff) are given surveys and also asked to participate in in-depth interviews. The design is essentially concurrent with the data collection for all the phases of the project occurring in quick succession. The survey questions were not developed based on answers to prior interviews; instead, the interview and survey questions are complementary. The qualitative data are used to add depth to the quantitative findings and to illuminate important themes not captured in the quantitative data.

Data

In their study of volunteer and staff attitudes and behaviors, Laczo and Hanisch (2000, 457) argue, "one way in which the interaction between volunteer workers and paid employees can be understood is to determine the perception each type of worker has of the other." To understand these mutual perceptions among library volunteers and staff, in March 2012 we collected survey data. We invited all current volunteers and staff members within the library system to participate in an anonymous, confidential electronic survey. A total of 119 staff members and 172 volunteers responded to the survey invitation (response rates of 35 percent and 34 percent, respectively). The information provided by one of the volunteer respondents had to be dropped due to response entry issues, bringing the total to 171 volunteer respondents. Of the respondents, 22 of the staff (18 percent) and 137 of the volunteers (80 percent) began work at the library during or after the volunteer ramp-up.

The electronic surveys included core sets of identical questions that queried both staff members and volunteers about their perceptions of the library's volunteer program and its effectiveness, beliefs about volunteer/staff relationships, self-reports of internal motivations, and demographic characteristics. Surveys contained additional questions relevant to specific respondent groups: staff members described the frequency of their interactions with volunteers,

perceptions of volunteers at their library location, and perspectives on the adequacy of library system support for the volunteer program; whereas volunteers indicated their motivations for volunteering, personal impacts of volunteering, and the major tasks they performed for the library. The lead researchers developed the survey questions based on a review of the literature and discussions with the central volunteer coordinator at the library. Table 16.1 presents basic demographic information for both staff and volunteer survey respondents.

In addition to the survey data, we conducted thirty-four in-depth, semi-structured interviews with staff members who were currently, or had recently been, responsible for supervising volunteers at their respective library locations (response rate 100 percent). Two of these volunteer managers had joined the library system after the volunteer ramp-up. Given the volunteer manager's unique position of acting as a liaison between volunteers and other staff members, we expected these interviewees to be cognizant of both staff members' and volunteers' concerns with the volunteer program. These interviews took place in January and February 2012.

With the exception of education level, the volunteer managers have a demographic profile that is similar to the rest of the library staff; Table 16.2 presents this information.

Although the bulk of our analysis in this article focuses on the survey data and on the volunteer manager interviews described above, both of which are representative of the entire library system, we also draw on some qualitative data collected in an earlier phase of the larger research project. The earlier phase was conducted in fall 2011 and involved an in-depth investigation of three of the twenty library locations. In this phase we collected a combination of information from in-person volunteer interviews (six volunteers at two library locations, all of whom had joined the library after the volunteer ramp-up), a focus group (nine volunteers at one library location, about half of whom

TABLE 16.1 Library Staff and Volunteer Characteristics

	Mean	SD	Min	Max
Staff Characteristics (n = 119)				
Female	0.85	0.36	0	1
Age	45.61	12.69	25	72
Years of service	8.28	6.53	0	29
Some college	0.08	0.28	0	1
Associate's degree	0.08	0.28	0	1
Bachelor's degree	0.39	0.49	0	1
Master of library science	0.35	0.48	0	1
Other graduate degree	0.09	0.29	0	1
Hours/Week with vols.	5.22	6.23	0	30
Volunteer Characteristics (n =171)				
Female	0.81	0.39	0	1
Age	58.8	17.6	15	84
Years of service	2.67	3.63	1	30
Less than high school	0.07	0.25	0	1
High school	0.07	0.26	0	1
Some college	0.11	0.32	0	1
Associate's degree	0.05	0.21	0	1
Bachelor's degree	0.43	0.50	0	1
Graduate degree	0.27	0.45	0	1
Volunteer hours/week	2.95	2.93	0	30

TABLE 16.2 Volunteer Manager Characteristics

	Mean	Min	Max
Volunteer Manager Characteristics (n = 34)			
Female	0.88	0	1
Age	47	29	64
Years as vol. mgr.	2.6	.33	12
Years at library	11.7	1	34
Some college	0.12	0	1
Associate's degree	0.09	0	1
Bachelor's degree	0.35	0	1
Master of library science	0.35	0	1
Other graduate degree	0.09	0	1

had started volunteering after the ramp-up), and in-person staff interviews (fourteen general staff with no volunteer supervision duties, all of whom had been with the library prior to the volunteer ramp-up). Although not the central focus of our analysis, we utilize this additional interview data to add depth to our survey data as well as to offer guidance as to whether volunteer manager interviews describe both volunteer and staff perspectives adequately.

One member of our research team completed all coding of the data from interviews and focus groups. The coder employed an iterative, thematic coding process, beginning first with a deductive approach, directed by key concepts in the literature. The researcher then processed the qualitative data again, this time using inductive coding, to allow for the emergence of new themes. After conducting deductive and inductive coding, the researcher organized these themes by the frequency of their appearance across all interviews. . . .

Findings

Our findings reflect on and add nuance to the themes of satisfaction and conflict identified in our initial literature review. In the following sections we discuss the overarching themes, first from the volunteers' perspectives, followed by staff members' perspectives. Our analysis reveals two new categories of conflict emergent in our data: unsuccessful workflow integration and lack of trust, which we discuss in turn. To depict these and other themes, we use illustrative quotes from open-ended survey responses as well as interview questions, identified according to the respondent's role: general staff (GS), volunteer manager (VM), or volunteer (V) and a respondent number.

Satisfaction: Volunteer Perspectives

We find that volunteers generally express high levels of satisfaction regarding their interactions with library staff members. Electronic surveys asked volunteers to indicate, on a 7-point scale

ranging from strongly disagree to strongly agree, their level of agreement with a list of statements that described volunteer-staff interactions. These statements included whether the respondent feels that staff appreciate volunteer work, work effectively with volunteers, listen to volunteer input, make volunteers feel important, provide helpful feedback, communicate promptly, and enjoy working with volunteers. Table 16.3 shows the average scores for volunteers' responses to these items. The volunteer interviews and focus group also identify a general sense of satisfaction among participants. All volunteer interviewees expressed some degree of satisfaction regarding their relationships with library staff, represented by statements such as "They [the staff] are very positive about my work here and I enjoy it" (V1).

Satisfaction: Staff Perspectives

Staff members' survey response patterns also indicate a tendency toward satisfaction with volunteer-staff interactions. Staff members answered a set of questions identical to the ones posed to volunteers, and for the majority of statements, more than 50 percent of staff respondents indicated agree or strongly agree. These response patterns are depicted in Table 16.4.

Similarly, general staff who were interviewed indicated feelings of satisfaction regarding volunteer-staff relationships, although not to the same degree as reported by most volunteers. For instance, one staff member shares, "they've [the volunteers] made it a better place for us, I think by, as I was saying, doing the little things" (GS14). These findings are corroborated by interview data from volunteer managers who indicate that, from their perspective, the reciprocal relationship between volunteers and staff is beneficial to both parties: "Most of them [the volunteers], I think they stay because they like it and there's good camaraderie between staff. So they're getting something out of it as well as we're getting something out of it" (VM7).

TABLE 16.3 Volunteer Perceptions Regarding Volunteer/Staff Interactions

	Percentage Somewhat Agree–Strongly Agree	Percentage Neutral	Percentage Somewhat Disagree–Strongly Disagree
Volunteer Perceptions			
Staff appreciate volunteer work	98.8	0.6	0.6
Staff work effectively with volunteers	89.7	9.1	1.2
Staff listen to volunteer ideas and input	71.9	24.0	4.1
Staff make volunteers feel that their roles are important and valuable	96.4	3.0	0.6
Staff provide helpful feedback	81.7	14.2	4.2
Staff communicate promptly	92.9	3.0	4.1
I enjoy working with staff	97.6	1.8	0.6

TABLE 16.4 Staff Perceptions Regarding Volunteer/Staff Interactions

	Percentage Somewhat Agree–Strongly Agree	Percentage Neutral	Percentage Somewhat Disagree–Strongly Disagree
Staff Perceptions			
Staff appreciate volunteer work	92.4	2.5	5.0
Staff work effectively with volunteers	88.2	6.7	5.0
Staff listen to volunteer ideas and input	65.3	22.9	11.9
Staff make volunteers feel that their roles are important and valuable	88.2	3.4	8.4
Staff provide helpful feedback	72.3	17.7	10.1
Staff communicate promptly	81.5	10.9	7.6
Staff enjoy working with volunteers	79.5	14.5	6.0

Conflict: Volunteer Perspectives

Survey data show that volunteers and staff exhibit agreement regarding the facets of volunteer-staff interactions that are less satisfactory than others. We highlight these as areas where volunteer-staff conflict may be more likely to occur. For both groups the statements "staff listen to volunteer ideas and input" and "staff provide helpful feedback to volunteers" receive the lowest levels of agreement (see Tables 16.3 and 16.4). In an open-ended question asking about most needed improvements for the volunteer program, 10 percent of all volunteers who responded to the survey listed elements of feedback and training. In other responses to the open-ended survey item, volunteers indicated that handling elements of diversity, such as physical disabilities, is a weakness in the library system, another area of potential conflict. We discuss each of these points below under subheadings reflecting their alignment with the subthemes from our literature review.

Communication Issues: Lack of Feedback

Regarding communication failures in the area of feedback, one volunteer shared that the program could be improved by incorporating a "regular review of my contribution with the volunteer coordinator—don't wait to talk to me until something is wrong" (V104). Another volunteer stated, "I want to help, but I don't know what to do, so I just put books back on the shelf like I always do. Nobody seems to want to take the time to tell me how to do anything else" (V69). These comments reflect the current state of feedback processes within the library system. Three-quarters of the library branches provide feedback to volunteers solely through informal, verbal channels, if at all. In addition to supervision of volunteer performance to ensure accurate and efficient service delivery, feedback can help to protect volunteers and make sure that they are able to perform their roles comfortably. One volunteer manager relayed a story about a volunteer who was treated poorly by patrons, unbeknownst to library staff:

> For example, we had the most wonderful volunteer who was treated so poorly by the public on more than one occasion that she just said, "I can't do this anymore." So . . . she had to take a break because of some pretty bad experiences.
>
> (VM3)

Established feedback processes may help to mitigate these types of situations.

Divergent Expectations: Lack of Accommodation for Diversity

The library branches have also struggled to accommodate volunteers' physical limitations. For instance, the library attracts many retirees as volunteers. Bending and stooping to perform shelving activities, the main volunteer task at most of the branches, is very physically demanding. One volunteer states, "Many of the volunteers have physical disabilities. It would be helpful to recruit and/or keep volunteers if there were more sit-down jobs, or jobs that did not require lower shelving" (V50). To their credit, some branches have made attempts to find ways to incorporate these volunteers, but other branches indicate that they expect volunteers to self-select and opt out of volunteering if they find that the physical demands are more than they can handle. Although seeming to avoid conflict, failure to address these concerns directly may instead invite it.

Conflict: Staff Perspectives

In both surveys and interviews the staff members in our study tend to paint a less rosy picture of volunteer-staff relationships than do the volunteers. For example, t-tests in Table 16.5 demonstrate that staff score significantly lower than volunteers on each survey item related to volunteer-staff interactions.

Additionally, both survey and interview data indicate a lack of confidence on the part of paid staff regarding their competence to engage volunteers successfully. Table 16.6 shows evidence from the survey data that staff members' lowest scores are related to whether they felt prepared to interact with volunteers. Less than one-quarter of staff survey respondents (23 percent) agree or strongly agree that their previous education prepared them for the types of interactions that they would have with volunteers. Moreover, they rate the training they received through the library system even lower with respect to providing adequate preparation.

Communication Issues: Inadequate Feedback Processes and Infrastructure

Staff responses to surveys and interviews echo the volunteers' perspective that the volunteer

TABLE 16.5 *T*-Tests for Equality of Means

| | Group | | | | | | | |
| | Staff | | | Volunteer | | | | |
Statement	M	SD	n	M	SD	n	t	df
Staff appreciate volunteer work	6.03	1.29	119	6.55	.76	168	−4.30***	285
Staff work effectively with volunteers	5.80	1.24	119	6.25	1.02	165	−3.40***	282
Staff listen to volunteer ideas and input	515	1.45	118	5.58	1.35	167	−2.56*	283
Staff feel that the volunteer role is important and valuable	5.71	1.42	119	6.48	.86	167	−5.66***	284
Staff provide helpful feedback	5.20	1.38	119	5.92	1.34	169	−4.52***	286
Staff communicate promptly	5.58	1.34	119	6.30	1.13	169	−4.90***	286
I enjoy working with staff/volunteers	5.57	1.39	117	6.57	.78	167	−7.76***	282

Note: $^{*}p < .05;$ $^{***}p < .0001.$

TABLE 16.6 Staff General Beliefs about the Volunteer Program

	Percentage Somewhat Agree– Strongly Agree	Percentage Neutral	Percentage Somewhat Disagree–Strongly Disagree
Staff Beliefs			
My experience working with volunteers will be helpful to my career	56.3	31.1	12.6
My education prepared me to work with volunteers	38.1	34.8	27.1
Training from the library's central coordinator prepared me to work with volunteers	32.3	37.3	30.5
The benefits of using volunteers outweigh the costs	68.1	17.7	14.3
Staff members at my location value the work of volunteers	84.0	8.4	7.6

program's feedback infrastructure and processes are problematic and vulnerable to conflict. Most staff survey respondents (58 percent) report that their daily interactions with volunteers consist typically of giving praise and answering questions. However, they also indicate that less frequently, staff supervise volunteers. Sixty-three percent of staff survey respondents indicate that they help to supervise volunteers once per month or less. This situation alone can breed conflict due to the confusion that these role ambiguities might generate. Volunteers may expect supervisory advice from a staff member and not receive it, or they may be confused when they receive performance feedback sporadically from multiple sources.

Problems are likely exacerbated by the hands-off approach to supervision and feedback taken by most volunteer managers. Of the thirty-four volunteer managers interviewed, only four describe utilizing any formal mechanisms for providing volunteers with feedback related to their job performance. Five managers report never giving intentional feedback to volunteers about their work, and twenty-five state that any feedback given is usually informal and verbal. Importantly, and reflective of previously discussed volunteer and staff beliefs that this feedback is not always helpful, some of these managers shared that they and their staff avoid giving any critical feedback:

> Well, I think we did a lot of verbal feedback [such as] thank you for coming; we're glad you came today . . . and very rarely do we have to do negative feedback. But mainly it was positive feedback, and it was more in the way of saying thank you.
>
> (VM32)

In their efforts to avoid sounding accusatory, the paid staff may not provide enough guidance for volunteers to correct problems, allowing situations to become worse until outright conflict may become unavoidable.

In addition to breakdowns in staff-to-volunteer feedback processes, the library system exhibits a lack of communication infrastructure for volunteer-to-staff feedback. Data from volunteer manager interviews show that only four of the library branches employ a formal means for collecting volunteer input, three of which utilize periodic surveys. One volunteer manager reported that, through the survey, she was able to understand better and address some problems with volunteer-staff relationships:

> I found that out when I did the feedback questionnaire . . . they [the volunteers] would say, you know, people don't speak to me when I come in and out. And . . . sometimes they were made to feel . . . [that] the staff was condescending . . . and [were] made to feel stupid if they didn't know how to do something or they'd done something incorrectly.
>
> (VM12)

More typically, volunteer managers expressed that they were willing to listen to volunteers' ideas, but they had not thought to encourage volunteers to formally share their insights about potential improvements or changes to library services. One manager explained that she felt reluctant to encourage volunteers to share their thoughts and opinions because it could create conflict if it was seen as criticism of the status quo or of paid staff members:

> I think . . . people [staff] are getting upset about them [the volunteers] making suggestions. But a suggestion is all in the way you present it . . . I think when you're first starting, you have got to consider . . . [yourself] like a new employee, and your credibility is not there. If you had a volunteer that had been there maybe a couple, maybe three months and has an idea, then you should . . . at least listen to it and maybe tell them yes or no, or we'll see. That's not really something that's been fostered.
>
> (VM19)

Volunteers can offer insight and a fresh perspective on many organizational activities and are an important stakeholder in the work of an organization. Within library systems, volunteers are typically also patrons and may be able to offer staff an accessible means of understanding and responding to patrons' opinions and complaints. Inability to solicit and direct volunteer input to appropriate channels and utilize it effectively breeds frustration for both groups.

Behavioral/Emotional Discord: Indirect Responses to Problematic Behavior

Another area that troubles volunteer managers and staff members alike is handling situations in which troublesome behavioral or performance-related issues must be addressed. Paid staff often report attempting to resolve the situation through indirect means. One volunteer manager relays,

> I'll be honest with you, library staff are probably the least likely to engage in conflict of any sort. So we would probably more likely try to find something else for them to do. Invariably they just go away on their own accord because I think they're just so bored by the work.
>
> (VM29)

Of the twenty-five reports of these types of issues in the volunteer manager interview data, interviewees describe using indirect means to solve fourteen of them. For example, rather than dismissing a problem volunteer directly, a volunteer manager may schedule fewer and fewer hours for the volunteer or leave the problem volunteer off the schedule until he or she "self-selects" and stops coming to the library. One manager shares such a story:

> I had a volunteer that . . . would come in and he would work in the department . . . He would . . . mock people in different religious

groups and political groups. . . . [The central system volunteer coordinator] didn't have me . . . outright dismiss him. She had me just say, I'm sorry we don't have any volunteer opportunities at this time for you, and it just went away over time.
>
> (VM26)

While these indirect approaches to problem behavior may seem to avoid conflict, they likely intensify it by allowing untenable actions to linger indefinitely, as well as forcing both volunteers and staff into situations in which they have no formal mechanisms for recourse or other outlets for their concerns.

Divergent Expectations: Lack of Capacity for Incorporating Diversity

Effectively utilizing volunteers with disabilities is also a challenge with the potential for stirring volunteer-staff conflict. In addition to the issues reported by volunteers regarding providing meaningful work for volunteers with physical disabilities, several of the interviews with volunteer managers reveal instances of difficulty accommodating a volunteer with a mental disability. For example, an interviewee states:

> We had a young man who was challenged. And he would come in, and he was really excited about being a volunteer, but he couldn't follow directions. . . We would give him jobs to do in each department, and he would begin and then stop and then go over to the computers and look up things like . . . books on dragons. . . And he'd get all excited and want people to help him with it and everything . . . and the mother explained a bit of it, but it got really, really bad, so we had to let him go.
>
> (VM7)

This situation exemplifies issues that untrained staff are ill-prepared to handle and that can result in job stress and unpleasant experiences for both volunteers and staff.

Workflow Integration Hurdles

Staff and volunteer managers also describe ineffective integration of volunteers into the library's workflow as contributing to conflict between the two groups. This problem seems to be associated more strongly with the dramatic increase in volunteer use than the other issues we discuss above. We encounter reports of tension as library branches endeavor to accommodate so many new and untrained volunteers. One interviewee describes the situation:

> Before we knew it, we had a hundred volunteers . . . and so just the physical crowdedness that we experienced was, you could tell, was a little stressful for people. . . . The volunteers . . . they were kind of hovering a little bit, waiting to be trained, or, having just been trained, not quite sure what to do first.
>
> (GS2)

These growing pains are noteworthy for other organizations that might be considering increased volunteer reliance.

Lack of Trust

The final issue evident in our case that has the potential to foment volunteer-staff conflict is a lack of trust between volunteers and staff members. Although no volunteer mentioned this issue, both general staff and volunteer managers discussed it in their interviews. A general staff member pointed out that trust issues are related to work reliability:

> I figured if there wasn't a paycheck involved, they wouldn't have any incentive to show up on time, show up consistently, or work at a level that we were probably going to require.
>
> (GS8)

Others also discussed the level of training that paid staff undertake in order to perform their job functions. They felt that trusting laypeople (volunteers) with these same tasks after a short training period could be considered unwise:

> It's always concerning to hear that unpaid staff are going to be made responsible for tasks that we take very seriously, for things that we've always thought of as being important for paid staff to handle.
>
> (GS12)

Given the role that trust has been found to play in supervisor-subordinate relationships in the general management literature (Gerstner and Day 1997), the lack of trust displayed here may undermine effective working relationships between the two groups.

Discussion: Managerial and Policy Implications

Our findings highlight the pitfalls of ad hoc management and supervision of volunteers. In general, paid staff lack the training and preparation to handle these types of situations confidently and competently, which may hinder their ability to contribute to volunteer development and, ultimately, may be detrimental to effective service delivery. Clear volunteer supervision practices should be explicitly included in the organization's human resource management strategies. Organization leaders must recognize that staff members need specific skill sets and abilities to work effectively with volunteers. A professional, trained volunteer manager should know how to handle problem volunteers, be willing to discipline or fire a problem volunteer, and support training and evaluation activities that minimize the drain on staff time that these situations may provoke. Lack of investment in an organizational infrastructure to manage volunteers can also have a negative impact on the volunteers, which can ultimately increase turnover (Rehnborg et al. 2009).

Few organizations employ a dedicated, full-time paid volunteer manager (Hager and Brudney 2004; Machin and Paine 2008). In these situations—where hiring a professional volunteer manager is not feasible (or even desirable)—the executive director's role in championing the volunteer program becomes more crucial (see Ellis 1996 for an extensive discussion of the executive director's role in the volunteer program). The director must ensure that someone who has received appropriate training and support is accountable for the volunteer program. In our view, too many organizations fail to make a sufficient investment in training staff to supervise or manage volunteers. Many of these organizations might also fail to account for the issue of staff resistance to taking on a volunteer supervision role (Follman, Cseh, and Brudney 2016).

Our study also hints at the difficulties organizations face when trying to engage volunteers with physical or mental disabilities. Many organizations have prescribed volunteer positions that preclude involvement by individuals with such challenges. Because so many organizations do not make a sufficient investment in volunteer management (Hager and Brudney 2004; Machin and Paine 2008), these organizations often do not have the capacity to be more creative in designing volunteer positions that fit the needs and interests of individuals with disabilities (Choma and Ochocka 2005). To integrate volunteers with disabilities successfully, organizations might need to seek advice and help from other organizations who have successfully done so or partner with organizations that serve individuals with disabilities to learn more about designing work suited to these potential volunteers.

A defining aspect of this case study is the use of volunteers to attempt to compensate for shortfalls in staff time after major cuts to the organization's budget. This situation raises important practical and ethical questions about the deployment of paid and unpaid staff members and how changes in deployment might affect the relationships and satisfaction of both groups. Although our data did not indicate any major, overt conflict in this instance, staff members did acknowledge concerns about job vulnerability linked to the increased use of volunteers in the library system. Conflict stemming from these concerns could manifest in subtle ways—including lack of communication between staff and volunteers, which might be evidenced by the breakdown in the feedback systems between volunteers and their volunteer managers that we saw in this case. This situation highlights the importance of clearly defining (and separating) staff and volunteer roles to avoid turf issues and feelings of insecurity in both groups.

Another managerial implication emerging from this study is that organizations need to be proactive about assessing the quality of relationships between volunteers and staff. Macduff (2012) argues that organizations should regularly survey volunteers, staff, and clients in order to stay abreast of the volunteer-staff climate and make changes should any of these symptoms of poor volunteer-staff relations or other red flags emerge. We also encourage organizations to collect both qualitative and quantitative data to describe these relationships; many important comments emerged in our interviews and open-ended survey questions that would not have been apparent in the quantitative survey data alone.

Our primary managerial and policy recommendation is that community and nonprofit leaders need to do more to support and encourage organizations in developing greater volunteer management capacity. When an individual has a negative experience as a volunteer, that person is less likely to volunteer again at any organization. Organizations that misuse volunteers or those that make an insufficient investment in volunteer management can potentially deplete their community's pool of volunteers by inadvertently creating an unsatisfactory volunteer experience that will drive people away from volunteering.

References

Brodie, E., T. Hughes, V. Jochum, S. Miller, N. Ockenden, and D. Warburton. 2011. *Pathways through Participation*. London: National Council for Voluntary Organizations, Institute for Volunteering Research, and Involve.

———. 1990. *Fostering Volunteer Programs in the Public Sector*. San Francisco: Jossey-Bass.

Brudney, J. L. 1993. "Volunteer Involvement in the Delivery of Public Services: Advantages and Disadvantages." *Public Productivity & Management Review* 16 (3): 283–97.

Bryman, A. 2006. "Integrating Quantitative and Qualitative Research: How Is It Done?" *Qualitative Research* 6 (1): 97–113.

Choma, B. L., and J. Ochocka. 2005. "Supported Volunteering: A Community Approach for People with Complex Needs." *Journal on Developmental Disabilities* 12 (1): 1–18.

Dover, G. J. 2010. "Public Sector Volunteering: Committed Staff, Multiple Logics, and Contradictory Strategies." *Review of Public Personnel Administration* 30 (2): 235–56.

Ellis, S. J. 1996. *From the Top Down: The Executive Role in Volunteer Program Success*. Philadelphia: Energize, Inc.

Follman, J., M. Cseh, and J. L. Brudney. 2016. "Structures, Challenges, and Successes of Volunteer Programs Co-managed by Nonprofit and Public Organizations." *Nonprofit Management and Leadership* 26 (4): 453–70.

Galindo-Kuhn, R., and R. M. Guzley. 2002. "The Volunteer Satisfaction Index: Construct Definition, Measurement, Development, and Validation." *Journal of Social Service Research* 28 (1): 45–68.

Garner, J. T., and L. T. Garner. 2011. "Volunteering an Opinion: Organizational Voice and Volunteer Retention in Nonprofit Organizations." *Nonprofit and Voluntary Sector Quarterly* 40 (5): 813–28.

Gerstner, C. R., and D. V. Day. 1997. "Meta-Analytic Review of Leader-Member Exchange Theory: Correlates and Construct Issues." *Journal of Applied Psychology* 82 (6): 827–44.

Gidron, B. 1985. "Predictors of Retention and Turnover among Service Volunteer Workers." *Journal of Social Service Research* 8 (1): 1–16.

Hackman, J. R., and G. R. Oldham. 1975. "Development of the Job Diagnostic Survey." *Applied Psychology* 60 (2): 159–70.

Hager, M. A., and J. L. Brudney. 2004. *Volunteer Management Practices and Retention of Volunteers*. Washington, DC: The Urban Institute.

Handy, F., and L. Mook. 2011. "Volunteering and Volunteers: Benefit-Cost Analyses." *Research on Social Work Practice* 21 (4): 412–20.

Hirschman, A. O. 1970. *Exit, Voice, and Loyalty*. Cambridge, MA: Harvard University Press.

Hobson, C. J., and K. Heler. 2007. "The Importance of Initial Assignment Quality and Staff Treatment of New Volunteers: A Field Test of the Hobson-Heler Model of Nonprofit Agency 'Volunteer-Friendliness.'" *International Journal of Volunteer Administration* 14 (6): 47–56.

Judge, T. A., C. J. Thoresen, J. E. Bono, and G. K. Patton. 2001. "The Job Satisfaction–Job Performance Relationship: A Qualitative and Quantitative Review." *Psychological Bulletin* 127 (3): 376–407.

Kreutzer, K., and U. Jäger. 2011. "Volunteering versus Managerialism: Conflict over Organizational Identity in Voluntary Associations." *Nonprofit and Voluntary Sector Quarterly* 40 (4): 634–61.

Kulik, L. 2006. "Burnout among Volunteers in the Social Services: The Impact of Gender and Employment Status." *Journal of Community Psychology* 34 (5): 541–61.

Laczo, R. M., and K. A. Hanisch. 2000. "An Examination of Behavioral Families of Organizational Withdrawal in Volunteer Workers and Paid Employees." *Human Resource Management Review* 9 (4): 453–77.

Macduff, N. 2012. "Volunteer and Staff Relations." In *The Volunteer Management Handbook: Leadership Strategies for Success*. 2nd ed., edited by T. D. Connors. Hoboken, NJ: John Wiley & Sons, Inc.

Machin, J., and A. E. Paine. 2008. *Management Matters: A National Survey of Volunteer Management*

Capacity. London: Institute for Volunteering Research.

Nesbit, R., H. Rimes, R. K. Christensen, and J. L. Brudney. 2016. "Inadvertent Volunteer Managers: Exploring Perceptions of Volunteer Managers' and Volunteers' Roles in the Public Workplace." *Review of Public Personnel Administration* 36 (2): 164–87.

Nicol, E. A., and C. M. Johnson. 2008. "Volunteers in Libraries: Program Structure, Evaluation, and Theoretical Analysis." *References & User Services Quarterly* 48(2): 154–63.

Pearce, J. L. 1993. *Volunteers: The Organizational Behaviour of Unpaid Workers*. New York: Routledge.

Rehnborg, S. J., W. L. Bailey, M. Moore, and C. Sinatra. 2009. *Strategic Volunteer Engagement: A Guide for Nonprofit and Public Sector Leaders*. Austin, TX: RGK Center for Philanthropy & Community Service.

Rogelberg, S. G., J. A. Allen, J. M. Conway, A. Goh, L. Currie, and B. McFarland. 2010. "Employee Experiences with Volunteers." *Nonprofit Management and Leadership* 20 (4): 423–44.

Roy, L. 1984. "Volunteers in Public Libraries: Issues and Viewpoints." *Public Library Quarterly* 5 (4): 29–40.

Scheier, I. 2003. *Building Staff/Volunteer Relations*. Philadelphia, PA: Energize, Inc.

Small, M. L. 2011. "How to Conduct a Mixed Methods Study: Recent Trends in a Rapidly Growing Literature." *Annual Review of Sociology* 37 (1): 57–86.

Smith, P. C., L. M. Kendall, and C. L. Hulin. 1969. *The Measurement of Satisfaction in Work and Retirement: A Strategy for the Study of Attitudes*. Chicago, IL: Rand McNally.

Studer, S., and G. von Schnurbein. 2013. "Organizational Factors Affecting Volunteers: A Literature Review on Volunteer Coordination." *VOLUNTAS: International Journal of Voluntary and Nonprofit Organizations* 24 (2): 403–40.

Taylor, T., S. Darcy, R. Hoye, and G. Cuskelly, 2006. "Using Psychological Contract Theory to Explore Issues in Effective Volunteer Management." *European Sport Management Quarterly* 6 (2): 123–47.

Wandersman, A., and J. Alderman. 1993. "Incentives, Costs, and Barriers for Volunteers: A Staff Perspective on Volunteers in One State." *Review of Public Personnel Administration* 13 (1): 67–76.

CHAPTER 17

Volunteers as Boundary Workers

Negotiating Tensions Between Volunteerism and Professionalism in Nonprofit Organizations

Kirstie McAllum

Both nonprofit practitioners and scholars face the vexed question of whether collapsing boundaries between the nonprofit, government, and corporate sectors is a desirable outcome for volunteers. For most of the 20th century, analyses clearly differentiated between the corporate world (the first sector), government (the second sector), and the nonprofit or "third" sector (Frumkin, 2002). Sectorial distinctiveness came under fire in the early 1980s, as neoliberal policy makers slashed universal access to education, welfare, and health services, retaining only a thin safety net for society's most vulnerable individuals (Baines, 2010). To ensure that base-line services did not exacerbate ballooning fiscal debt, many governments divested themselves of direct service provision, devolving these functions to nonprofit organizations (NPOs; Henriksen, Rathgeb Smith, & Zimmer, 2012). Governments simultaneously adopted short-term, competitive contracts and business-like accountability mechanisms to identify "efficient" NPOs, able to deliver more

services with fewer resources (Salamon, 2015). Such shifts in responsibility blurred sector boundaries.

Internationally, institutional and cultural trends have also contributed to decreased sectorial distinctiveness. Although Northern and Western European countries have been in the vanguard of new institutional forms such as "social enterprises" that combine volunteer contributions, sales/fees from users, and public subsidies (Nyssens, 2006), other countries are experimenting with organizational configurations that integrate for-profit and nonprofit practices (Berzin & Camarena, 2018). These hybrids with varied appellations—fourth sector organizations, for-benefit organizations, blended value organizations, for-profits with a nonprofit soul—reject an organizational ethos that "denigrates" commercial activity (Katz & Page, 2010, p. 61). Cultural shifts such as the rise of corporate volunteering, NPO use of for-profit financial success indicators, and consumer expectations of corporate social responsibility have also contributed to blending for-profit and nonprofit principles.

DOI: 10.4324/9781003387800-39

Despite the seeming inevitability of "sector bending" (Dees & Anderson, 2003), nonprofit managers, think tank representatives, and researchers have raised alarm bells about professionalism's[1] encroachment in the nonprofit sector. Criticisms include sector-level differences in goals and values that create mission drift (Lewis, 2005), cuts in services to difficult, unresponsive or resource-intensive clients (Weisbrod, 2004), reduced advocacy-related work (Eliasoph, 2009), and conflict over identity change (Kreutzer & Jäger, 2011). The disjuncture between mission and market, framed as threatening the voluntary spirit, is particularly pronounced in the human services sector, which provides health, education, and welfare services. Volunteer-dependent NPOs have suffered most, because volunteers' dissatisfaction with "unreasonable" tasks or rigid organizational practices that make volunteering "better organized but too much like paid work" (Paine, Ockenden, & Stuart, 2010, p. 101) has adversely impacted recruitment and retention (Van Schie, Güntert, & Wehner, 2014). Professionalism, then, has become a dirty word, extinguishing "passion, . . . the human element and sense of what organisations 'really stand for'" (Tennant, O'Brien, & Sanders, 2008, p. 27).

The few studies documenting volunteers' perspectives on institutional blurring have probed reasons underpinning their negative reactions to professionalism. Yet, as Child, Witesman, and Spencer (2016) explained, this research takes incompatible worldviews for granted, "without [qualitatively] scrutinizing what it looks like from the perspectives of individuals working in blended spaces" (p. 1832). Rather than dichotomizing volunteers' reactions according to their acceptance or rejection of professionalized role expectations, this study uses the concepts of boundary crossing, passing, and boundary spanning to explore how volunteers for two human services NPOs managed the tensions between volunteerism

and professionalism on the ground (Maier, Meyer, & Steinbreitner, 2014).

Boundaries and Boundary Work

Most of the nonprofit management literature conceptualizes boundaries as fixed borders or barriers between discrete social systems (e.g., Tsasis, 2009). However, given the blurring of organizational structures, practices, and missions that has characterized intersectorial hybrids, conceptual approaches from fields such as activity theory and organizational learning that view boundaries as interactional spaces offer a useful theoretical lens to understand boundaries. The premises of this interactional approach are twofold. First, boundaries create opportunities for diverse individuals to engage in collective projects. Akkerman and Bakker (2011), for instance, contended that although boundaries pinpoint the existence of "a sociocultural difference leading to discontinuity" (p. 133), the domains already possess elements of sameness due to the common interests that lead members to interact together. Star (2010) also insisted that boundaries are not an "edge" or "periphery" but a "shared space" (pp. 602–603) where members of distinct but intersecting social worlds interact. According to Star and Griesemer (1989), individuals from diverse social worlds create these spaces by negotiating the meanings of boundary objects with the requisite interpretive flexibility. Even if groups give different meanings to boundary objects (in their study, field notes and maps), they can work together if the boundary object meets their respective information and work requirements.

Second, this more interactional approach suggests that boundaries are not solid or fixed, but upheld, contested, or modified through interaction. For example, Valentinov (2012) posited that critiquing others' interpretations might enlarge a reference system to include previously rejected phenomena and concluded that "boundary critique is a boundary spanning exercise" (p. 356). Because boundaries are intersubjectively constructed in interaction, boundary work is a dynamic, inherently communicative accomplishment. Individuals can enact boundary work in three different ways: by boundary crossing, passing, and/or boundary spanning. Boundary crossing implies that individuals must *oscillate* between "multiple parallel activity contexts . . . with different cognitive tools, rules, and patterns of social interaction" (Engeström, Engeström, & Kärkkäinen, 1995, p. 319). Passing occurs when individuals are so "multilingual" that they can *adopt* the practices and identities of the other social system as if they were native members (Hogg, 2016). Boundary spanning, by contrast, focuses on individuals' ability to understand and disseminate the "contextual information on both sides of the boundary" (Tushman & Scanlan, 1981, pp. 291–292). To avoid semantic boundary problems (lack of common vocabulary and shared meanings) and pragmatic boundary issues (lack of common interests, motivations, or goals), boundary spanners must *translate* concepts to connect distinctive social systems together (Carlisle, 2004). At times, translating implies creating hybrid meanings that integrate elements from both social systems (Engeström, 2001).

Volunteerism and Professionalism as Distinctive Social Systems

Studies of boundary crossing, passing, and boundary spanning require an analysis of the systems that are loosely connected together yet have different sets of requirements and objects of interest (Akkerman & Bakker, 2011). I begin by defining professionalism and explain how professionalism and volunteerism constitute discrete systems.

Professionalism

I chose to hone in on professionalism rather than related concepts such as managerialism, which refers to the use of corporate principles such as performance-based measurement, competition, and efficiency to coordinate and control organizational practices. While managerialism has left a significant mark on NPOs, professionalism more usefully conceptualizes how workers enact and react to *occupational* practices and knowledge demands (Hvenmark, 2016). Poutanen and Kovalainen (2016) argue that, similar to managerialism, professionalism acts as a "distinctive way of controlling and organizing work and workers" (p. 119), an ideological frame that specifies the "conditions under which knowledge is *produced and applied* in ways that make a difference for the life of others" (Larson, 1990, p. 32). Control mechanisms include the promulgation of codified and authoritative knowledge, criteria for the inclusion and exclusion of particular types of workers, and evaluation by performance by other professionals. By deciding who and what counts, professionalism shapes occupational norms, work practices, and personal, organizational, and social relationships (Ganesh & McAllum, 2012) and acts as a form of regularizing control that guides behavior (Flyverbom, Christensen, & Hansen, 2015).

Perhaps due to the ubiquity of the term *professional*, professionalism tends to be used as an all-encompassing term that embraces multiple practices (Cheney & Ashcraft, 2007). Here, I pause to distinguish among three processes that have created distinctive forms of professionalism: rationalization, marketization, and bureaucratization. I take *rationalization* to refer to social action that is evaluated in terms of *practical rationality*. That is, "practical ends are attained by careful weighing and increasingly precise calculation of the most adequate means" (Kalberg, 1980, p. 1152). Extraneous processes that impede organizational members from efficiently attaining desired outcomes become obsolete. *Bureaucratization* emphasizes *formal rationality* or the process of standardizing, formalizing, and institutionalizing systems, rules, and documentation requirements to ensure due process and fair outcomes. *Marketization* can be understood as the adoption of a particular type of *substantive rationality* or cluster of monetary values that guide social behavior. Marketized values such as flexibility, ease of exchange, and cost-benefit analyses inform and increasingly dominate various life spheres and become the touchstone against which other events and values are evaluated (Kalberg, 1980).

Viewed through these three lenses, professionalism is not limited to what Noordegraaf (2007) termed "control over content" (p. 761), whereby professional bodies codify occupational knowledge and engage in occupational closure (Abbott, 1988; Freidson, 1994). It refers more broadly to the "content of control" or "ways of ordering and controlling collective conduct" (Noordegraaf, p. 781). As in this study, the acceptability of visible emotional expression often exerts considerable control over participants' conduct. Rationalized professionalism, for instance, tends to leave little place for emotional expression in task performance. Professionalism thus involves "clean" cerebral work that is detached and clinical rather than nurturing, emotionally close, or hands-on (Morgan & Krone, 2001). Kramer and Hess's (2002) participants categorized both excessive positive or negative emotional expression in the workplace as "unprofessional." Webley and Duff (2007) also differentiated between the emotional, caring behaviors associated with "being present" and efficient, outcome-focused behaviors required to "do" professional work. A marketized form of professionalism controls conduct by specifying a series of "desirable" behaviors such as personal responsibility, ability to interact with colleagues and clients in appropriate, impartial

ways, flexibility, openness to change, and self-improvement (Lair, Sullivan, & Cheney, 2005).

Professionalism and Volunteerism

When professionalism is applied as an overarching frame to human services' volunteering, success requires that volunteers measure up to criteria that are used to evaluate professionals in for-profit settings. Certainly, those whom Giddens (1994) called "clever volunteers" (p. 94), who deploy knowledge from paid work contexts to benefit an NPO, sometimes as part of corporate volunteering initiatives or pro bono work, continue to be "professional" accountants, lawyers, web designers, and so on. However, the vast majority of volunteers, whose activities are not linked to their workplace expertise, are rarely attributed professional status.

Limited Control of Volunteers' Prior Knowledge

While professional associations demand mastery of complex knowledge and specialist skills and oversee how these principles should be applied to unique cases, NPOs seldom if ever require evidence of prior knowledge or demand preentry testing (Geoghegan & Powell, 2006). One reason is that volunteers usually "[supplement] professionally planned and delivered services" (Anheier & Salamon, 1999, p. 43). Handy, Mook, and Quarter's (2008) study of the potential replacement of paid staff by volunteers in cash-strapped Canadian NPOs confirmed volunteers' position as nonprofessionals. Although volunteers did replace paid staff in some customer service or advocacy roles, "professional" paid staff had been employed in lieu of volunteers within the *same* organization when skill level, legal liability, and reliability were important.

Moreover, although statistical analyses show that organizational volunteers have completed more formal education and engage in paid employment in greater numbers than nonvolunteers (Musick & Wilson, 2008), organizations rarely use specialist knowledge as a criterion for including/excluding volunteers. Instead, recruitment materials mention qualities such as "good intentions" (Wuthnow, 1998), "local knowledge," and "energy" (Hodgkinson, 2003, p. 36). Because volunteering requires general knowledge of place, space, and culture rather than occupational expertise, NPOs generally seek to encourage participation by as many volunteers as possible (Hwang & Powell, 2009). Haski-Leventhal, Meijs, and Hustinx (2009) proposed that, "Everyone is capable of volunteering in some role or another" (p. 142). In marked contrast to professional settings, volunteer managers, policy makers, and scholars usually brand volunteering as a means to *acquire* specific skills and knowledge rather than the expression of a preexisting knowledge base (Clary et al., 1998).

Lack of Regulation and Control of Volunteers' Practice

Professionalism has a broader conceptual scope than the narrow set of attributes that characterize traditional liberal professions such as law and medicine: expertise in dealing with complex, nonstandardized problems; internal occupational autonomy; and regulation by an independent professional body (Freidson, 1994). It is in their shared concern with regulation of members' behavior that the professions overlap conceptually with professionalism, which acts as an ideological form of occupational control. Deetz (1992), for example, claimed that collective conformity to professional norms stifles individual autonomy by structuring the range of possible responses to such an extent that individuals take "greater care to not make a mistake than to make a creative decision" (p. 226).

In stark contrast, volunteers are not professional in either sense. They do not belong to an overarching professional body and the NPOs with whom they engage are unable to effectively control them. Because volunteers often carry out their role within the community outside the NPO's fixed working hours, NPOs are unable to assess volunteers' performance and conformity to organizational policies and practices. Furthermore, even when volunteers "express dissent, resist directives, and create conflict" (McAllum, 2013, p. 387), NPOs lack disciplinary measures, because volunteers can leave the organization at will.

However, most nonprofit scholars view this lack of surveillance, control, and internal discipline positively. They argue that volunteers do not *want* to be professional, because professionalism controls the production and circulation of knowledge and suppresses emotional authenticity. Skocpol (2003), for instance, connected professionalism with diminished capacity for expressive goals. The lack of tight, repressive knowledge frameworks gives volunteers considerable latitude to innovate and experiment with new ideas and practices outside of organizational control. Kreutzer and Jäger's (2011) study of volunteer-based patient associations, for example, described the importance of "creative chaos" (p. 13), inventiveness, and informal networks, which enabled volunteers to organize large-scale information evenings for patients. Freedom from the constraints of professionalism and expectations of emotional neutrality also allows volunteers to construct rich, emotionally close relationships (Ronel, 2006). Indeed, detachment from nurturing behaviors is often positioned as inappropriate: Volunteers in Onyx's (2013) study "broke the rules" contained in risk management procedures and professional codes of conduct to care.

In common parlance, volunteers are perceived to be amateurs, who are, as the word's etymology indicates *(amare* being the Latin verb "to love"), moved by the heart and personally invested, whether for other- or self-oriented motives (see Clary et al., 1998, for a discussion of volunteer motivations such as social connection, value expression, career development, and enhanced understanding). Other-oriented motives may include the desire to "bend over backwards" (Knutsen, 2012, p. 994) to give time, resources, and energy to community causes. However, individuals can also be enthused by what they receive from volunteering: skill development, enjoyable leisure, meaningful relationships with beneficiaries or other volunteers, and opportunities to participate in "spectacular and entertaining" activities (Hustinx & Lammertyn, 2003. p. 168). This underlying emotional dimension is a third element distinguishing volunteerism from professionalism.

Most scholarship presents professionalism and volunteerism as incompatible social systems with divergent norms and practices (see Table 17.1) and denigrates the imposition of professional ideologies and practices on volunteers (Ganesh & McAllum, 2012).

The underlying premise is that professionalism undermines volunteerism and that volunteers will resist professionalism. Child et al. (2016) foregrounded the possibility of stakeholder challenges to professionalism, explaining that "the pressures causing organizations to look alike are obstructed—even if unwittingly—by the actors who orient themselves according to sectors because of the meanings and values that they attach to different kinds of organizations" (p. 1835). This categorical opposition is unsurprising

from a boundary work perspective. Boundary spanning, which involves translating between systems or integrating meanings and practices to create hybrids, is only possible when a group (i.e., volunteers) is not "*overly*-disciplined" to conform to the practices of another group (i.e., professionals; Star & Griesemer, 1989, p. 407). Insisting on standardization between social systems, they argued, is counterproductive because it leads to conflict and splinters social systems into separate communities of practice, such as traditional volunteers, professional(ized) volunteers, and professionals (Hustinx & Lammertyn, 2003).

However, these critiques assume that professionalism and volunteerism generate highly distinctive identities and practices. This dichotomy may be less rigid in the case of high-stakes volunteers who engage in complex activities that have "significant implications for the volunteers, their organizations, and the people they serve" (McNamee & Peterson, 2014, p. 6). Volunteers in McNamee and Peterson's (2014) study, for instance, dedicated themselves to firefighting, victim support services, and youth outreach programs that were core rather than peripheral to organizational mission. The tension, presented earlier in the literature review, between many NPOs' low expectations of volunteers' capabilities and volunteers' actual skill sets does not seem to hold here. Organizations hold high-stakes volunteers accountable, because what they do matters a great deal. High-stakes volunteers may interpret demands

TABLE 17.1 Professionalism and Volunteerism

Professionalism	Volunteerism
Complex tasks, specialist knowledge	Day-to-day tasks, general knowledge
Strong internal control mechanisms: consensus, group norms of excellence	Lack of internal control: flexibility, experimentation
Cerebrally driven; task-oriented	Heart-driven; person-oriented

for professionalism in two contradictory ways: Insisting on professionalism can reinforce the idea that the volunteer role has an importance "similar to paid work commitments" (McNamee & Peterson, 2014, p. 5) or it may imply that irresponsible volunteers require extensive supervision to perform as needed. Because we know little about how these volunteers experience organizational demands for professionalism or how they hold them in a productive organizing tension, I ask the following research questions:

> **Research Question 1:** How do high-stakes volunteers react to NPO demands for professionalism?
>
> **Research Question 2:** How do volunteers communicatively navigate the tensions between professionalism and volunteerism when these occur?

Method

Because volunteers' reactions to professionalism depend on organizational context, the first step involved gathering data from two human services' NPOs in New Zealand that use high-stakes volunteers. The human services' sector has tended to vociferously denounce the perceived tension between market and mission, making these NPOs a relevant site to explore the relationship between volunteerism and professionalism. As I describe in more detail, one organization monitors professionalism by assessing volunteers' compliance with business tools and reporting requirements, while in the other, paid staff who work alongside volunteers give feedback on their performance. Given New Zealand's size, organizational representatives agreed that the NPOs could be named, as concealing their identity would require removing all references to volunteers' tasks and responsibilities. I first outline organizational expectations about professionalism at the Royal

New Zealand Plunket Society and St John Ambulance (henceforth, Plunket and St John), before describing the data collection and analysis strategies.

Distinctive Views of Organizational Professionalism at Plunket and St John

To recognize specific forms of organizational professionalism, I created codes for rationalized, bureaucratized, and marketized professionalism, using definitions drawn from the literature. I then combed codes of conduct (recruitment posters, training videos, PowerPoint presentations, handbooks, rules, and protocols) and the transcripts of 60 to 90 min interviews with regional and national representatives for examples of organizational expectations of volunteer practice that flowed from a particular variant of professionalism.

The first organization, Plunket, has promoted children's health in New Zealand for over 100 years. Paid nurses provide free health checks for children below 5 years. Eight thousand volunteers across 660 communities run support groups, participate in and recruit others for fund-raising events, organize monthly branch meetings, oversee the building and maintenance of clinics, and report on the efficacy of initiatives at the regional area and national level. Most volunteers put in about 5 to 6 hr a week, but office holders such as committee presidents can end up spending 2 to 3 hr a day on Plunket-related work. Although early Plunket documents stated that "womanly instincts" should override "bureaucratic formalism" (Bryder, 2003, p. 31), in 1992 government pressures led Plunket to appoint a predominantly male, commercially oriented management team. One consequence of this change was the requirement that local committees submit a yearly business plan outlining their goals and send monthly financial accounts to the National Office.

Somewhat unsurprisingly, Plunket's codes of conduct operationalize a marketized version of professionalism. According to organizational interview data and documents such as officeholder booklets, materials for training workshops, and the official Society Rules, professionalism requires an entrepreneurial attitude and the use of business tools to ensure that choices reflect community needs. As the National Volunteer Education Advisor explained, the business plan offers volunteers the chance to indicate local priorities, so that committees "raise money for what it is that their community wants." Volunteers act as citizen professionals who "'translate' policies to suit local contexts" (Tonkens, 2016, p. 46) and promote public goals. In the context of marketized professionalism, choice and voice become the key principles organizing volunteers' practices (Tonkens, 2016).

St John, the second organization, has 2,700 ambulance volunteers who commit to at least one 12-hr shift every 2 weeks, although many do a weekly shift. The volunteers in this study all worked alongside paid staff to provide emergency ambulance services, especially at night and in rural areas. Volunteers' responsibilities include driving to jobs, treating patients according to their level of clinical expertise, and, when needed, transporting patients to hospital. St John managers describe volunteers as "health professionals" who wear the same uniform as paid staff and receive identical training. During organizational induction, new members are introduced to St John's core values. The Core Values' training kit describes professionalism as clinical excellence, "achieving outcomes and standards, and continuously developing," keeping a calm task focus and demonstrating emotional neutrality. The voiceover in the training DVD compares St John members to superheroes, concluding that, "There's something different about their stance and demeanor, as if a confidence and composure is being worn like an invisible cloak." Organizational professionalism

was both rationalized, with calmness a means to better service, and bureaucratized, with clinical expertise dictating the organization of ambulance crews.

Data Collection and Analysis

Data came from semistructured interviews with 30 volunteers, 15 from each organization. Participants were recruited using a snowball sampling strategy. All Plunket volunteers were women whose involvement ranged from 6 months to 50 years. Older volunteers grew up in an era where Plunket membership offered a platform from which women could contribute to public issues. More recent recruits, mothers of young children, intended to volunteer for 3 to 4 years before moving into school-related volunteer roles or returning to work. Three participants were retired, three worked part-time in service work, one studied full-time, and eight were at home full-time with their children. Of this last group, all had recently held jobs in a range of professional sectors: accountancy, banking, teaching, child care, science, and landscaping. Eight St John volunteers were men and seven were women. Average length of involvement was 6 years, the organizational average, although two had volunteered for over 25 years. Twelve of the 15 participants worked full-time: Their occupations ranged from managers, shop assistant, and business owner to farmer, scientist, and graphic artist. Of the remaining three, one was a student, one retired, and the other a full-time homemaker. None of the Plunket participants had ever been professional fundraisers and none of the St John volunteers interviewed had previous experience in a related medical field. Volunteering was distinct from their current or previous professional roles. In contrast to individuals doing pro bono or corporate volunteering, participants needed to "be professional" according to organizational directives, without being able to transfer their professional knowhow to the volunteer context.

Interviews lasted from 1 to 1½ hours and were audio-recorded and transcribed verbatim, generating 624 typed single-spaced pages. To explore participants' understandings of volunteerism, questions focused on preconceptions of volunteering and how their actual experiences challenged these. I also asked participants to create detailed descriptions of a typical day spent volunteering. Questions about particularly positive or negative experiences of volunteering elicited accounts about organizational policies and demands for professionalism. Because the literature assumes that volunteerism and professionalism constitute oppositional social systems, I focused on how participants had reacted to organizational insistence on professionalism, and specifically if they positioned these demands as (in)compatible with their volunteer status.

I then engaged in close reading of transcripts to identify practices, objects, and goals that were problematic due to a clash in the demands of volunteerism and professionalism. According to Kerosuo (2004), practices that cause boundary disputes can be "traced" by searching participants' transcripts for divisive *social relations*, different *locations*, and *temporal* distinctions. The Plunket transcripts, for instance, described two types of actors with highly distinctive interests, knowledge, and roles: *non-specialists* (based on in-vivo codes such as "normal people," "ordinariness," "all walks of life," and "varied family situations") based in local communities and *professionals* (expressed by codes such as "jargon," "job," and "SWOT analysis") who sent documentation to National Office. Objects, or "something people act toward and with" (Star, 2010, p. 603), were chosen for analysis when they took on "a different type of role for the different actors . . .—an object being a motivator for some while at the same time being a background for others" (Nicolini, Mengis, & Swan, 2012, p. 612). Objects are not just physical things but emblematic of what Nicolini et al. (2012) named an "object(ive)" or goal that orients the collective activity of a particular

knowledge community. In the case of Plunket, the business plan was not just a tangible object but shaped how volunteers managed community development.

The next step involved using Saldaña's (2009) notion of *versus codes* to analyze how participants used boundary work to manage perceived binaries between two mutually exclusive social systems with conflicting practices and philosophies (p. 95). Versus codes are assigned to (a) stakeholders (identified by looking at pronouns and articles such as "us," "them," and "our"); (b) issues at stake; and (c) actions taken to manage conflicts. Versus codes for Plunket, for example, included (a) "we," community based volunteers *versus* "them," staff at National Office; (b) ground-up decision making by volunteers who could identify locally relevant needs ("We know what families need") *versus* imposition of centrally imposed top down evaluation tools ("They [National Office] kept saying, 'If you don't have these things in your business plan, you can't do it'"); and (c) avoidance of/anger about constraining tools ("Wow, we've got to do a business plan . . . ?! It's just *crazy*") *versus* appreciation of tools which could be used as a resource ("If we have a business plan, it's easier for us, we can prioritize").

The following section examines how both Plunket and St John volunteers navigated these tensions.

Findings

The findings document how Plunket and St John volunteers used boundary work to navigate the tensions between professionalism and volunteerism. The Plunket role required volunteers to be boundary spanners, able to leverage local relationships to identify community education needs and convert them into actionable outcomes. St John volunteers attempted to boundary cross between excellent clinical care and patient-centered personal connection.

Volunteerism and Professionalism at Plunket

All but three Plunket participants rejected organizational understandings of a marketized form of professionalism based on evaluation-based tools and entrepreneurialism. They discursively positioned themselves as ordinary folk "from all walks of life" who could not be expected to understand business documents that did not contain "words that *normal people* actually understand and recognize." These participants were convinced that being women who were "just Mums," "trying to fit in stuff in our spare time while juggling the children," was antithetical to being professionals. Instead, their role involved working alongside other volunteers and establishing contact with members of the community:

> I enjoy the catering. Two of us did the dishes for the Wild Food Feast . . . and they had a big screen for the rugby and we were watching that. We had an absolute ball. I love doing that. You get to meet all the people. We do the fireworks fiesta every year, and we are only serving cups of tea and cakes and that sort of thing.

From this perspective, volunteer activities ought to promote patterns of social interaction based on manifestations of nurturing and hosting such as baking cakes, cooking, and serving cups of tea. These activities, produced and consumed in the present moment, generated positive emotions ("enjoyment," "love," and "having a ball") and a sense of fun. Participants' descriptions of how they presented the Plunket role to potential recruits reinforced this interpretation of volunteerism. New volunteers were not invited to meetings which "put them off, because it was so business-oriented and we just talked about all the work that we had to do." Instead, they were asked to attend "an actual event, so they're actually helping us out doing what most people *imagine* volunteers would do rather than just sitting at a desk talking about finances."

This relational, nurturing approach also structured the organization of Plunket events where participants worked alongside other volunteers to meet the needs of mothers and babies. One key way volunteers contributed to new Mums' needs was by facilitating informal get-togethers or "coffee groups." Participants mentioned the importance of developing spaces where women could interact and feel comfortable asking questions about their worries: "My son's got a rash," "My daughter's up all night crying," "Should I be starting on solids?" A participant explained that, "They might just think they're having a talk! But they go home and think, 'I feel so much better now.'" Several participants mentioned that attendees with premature babies or postnatal depression thanked them "for listening," highlighting the importance of simply "being there." Volunteers also ran playgroups where mothers "at a similar stage in their lives" could interact and spend time playing with their toddlers.

Another way to help women to meet their babies' needs involved coordinating the buying and selling of secondhand clothes in Plunket-organized baby gear sales. Similar to coffee groups and playgroups, support was not just informational but emotional, as encounters created links with others. A participant recalled that

> Oh, there was this girl, she didn't have a car, she had all this stuff to sell and no way of getting there. She'd phoned so many other people to try and sell her stuff, met dead ends and no-one was interested. And I was like "Oh, we can do that."

Several committees also supplied clothing by building networks with local rest homes, where they recruited

> a whole lot of grannies to knit blankets for us and it was a lot of fun. We were also were able to purchase a whole lot of woollen vests

for babies, for the nurses to give out to those in need.

In line with the value that these participants accorded to nurturance within this social system, seven volunteers specified that meeting these immediate physical needs felt like what volunteers

> are *supposed* to be doing. I mean, we do all the activities for the Mums and all the educational courses as well, but this felt like something that we were doing for the babies. You know, helping them out and keeping them warm and toasty.

Plunket volunteers' other core responsibility was the provision of a safe, accessible, and attractive clinic for child health checks and parent education. Activities associated with funding clinics were wide-ranging: Volunteers organized cake sales, sausage sizzles, and catering events to raise funds for courses in parenting, baby cardiopulmonary resuscitation (CPR), and infant massage. During working bees to upgrade playgrounds, participants co-opted husbands and partners, "supervising" them as they ripped out fences, chopped down trees, and moved playhouses. All of these activities involved considerable interaction among committee members, consolidating their relationships and allowing them to look after each other as well as community members.

Obtaining grants to build new clinics or maintain existing ones, however, implied a considerably greater investment of time and money and meant "answering back" to Plunket about "what happens with money that's raised." As one of New Zealand's oldest charities, Plunket has always had rules about recording financial transactions. The *President and Vice President Resource Booklet* reminds those in charge that committees are the "guardians/stewards of the community resource in their location" (p. 1). However, the "turnaround" in the accountability requirements of the government's Charities

Commission meant that committees had to send regular financial accounts to National Office so that Plunket retains its charity status. For most, completing accounts ran counter to the collegial, nurturing interactional style that characterized other volunteer activities, since participants frequently had to balance the books alone at home:

> You get a bank statement and you get a form and you send it through. You do copies and then it's through to centralized accounts. That's a monthly thing. And every half a year, you've got the grants to do, which is for the Ministry of Education. Then you do the Year-end thing. So you've got two grants plus Year-end, plus the monthly reports every month. [Seeing my expression of horror, this participant consoled me] I mean *you* could do the monthly reports, they're easy.

She concluded that Plunket was "a bit cheeky" to offload paperwork onto volunteers and that their role should be limited to "helping Plunket out." Other participants complained that bureaucratic "red tape" and "grants are a big fat pain" and that "we've got so much bookwork to do that we're really not getting on to do what we're trained to do. You know, we're trained *to be there and to look after the mothers*."

The main issue, then, involved decisions about appropriate activities for volunteers: tangible, person-centric activities that enabled volunteers to connect with others, or paper-based, task-focused activities that facilitated planning new initiatives. Organizational resources such as the *President and Vice President Resource Booklet* did recognize possible tensions between "process-" and "task-oriented" volunteers, specifying that the president of each committee had the arduous job of reconciling the needs of volunteers who wanted to fulfill "social needs," experience "harmony" (p. 6) and develop "long-term friendships" (p. 1) and those focused on "outcomes" who like to "tick things off" (p. 6).

However, the booklet offered no suggestions about how to manage such tensions.

The first group tolerated bureaucratic reporting as an annoying but necessary justification of monies spent during volunteering, but they took issue with demands that committees complete a business plan. A volunteer insisted that she "didn't want to have to run a mini-business. It's taken the joy out of it [volunteering] for me." Another stated, "There's nothing about it that I don't like except that business plan. I will do anything else." Participants resisted professionalism in two ways: insisting that the lack of a business plan in the past had not impeded effective organizing and positioning the business plan itself as unprofessional. In the first instance, a participant explained, "I don't want to do it. We don't *need* to do this. We've never done it before." In the second, volunteers dissociated the business plan from the knowledge base of "real" professionals. A participant with over 40 years of involvement with Plunket explained that, "My husband is a businessman and he's been saying, 'It's time you got out.' He couldn't understand half of what is in that thing. He couldn't believe it."

The second, smaller group of participants embraced professionalism. These participants discursively positioned themselves as solution-oriented, proactive rather than reactive, and calm when faced with challenges. Two of these volunteers framed the business plan as a way to increase committees' control over plans for community development and as a tool that fostered "organizational skills, forward planning, looking to the future, and looking at the bigger picture, being more professional." These characteristics enabled volunteers to overcome inefficient committee decision-making: "Rather than us going, 'Oh, we need a wall heater. We'll discuss it next meeting,' and then in the winter with the first cold snap, it's like 'Oh! We really need a wall heater!'" According to the third participant, who worked part-time as a housekeeper, professionalism was beneficial because it

acted as a buffer from the emotions and stress of home and family:

> You can have a really stressful day. It's crazy at home and you're ready to go "Aaagh!" but then you've sort of got to put—not professional but a professional hat if you like. Yeah, that's it, you can go to a meeting and it's a whole different focus. You can forget about all of that for an hour, two hours, because you're thinking about things that are not necessarily your life—sometimes it's escapism.

From her perspective, professionalism was an intellectual pursuit that helped to manage runaway emotions.

Consequently, she managed the tension between volunteerism and professionalism by attempting to convince other committee members that opposition to new business tools was exaggerated and even irrational. She criticized "some people," volunteers whose hyper-emotionality inhibited problem solving, for magnifying the quantity and difficulty of tasks and not using the resources and skills at hand to get the job done:

> Some people make things *look* scary, but it's not a biggie when you break it down. It's work to do, but it's not a huge amount. Some people make more of a job than other people. Then, when National Office sends you forms and you don't know what you're looking at and you see big fancy words, you just freak out, but there are people to help you.

Time commitment and tasks that might seem initially overwhelming were reframed as entirely manageable by professionals who could view them with appropriate perspective and use strategies such as breaking large tasks into chunks, asking for help, and being realistic about the workload.

More commonly, participants who did not appreciate professionalism managed the tension between volunteerism and professionalism by segmenting their role, focusing on the "nice bits" such as catching up with friends, connecting a struggling mother with appropriate support, and enjoyable fundraisers. In another interview, a participant suggested to her committee that they focus on the "*gory bits* for the first half hour and the next hour you can do whatever you want." The role was also segmented according to skill sets. One of the accountants split the Plunket role into tasks suitable for those with training due to their profession or Plunket role from activities that were suitable for those without this formation. She explained that because "the girls hated it," she limited their participation to a brainstorming session and filled out the forms later.

Boundary Spanning and Passing at Plunket

Boundary spanning across volunteer and professional systems seemed stymied by three groups of people: volunteers who adapted their workplace skills to deal with the business plan; National Office staff; and members of the public. In each case, volunteerism was reinforced. Volunteers whose paid jobs as accountants and managers meant that they were familiar with cost–benefit analyses seemed capable of "passing" in both systems. Although these volunteers seemed ideally placed to help other volunteers become boundary spanners, their insistence during meetings that they take responsibility for the business plan meant that other volunteers could opt out and reified the boundaries between the two social systems.

National Office also reduced participants' ability to boundary span by responding to business plans submitted by the accountants with criticism and corrections. If not even the "professionals" could get it right, volunteers who were just Mums decided to avoid the process altogether,

> because it's all too scary . . . we don't have the right person on our committee . . . We don't

know what to do, so we'll push it under the table. We won't be involved in anything.

Finally, conversations with members of the public during fund-raising drives confirmed a vision of Plunket's activities as nonprofessional. As a participant who embraced professionalism highlighted, "When we explain that we are Plunket volunteers, people tend to think we bake cakes and knit woollen vests for new-born babies. They don't see us as a professional entity, and that is what we are striving to become." Interestingly, this participant used a woollen vest, the same object chosen to epitomize and defend a "traditional" understanding of volunteerism, to summarize this identity challenge.

In sum, volunteers chose which system to operate in, depending on their skill set and prior experience, with most opting for volunteerism. Although Plunket policy documents expressed hope that its volunteers would be able to link the two social systems together by professionally managing community development initiatives, organizational critiques of individuals who did attempt to boundary span made this less likely. St John volunteers managed the volunteerism–professionalism tension quite differently.

Professionalism and Volunteerism at St John

During emergency callouts, participants described the importance of professionalism, manifest by excellent clinical service, a calm task focus, and personal responsibility for one's actions. Participants' descriptions often repeated word for word ideas contained in the Core Values pack. A participant asked a facetious question to underline the importance of professionalism, distancing his performance from that of an inept volunteer:

> If you're critically ill or you've had an accident, should you be entitled to substandard care because it's a volunteer that's giving it?

I would expect the best service I can get.
I don't care if they volunteer or not.

Definitions reflected rationalized and bureaucratized forms of professionalism. Rationalization meant streamlining processes to provide the most efficient emergency care possible, while bureaucratization manifest in strict adherence to codified medical practices and insistence on impartial treatment for all community members. In line with the Core Values' PowerPoint, which listed professional attitudes such as "skillful, calm and authoritative behaviour, energy and urgency," participants specified that ambulance crews that were able to rationalize their activity by setting aside nonproductive emotions such as sympathy and compassion would be better able to meet clinical standards. Participants also criticized the volunteer tendency to become too personally involved and specified that emotional detachment and a cool, rational reading of the situation ("knowing" rather than "feeling") were essential to actually help patients. Appropriate interactional styles involved "curing" rather than "caring":

> You've got to stand back a bit. Yeah, this person is screaming in pain, but all I can do this for this person is X, Y and Z. If I keep a level head, I can do this procedure, I can get the appropriate backup, keep them calm. And that's actually helping them, whereas if you think, "Oh crap, I can't do that! I'm sorry! I'm sorry! I don't want to!"

While participants linked volunteerism to panicking, freezing, and inability to act, professionalism enabled selecting procedures and equipment that could make a difference in the situation. A focus on clinical processes also meant that even when interventions did not save patients, volunteers could still maintain a positive sense of their ability if they had exerted all their skill and effort.

Other volunteers reported using professionalism to suspend personal value judgments when carrying out tasks that were "unpredictable, identity-threatening, [and] tragic" (Tracy, Myers, & Scott, 2006, p. 284). Participants adopted a professional persona when they entered homes with domestic violence and gang activity or that were dirty, lacked electric lighting, and had mattresses strewn over the floor. A participant reiterated that, "I've held people that have been dying and seriously injured, and possibly people that in my 'real' job, in my 'real' life, I wouldn't give the time of day to." Here, in line with a bureaucratized approach to professionalism, task and role requirements took precedence over personal value judgments.

In contrast, when the technical or medical aspects of the job receded, participants reverted to the "volunteer" way: creating personal connections, expressing sympathy, and meeting patients' emotional needs. A volunteer described how she ignored the paperwork and held the hand of a dying cancer patient:

> I just sat with her, and you knew that this was the last time . . . that she was going to hospital to die. She knew that, and she was talking about the old days and her children. It was touching.

Five participants explained how they chose to reveal their volunteer status to patients during nonemergency ambulance journeys:

> Sometimes you pick someone up, they are like "Oh, what time are you on till?" "Seven o'clock tomorrow morning." "Oh, that's a long night." "Yes, and I do it all for love!" And they are like, "Really? Wow!" and their whole perception of you changes. They think, "Hey, she's doing it because she wants to help me."

Members of the public thus confirmed the value of the volunteer contribution, which was framed as an appropriate form of "helping" when genuine emotion work was needed. It also permitted volunteers to distance themselves from paid officers who were unable to lay aside a hardened emotional shell: "There are ambulance officers out there that are a bit bitter and twisted, and I think, 'I don't want to be that person.'"

Boundary Crossing at St John

Participants engaged in constant boundary crossing, depending on the type of call and the state of the patient. A participant who insisted that ambulance work required "composure" and the ability to "take control" and not be "phased by seeing a really bad motor vehicle accident, somebody who has fallen off scaffolding or committed suicide" also reiterated the importance of reassurance and empathy when life and death were not hanging in the balance. When responding to a call where a toddler's penis had caught in his trouser zip, she inferred that his mother was "in more agony" than the little boy, and that consequently her role involved "looking at me being a Mum, putting myself into *her* situation, how she felt." Deciding which system to operate in required participants to "look at the situation, and say, 'Okay, what is the best approach?'" However, when the situation was less clear-cut, some participants did not always manage to align with paid staff's enactment of professionalism. A volunteer assisting a paid crew to move a dead man from the shed where he had been chopping wood to a bed in the farm homestead oriented to the personal dignity of the person, while the paid staff focused on the difficulty of laying out the body:

> The paid guys were saying, "You're a woman. You should know how to make a bed" and I was more worried about the dead guy and they started laughing because we really couldn't figure out how the cover went. I initially felt that we were quite disrespectful, but then looking back on it now, we couldn't have really done anything different and that was just how the guys were dealing

with it, and I sort of learnt that this is how you deal with it. You have a bit of a laugh because it *is* sad.

Similar to the firefighters in Tracy et al.'s (2006) study, paid officers created role distance by using black humor. The volunteer, however, interpreted their laughter as "disrespectful." Her attempts to boundary cross by comparing earlier reactions with how she reframed sad situations now ("initially" versus "looking back on it now") were only partially successful, as she concluded, "I *sort of* learnt."

The other challenge was that volunteers' continual oscillation between establishing emotional connections with patients and enacting clinical detachment in emergencies made it harder for paid staff to know which system volunteers were currently working in. A volunteer who criticized a television commercial that presented ambulance officers tucking a "little old lady who had a fall into bed" noted less than 10 min later how much the public appreciated the "extra things we do for people that really make the difference. We lock the house. We make sure the cat's out, that kind of thing." The decision to switch between professionalism and volunteerism front stage was also risky, because paid staff who feared that a volunteer workforce jeopardized their job security could emphasize their superior skill relative to volunteers' contribution, amplifying their anxiety.

Participants' ability to "pass" as professionals was relatively easy in front of patients and their families, who could not distinguish between volunteers and paid staff. Paid staff, however, could call volunteers' professionalism into question, disparaging their knowledge and skills through criticism, invisibility treatment, and lack of gratitude. Criticism, such as being yelled at for not finding equipment quickly, exacerbated volunteers' sense of knowing "this much about first aid" [indicating space between thumb and forefinger], whereas paramedics know "thiiiiiiis much" [arms extended wide].

Another participant described the "wrath" of a paramedic when volunteers failed to measure up: "it's her way or the highway. We're expected to know everything even though we're only first aid level." Another reported that a paramedic who had asked that she take a blood pressure interrupted her shortly afterward with the instruction to "shut up and sit in the corner." In other cases, some paid staff ignored volunteers, by not speaking to them during shifts, grunting in reply to questions, or in one case screwing up and throwing away the patient report form the volunteer had filled out without looking at it. After a year of weekly 12-hr shifts, a volunteer noted that "very rarely do the paid staff say thank you," specifying that this had only occurred twice.

Paid staff's feedback on clinical interventions was of critical importance, as positive comments moderated volunteers' sense of responsibility. A new volunteer described how paid staff coached him through the treatment of an unconscious cardiac arrest patient whose face had already turned purple. When his heart rate stabilized after 10 min of CPR, they "gave me a pat on the back: 'Well done, Greg! You've just saved this guy's life!'" Another mentioned how paid staff "were 100% supportive. They just reassured me the whole time that no matter how inadequate I felt, it was a natural—every volunteer felt like that when they first started." Even more experienced volunteers appreciated comments such as "I couldn't have done any-more for that patient than you did" and "We did all that we could." Without this validation or in the face of criticism that "knocks your confidence down," closure on incidents became more difficult: "That's to me when it is really bad, because then it gets you thinking, 'Did I do the right thing? Did I not?' 'Yes, I did. No, I didn't.'" Eight participants gave vivid examples of moments where their sense of responsibility for negative patient outcomes was overwhelming, to such an extent that "Sometimes, I've gone through self-doubt, and I've thought

I don't think I can handle the responsibility of having someone's life in my hands."

The data indicate that St John volunteers wanted to move smoothly between social systems depending on the type of job they were called to. Some paid staff facilitated boundary crossing by commending volunteers' contribution, while others erected symbolic boundaries that led volunteers to doubt their competence.

Discussion and Conclusion

Rather than rejecting professionalism a priori as an inappropriate logic for the nonprofit sector, this study examined how volunteers managed organizational demands for professionalism by boundary crossing, passing, and boundary spanning between professional and volunteer systems. The study thus contributes to the literature on the professionalization of the nonprofit sector by (a) describing how organizational volunteers communicatively negotiated the tensions between professionalism and volunteerism and (b) identifying conditions that constrained or enabled boundary work.

The findings pointed to two distinctive ways of navigating between the two social systems. At Plunket, participants did not engage in boundary spanning but dichotomized volunteerism and professionalism as incompatible social systems and managed the disjuncture between them by segmenting and privileging one or the other system. Most participants rejected external accountability measures such as the business plan while a smaller number, who relished the development of efficient planning processes, embraced them. The decision as to which social system to operate in reflected personal preferences rather than organizational directives. Despite the promotion of professionalism in organizational documents, policies, and legal reporting requirements and prodding by volunteers who touted the benefits of forward planning, committee-level conversations and decision-making processes, negative National Office feedback, and interactions with the public confirmed most participants' desire to be "just" volunteers.

Two key reasons that explain Plunket volunteers' relative autonomy from organizational control are task design and organizational structure. In terms of task distribution, planning for and carrying out fund-raising activities were not simultaneous, but separated in time and space. Committees were thus able to function effectively by creating a division of labor. Volunteers who enjoyed relationships, being together, and connecting with the community could offer to take charge of catering and other fund-raising events. They could also delegate planning tasks that they did not like to volunteers who valued professional tools, emotional neutrality, and future-oriented thinking.

Both groups could feel that they were contributing, albeit differently, to community development. As Aldridge and Evetts (2003) pointed out, polyvalent terms—such as community development—provide an "operating space in which parties to large-scale occupational and organizational change can pursue multiple, perhaps opposed, goals without fully acknowledging what is happening" (p. 558).

More importantly, the geographical separation between National Office and local committees meant that on-the-spot surveillance and oversight by paid staff was nonexistent. Volunteers could thus avoid or ignore professional directives with relative ease (McAllum, 2013). This finding would seem to be a fairly common occurrence in advocacy-oriented NPOs with a dispersed volunteer workforce. These NPOs can only influence volunteers' behavior by appealing to a shared vision of organizational mission. However, most Plunket participants situated professionalism as an inappropriate social system due to the type of work involved. For volunteers focused on children's health, parenthood sat more comfortably in the sphere of home and family than in the public sphere

of professionalism. These findings align with Meisenbach's (2008) study of higher education fundraisers who rejected traditional notions of professionalism, managing the taint associated with asking for money by situating relationship development as core to their occupational identity.

Consequently, insistence on boundary spanning was ineffectual, because the cognitive and practical demands of conforming to a professional understanding of community development precluded volunteers' vision of what meeting the needs of mothers and babies meant. Most participants felt that community development did not require a business plan and refused to buy into the hybrid "volunteer professional" model. National Office's overemphasis on "how" community development was to be reported splintered the group. Star (2010) confirmed that attempts to impose administrative or regulatory standards generate "residual categories" (p. 615) of others who create alternative communities of practice.

St John volunteers managed the tension between professionalism and volunteerism by boundary crossing. The social system in which volunteers operated depended on several contextual factors, rather than individual choice, as was the case for Plunket volunteers. The first contextual factor was the type of work needed to meet patient needs. In emergencies, participants wanted to enact professionalism based on clinical capability and emotion management. In this setting, forging emotional connections interfered with ability to treat patients and could lead to trauma if patient outcomes were negative. In nonemergency contexts, participants wanted to create more compassionate encounters, without relational partners linking their conduct to incompetence. Feedback also influenced participants' choice of "appropriate" social systems. Because emergency work is in situ with no separation between the planning and execution of care, volunteers' work is visible to patients, their families, and paid crew.

Through comments made on or after each job, paid staff gave feedback about what constituted acceptable task- or relationship-focused performance.

However, for individuals to cross between volunteer and professional systems with ease, organizations must encourage permeable boundaries. Given the importance of the medical hierarchy at St John, boundaries were often reified. Indeed, paid staff members who resented volunteers' attempts to become "professional" without having passed through the ranks from novice to expert could make use of the "knowledge-power knot of traditional professional authority" (Tonkens, 2016, p. 50). One way of doing so was to withhold the informational, emotional, and social support that volunteers needed to remain emotionally detached and professional. As Akkerman and Bakker (2011) pointed out, "knowledge processes, personal and professional relations" affect "who experiences a particular discontinuity [between social systems] in which interactions" (p. 153).

These findings have practical implications for NPOs wanting to professionalize their volunteer workforce. First, because only volunteers with pre-existing skill sets were able to pass in both systems, we need to think about how volunteering works as a trampoline for skill development and employability or the consequences of shifting from a volunteer to paid status within an organization. Second, the study indicates that NPOs cannot demand that volunteers be "professional" unless the organizational structure supports this change. Specifically, managers need to consider the types of relationships that volunteers would like to establish with each other and with paid staff, volunteers' proximity or distance from beneficiaries, and organizational ability to follow-up the use of tools and protocols.

This study also made several theoretical contributions. First, by applying a boundary work lens to larger occupational systems (professionalism and volunteerism), it contributed

to the boundary work literature which usually analyzes how specific organizational or occupational work groups such as hospital-based/primary care practitioners (Engeström, 2001) and social workers/physicians (Engeström et al., 1995) manage divergent work rules, practices, and tools. Second, instead of conceptualizing professionalism and volunteerism as fundamentally oppositional, this study demonstrated multiple ways of moving dynamically between the two systems, by boundary crossing, passing, or spanning. Moreover, the ways individuals engaged in boundary work produced particular types of organizational practices. Rather than simply reacting to institutional blurring, volunteers who craft "new working rules or organizational arrangements to work together" may create new forms of boundary organizations (O'Mahoney & Bechky, 2008, p. 451).

Third, and somewhat surprisingly, the study showed that participants reproduced the dominant gender assumptions underpinning professionalism and volunteerism. In line with Ganesh and McAllum's (2012) assertion that "masculine, 'professional' work emphasizes efficiency and getting things done" (p. 3), professionalism involved manipulating objects (a plan, equipment, or a human body); rationally, reflexively managing the self; and taking on a distinctive "other" persona that allowed for emotional detachment (Clarke, Brown, & Hailey, 2009). Volunteerism, in contrast, was a feminized form of social engagement that built up strong communities due to volunteers' capacity to connect with people as persons, emotional expansiveness, and attachment. Participants in this study invoked home-based objects (home baking, hand-knitted vests) and actions (holding someone's hand, making beds, tucking someone in) as emblematic of what it meant to be a volunteer, even if such behavior linked volunteerism to lower-status, invisible women's work (Petrzelka & Mannon, 2006).

The study thus reinforced Mumby and Putnam's (1992) argument that rationality and emotionality are fundamentally gendered concepts. Interestingly, the all-female Plunket committees held professionalism, understood as requiring a (male-centered) cognitive evaluation of possible decisions, in tension with emotional experience. Despite the means-end logic that dominated emergency settings, the St John data offered a glimmer of hope that bounded emotionality might inform volunteers' "affective responses to organizational situations" (p. 471). Instead of separating emotions from task performance, volunteers used work feelings to intuit patient needs and normalized the need for supportive forms of teamwork to manage anxiety about responsibility for patients.

The study has several limitations that point toward future research trajectories. First, both organizations were what Hustinx and Lammertyn (2003) called "traditional" human services' NPOs. Future research might examine how other types of volunteers react to NPO demands for professionalism. For instance, how are "low-stakes" volunteers different or similar to high-stakes volunteers? How do volunteers who perform their professional job in nonprofit settings navigate the boundaries? Further empirical studies of volunteers involved in sport, culture, and environmental activities in public, nonprofit, for-profit, and social enterprise settings would allow us to better understand the influence of tasks and sector on volunteers' reactions to professionalism. Second, like other scholars and NPO practitioners, this study described the attributes of professionalism in terms that reflect for-profit than nonprofit contexts. Future studies could examine what happens when professionalism itself hybridizes and in particular what a specifically "nonprofit" version of professionalism might look like.

Note

1. The sociology of professions literature has documented how "classic" professions like medicine, law,

and engineering have developed proprietary rights over specialist knowledge, with publicly recognized expertise conferring authority and autonomy from external influence. Because professionalism increases the prestige of the occupational collective to which individuals belong, with some foresight Wilensky (1964) predicted the "professionalization of nearly everyone." Groups such as accountants, management consultants, IT specialists, and even aromatherapists have laid claim to niche expertise and thus professional status. Other more interdisciplinary groups such as nurses and social workers have been less successful. The nonprofit sector is reasonably singular in its disdain for professionalism.

References

Abbott, A. (1988). *The system of professions: An essay on the division of expert labor.* Chicago, IL: The University of Chicago Press.

Akkerman, S. F. & Bakker, A. (2011). Boundary crossing and boundary objects. *Review of Educational Research, 81,* 132–169.

Aldridge, M., & Evetts, J. (2003). Rethinking the concept of professionalism: The case of journalism. *British Journal of Sociology, 54,* 547–564.

Anheier, H. K., & Salamon, L. M. (1999). Volunteering in cross-national perspective: Initial comparisons. *Law and Contemporary Problems, 62,* 43–65.

Baines, D. (2010). Neoliberal restructuring, activism/participation, and social unionism in the nonprofit social services. *Nonprofit and Voluntary Sector Quarterly, 39,* 10–28.

Berzin, S. C., & Camarena, H. (2018). *Innovation from within: Redefining how nonprofits solve problems.* New York, NY: Oxford University Press.

Bryder, L. (2003). *A voice for mothers: The Plunket Society and infant welfare 1907–2000.* Auckland, New Zealand: Auckland University Press.

Carlisle, P. R. (2004). Transferring, translating and transforming: An integrative framework for managing knowledge across boundaries. *Organization Science, 15,* 555–568.

Cheney, G., & Ashcraft, K. (2007). Considering "the professional" in communication studies: Implications for theory and research within and beyond the boundaries of organizational communication. *Communication Theory, 17,* 146–175.

Child, C., Witesman, E., & Spencer, R. (2016). The blurring hypothesis reconsidered: How sector still matters to practitioners. *Voluntas, 27,* 1–22.

Clarke, C. A., Brown, A. D., & Hailey, V. H. (2009). Working identities? Antagonistic discursive resources and managerial identity. *Human Relations, 62,* 323–352.

Clary, E. G., Ridge, R. D., Stukas A. A., Snyder, M., Copeland, J., Haugen, J., & Miene, P. (1998). Understanding and assessing the motivations of volunteers: A functional approach. *Journal of Personality and Social Psychology, 74,* 1516–1530.

Dees, J. G., & Anderson, B. B. (2003). Sector-bending: Blurring lines between nonprofit and for-profit. *Society, 40,* 16–27.

Deetz, S. (1992). *Democracy in an age of corporate colonization: Developments in communication and the politics of everyday life.* Albany, NY: State University of New York Press.

Eliasoph, N. (2009). Top-down civic projects are not grassroots associations: How the differences matter in everyday life. *Voluntas, 20,* 291–308.

Engeström, Y. (2001). Expansive learning at work: Toward an activity theoretical reconceptualization. *Journal of Education and Work, 14,* 133–156.

Engeström, Y., Engeström, R., & Kärkkäinen, M. (1995). Polycontexturality and boundary crossing in expert cognition: Learning and problem solving in complex work activities. *Learning and Instruction, 5,* 319–336.

Flyverbom, M., Christensen, L. T., & Hansen, H. K. (2015). The transparency power nexus: Observational and regularizing control. *Management Communication Quarterly, 29,* 385–410.

Freidson, E. (1994). *Professionalism reborn: Theory, prophecy and policy.* Chicago, IL: The University of Chicago Press.

Frumkin, P. (2002). *On being nonprofit: A conceptual and policy primer.* Cambridge, MA: Harvard University Press.

Ganesh, S., & McAllum, K. (2012). Volunteering and professionalization: Trends in tension? *Management Communication Quarterly, 26,* 152–158.

Geoghegan, M., & Powell, F. (2006). Community development, partnership governance and dilemmas of professionalization: Profiling and assessing the case of Ireland. *British Journal of Social Work, 36,* 845–861.

Giddens, A. (1994). *Beyond left and right: The future of radical politics.* Cambridge, UK: Polity Press.

Handy, F., Mook, L., & Quarter, J. (2008). The interchangeability of paid staff and volunteers in nonprofit organizations. *Nonprofit and Voluntary Sector Quarterly, 37,* 76–92.

Haski-Leventhal, D., Meijs, L. C. P. M., & Hustinx, L. (2009). The third-party model: Enhancing volunteering through governments, corporations and educational institutes. *Journal of Social Policy, 39,* 139–158.

Henriksen, L. S., Rathgeb Smith, S., & Zimmer, A. (2012). At the eve of convergence? Transformations of social service provision in Denmark, Germany, and the United States. *Voluntas, 23,* 458–501.

Hodgkinson, V. A. (2003). Volunteering in global perspective. In P. Dekker & L. Halman (Eds.), *The values of volunteering: Cross-cultural perspectives* (pp. 35–54). New York, NY: Kluwer Academic.

Hogg, M. A. (2016). Social identity theory. In S. McKeown, R. Haji, & N. Ferguson (Eds.). *Understanding peace and conflict through social identity theory.* Retrieved from https://link.springer.com/chapter/10.1007/978-3-319-29869-6_1.

Hustinx, L., & Lammertyn, F. (2003). Collective and reflexive styles of volunteering: A sociological modernization perspective. *Voluntas, 14,* 167–187.

Hvenmark, J. (2016). Ideology, practice, and process? A review of the concept of managerialism in civil society studies. *Voluntas, 27,* 2833–2859.

Hwang, H., & Powell, W. W. (2009). The rationalization of charity: The influences of professionalism in the nonprofit sector. *Administrative Science Quarterly, 54,* 268–298.

Kalberg, S. (1980). Max Weber's types of rationality: Cornerstones for the analysis of rationalization processes. *American Journal of Sociology, 85,* 1145–1179.

Katz, R. A., & Page, A. (2010). The role of social enterprise. *Vermont Law Review, 35,* 59–103.

Kerosuo, H. (2004). Examining boundaries in health care—Outline of a method for studying organizational boundaries in interaction. *Outlines: Critical Social Studies, 6,* 35–60.

Knutsen, W. L. (2012). Value as a self-sustaining mechanism: Why some nonprofit organizations are different from and similar to private and public organizations. *Nonprofit and Voluntary Sector Quarterly, 42,* 985–1005.

Kramer, M. W., & Hess, J. A. (2002). Communication rules for the display of emotions in organizational settings. *Management Communication Quarterly, 16,* 66–80.

Kreutzer, K., & Jäger, U. (2011). Volunteering versus managerialism: Conflict over organizational identity in voluntary associations. *Nonprofit and Voluntary Sector Quarterly, 40,* 634–661.

Lair, D. J., Sullivan, K., & Cheney, G. (2005). Marketization and the recasting of the professional self: The rhetoric and ethics of personal branding. *Management Communication Quarterly, 18,* 307–343.

Larson, M. S. (1990). In the matter of experts and professionals, or how impossible it is to leave nothing unsaid. In R. Torstendahl & M. Burrage (Eds.), *The formation of professions: Knowledge. state and strategy* (pp. 24–50). London, England: SAGE.

Lewis, L. K. (2005). The civil society sector: A review of critical issues and research agenda for organizational communication scholars. *Management Communication Quarterly, 19,* 238–267.

Maier, F., Meyer, M., & Steinbreitner, M. (2014). Nonprofit organizations becoming business-like: A systematic review. *Nonprofit and Voluntary Sector Quarterly, 45,* 64–86.

McAllum, K. (2013). Challenging nonprofit praxis: Organizational volunteers and the expression of dissent. In M. W. Kramer, L. K. Lewis, & L. M. Gossett (Eds.), *Volunteering and communication: Studies from multiple contexts* (pp. 383–404). New York, NY: Peter Lang.

McNamee, L. G., & Peterson, B. L. (2014). Reconciling "third space/place": Toward a complementary dialectical understanding of volunteer management. *Management Communication Quarterly, 28,* 214–243.

Meisenbach, R. J. (2008). Working with tensions: Materiality, discourse, and (dis)empowerment in occupational identity negotiation among higher education fund raisers. *Management Communication Quarterly, 22,* 258–287.

Morgan, J. M., & Krone, K. J. (2001). Bending the rules of "professional" display: Emotional improvisation in caregiver performances. *Journal of Applied Communication Research, 29,* 317–340.

Mumby, D. K., & Putnam, L. L. (1992). The politics of emotion: A feminist reading of bounded rationality. *Academy of Management Review, 17,* 465–486.

Musick, M. A., & Wilson, J. (2008). *Volunteers: A social profile.* Bloomington, IN: Indiana University Press.

Nicolini, D., Mengis, J., & Swan, J. (2012). Understanding the role of objects in cross-disciplinary collaboration. *Organization Science, 23,* 612–629.

Noordegraaf, M. (2007). From "pure to hybrid" professionalism: Present-day professionalism in ambiguous public domains. *Administration & Society, 39,* 761–785.

Nyssens, M. (Ed.). (2006). *Social enterprise: At the crossroads of market, public policies and civil society.* London, UK: Routledge.

O'Mahoney, S., & Bechky, B. A. (2008). Boundary organizations: Enabling collaboration among unexpected allies. *Administrative Science Quarterly, 53,* 422–459.

Onyx, J. (2013). Breaking the rules: The secret of successful volunteering in a caring role. In M. W. Kramer, L. K. Lewis, & L. M. Gossett (Eds.), *Volunteering and communication: Studies from multiple contexts* (pp. 343–364). New York, NY: Peter Lang.

Paine, A. E., Ockenden, N., & Stuart, J. (2010). Volunteers in hybrid organizations: A marginalized majority? In D. Billis (Ed.), *Hybrid organizations and the third sector: Challenges for practice, theory and policy* (pp. 93–113). Basingstoke, UK: Palgrave Macmillan.

Petrzelka, P., & Mannon, S. E. (2006). Keepin' this little town going: Gender and volunteerism in rural America. *Gender and Society, 20,* 236–258.

Poutanen, S., & Kovalainen, A. (2016). Professionalism and entrepreneurialism. In M. Dent, I. L. Bourgeault, J. L. Denis, & E. Kuhlmann (Eds.)., *The Routledge companion to the professions and professionalism* (pp. 116–128). London, UK: Routledge.

Ronel, N. (2006).' When good overcomes bad: The impact of volunteers on those they help. *Human Relations, 59,* 1133–1153.

Salamon, L. M. (2015). Introduction: The nonprofitization of the welfare state. *Voluntas, 26,* 2147–2154.

Saldaña, J. (2009). *The coding manual for qualitative researchers.* Thousand Oaks, CA: SAGE.

Skocpol, T. (2003). *Diminished democracy: From membership to management in American civic life.* Norman: University of Oklahoma Press.

Star, S. L. (2010). This is not a boundary object: Reflections on the origin of a concept. *Science, Technology, & Human Values, 35,* 601–617.

Star, S. L., & Griesemer, J. R. (1989). Institutional ecology, "translation" and boundary objects: Amateurs and professionals in Berkeley's Museum of Vertebrate Zoology, 1907–1939. *Social Studies of Science, 19,* 387–420.

Tennant, M., O'Brien, M., & Sanders, J. (2008). *The history of the non-profit sector in New Zealand.* Wellington, New Zealand: Office for the Community and Voluntary Sector.

Tonkens, E. (2016). Professions, service users and citizenship. In M. Dent, I. L. Bourgeault, J. L. Denis, & E. Kuhlmann (Eds.), *The Routledge companion to the professions and professionalism* (pp. 45–56). London, UK: Routledge.

Tracy, S. J., Myers, K. K., & Scott, C. W. (2006). Cracking jokes and crafting selves: Sensemaking and identity management among human service workers. *Communication Monographs, 73,* 283–308.

Tsasis, P. (2009). The social processes of interorganizational collaboration and conflict in nonprofit organizations. *Nonprofit Management & Leadership, 20,* 5–21.

Tushman, M. L., & Scanlan, T. J. (1981). Boundary spanning individuals: Their role in information transfer and their antecedents. *Academy of Management Journal, 24,* 289–305.

Valentinov, V. (2012). Toward a critical systems perspective on the nonprofit sector. *Systemic Practice and Action Research, 25,* 355–364.

Van Schie, S., Güntert, S. T., & Wehner, T. (2014). How dare to demand this from volunteers! The impact of illegitimate tasks. *Voluntas, 25,* 851–868.

Webley, L., & Duff, L. (2007). Women solicitors as a barometer for problems within the legal profession—Time to put values before profits? *Journal of Law and Society, 34,* 374–402.

Weisbrod, B. A. (2004). The pitfalls of profits. *Stanford Social Innovation Review, 2,* 40–47.

Wilensky, H. L. (1964). The professionalization of everyone? *American Journal of Sociology, 70,* 137–158.

Wuthnow, R. (1998). *Loose connections: Joining together in America's fragmented communities.* Cambridge, MA: Harvard University Press.

Changing of the Guard
Leadership Change in Nonprofit Organizations

BETSY HULL, BENJAMIN S. BINGLE AND C. KENNETH MEYER

The staff of Safe Haven recently learned that their beloved Executive Director and founder, Don Jones, was planning to retire at the end of the year. Safe Haven is a large nonprofit organization with a mission to provide suicide counseling services and prevention programs to at-risk teens and adults. The idea for Safe Haven surfaced after Don, a seasoned family counselor, experienced suicide first-hand when his wife took her own life. It became Don's personal mission to assist others suffering from the same mental health challenges.

Don established Safe Haven fifteen years ago and was instrumental not only in its creation, but in its evolution from a small three-counselor organization to a highly respected social service agency in the region. Safe Haven now employs over 40 individuals with counselors and program directors serving a large urban population.

Prior to announcing his retirement to his staff, Don approached Safe Haven's board of directors with the news. The board had the difficult job of replacing Don with a competent individual that could lead Safe Haven's staff and constituents in a manner that would emulate Don's good work. Prior to Don's retirement plans, the board was also considering a new direction for Safe Haven including a capital campaign and strengthening its development presence in the region. After much discussion and an extensive search process, the board hired Federickia Williams, an experienced leader in nonprofit operations, strategic planning, and leadership. The board was pleased with her proven track record of success, and while Don was not a direct contributor in the selection committee, he felt confident that the board had made an excellent decision.

Don shared his retirement news in person with the staff alongside the board president who also announced the new Executive Director. After the initial shock, some Safe Haven staff members were not as confident as Don when they heard about the new hire. There were mixed emotions among long-time personnel who were disappointed that they were not considered for the position and others who were angry with the board for not including staff in the search process. Additionally, counseling and program staff in particular were concerned about a leader who lacked subject matter expertise in suicide. There were, however, several administrative

DOI: 10.4324/9781003387800-40

staff members who were thrilled with the idea that a proven leader was coming onboard and could help direct the operations of the organization, which was not necessarily one of Don's strengths.

As Safe Haven prepared for the 'changing of the guard' Don and Federickia worked with the board and staff to ensure a smooth transition. Although nearly everyone was anxious about the transition, they were also committed to furthering the mission of Safe Haven.

Discussion Questions

1. How involved should staff be in the selection of leadership of nonprofits? Should rank and file volunteers be included in the process? Where does the responsibility fall between board and staff?

2. Can a nonprofit leader be effective if they do not possess subject matter expertise?

3. What traits would a good leader for Safe Haven need to have? Why?

4. Define and discuss succession planning in nonprofit organizations. How might a succession plan have benefited Safe Haven in this case?

Turning the Tide
Transitioning from Volunteers to Paid Staff

JULIE ANN O'CONNELL, BENJAMIN S. BINGLE
AND C. KENNETH MEYER

Long Lake Caring (LLC) quickly became an important community asset during its first five years of existence. It grew from a small, informal group that provided winter coats to those in need to a registered 501(c)(3) organization that stayed open five days a week to provide used clothing to more than 1,000 families each year. As LLC grew, its cadre of volunteers expanded as well.

This growth caused the volunteer coordinator to voice his concerns about LLC's unsustainable model to the board of directors. He told them that by the end of the year his position needed to become a paid position—or he would have to leave.

Organization Overview

LLC had humble beginnings. Three friends, each of whom attended a different church in the Long Lake area, noticed that young children at the local elementary school lacked adequate coats and hats to protect them from the harsh winter weather. Each woman convinced her church leaders to hold a Thanksgiving coat drive to provide coats for the children in need.

Little did the women know that they would collect nearly 500 winter coats (along with hats and gloves) during the first coat drive, and they certainly had no idea how much work it would take to prepare the coats for distribution!

Fortunately, one of the church pastors let the women use a large multipurpose room where they could categorize all the donations based on size and make preparations to distribute the coats. Each of the three women gathered groups of volunteers from her church to host the first Long Lake Coat Fair. In just one afternoon, all of the 500 coats were claimed.

After the initial coat distribution, the volunteers from each church gathered to discuss the event. They noted that the migrant workers who had long shown up in Long Lake each summer to fill low-paying agricultural jobs in the surrounding region had begun in recent years to stay in the area year-round. The volunteers also talked about the impact of the recent economic downturn, which had increased the divide between the "haves" and "have-nots." Both of these factors had contributed to the growing need for affordable clothing—beyond winter coats—in Long Lake. In short, the volunteers decided that the community would benefit

 DOI: 10.4324/9781003387800-41

significantly from an organization that collected gently used clothing for people in need. Thus, Long Lake Caring was born.

Organization Growth

During the first year, the teams of volunteers planned multiple clothing drives and distributions. Members of the community appreciated having a place to donate excess bedding and clothing, while people in need benefited from the high-quality, affordable items, which helped them stretch their meager budgets to cover other necessary expenses. It was a win-win situation all around.

The second year of operation saw increased cooperation with local businesses. Lee Hopkins, one such businessperson, donated a small building just off the town's main street. The original team of two dozen volunteers agreed to staff the building each Saturday for donation intake and distribution, and the building was also open on Wednesdays so that volunteers could sort and organize the clothing. Volunteers indicated their availability to serve on a sign-up sheet posted in the LLC kitchen, and this very informal system seemed to work quite well for all involved. It was during this time of growth that one person from each of the three churches agreed to serve on the executive board of the organization, and papers were drawn up to officially register the group as a 501(c)(3) nonprofit organization.

By the end of the second year, however, it became apparent that having the building open to volunteers just one day a week was not enough. Heavy traffic on Saturday mornings became the norm around the LLC building, and volunteers had to park blocks away in order to allow customers to use the facility. In addition, the original group of volunteers was starting to grow weary, especially when faced with the prospect of increased operating hours. A newer member of the volunteer team, Neil Henderson, agreed to become volunteer coordinator,

an unpaid position. He was a recently retired banker who enjoyed volunteering at LLC, and he had a keen interest and background in organizational software. With his expertise, he was able to supplement existing software to develop an easy-to-use volunteer registry that was accessible to prospective volunteers online.

As demand for the organization's services grew, so did its need for volunteers. After just three years, LLC was open five days a week and utilizing more than fifty volunteers each week in order to keep the doors open. Meanwhile, Neil continued to tweak the software system to make it more user-friendly. He also introduced both volunteer recruitment and retention programs so that LLC could continue to attract the large numbers needed to ensure that it remained a viable community organization. Volunteer training was added to the mix, and LLC was able to continue staffing the facility five days a week with a trained, reliable network of support.

Volunteers or Paid Staff?

After another full year of organizing volunteers, Neil's wife commented that he spent as much time at LLC as he had at his full-time job—except without a paycheck. What had begun as an enjoyable, part-time position to occupy his spare time had turned into a full-time job that was a linchpin of the organization. Living on a retirement income was not as easy as Neil and his wife had hoped, but his demanding responsibilities at LLC had made looking for a part-time job nearly impossible. As LLC continued to grow and began to experience a steady flow of both in-kind and monetary donations, Neil wondered if there was room in the budget to pay him a stipend.

Neil voiced his concerns at the next LLC board meeting. In noting that there were other people who also donated a great deal of time to the organization and who were deserving of compensation, he reminded the board of the dangers an all-volunteer staff can pose. He told them that as much as he loved organizing the volunteers, if his position was not paid by the beginning of the next fiscal year, he would be forced to step down.

The board was stunned. Never before had they discussed or considered hiring a paid staff. They had always been an entirely volunteer-run organization, and the organization's success using that model was substantial. Nevertheless, the board recognized the gravity of Neil's proposal and saw that it would soon need to discern whether LLC had outgrown its all-volunteer model. Deliberation continued during the next several board meetings. Most board members conceded that the organization had reached a pivotal point where it needed to begin offering compensation to those in key positions if it was to continue to grow. A few others, however, remained firm in their belief that the organization could move ahead with an all-volunteer staff. They suggested that perhaps it was time to find another person to fill the volunteer coordinator position so that Neil could find a paid position elsewhere.

The tide was turning, and LLC had to decide what to do next. Choosing to hire a paid staff, even a small one, would be a big commitment for Long Lake Caring—and one that would have serious implications for the young organization's future.

Questions and Instructions

1. Please identify and discuss some factors that should be considered when a nonprofit transitions from a volunteer to a paid staff.

2. How should LLC's board of directors determine which jobs become paid positions? Please explain your response.

3. The organization currently had no stable source of funding, although the annual budget was sound. What did the board of directors need to do to ensure the level of funding required to cover salaries?

4. Identify and discuss some of the benefits and drawbacks of using a volunteer staff. Are volunteers a renewable resource? Please explain.

5. At the end of the case, some board members were in favor of transitioning to paid staff while others wanted to retain the volunteer model. Based on the information available, which option do you think would be best for LLC? Please justify your response.

PART IX

ACCOUNTABILITY AND EVALUATION

The needs, purposes, and concepts of *accountability* and *evaluation* have been written about extensively since at least the 1970s, but our ability to obtain and analyze accurate information needed to evaluate programs and achieve accountability has improved dramatically in recent years.[1] But, let's start with basic definitions:

> *Accountability* means *answerability* for one's actions or behavior.[2]
>
> Evaluation, on the other hand, determines the value or effectiveness of an activity for the purpose of decision making.[3]

Both accountability and evaluation present measurement difficulties and reporting challenges for nonprofit organizations. These arise, in part, from internal and external environments with multiple stakeholders and the very real possibility that it may not be feasible to satisfy them all.

The problem that we face in the implementation of performance measurement is not how to build an effective performance measurement system, but for whom we are building that effective system. Often, we get so wrapped up in the measuring of performance that we forget to examine the purposes for which we measure.[4]

Thus, the difficult questions for nonprofit organizations begin at the outset: accountable to whom and accountable for what?

Accountable to Whom?

Within any organization, the primary accountability is up to the organization's higher levels of management, the executive director, and the board of trustees. This, however, is only a limited view of accountability in and around nonprofit organizations and for the people who work and volunteer in them. A nonprofit organization and its volunteers, staff, executives, and board members are accountable to all individuals, groups, and organizations to which they are answerable—at least for some things and to some extent. Thus, a performing arts nonprofit is accountable to its many types of paying and nonpaying audiences; the rising and established performers; high schools and universities that provide interns; individual, family, corporate, and nonprofit donors and sponsors; government grant-making agencies; and the "community" including community influencers, elected

DOI: 10.4324/9781003387800-42

officials, and the print and electronic media. For a nonprofit organization, accountability truly is *answerability* to individuals and groups with stakes in the organization and its activities.

Accountable for What?

People who own stock in corporations regularly scrutinize the fine print in the stock market reports because stockholders want to know how their investments are doing. For a business, trends in its stock price, profits, earning ratios, market penetration, and dividends serve as measures of organizational performance—its efficiency and effectiveness. Thus, a business can satisfy most of its accountability requirements by regularly publishing data about these performance measures for its shareholders, government regulators, and the general public. Likewise, publishing data in an open and easily accessible manner allows a nonprofit to demonstrate accountability and its corollary: transparency. Transparency is a mechanism for allowing the public to scrutinize meaningful information, and it is an expected part of being accountable. When an investigation shows a lack of transparency or dishonest practices by a nonprofit organization, a shadow is cast over the others. The usefulness of transparency is reduced when information overload or overly technical terminology hinders meaningful evaluations. As was the case with Enron in the early 2000s, information was publicly available, but it was undecipherable except by a select few accounting experts.[5] As the *Nonprofit Quarterly* reported in 2014, a number of foundations and charities established by professional football players were facing heightened scrutiny due to accusations of fraud or, at best, poor accounting practices.[6] Such publicity draws the attention of the IRS and other stakeholders to the accountability practices of all foundations and charities in the nonprofit sector.

In nonprofit organizations, *efficiency*—the quantity of resources consumed in the production of services or outputs to the public or its members—should serve as a clear and useful measure of performance. Demonstrating accountability for efficiency does not raise unique problems for most nonprofits. Accountability for *effectiveness*, however, is a different story; it is far more complex for reasons that cannot be resolved easily. Effectiveness "for what" is relevant beyond internal programmatic concerns. For example, some nonprofits are increasingly being asked to account for the quality of their capacities. For example, a 2007 study of nonprofit accountability focused not on program effectiveness per se, but rather on the composition, best practices, and governance capabilities of their organizations' boards.[7] By 2023, effectiveness continues to focus on these concerns.

The Importance of "Felt Accountability"

Overman and Schillemans argue persuasively that unless employees in government agencies and nonprofit organizations understand and accept that they are individually responsible for accountability—that they will be held accountable for their behavior and performance in the future—accountability will remain nothing more than a hoped-for concept.[8] *Felt accountability* is defined as a clear expectation that a person's decisions or actions will potentially lead to rewards or punishments.[9] "In psychology, accountability is understood as potentially the most powerful source of external social influence on individual behaviors."[10] In sum, unless employers communicate their full commitment to accountability to their service providers, their employees and contractors will not experience *felt accountability*, and therefore accountability is unlikely to become an organizational reality.

Effectiveness as Seen Through Whose Eyes?

Effectiveness seldom, if ever, means the same thing to all stakeholders.[11] Effectiveness is not "a thing." It is instead a subjective phenomenon that is constructed differently by different constituencies. Effectiveness is defined from the divergent perspectives of many beholders. Each of the many constituencies of an organization shares some goals with others but also has its own specific and sometimes changing goals and priorities and thus also criteria of organizational effectiveness.[12] Because each constituency brings its own interests and expectations into its relationship with a nonprofit organization, some priorities are almost always in competition with others for scarce organizational resources and attention. Thus, nonprofit organizations are webs of fluid interactions, constantly changing interests, and forever shifting balances of power among coalitions of constituencies.

For example, nonprofit organizations that house and provide services to troubled youths, adults on parole, and individuals who have been in mental hospitals provide not-uncommon examples. These "halfway house" programs help individuals reintegrate into society but, in doing so, often cause neighbors to believe that they and their children have been placed at risk ("not in my backyard"). What is effectiveness for these types of programs? Whose perspective should have priority? Depending on the answers to these questions, the answer to what measure(s) should be used to determine effectiveness become obvious.

How effective is a symphony orchestra that fills its halls for performances but performs only well-known works by long-established composers? If this orchestra offered some performances by up-and-coming local composers that only filled one-third of the hall, would this programming change increase or decrease its effectiveness? Or how would effectiveness change if the orchestra were to decrease the frequency of its symphony hall performances and initiate instructional activities and performances in elementary and secondary schools across the state? Different stakeholders would have different opinions.

Nonprofit organizations sometimes face difficult decisions about which of several competing constituencies' interests will have priority. When this occurs, the interests of some stakeholders must be set aside either temporarily or permanently. They may decide to "fight" or to withdraw their support from the organization, either of which may weaken it.[13] Interestingly, when it comes to effectiveness, sometimes it is not organizational outputs or outcomes that are recognized by stakeholders, but rather it is a subjective assessment of board effectiveness that becomes "the most important determinant of evaluating organizational effectiveness."[14]

Difficulties Measuring Effectiveness

Many of the services that nonprofit organizations provide can also be difficult to measure.[15] For example, how can and should we measure the effectiveness of programs that strive to improve the quality of life for persons with lifelong disabilities or chronic mental illness—including changes in beliefs, attitudes, and behaviors that are coproduced by the service providers and the recipients of services?[16] The mission of most nonprofit organizations is to change the lives of individuals in some way—make lives better somehow or prevent deterioration of the current quality of life. Collecting information to evaluate the effectiveness of programs sometimes requires unwanted intrusion into sensitive personal areas.[17]

Consider the privacy problems involved, for example, in collecting data to evaluate the effectiveness of a program that is trying to prevent teenage pregnancies. Few of us would accept pregnancy rates—the ultimate outcome measure—as an adequate single measure of effectiveness. We also would want to know at least something about sensitive private behaviors, including frequency and patterns of sexual activity, prevention methods used and not used, STD prevalence, and abortions performed. Even if we were able to collect information of this type, how would we know whether or not the information was accurate, and could we convince others of its accuracy?

Evaluation measurements are less difficult when the important processes, outputs, and/or outcomes can be quantified or observed objectively: for example, it is not difficult to measure how many pregnant women attend prenatal classes, how many contact hours there are between service providers and patients with Alzheimer's disease, or how many people are removed from the welfare rolls during a given year. All too frequently, however, the variables that can be measured are not particularly important. Does anyone truly care how many pregnant mothers attend classes if they do not change their unhealthy lifestyles, or if the individuals who are removed from the welfare rolls have nowhere to live except on the streets and are not eligible for health care services?

Usually, it is not especially difficult to measure the quantity of inputs, activities, and outputs of a nonprofit's services, but it is often very difficult to measure the quality of activities and outputs and either the quantity or the quality of outcomes. It is yet more difficult and much more expensive to measure and establish cause-effect relationships between activities and outcomes, especially with coproduced services whose activities only influence outcomes and do not cause them.[18] When changes in behavior or lifestyle are the desired outcome (for example, programs to improve the outcome of pregnancies or to treat individuals with chemical dependencies), the timeliness of measurements often poses additional serious problems. Outcomes can take years or even decades to establish.[19]

Despite difficulties, evaluation activities are an expected responsibility of nonprofit organizations, and in recent years, some evaluation efforts have been facilitated by funders. For example, United Way of America[20] has worked with local affiliates to help United Way–funded agencies learn to evaluate and report on program and performance outcomes. Three major forces are behind the move:

- Local UWs want to ensure that they can direct money to demonstrably effective programs and demonstrate to donors the results of their financial contributions;
- Measuring outcomes reflects the logical evolution of performance measurement; and,
- Since the early 1990s, the government and business sectors of US society have also been in an era when results and accountability are expected.

Not surprisingly, there is a connection between service providers' conducting performance evaluations and the ability to raise funds from outside sources.[21] Obviously, funders of all types want to know whether their investments are paying off and in what ways lives are being improved.

The limited abilities of the populations served by many nonprofits introduce another difficulty when measuring program effectiveness, however. Many nonprofit programs use some aspects of quality of life or changes in the quality of life as indicators of program effectiveness. Evaluators attempt to measure quality of life through surveys administered to recipients of services, people who know them, or the public. Surveying for quality of life has many difficulties and limitations in and of itself; with recipients of services who have severe cognitive, emotional, or communication challenges, these difficulties are compounded. How should quality of life be determined for people with severe intellectual challenges? Answers to this type of question require difficult value judgments, not technical solutions. Are the judgments of family members or professionals acceptable as proxy measures? Should we accept the judgment of professionals who provide services to the clients, only professionals who represent supposedly neutral and objective funding agencies, or groups that advocate for the clients and their families? Can family members always be trusted to make decisions that are in the best interests of their relatives/clients? These questions are far from hypothetical; they reflect some of the difficult realities of being accountable for effectiveness in nonprofit organizations.

Wrapping Up Accountability and Evaluation

Accountability has at least five often-competing dimensions: hierarchical, legal, professional, political, and moral or ethical.[22] The evaluation methods that are used most commonly today are best able to achieve and verify hierarchical, legal, and political accountability and least able to achieve and verify ethical or moral accountability—the dimension of accountability most directly associated with quality of services. Accountability thus means far more than compliance with contractual, legal, or financial reporting requirements.[23] Accountability also includes responsibility for moral, professional, and ethical dimensions of service, which means that service providers need to be answerable for the quality as well as the quantity of services.[24]

Accountability problems of this nature and complexity are not limited to nonprofit organizations. They cross sector boundaries. Far too much attention has been paid to traditional or compliance accountability and process accountability and far too little to managerial accountability (which focuses on the judicious use of public resources), program accountability (which is concerned with the outcomes or results of operations), and social accountability (which attempts to determine the societal impacts of government programs).[25] Likewise, using performance evaluations for the purpose of satisfying the multiple expectations of diverse stakeholders is not a one-size-fits-all proposition. "When different funders use their own approaches, terms, definitions, time frames, and reporting requirements, local agencies are forced to change their procedures for each funder. This harms the agencies and undermines each funder's intentions."[26] To begin to solve this problem will, at the very least, require the time and willingness to compromise from all invested stakeholders.[27]

Readings Reprinted in Part IX

Gregory D. Saxton and Chao Guo's "Accountability Online: Understanding the Web-Based Accountability Practices of Nonprofit Organizations" reports on the online accountability practices of 117 community foundations in the US. Not unexpectedly, nonprofit community foundations with strong financial capacity and highly effective boards of directors are most likely to use the web for accountability purposes.

The idea of accountability as simply being transparent in reporting financial documents or demonstrating conformity to performance expectations is fast becoming outdated, however. As Saxton and Guo show, web-based technology has opened the door to a more interactive interpretation of the notion of accountability or "being accountable." "Web-based accountability practices include not only *disclosure* (transparency in documentation), but also *dialogue* "which encompasses and solicits the input and active engagement of core stakeholders."[28]

To the dismay of Saxton and Guo, however, although web-based approaches provide an ideal medium for two-way engagement, it is the approach least likely to be used by community foundations.

The second reading in Part IX is an excerpt from "Measuring the Networked Nonprofit: Using Data to Change the World" by Beth Kanter and Katie Delahaye Paine,[29] who discuss the importance of using data as part of a nonprofit's web-based strategic efforts to reach new markets and achieve and evaluate mission-related goals. The networked nonprofit is described as a new type of nonprofit organization that leverages the power of social media to expand its network of supporters and thereby greatly increases its capacity and success. The authors argue that measurement is a powerful tool that provides feedback, stimulates ideas, helps with documentation, offers credibility, saves time (since wasted activities can be avoided), and fuels passion for the work. In an era when nonprofits are using social media to appeal to a younger demographic, this medium requires the same care as any other outreach tactic. If appropriately understood, staffed, and funded—all big *ifs*—social media can serve as an effective method of two-way communications between administrators and employees, citizens, clients, consumers, audiences, and a myriad of other stakeholders. There are no shortcuts when seeking to be innovative. As with all managerial strategies, using social media requires resources and careful attention to the relationships that these tools can help create.

Cases in Part IX

The cases in Part IX present transparency, accountability, and evaluation dilemmas. The first case, "Technology and Transparency at the Museum," introduces a nonprofit that may not be comfortable sharing financial or performance data on the web. Regardless of comfort level, however, nonprofits are required to conform to the public's expectations regarding the availability of data, online or otherwise. When expectations are not met, there may be unpleasant or unexpected ramifications. The second case, Measure Twice, Cut Once: Performance Evaluation in Nonprofit Organizations, provides the reader with a not-uncommon circumstance—budgetary pressures that require decisions about where to cut expenses. Here, the case asks the reader to consider the evaluative processes needed to recommend adjustments in programming and/or personnel.

Notes

1. Edward A. Suchman, *Evaluative Research: Principles and Practice in Public Service and Social Action Programs* (New York: Russell Sage Foundation, 1967); also, Yaser Hasan Al-Mamary, Alina Shamsuddin, and Nor Aziati, "The Relationship between System Quality, Information Quality, and Organizational Performance," *International Journal of Knowledge and Research in Management & E-Commerce*, 4, no. 3 (July 2014), 7–10.

2. Kevin P. Kearns, *Managing for Accountability: Preserving the Public Trust in Public and Nonprofit Organizations* (San Francisco: Jossey-Bass, 1996), 11.

3. American Evaluation Association, *What is Evaluation?* www.eval.org/About/What-is-Evaluation (accessed February 16, 2022).

4. Daniel Bromberg, "Performance Measurement: A System with a Purpose or a Purposeless System?" *Public Performance & Management Review* 33 no. 2 (December 2009), 214–221.

5. Stuart C. Gilman and Howard Whitton, "When Transparency Becomes the Enemy of Accountability: Reflections from the Field," *PA Times* (2013) http://patimes.org/transparency-enemy-accountability-reflections-field/

6. John Brothers, "As NFL Suffers Ethical Lapses, Player Charities also Under Scrutiny," *The Nonprofit Quarterly* (October 9, 2014) www.nonprofitquarterly.org

7. Francie Ostrower, "Nonprofit Governance in the United States. Findings on Performance and Accountability from the First National Representative Study," The Urban Institute (June 2007).

8. Sjors Overman and Thomas Schillemans, "Toward a Public Administration Theory of Felt Accountability," *Public Administration Review*, 82 no. 1 (January/February 2022), 12.

9. Jennifer S. Lerner and Philip E. Tetlock, "Accounting for the Effects of Accountability," *Psychological Bulletin, 125*(2) (1999). 255–275.

10. Philip E. Tetlock, "The Impact of Accountability on Judgment and Choice: Toward a Social Contingency Model," *Advances in Experimental Social Psychology*, 25 no. 1 (1992), 333.

11. For more information about the multiple constituency theory approach to organizations and their effectiveness, see Robert D. Herman and David O. Renz, "Multiple Constituencies and the Social Construction of Nonprofit Organization Effectiveness," *Nonprofit and Voluntary Sector Quarterly* 26 no. 2 (June 1997),185–206; David Campbell and Kristina T. Lambright, "Program Performance and Multiple Constituency Theory," *The Open Repository—Binghamton*, February 1, 2016. https://orb.binghamton.edu/public_admin_fac/54/; and Thomas Connolly, Edward J. Conlon, and Stuart J. Deutsch, "Organizational Effectiveness: A Multiple-Constituency Approach," *Academy of Management Review* 5 (1980), 211–217

12. Examples include Herman and Renz, "Multiple Constituencies," 185–206.

13. J. Steven Ott, "Perspectives on Organizational Governance: Some Effects on Government-Nonprofit Relations," *Southeastern Political Review* 21 no. 1 (Winter 1993), 3–21.

14. Robert D. Herman and David O. Renz, "Multiple Constituencies and the Social Construction of Nonprofit Organization Effectiveness," *Nonprofit and Voluntary Sector Quarterly* 26 no. 2 (June 1997), 185–206.

15. Vermont Agency of Human Services, "Results-Based Accountability," https://humanservices.vermont.gov/our-impact/results-based-accountability (accessed February 16, 2022) and J. Steven Ott and Lisa A. Dicke, "Important but Largely Unanswered Questions About Accountability in Contracted Public Human Services," *International Journal of Organization Theory & Behavior* 3, nos. 3 and 4 (Summer 2000), 283–317.

16. James F. Mensing, "The Challenges of Defining and Measuring Outcomes in Nonprofit Human Service Organizations," *Human Service Organizations: Management, Leadership & Governance* 41 no. 3 (2017) 207–212; and Bruce B. Clary, "Coproduction," in J. M. Shafritz, ed., *International Encyclopedia of Public Policy and Administration* (Boulder, CO: Westview Press, 1998), 531–536.

17. J. Steven Ott and Lisa A. Dicke, "Challenges Facing Public Sector HRM in an Era of Downsizing, Devolution, Diffusion, and Empowerment . . . and Accountability??" in Ali Farazmand, ed., *Strategic Public Personnel Administration/HRM: Building Human Capital for the 21st Century* (Westport, CT: Greenwood Press, 2007).

18. Edward A. Suchman, *Evaluative Research: Principles and Practice in Public Service and Social Action Programs* (New York: Russell Sage Foundation, 1967); also Mithila Fox, "Evaluative Research: Definition, Methods, and Types," Maze, https://maze.co/guides/ux-research/evaluative/ (accessed February 16, 2022).

19. Except through indirect and/or proxy measures, which introduce additional measurement difficulties. See Emil J. Posavac and Raymond G. Carey, "Program Evaluation: An Overview," in E. J. Posavac and R. G. Carey, *Program Evaluation: Methods and Case Studies*, 8th ed. (Upper Saddle River, NJ: Prentice-Hall, 2011).

20. Michael Hendricks, Margaret C. Plantz, and Kathleen J. Prichard, "Measuring Outcomes of United Way–Funded Programs: Expectations and Reality," in J.G. Carman and K. A. Fredericks, eds., *Nonprofits and Evaluations: New Directions for Evaluation* (2008), 119, 13–35.

21. Joanne G. Carman, "Nonprofits, Funders, and Evaluations: Accountability in Action," *American Review of Public Administration* 39 no. 4 (July 2009), 374–390.

22. Lester M. Salamon, *Partners in Public Service: Government-Nonprofit Relations in the Modern Welfare State* (Baltimore: Johns Hopkins University Press, 1995).

23. See, for example, Ruben Berrios and Jerome B. McKinney, "Contracting and Accountability Under Leaner Government," *Public Integrity* 19 no. 6, 559–575 and Lisa A. Dicke and J. Steven Ott, "Public Agency Accountability in Human Services Contracting," *Public Productivity & Management Review* 22, no. 4 (June 1999), 502–516.

24. Gene E. Caiden, "The Problem of Ensuring the Public Accountability of Public Officials," in J. G. Jabbra and O. P. Dwivedi, eds., *Public Service Accountability* (West Hartford, CT: Kumarian Press, 1988), 23–24.

25. Michael Hendricks, Margaret C. Plantz, and Kathleen J. Pritchard, "Measuring Outcomes of United Way-–Funded Programs: Expectations and Reality," in J. G. Carman and K. A. Fredericks, eds., *Nonprofits and Evaluations: New Directions for Evaluation* (2009), 13–35, 119.

26. Daniel Bromberg, "Performance Measurement: A System with a Purpose or a Purposeless System?" *Public Performance & Management Review* 33 no. 2, (December 2009), 214–221.

27. Saxton and Guo, "Accountability Online: Understanding the Web-Based Accountability Practices of Nonprofit Organizations." Reprinted as Chapter 18.

28. Gijs Jan Brandsma and Thomas Schillemans, "The Accountability Cube: Measuring Accountability," *Journal of Public Administration Research and Theory* 23 no. 4 (September 2013), 953–975.

29. Measuring the Networked Nonprofit: Using Data to Change the World, Beth Kanter and Katie Delahaye Paine.

Accountability Online
Understanding the Web-Based Accountability Practices of Nonprofit Organizations

GREGORY D. SAXTON AND CHAO GUO

From Gregory D. Saxton and Chao Guo, "Accountability Online: Understanding the Web-Based Accountability Practices of Nonprofit Organizations," *Nonprofit and Voluntary Sector Quarterly* 40, no. 2, 270–289. Copyright © 2011 by SAGE Publications. Reprinted by permission of SAGE Publications.

The idea of holding organizations and their leaders accountable for their actions has long been a matter of concern in the nonprofit sector. In recent years, the rapid diffusion of advanced Internet-based technologies among nonprofit organizations has brought with it considerable potential for demonstrating and promoting organizational accountability. How are nonprofit organizations taking advantage of this potential?

And what is driving their use of the Internet as an accountability- and public trust-building tool? In this article, we examine these questions in reporting the results of the first comprehensive study of nonprofit organizations' adoption of Web-based accountability practices.

Our central aims here are, first, to present a framework for conceptualizing and operationalizing Web-based accountability practices and, second, to present and test a theoretical model that can account for variation in these practices. Specifically, building on existing literature, we propose to understand the Web-based

accountability practices of nonprofit organizations through two key dimensions: (a) disclosure, which concerns the transparent provision of key information on organizational finances and performance, and (b) dialogue, which encompasses the solicitation of input from and interactive engagement with core stakeholders. We then present a theoretical model in which four groups of factors—strategy, capacity, governance, and environment—are posited to affect the extent to which organizations vary in their adoption of Web-based accountability practices along our two dimensions.

In providing a generalized test of Web-based accountability, this article represents an important first step toward understanding the role of information technology in enhancing nonprofit accountability. Using our four-factor model and new data collected through a content analysis of 117 US community foundation[1] Web sites in conjunction with survey and financial data, we demonstrate that organizations vary greatly in the extent to which they adopt Web-based

DOI: 10.4324/9781003387800-43

accountability practices along the dimensions of disclosure and dialogue. Though the typical community foundation takes care to disclose at least minimal financial- and performance-related information, many community foundations' Web sites are, it appears, mostly information-only brochureware; they provide few mechanisms to facilitate input from or interactively engage with key stakeholders. The dialogue dimension is hence severely lacking in the typical community foundation. Our multivariate analyses, in turn, provide some support for the validity of the four-factor model we identified, with the governance- and capacity-related factors tending to dominate the results. . . .

Web-Based Accountability: A Two-Dimensional View

In the most general of terms, we might refer to a nonprofit organization's Web-based accountability practices as any online reporting, feedback, and/or stakeholder input and engagement mechanisms that serve to demonstrate or enhance accountability . . .

There are both demand and supply forces at work. On the demand side, Internet-based technologies are providing citizens with the increasing ability and interest to gain access to information they deem important.[2] According to a Pew Internet & American Life Project (2008) survey, as of May 2008, 73 percent of Americans use the Internet. More and more people are getting their information from the Web—and in such a way that it is affecting how they volunteer with, give to, and otherwise interact with charitable organizations (e.g., see Gordon, Knock, and Neely 2008). On the supply side, in turn, Internet-based technologies have led to an increased ability of organizations to disclose financial and operational information. Through the use of interactive electronic networking capabilities, the technology also

facilitates stakeholder inclusion in organizational decision making by lowering participation costs.

In short, with the diffusion of Internet technology, there is both an increased need as well as ability to use the Web to address organizational accountability . . . . We posit that there are two fundamental dimensions to Web-based accountability practices: *disclosure* and *dialogue*.

Disclosure

. . . [A]n organization's online efforts in the areas of both accountability for finances and accountability for performance essentially amount to demonstrating accountability through the voluntary disclosure of key organizational information.[3] . . .

Financial Disclosure

. . . [W]e conceptualize financial disclosure as the extent of financial information a nonprofit organization discloses on its Web site. Such disclosure aims at demonstrating accountability for finances, and in the online environment involves posting such content as budgeting materials, reporting on the utilization of financial resources, and compliance-related documents—including information on administrative fees for funds; fund investment, management, and spending policies; investment philosophies; investment performance and asset growth; audited and unaudited financial reports; Internal Revenue Service (IRS) 990 forms; overhead costs; annual reports; codes of ethics and conflict-of-interest policies; and adherence to best practice standards.

Performance Disclosure

. . . [W]e conceptualize performance disclosure as the extent of goal- and outcome-oriented information a nonprofit organization discloses on its Web site. Such disclosure aims at demonstrating accountability for performance, which . . . covers both the organization's mission and its results. Performance disclosure thus involves an organization making available online any information, first, on what it is trying to achieve—such as its mission statement, history, vision, plans, values, and goals—and, second, on what it has achieved in terms of outputs, outcomes, and broader community impacts.

Dialogue

The second dimension of Web-based accountability concerns mechanisms for stakeholder input and interactive engagement . . . . [W]e refer to this dimension as dialogue. Although preliminary evidence suggests the disclosure element can be critical to organizational outcomes (e.g., Gordon et al. 2008), it is on this second dimension that the Web holds special promise.

Solicitation of Stakeholder Input

. . . [D]ialogue includes two related but distinct components. The first refers to the solicitation of stakeholder input, and includes any Web-based mechanism that can tap stakeholders' preferences, needs, and demands in such a way that, ultimately, stakeholders have some degree of say in the organization's decision making regarding policies and programs. In addition to simple feedback forms, discussion lists, and bulletin boards, the recent development and growth of collaborative wikis, online surveying and polling tools, and tagging and social bookmarking projects has opened up new opportunities for intense, decentralized, and highly participatory problem-solving, decision-making, brainstorming, and knowledge-creation efforts. Collectively, the architecture of participation (O'Reilly 2005) in these technologies has dramatically increased organizations' ability to obtain meaningful stakeholder input.

Interactive Engagement

Although the first component of dialogue can be seen as the input of stakeholder preferences, this second component can be seen as an output of those preferences in the form of interactive content, tools, and services specifically designed for and targeted at particular stakeholder groups. This component is built on the notion that what best distinguishes second-generation Web technologies is precisely the ability to facilitate intense interactions between actors and, moreover, that highly interactive content targeted at core stakeholders is a key component of an organization's attempts to be accountable to those stakeholders by responding to their preferences.[4] . . .

Strategy, Capacity, Governance, and Environment: A Model of Web-Based Accountability Practices

We propose that a nonprofit organization's level of Web-based accountability derives from four sets of factors familiar to nonprofit organizational scholars: strategy, capacity, governance, and environment. In particular, an organization's adoption of Web-based accountability practices is a function of (a) the extent to which the organization's strategy is focused on certain stakeholder groups or geographic service areas; (b) the degree to which the organization has the capacity to sustain strategic-level projects, especially with regard to the utilization of information technology; (c) the degree to which the organization is well governed; and (d) the degree to which the external environment is receptive to or demanding of Web-based organizational practices.

In this section, we lay out specific hypotheses about these relationships. It is our assertion that all of these determinants—strategy, capacity, governance, and environment—must be considered when explaining a nonprofit organization's level of Web-based accountability. See Figure 18.1.

Strategy

The particular strategy that a nonprofit organization develops to accomplish its social mission has important implications for its adoption of Web-based accountability mechanisms. We consider two elements here, the first of which is stakeholder focus. Community foundations' strategies are often categorized according to whether the dominant stakeholder focus is on donor services or community leadership (Graddy and Morgan 2006). . . . The community-focused model emphasizes community leadership, participation in community collaborative initiatives, and raising unrestricted funds to target high-priority needs. The donor-focused model, on the other hand, focuses on fulfilling the charitable interests of individual donors and on managing donor-advised funds. These two models have led to distinct views regarding community foundations' accountability relationships. In line with the community-focused model, the foundation should be accountable to the community where it operates and responsive to the needs and concerns of that community. In line with the donor-focused model, however, the community foundation should be accountable to its donors and facilitate each donor's individual charitable interests.

Taking the important differences between these two models into account, we posit that donor-focused foundations will adopt a higher level of Web-based accountability practices than community-focused foundations because of the stronger influence of and closer monitoring by donors . . . . In recent years, donor-advised funds have grown in popularity as a major funding source for many community foundations (Luke and Feurt 2002). This more restrictive type of funds, while offering hope of accumulating assets at a much faster pace than unrestricted funds, allows donors to have stronger control over the use of funds. It is thus reasonable to expect that a foundation that relies on donor-advised funds is more likely to demonstrate a higher level of online accountability or, conversely, that a foundation with greater amounts of unrestricted funds in its endowment will have lower levels of Web-based accountability. This leads to our first hypothesis:

> *Hypothesis 1:* Online accountability is negatively associated with the percentage of unrestricted funds.

The second strategy-related factor is geographic service area. Each community foundation serves a specific geographic area that often does not overlap with others. In a recent study (Guo and Brown 2006), those foundations serving smaller or more-defined geographic or sociopolitical regions are defined as *specialist* foundations, and those serving larger and more heterogeneous regions as *generalist* foundations . . . . The authors suggest that specialist foundations can make fuller use of local knowledge and experience to connect donors with effective providers. Following this line of reasoning, it seems reasonable to expect that specialist foundations will demonstrate a higher level of online accountability than generalist foundations:

> *Hypothesis 2:* Online accountability is negatively associated with the size of geographic service area.

Capacity

The capacity the organization has to undertake strategically driven initiatives also has implications for the adoption of Web-based accountability practices. One of the most consistently important capacity factors cited in the literature is organizational size. Size is a particularly important determinant of nonprofit accountability. As an organization grows, it becomes more visible and therefore attracts greater attention and scrutiny by multiple external constituencies, such as the state, the media, and the general public (Luoma and Goodstein 1999).

The literature also demonstrates a strong relationship between size and access to technology (Berlinger and Te'eni 1999; McNutt and Boland 1999; Schneider 2003); more importantly, there appears to be a critical connection between wealth and the ability to exploit technology for specifically mission-related purposes (Hackler and Saxton 2007).[5] In effect, size predicts an organization's capacity to employ information technology for strategic functions—such as boosting accountability—as opposed to purely administrative functions. Recent nonprofit research has also found a positive relationship between size and voluntary disclosure (e.g., Behn, DeVries, and Lin 2007; Gordon, Fisher, Malone, and Tower 2002). Accordingly, we submit the following hypothesis:

> *Hypothesis 3:* Online accountability is positively associated with organizational size.

We also posit that younger organizations will be more likely to resort to Web-based accountability mechanisms. The literature denotes several reasons for this. First, accounting scholars have argued that there is a greater information asymmetry between insiders and outsiders in new organizations, which spurs younger organizations to greater voluntary disclosure to bridge the gap (e.g., Trabelsi, Labelle, and Dumontier 2008). Management scholars, in turn, are likely to cite organizational age as a factor that increases inertia and weakens discretion (Ham-brick and Fin-kelstein 1987), rendering older organizations less likely to be innovative in the adoption of new technology. This leads us to the following hypothesis:

> *Hypothesis 4:* Online accountability is negatively related to organizational age.

Governance

The upper-echelons perspective (Hambrick and Mason 1984) attributes major influence (in terms of both strategic choices and organizational performance) to organizational leadership. We present propositions for two specific governance characteristics. The first is board performance. In the United States, the law ultimately holds the board of directors accountable for the affairs and conduct of the organization. . . .

Brody (2002) . . . described the role of a nonprofit's board as the "classical model of nonprofit accountability" (p. 476). Given the board's ultimate responsibility for a foundation's mission, direction, and policies (Bothwell 1989), we expect that those organizations with a high-performing board will demonstrate a greater level of online accountability than those with a low-performing board:

> *Hypothesis 5:* Online accountability is positively associated with board performance.

Financial stewardship is one of the most important responsibilities of the nonprofit board. It refers to "the degree to which the board scrutinizes finances and the existence of sound financial practices as well as the extent to which the board maintains a degree of objectivity and independence from management" (Gill, Flynn, and Reissing 2005, 278). . . .

. . . [W]e posit it as a direct determinant of an organization's willingness to invest in technology-enabled accountability practices. This leads to the following hypothesis:

> *Hypothesis 6:* Online accountability is positively related to financial stewardship.

Sample and Data Gathering

To investigate the prevalence and determinants of Web-based accountability, we utilize data gathered in September and October of 2005 on 117 US community foundations that had in a previous study (Guo and Brown 2006) completed a questionnaire and follow-up telephone interviews.[6] Our Web site data-gathering method consisted of a multicoder analysis of the complete content on each of the 117 community foundations' Web sites.[7] Our approach

FIGURE 18.1 Generic Model of Causal Factors Determining an Organization's Online Accountability Practices

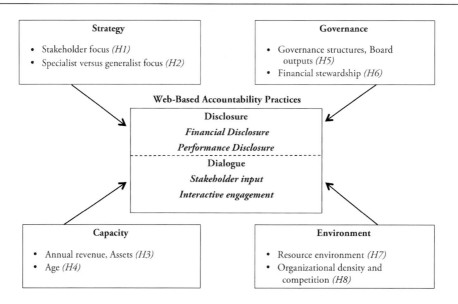

FIGURE 18.2 Financial Disclosure

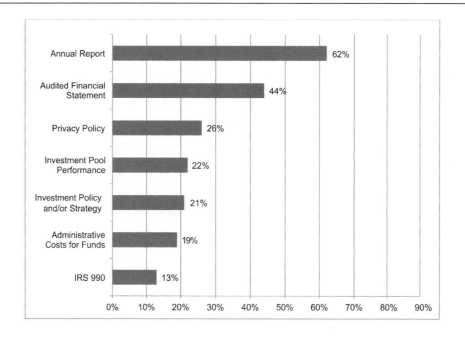

was to search for and code any Web site content that conformed to our literature-grounded conceptualizations of financial disclosure, performance disclosure, solicitation of stakeholder input, and interactive engagement.[8] We then combine these data with questionnaire responses data and IRS form 990 data to test our hypotheses.

The average community foundation in our sample was 28 years old in 2005 and had US$58.6 million in assets, of which 24.4 percent were discretionary funds. It generated revenues of US$5.7 million a year, and granted, on average, 9 percent of its assets.[9] Our content analysis showed 113 of the 117 foundations to have meaningful Web sites.[10] In terms of accountability-related content, 92 percent of the organizations made available online at least minimal information relevant to performance-related disclosure, 77 percent had information relevant to financial disclosure, 78 percent had at least simple feedback/stakeholder input mechanisms in place, and 85 percent made available some form of nonstatic interactive engagement mechanism with one or more core stakeholder group.

Operationalization

We operationalize five dependent variables that conform to our conceptual specifications of Web-based accountability: For the disclosure element, we create indices of both financial- and performance-related disclosure, for the dialogue dimension, we measure both the solicitation of input and the interactive engagement with key stakeholders, and to capture overall effort, we create a composite online accountability index.

In this section, we describe our measurement procedures for these variables before turning to a brief description of our specification of the eight independent variables we use to test our hypotheses.

Dependent Variables: Measuring Web-Based Accountability
Financial Disclosure Index (FDI)

Following the data-gathering approach noted above, for this measure we coded content found anywhere on the site that was targeted at demonstrating financial responsibility. As shown in Figure 18.2, we found seven items that indicate a community foundation's online financial disclosure efforts: annual report, audited financial statement, privacy policy, data on investment pool performance, investment policy and/or strategy, information on administrative costs for funds, and IRS 990 form. . . .

Performance Disclosure Index (PDI)

In the area of performance disclosure, we coded any material on the Web site related to the organization's fulfillment of its social mission. In line with our literature review, such disclosure includes any information related to the foundation's mission, or what it is trying to achieve, along with its results, or the outputs, outcomes, and broader community impacts of its grant-making activity.[11] Figure 18.3 shows the eight items we found that indicate community foundations' online performance disclosure in these areas—a mission statement, list of recent grant awards, dollar amounts of individual grants awarded, description of community foundations' general purpose, summaries of funded projects, reporting on program or grant impact, community impact reporting, and grantee success stories. . . .

Solicitation of Stakeholder Input

With this first component of dialogue, we are interested in how community foundations use Web-based technologies to solicit feedback from their stakeholders, assess their preferences

FIGURE 18.3 Performance Disclosure

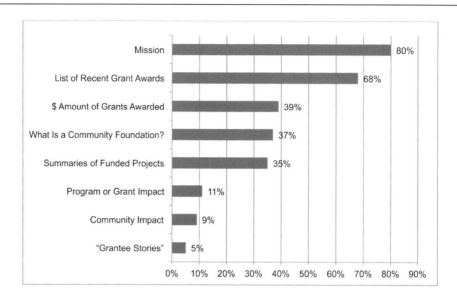

and needs, or engage them in discussions that will help the organization make important program-related decisions. As shown in Figure 18.4, we found a few exemplary practices along this dimension that one or two organizations were using, such as a Nonprofit Listserv or an Interactive Message Center. However, the number of organizations availing themselves of such tools is very low; besides the ubiquitous contact-us links, the great majority of sites had no means of soliciting information on stakeholder concerns. . . .

Interactive Engagement (Interactivity)

We are interested here in how community foundations are using the Internet to be responsive to the needs and demands of donors, grant seekers, and the community—their three core stakeholders—through the provision of high-level interactive Web site content. Our framework for evaluating the level of interactive engagement is the information-transaction-interaction

hierarchy developed by Saxton, Guo, and Brown (2007). In this framework, an organization that has, for instance, only informational content available for donors cannot have great intensity in its online relationships with this key group. In contrast, an organization that allows online transactions to take place, such as e-donations, newsletter sign-ups, content downloads, or information uploads, has permitted more intense and important interactions with its contributors. And a site that has a variety of interactive,[12] Web 2.0–type content targeted at donors—such as a customizable donor/advisor extranet, interactive blogs, Web-enabled databases, online training, virtual conferences, and social networking applications—will have the most meaningful donor interactions and thus the highest levels of interactive engagement. Based on this hierarchy, Figure 18.5 shows the proportion of foundations with low-level informational content, higher-level transactional content, and highest-level interactive content targeted at donors, grant seekers, and the community, respectively.

FIGURE 18.4 Solicitation of Stakeholder Input

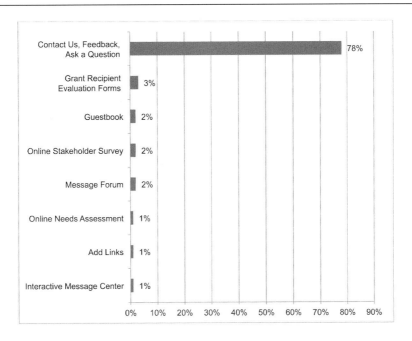

To create our measure of interactive engagement, we first assigned each community foundation three provisional scores based on the information shown in the figure. Specifically, with regard to donors, a community foundation received a score of 3 if it provided any donor-related services on its Web site that allow for interaction; it received a score of 2 if it provided services that allow for transactions but no interactive content; it received a score of 1 if it provided only basic informational content to donors; and it received a score of 0 if it provided no donor-related content. We did the same with regard to grant seekers and the community. Our final composite scale, Interactivity, is then the sum of these three values, such that each community foundation's score can range from a low of 0 to a high of 9.[13]

Online Accountability Index

Last, we created a composite index of online accountability by summing each organization's scores on the FDI, PDI, and Interactivity variables. A Cronbach's alpha of .82 indicates a high level of internal consistency.[14]

Independent Variables

As discussed earlier, we operationalize our hypotheses through eight independent variables, two for each of the four factors (strategy, capacity, governance, and environment) in our explanatory model. First, with regard to strategy, Discretionary Income is the natural logarithm of the percentage of permanent unrestricted funds in a foundation's total assets, as reported by the chief executive (Community Foundation CEO survey, Guo and Brown 2006). Size of Service Area, in turn, measures the size of geographical area that a community foundation serves; it is defined as a binary variable with a value of 1 for specialist foundations that serve a small-sized community (i.e., local community such as city or county) and 2 for generalist foundations that serve a medium- to large-sized community (i.e., a regional or statewide foundation). In terms of capacity, we

FIGURE 18.5 Interactive Engagement with Stakeholders

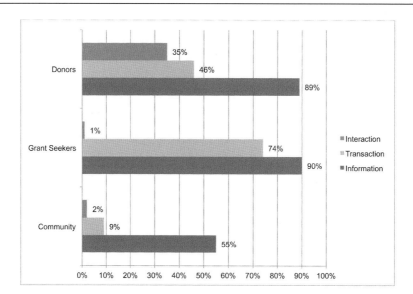

include Asset Size, the natural log of a given foundation's assets from the 2004FY IRS form 990, and Age, the age of the organization in years. To examine governance, we first use our CEO survey data (Guo and Brown 2006) to measure the chief executive's perception of Board Performance on a 1 to 5 scale; this is a composite measure that covers resource acquisition, stewardship, donor service, grant making, marketing, and mission and strategy. We also measure the organization's Net Working Capital as current assets less current liabilities (2004FY IRS form 990); this serves as the proxy for financial stewardship.[15] Last, we measure environment via Community Poverty, the percentage of residents below the poverty line in the foundation's primary county in 2001 (US Census Bureau), and Organizational Density, the ratio of the number of community foundations in a given state over the state's gross state product.[16]

Data Analysis and Results

Because the dependent variables in this study involve counts of services and content on a community foundation's Web site, we use a Poisson regression analysis[17] to estimate the following four models:

FDI = $\exp(\beta_0 + \beta_1$ Discretionary Income + β_2 Size of Service Area + β_3 Asset Size + β_4 Age + β_5 Board Performance + β_6 Net Working Capital + β_7 Community Poverty + β_8 Organizational Density)

PDI = $\exp(\beta_0 + \beta_1$ Discretionary Income + β_2 Size of Service Area + β_3 Asset Size + β_4 Age + β_5 Board Performance + β_6 Net Working Capital + β_7 Community Poverty + β_8 Organizational Density)

Interactivity = $\exp(\beta_0 + \beta_1$ Discretionary Income + β_2 Size of Service Area + β_3 Asset Size + β_4 Age + β_5 Board Performance + β_6 Net Working Capital + β_7 Community Poverty + β_8 Organizational Density)

Online Accountability Index = $\exp(\beta_0 + \beta_1$ Discretionary Income + β_2 Size of Service Area + β_3 Asset Size + β_4 Age + β_5 Board Performance + β_6 Net Working Capital + β_7 Community Poverty + β_8 Organizational Density)

Table 18.1 displays the results of these regression analyses. The coefficients in Models 1 through

TABLE 18.1 Factors Associated with Online Accountability of Community Foundations: Poisson Regression Analyses

Hypothesis	Independent Variable	Hypothesized Direction	Model 1 Financial Disclosure Index (FDI)	Model 2 Performance Disclosure Index (PDI)	Model 3 Interactive Engagement Scale (Interactivity)	Model 4 Composite Online Accountability Index
1	Discretionary income	−	−0.03 (0.06)	−0.08 (0.05)	−0.03 (0.04)	−0.05** (0.02)
2	Size of service area	−	.23 (0.15)	−0.10 (0.13)	−0.17 (0.11)	−0.15*** (0.05)
3	Asset size	+	0.29*** (0.06)	0.15*** (0.05)	0.13*** (0.04)	0.17*** (0.02)
4	Age	−	−0.003 (0.004)	−0.001 (0.003)	−0.001 (0.003)	−0.000 (0.000)
5	Board performance	+	0.29** (0.14)	0.19* (0.12)	0.12 (0.09)	0.13** (0.05)
6	Net working capital	+	−0.66 (0.47)	−0.46 (0.44)	−0.17 (0.31)	−0.55*** (0.18)
7	Community poverty	−	−0.01 (0.02)	−0.01 (0.01)	0.02* (0.01)	−0.00 (0.01)
8	Organizational density	−	−1.51* (0.80)	−0.36 (0.64)	0.07 (0.51)	−0.58** (0.27)
	Intercept		−4.42*** (1.07)	−1.65** (0.83)	−1.07 (0.66)	−0.04 (0.34)
	n		113	113	113	113
	Log likelihood		−193.82	−204.34	−217.67	−378.32
	χ^2		48.13***	23.56***	21.37***	124.60**

*p < 0.1. **p < 0.05. ***p < 0.01. Standard errors are shown in parentheses.

4 (with standard errors in parentheses) indicate the effects of each independent variable on the financial disclosure index (FDI), performance disclosure index (PDI), interactive engagement scale (Interactivity), and composite online accountability index, respectively.

To recap, each of the eight independent variables is associated with a specific hypothesis related to one of the four primary factors in our explanatory model. In line with our hypothesis testing, we present our results here briefly factor by factor before discussing the most important implications of these findings in the Conclusions.

First, in Hypotheses 1 and 2, we proposed that two strategy-related variables—the percentage of unrestricted funds and the size of the geographic service area—would be negatively associated with Web-based accountability practices. The regression analyses revealed no significant relationship between either of these variables and the disclosure and dialogue measures of accountability (FDI, PDI, and Interactivity). However, both obtained a strong, negative relationship with the composite measure of accountability, thus providing partial support for our hypotheses.

Next, we created two hypotheses to tap organizational capacity: Hypothesis 3 described a positive relationship between asset size and Web-based accountability practices, whereas Hypothesis 4 posited a negative relationship between age and accountability. The results were mixed. The analyses revealed a strong positive relationship between asset size and all four of the accountability measures; yet, age failed to obtain significance in any of the models.

Hypotheses 5 and 6 then proposed that two governance-related factors—board performance and financial stewardship—were expected to obtain a positive relationship with online accountability. The regression analyses revealed no significant relationship between net working capital, our proxy for financial stewardship, and the disclosure and dialogue measures of Web-based accountability (i.e., FDI, PDI,

and Interactivity). Yet, it did obtain a strong negative association with the composite online accountability index. The analyses also revealed a significant, positive relationship between board performance and three of the measures of accountability (FDI, PDI, and the composite index).

Last, in Hypotheses 7 and 8 we posited that community poverty and organizational density, our two environment-related measures, would be negatively associated with Web-based accountability practices. Surprisingly, regional poverty was found to be positively associated with the dialogue dimension of accountability (Interactivity) but not with the other accountability measures. However, consistent with our prediction, the analyses revealed a significant and negative relationship between organizational density and both the FDI and the composite index of online accountability.

Implications and Conclusions

In this article, we have examined the extent to which nonprofit organizations adopt Web-based accountability practices through an analysis of the content of 117 diverse US community foundation Web sites. . . . We believe the spread of interactive second-generation Web technologies has effectively increased organizations' potential for communicating with, strategically engaging, and being responsive to their core constituents.

However, what do our findings suggest about nonprofit organizations' realization of this potential? The strong implication is that community foundations in particular are failing to maximize the opportunity to use the Web to engage stakeholders. For instance, while 78 percent of the community foundations had the most basic contact-us, feedback, or ask-a-question features on their Web sites, only 7 percent of the community foundations in our sample had any higher-level mechanism for the solicitation of stakeholder preferences, needs, and demands—such as an online stakeholder survey, an interactive message forum, an online grant recipient evaluation form, a guestbook, or an online needs assessment. We also found great variability in the extent to which foundations avail themselves of financial accountability mechanisms. . . .

This severe underutilization of the technology deserves further attention—the nonprofit sector may need a resource-rich "accountability entrepreneur" to help nonprofits redefine what is considered good governance with respect to accountability, both on the Web and off. Our findings, however, cast some doubts on whether community foundations are willing and capable of playing this role of accountability entrepreneur, even in the online environment. . . .

Our findings show that capacity, and particularly asset size, stands out as the predominant factor in our model. As with many nonprofit phenomena, resources matter. Moreover, we found that higher levels of community poverty are not generally associated with increased online accountability, except in terms of interactive engagement. On the positive side, we do find that governance in the form of board performance is important. We would like to think that this link between board traits and accountability outputs is causal in nature; practitioners might thus want to look into further institutionalizing the accountability-building function of the board. We also found some evidence that community foundations respond to increases in organizational density by decreasing the amount of financial disclosure. This lends credence to the idea that disclosure is a tool organizations use to boost legitimacy in low-density (i.e., low-legitimacy) industries. . . .

As there is no one typical nonprofit organization, community foundations being no exception, we cannot argue that the same pattern of online accountability practices will necessarily exist in other types of nonprofits. Therefore, caution must be exercised in generalizing the

findings of this study to a different industry context. Still, we believe that the two-dimensional view of Web-based accountability and the four broad sets of influencing factors identified in our model should work similarly in the rest of the nonprofit world.

Notes

1. Community foundations are 501(c)(3) public charities that work to improve the quality of life of a specific geographic community by pooling funds from a wide range of individual, family, and corporate donors and allocating grants to targeted program areas that meet specific local needs. For more on community foundations, see Grønbjerg (2006).

2. An excellent example is the GuideStar Web site, which provides financial and operational information on more than one million nonprofit organizations throughout the United States.

3. The disclosure of financial and performance information has been increasingly identified as an important aspect of nonprofit accountability (e.g., Brody 2002; Melendez 2001).

4. For a complete account of this argument, see Saxton, Guo, and Brown (2007).

5. Similar results have obtained in the for-profit literature, where size has been identified as one of the critical prerequisites or antecedents that enable an organization to exploit technology for mission-related purposes (e.g., Aral and Weill 2004; Buhalis 1998).

6. The authors of the earlier study (Guo and Brown 2006) began with an original sample of 677 US community foundations, obtained from the Council on Foundations Web site, which essentially represented the population of community foundations in the country. They then contacted chief executives of all 677 community foundations in May and June of 2004. Follow-up e-mails and telephone calls resulted in a final sample of 117, which is a response rate of 17 percent.

7. Several steps were made to ensure the reliability of the analysis. First, we conducted an exhaustive search of the 117 Web sites rather than a limited examination of specific sections of the sites as financial-disclosure items, for example, can be found in a wide variety of differently named Web

site sections. Second, in terms of coding, each of the two principal investigators started by analyzing and coding the same 10 community foundation Web sites. This helped standardize the terminology used to code certain generic features (e.g., administrative costs for funds or online stakeholder survey) that were found on multiple sites but under different names. The two principal investigators and a graduate assistant then each coded a third of the remaining sites. Given the comprehensive nature of the examination of the sites and the multicoder review of the initial data-gathering efforts, there were few ambiguous codings at this stage, such as questions about whether an item counted as financial disclosure or performance disclosure. Nevertheless, an additional crucial step was taken to ensure intercoder reliability. Each of the two principal investigators reviewed half of the graduate assistant's sites in addition to half of the other investigator's sites. This step helped discover various minor coding errors and/or discrepancies that were found in less than 10 percent of the sites.

8. Beginning deductively with our theoretically grounded conceptualizations of the types of content implied by the two dimensions of online accountability, we approached the coding process with a fair amount of inductive reasoning in mind, given that we did not know precisely which features (some of which might be unique to the Web) we would find under each of these categories. For instance, we would have no way of knowing a priori that, related to community foundations' solicitation of stakeholder input, we would find such material as online stakeholder surveys, interactive message forums, or online needs assessments.

9. To check for any potential nonresponse bias, we compared these key characteristics with those of the entire population of 677 community foundations then operating in the United States. We found that the average community foundation in the population at large was 22 years old and had US$43.2 million in assets. It generated revenue of US$5.2 million a year and granted, on average, 8 percent of its assets. In brief, the organizations in our final sample are slightly older and wealthier but overall quite representative of the population at large.

10. Interestingly, two of the foundations had no Web site, and another two had simplistic sites with no meaningful content.

11. It is on this component that community foundations seem to be making better use of Web technologies and providing more imaginative content to their key stakeholders—such as the regularly updated, hyperlinked photo galleries highlighting grant recipient success stories provided by the Lexington Community Foundation of Nebraska or the Madison Community Foundation of Wisconsin. Other organizations, such as the Community Foundation of Jackson Hole, provide copious details of their grant-making activities in a way that is both educational for the general public and instructive to grant-seeking organizations. The organization's Web site also serves a convening function by incorporating a nonprofit community event calendar and information on workshops, talks, and nonprofit executive meet-and-greet sessions. Last, several organizations were using their Web sites to provide extensive assistance in the area of project evaluation and outcome measurement. The Maine Community Foundation, for example, allows grant recipients to submit online a Project Evaluation Report to provide their results and feedback to the foundation on what contributed to the success of their project as well as reasons that made other aspects of their project more difficult or impossible to achieve. The Gulf Coast Community Foundation, meanwhile, provides a free online outcomes-tracking program called Impact Manager that comes bundled with how-to documents, outcome workbooks, links to external sites, online technical assistance documents, frequently asked questions (FAQs), and an online library.

12. As its name suggests, this highest level of content involves some form of interaction—the two-way exchange of ideas, opinions, data, or information between two or more parties.

13. Though a PFA returned a single factor (eigenvalue = 0.64) with a low Cronbach's alpha (.49) score, we decided on theoretical grounds to include the scale in our analyses.

14. A PFA returned a single factor (eigenvalue = 2.06) on which all items load at 0.6 or better.

15. Similar to the current ratio, net working capital is a method of assessing a nonprofit's ability to pay its short-term obligations. For the purpose of measuring financial stewardship, we decided to use net working capital instead of the current ratio because the latter has more missing observations in our sample.

16. We use this ratio instead of the actual number of community foundations to control for the effect of a state's wealth on organizational density.

17. With count variables, the ordinary least squares (OLS) method would tend to result in biased, inefficient, and inconsistent estimates (Long 1997). To deal with this problem, researchers have developed various nonlinear models based on the Poisson and negative binomial distributions. Both analyses were conducted here and produced similar results; since a likelihood ratio test showed that the negative binomial regression model is not a significantly better fit than the Poisson regression model, we only present here the results from the latter. We also ran an ordered logit regression for Interactivity and both an ordered logit and an OLS regression for our composite index. In all cases, there were no changes in sign or significance for any of the variables; thus we do not report the results further.

References

Aral, S., and P. Weill. 2004. *IT Assets, Organizational Capabilities and Firm Performance: Asset and Capability Specific Complementarities.* MIT Sloan CISR Working Paper No. 343. Boston: Massachusetts Institute of Technology.

Behn, B. K., D. DeVries, and J. Lin. 2007. *Voluntary Disclosure in Nonprofit Organizations: An Exploratory Study.* Retrieved June 15, 2009, from http://ssm.com/abstract=727363.

Berlinger, L. R., and D. Te'eni. 1999. "Leaders' Attitudes and Computer Use in Religious Congregations." *Nonprofit Management and Leadership* 9: 399–412.

Bothwell, R. O. 1989. "Are They Worthy of the Name? A Critic's View." In R. Magat, ed., *An Agile Servant: Community by Community Foundations,* 155–165. New York: Foundation Center.

Brody, E. 2002. "Accountability and Public Trust." In L. M. Salamon, ed., *The State of Nonprofit America,* 471–498. Washington, DC: Brookings Institution.

Buhalis, D. 1998. "Strategic Use of Information Technologies in the Tourism Industry." *Tourism Management* 19: 409–421.

Gill, M., R. J. Flynn, and E. Reissing. 2005. "The Governance Self-Assessment Checklist: An Instrument for Assessing Board Effectiveness." *Nonprofit Management and Leadership* 15: 271–294.

Global Accountability Project Framework. 2005. *London, UK: One World Trust.* Retrieved June 15, 2009, from www.oneworldtrust.org/?display=gap framework.

Gordon, T., M. Fisher, D. Malone, and G. Tower. 2002. "A Comparative Empirical Examination of Extent of Disclosure by Private and Public Colleges and Universities in the United States." *Journal of Accounting and Public Policy* 21: 235–275.

Gordon, T. P., C. L. Knock, and D. G. Neely. 2008. *The Role of Rating Agencies in the Market for Charitable Contributions: An Empirical Test.* Working Paper. Moscow: University of Idaho.

Graddy, E. A., and D. L. Morgan. 2006. "Community Foundations, Organizational Strategy, and Public Policy." *Nonprofit and Voluntary Sector Quarterly* 35: 605–630.

Grønbjerg, K. A. 2006. "Foundation Legitimacy at the Community Level: The Case of Community Foundations in the US." In K. Prewitt, M. Dogan, S. Heydemann, and S. Toepler, eds., *Foundations and the Challenge of Legitimacy in Comparative Perspective,* 150–174. New York: Russell Sage Foundation.

Guo, C., and W. A. Brown. 2006. "Community Foundation Performance: Bridging Community Resources and Needs." *Nonprofit and Voluntary Sector Quarterly* 35: 267–287.

Hackler, D., and G. D. Saxton. 2007. "The Strategic Use of Information Technology by Nonprofit Organizations: Increasing Capacity and Untapped Potential." *Public Administration Review* 67: 474–487.

Hambrick, D. C., and S. Finkelstein. 1987. "Managerial Discretion: A Bridge Between Polar Views of Organizational Outcomes." *Research in Organizational Behavior* 9: 369–406.

Hambrick, D. C., and P. A. Mason. 1984. "Upper Echelons: The Organization as a Reflection of Its Top Managers." *Academy of Management Review* 9: 193–206.

Hannan, M. T., and J. Freeman. 1987. "The Ecology of Organizational Founding Rates: The Dynamics of Foundings of American Labor Unions, 1836–1975." *American Journal of Sociology* 92: 910–943.

Luke, J. L., and S. L. Feurt. 2002. *A Flexible and Growing Service to Donors: Donor-Advised Funds in Community Foundations*. Available at Council on Foundations' Web site, www.cof.org.

Luoma, P., and J. Goodstein. 1999. "Stakeholders and Corporate Boards: Institutional Influences on Board Composition and Structure." *Academy of Management Journal* 42: 553–563.

McNutt, J. G., and K. M. Boland. 1999. "Electronic Advocacy by Nonprofit Organizations in Social Welfare Policy." *Nonprofit and Voluntary Sector Quarterly* 28: 432–451.

Melendez, S. E. 2001. "The Nonprofit Sector and Accountability." *New Directions for Philanthropic Fundraising* 31: 121–132.

O'Reilly, T. 2005. What Is Web 2.0? Design Patterns and Business Models for the Next Generation of Software. *Available from www.oreillynet.com.*

Pew Internet & American Life Project. 2008. *April 8–May 11, 2008 Tracking Survey.* Available from www.pewinternet.org.

Saxton, G. D., C. Guo, and W. A. Brown. 2007. "New Dimensions of Nonprofit Responsiveness: The Application and Promise of Internet-Based Technologies." *Public Performance and Management Review* 31: 144–171.

Schneider, J. A. 2003. "Small, Minority-Based Nonprofits in the Information Age." *Nonprofit Management and Leadership* 13: 383–399.

Trabelsi, S., R. Labelle, and P. Dumontier. 2008. "Incremental Voluntary Disclosure on Corporate Web Sites: Determinants and Consequences." *Journal of Contemporary Accounting and Economics* 4: 120–155.

CHAPTER 19

Measuring the Networked Nonprofit
Using Data to Change the World

BETH KANTER AND KATIE DELAHAYE PAINE

The Keys to Nonprofit Success: Networking and Measurement

Two key processes lead to tremendous success for nonprofits: becoming networked and using measurement. . . .

A *networked nonprofit* is an organization that uses social networks and the technology of social media to greatly extend its reach, capabilities, and effectiveness. *Measurement* is the process of collecting data on your communications results and using the data to learn and improve your programs. An organization with a *data-informed culture* uses data to help make decisions and uses measurement to continuously improve and refine its systems.

Most nonprofit organizations use at least some sort of informal measurement and some form of social media-enabled networking. Many nonprofits are striving to build a data-informed culture and networked mindset. But few organizations use these powerful techniques to their greatest potential. One of these is MomsRising.

org, a poster child for networked nonprofits and nonprofit measurement mavens.

MomsRising: A Superstar of Networked Nonprofits Knows the Joys of Measurement

Kristin Rowe-Finkbeiner and Joan Blades founded MomsRising in 2006. To design this nonprofit, they combined their experience in grassroots organizing and social media with successful ideas from organizations like Move On, Color OfChange, League of Conservation Voters, and others. The result was an organization that embraces constant learning from experience and embeds this powerful concept in its organizational culture and processes. It has fueled the organization's growth from zero members in May 2006 to over a million active members—moms, dads, grandparents, aunts, and uncles—today.

MomsRising uses measurement to achieve tremendous success . . . and there are several

DOI: 10.4324/9781003387800-44

themes concerning measurement and how it is used. . . .

Theme 1: "Likes" on Facebook Is Not a Victory—Social Change Is

Proper measurement keeps organizations focused on results rather than the tools they use. . . . MomsRising, for instance, does not simply count "likes" on Facebook. Instead, it uses social change to define its successes and develops metrics accordingly. Its most important goals generally include these:

- Getting policies passed on family-related issues
- Increasing capacity
- Increasing the movement size by increasing membership
- Working with aligned partner organizations
- Garnering attention from all media through creative engagement

For MomsRising, the holy grail of results is getting legislatures to pass family-friendly policies. This requires grabbing the attention of policymakers. As one indicator of progress toward that goal, it counted an invitation to bring mothers to the White House to talk with policymakers about their experience with Medicaid. The White House blogged about the power of people's stories, and MomsRising members blogged about their White House experience, resulting in even greater exposure for their messages. Says Rowe-Finkbeiner, "The after-story is just as important because it will often get picked up by mainstream media outlets like NPR or the Huffington Post."[1]

Theme 2: Measurement Helps Nonprofits Understand and Improve Their Social Networks

Another theme is that measurement helps nonprofits listen to and engage with their constituents. Measurement enables organizations to assess and improve their relationships with their members and stakeholders. . . .

An important part of MomsRising's decision making is the use of member feedback in the form of stories or comments on social channels or e-mail and in more structured ways such as surveys. Says Rowe-Finkbeiner, "We are in constant dialogue with our members to figure out what works and what doesn't. The data keeps us focused on our mission of building a movement for family economic security, while listening and engaging with our members breathes life into our movement."

Theme 3: Measurement Means Data for Decisions, Not for Data's Sake

Unfortunately, many organizations see measurement as collecting data to dump on the boardroom table or the executive director's desk. But measurement isn't about justifying one's existence or budget, and it isn't about filling spreadsheets with lots of "just-in-case" data to throw over the fence.

Measurement is about using data to learn to become more effective and more efficient. It's about doing your job better, and helping your organization achieve its mission with fewer resources. It's about reaching more people, and becoming better at saving the world.

Theme 4: Measurement Makes You Plan for Success

More and more nonprofits are making larger investments in social media: hiring dedicated staff, upgrading Web sites to incorporate social features, and using more powerful professional tools to do the work. Measurement helps you make smarter investments and helps you use those investments in a smarter way. Having a social media measurement plan and approach is no longer an afterthought. It's the smart way to run an organization.

Theme 5: Good Measurement Is Good Governance

As networked nonprofits become more skilled in their social media practice, their boards and senior management are becoming more knowledgeable about this area. They expect reports showing social media results, and they expect results expressed in the kind of language that measurement provides. In addition, foundations and other funders want credible evaluation reports and demonstrations of impact. Today boards and foundations increasingly include executives from the for-profit world who have come to expect actionable data and standardized measurement systems.

Theme 6: Data Without Insight Is Just Trivia

The key to MomsRising's success is that it uses data to refine its strategies and tactics. It has achieved its success not by luck or gut instinct but by using measurement to make decisions.

MomsRising holds a weekly staff meeting, nicknamed "Metrics Monday." Prior to this meeting each program and campaign staff person reviews his or her results as part of an explicit process of preparation. The meeting is actually a group conversation about what actions to reinforce, how to refine messages, and what other improvements need to be made. Says Rowe-Finkbeiner, "Our dashboards have multiple views: a high-level view and the ability to drill down into specific campaigns. This informs our discussion."

Theme 7: Measuring Failure Is Part of the Path to Success

Some experiments bomb. Some projects or ideas seem brilliant at first, but when the results come in the data shows that they simply didn't work. The staff at MomsRising give themselves permission to kill these. To remove the stigma of failure, they do this with humor, calling it a "joyful funeral." To learn from the experience, they reflect on why it didn't work.

Theme 8: Incremental Success is Not Failure

Many organizations experiment with social media. Networked nonprofits are expert at setting up and measuring low-risk experiments and pilots. What sets MomsRising apart is that the staff don't do aimless experiments; they set realistic expectations for success and measure along the way.

Some experiments, actions, or issues provide dramatic results. For example, a MomsRising interactive educational video garnered over 12 million views, hundreds of comments, and thousands of new members who signed up or took action. Rowe-Finkbeiner says, "That type of success does not happen every day, but we need to try for that kind of success every day. We can do it only if we decide not to pursue things that don't work." They analyze these game-changing successes to understand how they can be replicated and to make sure they weren't accidents.

Theme 9: Measurement is Valuable at Every Level of Functioning

Any nonprofit can learn to use measurement to make its social media more effective. It is not hard to get started and doesn't require expensive software, a graduate degree, or even an aptitude for mathematics. The trick is to start simple and grow from there. . . .

Seven Vital Characteristics of Networked Nonprofits

Knowing how to use social media well is not just about knowing which button to push or what technological wizardry to employ. The power of a networked approach is its ability to connect people to one another and help build strong, resilient, trusting relationships that lead to real on-the-ground social change. We see seven characteristics as vital in this approach:

1. Networked nonprofits know their organizations are part of a much larger ecosystem of organizations and individuals that provides valuable resources. *They understand that they don't need to own the to-do list, only the results.*

2. Networked nonprofits know that relationships are the result of all the interactions and conversations they have with their networks. *They are comfortable doing their work transparently. It makes them open to serendipity and new ideas.*

3. *Networked nonprofits experiment and learn from experience.* They are masters at experimenting their way into dramatic wins. They don't shy away from failure because it leads them to innovation and success.

4. *Networked nonprofits have data-informed cultures.* They use data to develop strategy, measure success, assess their experiments, and then make decisions on how best to move forward with new strategies.

5. *Networked nonprofits know how to inspire people.* They motivate their networks of support to help shape the organization's programs, share stories in order to raise awareness of social issues, change attitudes and behavior, and organize communities to provide services or advocate for legislation.

6. *Networked nonprofits work differently from other organizations.* They enjoy a social culture that encourages everyone in and outside the organization to participate and spread their mission. They challenge deeply held assumptions about leadership, roles, and structures. They have broken down departmental silos. They are comfortable sharing control or cocreating with their networks—whether that means allowing people to retell the organization's story in their own words or scaling programs.

7. *Networked nonprofits are masters at using social media.* They are adept at using tools that encourage conversations and building

relationships between people and between people and organizations. They are able to scale their efforts quickly, easily, and inexpensively. They are adept at blending tried-and-true methods with new digital tools. . . .

Becoming a Networked Nonprofit: The Crawl, Walk, Run, Fly Model

Learning to use social media and other emerging technologies and putting the ideas into practice will be successful only if nonprofits take small, incremental, and strategic steps. Our model incorporates four levels of social media practice: crawl, walk, run, and fly. Each level indicates where the organization is with respect to becoming a networked nonprofit.

It is important to note that reaching the highest level of networked nonprofit practice takes months, if not years. Even an organization like MomsRising, which was born as a networked nonprofit and has several years of social media experience, has not won its dramatic victories over night. . . .

Not every nonprofit will go through the levels at the same pace because different organizations have different cultures, capacities, communication objectives, program designs, and target audiences. Moreover, the reality will be messy; an organization might not precisely fit the profile in any specific category. But every organization can take pride in its success at whatever level it has achieved. . . .

[Below,] . . . we set out a crawl, walk, run, fly self-assessment checklist that any organization can use to evaluate where it is in its development as a networked nonprofit.

Crawl

Organizations in the crawl stage of becoming networked nonprofits are not using social media or emerging technology at all or, if they are using it, are not using it consistently. These organizations lack a robust communications strategy or program plan that can be scaled using a networked approach. Crawlers are not just smaller nonprofits; they include larger institutions that have all the basics in place but lack a social culture or are resisting transforming from a command-and-control style to a more networked mindset. These nonprofits need to develop a basic communications strategy or program plan. . . . The first measurement step at this level is setting up a listening process and integrating listening on social channels into planning research.

Walk

Nonprofits at the walk stage (dubbed "the walkers") are using one or more social media tools consistently, but this use isn't linked to a communications strategy, campaign, or program plan. They have in place best practices on tools and techniques as part of the organizational skill set but may need assistance in developing a social media strategy to support short- and long-term SMART (specific, measurable, achievable, realistic, and time) objectives. They may also need help to correctly identify the audiences they need to target.

Walkers have internalized listening and are able to use the data they collect to improve engagement and content best practices. At this stage, leaders may not fully understand social media and networked ways of working. Often the question "What's the value?" surfaces. Nonprofits in the walk stage need to avoid spreading the organization's resources too thin. They should instead focus on one or two social media tools, going deep on tactics, and generating tangible results to demonstrate value.

Walkers must identify low-cost ways to build capacity internally, for example, by using interns or volunteers effectively and integrating social media tasks into existing job descriptions. Staff members should evaluate their job tasks and identify what they don't need to do in order to make time for social media and other emerging technologies, all with support from leaders. They must also enlist the help of their social networks outside their organization.

A nonprofit's social media policy in the walk stage formalizes the value and vision for social media use and networked approach and encourages free agent outsiders to help with implementation. The organization integrates simple measurement techniques and learning as an organizational habit that helps improve practice.

Run

Nonprofits at the run stage use one or more social media tools and are strategic, identifying key result areas and key performance metrics that drive everything they do. They also have a formal ladder of engagement and know how to measure it. They understand the importance of visualizing their networks and measuring their relationships.

In these organizations, social media are not in a silo or guarded by one person or department. With a social media policy in place and a more social culture, the organization is comfortable with working transparently and working with people outside its organization. . . . They know how to use measurement to identify these influencers. The board is also using social media as part of its governance role.

The main problem at this stage is scaling. To build internal capacity, organizations may need to bring on a half- or full-time staff person who serves as a community manager, building relationships with people on social media or new technology platforms. This social media point person also works internally as a network weaver or trainer to help departments and individuals use social media to support the organization's programs.

These runners effectively integrate social media and emerging technologies such as mobile messaging across all communications channels and know the right combination of measurement tools to evaluate their performance. They have strong capacity in content creation as well as repurposing or remixing across channels and use crowdsourcing to create and spread content. Runners also incorporate social fundraising, knowing that community engagement is as important to measure as dollars raised.

For program strategy, runners use crowdsourcing to help design pilots, generate feedback on an evaluation, or rethink programs. They know how to measure the impact of the crowd. . . . The organization has adequately engaged and built relationships with key influencers—both organizations and individuals. The organization has codified and shared its program work flow and has made all program tools and

materials available so its network can assist with implementation.

Fly

Organizations at the fly stage have mastered everything at the running stage and internalized it. These "flyers" create a culture of public learning for both individuals and the entire organization. They embrace failure and success alike and learn from both. The organization uses data to make decisions, but leaders understand how to lead from the heart as well as the head. The organization has documented and shared dramatic results with its stakeholders and peer organizations. Flyers are part of a vibrant network of people and organizations focused on social change.

TABLE 19.1 Crawl, Walk, Run, Fly (CWRF) Assessment Tool

Practice	Indicator	CWRF Rating
Strategy		
Identifies goals and measurable objectives	Identifies the most important overall results and creates measurable objectives based on those.	
Identifies specific target audience	Identifies specific audience target groups, including key stakeholders and influencers.	
Identifies success and value	Identifies what success looks like and the value it brings to the organization.	
Networked mind-set	Management understands and supports social media and networked approaches as part of the overall communications or program plan.	
Social media policy	Has formally identified appropriate personal and organizational use.	
Listening and influencer research	Has done research to learn what other organizations are doing and what the conversations are. Has done research to identify influencers and free agents.	
Allocates sufficient resources	Understands the capacity to implement by hiring staff or having social media tasks in job description or recruits volunteers. Tracks investment of time against results.	

Practice	Indicator	CWRF Rating
Implementation		
Tool selection	Uses best practices on a selective number of social media tools that match audience and capacity to implement.	
Engagement	Takes steps to foster online engagement and conversations related to strategic objectives. Has a formal ladder of engagement and uses it to guide strategy and measurement.	
Transparency	Works in a transparent way and has measured trust and other factors.	
Content	Has an editorial calendar and strategy for linking, producing, and distributing content across social media and other channels.	
Network building	Takes steps to foster online community or networked effects, with linkages to other organizations and free agents.	
Crowdsourcing	Gets feedback from network on ideas and strategies as appropriate and has a process to measure the value of feedback.	
Job description and training	Provides appropriate training to those responsible for implementation.	
Involves all staff	Social media are not isolated function. Most, if not all, staff or volunteers have some knowledge or participate as appropriate.	
Builds valuable partnerships	Relationships have been made with stakeholders and other organizations to achieve goals. Measures relationships on a regular basis.	
Measures, monitors, evaluates	Activities are monitored, measured, and evaluated for improvement. A formal process for reflecting on data and improving is in place.	
Integration		
Website	Strategic linkages and integration between social media and website include link, content, and distribution.	
Other social channels	Strategic cross-promotion and integration among social channels.	

(Continued)

TABLE 19.1 (Continued)

Practice	Indicator	CWRF Rating
Print materials	Strategic links between social media and printed materials.	
E-mail marketing	Strategic links between social media and e-mailed newsletters.	
Mobile	Strategic links between social media and mobile.	
Offline	Strategic links between offline activities and social media channels.	

Organizations in this category have adopted sophisticated measurement techniques, tools, and processes. This may include benchmarking, testing, shared organizational dashboards, and linking results to job compensation for larger institutions. Above all, measurement is not viewed as an afterthought. It is part of an ongoing decision-making process that helps the organization continuously improve its programs.

Crawl, Walk, Run, Fly Assessment Tool for Networked Nonprofits

The assessment tool lists the ideal best practices for networked nonprofits. Review each practice and self-assess whether you are crawling, walking, running, or flying. Where could you improve current practice?

This assessment tool builds on and adapts the work of Ash Shepherd, who created an integrated communications audit and, with Beth Kanter's encouragement, set up a wiki to share the documents and encourage people to "remix it."[2]

Notes

1. In Beth Kanter and Katie Delahaye Paine, *Measuring the Networked Nonprofit* (San Francisco: Jossey-Bass, 2012), 8.

2. "Nonprofit Social Media Audit," http://nonprofitsocialmediaaudit.wikispaces.com/, in Kanter and Paine, *Measuring the Networked Nonprofit*, 279.

Technology and Transparency at the Museum

AMANDA R. INSALACO, BENJAMIN S. BINGLE
AND C. KENNETH MEYER

"How am I going to get all this work done?" Ted Hamilton asked, not expecting an answer in return. He was alone in his second-floor office pondering the coming fiscal year's budget. The sensor on the visitors' center front door released yet another deafening buzz. The museum simply needs more staff, there is no denying it, he thought as he scurried downstairs to greet museum guests.

As the executive director of the local historic house museum, it was Ted's duty to impress upon the board the gravity of the museum's need. Surely they would understand. After all, the board had recently initiated a campaign that was thus far successful in increasing admission ticket sales. The only problem: they now had to find the resources necessary to absorb the additional guests! Ted and his small staff were already working nearly seven days a week; clearly this was an unsustainable arrangement.

While Ted acted as host to museum guests in the lobby, his computer monitor dimmed on forgotten windows—Facebook, Twitter, and the museum website remained unattended. Meanwhile, the director of visitor services, Shanna Hernandez, conducted a tour and the programs coordinator, Dan Weber, cleaned bathrooms. The docent who typically volunteered on Tuesday afternoons had called in sick, again.

Background

The Highside House had been operating as a museum and cultural center for more than fifty years. A prominent component of the arts landscape in the region, the museum frequently served as host to a wide variety of events. Weddings had been held in its gardens, employee trainings in its facilities, and art shows in its vast expanses. Plaques had been carefully placed on the grounds in remembrance of loved ones past. Even the governing board visibly demonstrated the value it placed on the organization. Board members were not reluctant to get their hands dirty, frequently rolling up their sleeves to repair trodden flowerbeds and tend to overgrown terraces.

The Highside House had been donated to the municipal park district by the grandchildren of Ivan and Mary Hinters in the late 1960s. Ivan, originally from modest means, made his fortune in the late nineteenth century raising

 DOI: 10.4324/9781003387800-45

draft horses on the hundreds of acres surrounding the estate. It was these riches that the Highside House was built upon.

Ivan and Mary had three children, and their youngest daughter and her husband eventually inherited the estate. In their will, they declared that the mansion and land would be donated to the municipal park district. Had the Hinters' descendants not graciously donated the property, it was likely that the historic structures would have been demolished long ago, the land swallowed up by housing developers. Through a unique arrangement, the property and structures were owned by the park district while the items within the structures were owned and managed by a nonprofit, the Highside House Association. The Association also provided the funds necessary for operating expenses.

With just three staff members, the museum maintained a relatively modest operating budget. Collections management and restoration services accounted for a significant portion of the organization's expenses, after salaries and employee benefits. Total annual expenses frequently fell below $200,000, though expenses could be expected to rise when the museum periodically undertook a restoration project.

Priorities and Challenges

The museum charged a modest fee for its tours, providing senior and student discounts. Other sources of revenue included membership dues and fees for facility rentals. Although the organization's budget was in good health, staff members remained overworked and special exhibits were frequently put on hold, owing to a lack of surplus resources.

The Highside House relied heavily on volunteers to provide tours to the public. They were often expected to manage the museum gift shop as well. Unfortunately, volunteers were at times unable to commit their time; when this happened, staff had to provide these

basic services. Frequently overlooked were the standard operational and governance responsibilities. The museum had struggled in years past, for example, to even compile financials for review by the board. As executive director, Ted insisted that staff prioritize direct service to the public over "fancy financial reports."

> "After all," said Ted, "the doors stay open, and the public is happy. Why should we concentrate on that stuff when there are tours to give, weddings to book, and exhibits to develop?"

Although museum guests had certainly been pleased in the past, the museum's online reputation had suffered as a result of the disproportionate emphasis on direct service. The website was infrequently updated by overburdened staff, and the number of Facebook followers on the museum page had remained stagnant.

Meanwhile, an online "2-for-1" admission coupon and a targeted marketing campaign had proved successful, resulting in a noticeable increase in tours. Given the steady rise in patrons, Ted could no longer deny the need for additional human resources.

Online Presence and Transparency

The higher number of guests yielded increased revenue from ticket sales, but also increased attention, some of which was unpopular. Specifically, the online coupon campaign brought unprecedented scrutiny of the organization's online presence—or lack thereof. As more people visited the website, it became clear that having an online presence had never been a priority at the Highside House. Calls began to trickle in inquiring about issues on the website, outdated information, and a lack of solid details related to the museum's finances. Potential donors and members alike asked, "Why isn't your website updated?" and, "How is my donation being used?" and, "Why is there no financial information online?"

In an era when the misuse of funds is commonplace and the best organizations use their websites as avenues for transparency, it appeared that donors and members had finally decided to hold the Highside House accountable. They demanded that more information—including financial data—be made available to the public and that the website be made more professional, appealing, and user-friendly. Embarrassed, Ted reluctantly approached the board.

More staff were needed to ensure that the organization could cater to a culture of transparency. Gradually, the board accepted the severity of the need as well, though some recognized the value of transparency more than others. It was determined that the organization would search for grants to help alleviate the financial strain, shore up operations, stabilize programming, and put the museum in a position to hire additional staff.

Ted located a funding opportunity aimed at providing support for community-based education initiatives. It was a perfect fit! He soon discovered, however, that the funding organization would also insist upon transparency. The museum would have to address five questions:

- Why should grant funds be given to the museum?
- What will the museum do with the grant funding?
- How will results be measured and communicated?
- How will the impact of this grant be shared with the public?
- How will the museum sustain transparent and responsible programming after the grant funding has concluded?

The museum could linger no longer. The pressure from donors, members, potential funders, and even a few board members made it clear that more transparency was necessary.

The Funding Pursuit

Ted looked at the five primary questions that he was required to answer in the grant application. The first two were pretty straightforward, he thought as he began jotting notes on the grant guidelines and application document. The remaining questions all centered on transparency, measuring results, and sharing results. He had never been forced to think about these matters in such a structured way. "It's much easier to lead a couple tours or recruit some volunteers," Ted muttered. Furthermore, the idea of making financial data widely available still made him, and some board members, uncomfortable. After all, the organization had never even produced an annual report. Instead, all financial reporting was kept in-house and also kept to the bare minimum as required by law.

In the end, the need for financial support overpowered his concerns about financial privacy. Carrying the grant application materials in an overstuffed envelope, he released the package into the mailbox with bated breath and hoped for the best.

Funding Decision

While waiting for a funding decision, Ted got back to the daily operations of the Highside House. During this time, Ted and his staff did nothing to shore up the website deficiencies. In fact, their only online activity was a few social media posts.

Two months had passed since he submitted the grant proposal, and Ted finally received a letter in the mail from the funding agency. He slowly read through its contents while sitting at his desk. What he read came as a surprise.

The grant allocation committee noted the worthiness of Ted's proposal, but suggested that certain areas of the application were woefully underdeveloped. Namely, the committee thought that Ted had skirted around the transparency clause of the application, using vague descriptions and convoluted wording. Moreover, in their review of applicant websites, the allocation committee had noticed inaccuracies, inconsistencies, and outdated information on the Highside House site. This did not inspire confidence among committee members. The letter said, "As funding partners, the websites of our grantees must not only exemplify their organizational values, but also our own. In essence, our grantees are an extension of us because they carry out the vital programs that we financially support."

Combining these website concerns with its concern about the Highside House's lack of an emphasis on transparency, the committee had decided to deny Ted's grant request this funding cycle. The letter ended, however, on an encouraging note: "The committee is excited by the possibilities you have outlined, and we encourage you to apply for funding again in the future after the Highside House staff has had an opportunity to reevaluate the transparency clause and reinforce its online presence."

Slightly embarrassed, somewhat defeated, and a little insulted, Ted folded the letter and placed it on his desk. Just then, a group of patrons entered the visitors' center and the familiar buzz sound rang out, alerting Ted that it was time to get back to work.

Questions and Instructions

1. How much emphasis should nonprofit organizations place on accountability, evaluation, and transparency efforts? Are these vital considerations or are they secondary to programming and services? Please elaborate.

2. Putting yourself in the place of the executive director, what would you do to make the Highside House more transparent as an organization? How could technology be used to enhance transparency in this case?

3. How might you persuade a reluctant staff member that it would be advantageous to share the organization's financial information online? Would your strategy change if it was a board member you were attempting to persuade? If so, how?

4. The push for transparency in this case was primarily externally motivated. Do you think the museum would be likely to embrace and support a transparency initiative under these circumstances? What can an understaffed organization realistically do to meet the accountability expectations of the public or other stakeholders? Is there a need to prioritize accountability expectations under such circumstances? If so, what are the potential costs involved? If not, how would you manage this process?

Measure Twice, Cut Once
Performance Evaluation in Nonprofit Organizations

Benjamin S. Bingle and C. Kenneth Meyer

A serious dilemma had come up at the Center for Community Action (CCA). The 25 year old nonprofit organization provided vital human services programming for the local community, including group therapy, mental health counseling, youth mentoring, and much more. Yet, their financial model had not kept up with the evolving organization and was overly reliant on uncertain grant funding. The CCA board of directors saw the writing on the wall. Difficult decisions needed to be made; but first, the board wanted data to help inform their decisions.

Alexander Garcia served as CCA's Assistant Director. He was well-liked by the other employees, their patrons, donors, and the board. He was viewed as an effective leader, a collaborator, and a capable professional. He also had a productive relationship with CCA's Executive Director, Trisha Edwards.

One Friday afternoon, after a particularly difficult board meeting the night before, Trisha stopped by Garcia's office. She informed him that the board sought data to help them decide which program(s) and/or staff position(s) to eliminate. This caught Garcia off-guard. He

knew CCA was struggling, but had no idea their financial position had deteriorated so significantly. Trisha explained to Garcia that he would lead an effort to collect, analyze, and report on the data that would be used to make these strategic decisions. He had two months to develop his report and prepare his recommendations.

Over the weekend, Garcia could hardly think of anything other than this new assignment. He had taken courses on performance management, data analysis, and program evaluation, but had not truly put these skills to use outside of the classroom. He also knew that every individual program that CCA administered had different data collection requirements and reporting standards based on which grant was funding the program. He wondered how to effectively organize all of this disparate information and whether or not he could even make sense of some of the data points.

On Monday morning, he started early and outlined a framework that could evaluate the effectiveness of programs *and* staff members. Evaluation would focus on the following key indicators:

 DOI: 10.4324/9781003387800-46

Indicator Category	Programs	Staff
Transactional	Number of People Served	Number of Staff Per Program
	Cost Per Person Served	Total Salary Per Program
	Total Revenue Generated Per Program	Revenue Per Person (revenue generated divided by total number of staff)
Transformative	Mission Alignment	Annual Performance Evaluation Summary
	Public Perception	360 Performance Review
	SWOT Analysis	Personnel Assessment

Admittedly, Garcia had no experience with this type of project. Yet, he thought he had developed an effective way to capture data relevant to the board's upcoming decisions. After all, he only had two months to complete this project and he had to keep up with his everyday tasks as well. Using this framework, Garcia figured he could rely on existing data for every key indicator in the *Transactional* category. For *Transformative* indicators, he planned to assess the program's alignment with CCA's mission, the public's perception of each program, and he would also conduct a SWOT analysis for each program. Regarding Transformative indicators for staff, Garcia would summarize each staff member's annual performance, he would carry out a 360 review to understand how others perceive each staff member's performance, and he would develop a qualitative narrative about each staff member to summarize their contributions to CCA.

With just eight weeks to carry out this work, Garcia started in with vigor. Unfortunately, his daily duties consumed much more time than he anticipated; especially when word got out that CCA had not received funding to support a new counseling program they hoped to launch soon. This meant Garcia was called upon to attend more donor meetings than usual and to seek out new grant opportunities to potentially fund the planned initiative.

As the deadline approached, Garcia began to doubt his process. Was this framework effective at actually capturing the performance of programs and staff and would it lead to meaningful information the board could use in their decision-making? Should he split the two and create models to evaluate programs separate from staff? He recognized his evaluation included no reference to outcomes or the *actual impact* of these programs and staff performances. How could he claim that he had conducted a thorough evaluation with no reference to outcomes?

In the end, too much time had passed to change his approach. The board meeting was looming and he had to prepare. Still, he lacked confidence in his process and the data he had compiled; mainly because this information would be used to eliminate programs and possibly to cut staff. Alexander Garcia wished he had more time and had gained a new appreciation for the old saying: "Measure twice, cut once." He wanted to measure and evaluate again and to consider new data points before decisions were made about cutting programs or staff.

Uncertain about his process, his data, or his findings, Garcia walked into the board room to deliver a presentation that would significantly impact the future of CCA.

Discussion Questions

1. Evaluate and discuss Garcia's process and the framework he developed. Do you agree with his approach? Why or why not? Outline the framework you would use if you were given this task.

2. Alexander Garcia had a reputation as a capable professional, but had no practical experience in conducting performance evaluations. Did the Executive Director Trisha Edwards make the right decision to delegate the project to Garcia? Why or why not?

3. Define and discuss outcomes evaluation. What are the benefits and challenges that accompany outcomes evaluation? Do you believe Alexander Garcia should have attempted to incorporate outcomes into his evaluation framework? Why or why not?

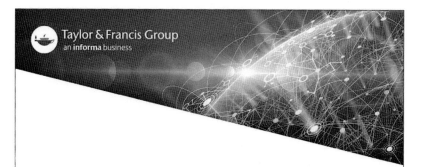